# AMERICAN MUSEUM OF NATURAL HISTORY

# BIRDS
## OF NORTH AMERICA
## AMERICA
### WESTERN REGION

AMERICAN MUSEUM
OF NATURAL HISTORY

# BIRDS
## OF NORTH
## AMERICA
### WESTERN REGION

Editor-in-Chief
François Vuilleumier

Content previously published in
*Birds of North America*

**DK | Penguin Random House**

## AMERICAN MUSEUM OF NATURAL HISTORY

**Editor-in-chief**
François Vuilleumier, Ph.D.
**Consultant**
Paul Sweet
**Project Coordinators**
Alex Navissi, Caitlin Roxby,
Molly Leff
**Global Business Development**
Joanna Hostert

### DEDICATION
We dedicate this book to the memory of John Bull, John Farrand, and Stuart Keith, top birders, field guide authors, AMNH colleagues, first-rate ornithologists, and friends.

## DORLING KINDERSLEY

**Senior Art Editors**
Caroline Hill, Ina Stradins
**Senior Editor**
Angeles Gavira Guerrero
**US Senior Editors**
Shannon Beatty, Jill Hamilton
**Project Editor**
Nathan Joyce
**Designers**
Sonia Barbate, Helen McTeer
**Editors**
Jamie Ambrose, Lori Baird,
Tamlyn Calitz, Marcus Hardy,
Lizzie Munsey, Patrick Newman,
Siobhan O'Connor, David
Summers, Cressida Tuson,
Miezan van Zyl, Rebecca Warren
**Design Assistant**
Becky Tennant
**Editorial Assistant**
Jaime Tenreiro
**Creative Technical Support**
Adam Brackenbury,
John Goldsmid
**Production Editors**
Joanna Byrne, Maria Elia
**Production Controllers**
Erika Pepe, Rita Sinha
**Jacket Designer**
Mark Cavanagh
**Illustrators**
John Cox, Andrew Mackay
**Picture Editor**
Neil Fletcher
**Picture Researchers**
Laura Barwick, Will Jones
**Managing Art Editor**
Michelle Baxter
**Managing Editor**
Sarah Larter
**Publishing Manager**
Liz Wheeler
**Art Directors**
Phil Ormerod, Bryn Walls
**Publisher**
Jonathan Metcalf

## DK INDIA

**Editors**
Megha Gupta, Rukmini Kumar,
Garima Sharma, Dipali Singh
**Project Designer**
Mahua Mandal
**Senior Designer**
Mini Dhawan
**Editorial Manager**
Glenda Fernandes
**DTP Designers**
Shanker Prasad, Arjinder Singh,
Jaypal Singh, Bimlesh Tiwary,
Anita Yadav, Tanveer Abbas Zaidi
**Senior DTP Designer**
Harish Aggarwal
**DTP Manager**
Balwant Singh
**Picture Researcher**
Sakshi Saluja

### FOR SECOND EDITION

## DK LONDON

**US Editor**
Jill Hamilton
**Managing Editor**
Angeles Gavira Guerrero
**Managing Art Editor**
Michael Duffy
**Jacket Design Development Manager** Sophia MTT
**Production Editor**
George Nimmo
**Senior Production Controller**
Meskerem Berhane
**Associate Publishing Director**
Liz Wheeler
**Publishing Director**
Jonathan Metcalf
**Art Director**
Karen Self

## DK INDIA

**Project Editor**
Tina Jindal
**Project Art Editor**
Meenal Goel
**Editor**
Kanika Praharaj
**Assistant Editor**
Chhavi Nagpal
**Assistant Art Editors**
Aarushi Dhawan, Arshti Narang
**Senior Managing Editor**
Rohan Sinha
**Managing Art Editor**
Sudakshina Basu
**DTP Designers**
Rakesh Kumar, Tanveer
Abbas Zaidi
**Pre-production Manager**
Balwant Singh
**Production Manager**
Pankaj Sharma
**Senior Jacket Designer**
Suhita Dharamjit

Content first published in
*Birds of North America* 2009.

This American edition, 2021
First American Edition, 2011
Published in the United States by DK Publishing
1450 Broadway, Suite 801, New York, NY 10018

Copyright © 2009, 2011, 2016, 2020, 2021
Dorling Kindersley Limited
DK, a Division of Penguin Random House LLC

21 22 23 24 25 10 9 8 7 6 5 4 3 2 1
001—319127—February 2021

A catalog record for this book is available from the Library of Congress.

ISBN 978-0-7440-2737-2

DK books are available at special discounts when purchased in bulk for sales promotions, premiums, fund-raising, or educational use. For details, contact: DK Publishing Special Markets,
1450 Broadway, Suite 801, New York, NY 10018
SpecialSales@dk.com

Printed and bound in China

**For the curious**
**www.dk.com**

MIX
Paper from responsible sources
FSC™ C018179

This book was made with Forest Stewardship Council ™ certified paper – one small step in DK's commitment to a sustainable future. For more information go to www.dk.com/our-green-pledge

## CONTRIBUTORS

David Bird, Ph.D.; Nicholas L. Block; Peter Capainolo; Matthew Cormons; Malcolm Coulter, Ph.D.; Joseph DiCostanzo; Shawneen Finnegan; Neil Fletcher; Ted Floyd; Jeff Groth, Ph.D.; Paul Hess; Brian Hiller; Rob Hume; Thomas Brodie Johnson; Kevin T. Karlson; Stephen Kress, Ph.D.; William Moskoff, Ph.D.; Bill Pranty; Michael L. P. Retter; Noah Strycker; Paul Sweet; Rodger Titman, Ph.D.; Elissa Wolfson

**Map Editor**
Paul Lehman

**Project Coordinator**
Joseph DiCostanzo

**AMERICAN BITTERN**
A typically solitary bird, the American Bittern has a cryptic coloration and a still, vertical posture that help camouflage it in reed beds.

# CONTENTS

## AMERICAN MUSEUM OF NATURAL HISTORY

The American Museum of Natural History, founded in 1869 and currently celebrating its 150th anniversary, is one of the world's preeminent scientific, educational, and cultural institutions. The Museum encompasses 45 permanent exhibition halls, including the Rose Center for Earth and Space and the Hayden Planetarium, as well as galleries for temporary exhibitions. The Museum's scientists draw on a world-class research collection of more than 34 million artifacts and specimens, some of which are billions of years old, and on one of the largest natural history libraries in the world. Through its Richard Gilder Graduate School, the Museum grants the Ph.D. degree in Comparative Biology and the Master of Arts in Teaching (MAT) degree, the only such free-standing, degree-granting programs at any museum in the United States. In addition to its campus, the Museum's exhibitions and Space Shows can be seen in venues on six continents, and its website, digital videos, and apps for mobile devices extend its collections, exhibitions, and educational programs to millions more around the world. Visit amnh.org for more information.

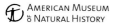

AMERICAN MUSEUM OF NATURAL HISTORY

### EDITOR-IN-CHIEF

Lifelong studies of birds made François Vuilleumier (1938–2017) uniquely qualified to be Editor-in-Chief of *Birds of North America*. After obtaining a Ph.D. at Harvard University, he started a long association with the American Museum of Natural History in New York City. He served as the Chairman of the Department of Ornithology from 1987 to 1992 and was Curator when he retired in 2005. His research took him all over the world, especially South America. Author of about 250 papers and one book, Dr. Vuilleumier taught ornithology at the College of the Atlantic, Bar Harbor, Maine. He watched birds from the Canadian High Arctic and south to Mexico. His life list was about 4,000 species, and he was familiar in the field with all but a handful of the species treated in this book.

### CONSULTANT

Paul Sweet was born in Bristol, England, and has been interested in natural history for as long as he can remember. After completing a degree in zoology at the University of Liverpool, he worked at the Raffles Museum in Singapore. In 1991 he moved to the American Museum of Natural History, where he is now the Collection Manager of the Ornithology Department, the largest bird collection in the world.

## DK BIRD SOUNDS APP

The songs and calls of more than 200 species of birds are featured on the new DK Bird Sounds app. Bird calls are usually short and simple, and are used to pass on information, such as an alarm call that warns of a predator or a contact call that helps birds stay in touch with each other. Songs are longer and made up of a complex set of notes, and are used by males to defend a territory or attract a mate. A bird may have several sounds in its repertoire, but each type is usually constant and unique to a species. As bird sounds carry a long way, you will often hear a bird before you can see it, and this app will help you identify it.

To download the app, go to:

www.dk.com/bird-sounds-na

The birds featured on the app have this symbol next to their common name in this book.

# PREFACE

With its eastern and western volumes, *Birds of North America* attempts to fill a gap in the North American bird book market. No other work offers, for every North American bird species, the same combination of stunning iconography, including beautiful photographs and precise distribution maps; scientifically accurate and readable accounts of salient characteristics; data on identification, behavior, habitat, voice, social structure, nest construction, breeding season, food, and conservation status; diagrams of flight patterns; statistics of size, wingspan, weight, clutch size, number of broods per year, and lifespan; and geographic information about breeding, wintering, and migration. Furthermore, no other bird book introduces, in such an up-to-date and lavishly illustrated manner, general material about birds: their evolution, classification, anatomy, flight, migration, navigation, courtship, mating, nests, and eggs. Scientific jargon has been avoided, but a glossary identifies concepts that benefit from an explanation. With their user-friendly format, these eastern and western guides to *Birds of North America* should permit readers either to enjoy studying one species account at a time, or browse to make cross comparisons.

Many field guides exist, as well as treatises on groups like gulls, hummingbirds, or sparrows; other books are dictionary-like, or focus on species of conservation concern. However, no bird book today can be called a "handbook," a concise reference work that can be conveniently carried around. I hope that these books will be useful in this role to all persons interested in birds, whether young or older, enthusiastic birder or beginner.

Historically, *Birds of North America* can be viewed as a successor to Frank M. Chapman's epochal *Handbook of the Birds of Eastern North America*, published in 1895. During his 54 years at the American Museum of Natural History in New York City, Chapman, dean of American ornithologists, blazed a trail that contributed substantially to what American ornithology, bird conservation, and birding have become. The facts that the new book has the imprint of the American Museum of Natural History, and that I, as its Editor-in-Chief, have worked there for 31 years as Curator of Ornithology and as Chairman of its Department of Ornithology, are not coincidental.

In his Handbook, Chapman treated all birds found in Eastern North America. The description of each species was followed by data on distribution, nest, and eggs, and a readable, often even brilliant text about habitat, behavior, and voice. The illustrations included plates by two pioneer American wildlife artists, Louis Agassiz Fuertes and Francis Lee Jaques, whose style inspired all those who followed them. Some of these

**THRUSHES**
Back in the early 1900s, the great wildlife artist Louis Agassiz Fuertes already painted birds in the style of modern field guides, as shown in this plate from Chapman's *Handbook of the Birds of Eastern North America.*

## EASTERN AND WESTERN REGIONS

In a pioneering essay from 1908, Frank Chapman realized, on the basis of his own fieldwork, that the 100th Meridian corresponded to a rather clear-cut division of North American bird faunas into an Eastern and a Western region. Of course there are exceptions and the 100th Meridian line is not something that the birds themselves recognize. The invisible barrier is located in a transitional zone between habitats that represent, respectively, Eastern versus Western landscape types or biomes. Some, but not all, modern field guides use the 100th Meridian as a division between East and West.

*Arctic Circle*

*Western Region*

*Eastern Region*

*Tropic of Cancer*

*100° W*

plates were, already then, executed in field guide fashion. Anybody who examines Chapman's *Handbook* today is struck by how modern it is. "Museum man" and "birder," Chapman was also a gifted educator and a good writer: a rare combination. Museum research gave him the taxonomic background, and fieldwork throughout North America sharpened his birding skills. As Editor-in-Chief of *Birds of North America*, working in the department Chapman created, enjoying the same extraordinary collection and library resources, and traveling as widely as he did, I have endeavored to make this new book a work of which he would have been proud. Don't leave home without it—and bring along binoculars and a pencil to jot down notes.

*François Vuilleumier*

**François Vuilleumier**
American Museum of Natural History,
New York City
February 2011

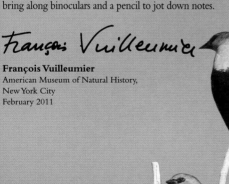

**YELLOW GARLAND**
Abundant in Western marshes, the Yellow-headed Blackbird is not only conspicuous because of the yellow head of males, but also because of their loud and strange vocalizations.

7

# HOW THIS BOOK WORKS

This guide covers over 600 Western North American bird species. The species are arranged into three sections: the first profiles common species, each being given full-page treatment; the second covers rarer birds in quarter-page entries; the third section consists of a list of rare visitors.

## ▽ INTRODUCTION

The species are organized conventionally by order, family, and genus. Related birds appear together, preceded by a group introduction. The book follows the most up-to-date avian classification system, based on the latest scientific research.

**Family Icteridae**

### ORIOLES AND BLACKBIRDS

### MAPS

In this book, North America is defined as the area from the southern tip of Florida and the US–Mexico border northward to the Canadian High Arctic. Each species profile includes a map showing its range, with different colors reflecting seasonal movements.

**KEY**

- Resident all year
- Breeding distribution
- Nonbreeding distribution
- During migration

**GROUP NAME**
The common name of the group each species belongs to is at the top of each page.

**COMMON NAME**

**IN FLIGHT**
Illustrations show the bird in flight, from above and/or below —differences of season, age, or sex are not always visible.

**DESCRIPTION**
Conveys the main features and essential character of the species including:

**VOICE**
A description of the species' calls and songs, given phonetically where possible.

**NESTING**
The type of nest and its usual location; the number of eggs in a clutch; the number of broods in a year; the breeding season.

**FEEDING**
How, where, and what the species feeds on.

**SIMILAR SPECIES**
Similar-looking species are identified and key differences pointed out.

**LENGTH, WINGSPAN, AND WEIGHT**
Length is tip of tail to tip of bill; measurements and weights are averages or ranges.

**SOCIAL**
The social unit the species is usually found in.

**LIFESPAN**
The length of life, in years, obtained from either zoo birds or from banding and recovery records of wild birds. The actual average or maximum life expectancy of many bird species is still unknown.

**STATUS**
The conservation status of the species; (p) means the data available is only provisional. "Localized" means the species may be widespread but restricted to smaller areas of suitable habitat and climatic conditions.

**SYMBOLS**

| | | | |
|---|---|---|---|
| ♂ | Male | ☘ | Spring |
| ♀ | Female | ☼ | Summer |
| ☾ | Juvenile | 🍂 | Autumn |
| ☻ | Immature | ❄ | Winter |

## ▽ COMMON SPECIES

The main section of the book features the 371 most commonly seen bird species in Western North America. Each entry is clear and detailed, following the same format.

ORIOLES AND BLACKBIRDS

Order **Passeriformes**     Family **Icteridae**

# Bullock's Oriole

large white wing patch

MALE

black back and wings

conspicuous white wing patch

IN FLIGHT

orange underparts     MALE

black tail with orange outer feathers

gray and

Bullock's Oriole is the western counterpart of in both behavior and habitat. The two were to belong to a single species, the Northern Oriol because they interbreed where they overlap in th Recent studies, however, suggest that they are sep Unlike many other orioles, Bullock's is more resi parasites and removes cowbird eggs from its nest.
**VOICE** Varied string of one- and two-part notes at the end; similar to, but less melodious, than the
**NESTING** Hanging basket of woven plant strips l branches; 4–5 eggs; 1 brood; March–June.
**FEEDING** Forages for insects, in particular grasshoppers and caterpillars, but also ants, beetle and spiders; nectar and fruit when available.

### SIMILAR SPECIES

**HOODED ORIOLE** see p.465
orange head
long, slender black tail

**BALTIMORE ORIOLE** see p.465
black hood
black face
less white in wings

| Length 6½–7½in (16–19cm) | Wingspan **10–1.** |
|---|---|
| Social **Pairs/Flocks** | Lifespan **Up to 8** |

| DATE SEEN | WHERE |
|---|---|
| | |
| | |
| | |
| | |

378

**HABITAT/BEHAVIOR**
Photographs reveal the species in its habitat or show interesting behavior.

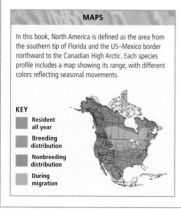

## CLASSIFICATION
The top band of each entry provides the scientific names of order, family, and species (see glossary, pp. 472–473, for full definitions of these terms).

RARE SPECIES

Family Icteridae    Species *Icterus cucullatus*

### Hooded Oriole
Tall palms trees in suburban gardens and urban parks, especially in California, have become popular nesting sites for the Hooded Oriole. Increasing numbers of palm trees, combined with the offerings of nectar intended for hummingbirds have contributed to the expansion of its range from California to the Southwest. By contrast, its numbers in Texas have been shrinking, in part because of its susceptibility to brood parasitism by Brown-headed and Bronzed Cowbirds.
**OCCURRENCE** Breeds in open woodlands along water courses, especially those containing palm trees. Winters in Mexico.
**VOICE** A harsh *sneek* call; song a weakly whinned and rapid series of whistles interspersed with notes often run together; imitates other birds.

MALE (BREEDING)

Length 7–8in (18–20cm)    Wingspan 9–11in (23–28cm)

Family Icteridae    Species *Icterus galbula*

### Baltimore Oriole
The brilliantly colored Baltimore Oriole, the eastern counterpart of the Bullock's Oriole, ranges westward in Canada to Alberta and locally, where British Columbia. At the edge of their respective distributions, in the Great Plains, Baltimore and Bullock's Orioles interbreed. Ornithologists have, at times, considered them to be a single species.
**OCCURRENCE** A variety of woodlands, also parks and gardens. Most winter in Central and South America.
**VOICE** Loud, clear, melodious song comprising several short notes in series, often of varying lengths.

MALE

Length 8–10in (20–24cm)    Wingspan 10–13in (26–30cm)

Species *Icterus bullockii*

black eye stripe
black bib
pale yellow underparts
MALE (1ST FALL)
yellow face, throat, and breast
olive-brown back and wings
olive...
buffy gray belly and rump
FEMALE

Family Icteridae

### Tricolored Blackbird
A close relative of the widespread Red-winged Blackbird, the Tricolored occurs primarily in California, where it breeds in marshes in large colonies, sometimes containing more than 100,000 pairs. After breeding, flocks of Tricolored Blackbirds move to agricultural areas.
**OCCURRENCE** Found in cattail marshes, also in a variety of human-altered upland and wetland habitats, found in western California, northward to Washington State and southward to Baja California.
**VOICE** Both utters call a chip, chunk, and chu-uhk when alarmed; male song a grave, nasal kon-eeeee or krrrreaaaa.

MALE

Length 7–8in (18–24cm)    Wingspan 10–13in (26–33cm)

Family Icteridae    Species *Molothrus aeneus*

### Bronzed Cowbird
The range of this species has been expanding in the US ever since it was first recorded in the early 1900s. This could be the result of human clearing of native habitat and replacing them with agricultural crops. A brood parasite, it has been recorded to lay its eggs in the nests of more than 80 bird species, and their young have fledged from more than 30 of these. The females may work cooperatively to identify and parasitize the nests of other birds.
**VOICE** High and metallic; with short notes, can be described as *gug-gub-buh-tzee-po-tzee*.

MALE

Length 8in (20cm)    Wingspan 13–14in (33–36cm)

RARE SPECIES
Over 200 less common birds are presented on pages 418–469. Arranged in the same group order used in the main section, these entries consist of one photograph of the species accompanied by a description of the bird. Information on geographical distribution, occurrence, and voice is also given.

# VAGRANTS AND ACCIDENTALS

The LIST THAT FOLLOWS includes species that occur rarely in western North America (defined in this book as Canada and the continental United States west of the 100th Meridian). These species can reach North America from Eurasia, Central or South America, Africa, and even Oceania, and Antarctica. The US and Canada can receive birds that drift off course, during migration, from eastern Asia across the Pacific Ocean, or from Europe across the Atlantic. Western Alaska has a high concentration of "vagrants" because the southwesternmost tip of the state forms a series of islands, the Aleutians, that reach almost all the way across the Bering Sea to the Russian Far East.

The occurrence of "vagrant" species is classified by the American Birding Association, depending on their relative frequency, and this terminology is followed in the "status" column for each species. **Rare** species are reported every year in small numbers. **Casual** visitors have been reported at least a dozen times. **Accidental** species have been recorded no more than five times. However, because of climatological, biological, and other factors, the status of "vagrant" species is constantly changing.

| COMMON NAME | SCIENTIFIC NAME | FAMILY NAME | STATUS |
|---|---|---|---|
| **Ducks, Geese, and Swans** | | | |
| Whooper Swan | *Cygnus cygnus* | Anatidae | Rare visitor from Eurasia to Aleutians, south to California |
| Garganey | *Spatula querquedula* | Anatidae | Rare visitor from Eurasia to the Pribilofs, casual in California |
| Eurasian Wigeon | *Mareca penelope* | Anatidae | Rare visitor from Eurasia to West Coast |
| American Black Duck | *Anas rubripes* | Anatidae | Introduced to British Columbia and Washington state |
| Tufted Duck | *Aythya fuligula* | Anatidae | Rare visitor from Eurasia to Alaska, casual along the West Coast |
| Smew | *Mergellus albellus* | Anatidae | Rare visitor from Eurasia to Alaska, casual to California |
| **Cuckoos** | | | |
| Common Cuckoo | *Cuculus canorus* | Cuculidae | Casual visitor from Eurasia to islands off Alaska |
| Oriental Cuckoo | *Cuculus optatus* | Cuculidae | Casual visitor from Asia to Aleutian and Pribilof Islands |
| **Hummingbirds** | | | |
| Xantus's Hummingbird | *Hylocharis xantusii* | Trochilidae | Accidental from Baja California to S California and British Columbia |
| **Shorebirds, Gulls, Auks, and Relatives** | | | |
| Common Ringed Plover | *Charadrius hiaticula* | Charadriidae | Casual visitor from Eurasia to the Aleutian and Pribilof Islands |
| Lesser Sand Plover | *Charadrius mongolus* | Charadriidae | Rare visitor from Asia to West Alaska and Pacific Coast |
| Red-necked Stint | *Calidris ruficollis* | Scolopacidae | Rare visitor from Siberia to both coasts in summer and fall |
| Temminck's Stint | *Calidris temminckii* | Scolopacidae | Rare visitor from Eurasia to Alaska and Pacific Northwest |
| Long-toed Stint | *Calidris subminuta* | Scolopacidae | Rare visitor from Asia to Aleutians, Pribilofs, Pacific Coast to California |
| Sharp-tailed Sandpiper | *Calidris acuminata* | Scolopacidae | Rare visitor from eastern Asia to Alaska and Pacific Coast to California |
| Curlew Sandpiper | *Calidris ferruginea* | Scolopacidae | Rare visitor from Eurasia to Alaska and Pacific Coast |
| Ruff | *Calidris pugnax* | Scolopacidae | Rare visitor from Eurasia to Alaska and Pacific Coast |
| American Woodcock | *Scolopax minor* | Scolopacidae | Rare visitor from the East to the West and Southwest |
| Common Sandpiper | *Actitis hypoleucos* | Scolopacidae | Casual visitor from Eurasia to western Alaska and the Aleutian Islands |
| Black-tailed Godwit | *Limosa limosa* | Scolopacidae | Casual visitor from Eurasia to the Aleutian and Pribilof Islands |
| Wood Sandpiper | *Tringa glareola* | Scolopacidae | Rare visitor from Eurasia to Alaska and south to California |
| Gray-tailed Tattler | *Tringa brevipes* | Scolopacidae | Rare visitor from Asia to Alaska, southward to California |
| Great Black-backed Gull | *Larus marinus* | Laridae | Casual visitor from the East to several western states |
| Laughing Gull | *Leucophaeus atricilla* | Laridae | Rare visitor from Mexico to SouthCalifornia, casual from the East to Colorado and West Coast |
| Slaty-backed Gull | *Larus schistisagus* | Laridae | Casual visitor from Asia to Alaska and West Coast |
| Ivory Gull | *Pagophila eburnea* | Laridae | Casual visitor from the Arctic to Colorado, California, and British Columbia |

470

## COLOR BAND
The information bands at the top and bottom of each entry are color-coded for each family.

## PHOTOGRAPHS
These illustrate the species in different views and plumage variations. Significant differences relating to age, sex, and season (breeding/nonbreeding) are shown and the images labeled accordingly; if there is no variation, the images have no label. Unless stated otherwise, the bird shown is an adult.

## FLIGHT PATTERNS
This feature illustrates and briefly describes the way the species flies. See panel below.

VAGRANTS
Very rare and accidental visitors are listed at the back of the book with a brief indication of the species' status.

...GHT: full, powerful wingbeats, resulting "heavier" flight aspect than similar species.

...rred
...ng.

## OCCURRENCE
Found in the western US; breeds commonly in riverside woodlands with willows and cottonwoods; also mixed hardwood forests, mesquite woodland, and groves of fruit trees. After breeding, Bullock's Orioles migrate southward and spend the winter from Mexico to Nicaragua.

...HORNS
...riole
...with long
...erturbed.

Weight 1⅛–1⅝oz (30–45g)
Status Secure

## MAPS
See panel, left. The occurrence caption describes the bird's preferred habitats and range within North America.

---

## FLIGHT PATTERNS

Simple line diagrams are used to illustrate eight basic flight patterns.

wingbeats

**Woodpecker-like:** bursts of wingbeats between deeply undulating glides.

**Finch-like:** light, bouncy action with flurries of wingbeats between deep, undulating glides.

**Grouse-like:** bursts of wingbeats between short, straight glides.

**Accipiter Hawk-like:** straight, with several quick, deep beats between short glides.

**Gull-like:** continually flapping, with slow, steady wingbeats; also glides.

**Duck-like:** continually flapping, with fast wingbeats.

**Buteo-like:** deep, slow wingbeats between soaring glides.

**Swallow-like:** swooping, with bursts of wingbeats between glides.

# EVOLUTION

ORNITHOLOGISTS AGREE THAT BIRDS evolved from dinosaurs about 150 million years ago, but there is still debate about the dinosaur group from which they descended. Around 10,000 species of birds exist today, living in many different kinds of habitats across the world, from desert to Arctic tundra. To reconstruct how avian evolution occurred, from *Archaeopteryx* on up to the present, scientists use many clues, especially fossil birds, and now DNA.

**MISSING LINK?**
*Archaeopteryx*, shown here, is a 145-million-year-old fossil. It had dinosaur-like teeth, but bird-like feathers.

## SPECIATION

What are species and how do they evolve? Species are biological entities. When two species of a genus overlap they rarely interbreed and produce hybrids. The Northern Flicker has an eastern (yellow-shafted) and a western (red-shafted) form; after the discovery that these two forms interbreed in the Great Plains, the flickers, which were formerly "split" into two species, are now considered one. In other cases, a previously single species, such as the Sage Grouse, has been divided. Such examples illustrate how species evolve, first by geographic separation, followed in time by overlap. This process can take from tens of thousands to millions of years.

### BIRD GENEALOGY

The diagram below is called a phylogeny, and shows how selected groups of birds are related to each other. The timescale at the top of the diagram is derived from both fossil and DNA evidence, which allows ornithologists to estimate when different lineages of birds diverged. The names of groups shown in bold are those living in North America.

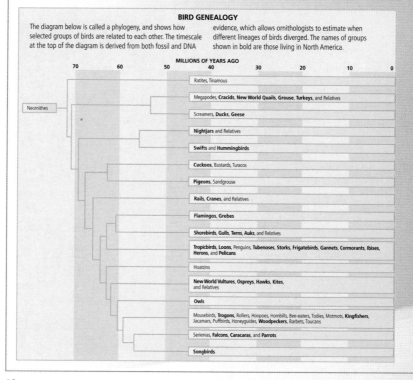

**MILLIONS OF YEARS AGO**

| 70 | 60 | 50 | 40 | 30 | 20 | 10 | 0 |

Neornithes

- Ratites, Tinamous
- Megapodes, **Cracids**, **New World Quails**, **Grouse**, **Turkeys**, and Relatives
- Screamers, **Ducks**, **Geese**
- **Nightjars** and Relatives
- **Swifts** and **Hummingbirds**
- **Cuckoos**, Bustards, Turacos
- **Pigeons**, Sandgrouse
- **Rails**, **Cranes**, and Relatives
- **Flamingos**, **Grebes**
- **Shorebirds**, **Gulls**, **Terns**, **Auks**, and Relatives
- **Tropicbirds**, **Loons**, Penguins, **Tubenoses**, **Storks**, **Frigatebirds**, **Gannets**, **Cormorants**, **Ibises**, **Herons**, and **Pelicans**
- Hoatzins
- **New World Vultures**, **Ospreys**, **Hawks**, **Kites**, and Relatives
- **Owls**
- Mousebirds, **Trogons**, Rollers, Hoopoes, Hornbills, Bee-eaters, Todies, Motmots, **Kingfishers**, Jacamars, Puffbirds, Honeyguides, **Woodpeckers**, Barbets, Toucans
- Seriemas, **Falcons**, **Caracaras**, and **Parrots**
- **Songbirds**

**BLENDING IN**
This magnificent species is diurnal, unlike most other owls, which are nocturnal. The Snowy Owl breeds in the Arctic tundra, and if the ground is covered with snow, it blends in perfectly.

## CONVERGENCE

The evolutionary process during which birds of two distantly related groups develop similarities is called convergence. Carrion-eating birds of prey are one example. Old World vultures belong to the hawk family (Accipitridae), while New World vultures are more closely related to storks. However, both groups are characterized by hooked bills, bare heads, and weak talons. Convergence can involve anatomy and behavior, as in the vultures, or other traits, including habitat preference.

**PARALLEL EVOLUTION**
The African longclaws (family Motacillidae) and North American meadowlarks (family Icteridae) show convergence in plumage color and pattern. Both groups live in grasslands.

**CAPE LONGCLAW**

**WESTERN MEADOWLARK**

## EXTINCTION

During the last 150 years, North America has lost the Passenger Pigeon, the Great Auk, the Carolina Parakeet, the Labrador Duck, and the Eskimo Curlew. Relentless hunting and habitat destruction are the main factors that have led to extinction. Some species that seemed doomed have had a reprieve. Thanks to a breeding and release program, the majestic California Condor soars once again over the Grand Canyon.

**OVERHUNTING**
The Passenger Pigeon was eradicated as a result of over-hunting.

### CLASSIFYING BIRDS

All past and present animal life is named and categorized into groups. Classifications reflect the genealogical relationships among groups, based on traits such as color, bones, or DNA. Birds make up the class "Aves," which includes "orders;" each "order" is made up of one or more "families." "Genus" is a subdivision of "family," and contains one or more "species." A species is a unique group of similar organisms that interbreed and produce fertile offspring. Some species have distinct populations, which are known as subspecies.

| | |
|---|---|
| Aves (Birds) | Class |
| Passeriformes (Songbirds) | Order |
| Parulidae (Wood Warblers) | Family |
| Setophaga | Genus |
| Setophaga castanea — Setophaga palmarum — Setophaga tigrina | Species |
| S. p. palmarum | Subspecies |

# ANATOMY AND FLIGHT

IN SPITE OF THEIR EXTERNAL DIVERSITY, birds are remarkably similar internally. To allow flight, birds have a skeleton that is both rigid and light. Rigidity is achieved by the fusion of some bones, especially the lower vertebrae, while lightness is maintained by having hollow limb bones. These are connected to air sacs, which, in turn, are connected to the bird's lungs.

**SKELETON**
Avian skeletal features include the furcula (wishbone), the keeled sternum (breastbone), and the fused tail vertebrae.

## FLIGHT ADAPTATIONS
For birds to be able to fly, they need light and rigid bones, a lightweight skull, and hollow wing and leg bones. In addition, pouch-like air sacs are connected to hollow bones, which reduce a bird's weight. The air sacs also function as a cooling system, which birds need because they have a high metabolic rate. The breast muscles, which are crucial for flight, attach to the keeled sternum (breastbone). Wing and tail feathers help support birds when airborne. Feathers wear out, and are regularly replaced during molt.

**BIRD BONE STRUCTURE**
Most bird bones, except those of penguins and other flightless birds, are hollow, which reduces their weight. A honeycomb of internal struts makes the bones remarkably strong.

## LEGS, FEET, AND TOES
When you look at a bird's leg, you do not see its thigh, which is inside the body cavity, but the leg from the knee down. When we talk about a bird's feet we really mean its toes. The shin is a fused tibia and fibula. This fused bone plus the heel are known as the "tarso-metatarsus." The four examples below illustrate some toe arrangements.

**UNDERPARTS**
Underwing coverts have a regular pattern of overlapping rows. Short feathers cover the head, breast, belly, and flanks. In most birds, the toes are unfeathered.

*neck vertebrae*
*"forearm"*
*"har*
*bill*
*furcula*
*fused t vertebr*
*keeled sternum*
*secondaries*
*tail feathers*
*uppertail coverts*
*rump*
*tertials*
*scapulars*
*primaries*
*axillaries*
*breast*
*belly*
*toes*
*undertail coverts*

*enables grip on ground*

**WALKING**
Ground-foraging birds usually have a long hind claw.

*enables strong grip on branches*

**CLIMBING**
Most climbers have two toes forward and two backward.

*webbing provides thrust in water*

**SWIMMING**
Waterbirds have webbing between their toes.

*used to grasp prey*

**HUNTING**
Birds of prey have powerful toes and strong, sharp claws.

## FEATHERS

All birds, by definition, have feathers. These remarkable structures, which are modified scales, serve two main functions: insulation and flight. Special muscles allow birds to raise their feathers or to flatten them against the body. In cold weather, fluffed-out feathers keep an insulating layer of air between the skin and the outside. This insulating capacity is why humans often find wearing "down" jackets so effective against the cold. The first feathers that chicks have after hatching are down feathers. The rigidity of the flight feathers helps create a supporting surface that birds use to generate thrust and lift.

**TYPES OF FEATHERS**
Birds have three main kinds of feathers: down, contour, and flight feathers. The rigid axis of all feathers is called the "rachis."

**DOWN FEATHER** **CONTOUR FEATHER** **FLIGHT FEATHER**

## WING FUNCTIONS

Flapping, soaring, gliding, and hovering are among the ways birds use their wings. They also exhibit colors or patterns as part of territorial and courtship displays. Several birds, such as herons, open their wings like an umbrella when foraging in water for fish. An important aspect of wings is their relationship to a bird's weight. The ratio of a bird's wing area to its weight is called wing loading, which may be affected also by wing shape. An eagle has a large wing area to weight ratio, which means it has lower wing loading, whereas a swallow has a small wing area to weight ratio, and therefore high wing loading. This means that the slow, soaring eagle is capable of much more energy-efficient flight than the fast, agile swallow.

**LONG AND BROAD**
The broad, long, rectangular wings of an eagle allow it to soar. The outstretched alulae (bastard wings) give it extra lift.

**POINTED**
Broad at their base and tapering toward a point, and bent at the wrist, a swallow's wings enable fast flight and sharp turns.

**SHORT AND ROUND**
Short, broad, and round wings permit warblers to move easily in dense vegetation.

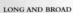

primary coverts

secondary coverts

coverts

neck

nape

crown

chin

throat

mantle

alula (bastard wing)

**UPPERPARTS**
The wing feathers from the "hand" of the bird are the primaries, and those on the "forearm" are the secondaries. Each set has its accompanying row of coverts. The tertials are adjacent to the secondaries.

### WING AERODYNAMICS

The supporting surface of a bird's wing enables it to takeoff and stay aloft. Propulsion and lift are linked in birds—which use their wings for both—unlike in airplanes in which these two functions are separate. Large and heavy birds, like swans, flap their wings energetically to create propulsion, and need a long, watery runway before they can fly off. The California Condor can takeoff from a cliff with little or no wing flapping, but Black and Turkey Vultures hop up from carrion, then flap vigorously, and finally use air flowing across their wings to soar. This diagram shows how airflow affects lift.

faster airflow

low air pressure

slower airflow

high air pressure

cross section of bird's wing

# MIGRATION

U NTIL RECENTLY, THE MECHANICS, or the "how" of
migration, was poorly understood. Today, however,
ornithologists know that birds use a variety of cues
including visual and magnetic, whether they migrate
by day or by night. Birds do not leave northern breeding
areas because of the winter cold, but because day-length
is getting shorter and food scarcer.

**NIGHT MIGRANTS**
During migration, ornithologists can point
a telescope on the moon and count the birds
that cross its surface.

**REFUELING**
Red Knots stop on their journey
from Tierra del Fuego to the Arctic
to eat horseshoe crab eggs.

## INSTINCTIVE MOVE

Even though many birds use visual cues and landmarks during their migration,
for example, birds of prey flying along the Appalachians, "instinctive" behavior
must control much of how and where they move. Instinct is a loose term that
is hard to define, but ornithologists generally understand it as a genetically
programmed activity. They assume that natural selection has molded a behavior
as complex as migration by acting on birds' DNA; this hypothesis is reasonable,
but hard to prove. Nevertheless, it would seem to be the only explanation why
many juvenile shorebirds leave their breeding grounds after their parents, and
yet find their way to their final destination.

## NAVIGATION

One of the most puzzling aspects of migration
is understanding how birds make their way
from their summer breeding grounds to their
winter destination. Ornithologists have devised
experiments to determine the different
components. Some of these components are
innate, others learned. For example, if visual
landmarks are hidden by fog, a faint sun can give
birds a directional clue; if heavy clouds hide the
sun, then the birds' magnetic compass may be
used to ascertain their direction.

**FINDING THE WAY**
Birds coordinate information their brains receive
from the sun, moon, stars, landmarks, and
magnetite, or iron oxide, and use it as a compass.

**OVERLAND FLIERS**
Sandhill Cranes migrate over hills and
mountains, from their Arctic tundra
breeding grounds to the marshes of
the Platte River in the midwestern US.

# GLOBETROTTERS

Some bird species in North America are year-round residents, although a few individuals of these species move away from where they hatched at some time in the year. However, a large number of North American species are migratory. A few species breed in Alaska, but winter on remote southwest Pacific islands. Others breed in the Canadian Arctic Archipelago, fly over land and the Pacific Ocean, and spend the winter at sea off the coast of Peru. Many songbirds fly from the Gulf Coast to northern South America. The most amazing globetrotters, such as the Red Knot, fly all the way to Tierra del Fuego, making only a few stops along the way after their short breeding season in the Arctic tundra. The return journeys of some of these travelers are not over the same route— instead, their entire trip is elliptical in shape.

**EPIC JOURNEY**
The Arctic Tern is a notorious long-distance migrant, breeding in Arctic and subarctic regions, and wintering in the pack ice of Antarctica before returning north, a round-trip distance of at least 25,000 miles (40,000km).

**KEY**
→ Trans-Pacific route
→ Coastal Pacific route
→ Arctic to Pacific route
→ Trans-Gulf route
→ Atlantic to Caribbean route
→ Argentina to Arctic route
→ Arctic-Atlantic Neotropical route

**NEOTROPICAL MIGRANT**
Many wood warblers, such as this Blackpoll Warbler, breed in boreal forests, before migrating to their wintering grounds in the Caribbean, or Central or South America.

**MIGRATION ROUTES**
The map above shows the range of migration routes that some North American species take to and from their breeding grounds.

**V-FORMATION**
Geese and other large waterbirds fly in a V-formation. The leader falls back and is replaced by another individual, saving energy for all the birds.

**PARTIAL MIGRANT**

The American Robin is a good example of a partial migrant, a species in which the birds of some populations are resident, whereas others migrate out of their breeding range. Most Canadian populations of the American Robin fly south, US populations are largely resident, and quite a few birds from either population spend the winter in the Southwest, Florida, or Mexico.

**KEY** ▪ Breeding distribution
▪ Resident all year
▪ Nonbreeding distribution

# COURTSHIP AND MATING

WHETHER MONOGAMOUS OR NOT, males and females need to mate for their species to perpetuate itself. With most species, the male plays the dominant role of advertising a territory to potential mates using vocal or visual displays. Females then select a male, and if the two respond positively to each other, a period of courtship follows, ending in mating. The next steps are nest building, egg laying, and rearing the young.

**DANCING CRANES**
During courtship, Sandhill Cranes perform spectacular dances, the two birds of a pair leaping into the air with wings opened and legs splayed.

## DISPLAYS

Mutual attraction between the sexes starts with some sort of display, usually performed by the male. These displays can take a number of forms, from flashing dazzling breeding plumage, conducting elaborate dancing rituals, performing complex songs, offering food or nesting material, or actually building a nest. Some birds, such as grebes, have fascinatingly intricate ceremonies, in which both male and female simultaneously perform the same water-dance. Because they are usually very ritualized, displays help ornithologists understand relationships among birds.

**WELCOME HOME**
Northern Gannets greet their mates throughout the breeding season by rubbing bills together and opening their wings.

**LADIES' CHOICE**
On a lek (communal display area), male Sage-Grouse inflate chest pouches while females flock around them and select a mate.

## COURTSHIP FEEDING

In some species, males offer food to their mate to maintain the pair-bond. For example, male terns routinely bring small fish to their mates in a nesting colony, spreading their wings and tail until the females accept the fish.

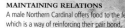

**MAINTAINING RELATIONS**
A male Northern Cardinal offers food to the female, which is a way of reinforcing their pair bond.

## BREEDING

After mating, a nest is made, often by the female, where she lays from one to a dozen eggs. Not all birds make nests, however. Nightjars, for example, lay their eggs directly on the ground. In many species, incubation doesn't start until the female has laid all the eggs. Incubation, usually done by the female, varies from 12 days to about 45 days. Songbirds breeding from the temperate zone northward to the Arctic show a range in clutch size with more eggs produced in the North than in the South. The breeding process can fail at any stage, for example, a predator can eat the eggs or the chicks. Some birds will nest again after such a failure, but others give up breeding for the season.

**MATING TERNS**
Mating is usually brief, and typically takes place on a perch or on the ground, but some species, like swifts, mate in the air. This male Black Tern balances himself by opening his wings.

**MUTUAL PREENING**
Many species of albatrosses, like these Black-footed Albatrosses from the Pacific, preen each other, with one bird softly nibbling the feathers on the other's head.

**POLYGAMY**
This Winter Wren collects nesting material for one of the several nests he will build.

**MONOGAMOUS BONDS**
Some birds, such as Snow Geese, remain paired for life after establishing a bond.

**SINGLE FATHER**

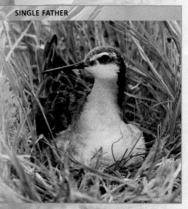

A male Red-necked Phalarope incubates eggs in the Arctic tundra. Phalaropes are well known for their reversal of breeding roles. The female, who is the larger and more colorful of the two sexes, aggressively competes for males, and after mating with several of them, plays no role in nest building, incubation, or caring for chicks, but tends to her territory instead. Although the chicks can feed by themselves immediately after hatching, they remain with a male before growing feathers and living on their own.

17

# NESTS AND EGGS

**M**OST BIRD SPECIES BUILD THEIR OWN NEST, which is a necessary container for their eggs. Exceptions include some species of cuckoos and cowbirds, that lay their eggs in other species' nests. Nest-building is often done by the female alone, but in some species the male may help or even build it himself. Eggs are incubated either by females only, or by males and females, depending on the species. Eggs, consisting of 60 percent water, contain a fatty yolk for nourishment of the embryo, as well as sugars and proteins. Eggshells are hard enough to sustain the weight of incubating parents, yet soft enough for a chick to break its way out. Hatching is an energy-draining process, and can last for several hours.

## NEST TYPES

In addition to the four types shown below, nests range from a simple scrape in the ground with a few added pebbles to an elaborate woven basket-like structure. Plant matter forms basic nest material. This includes twigs, grass stems, bark, lichens, mosses, plant down, and rootlets. Some birds add mud to their nest for strength. Others incorporate animal hair or feathers to improve its softness and insulation. Female eider ducks line their nest with down feathers plucked from their belly. Some birds include bits of plastic or threads in their nests. Several species of flycatchers add shed snakeskins to their nests. Many birds make their nest or lay their eggs deep inside the empty burrows of other animals. Burrowing Owls nest in prairie dog burrows, where they coexist with the rodents.

**UNTIDY NEST**
Huge stick nests, built on top of dead trees, are the hallmark of Ospreys. They also readily use custom-made nesting platforms erected by humans specifically for them.

**EGG CUP**
A clutch of three Blue Robin's eggs rest in a cup lined with grass stems and strengthened with mud. Robins build their nests either in shrubs or trees.

**NATURAL CAVITY**
This Northern Saw-whet Owl is nesting at the bottom of a cavity, in a tree that has probably been excavated by a woodpecker.

**NEST BOX**
Cavity-nesting bluebirds have been affected by habitat loss, and compete with other birds for nest sites, which may include manmade structures.

**COMPLEX WEAVE**
New World orioles weave intricate nests from dried grass stems and other plant material, and hang them from the tip of branches, often high up in trees.

## EGG SHAPES

There are six basic egg shapes among birds, as illustrated to the right. The most common egg shapes are longitudinal or elliptical. Murres lay pear-shaped eggs, an adaptation for nesting on the narrow ledges of sea cliffs; if an egg rolls, it does so in a tight circle and remains on the ledge. Spherical eggs with irregular red blotches are characteristic of birds of prey. Pigeons and doves lay white oval eggs, usually two per clutch. The eggs of many songbirds, including sparrows and buntings, are conical and have a variety of dark markings on a pale background.

**COLOR AND SHAPE**
Birds' eggs vary widely in terms of shape, colors, and markings. The American Robin's egg on the left is a beautiful blue.

**PEAR SHAPED**    **LONGITUDINAL**    **ELLIPTICAL**

**OVAL**    **CONICAL**    **SPHERICAL**

**NEAT ARRANGEMENT**
Many shorebirds, such as plovers and sandpipers, lay four conical eggs with the narrow ends pointed in toward each other.

## HATCHING CONDITION

After a period of incubation, which varies from species to species, chicks break the eggshell, some of them using an egg tooth, a special bill feature that falls off after hatching. After a long and exhausting struggle, the chick eventually tumbles out of the shell fragments. The transition from the watery medium inside the egg to the air outside is a tremendous physiological switch. Once free of their shell, the hatchlings recover from the exertion and either beg food from their parents or feed on their own.

**FOOD DELIVERY**
Tern chicks, although able to move around, cannot catch the fish they need to survive, and must rely on their parents to provide food until they can fly.

**PARENTAL CARE**
Birds of prey, such as these Snowy Owl owlets, need their parents to care for them longer than some other bird species, and do not leave the nest until their feathers are sufficiently developed for their first flight.

**FAST FEEDER**
Coots, gallinules, and rails hatch with a complete covering of down, and can feed by themselves immediately after birth.

### BROOD PARASITISM

Neither cowbirds in the New World nor cuckoos in the Old World make a nest. Female cowbirds deposit up to 20 eggs in the nests of several other species. If the foster parents accept the foreign egg, they will feed the chick of the parasite until it fledges. In the picture below, a tiny wood warbler feeds its adopted chick, a huge cowbird hatchling that has overgrown the nest. Whereas some host species readily incubate the foreign egg, others reject it or abandon the nest.

# IDENTIFICATION

$S$OME SPECIES ARE EASY TO IDENTIFY, but in many other cases, species identification is tricky. In North America, a notoriously difficult group in terms of identification is the wood warblers, especially in the fall, when most species have similar greenish or yellowish plumage.

**BLUEBIRD VARIATIONS**
Species of the genus *Sialia*, such as the Mountain Bluebird above, and the Eastern Bluebird left, are easy to identify.

## GEOGRAPHIC RANGE

Each bird species in North America lives in a particular area that is called its geographic range. Some species have a restricted range; for example, Kirtland's Warbler occurs only in Michigan. Other species, such as the Red-tailed Hawk, range from coast to coast and from northern Canada to Mexico. Species with a broad range usually breed in a variety of vegetation types, while species with narrow ranges often have a specialized habitat; Kirtland's Warblers' is jack pine woodland.

bright blue wings

white belly

chestnut flanks

## SIZE AND WEIGHT

From hummingbird to Tundra Swan and from extra-light (1/16oz) to heavy (15 lb), such is the range of sizes and weights found among the bird species of North America. Size can be measured in several ways, for example the length of a bird from bill-tip to tail-tip, or its wingspan. Size can also be estimated for a given bird in relationship with another that is familiar. For example, the less familiar Bicknell's Thrush can be compared with the well-known American Robin.

**SIZE MATTERS**
Smaller shorebirds, with shorter legs and bills, forage in shallow water, but larger ones have longer legs and bills and can feed in deeper water.

**SEMIPALMATED PLOVER**   **LESSER YELLOWLEGS**   **HUDSONIAN GODWIT**   **LONG-BILLED CURLEW**

## GENERAL SHAPE

Just as birds come in all sizes, their body shapes vary, but size and shape are not necessarily correlated. In the dense reed beds in which it lives, the American Bittern's long and thin body blends in with stems. The round-bodied Sedge Wren hops in shrubby vegetation or near the ground where slimness is not an advantage. In dense forest canopy, the slender and long-tailed Yellow-billed Cuckoo can maneuver easily. Mourning Doves inhabit rather open habitats and their plumpness is irrelevant when it comes to their living space. The relative shape and length of wings and tail are often, but not always, an important component of how a particular bird species behaves.

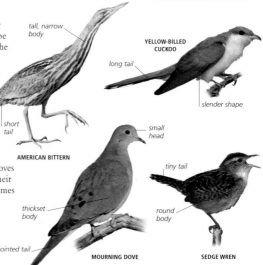

tall, narrow body

**YELLOW-BILLED CUCKOO**

long tail

slender shape

short tail

**AMERICAN BITTERN**

small head

tiny tail

thickset body

round body

long, pointed tail

**MOURNING DOVE**   **SEDGE WREN**

## BILL SHAPE

These images show a range of bill shapes and sizes relative to the bird's head size. In general, bill form, including length or thickness, corresponds to the kinds of food a birds consumes. With its pointed bill, the Mountain Chickadee picks tiny insects from crevices in tree bark. At another extreme, dowitchers probe mud with their long thin bills, feeling for worms. The avocet swishes its bill back and forth in briny water in search of shrimp.

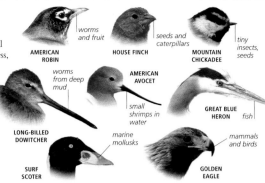

worms and fruit
**AMERICAN ROBIN**

seeds and caterpillars
**HOUSE FINCH**

**MOUNTAIN CHICKADEE**
tiny insects, seeds

worms from deep mud
**AMERICAN AVOCET**
small shrimps in water

**LONG-BILLED DOWITCHER**

**GREAT BLUE HERON** fish

marine mollusks
**SURF SCOTER**

mammals and birds
**GOLDEN EAGLE**

## WING SHAPE

Birds' wing shapes are correlated with their flight style. The long, round-tipped wings of the Red-tailed Hawk are perfect for soaring, while the tiny wings of hummingbirds are exactly what is needed to hover in front of flowers and then to back away after a meal of nectar. When flushed, quails flutter with their round wings and quickly drop down.

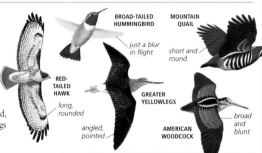

**BROAD-TAILED HUMMINGBIRD**
just a blur in flight

**MOUNTAIN QUAIL**
short and round

**RED-TAILED HAWK**
long, rounded

**GREATER YELLOWLEGS**
angled, pointed

**AMERICAN WOODCOCK**
broad and blunt

## TAIL SHAPE

It is not clear why some songbirds, like the American Goldfinch, have a notched tail while other similar-sized birds do not. Tail shapes vary as much as wing shapes, but are not so easily linked to a function or to the habitat in which a given species lives. Irrespective of shape, tails are needed for balance. In some birds, tail shape, color, and pattern are used in courtship displays or in defensive displays when threatened.

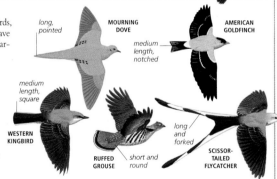

long, pointed
**MOURNING DOVE**

medium length, notched
**AMERICAN GOLDFINCH**

medium length, square
**WESTERN KINGBIRD**

**RUFFED GROUSE** short and round

long and forked
**SCISSOR-TAILED FLYCATCHER**

## COLORS AND MARKINGS

Melanin and carotenoid pigments determine color. Gray and brown birds have melanin (under hormonal influence), yellow and red ones have carotenoid (derived from food). Flamingos are pink because they eat carotenoid-rich crustaceans. Diversity in color and markings also results from scattering of white light by feathers (producing blue colors) and optical interference (iridescence) because of the structural properties of some feathers (as in hummingbirds). Bare patches of skin are often used in displays.

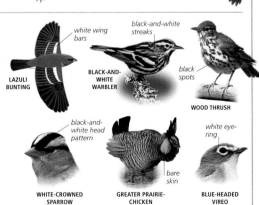

white wing bars
**LAZULI BUNTING**

black-and-white streaks
**BLACK-AND-WHITE WARBLER**

black spots
**WOOD THRUSH**

black-and-white head pattern
**WHITE-CROWNED SPARROW**

**GREATER PRAIRIE-CHICKEN**
bare skin

white eye-ring
**BLUE-HEADED VIREO**

# DUCKS, GEESE, AND SWANS

RECENT GENETIC studies indicate that waterfowl are most closely related to members of the order Galliformes. Most species of waterfowl molt all their flight feathers at once after breeding, making them flightless for several weeks until they grow new ones.

## GEESE
Ornithologists group geese and swans together into the subfamily Anserinae. Geese are generally intermediate between swans and ducks in body size and neck length. They are more terrestrial than either swans or ducks, often being seen grazing on dry land. Like swans, geese pair for life. They are highly social, and most species are migratory, flying south for the winter in large flocks.

## SWANS
Swans are essentially large, long-necked geese. Their heavier weight makes them ungainly on land, and they tend to be more aquatic than their smaller relatives. On water, however, they are extremely graceful. When feeding, a swan stretches its long neck to reach water plants at the bottom, submerging up to half its body as it does so. The Trumpeter Swan of the Northwest is North America's largest native waterfowl, growing up to 5ft (1.5m) long, and weighing up to 25lb (12kg).

## DUCKS
Classified into several subfamilies, ducks are more varied than swans or geese, with many more species. They are loosely grouped by their feeding habits. Dabblers, or puddle ducks, such as the Mallard, teals, and wigeons, eat plants and invertebrates. They feed by upending "on the surface of shallow water. By contrast diving ducks, a group that includes scaups, scoters, eiders, mergansers, and the Ruddy Duck, dive deep underwater for their food.

**INSTANT TAKEOFF**
Puddle ducks like the Mallard can shoot straight out of the water and into the air.

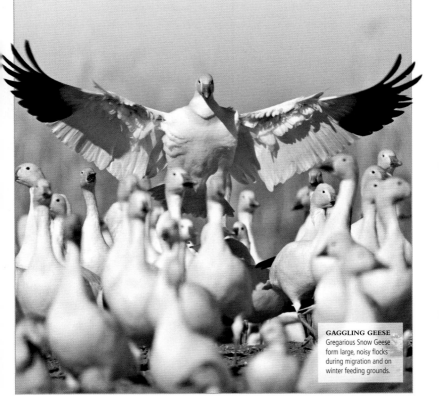

**GAGGLING GEESE**
Gregarious Snow Geese form large, noisy flocks during migration and on winter feeding grounds.

| Order **Anseriformes** | Family **Anatidae** | Species *Anser caerulescens* |

# Snow Goose 🔊

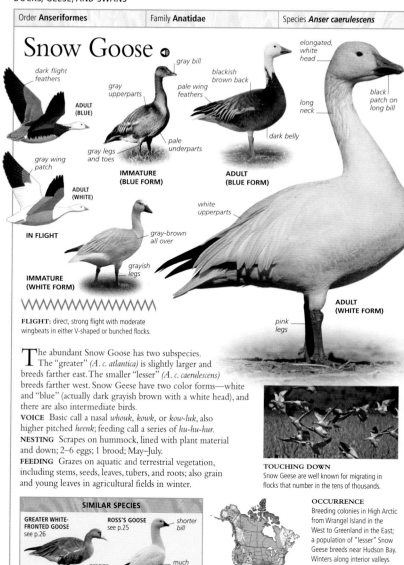

dark flight feathers

**ADULT (BLUE)**

gray bill

gray upperparts

blackish brown back

pale wing feathers

elongated, white head

black patch on long bill

long neck

dark belly

gray legs and toes

pale underparts

**IMMATURE (BLUE FORM)**

**ADULT (BLUE FORM)**

gray wing patch

**ADULT (WHITE)**

**IN FLIGHT**

gray-brown all over

grayish legs

**IMMATURE (WHITE FORM)**

white upperparts

white upperparts

**ADULT (WHITE FORM)**

pink legs

**FLIGHT:** direct, strong flight with moderate wingbeats in either V-shaped or bunched flocks.

The abundant Snow Goose has two subspecies. The "greater" (*A. c. atlantica*) is slightly larger and breeds farther east. The smaller "lesser" (*A. c. caerulescens*) breeds farther west. Snow Geese have two color forms—white and "blue" (actually dark grayish brown with a white head), and there are also intermediate birds.

**VOICE** Basic call a nasal *whouk*, *kowk*, or *kow-luk*, also higher pitched *heenk*; feeding call a series of *hu-hu-hur*.
**NESTING** Scrapes on hummock, lined with plant material and down; 2–6 eggs; 1 brood; May–July.
**FEEDING** Grazes on aquatic and terrestrial vegetation, including stems, seeds, leaves, tubers, and roots; also grain and young leaves in agricultural fields in winter.

**TOUCHING DOWN**
Snow Geese are well known for migrating in flocks that number in the tens of thousands.

### SIMILAR SPECIES

**GREATER WHITE-FRONTED GOOSE** see p.26

orange legs

**ROSS'S GOOSE** see p.25

shorter bill

much smaller overall

**OCCURRENCE**
Breeding colonies in High Arctic from Wrangel Island in the West to Greenland in the East; a population of "lesser" Snow Geese breeds near Hudson Bay. Winters along interior valleys westward to coastal lowlands and central plateau of Mexico; Atlantic populations winter in coastal marshes.

| Length **27–33in (69–83cm)** | Wingspan **4¼–5½ft (1.3–1.7m)** | Weight **3¾–6½lb (1.7–3kg)** |
| Social **Flocks** | Lifespan **Up to 27 years** | Status **Secure** |

| DATE SEEN | WHERE | NOTES |
|---|---|---|
| | | |
| | | |
| | | |
| | | |
| | | |

| Order **Anseriformes** | Family **Anatidae** | Species *Anser rossii* |

# Ross's Goose

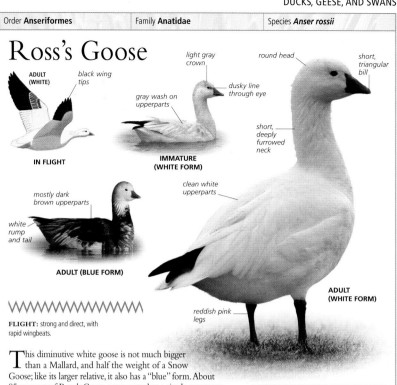

**ADULT (WHITE)** black wing tips

**IN FLIGHT**

light gray crown

gray wash on upperparts

dusky line through eye

**IMMATURE (WHITE FORM)**

round head

short, triangular bill

short, deeply furrowed neck

clean white upperparts

mostly dark brown upperparts

white rump and tail

**ADULT (BLUE FORM)**

**ADULT (WHITE FORM)**

reddish pink legs

**FLIGHT:** strong and direct, with rapid wingbeats.

This diminutive white goose is not much bigger than a Mallard, and half the weight of a Snow Goose; like its larger relative, it also has a "blue" form. About 95 percent of Ross's Geese once nested at a single sanctuary in Arctic Canada, but breeding pairs have spread eastward along Hudson Bay and in several island locations. Hunting reduced numbers to just 6,000 in the early 1950s, but since then numbers have increased to around 2 million individuals.

**VOICE** Call a *keek keek keeek*, higher pitched than Snow Goose; also a harsh, low *kork* or *kowk*; quiet when feeding.

**NESTING** Plant materials placed on ground, usually in colonies with Lesser Snow Geese; 3–5 eggs; 1 brood; June–August.

**FEEDING** Grazes on grasses, sedges, and small grains.

**TRAVELING IN FAMILIES**
Groups migrate thousands of miles together, for example from northern Canada to central California.

**OCCURRENCE**
Breeding grounds are amid tundra in scattered, High Arctic locations. Main wintering areas in California. On the wintering grounds, it feeds in agricultural fields, and also grasslands. Roosts overnight in several types of wetlands.

| SIMILAR SPECIES | | |
|---|---|---|
| **SNOW GOOSE** white form; see p.24 | larger bill | |
| | longer neck | |
| pink legs | | |
| **SNOW GOOSE** blue form; see p.24 | longer neck | black patch on bill |

| Length **22½–25in (57–64cm)** | Wingspan **3¼ft (1.1m)** | Weight **1¾–4½lb (0.85–2kg)** |
| Social **Flocks** | Lifespan **Up to 21 years** | Status **Secure** |

| DATE SEEN | WHERE | NOTES |
|---|---|---|
| | | |
| | | |
| | | |
| | | |
| | | |

| Order **Anseriformes** | Family **Anatidae** | Species *Anser albifrons* |

# Greater White-fronted Goose

gray wing feathers

**ADULT**

**IN FLIGHT**

white rump band

white tip to tail

chocolate-brown upperparts

pale brownish gray head

pale pink bill with narrow white base

black belly patches

*A. a. gambeli* (TULE)

larger body

dull yellowish orange bill

no belly barring

**JUVENILE**

white flank streak

orange legs

brownish gray head

**MALE**
*A. a. frontalis* (TUNDRA)

The Greater White-fronted Goose is the most widespread goose in the Northern Hemisphere. It is easily distinguished by its black-barred belly and the patch of white at the base of its bill. There are five subspecies, two of which are commonly seen in North America. The "tundra" (*A. a. frontalis*) makes up the largest population, breeding in extreme northwestern Canada and Alaska. The "tule" (*A. a. gambeli*), while the larger, occurs in smaller numbers, and is restricted in range to north-central Canada.

**VOICE** Laugh-like *klow-yo* or *kleu-yo-yo;* very musical in a flock.
**NESTING** Bowl-shaped nest made of plant material, lined with down, constructed near water; 3–7 eggs; 1 brood; May–August.
**FEEDING** Eats sedges, grasses, berries, and plants on both land and water in summer; feeds on grasses, seeds, and grains in winter.

**FLIGHT:** strong, direct flight; flies alone, in multiple lines, or in a V-formation.

**FLIGHT FORMATIONS**
This heavy-bodied, powerful flier can often be seen in tightly packed flocks.

### SIMILAR SPECIES

**CANADA GOOSE**
see p.28

black head, neck, and bill

white chin strap

**HEAVY GRAZER**
Grass is the major component of this goose's diet.

**OCCURRENCE**
Different habitats are utilized for breeding and wintering. Nesting areas include tundra ponds and lakes, dry rocky fields, and grassy slopes in Alaska and northern Canada. In winter, coastal marshes, inland wetlands, agricultural fields, and refuges are used along Pacific Coast and Mexico.

| Length **25–32in (64–81cm)** | Wingspan **4¼–5¼ft (1.3–1.6m)** | Weight **4–6½lb (1.8–3kg)** |
| Social **Flocks** | Lifespan **Up to 22 years** | Status **Secure** |

| DATE SEEN | WHERE | NOTES |
|---|---|---|
| | | |
| | | |
| | | |
| | | |
| | | |

| Order **Anseriformes** | Family **Anatidae** | Species *Branta bernicla* |

# Brant 🔊

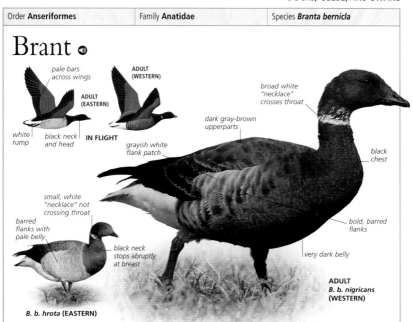

*pale bars across wings*

**ADULT (WESTERN)**

**ADULT (EASTERN)**

*white rump*

*black neck and head*  **IN FLIGHT**

*grayish white flank patch*

*broad white "necklace" crosses throat*

*dark gray-brown upperparts*

*black chest*

*small, white "necklace" not crossing throat*

*barred flanks with pale belly*

*black neck stops abruptly at breast*

*bold, barred flanks*

*very dark belly*

**ADULT**
*B. b. nigricans*
**(WESTERN)**

*B. b. hrota* **(EASTERN)**

A small-billed, dark, stocky sea goose, the Brant winters on both the East and West Coasts of North America. There are two subspecies in the US (three overall)—the pale-bellied "Atlantic" Brant (*B. b. hrota*), found in the East, and the darker "black" Brant (*B. b. nigricans*), in the West. In addition, there is an intermediate gray-bellied form that winters in the Puget Sound region along the Washington State Coast. Unlike other North American geese, the Brant feeds mainly on eelgrass in winter.
**VOICE** Nasal *cruk*, harsh-sounding in tone; rolling series of *cut cut cut cronk*, with an upward inflection at end.
**NESTING** Scrape lined with grass, plant matter, and down on islands or gravel spits; 3–5 eggs; 1 brood; May–July.
**FEEDING** Eats grass and sedges when nesting; eelgrass in winter; also green algae, saltmarsh plants, and mollusks.

**FLIGHT:** rapid and strong; low, irregular flight formations.

**GRASSY MEAL**
In winter, Brants forage almost exclusively on eelgrass between the high and low tide marks.

### SIMILAR SPECIES

**SNOW GOOSE (BLUE FORM)** 🔊
see p.24

*pale wing feathers*

**CACKLING GOOSE**
see p.419

*broad, white chin strap*

*darker underparts*

*browner coloration*

**OCCURRENCE**
Breeds in colonies in northern Canada and Alaska, and winters along both Pacific and Atlantic Coasts. The western breeding population of the Brant ("black") winters from the Aleutian Islands to northern Mexico, while the pale-bellied form ("Atlantic") is restricted in range to the East Coast.

| Length **22–26in (56–66cm)** | Wingspan **3½–4ft (1.1–1.2m)** | Weight **2½–4lb (1–1.8kg)** |
| Social **Flocks** | Lifespan **Up to 25 years** | Status **Secure** |

| DATE SEEN | WHERE | NOTES |
|---|---|---|
| | | |
| | | |
| | | |
| | | |

| Order **Anseriformes** | Family **Anatidae** | Species *Branta canadensis* |
|---|---|---|

# Canada Goose 🔊

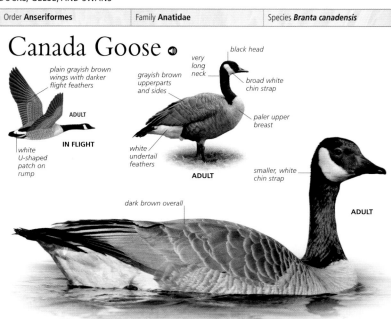

*plain grayish brown wings with darker flight feathers*

**ADULT**

**IN FLIGHT**

*white U-shaped patch on rump*

*grayish brown upperparts and sides*

*very long neck*

*black head*

*broad white chin strap*

*paler upper breast*

*white undertail feathers*

**ADULT**

*smaller, white chin strap*

**ADULT**

*dark brown overall*

The Canada Goose is the most common, widespread, and familiar goose in North America. Given its vast range, it is not surprising that the Canada Goose should have much geographic variation. Twelve subspecies have been recognized. With the exception of the Cackling Goose, which has recently been separated, it is difficult to confuse it, with its distinctive white chin strap, black head and neck, and grayish brown body, with any other species of goose. It is a monogamous species, and once pairs are formed, they stay together for life.

**VOICE** Male call *honk* or *bark*; females have higher pitched *hrink*.
**NESTING** Scrape lined with available plant matter and down, near water; 1–2 broods; 2–12 eggs; May–August.
**FEEDING** Grazes on grasses, sedges, leaves, seeds, agricultural crops, and berries; also insects.

**FLIGHT:** strong and direct with fairly slow, deep wingbeats; often flies in V-formation.

**TRICK OF THE LIGHT**
A low sun can play tricks—these birds are actually pale grayish underneath.

**SIMILAR SPECIES**

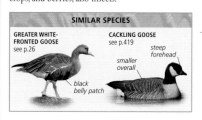

**GREATER WHITE-FRONTED GOOSE**
see p.26

*black belly patch*

**CACKLING GOOSE**
see p.419

*smaller overall*

*steep forehead*

**OCCURRENCE**
Variety of inland breeding habitats near water, including grassy urban areas, marshes, prairie, parkland, coastal temperate forest, northern coniferous forest, and Arctic tundra. Winters in agricultural fields, mudflats, saltwater marshes, lakes, and rivers.

| Length 2¼–3½ft (0.7–1.1m) | Wingspan 4¼–5½ft (1.3–1.7m) | Weight 6½–9¾lb (3–4.4kg) |
|---|---|---|
| Social **Flocks** | Lifespan **Up to 25 years** | Status **Secure** |

| DATE SEEN | WHERE | NOTES |
|---|---|---|
| | | |
| | | |
| | | |
| | | |
| | | |

| Order **Anseriformes** | Family **Anatidae** | Species **Cygnus columbianus** |
| --- | --- | --- |

# Tundra Swan

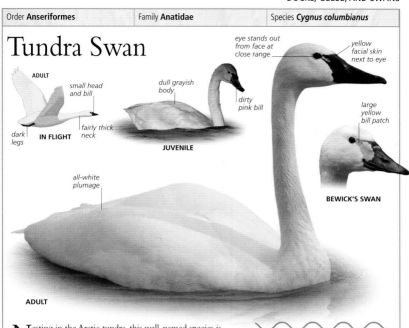

*eye stands out from face at close range*

*yellow facial skin next to eye*

**ADULT**

*small head and bill*

*dull grayish body*

*dirty pink bill*

*dark legs* **IN FLIGHT** *fairly thick neck*

**JUVENILE**

*large yellow bill patch*

**BEWICK'S SWAN**

*all-white plumage*

**ADULT**

Nesting in the Arctic tundra, this well-named species is North America's most widespread and smallest swan. Two populations exist, with one wintering in the West, and the other along the East Coast. The Tundra Swan can be confused with the Trumpeter Swan, but their different calls immediately distinguish the two species. When they are silent, weight and bill structure are the best way to tell them apart. In Eurasia, this species is known as Bewick's Swan and possesses a larger yellow patch at the base of its bill.

**VOICE** Clear, high-pitched yodeling *whoo-hooo* calls mixed with garbles, yelping, and barking sounds.

**NESTING** Mound-shaped nest made of plant matter near water; 3–6 eggs; 1 brood; May–September.

**FEEDING** Eats aquatic vegetation, insects, mollusks; also grain.

**FLIGHT:** flight pattern like that of other swans but with slightly faster wingbeats.

**WINTER FLOCKS**
Its size, white plumage, and flocking habits make the Tundra Swan a conspicuous species.

### SIMILAR SPECIES

**MUTE SWAN** ♂

*pointed tail*

*heavier bodied*

**TRUMPETER SWAN** see p.419

*all-black bill*

*more curved neck*

*straighter edge from eye to bill*

**OCCURRENCE**
Nests around lakes and pools in northern tundra from the Aleutians to the Yukon, and east to northwest Québec. Winters in southern British Columbia, western US, and mid-Atlantic states, mostly New Jersey to South Carolina. Winter habitat includes shallow coastal bays, ponds, and lakes.

| Length **4–5ft (1.2–1.5m)** | Wingspan **6¼–7¼ft (1.9–2.2m)** | Weight **12–18lb (5.5–8kg)** |
| --- | --- | --- |
| Social **Flocks** | Lifespan **Up to 21 years** | Status **Secure** |

| DATE SEEN | WHERE | NOTES |
| --- | --- | --- |
| | | |
| | | |
| | | |
| | | |
| | | |

| Order **Anseriformes** | Family **Anatidae** | Species **Aix sponsa** |
|---|---|---|

# Wood Duck 🔊

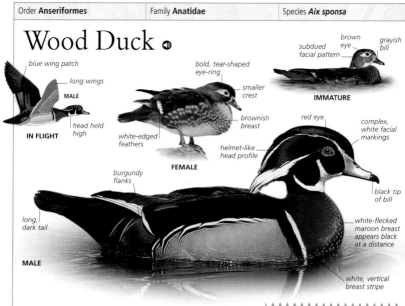

**MALE**

blue wing patch

long wings

**IN FLIGHT**

head held high

brown eye

subdued facial pattern

grayish bill

**IMMATURE**

bold, tear-shaped eye-ring

smaller crest

brownish breast

white-edged feathers

helmet-like head profile

**FEMALE**

red eye

complex, white facial markings

black tip of bill

burgundy flanks

long, dark tail

white-flecked maroon breast appears black at a distance

**MALE**

white, vertical breast stripe

The male Wood Duck is perhaps the most striking of all North American ducks. With its bright plumage, red eye and bill, and its long sleek crest that gives its head a helmet-shaped profile, the male is unmistakable. It is related to the Mandarin Duck of Asia. The Wood Duck is very dependent on mature swampy forestland. It is typically found on swamps, shallow lakes, ponds, and park settings that are surrounded by trees. Although it adapts to human activity, it is quite shy. When swimming, the Wood Duck can be seen jerking its head front to back. Of all waterfowl, this is the only species that regularly raises two broods each season.
**VOICE** Male gives a wheezy up-slurred whistle *zweeet*; female's call a double-note, rising *oh-eek oh-eek*.
**NESTING** Nests in natural tree cavities or nest boxes in close proximity to water; 10–13 eggs; 2 broods; April–August.
**FEEDING** Forages for seeds, tree fruit, and small acorns; also spiders, insects, and crustaceans.

**FLIGHT:** rapid flight with deep wingbeats; flies with head up; leaps straight off the water.

**PLAIN BELLY**
Wings raised, a male reveals one of the only plain areas of its plumage—its pale belly and underwing.

**SIMILAR SPECIES**

**BUFFLEHEAD ♀**
see p.48

white on cheek

shorter neck

shorter tail

**HOODED MERGANSER ♀**
narrower wings;
see p.51

long, tan crest

no eye-ring

**OCCURRENCE**
Usually found throughout the year, along rivers, streams, and creeks, in swamps, and marshy areas. Has a preference for permanent bodies of water. If good aquatic feeding areas are unavailable, the Wood Duck feeds in open areas, including agricultural fields.

| Length **18½–21½in (47–54cm)** | Wingspan **26–29in (66–73cm)** | Weight **16–30oz (450–850g)** |
|---|---|---|
| Social **Small flocks** | Lifespan **Up to 18 years** | Status **Secure** |

| DATE SEEN | WHERE | NOTES |
|---|---|---|
| | | |
| | | |
| | | |
| | | |
| | | |

| Order **Anseriformes** | Family **Anatidae** | Species *Spatula discors* |

# Blue-winged Teal 🔊

powdery blue forewing with green patch

**MALE (BREEDING)**

white facial crescent

white underwing stripe

**IN FLIGHT**

broken, contrasting, dark eye-ring

grayish brown overall

pale eyebrow, white eye-line

pale spot at base of bill

**FEMALE**

white facial crescent

dark grayish head

black bill

**MALE (FALL)**

black spots on rich, buff-brown breast and flanks

white facial crescent

dark cape, and eye-line

long blackish bill

rich tan flanks

warmer brown overall

**MALE (BREEDING)**

conspicuous white patch

This small dabbling duck is a common and widespread North American breeding species. With a bold white crescent between bill and eye on its otherwise slate-gray head and neck, the male Blue-winged Teal is quite distinctive. The Blue-winged and Cinnamon Teals, together with the Northern Shoveler, constitute the three "blue-winged" ducks; this is a feature that is conspicuous when the birds are flying. The Cinnamon and the Blue-winged Teals are almost identical genetically and interbreed to form hybrids. The Blue-winged Teal winters mostly south of the US and migrates back north in spring.

**VOICE** Male a high-pitched, raspy *peew* or low-pitched *paay* during courtship; female a loud single *quack*.

**NESTING** Bowl-shaped depression lined with grasses, close to water's edge, in meadows; 6–14 eggs; 1 brood; April–September.

**FEEDING** Eats seeds of a variety of plants; feeds heavily on insect larvae, crustaceans, and snails, when breeding.

**FLIGHT:** fast, twisting flight; flies in compact, small groups.

**OUTSTRETCHED WING**
Wing stretch behavior shows the white feathers between the blue forewing and green speculum.

### SIMILAR SPECIES

**CINNAMON TEAL ♀**
see p.32

plain face

warmer brown

**GREEN-WINGED TEAL ♀**
see p.38

different wing pattern

streaked rump

smaller, more compact body

smaller bill

**OCCURRENCE**
Nests across North America, with highest numbers in the prairie and parkland regions of the midcontinent. Prefers shallow ponds or marshes during nesting; freshwater to brackish water and (less so) saltwater marshes during migration. In winter, prefers saline environments, including mangroves.

| Length **14½–16in (37–41cm)** | Wingspan **23½–25in (60–64cm)** | Weight **11–18oz (300–500g)** |
| Social **Flocks** | Lifespan **Up to 17 years** | Status **Secure** |

| DATE SEEN | WHERE | NOTES |
|---|---|---|
| | | |
| | | |
| | | |
| | | |
| | | |

| Order **Anseriformes** | Family **Anatidae** | Species *Spatula cyanoptera* |

# Cinnamon Teal

*powdery blue forewing*

**MALE**

**IN FLIGHT**

*white underwing stripe*

*warm brown, upperparts with rust tinge*

*plain face pattern*

*shoveler-like bill*

**FEMALE**

*dull yellow legs*

*solid cinnamon color*

*conspicuous orange to red eye*

*long, spoon-shaped, black bill*

**MALE**

True to his English name, the male Cinnamon Teal is unmistakable in its rusty brown color adorned with blazing red eyes. A small duck, the Cinnamon Teal is the only North American dabbling duck that does not breed in the Great Plains and prairies of the midcontinent. It winters mostly in the coastal marshes and interior wetlands of Mexico. Common in the West, it is even seen in tiny roadside pools. Closely related to the Blue-winged Teal, the Cinnamon Teal shares with it its wing pattern. The latin name *cyanoptera* means "blue-winged."

**VOICE** Male a snuffled *chuk chuk chuk*; female a loud single *quack* and soft *gack gack gack ga*.

**NESTING** Shallow depression lined with grass near water; 4–16 eggs; 1 brood; March–September.

**FEEDING** Feeds on seeds of many plant species; adds aquatic insects, crustaceans, and snails, when breeding; omnivorous.

**FLIGHT:** rapid wingbeats; very agile, making sharp turns.

**FLOCKING TOGETHER**
The cinnamon-colored males and tan females are often found together in flocks.

### SIMILAR SPECIES

**BLUE-WINGED TEAL** ♀
see p.31

*darker cap and eye-line*

*colder, brown-gray overall*

**NORTHERN SHOVELER** ♀
see p.33

*longer, thinner wings*

*white on flanks and upper breast*

*longer, paler bill*

**OCCURRENCE**
Found in freshwater and brackish habitats of various sizes, such as marshes, reservoirs, flooded fields, ponds, ditches, and stock ponds. In the southern part of its wintering range, can also be found in tidal estuaries, saltmarshes, and mangrove forests. Widespread in Central and South America.

| Length **14–17in (36–43cm)** | Wingspan **22in (56cm)** | Weight **10–17oz (275–475g)** |
| Social **Winter flocks** | Lifespan **Up to 12 years** | Status **Secure** |

| DATE SEEN | WHERE | | NOTES |
| --- | --- | --- | --- |
| | | | |
| | | | |
| | | | |
| | | | |
| | | | |

Order **Anseriformes** | Family **Anatidae** | Species *Spatula clypeata*

# Northern Shoveler 🔊

dark, narrow eye-line

brown overall

dusky olive-gray to orange bill

**FEMALE**

grayish blue wing patch

pale blue wing patch

**IN FLIGHT**

whitish tail

long bill

**FEMALE**

heavy fronted

**MALE**

pale-edged, brown flank feathers

dark green head

yellow eye

large, dark spatula-shaped bill

**MALE**

white breast

chestnut belly and flanks

black-and-white rump

The Northern Shoveler is a common, medium-sized, dabbling duck found in North America and Eurasia. It is monogamous—pairs remain together longer than any other dabbler species. Its distinctive long bill is highly specialized; it is wider at the tip and contains thin, comb-like structures (called "lamellae") along the sides, used to filter food items from the water. Shovelers often form tight feeding groups, swimming close together as they sieve the water for prey.

**VOICE** Male call a nasal, muffled *thuk thuk…thuk thuk*; also a loud, nasal *paaaay*; female call a variety of *quacks*, singly or in a series of 4–5 descending notes.

**NESTING** Scrape lined with plant matter and down, in short plants, near water; 6–19 eggs; 1 brood; May–August.

**FEEDING** Forages for seeds; filters small crustaceans and mollusks out of the water.

**FLIGHT:** strong direct flight; male's wings make a rattling noise when taking off.

**UPSIDE DOWN FEEDER**
This male upends to feed below the water's surface, revealing his orange legs.

**FILTER FEEDING**
Their bills open, these ducks sieve small invertebrates from the water.

**OCCURRENCE**
Widespread across North America, south of the tundra. Breeds in a variety of wetlands, in edges of shallow pools with nearby tall and short grasslands. Occurs in fresh- and saltmarshes, ponds, and other shallow bodies of water in winter; does not feed on land.

## SIMILAR SPECIES

**MALLARD ♀**
larger; see p.36

darker blue wing patch

**CINNAMON TEAL ♀**
see p.32

slimmer bill

plainer plumage

plainer face

longer tail

| Length **17½–20in (44–51cm)** | Wingspan **27–33in (69–84cm)** | Weight **14–29oz (400–825g)** |
|---|---|---|
| Social **Flocks** | Lifespan **Up to 18 years** | Status **Secure** |

| DATE SEEN | WHERE | NOTES |
|---|---|---|
| | | |
| | | |
| | | |
| | | |

| Order **Anseriformes** | Family **Anatidae** | Species *Mareca strepera* |

# Gadwall 🔊

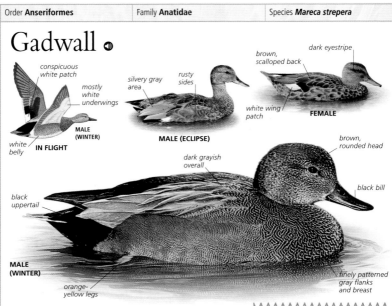

conspicuous white patch

mostly white underwings

**MALE (WINTER)**

white belly **IN FLIGHT**

silvery gray area

rusty sides

**MALE (ECLIPSE)**

white wing patch

brown, scalloped back

dark eyestripe

**FEMALE**

dark grayish overall

brown, rounded head

black bill

black uppertail

**MALE (WINTER)**

orange-yellow legs

finely patterned gray flanks and breast

Although the Gadwall's appearance is somewhat somber, many birders consider this duck one of North America's most elegant species because of the subtlety of its plumage. Despite being common and widespread, Gadwalls are often overlooked because of their retiring behavior and relatively quiet vocalizations. This dabbling duck is slightly smaller and more delicate than the Mallard, yet female Gadwalls are often mistaken for female Mallards. Gadwalls associate with other species, especially in winter.

**VOICE** Low, raspy *meep* or *reb* given in quick succession; female *quack* similar to that of female Mallard, but higher pitched and more nasal; high-pitched *peep*, or *pe-peep*; both sexes give *tickety-tickety-tickety* chatter while feeding.

**NESTING** Bowl nest made of plant material in a scrape; 8–12 eggs; 1 brood; April–August.

**FEEDING** Dabbles on the surface or below for seeds, aquatic vegetation, and invertebrates, including mollusks and insects.

**FLIGHT:** direct flight with fast wingbeats; leaps straight off the water.

**BROOD ON THE MOVE**
Females lead their ducklings from their nest to a brood-rearing habitat that provides cover and ample food for the ducklings to forage.

**SIMILAR SPECIES**

**MALLARD ♀** see p.36

darker eye-line

thicker, longer bill

whitish tail

**MOTTLED DUCK ♀**

olive to yellow bill

buffier face

**OCCURRENCE**
From the western prairie pothole country of Canada and the northern US, the Gadwall's range has expanded as it has adapted to manmade bodies of water, such as reservoirs and ponds. In winter, mostly found on lakes, marshes, and along rivers.

| Length **18–22½in (46–57cm)** | Wingspan **33in (84cm)** | Weight **18–45oz (500–1,250g)** |
| Social **Winter flocks** | Lifespan **Up to 19 years** | Status **Secure** |

| DATE SEEN | WHERE | NOTES |
| --- | --- | --- |
| | | |
| | | |
| | | |
| | | |
| | | |

| Order **Anseriformes** | Family **Anatidae** | Species *Mareca americana* |

# American Wigeon 🔊

**MALE (BREEDING)**

white underwing patch

**IN FLIGHT**

long, pointed tail

gray head contrasts with pinkish brown breast and flanks

rufous-edged wing feathers

dark smudge around eye

gray head

narrow, black line along bill

warm brown breast and flanks

**FEMALE**

cream forehead and crown

green band from eye to nape

**MALE (BREEDING)**

black rump

pinkish brown flanks

black-tipped bill

Often found in mixed flocks with other ducks, the American Wigeon is a common and widespread, medium-sized dabbling duck. This bird is an opportunist that loiters around other diving ducks and coots, feeding on the vegetation they dislodge. It is more social during migration and in the nonbreeding season than when breeding.

**VOICE** Slow and fast whistles; male's most common call a slow, high-pitched, wheezy, 3-syllable *whew-whew-whew*, with middle note loudest; also, a faster *whee* whistle.

**NESTING** Depression lined with plant material and down, usually in tall grass away from water; 5–10 eggs; 1 brood; May–August.

**FEEDING** Grazes on grass, clover, algae, and, in agricultural fields; feeds on many seeds, insects, mollusks, and crustaceans during the breeding season.

**FLIGHT:** rapid, fairly deep wingbeats; leaps almost vertically off the water.

**COMING IN FOR LANDING**
This male's cream-colored forehead is clearly visible, as is the sharp contrast between the white belly, and the pinkish breast and flanks.

**FLAPPING WINGS**
This bird has a white patch on its underwing, while the Eurasian Wigeon has a gray patch.

### SIMILAR SPECIES

**GADWALL ♀**
see p.34

white patch

**GREEN-WINGED TEAL ♂**
see p.38

dark line through eye

black-and-orange bill

longer bill

green patch on wing

**OCCURRENCE**
The northernmost breeder of the dabbling ducks, occurs from Alaska to the Maritimes. Prefers pothole and grassland habitats; found almost anywhere near water in winter. Winters south to northern South America and the Caribbean, in freshwater and coastal bay habitats.

| Length **17½–23in (45–58cm)** | Wingspan **33in (84cm)** | Weight **1⅛–3lb (0.5–1.3kg)** |
| Social **Flocks** | Lifespan **Up to 21 years** | Status **Secure** |

| DATE SEEN | WHERE | NOTES |
| --- | --- | --- |
| | | |
| | | |
| | | |
| | | |
| | | |

| Order **Anseriformes** | Family **Anatidae** | Species *Anas platyrhynchos* |

# Mallard 🔊

broad-based wings

short, round, pale tail

**MALE (WINTER)**

heavy body

**FEMALE**

dark eye-line and cap

yellowish brown back

orange bill with blackish patch

grayer head

olive-yellow bill

**MALE (SUMMER)**

rusty underparts

mottled brown belly

metallic green head

**FEMALE**

blue wing patch

warm gray body

bright yellow bill

narrow, white neck collar

**IN FLIGHT**

brown underparts

whitish outer tail feathers

short, black curls above white tail

**MALE (WINTER)**

chestnut-brown breast

The Mallard is perhaps the most familiar of all ducks, and occurs in the wild all across the Northern Hemisphere. It is the ancestor of most domestic ducks, and hybrids between the wild and domestic forms are frequently seen in city lakes and ponds, often with patches of white on the breast. Mating is generally a violent affair, but outside the breeding season the wild species is strongly migratory and gregarious, sometimes forming large flocks that may join with other species.

**VOICE** Male's call a quiet raspy *raab*; during courtship a high-pitched whistle; female call a *quack* or repeated in series.

**NESTING** Scrape lined with plant matter, usually near water, often on floating vegetation; 6–15 eggs; 1 brood; February–September.

**FEEDING** Feeds omnivorously on insects, crustaceans, mollusks, and earthworms when breeding; otherwise largely vegetarian; takes seeds, acorns, agricultural crops, aquatic vegetation, and bread.

**FLIGHT:** fast, shallow, and regular; often flies in groups.

**STICKING TOGETHER**
The mother leads her ducklings to water soon after they hatch. She looks after them until they can fend for themselves.

**SIMILAR SPECIES**

**GADWALL ♀**
see p.34

slimmer body

steeper forehead

white wing patch

orange strip on bill

**AMERICAN BLACK DUCK ♀**
see p.470

dark tail

dark olive bill

darker brown overall

**OCCURRENCE**
Occurs throughout the region, choosing shallow water in natural wetlands, such as marshes, prairie potholes, ponds, and ditches; can also be found in manmade habitats such as city parks and reservoirs, preferring more open habitats in winter.

| Length 19½–26in (50–65cm) | Wingspan 32–37in (82–95cm) | Weight 1⅞–3lb (0.9–1.4kg) |
| Social **Flocks** | Lifespan **Up to 29 years** | Status **Secure** |

| DATE SEEN | WHERE | NOTES |
|---|---|---|
| | | |
| | | |
| | | |
| | | |
| | | |

| Order **Anseriformes** | Family **Anatidae** | Species *Anas acuta* |

# Northern Pintail 🔊

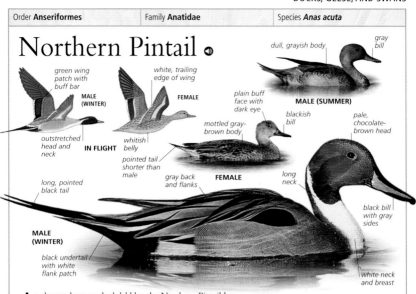

MALE (WINTER)
green wing patch with buff bar

FEMALE
white, trailing edge of wing

IN FLIGHT
outstretched head and neck
whitish belly
pointed tail shorter than male

dull, grayish body
gray bill

MALE (SUMMER)

plain buff face with dark eye
blackish bill
mottled gray-brown body

pale, chocolate-brown head

gray back and flanks
FEMALE
long neck

long, pointed black tail

MALE (WINTER)
black undertail with white flank patch

black bill with gray sides

white neck and breast

An elegant, long-necked dabbler, the Northern Pintail has extremely distinctive marking and a very long tail—in fact, the longest tail to be found on any freshwater duck. One of the earliest breeders in the year, these ducks begin nesting soon after the ice thaws. Northern Pintails were once one of the most abundant prairie breeding ducks. However, in recent decades, droughts, combined with the reduction of habitat on both their wintering and breeding grounds, have resulted in a significant decline in their population.

**VOICE** Male call a high-pitched rolling *prrreep prrreep;* lower pitched wheezy *wheeeee,* which gets louder then drops off; female call a quiet, harsh *quack* or *kuk* singularly or as short series; also a loud *gaak,* often repeated.

**NESTING** Scrape lined with plant materials and down, usually in short grass, brush, or even in the open; 3–12 eggs; 1 brood; April–August.

**FEEDING** Feeds on grains, rice, seeds, aquatic weeds, insect larvae, crustaceans, and snails.

**FLIGHT:** fast, direct flight; can be very acrobatic in the air.

**FEEDING TIME**
Even when tipping up to feed, these pintails can be identified by their long, black, pointed tails.

### SIMILAR SPECIES

**GADWALL ♀**
see p.34
shorter tail
orange-sided bill
white wing patch

**AMERICAN WIGEON ♀**
see p.35
darker gray head
shorter tail
chestnut breast and flanks

**OCCURRENCE**
Widely distributed in North America; breeding in open country in shallow wetlands or meadows in mountainous forest regions. Found in tidal wetlands and saltwater habitats in migration and winter; dry harvested and flooded agricultural fields in autumn and winter.

| Length **20–30in (51–76cm)** | Wingspan **35in (89cm)** | Weight **18–44oz (500–1,250g)** |
| Social **Flocks** | Lifespan **Up to 21 years** | Status **Declining** |

| DATE SEEN | WHERE | NOTES |
| --- | --- | --- |
| | | |
| | | |
| | | |
| | | |
| | | |

| Order **Anseriformes** | Family **Anatidae** | Species *Anas crecca* |
|---|---|---|

# Green-winged Teal 🔊

**MALE**

green-and-black patch on hindwing

short neck

**IN FLIGHT**

gray flanks

rufous head

dark green ear patch

horizontal, white line on sides

lacks white vertical bar

small, narrow, black bill

black-spotted breast

white vertical bar

finely detailed pattern

yellowish buff undertail feathers

**MALE**

**A. c. crecca (EURASIAN; RARE)**

steeper forehead

darker face

**FEMALE**

shoulder feathers with narrow pale edges

weaker face pattern

**JUVENILE**

The Green-winged Teal, the smallest North American dabbling duck, is slightly smaller than the Blue-winged and Cinnamon Teals, and lacks their blue wing patch. Its population is increasing, apparently because it breeds in more pristine habitats, and farther north, than the prairie ducks. The species has three subspecies, *A. c. crecca* (Eurasia), *A. c. carolinensis* (North America), and *A. c. nimia* (Aleutian Islands). *Carolinensis* males have a conspicuous vertical white bar, whereas Eurasian *crecca* males do not.

**VOICE** Male call a high-pitched, slightly rolling *crick crick*, similar to cricket; female call a quiet *quack*.

**NESTING** Shallow scrape on ground lined with nearby vegetation, often placed in dense vegetation near water; 6–9 eggs; 1 brood; April–September.

**FEEDING** Eats seeds, aquatic insects, crustaceans, and mollusks year-round; also feeds in grain fields in winter.

**FLIGHT:** fast flight; often flying in twisting, tight groups reminiscent of shorebird flocks.

**SINGLE PARENT**
The female duck is deserted by her partner during incubation, so she must provide all parental care.

### SIMILAR SPECIES

**BLUE-WINGED TEAL ♀**
larger overall; see p.31
different wing pattern

whitish spot at base of bill

**CINNAMON TEAL ♀**
larger overall; see p.32
rich brown overall

longer bill

yellowish legs

**OCCURRENCE**
Breeds from central US northward to Canada and Alaska; around ponds in forests and deciduous woodlands. Prefers shallow vegetated wetlands. In winter and migration, inland and coastal marshes, sloughs, and agricultural fields. Winters south of the Caribbean and in southern Mexico.

| Length **12–15½in (31–39cm)** | Wingspan **20½–23in (52–59cm)** | Weight **7–16oz (200–450g)** |
|---|---|---|
| Social **Flocks** | Lifespan **Up to 20 years** | Status **Secure** |

| DATE SEEN | WHERE | NOTES |
|---|---|---|
| | | |
| | | |
| | | |
| | | |
| | | |

| Order **Anseriformes** | Family **Anatidae** | Species **Aythya valisineria** |

# Canvasback

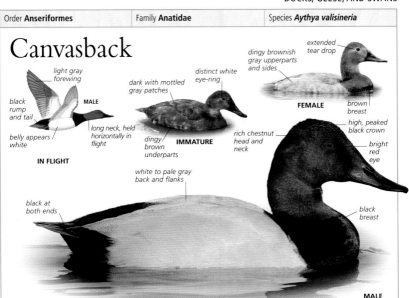

**IN FLIGHT**

light gray forewing

black rump and tail

**MALE**

belly appears white

long neck, held horizontally in flight

dark with mottled gray patches

distinct white eye-ring

dingy brown underpants

**IMMATURE**

dingy brownish gray upperparts and sides

extended tear drop

**FEMALE**

brown breast

rich chestnut head and neck

white to pale gray back and flanks

high, peaked black crown

bright red eye

black at both ends

black breast

**MALE**

A large, elegant, long-billed diving duck, the Canvasback is a bird of prairie pothole country. Its specialized diet of aquatic plants has resulted in a smaller population than other ducks. With legs set toward the rear, it is an accomplished swimmer and diver, and is rarely seen on land. Weather conditions and brood parasitism by Redheads determine how successful the Canvasback's nesting is from year to year.
**VOICE** Mostly silent except during courtship when males make soft *cooing* noises; females emit a grating *krrrrr krrrrrr krrrrrr*; females give loud *quack* when taking off; during winter, both sexes make soft wheezing series of *rrrr rrrr rrrr* sounds.
**NESTING** Platform over water built of woven vegetation; occasionally on shore; 8–11 eggs; 1 brood; April–September.
**FEEDING** Mainly eats aquatic tubers, buds, root stalks, and shoots, particularly those of wild celery; also eats snails when preferred plants are unavailable.

**FLIGHT:** direct strong flight; one of the fastest ducks; forms V-shaped flocks.

**DEEP WATER**
Canvasbacks prefer deeper-bodied waters that support the aquatic vegetation they eat.

### SIMILAR SPECIES

**REDHEAD** ♂
see p.40
shorter gray, black-tipped bill
yellow eye

**LESSER SCAUP** ♂
see p.42
darker gray on back
smaller overall
yellow eye

**OCCURRENCE**
Found in potholes, marshes, and ponds in prairie parkland, tundra; northerly forests preferred where their favorite foods grow. Winters in large numbers in large bays and lakes, and deltas, with smaller numbers scattered across North America and Mexico.

| Length **19–22in (48–56cm)** | Wingspan **31–35in (79–89cm)** | Weight **1¾–3½lb (0.8–1.6kg)** |
| Social **Flocks** | Lifespan **Up to 22 years** | Status **Secure** |

| DATE SEEN | WHERE | NOTES |
| --- | --- | --- |
| | | |
| | | |
| | | |
| | | |
| | | |

| Order **Anseriformes** | Family **Anatidae** | Species **Aythya americana** |
|---|---|---|

# Redhead

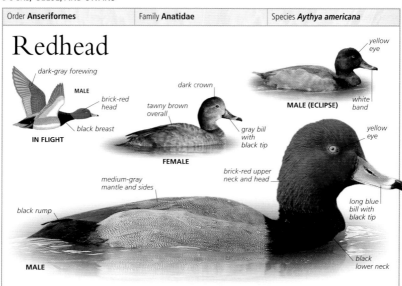

**MALE**
- dark-gray forewing
- brick-red head
- black breast
- **IN FLIGHT**

**FEMALE**
- dark crown
- tawny brown overall
- gray bill with black tip

**MALE (ECLIPSE)**
- yellow eye
- white band

**MALE**
- yellow eye
- brick-red upper neck and head
- medium-gray mantle and sides
- black rump
- long blue bill with black tip
- black lower neck

The Redhead, a medium-sized diving duck belonging to the Pochard group, is native only to North America. Only when seen up close is it apparent that the male's seemingly gray upperparts and flanks are actually white, with dense, black, wavy markings. The Redhead often feeds at night and forages mostly around dusk and dawn, drifting during the day. It parasitizes other duck nests more than any other duck species, particularly those of the Canvasback and even other Redheads.

**VOICE** Male courtship call a wheezy rising then falling *whee ough*, also *meow*; female call a low, raspy *kurr kurr kurr*.

**NESTING** Weaves solid nest over water in dense vegetation such as cattails, lined with down; 7–14 eggs; 1 brood; May–September.

**FEEDING** Omnivorous; feeds on aquatic plants, seeds, tubers, algae, insects, spiders, fish eggs, snails, and insect larvae; diet is variable depending on location.

**FLIGHT:** direct flight; runs on water prior to takeoff.

**MALE DISPLAY**
This male is performing a spectacular courtship display called a head throw, while remaining otherwise completely still on the water.

**EASY IDENTIFICATION**
The long blue bill with a whitish band and black tip is clearly visible in males.

**OCCURRENCE**
Breeds in shallow wetlands across the Great Basin and Prairie Pothole region, very densely in certain marsh habitats. The bulk of the population winters in coastal lagoons along the Atlantic Coast and the Gulf of Mexico.

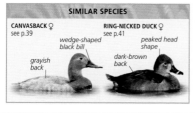

**SIMILAR SPECIES**

**CANVASBACK ♀** see p.39
- wedge-shaped black bill
- grayish back

**RING-NECKED DUCK ♀** see p.41
- peaked head shape
- dark-brown back

| Length **17–21in (43–53cm)** | Wingspan **30–31in (75–79cm)** | Weight **1⅜–3¼lbs (0.6–1.5kg)** |
|---|---|---|
| Social **Flocks** | Lifespan **Up to 21 years** | Status **Secure** |

| DATE SEEN | WHERE | NOTES |
|---|---|---|
| | | |
| | | |
| | | |
| | | |
| | | |

| Order **Anseriformes** | Family **Anatidae** | Species *Aythya collaris* |

# Ring-necked Duck 🔊

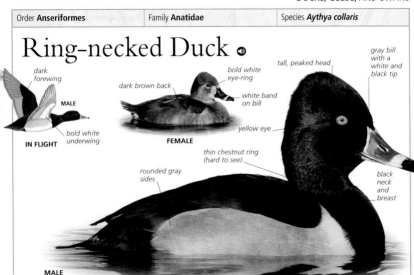

dark forewing

**MALE**

bold white underwing

**IN FLIGHT**

dark brown back

bold white eye-ring

white band on bill

yellow eye

**FEMALE**

tall, peaked head

gray bill with a white and black tip

thin chestnut ring (hard to see)

rounded gray sides

black neck and breast

**MALE**

A resident of freshwater ponds and lakes, the Ring-necked Duck is a fairly common medium-sized diving duck. A more descriptive and suitable name might have been Ring-billed Duck as the bold white band on the bill tip is easy to see whereas the thin chestnut ring around the neck can be very difficult to observe. The tall, pointed head is quite distinctive, peaking at the rear of the crown. When it sits on the water, this bird typically holds its head high.

**VOICE** Male normally silent; female makes low *kerp kerp* call.

**NESTING** Floating nest built in dense aquatic vegetation, often in marshes; 6–14 eggs; 1 brood; May–August.

**FEEDING** Feeds in water at all times, either by diving, tipping up, or dabbling for aquatic plant tubers and seeds; also eats aquatic invertebrates such as clams and snails.

**FLIGHT:** strong flier with deep, rapid wingbeats; flight somewhat erratic.

**UNIQUE BILL**
A white outline around the base of the bill and the white band on the bill are unique markings.

**FLAPPING WINGS**
Bold white wing linings are apparent when the Ring-necked Duck flaps its wings.

### SIMILAR SPECIES

**LESSER SCAUP ♂**
see p.42

rounded head

wavy-patterned gray mantle

**TUFTED DUCK ♂**
see p.470

crested tufts

white sides

**OCCURRENCE**
Breeds across Canada, south of the Arctic zone, in shallow freshwater marshes and bogs; sporadically in the western US. Winters in freshwater and brackish habitats such as swamps, lakes, estuaries, reservoirs, and flooded fields. Migrants are found in the Midwest near stands of wild rice.

| Length **15–18in (38–46cm)** | Wingspan **24–25in (62–63cm)** | Weight **1⅛–2lbs (500–900g)** |
| Social **Flocks** | Lifespan **Up to 20 years** | Status **Secure** |

| DATE SEEN | WHERE | NOTES |
| --- | --- | --- |
| | | |
| | | |
| | | |
| | | |
| | | |

| Order **Anseriformes** | Family **Anatidae** | Species *Aythya affinis* |

# Lesser Scaup 🔊

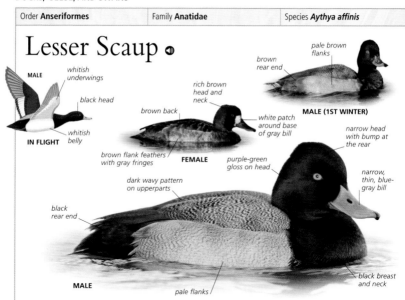

**MALE**
whitish underwings
black head
**IN FLIGHT** whitish belly

pale brown flanks
brown rear end
**MALE (1ST WINTER)**

rich brown head and neck
brown back
white patch around base of gray bill
brown flank feathers with gray fringes **FEMALE**
purple-green gloss on head

narrow head with bump at the rear
narrow, thin, blue-gray bill

dark wavy pattern on upperparts
black rear end

black breast and neck

**MALE**
pale flanks

The Lesser Scaup, far more numerous than its somewhat larger relative (their size and weight ranges overlap), is also the most abundant diving duck in North America. The two species are very similar in appearance and are best identified by shape. Identification must be done cautiously as head shape changes with position. For example, the crown feathers are flattened just before diving in both species; thus, scaups are best identified when they are not moving.
**VOICE** Males mostly silent except during courtship when they make a wheezy *wheeow wheeow wheeow* sound; females give repetitive series of grating *garrrf garrrf garrrf* notes.
**NESTING** Nest built in tall vegetation or under shrubs, sometimes far from water, also on islands and mats of floating vegetation; 8–11 eggs; 1 brood; May–September.
**FEEDING** Feeds mainly on leeches, crustaceans, mollusks, aquatic insects, and aquatic plants and seeds.

**FLIGHT:** rapid, direct flight; can jump off water more easily than other diving ducks.

**PREENING SCAUP**
Ducks are meticulous preeners, and the Lesser Scaup is no exception.

### SIMILAR SPECIES

**RING-NECKED DUCK ♀**
see p.41
prominent white eye-ring
solid dark back

**GREATER SCAUP ♀**
see p.419
more tawny brown upperparts
more white around bill

**OCCURRENCE**
Breeds inland from Alaska to eastern Canada in open northern forests and forested tundra. Winters in the Caribbean, southern US, and south to northern South America. Majority winter along coasts; others winter inland on lakes and reservoirs.

| Length **15½–17½in (39–45cm)** | Wingspan **27–31in (68–78cm)** | Weight **1–2¾lb (0.45–1.2kg)** |
| Social **Flocks** | Lifespan **Up to 18 years** | Status **Secure** |

| DATE SEEN | WHERE | NOTES |
| --- | --- | --- |
|  |  |  |
|  |  |  |
|  |  |  |
|  |  |  |
|  |  |  |

| Order **Anseriformes** | Family **Anatidae** | Species *Histrionicus histrionicus* |
|---|---|---|

# Harlequin Duck

**MALE**

dark wings above and below

short neck

pointed tail · **IN FLIGHT**

dark sooty brown overall

broad face with whitish patches

scaly, pale brown lower breast and belly

**FEMALE**

slate-blue with bright rusty sides

two white bands perpendicular to breast and neck

two white facial spots

rust crown stripes

very round head

steep forehead

white bands down either side of back

small dark bill

white crescent

**MALE**

This small, hardy duck is a superbly skilful swimmer, diving to forage on the bottom of turbulent streams for its favorite insect prey. Despite the male's unmistakable plumage at close range, it looks very dark from a distance. With head and long tail held high, in winter it can be found among crashing waves, alongside larger and bigger-billed Surf and White-winged Scoters, who feed in the same habitat.

**VOICE** Male a high-pitched squeak earning it the nickname "sea mice"; female's call a raspy *ekekekekekek*.

**NESTING** Nests near water under vegetation or base of tree; also tree cavities; 3–9 eggs; 1 brood; April–September.

**FEEDING** Dives for insects and their larvae, and fish roe when breeding; in winter, eats mollusks, crustaceans, crabs, snails, fish roe, and barnacles.

**FLIGHT:** rapid and regular wingbeats; usually flies low over water, in pairs or small groups.

**MALE GROUPS**
After the breeding season, many males may gather and forage together.

**PAIR IN FLIGHT**
Note the crisp white markings on the slate-blue male in flight.

**OCCURRENCE**
Breeds near rushing coastal and mountain streams. During winter, found in small groups or mixed in with other sea ducks close to the shore, particularly along shallow rocky shorelines, jetties, rocky beaches, and headlands. Western populations are widespread, unlike Eastern ones. Also breeds in Iceland.

| SIMILAR SPECIES | | |
|---|---|---|

**SURF SCOTER ♀** see p.44 — large, triangular bill

flatter head

elongated body

**BUFFLEHEAD ♀** see p.48 — larger head

oblong patch on cheek

| Length **13–21½in (33–54cm)** | Wingspan **22–26in (56–66cm)** | Weight **18–26oz (500–750g)** |
|---|---|---|
| Social **Small flocks** | Lifespan **Unknown** | Status **Secure** |

| DATE SEEN | WHERE | NOTES |
|---|---|---|
| ................... | ................................... | ................................... |
| ................... | ................................... | ................................... |
| ................... | ................................... | ................................... |
| ................... | ................................... | ................................... |
| ................... | ................................... | ................................... |

| Order **Anseriformes** | Family **Anatidae** | Species *Melanitta perspicillata* |
|---|---|---|

# Surf Scoter

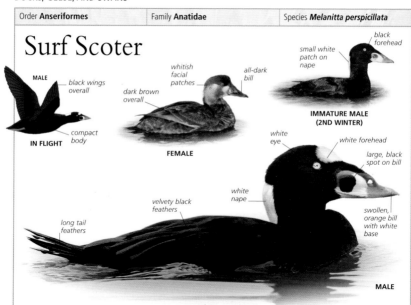

**MALE**

**IN FLIGHT**
black wings overall
compact body

dark brown overall
whitish facial patches
all-dark bill
**FEMALE**

black forehead
small white patch on nape
**IMMATURE MALE (2ND WINTER)**

white eye
white forehead
large, black spot on bill
white nape
velvety black feathers
long tail feathers
swollen, orange bill with white base
**MALE**

Surf Scoters, one of three species of scoters living in North America, migrate up and down both coasts, often with other species. They take their name from the way they dive for mollusks on the sea floor, in shallow coastal waters, through heavy surf. Groups often dive and resurface in unison. Black and Surf Scoters can be difficult to tell apart as both have all-black wings. The underside of the Surf Scoter's wings are uniform black, whereas the Black Scoter has gray flight feathers, which contrast with the black underwing feathers.

**VOICE** Normally silent; courting male's variety of calls includes liquid gurgled *puk-puk*, bubbled whistles, and low croaks; female call a harsh *crahh*, reminiscent of a crow.

**NESTING** Ground nest lined with down and vegetation on brushy tundra, often under low branches of a conifer tree; 5–10 eggs; 1 brood; May–September.

**FEEDING** Dives for mollusks and other aquatic invertebrates.

**FLIGHT:** strong wingbeats; flies in bunched up groups; male's wings hum or whistle in flight.

**DISTINGUISHING FEATURES**
The white forehead and bright orange bill, in addition to the red-orange legs and toes, identify male Surf Scoters.

| SIMILAR SPECIES | |
|---|---|
| **GREATER SCAUP** ♀ see p.419 | **WHITE-WINGED SCOTER** ♀ see p.45 |

no white patches on cheek
thinner bill
long, sloping forehead
longer bill

**OCCURRENCE**
Nests on lake islands in forested regions of interior Alaska and northern Canada. Nonbreeders in summer and adults in winter are strictly coastal, with numbers decreasing from north to south along the Pacific Coast. In the East, most overwinter in the mid-Atlantic Coast region.

| Length **19–23½in (48–60cm)** | Wingspan **30in (77cm)** | Weight **1¾–2¾lb (0.8–1.2kg)** |
|---|---|---|
| Social **Flocks/Pairs** | Lifespan **Unknown** | Status **Declining** |

| DATE SEEN | WHERE | NOTES |
|---|---|---|
| | | |
| | | |
| | | |
| | | |
| | | |

| Order **Anseriformes** | Family **Anatidae** | Species *Melanitta deglandi* |

# White-winged Scoter

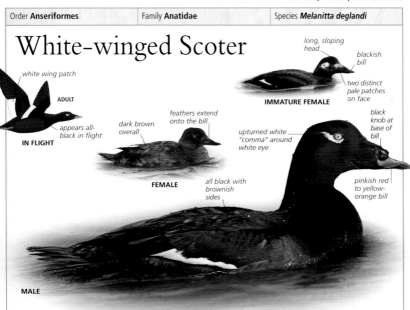

long, sloping head

blackish bill

two distinct pale patches on face

**IMMATURE FEMALE**

white wing patch

**ADULT**

appears all-black in flight

**IN FLIGHT**

dark brown overall

feathers extend onto the bill

**FEMALE**

upturned white "comma" around white eye

black knob at base of bill

pinkish red to yellow-orange bill

all black with brownish sides

**MALE**

The White-winged Scoter is the largest of the three scoters. When visible, the white wing patch makes identification easy. Females are quite similar to immature male and female Surf Scoters and can be identified by head shape, extent of bill feathering, and shape of white areas on the face. When diving, this scoter leaps forward and up, arching its neck, and opens its wings when entering the water. Underwater, White-winged Scoters open their wings to propel and stabilize themselves.

**VOICE** Mostly silent; courting males emit a whistling note; female call a growly *karr*.

**NESTING** Depression lined with twigs and down in dense thickets, often far from water; 8–9 eggs; 1 brood; June–September.

**FEEDING** Dives for mollusks and crustaceans; sometimes eats fish and aquatic plants.

**FLIGHT:** direct with rapid wingbeats; flies low over the water in small groups.

**WHITE FLASH IN FLIGHT**
Scoters often migrate or feed in mixed flocks. The white wing patches are striking in flight.

**SIMILAR SPECIES**

**SURF SCOTER ♂**
see p.44

white forehead

white nape

**BLACK SCOTER ♂**
see p.46

yellow-orange knob

black overall

**OCCURRENCE**
Majority breed in dense colonies in interior Alaska and western Canada on large freshwater or brackish lakes or ponds, sometimes on saltwater lakes. Winters along both coasts, large bays, inlets, and estuaries. Rarely winters inland, except on the Great Lakes.

| Length **19–23in (48–58cm)** | Wingspan **31in (80cm)** | Weight **2¾–4¾lb (0.9–1.9kg)** |
| Social **Flocks/Colonies** | Lifespan **Up to 18 years** | Status **Vulnerable** |

| DATE SEEN | WHERE | | NOTES |
|---|---|---|---|
| | | | |
| | | | |
| | | | |
| | | | |
| | | | |

| Order **Anseriformes** | Family **Anatidae** | Species **Melanitta americana** |

# Black Scoter

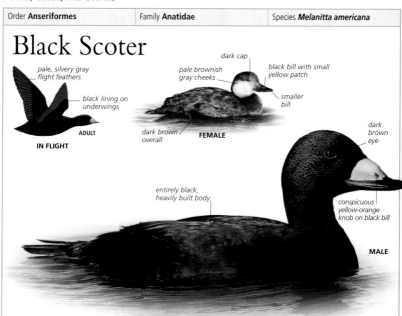

pale, silvery gray flight feathers

black lining on underwings

**ADULT**

**IN FLIGHT**

dark cap

pale brownish gray cheeks

black bill with small yellow patch

smaller bill

dark brown overall

**FEMALE**

dark brown eye

entirely black, heavily built body

conspicuous yellow-orange knob on black bill

**MALE**

Black Scoters, the most vocal of the scoters, are medium-sized sea ducks that winter along both coasts of North America. Riding high on the waves, they form dense flocks, often segregated by gender. While swimming, the Black Scoter sometimes flaps its wings and while doing so drops its neck low down, unlike the other two scoters. This scoter breeds in two widely separated subarctic breeding areas and is one of the least studied ducks in North America. The Common Scoter was once thought to be the Black Scoter's Eurasian subspecies, but it has now been split into a separate species.
**VOICE** Male call a high-whistled *peeew*; female a low raspy *kraaa*.
**NESTING** Depression lined with grass and down, often in tall grass on tundra; 5–10 eggs; 1 brood; May–September.
**FEEDING** Dives in saltwater for mollusks, crustaceans, and plant matter; feeds on aquatic insects and freshwater mussels.

**FLIGHT:** strong wingbeats; male's wings make whistling sound during takeoff.

**YELLOW BILL**
Male Black Scoters are distinctive with their black plumage and yellow bill-knob.

### SIMILAR SPECIES

**SURF SCOTER ♀**
see p.44

flatter crown

two whitish patches

larger bill

**WHITE-WINGED SCOTER ♀**
see p.45

more sloping head

longer bill

**OCCURRENCE**
Breeding habitat is somewhat varied, but is generally close to fairly shallow, small lakes. Winters along both coasts. Populations wintering farther north prefer water over cobbles, gravel, or offshore ledges, whereas in southern locations, sandier habitats are chosen.

| Length **17–21in (43–53cm)** | Wingspan **31–35in (79–90cm)** | Weight **1¾–2¾lb (0.8–1.2kg)** |
| Social **Flocks** | Lifespan **Unknown** | Status **Declining** |

| DATE SEEN | WHERE | | NOTES |
|---|---|---|---|
| | | | |
| | | | |
| | | | |
| | | | |
| | | | |

| Order **Anseriformes** | Family **Anatidae** | Species *Clangula hyemalis* |
|---|---|---|

# Long-tailed Duck

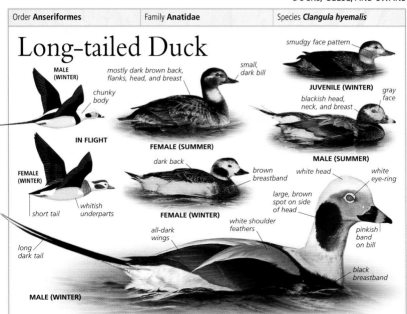

**MALE (WINTER)**

mostly dark brown back, flanks, head, and breast

small, dark bill

smudgy face pattern

chunky body

**JUVENILE (WINTER)**

gray face

blackish head, neck, and breast

**IN FLIGHT**

**FEMALE (SUMMER)**

**MALE (SUMMER)**

dark back

brown breastband

white head

white eye-ring

**FEMALE (WINTER)**

whitish underparts

short tail

large, brown spot on side of head

white shoulder feathers

all-dark wings

pinkish band on bill

long dark tail

black breastband

**MALE (WINTER)**

The Long-tailed Duck is a small, pudgy sea duck with a wide range of plumages depending on the season and the sex of the bird. The male has two extremely long tail feathers, which are often held up in the air like a pennant. The male's loud calls are quite musical, and, when heard from a flock, have a chorus-like quality, hence the name *Clangula*, which is Latin for "loud." This species can dive for a prolonged period of time, and can reach depths of 200ft (60m), making it one of the deepest diving ducks. Its three-part molt is more complex than that of other ducks.

**VOICE** Male call a *ang-ang-eeeooo* with yodeling quality; female barking *urk* or *uk* alarm call.

**NESTING** Shallow depression in ground lined with plant matter; 6–9 eggs; 1 brood; May–September.

**FEEDING** Dives to bottom of freshwater or saltwater habitats for mollusks, crustaceans, insects, fish, and roe.

**FLIGHT:** flies low over the water, somewhat erratically, with fast, fluttering wingbeats.

**UNMISTAKABLE MALE**
In winter, dark wings, a white body with black breast-band, and a long tail make this male unmistakable.

**OCCURRENCE**
Breeds in Arctic and subarctic, nesting in small groups on islands and peninsulas on lakes, less commonly on tundra and freshwater ponds on islands. Winters mostly along rocky coasts and headlands, protected bays, or on large freshwater lakes.

**SIMILAR SPECIES**

**BUFFLEHEAD ♀**
see p.48

white wing patch

white cheek patch

**BLACK GUILLEMOT ✳**
see p.433

pale rump

white wing patches

| Length **14–23in (35–58cm)** | Wingspan **28in (72cm)** | Weight **18–39oz (500–1,100g)** |
|---|---|---|
| Social **Flocks** | Lifespan **Up to 22 years** | Status **Declining** |

| DATE SEEN | WHERE | NOTES |
|---|---|---|
| .......... | ................... | .......................... |
| .......... | ................... | .......................... |
| .......... | ................... | .......................... |
| .......... | ................... | .......................... |
| .......... | ................... | .......................... |

| Order **Anseriformes** | Family **Anatidae** | Species **Bucephala albeola** |
|---|---|---|

# Bufflehead 🔊

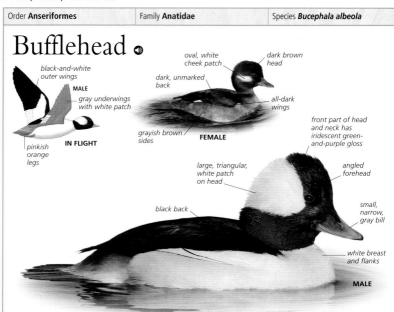

black-and-white outer wings

**MALE**

gray underwings with white patch

**IN FLIGHT**

pinkish orange legs

oval, white cheek patch

dark brown head

dark, unmarked back

all-dark wings

grayish brown sides

**FEMALE**

front part of head and neck has iridescent green-and-purple gloss

large, triangular, white patch on head

angled forehead

black back

small, narrow, gray bill

white breast and flanks

**MALE**

The smallest diving duck in North America, the Bufflehead is a close relative of the Common and Barrow's Goldeneyes. Males make a bold statement with their striking head pattern. In flight, males resemble the larger Common Goldeneye, yet the large white area on their head makes them easy to distinguish. The Common Goldeneye's wings create a whirring sound in flight whereas the Bufflehead's do not. The northern limit of the Bufflehead's breeding range corresponds to that of the Northern Flicker, as the ducks usually nest in abandoned Flicker cavities.

**VOICE** Male a low growl or squeal; chattering during breeding; female mostly silent except during courtship or calling to chicks.

**NESTING** Cavity nester, no nesting material added, near water; 7–9 eggs; 1 brood; April–September.

**FEEDING** Dives for aquatic invertebrates: usually insects in freshwater, mollusks and crustaceans in saltwater; also eats seeds.

**FLIGHT:** very rapid wingbeats; no flight sound, unlike Goldeneyes.

**IMMEDIATE TAKEOFF**
Unlike other diving ducks, the small, compact Bufflehead can takeoff almost vertically.

**OCCURRENCE**
Breeds in forest from Alaska to eastern Canada, in woodlands near small lakes and permanent ponds, where young are raised. Winters largely along the Pacific and Atlantic Coasts with lower densities scattered across the continent, south to northern Mexico, and in Bermuda.

## SIMILAR SPECIES

**HOODED MERGANSER ♂**
see p.51

smaller, with white cheek patch

**RUDDY DUCK ♂ ❄**
see p.54

dark cap

longer bill

larger size

| Length  12½–15½in (32–39cm) | Wingspan  21½–24in (54–61cm) | Weight  10–18oz (275–500g) |
|---|---|---|
| Social  **Flocks** | Lifespan  **Up to 15 years** | Status  **Secure** |

| DATE SEEN | WHERE | NOTES |
|---|---|---|
| | | |
| | | |
| | | |
| | | |
| | | |

| Order **Anseriformes** | Family **Anatidae** | Species ***Bucephala clangula*** |
| --- | --- | --- |

# Common Goldeneye

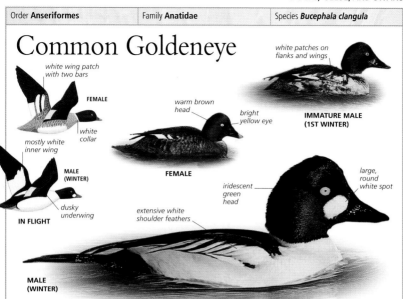

white wing patch with two bars

**FEMALE**

white collar

mostly white inner wing

**MALE (WINTER)**

dusky underwing

**IN FLIGHT**

warm brown head

bright yellow eye

**FEMALE**

white patches on flanks and wings

**IMMATURE MALE (1ST WINTER)**

large, round white spot

iridescent green head

extensive white shoulder feathers

**MALE (WINTER)**

Common Goldeneyes closely resemble Barrow's Goldeneyes. Found in North America and Eurasia, this is a medium-sized, compact diving duck. It is aggressive and very competitive with members of its own species, as well as other cavity-nesting ducks. It regularly lays eggs in the nests of other species—a behavior that is almost parasitic. Before diving, the Common Goldeneye flattens its feathers in preparation for underwater foraging. The female's head shape changes according to her posture.

**VOICE** Courting males make a faint *peent* call; females a harsh *gack* or repeated *cuk* calls.

**NESTING** Cavity nester in holes made by other birds, including Pileated Woodpeckers, in broken branches or hollow trees; also commonly uses nest boxes; 4–13 eggs; 1 brood; April–September.

**FEEDING** Dives during breeding season for insects; in winter, mollusks and crustaceans; sometimes eats fish and plant matter.

**FLIGHT:** rapid with fast wingbeats; male's wings make a tinkling sound in flight.

**MALE TAKING OFF**
Quite a long takeoff, involving energetically running on the water, leaves a trail of spray.

### SIMILAR SPECIES

**BUFFLEHEAD ♀**
see p.48

smaller overall

white oval patch behind eye

**BARROW'S GOLDENEYE ♂**
see p.50

smaller bill

large crescent on face

**OCCURRENCE**
Breeds along wetlands, lakes, and rivers with clear water in northern forests, where large trees provide appropriate nest cavities. Winters across continent, with highest densities located from north New England to the mid-Atlantic on coastal bays and in the West from coastal southeast Alaska to British Columbia.

| Length **15½–20in (40–51cm)** | Wingspan **30–33in (77–83cm)** | Weight **19–44oz (550–1,300g)** |
| --- | --- | --- |
| Social **Flocks** | Lifespan **Up to 15 years** | Status **Secure** |

| DATE SEEN | WHERE | NOTES |
| --- | --- | --- |
| | | |
| | | |
| | | |
| | | |
| | | |

| Order **Anseriformes** | Family **Anatidae** | Species ***Bucephala islandica*** |
|---|---|---|

# Barrow's Goldeneye

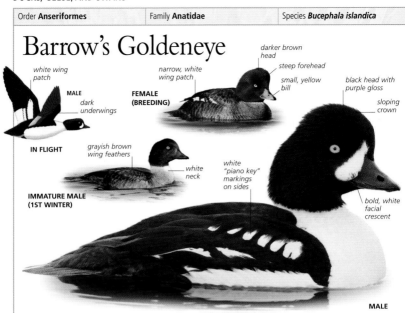

*darker brown head*

*steep forehead*

*white wing patch*

*narrow, white wing patch*

*small, yellow bill*

*black head with purple gloss*

**MALE**

*dark underwings*

**FEMALE (BREEDING)**

*sloping crown*

**IN FLIGHT**

*grayish brown wing feathers*

*white neck*

*white "piano key" markings on sides*

**IMMATURE MALE (1ST WINTER)**

*bold, white facial crescent*

**MALE**

B arrow's Goldeneye is a slightly larger, darker version of the Common Goldeneye. Although the female can be identified by her different head structure, her bill color varies seasonally and geographically. Eastern Barrow's have blacker bills with less yellow, and western populations have entirely yellow bills, which darken in summer. During the breeding season, the majority of Barrow's Goldeneyes are found in mountainous regions of northwestern North America.

**VOICE** Males normally silent; courting males grunt *ka-KAA*; females *cuc* call, slightly higher pitched than Common Goldeneye.
**NESTING** Tree cavity in holes formed by Pileated Woodpeckers, often broken limbs or hollow trees; also uses nest boxes; 6–12 eggs; 1 brood; April–September.
**FEEDING** Dives in summer for insects, some fish, and roe; in winter, mainly mollusks and crustaceans; some plant matter.

**FLIGHT:** rapid flight with fast, deep wingbeats; flies near water surface on short flights.

**COURTING DISPLAY**
A male thrusts his head back and gives a guttural call. His feet then kick back, driving him forward.

### SIMILAR SPECIES

**GREATER SCAUP ♀** browner overall; see p.419

*longer neck*

*white patch*

**COMMON GOLDENEYE ♀** see p.49

*warmer brown head*

*more triangular head*

**OCCURRENCE**
Winters along the Pacific Coast between southeast Alaska and Washington, with small populations in eastern Canada. Smaller numbers found inland from the lower Colorado River to Yellowstone National Park. Eastern population is localized in winter with the highest count in St. Lawrence estuary.

| Length **17–19in (43–48cm)** | Wingspan **28–30in (71–76cm)** | Weight **17–46oz (475–1,300g)** |
|---|---|---|
| Social **Flocks** | Lifespan **Up to 18 years** | Status **Secure** |

| DATE SEEN | WHERE | NOTES |
|---|---|---|
| | | |
| | | |
| | | |
| | | |
| | | |

| Order **Anseriformes** | Family **Anatidae** | Species **Lophodytes cucullatus** |

# Hooded Merganser

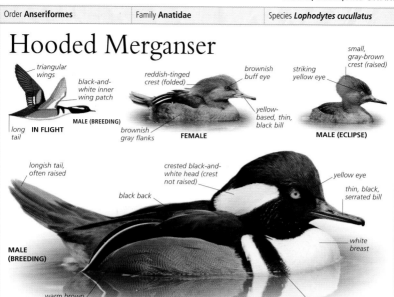

triangular wings

black-and-white inner wing patch

**MALE (BREEDING)**

long tail **IN FLIGHT**

reddish-tinged crest (folded)

brownish gray flanks

brownish buff eye

yellow-based, thin, black bill

**FEMALE**

striking yellow eye

small, gray-brown crest (raised)

**MALE (ECLIPSE)**

longish tail, often raised

crested black-and-white head (crest not raised)

black back

yellow eye

thin, black, serrated bill

white breast

**MALE (BREEDING)**

warm brown flanks

bold vertical bars

This dapper, miniature fish-eater is the smallest of the three mergansers. Both male and female Hooded Mergansers have crests that they can raise or flatten. When the male raises his crest, the thin horizontal white stripe turns into a gorgeous white fan, surrounded by black. Although easily identified when swimming, the Hooded Merganser and the Wood Duck can be confused when seen in flight since they both are fairly small with bushy heads and long tails.

**VOICE** Normally silent; during courtship, males produce a low, growly, descending *pah-hwaaaaa*, reminiscent of a frog; females give a soft *rrrep*.

**NESTING** Cavity nester; nest lined with down feathers in a tree or box close to or over water; 6–15 eggs; 1 brood; February–June.

**FEEDING** Dives for fish, aquatic insects, and crayfish, preferably in clear and shallow fresh waters, but also in brackish waters.

**FLIGHT:** low, fast, and direct; shallow wingbeats; quiet whirring noise produced by wings.

**FANHEAD SPECTACULAR**
The male's magnificent black-and-white fan of a crest is like a beacon in the late afternoon light.

**OCCURRENCE**
Prefers forested small ponds, marshes, or slow-moving streams during the breeding season. During winter, occurs in shallow water in both fresh- and saltwater bays, estuaries, rivers, streams, ponds, freshwater marshes, and flooded sloughs.

### SIMILAR SPECIES

**WOOD DUCK ♀**
see p.30

bold, white eye-ring

blue wing patch

**RED-BREASTED MERGANSER ♀**
see p.53

steel gray-and-white plumage

rustier head with ragged crest

| Length **15½–19½in (40–49cm)** | Wingspan **23½–26in (60–66cm)** | Weight **16–31oz (450–875g)** |
| Social **Small flocks** | Lifespan **Unknown** | Status **Secure** |

| DATE SEEN | WHERE | | NOTES |
|---|---|---|---|
| | | | |
| | | | |
| | | | |
| | | | |
| | | | |

| Order **Anseriformes** | Family **Anatidae** | Species *Mergus merganser* |
|---|---|---|

# Common Merganser

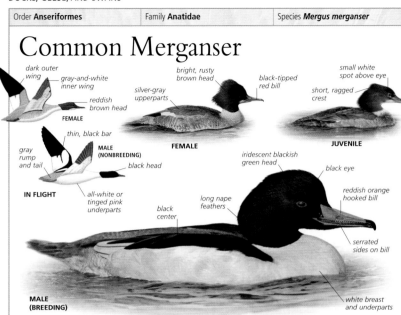

dark outer wing
gray-and-white inner wing
reddish brown head
**FEMALE**

bright, rusty brown head
silver-gray upperparts
black-tipped red bill

small white spot above eye
short, ragged crest

**JUVENILE**

gray rump and tail
thin, black bar
**MALE (NONBREEDING)**
black head
**FEMALE**

**IN FLIGHT**
all-white or tinged pink underparts

iridescent blackish green head
black eye
long nape feathers
black center
reddish orange hooked bill
serrated sides on bill
white breast and underparts

**MALE (BREEDING)**

The largest of the three merganser species in North America, the Common Merganser is called a Goosander in the UK. This large fish-eater is common and widespread, particularly in the northern portion of its range. It is often found in big flocks on lakes or smaller groups along rivers. It spends most of its time on the water, using its serrated bill to catch fish underwater.
**VOICE** Mostly silent, except when alarmed or during courtship; females give a low-pitched harsh *karr* or *gnuk*, the latter also given in series; during courtship, males emit a high-pitched, bell-like note and other twangy notes; alarm call a hoarse *grrr* or *uak*.
**NESTING** Cavity nester sometimes high in trees; uses nest boxes, nests on ground; 6–17 eggs; 1 brood; April–September.
**FEEDING** Eats mostly fish (especially fond of trout and salmon, but also carp and catfish), aquatic invertebrates, frogs, small mammals, birds, and plants.

**FLIGHT:** fast with shallow wingbeats; often flying low over the water.

**FEEDING ON THE MOVE**
This female Common Merganser is trying to swallow, head-first, a rather large fish.

**OCCURRENCE**
Breeds in the northern forests from Alaska to Newfoundland; winters south to north-central Mexico. It winters farther north than most other waterfowl as long as water remains open. Prefers fresh-to saltwater locations.

**SIMILAR SPECIES**

| COMMON GOLDENEYE ♂ see p.49 | RED-BREASTED MERGANSER ♀ see p.53 |
|---|---|
| white patch · black-and-white pattern | smaller, more lightly built · thinner bill |

| Length **21½–28in (54–71cm)** | Wingspan **34in (86cm)** | Weight **1¾–4¾lb (0.8–2.1kg)** |
|---|---|---|
| Social **Flocks** | Lifespan **Up to 13 years** | Status **Secure** |

| DATE SEEN | WHERE | NOTES |
|---|---|---|
| .................... | .................... | .................... |
| .................... | .................... | .................... |
| .................... | .................... | .................... |
| .................... | .................... | .................... |
| .................... | .................... | .................... |

| Order **Anseriformes** | Family **Anatidae** | Species **Mergus serrator** |

# Red-breasted Merganser

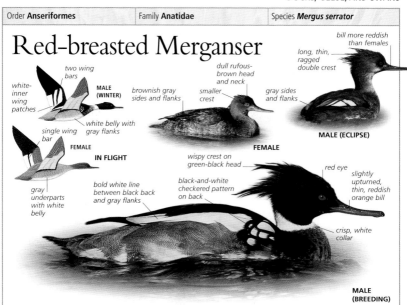

bill more reddish than females

long, thin, ragged double crest

two wing bars

**MALE (WINTER)**

white-inner wing patches

dull rufous-brown head and neck

brownish gray sides and flanks

smaller crest

gray sides and flanks

**MALE (ECLIPSE)**

white belly with gray flanks

single wing bar

**FEMALE**

**IN FLIGHT**

**FEMALE**

gray underparts with white belly

bold white line between black back and gray flanks

wispy crest on green-black head

black-and-white checkered pattern on back

red eye

slightly upturned, thin, reddish orange bill

crisp, white collar

**MALE (BREEDING)**

The Red-breasted Merganser, like the other saw-billed mergansers, is an elegant fish-eating duck. Both sexes are easily recognized by their long, sparse, somewhat ragged-looking double crest. Red-breasted Mergansers are smaller than Common Mergansers, but much larger than the Hooded. The Red-breasted Merganser, unlike the other two mergansers, nests on the ground, in loose colonies, often among gulls and terns, and is protected by its neighbors.

**VOICE** During courtship males make a raucous *yeow-yeow* call; females emit a raspy *krrr-krrr.*

**NESTING** Shallow depression on ground lined with down and plant material, near water; 5–11 eggs; 1 brood; May–July.

**FEEDING** Dives for small fish such as herring and minnows; also salmon eggs; at times flocks coordinate and drive fish together.

**FLIGHT:** fast flying duck with very rapid, regular, and shallow flapping.

**KEEPING CLOSE**
Red-breasted Mergansers are gregarious at all times of year, often feeding in loose flocks.

**SIMILAR SPECIES**

**HOODED MERGANSER ♀**
see p.51

fuller, cinnamon-tinged crest

darker back

smaller overall

**COMMON MERGANSER ♀**
see p.52

rusty red head

smaller bill

full crest

larger and more robust

white breast and chin

**OCCURRENCE**
Most northern range of all the mergansers, nests across Arctic and subarctic regions, tundra and northerly forests, along coasts, inland lakes, river banks, marsh edges, and coastal islands. Winters farther south than other mergansers, mostly in protected bays, estuaries, or on the Great Lakes.

| Length **20–25in (51–64cm)** | Wingspan **26–29in (66–74cm)** | Weight **1¾–2¾lb (0.8–1.3kg)** |
| Social **Flocks/Colonies** | Lifespan **Up to 9 years** | Status **Secure** |

| DATE SEEN | WHERE | NOTES |
| --- | --- | --- |
| | | |
| | | |
| | | |
| | | |
| | | |

| Order **Anseriformes** | Family **Anatidae** | Species *Oxyura jamaicensis* |
| --- | --- | --- |

# Ruddy Duck 🔊

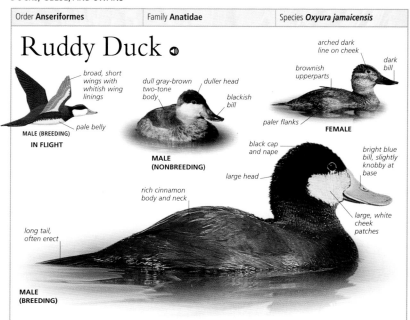

**MALE (BREEDING) IN FLIGHT**

broad, short wings with whitish wing linings

pale belly

dull gray-brown two-tone body

duller head

blackish bill

**MALE (NONBREEDING)**

arched dark line on cheek

dark bill

brownish upperparts

paler flanks

**FEMALE**

black cap and nape

large head

bright blue bill, slightly knobby at base

large, white cheek patches

rich cinnamon body and neck

long tail, often erect

**MALE (BREEDING)**

Small and stiff-tailed, the Ruddy Duck is comical in both its appearance and behavior. Both sexes often hold their tail in a cocked position, especially when sleeping. During courtship displays, the male points its long tail skyward while rapidly thumping its electric blue bill against its chest, ending the performance with an odd, bubbling sound. In another display, males make a popping sound by slapping their feet on the water's surface. Large feet, on legs set far back on its body, make the Ruddy Duck an excellent swimmer and diver; however, on land it is perhaps one of the most awkward of diving ducks. Females are known to push themselves along instead of walking.

**VOICE** Females give a nasal *raanh* and high pitched *eeek*; males vocally silent, but make popping noises with feet.

**NESTING** Platform, bowl-shaped nest built over water in thick emergent vegetation, rarely on land; 6–10 eggs; 1 brood; May–September.

**FEEDING** Dives for aquatic insects, larvae, crustaceans, and other invertebrates, particularly when breeding; during winter, also eats plants.

**FLIGHT:** rapid and direct, with fast wingbeats; not very agile in flight, which seems labored.

**HEAVY HEAD**
A female "sitting" on the water streamlines her body before she dives, making her head look large.

**SIMILAR SPECIES**

MASKED DUCK ♂

black tip to bill

black face

ruddy-colored back with black streaks

**OCCURRENCE**
Breeds in the prairie pothole region in wetland habitats; marshes, ponds, reservoirs, and other open shallow water with emergent vegetation and open areas. Majority winter on freshwater habitats from ponds to large lakes; smaller numbers found on brackish coastal marshes, bays, and estuaries.

| Length **14–17in (35–43cm)** | Wingspan **22–24in (56–62cm)** | Weight **11–30oz (300–850g)** |
| --- | --- | --- |
| Social **Flocks** | Lifespan **Up to 13 years** | Status **Secure** |

| DATE SEEN | WHERE | | NOTES |
| --- | --- | --- | --- |
| | | | |
| | | | |
| | | | |
| | | | |
| | | | |

| Order **Anseriformes** | Family **Anatidae** | Species *Alopochen aegyptiaca* |
|---|---|---|

# Egyptian Goose

white
forewing

long neck

black-and-white
underwing

**IN FLIGHT**

dark brown
face patch

stubby
pink
bill

large white
wing patch

pale
breast
and
underside

brown
with white
patches

gray bill

pale
breast
and
underside

long pink legs

**JUVENILE**

**ADULT**

**FLIGHT:** low, quick, powerful with regular deep wingbeats; may flutter up to a high perch such as the branch of a tree.

Originally from Africa, Egyptian Geese have become naturalized in North America following "escapes" from ornamental wildfowl collections. Many were imported in the late 19th century but breeding in the wild was not known until 1967 (California) and the 1980s (Florida). They have not spread very widely yet, but have become common in parts of Texas, where they are often seen on golf courses and near city-park lakes. While increasing numbers in the UK are a cause of concern, in North America, there is no evidence that they are a threat to native wildlife. Nevertheless, numbers are controlled in some districts.

**VOICE** Staccato, guttural quacking notes; noisy if disturbed near nest.
**NESTING** Nests in tree hole up to 65ft (20m) high; 6–10 eggs; 1 brood; May–June.
**FEEDING** Eats roots, shoots, seeds, and other vegetable matter from shallow water and margins of freshwater.

**PUZZLING NEWCOMERS**
Unexpectedly large, pale birds swimming in a lake or grazing on grassy spaces nearby can be mistaken for other species. The pale head and dark mask indicate Egyptian Geese.

**OCCURRENCE**
Found in wet grasslands and marshy areas with old trees, and in nearby areas of short grass; most common in southern Florida, southeastern Texas, and around Los Angeles, California.

| Length **25–29in (63–73cm)** | Wingspan **3½–4¼ft (1.1–1.3cm)** | Weight **3½–5½lb (1.5–2.3kg)** |
|---|---|---|
| Social **Small flocks** | Lifespan **10–20 years** | Status **Secure** |

| DATE SEEN | WHERE | NOTES |
|---|---|---|
| | | |
| | | |
| | | |
| | | |
| | | |

# QUAILS, GROUSE, TURKEYS, AND RELATIVES

THIS DIVERSE AND ADAPTABLE group of birds thrives in habitats ranging from hot desert to frozen tundra. Galliforms spend most of their time on the ground, springing loudly into the air when alarmed.

## NEW WORLD QUAILS

Among the most terrestrial of all galliforms, quails are renowned for their great sociability, often forming large family groups, or "coveys," of up to 100 birds. The Northern Bobwhite is the only quail species found in the East, and ranges over a variety of habitats. Each of the five species found in western North America lives in a specific habitat or at a particular elevation.

**DRESSED TO THRILL**
With its striking plumage, Gambel's Quail is one of the best-known desert birds in southwestern North America.

Prairie grouse, including the Sharp-tailed Grouse, are found throughout the middle of the continent. All three tundra and mountaintop grouse or ptarmigans are found in the extreme North and the Rockies. Grouse often possess patterns that match their surroundings, providing camouflage from both animal and human predators.

**GRASSLAND GROUSE**
The aptly named Sharp-tailed Grouse is locally common in western prairies. It searches for grasshoppers in the summer.

## PHEASANTS AND PARTRIDGES

These Eurasian galliforms were introduced into North America in the 19th and 20th centuries to provide additional targets for recreational hunters. While some introductions failed, species such as the colorful Ring-necked Pheasant adapted well and now thrive in established populations.

## GROUSE

The most diverse and widespread birds in the order Galliforms in North America, the 12 different species of grouse can be divided into three groups based on their preferred habitats. Forest grouse include the Ruffed Grouse in the East, the Spruce Grouse in the North, and the Sooty Grouse and Dusky Grouse in the West.

**SNOW BIRD**
The Rock Ptarmigan's white winter plumage camouflages it against the snow, helping hide it from predators.

| Order **Galliformes** | Family **Odontophoridae** | Species *Callipepla californica* |

# California Quail

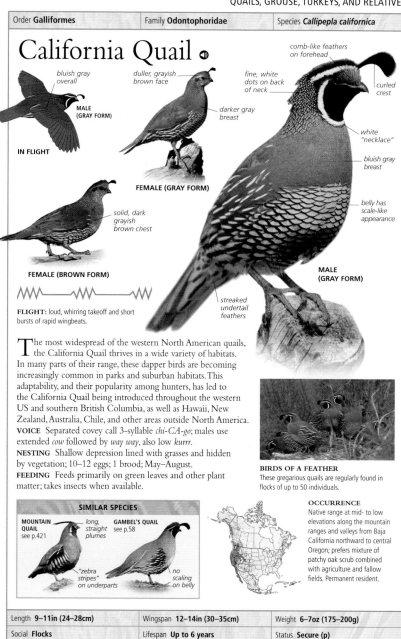

bluish gray overall

**MALE (GRAY FORM)**

**IN FLIGHT**

duller, grayish brown face

darker gray breast

**FEMALE (GRAY FORM)**

comb-like feathers on forehead

fine, white dots on back of neck

curled crest

white "necklace"

bluish gray breast

belly has scale-like appearance

solid, dark grayish brown chest

**FEMALE (BROWN FORM)**

**MALE (GRAY FORM)**

streaked undertail feathers

**FLIGHT:** loud, whirring takeoff and short bursts of rapid wingbeats.

The most widespread of the western North American quails, the California Quail thrives in a wide variety of habitats. In many parts of their range, these dapper birds are becoming increasingly common in parks and suburban habitats. This adaptability, and their popularity among hunters, has led to the California Quail being introduced throughout the western US and southern British Columbia, as well as Hawaii, New Zealand, Australia, Chile, and other areas outside North America.

**VOICE** Separated covey call 3-syllable *chi-CA-go*; males use extended *cow* followed by *way way*, also low *kurrr*.

**NESTING** Shallow depression lined with grasses and hidden by vegetation; 10–12 eggs; 1 brood; May–August.

**FEEDING** Feeds primarily on green leaves and other plant matter; takes insects when available.

**BIRDS OF A FEATHER**
These gregarious quails are regularly found in flocks of up to 50 individuals.

**SIMILAR SPECIES**

**MOUNTAIN QUAIL** see p.421

long, straight plumes

**GAMBEL'S QUAIL** see p.58

no scaling on belly

"zebra stripes" on underparts

**OCCURRENCE**
Native range at mid- to low elevations along the mountain ranges and valleys from Baja California northward to central Oregon; prefers mixture of patchy oak scrub combined with agriculture and fallow fields. Permanent resident.

| Length **9–11in (24–28cm)** | Wingspan **12–14in (30–35cm)** | Weight **6–7oz (175–200g)** |
| Social **Flocks** | Lifespan **Up to 6 years** | Status **Secure (p)** |

| DATE SEEN | WHERE | NOTES |
|---|---|---|
| | | |
| | | |
| | | |
| | | |
| | | |

| Order **Galliformes** | Family **Odontophoridae** | Species *Callipepla gambelii* |
|---|---|---|

# Gambel's Quail

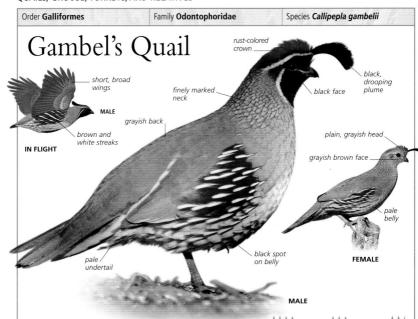

rust-colored crown

short, broad wings

**MALE**

**IN FLIGHT**

brown and white streaks

grayish back

finely marked neck

black face

black, drooping plume

plain, grayish head

grayish brown face

pale belly

pale undertail

black spot on belly

**FEMALE**

**MALE**

Gambel's Quail is a highly social bird of the low-elevation deserts and valley floors of the Southwest, particularly Arizona and northern Mexico, where it is often known as the Desert or Arizona Quail. While tolerant of hot, dry conditions, its breeding success depends entirely on local rainfall, which produces the green plants that make up most of its diet. Gambel's Quail is a popular galliform throughout its range, readily identified by its drooping black "topknot," or plume, in addition to its distinctive calls.
**VOICE** Most common call: *chi-CA-go-go*; males attract mates with *kaa* or *kaaow*; alarmed birds utter *chip-chip-chip*.
**NESTING** Small depression defined by twigs and lined with grass and leaves, usually within cover; 10–12 eggs; 1 brood; March–June.
**FEEDING** Feeds mainly on seeds, green leaves, and grasses, also berries, cactus fruit; insects eaten by young and breeding birds.

**FLIGHT:** prefers running; makes short, explosive flight of rapid wingbeats followed by glide.

**SHOWING OFF ITS CHEST**
This Gambel's Quail shows its distinctive blue, white, and blackish underparts.

### SIMILAR SPECIES

**MOUNTAIN QUAIL**
see p.421
long, thin, straight plume
chestnut-brown face
broadly striped flanks

**CALIFORNIA QUAIL ♂**
see p.57
buff forehead
scaly lower belly; no black spot

**OCCURRENCE**
Strongly associated with scrub/shrub river edge or gulley vegetation, including mesquite, various grasses, and a variety of cactus species, especially where these species border agricultural properties.

| Length **9½–11in (24–28cm)** | Wingspan **12½–14in (32–35cm)** | Weight **6oz (175g)** |
|---|---|---|
| Social **Flocks** | Lifespan **Up to 4 years** | Status **Secure** |

| DATE SEEN | WHERE | NOTES |
|---|---|---|
| | | |
| | | |
| | | |
| | | |
| | | |

| Order **Galliformes** | Family **Phasianidae** | Species *Alectoris chukar* |

# Chukar

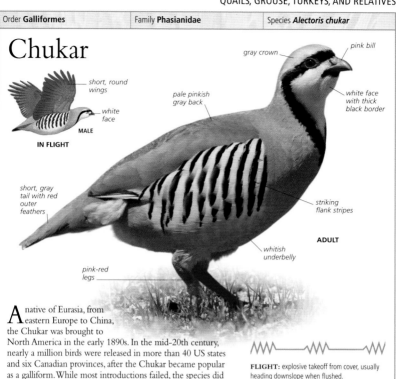

gray crown

pink bill

short, round wings

white face

**MALE**

**IN FLIGHT**

pale pinkish gray back

white face with thick black border

short, gray tail with red outer feathers

striking flank stripes

**ADULT**

whitish underbelly

pink-red legs

A native of Eurasia, from eastern Europe to China, the Chukar was brought to North America in the early 1890s. In the mid-20th century, nearly a million birds were released in more than 40 US states and six Canadian provinces, after the Chukar became popular as a galliform. While most introductions failed, the species did succeed in some areas, especially on steep mountain slopes in the West. Chukars form large communal groups, or crèches, of up to 100 young birds, with 10–12 adults overseeing them.

**VOICE** When flushed, a thin whistled *peee*, then a series of squeals *pittoo-pittoo-pittoo*; *chukka-chuka-chuka-chuka* reunites flushed or dispersed covey.

**NESTING** Shallow scrape lined with nearby dead vegetation, well-concealed among shrubs and rocks on hillside; 7–12 eggs; 1 brood; March–May.

**FEEDING** Eats mainly seeds from various grasses and green succulent plants; berries; also eats insects.

**FLIGHT:** explosive takeoff from cover, usually heading downslope when flushed.

### SIMILAR SPECIES

**MOUNTAIN QUAIL** see p.421
long, thin, straight head plume

brown face

brown flanks edged with black and white

**GRAY PARTRIDGE** see p.60
lighter gray body

rusty-orange face

dark chestnut bars on flanks

**MAKING AN EFFORT** Perched on a rock, this Chukar calls loudly, stretching its neck to increase vocal capacity.

**OCCURRENCE** Introduced to the West, released for shooting in the East; found on wide open areas and steep slopes at high elevation, up to 8,200ft (2,500m), with a mix of deep, brushy canyons and hillsides of loose rocks and boulders, sparse bush, low woody shrubs, grasses and aromatic herbs.

| Length **13½–15in (34–38cm)** | Wingspan **19–22in (48–56cm)** | Weight **18–23oz (500–650g)** |
| Social **Family groups** | Lifespan **Up to 3 years** | Status **Secure** |

| DATE SEEN | WHERE | NOTES |
|-----------|-------|-------|
| .......... | .......... | .......... |
| .......... | .......... | .......... |
| .......... | .......... | .......... |
| .......... | .......... | .......... |
| .......... | .......... | .......... |

| Order **Galliformes** | Family **Phasianidae** | Species **Perdix perdix** |
| --- | --- | --- |

# Gray Partridge

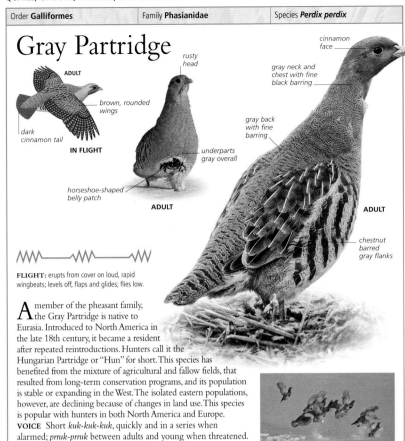

cinnamon face

gray neck and chest with fine black barring

gray back with fine barring

**ADULT**

rusty head

brown, rounded wings

dark cinnamon tail

**IN FLIGHT**

underparts gray overall

horseshoe-shaped belly patch

**ADULT**

**ADULT**

chestnut barred gray flanks

**FLIGHT:** erupts from cover on loud, rapid wingbeats; levels off, flaps and glides; flies low.

A member of the pheasant family, the Gray Partridge is native to Eurasia. Introduced to North America in the late 18th century, it became a resident after repeated reintroductions. Hunters call it the Hungarian Partridge or "Hun" for short. This species has benefited from the mixture of agricultural and fallow fields, that resulted from long-term conservation programs, and its population is stable or expanding in the West. The isolated eastern populations, however, are declining because of changes in land use. This species is popular with hunters in both North America and Europe.
**VOICE** Short *kuk-kuk-kuk*, quickly and in a series when alarmed; *prruk-prruk* between adults and young when threatened.
**NESTING** Shallow depression in soil lined with vegetation, usually in hedgerows; 14–18 eggs; 1 brood; March–May.
**FEEDING** Eats mostly seeds and row crops such as corn and wheat; succulent green leaves in spring; insects when breeding.

**NOISY TAKEOFF**
When the Gray Partridge takes flight its wings make a loud, whirring sound.

## SIMILAR SPECIES

**NORTHERN BOBWHITE ♀** see p.421
white streaks on rusty red body

**CHUKAR** see p.59
buffy throat and face
white face edged in black
red bill
black barring on white flanks

**OCCURRENCE**
Primarily agricultural fields of crops including corn, wheat, and oats, as well as associated hedgerows and fallow grasslands. Most birds are nonmigratory, but there is some movement by eastern birds after breeding.

| Length **11–13in (28–33cm)** | Wingspan **17–20in (43–51cm)** | Weight **12–18oz (350–500g)** |
| --- | --- | --- |
| Social **Family groups** | Lifespan **Up to 4 years** | Status **Declining** |

| DATE SEEN | WHERE | NOTES |
| --- | --- | --- |
| | | |
| | | |
| | | |
| | | |
| | | |

| Order **Galliformes** | Family **Phasianidae** | Species **Phasianus colchicus** |

# Ring-necked Pheasant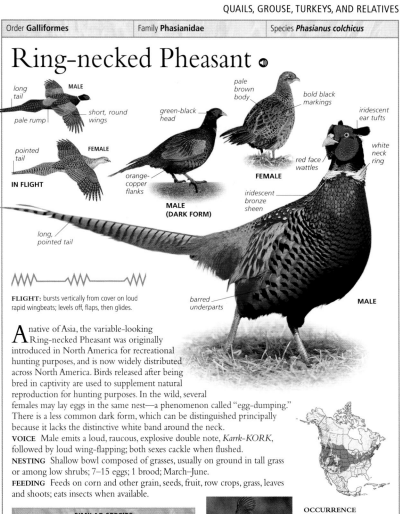

**MALE**
long tail
pale rump
short, round wings

**FEMALE**
pointed tail

**IN FLIGHT**

pale brown body
green-black head
bold black markings
orange-copper flanks

**MALE (DARK FORM)**

red face wattles
iridescent bronze sheen

iridescent ear tufts
white neck ring

**FEMALE**

long, pointed tail

**FLIGHT:** bursts vertically from cover on loud rapid wingbeats; levels off, flaps, then glides.

barred underparts

**MALE**

A native of Asia, the variable-looking Ring-necked Pheasant was originally introduced in North America for recreational hunting purposes, and is now widely distributed across North America. Birds released after being bred in captivity are used to supplement natural reproduction for hunting purposes. In the wild, several females may lay eggs in the same nest—a phenomenon called "egg-dumping." There is a less common dark form, which can be distinguished principally because it lacks the distinctive white band around the neck.

**VOICE** Male emits a loud, raucous, explosive double note, *Karrk-KORK*, followed by loud wing-flapping; both sexes cackle when flushed.

**NESTING** Shallow bowl composed of grasses, usually on ground in tall grass or among low shrubs; 7–15 eggs; 1 brood; March–June.

**FEEDING** Feeds on corn and other grain, seeds, fruit, row crops, grass, leaves and shoots; eats insects when available.

**SIMILAR SPECIES**

**GREATER SAGE-GROUSE** larger; see p.422
long, dark tail
dark belly
pale breast

**SHARP-TAILED GROUSE** slightly smaller; see p.69
shorter tail
darker brown overall

**FLUSHED OUT**
The Ring-necked Pheasant is a powerful flier when alarmed or flushed out of its cover.

**OCCURRENCE**
Widespread across southern Canada and the US; prefers mixture of active agricultural crops (especially corn fields), fallow fields, and hedgerows; also cattail marshes and wooded river bottoms. The Ring-necked Pheasant is native to Asia from the Caucasus east to China.

| Length **19½–28in (50–70cm)** | Wingspan **30–34in (76–86cm)** | Weight **1¼–6½lb (0.5–3kg)** |
| Social **Solitary/Flocks** | Lifespan **Up to 4 years** | Status **Secure** |

| DATE SEEN | WHERE | NOTES |
|---|---|---|
| | | |
| | | |
| | | |
| | | |
| | | |

| Order **Galliformes** | Family **Phasianidae** | Species *Bonasa umbellus* |
|---|---|---|

# Ruffed Grouse 🔊

**ADULT (RUFOUS FORM)**

**IN FLIGHT**

brown-barred
underparts

rusty tail
with black
band

dark patch
on neck

spotted gray
upperparts

heavy white
spotting on
brown
upperparts

raised
crest

gray-barred
underparts

**ADULT
(GRAY FORM)**

feathered
legs

**ADULT (RUFOUS FORM)**

The Ruffed Grouse is perhaps the most widespread galliform in North America. There are two color forms, rufous and gray, both allowing the birds to remain camouflaged and undetected on the forest floor, until they eventually burst into the air in an explosion of whirring wings. The male is well known for his extraordinary wing beating or "drumming" display, which he performs year-round, but most frequently in the spring.

**VOICE** Hissing notes, and soft *purrt, purrt, purrt* when alarmed, by both sexes; males "drumming" display when heard from distance resembles small engine starting, *thump...thump...thump...thump... thump...thuthuthuth.*

**NESTING** Shallow, leaf-lined bowl set against a tree trunk, rock or fallen log in forest; 6–14 eggs; 1 brood; March–June.

**FEEDING** Forages on ground for leaves, buds, and fruit; occasionally insects.

**FLIGHT:** an explosive takeoff, usually at close range, glides for a short distance before landing.

**OCCURRENCE**
Found in young, mixed forests throughout the northern US and much of Canada except tundra. Southern edge of range extends along higher elevations of the Appalachians and middle levels of the Rocky Mountains, if suitable habitat is available.

**WARM RED**
The rufous form of the Ruffed Grouse is more common in wetter parts of the continent.

**SIMILAR SPECIES**

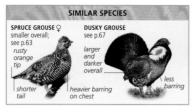

**SPRUCE GROUSE ♀**
smaller overall;
see p.63

rusty
orange
tip

shorter
tail

**DUSKY GROUSE**
see p.67

larger
and
darker
overall

heavier barring
on chest

less
barring

| Length **17–20in (43–51cm)** | Wingspan **20–23in (51–58cm)** | Weight **20–22oz (575–625g)** |
|---|---|---|
| Social **Solitary/Small flocks** | Lifespan **Up to 10 years** | Status **Secure** |

| DATE SEEN | WHERE | NOTES |
|---|---|---|
| | | |
| | | |
| | | |
| | | |
| | | |

| Order **Galliformes** | Family **Phasianidae** | Species *Falcipennis canadensis* |

# Spruce Grouse

**MALE (FRANKLIN'S)**
ADULT
**IN FLIGHT**
white spots on black tail

paler overall

**FEMALE**
*F. c. canadensis*
**(TAIGA)**
heavy barring on underparts

bright red comb above eye
black throat
black breast

gray upperparts
heavily barred underparts

triangular white spots on underparts

**FEMALE**
*F. c. franklinii*
**(FRANKLIN'S)**

**MALE**
*F. c. canadensis*
**(TAIGA)**

Perhaps because of the remoteness of their habitat and lack of human contact, Spruce Grouse are not afraid of humans. This lack of wariness when approached has earned them the name "fool hens." Their specialized diet of pine needles causes the intestinal tract to expand in order to accommodate a large volume of food to compensate for its low nutritional value. There are two groups of Spruce Grouse, the Taiga and the Franklin's, both of which have red and gray forms.
**VOICE** Mostly silent; males clap their wings during courtship display; females often utter long cackle at dawn and dusk.
**NESTING** Lined with moss, leaves, feathers; often at base of tree; naturally low area in forest floor 4–6 eggs; 1 brood; May–July.
**FEEDING** Feeds mostly on pine but also spruce needles; will eat insects, leaves, fruit, and seeds when available.

**FLIGHT:** generally avoids flying; when disturbed, bursts into flight on whirring wings.

**RUFOUS BAND**
The male "Taiga" form displays the thin rufous band on the tip of his tail.

**SIMILAR SPECIES**

**RUFFED GROUSE**
see p.62
spotted gray upperparts
gray-barred underparts

**DUSKY GROUSE**
see p.67
longer, charcoal-gray tail
much larger
grayer overall

**OCCURRENCE**
Present year-round in forests dominated by conifers, including jack, lodgepole, spruce, red spruce, black spruce, balsam fir, subalpine fir, hemlock, and cedar. Found from western Alaska to the Atlantic Coast.

| Length **14–17in (36–43cm)** | Wingspan **21–23in (53–58cm)** | Weight **16oz (450g)** |
| Social **Solitary** | Lifespan **Up to 10 years** | Status **Secure** |

| DATE SEEN | WHERE | NOTES |
|---|---|---|
| | | |
| | | |
| | | |
| | | |
| | | |

| Order **Galliformes** | Family **Phasianidae** | Species *Lagopus lagopus* |
|---|---|---|

# Willow Ptarmigan

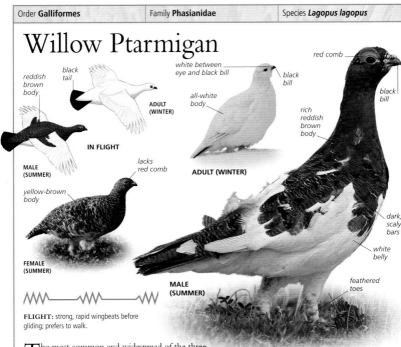

reddish brown body

black tail

**ADULT (WINTER)**

**IN FLIGHT**

**MALE (SUMMER)**

lacks red comb

yellow-brown body

**FEMALE (SUMMER)**

white between eye and black bill

black bill

all-white body

**ADULT (WINTER)**

red comb

black bill

rich reddish brown body

dark, scaly bars

white belly

**MALE (SUMMER)**

feathered toes

**FLIGHT:** strong, rapid wingbeats before gliding; prefers to walk.

The most common and widespread of the three ptarmigan species, the Willow Ptarmigan is the State Bird of Alaska. The Willow Ptarmigan is an unusual Galliform species, as male and female remain bonded throughout the chick-rearing process, in which the male is an active participant. The "Red Grouse" of British moors is a subspecies (*L. l. scoticus*) of the Willow Ptarmigan.

**VOICE** Variety of purrs, clucks, hissing, meowing noises; *Kow-Kow-Kow* call given before flushing, possibly alerting others.

**NESTING** Shallow bowl scraped in soil, lined with plant matter, protected by overhead cover; 8–10 eggs; 1 brood; March–May.

**FEEDING** Mostly eats buds, stems, and seeds, but also flowers, insects, and leaves when available.

**PERFECT BLEND-IN**
Its reddish brown upperparts camouflage this summer ptarmigan in the shrubby areas it inhabits.

**SIMILAR SPECIES**

**WHITE-TAILED PTARMIGAN** ☼ see p.66
browner plumage
smaller overall

**ROCK PTARMIGAN** ☼ see p.65
grayer plumage
darker

**OCCURRENCE**
Prefers tundra, in Arctic, subarctic, and subalpine regions. Thrives in willow thickets along low, moist river corridors; also in the low woodlands of the subarctic tundra.

| Length **14–17½in (35–44cm)** | Wingspan **22–24in (56–61cm)** | Weight **15–28oz (425–800g)** |
|---|---|---|
| Social **Winter flocks** | Lifespan **Up to 9 years** | Status **Secure** |

| DATE SEEN | WHERE | NOTES |
|---|---|---|
| | | |
| | | |
| | | |
| | | |
| | | |

| Order **Galliformes** | Family **Phasianidae** | Species **Lagopus muta** |
| --- | --- | --- |

# Rock Ptarmigan

brown-and-black barring

black tail

**MALE (WINTER)**

white wings

small, round head

red comb

mostly gray upperparts

small bill

all-white wings

mottled belly

**FEMALE (SUMMER)**

small, delicate bill

gray wing patch

**IN FLIGHT**

"salt-and-pepper" barring on gray upperparts

**MALE (SUMMER)**

white plumage

**FEMALE (WINTER)**

black line between eye and bill

white belly

**MALE (WINTER)**

feathered legs and toes

**MALE (SUMMER)**

**FLIGHT:** bursts into flight with rapid wingbeats, followed by gliding and shallow flapping.

The Rock Ptarmigan is the most northern of the three ptarmigan species found in North America. Although some birds make a short migration to more southern wintering grounds, many remain on their breeding grounds year-round. This species is well known for its distinctive seasonal variation in plumage, which helps to camouflage it against its surroundings. Ptarmigan are a common food of the Inuit, who inhabit the same Arctic habitat.

**VOICE** Quiet; male call a raspy *krrrh*, also growls and clucks.

**NESTING** Small scrape or natural depression, lined with plant matter, often away from cover; 8–10 eggs; 1 brood; April–June.

**FEEDING** Feeds on buds, seeds, flowers, and leaves, especially birch and willow; eats insects in summer.

**IN BETWEEN PLUMAGE**
Various transitional plumage patterns can be seen on the Rock Ptarmigan in spring and fall.

### SIMILAR SPECIES

**WHITE-TAILED PTARMIGAN** ☼
all-white tail in winter;
see p.66

smaller overall

**WILLOW PTARMIGAN** ☼
see p.64

larger overall

lighter brown upperparts

**OCCURRENCE**
Local in dry, rocky tundra and shrubby ridge tops; will use edges of open meadows and dense evergreen stands along fairly high-elevation rivers and streams during winter. Occurs throughout the Northern Hemisphere in Arctic tundra from Iceland to Kamchatka in the Russian Far East.

| Length **12½–15½in (32–40cm)** | Wingspan **19½–23½in (50–60cm)** | Weight **16–23oz (450–650g)** |
| --- | --- | --- |
| Social **Winter flocks** | Lifespan **Up to 8 years** | Status **Secure** |

| DATE SEEN | WHERE | NOTES |
| --- | --- | --- |
| .............. | .............................. | .............................. |
| .............. | .............................. | .............................. |
| .............. | .............................. | .............................. |
| .............. | .............................. | .............................. |
| .............. | .............................. | .............................. |

| Order **Galliformes** | Family **Phasianidae** | Species *Lagopus leucura* |

# White-tailed Ptarmigan

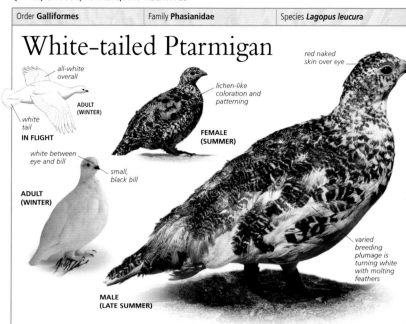

*all-white overall*

**ADULT (WINTER)**

*white tail*

**IN FLIGHT**

*red naked skin over eye*

*lichen-like coloration and patterning*

**FEMALE (SUMMER)**

*white between eye and bill*

*small, black bill*

**ADULT (WINTER)**

*varied breeding plumage is turning white with molting feathers*

**MALE (LATE SUMMER)**

The smallest and most southern of the three North American ptarmigan, the White-tailed Ptarmigan's native range is still largely intact. In the winter, its completely white plumage—unique among Galliform species—blends in perfectly with its icy mountain home. Its plumage is one of several adaptations to the inhospitable environment it inhabits. The feathers on its feet increase the surface area in contact with the ground, and so help to prevent the bird from sinking into the snow.

**VOICE** Males emit various cackling clucks, *cuk-cuk-cuuuk* during display; females cluck, purr, and growl softly.

**NESTING** Scrape in ground lined with plants and feathers; 4–8 eggs; 1 brood; May–June.

**FEEDING** Feeds heavily on willows, eating mostly leaves, buds, and twigs; insects when nesting.

**FLIGHT:** rarely flies unless pursued; flush on explosive wingbeats, then flap-and-glide sequence.

**WHITE ON WHITE**
Immobile on white snow, the male blends in superbly with the wintry surroundings.

### SIMILAR SPECIES

**ROCK PTARMIGAN** ☼
see p.65
*grayer summer plumage*
*larger overall*

**WILLOW PTARMIGAN** ☼
see p.64
*reddish brown summer plumage*
*red comb*
*white under-parts*
*larger overall*

**OCCURRENCE**
Has a more restricted distribution than Rock and Willow Ptarmigan, occurring from Alaska south to Idaho and Montana; small isolated populations exist in Colorado and New Mexico. Strongly associated with willow stands above tree-line; also meadows and evergreen stand mixtures.

| Length **12in (30–31cm)** | Wingspan **20–22in (51–56cm)** | Weight **12–16oz (350–450g)** |
| Social **Large flocks** | Lifespan **Up to 15 years** | Status **Secure** |

| DATE SEEN | WHERE | NOTES |
| --- | --- | --- |
| | | |
| | | |
| | | |
| | | |
| | | |

| Order **Galliformes** | Family **Phasianidae** | Species **_Dendragapus obscurus_** |

# Dusky Grouse

MALE

pale underwing

**IN FLIGHT**

plain tail tip

red wattle over eye

bare red or purple air sacs

broad, rounded black tail

barred crown and neck

mottled brown back

small bill

short, plain brown wings

**MALE (DISPLAY)**

gray belly

gray underparts

white scales on flanks

**FEMALE**

Once considered a single species, the Blue Grouse, the Dusky Grouse, and the Sooty Grouse are now considered distinct species. Male Dusky Grouse can be identified by their courtship displays, which are primarily ground-based and quieter than those of the Sooty Grouse, and by their reddish purple air sacs. The Dusky Grouse also has a plain tail, lacking the gray tip of the Sooty, and its chicks are more gray than brown.

**VOICE** A series of five soft hoots; also a hiss, growl, and cluck; females emit a whinnying cry.

**NESTING** Shallow scrape, usually lined with dead grass, leaves, or other plants, located under shrubs, against rocks or logs; 7–10 eggs; 1 brood; March–May.

**FEEDING** Feeds on leaves, flowers, fruit, also some insects; evergreen needles, buds, and cones in season.

**FLIGHT:** loud, short-distance flight with rapid wingbeats before gliding to the ground.

**FREEZING FOR SAFETY**
This female Dusky Grouse stands still as a statue, relying on camouflage, not flight, for protection.

### SIMILAR SPECIES

**SPRUCE GROUSE ♀**
see p.63

shorter tail

**SOOTY GROUSE**
see p.68

smaller overall

darker

yellow air sacs

**OCCURRENCE**
Found in the northern and central Rocky Mountains in Canada and US in high or mid-altitude open forests and shrublands. Typically uses older, denser, mixed, or evergreen forests at higher elevations in winter, more open-country, lighter forests at lower elevations in summer.

| Length **16–20in (41–51cm)** | Wingspan **25–28in (64–71cm)** | Weight **2½–2¾lb (1.1–1.3kg)** |
| Social **Solitary/Winter flocks** | Lifespan **Up to 14 years** | Status **Localized** |

| DATE SEEN | WHERE | NOTES |
|---|---|---|
| | | |
| | | |
| | | |
| | | |
| | | |

| Order **Galliformes** | Family **Phasianidae** | Species *Dendragapus fuliginosus* |

# Sooty Grouse

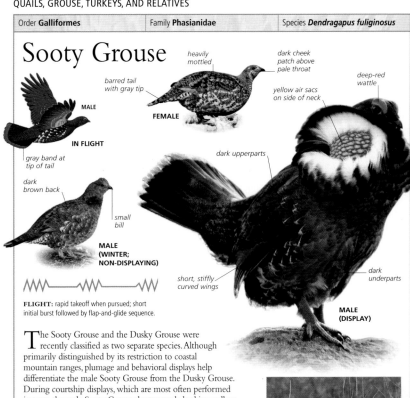

**MALE**

**IN FLIGHT**

barred tail with gray tip

heavily mottled

**FEMALE**

dark cheek patch above pale throat

yellow air sacs on side of neck

deep-red wattle

gray band at tip of tail

dark brown back

dark upperparts

small bill

**MALE (WINTER; NON-DISPLAYING)**

short, stiffly curved wings

dark underparts

**MALE (DISPLAY)**

**FLIGHT:** rapid takeoff when pursued; short initial burst followed by flap-and-glide sequence.

The Sooty Grouse and the Dusky Grouse were recently classified as two separate species. Although primarily distinguished by its restriction to coastal mountain ranges, plumage and behavioral displays help differentiate the male Sooty Grouse from the Dusky Grouse. During courtship displays, which are most often performed in trees, the male Sooty Grouse shows rough-looking, yellow air sacs. Females and chicks have a browner overall appearance to their plumage than those of the Dusky Grouse.

**VOICE** Loud 6-syllable hooting; also growl, hiss, cluck, *purrr*.
**NESTING** Shallow depression lined with dead vegetation, usually under small pine trees; 5–8 eggs; 1 brood; March–May.
**FEEDING** Feeds primarily on evergreen needles, especially douglas fir; will take leaves, grasses, fruit, and insects when seasonally available.

**CAUTIOUS PEEK**
Female Sooty Grouse disturbed on the ground peer up through grasses to check for danger.

### SIMILAR SPECIES

**SPRUCE GROUSE ♀**
see p.63

shorter tail

**DUSKY GROUSE**
see p.67

smaller browner overall

dull-red wattle

dark-red air sacs during display

**OCCURRENCE**
Found west of the Rocky Mountains in Canada and the US, from sea level to the timberline. Breeds at lower elevations in open areas with grassland, forest clearings, and shrubs, and moves up into thicker evergreen forests at higher elevations in winter.

| Length **16–20in (41–51cm)** | Wingspan **25–28in (64–71cm)** | Weight **2½–2¾lb (1.1–1.3g)** |
| Social **Solitary/Winter flocks** | Lifespan **Up to 14 years** | Status **Secure** |

| DATE SEEN | WHERE | NOTES |
|---|---|---|
| .................. | ...................... | .............................. |
| .................. | ...................... | .............................. |
| .................. | ...................... | .............................. |
| .................. | ...................... | .............................. |
| .................. | ...................... | .............................. |

| Order **Galliformes** | Family **Phasianidae** | Species *Tympanuchus phasianellus* |
|---|---|---|

# Sharp-tailed Grouse

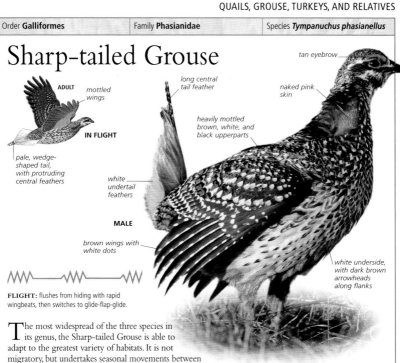

*tan eyebrow*

*naked pink skin*

**ADULT** *mottled wings*

*long central tail feather*

*heavily mottled brown, white, and black upperparts*

**IN FLIGHT**

*pale, wedge-shaped tail, with protruding central feathers*

*white undertail feathers*

**MALE**

*brown wings with white dots*

*white underside, with dark brown arrowheads along flanks*

**FLIGHT:** flushes from hiding with rapid wingbeats, then switches to glide-flap-glide.

The most widespread of the three species in its genus, the Sharp-tailed Grouse is able to adapt to the greatest variety of habitats. It is not migratory, but undertakes seasonal movements between grassland summer habitats and woodland winter habitats. These birds are popular with hunters and are legal quarry in most of their range. Elements of this grouse's spectacular courtship display have been incorporated into the culture and dance of Native American people, including foot stomping and tail feather rattling.
**VOICE** Male calls a variety of unusual clucks, cooing, barks, and gobbles during courtship; females cluck with different intonations.
**NESTING** Shallow depression lined with plant matter close at hand as well as some feathers from female, usually near overhead cover; 10–12 eggs; 1 brood; March–May.
**FEEDING** Forages primarily for seeds, leaves, buds, and fruit; also takes insects and flowers when available.

**PRAIRIE DANCER**
The courtship dance of the Sharp-tailed Grouse heralds the arrival of spring to the grasslands.

## SIMILAR SPECIES

**GREATER PRAIRIE-CHICKEN**
see p.422

*shorter, square tail*

*more heavily barred*

**RING-NECKED PHEASANT ♀**
see p.61

*light brown*

*longer tail*

*naked orange skin*

*scalloped pattern on underparts*

### OCCURRENCE
Has a northern and western distribution in North America, from Alaska (isolated population) southward to northern prairie states. Prefers a mixture of fallow and active agricultural fields combined with brushy forest edges and woodlots along river beds.

| Length **15–19in (38–48cm)** | Wingspan **23–26in (58–66cm)** | Weight **26–34oz (750–950g)** |
|---|---|---|
| Social **Flocks** | Lifespan **Up to 7 years** | Status **Declining (p)** |

| DATE SEEN | WHERE | NOTES |
|---|---|---|
| | | |
| | | |
| | | |
| | | |
| | | |

| Order **Galliformes** | Family **Phasianidae** | Species *Meleagris gallopavo* |
|---|---|---|

# Wild Turkey 🔊

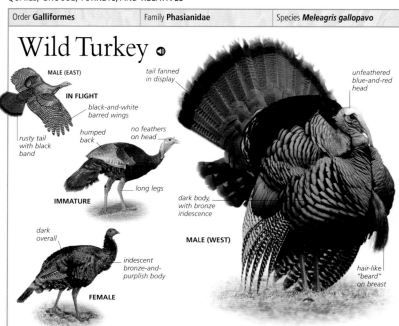

**MALE (EAST)**

**IN FLIGHT**

tail fanned in display

unfeathered blue-and-red head

black-and-white barred wings

rusty tail with black band

humped back

no feathers on head

long legs

**IMMATURE**

dark body, with bronze iridescence

**MALE (WEST)**

dark overall

iridescent bronze-and-purplish body

hair-like "beard" on breast

**FEMALE**

Once proposed by Benjamin Franklin as the national emblem of the US, the Wild Turkey—the largest galliform in North America—was eliminated from most of its original range by the early 1900s because of over-hunting and habitat destruction. Since then, habitat restoration and the subsequent reintroduction of Wild Turkeys has been very successful.

**VOICE** Well-known gobble, given by males especially during courtship; female makes various yelps, clucks, and purrs, based on mood and threat level.

**NESTING** Scrape on ground lined with grass; placed against or under protective cover; 10–15 eggs; 1 brood; March–June.

**FEEDING** Omnivorous, it scratches in leaf litter on forest floor for acorns and other food, mostly vegetation; also takes plants and insects from agricultural fields.

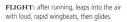

**FLIGHT:** after running, leaps into the air with loud, rapid wingbeats, then glides.

**COLLECTIVE DISPLAY**
Once the population expands into new areas, numerous males will be seen displaying together.

**SIMILAR SPECIES**

**GREATER SAGE-GROUSE**
see p.422

dark head

pointed tail

white breast

**TURKEY VULTURE**
see p.191

small red head

dark overall

**OCCURRENCE**
Found in mixed mature woodlands, fields with agricultural crops; also in various grasslands, close to swamps, but adaptable and increasingly common in suburban and urban habitats. Quite widespread, but patchily distributed across North America.

| Length **2¾–4ft (0.9–1.2m)** | Wingspan **4–5ft (1.2–1.5m)** | Weight **10–24lb (4.5–11kg)** |
|---|---|---|
| Social **Flocks** | Lifespan **Up to 9 years** | Status **Secure** |

| DATE SEEN | WHERE | NOTES |
|---|---|---|
| | | |
| | | |
| | | |
| | | |
| | | |

# GREBES

GREBES RESEMBLE LOONS and share many of their aquatic habits, but anatomical and molecular features show that they are actually unrelated; and they are placed in a different order—the Podicipediformes. Their bodies are streamlined, offering little resistance when diving and swimming. Grebes' toes have broad lobes that splay when the bird thrusts forward through the water with its feet. Underwater their primary means of propulsion is the sideways motion of their lobed toes. The legs are placed far back on the body, which greatly aids the bird when swimming above or below the surface. Grebes have short tails, and their trailing legs and

toes serve as rudders when they fly. The position of the legs makes it impossible, however, for grebes to stand upright for long or easily walk on land. Thus, even when breeding they are tied to water; and their nests are usually partially floating platforms, built on beds of water plants. They dive to catch fish with a short, forward-arching spring. Unusual among birds, they swallow feathers, supposedly to trap fish bones and protect their stomachs, then periodically disgorge them. Like loons, grebes can control their buoyancy by exhaling air and compressing their plumage so that they sink quietly below the surface. They are strong fliers and are migratory.

**SIDE BY SIDE**
A pair of Western Grebes display their elaborate courtship behavior.

# PIGEONS AND DOVES

THE LARGER SPECIES within the family Columbidae are known as pigeons, and the smaller ones as doves, although there is no actual scientific basis for the distinction. They are all fairly heavy, plump birds with relatively small heads and short necks. They also possess slender bills with their nostrils positioned in a fleshy mound at the base. Among other things, members of this family have strong wing muscles, making them powerful and agile fliers. When alarmed, they burst into flight, with their wings emitting a distinctive clapping or swishing sound. Pigeons and doves produce a nutritious "crop-milk," which they secrete to feed their young. Despite human activity having severely affected members of this family in the past (the leading cause of the Passenger Pigeon's extinction early in the 1900s is thought to be over-hunting), the introduced Rock Pigeon has adapted and proliferated worldwide, as has

the recently introduced Eurasian Collared-Dove, albeit on a smaller scale. The introduced Spotted Dove has not shown a similar tendency for explosive expansion, however, and remains limited to southern California and the islands of Hawaii. Among the species native to North America, only the elegant Mourning Dove is as widespread as the various species of introduced birds.

**DOVE IN THE SUN**
The Mourning Dove sunbathes each side of its body in turn, its wings and tail outspread.

| Order **Podicipediformes** | Family **Podicipedidae** | Species **Podilymbus podiceps** |
|---|---|---|

# Pied-billed Grebe 🔊

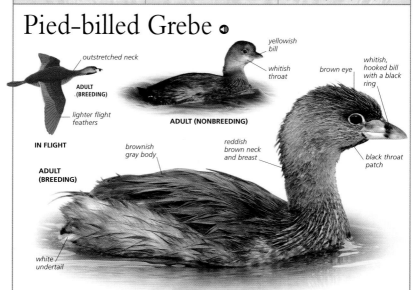

outstretched neck

**ADULT (BREEDING)**

yellowish bill

whitish throat

**ADULT (NONBREEDING)**

whitish, hooked bill with a black ring

brown eye

lighter flight feathers

**IN FLIGHT**

brownish gray body

reddish brown neck and breast

black throat patch

**ADULT (BREEDING)**

white undertail

The widest ranging of the North American grebes, the Pied-billed Grebe is tolerant of highly populated areas and is often seen breeding on lakes and ponds across North America. It is a powerful swimmer and can remain submerged for 16–30 seconds when it dives. In contrast to some of the elaborate displays from other grebe species, its courtship ritual is more vocal than visual and a pair usually duet-call in the mating season. Migration, conducted at night, is delayed until its breeding area ices up and food becomes scarce. The Pied-billed Grebe is capable of sustained flights of more than 2,000 miles (3,200km).

**VOICE** Various grunts and wails; in spring, call a cuckoo-like repeated gobble *kup-kup-Kaow-Kaow-kaow*, gradually speeding up.

**NESTING** Floating nest of partially decayed plants and clipped leaves, attached to emergent vegetation in marshes and quiet waters; 4–7 eggs; 2 broods; April–October.

**FEEDING** Dives to catch a variety of crustaceans, fish, amphibians, insects, and other invertebrates; also picks prey from emergent vegetation, or catches them mid-air.

**FLIGHT:** strong, direct flight with rapid wingbeats, but rarely seen.

**BACK OFF**
When alarmed, a Pied-billed Grebe may flap its wings in a defensive display.

### SIMILAR SPECIES

**LEAST GREBE** ✿

smaller bill

yellow eye

darker body

**OCCURRENCE**
Breeds on a variety of water bodies, including coastal brackish ponds, seasonal ponds, marshes, and even sewage ponds. Winters in the breeding area if food and open water are available, otherwise chooses still waters resembling its breeding habitat.

| Length **12–15in (30–38cm)** | Wingspan **18–24in (46–62cm)** | Weight **11–20oz (300–575g)** |
|---|---|---|
| Social **Pairs/Loose flocks/Colonies** | Lifespan **Up to 5 years** | Status **Declining** |

| DATE SEEN | WHERE | NOTES |
|---|---|---|
| .................... | .................... | .................... |
| .................... | .................... | .................... |
| .................... | .................... | .................... |
| .................... | .................... | .................... |
| .................... | .................... | .................... |

| Order **Podicipediformes** | Family **Podicipedidae** | Species *Podiceps auritus* |

# Horned Grebe

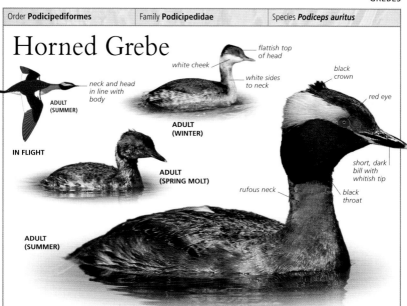

**IN FLIGHT**

ADULT
(SUMMER)

neck and head
in line with
body

white cheek

flattish top
of head

white sides
to neck

ADULT
(WINTER)

black
crown

red eye

ADULT
(SPRING MOLT)

rufous neck

short, dark
bill with
whitish tip

black
throat

ADULT
(SUMMER)

The timing of the Horned Grebe's migration depends largely on the weather—this species may not leave until its breeding grounds get iced over, nor does it arrive before the ice melts. Its breeding behavior is well documented since it is approachable on nesting grounds and has an elaborate breeding ritual. This grebe's so-called "horns" are in fact yellowish feather patches located behind its eyes, which it can raise at will.

**VOICE** At least 10 calls, but descending *aaanrrh* call most common in winter, ends in trill; muted conversational calls when birds are in groups.

**NESTING** Floating, soggy nest, hidden in vegetation, in small ponds and lake inlets; 3–9 eggs; 1 brood; May–July.

**FEEDING** Dives in open water or forages among plants, mainly for small crustaceans and insects, but also leeches, mollusks, amphibians, fish, and some vegetation.

**FLIGHT:** strong, rapid wingbeats; runs on water to become airborne; rarely takes off from land.

**HITCHING A RIDE**
In common with other grebes, Horned Grebe chicks often ride on the back of a swimming parent.

**SIMILAR SPECIES**

**RED-NECKED GREBE** ❋
see p.74

brownish
cap

darker eye

**EARED GREBE** ❋
see p.75

dark
cheek

upturned
bill

**OCCURRENCE**
Breeds in small freshwater, even slightly brackish, ponds and marshes, including manmade ponds. Prefers areas with open water and patches of sedges, cattails, and other wetland vegetation. Winters on saltwater close to shore; also on large bodies of freshwater.

| Length **12–15in (30–38cm)** | Wingspan **18–24in (46–62cm)** | Weight **11–20oz (300–575g)** |
| Social **Pairs/Loose flocks/Colonies** | Lifespan **Up to 5 years** | Status **Declining** |

| DATE SEEN | WHERE | NOTES |
|---|---|---|
| | | |
| | | |
| | | |
| | | |
| | | |

| Order **Podicipediformes** | Family **Podicipedidae** | Species *Podiceps grisegena* |
| --- | --- | --- |

# Red-necked Grebe

**IN FLIGHT**

**ADULT (BREEDING)**
head and neck in line with body
white-edged inner wing

**ADULT (NONBREEDING)**
pale, reddish brown crescent near ear
brownish cap

**JUVENILE**
broad stripes on cheek and ear
mostly yellowish bill

**ADULT (BREEDING)**
gray flanks
broad head with crest at rear
grayish white cheeks and throat
black cap
chestnut-brown neck and chest
yellow base of bill

The Red-necked Grebe is smaller than Western and Clark's Grebes, but larger than the other North American grebes. It migrates over short to medium distances and spends the winter along both coasts, where large flocks may be seen during the day. It runs along the water's surface to become airborne, although it rarely flies. This grebe doesn't come ashore often; it stands erect, but walks awkwardly, and prefers to sink to its breast and shuffle along.

**VOICE** Nasal, gull-like call on breeding grounds, evolves into bray, ends with whinny; also honks, rattles, hisses, purrs, and ticks.

**NESTING** Compact, buoyant mound of decayed and fresh vegetation in sheltered, shallow marshes and lakes, or artificial wetlands; 4–5 eggs; 1 brood; May–July.

**FEEDING** An opportunistic hunter, eats fish, crustaceans, aquatic insects, worms, mollusks, salamanders, and tadpoles.

**FLIGHT:** fast, direct, wingbeats, with head and outstretched neck mostly level with line of body.

**COURTSHIP DISPLAY**
This courting pair face each other, with outstretched necks and raised neck feathers.

**SIMILAR SPECIES**

**RED-THROATED LOON** ❊
see p.167
white spots on back
white neck
no yellow on bill

**HORNED GREBE** ❊
see p.73
reddish eye
paler neck

**OCCURRENCE**
Breeds from northern prairies and forests, almost to the tree line in the northwest; limited to suitable interior bodies of water such as large marshes and small lakes. Winters primarily in estuaries, inlets, bays, and offshore shallows along Atlantic and Pacific Coasts; can also be found on the Great Lakes.

| Length **16½–22in (42–56cm)** | Wingspan **24–35in (61–88cm)** | Weight **1¾–3½lb (0.8–1.6kg)** |
| --- | --- | --- |
| Social **Pairs/Loose flocks** | Lifespan **Up to 6 years** | Status **Vulnerable** |

| DATE SEEN | WHERE | NOTES |
| --- | --- | --- |
| | | |
| | | |
| | | |
| | | |
| | | |

| Order **Podicipediformes** | Family **Podicipedidae** | Species *Podiceps nigricollis* |
|---|---|---|

# Eared Grebe

darker flanks

white patch on wing

browner plumage

**ADULT (SUMMER)**

outstretched neck

**JUVENILE**

dusky cheek

upturned bill

dusky white flanks

large, wispy gold patch behind red eye

**IN FLIGHT**

grayish neck

dark back

black neck

**ADULT (WINTER)**

black crest

red eye

thin, upturned bill

rufous breast and sides

**ADULT (SUMMER)**

The most abundant grebe in North America, the Eared Grebe is quite remarkable in terms of physiology. After breeding, it undergoes a complex and drastic reorganization of body-fat stores, along with changes in muscle, heart, and digestive organ mass to prepare it for fall migration. All of this increases the bird's energy reserves and body mass, but renders it flightless. It may have the longest periods of flightlessness of any flying bird—up to 10 months.

**VOICE** Various trills during courtship, including squeaky, rising *poo-eep*; sharp *chirp* when alarmed; usually silent at other times.
**NESTING** Sodden nest of decayed bottom plants anchored in thinly spaced reeds or submerged vegetation in shallow water of marshes, ponds, and lakes; 1 brood; 1–8 eggs; May–July.
**FEEDING** Forages underwater for small crustaceans and aquatic insects; also small fish and mollusks; consumes worms in winter.

**FLIGHT:** flies with neck outstretched, held at a low angle; rarely flies except during migration.

**SALTY WATER**
The Eared Grebe prefers salty water at all times except when breeding.

**SIMILAR SPECIES**

**RED-NECKED GREBE** ❉
see p.74

browner cap

thicker bill

**HORNED GREBE** ❉
see p.73

white tip on bill

more distinct white cheek

**OCCURRENCE**
Breeds in marshes, shallow lakes, and ponds. After breeding, many birds seek saline waters, such as Mono Lake, or lakes in Utah where their favorite foods thrive—brine shrimp and alkali flies. Winters in coastal bays of Pacific Coast and is a vagrant on Atlantic Coast. Also breeds in Eurasia.

| Length **12–14in (30–35cm)** | Wingspan **22½–24in (57–62cm)** | Weight **7–26oz (200–725g)** |
|---|---|---|
| Social **Flocks** | Lifespan **Up to 12 years** | Status **Secure** |

| DATE SEEN | WHERE | NOTES |
|---|---|---|
| | | |
| | | |
| | | |
| | | |
| | | |

| Order **Podicipediformes** | Family **Podicipedidae** | Species *Aechmophorus occidentalis* |

# Western Grebe

black nape stripe

**ADULT**

whitish band on dark wing

**IN FLIGHT**

dark patch around eyes

light gray back

light white-gray neck

**CHICK**

black nape stripe

dark gray back

black crown extends below eye

distinctive red eye

long, slender, slightly upturned greenish yellow bill

**ADULT**

brilliant white throat, breast, and belly

Western and Clark's Grebes are strictly North American species. They share much of their breeding habitat and elaborate mating rituals, and were, until 1985, classified as different color forms of a single species. Interbreeding is uncommon, perhaps because of slight differences in calls, bill colors, and facial patterns. Although hybrids are rare, they appear to be fertile, and produce chicks of their own. Female Western Grebes are smaller than males and have smaller, thinner, slightly upturned bills. The Western Grebe dives more frequently than Clark's, and remains submerged for about 30 seconds.

**VOICE** Nine calls, each with a specific purpose, such as alarm, begging, and mating calls; advertising call is a harsh, rolling two-noted *krrrikk krrreek*.

**NESTING** Floating pile of available plants, attached to thick growth of submerged vegetation; occasionally constructed on land; 2–3 eggs; 1 brood; May–July.

**FEEDING** Mainly catches a wide variety of freshwater or saltwater fish; also crustaceans, worms, occasionally insects.

**FLIGHT:** fast and direct with rapid wingbeats; neck extended with feet stretched out behind.

**SELF-DEFENSE**
The posture of this Western Grebe shows that it is ready to defend itself when threatened.

## SIMILAR SPECIES

**CLARK'S GREBE**
see p.77

bright orange-yellow bill

white between crown and eye

**HIGHLY SOCIAL**
Western Grebes, much like Clark's Grebes, are highly gregarious in all seasons.

**OCCURRENCE**
Western North America, breeds from southern Canada to Mexico, in freshwater lakes and marshes with open water and emergent vegetation; rarely on tidewater marshes; also manmade marshes and artificial habitats. Winters along Pacific Coast, in bays and estuaries in the southwest US and Mexico.

| Length **21½–30in (55–75cm)** | Wingspan **30–39in (76–100cm)** | Weight **1¾–4lb (0.8–1.8kg)** |
| Social **Flocks** | Lifespan **At least 15 years** | Status **Declining** |

| DATE SEEN | WHERE | NOTES |
| --- | --- | --- |
| | | |
| | | |
| | | |
| | | |
| | | |

| Order **Podicipediformes** | Family **Podicipedidae** | Species *Aechmophorus clarkii* |

# Clark's Grebe

outstretched neck

**ADULT**

white throat, breast, and belly

distinct white band on wings

**IN FLIGHT**

red eye

black crown, slightly crested

white space between black crown and eye

bright orange-yellow bill

very thin, black nape stripe

long, thin, swan-like neck

moderately dark, gray back

whitish flanks

**ADULT**

Clark's and Western Grebes are closely related and very difficult to distinguish. They rarely fly except when migrating at night. Both species seldom come to land, where their movement is awkward because their legs and toes are located so far back, although they have been reported to run upright rapidly. Their flight muscles suffer wastage after their arrival on the breeding grounds, which also inhibits their ability to travel, but during the incubation period adults may feed several miles from the colony by following continuous water trails.

**VOICE** Variety of different calls, including a harsh, reedy, grating, 2-syllable, single, rising *kree-eekt* advertising call.

**NESTING** Floating pile of available plants, attached to thick growth of submerged vegetation; occasionally constructed on land; 2–3 eggs; 1 brood; May–July.

**FEEDING** Mainly catches saltwater or freshwater fish; also crustaceans.

**FLIGHT:** swift and direct with quick wingbeats; neck extended with feet trailing.

**HOW TO SWALLOW?**
It is not unusual for grebes to catch large fish; they crush the head first before swallowing.

**FORAGING IN DEEP WATER**
Clark's Grebe has a distinctive white S-shaped neck and black crown.

**SIMILAR SPECIES**

**WESTERN GREBE** ♂
see p.76

black crown extends below eye

dull greenish yellow bill

lighter upperparts

**WESTERN GREBE** ♀
see p.76

lighter nape

**OCCURRENCE**
Breeds in freshwater lakes and marshes with open water bordered by emergent vegetation; rarely tidewater marshes; has been nesting in manmade Lake Havasu marshes since 1960s. Winters along Pacific Coast, and in bays and estuaries in the southwest US and Mexico.

| Length **21½–30in (55–75cm)** | Wingspan **32in (82cm)** | Weight **1½–3¾lb (0.7–1.7kg)** |
| Social **Flocks** | Lifespan **At least 15 years** | Status **Declining** |

| DATE SEEN | WHERE | NOTES |
|---|---|---|
| | | |
| | | |
| | | |
| | | |
| | | |

| Order **Columbiformes** | Family **Columbidae** | Species *Columba livia* |
|---|---|---|

# Rock Pigeon 🔊

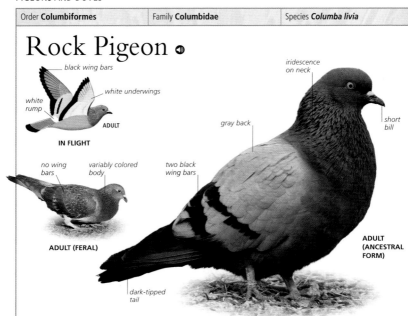

black wing bars

white underwings

white rump

**ADULT**

**IN FLIGHT**

iridescence on neck

gray back

short bill

no wing bars

variably colored body

two black wing bars

**ADULT (FERAL)**

**ADULT (ANCESTRAL FORM)**

dark-tipped tail

The Rock Pigeon was introduced to the Atlantic Coast of North America by 17th century colonists. Now feral, this species is found all over the continent, especially around farms, cities, and towns. This medium-sized pigeon comes in a wide variety of plumage colors and patterns, including bluish gray, checkered, rusty-red, and nearly all-white. Its wings usually have two dark bars on them—unique among North American pigeons. The variability of the Rock Pigeon influenced Charles Darwin as he developed his theory of natural selection.
**VOICE** Soft, gurgling *coo*, *roo-c'too-coo*, for courtship and threat.
**NESTING** Twig nest on flat, sheltered surface, such as caves, rocky outcrops, and buildings; 2 eggs; several broods; year-round.
**FEEDING** Eats seeds, fruit, and rarely, insects; human foods such as popcorn, bread, peanuts; various farm crops in rural areas.

**FLIGHT:** strong, direct; can reach speeds up to around 60mph (95kph).

**CITY PIGEONS**
Most Rock Pigeons in North America descend from domesticated forms and exhibit many colors.

**SIMILAR SPECIES**

**WHITE-CROWNED PIGEON**
mangroves

white crown

dark gray overall

white band on nape

**BAND-TAILED PIGEON**
western; see p.79

yellow bill with dark tip

**OCCURRENCE**
Across southern Canada and North America; nests in human structures of all sorts; resident. Original habitat in the Old World was (and still is) sea cliffs and inland canyons; found wild in some places, such as dry regions of North Africa, but feral in much of the world.

| Length **11–14in (28–36cm)** | Wingspan **20–26in (51–67cm)** | Weight **9–14oz (250–400g)** |
|---|---|---|
| Social **Solitary/Flocks** | Lifespan **Up to 6 years** | Status **Secure** |

| DATE SEEN | WHERE | NOTES |
|---|---|---|
| ....................... | ....................... | ....................... |
| ....................... | ....................... | ....................... |
| ....................... | ....................... | ....................... |
| ....................... | ....................... | ....................... |
| ....................... | ....................... | ....................... |

| Order **Columbiformes** | Family **Columbidae** | Species **Patagioenas fasciata** |
|---|---|---|

# Band-tailed Pigeon 🔊

dark-tipped
yellow bill

white band
on nape

iridescence
on hind neck

**ADULT**

wide
tail
band

dark gray
outer wings

light gray
inner wings

**ADULT**

**IN FLIGHT**

pale
tail tip

blue-gray
upperparts

uniform blue-gray
underparts

yellow
legs and
toes

gray tail

**FLIGHT:** direct, strong flight with powerful,
regular wingbeats.

The Band-tailed Pigeon
is similar to the Rock
Pigeon in its size, posture, body
movements, and breeding and
feeding behavior. However, in
North America the Band-tailed
Pigeon's distribution is limited
to the dry, mountain forests of
several southwestern states, and
the wet coastal forests of the West
Coast, from the southeastern tip of Alaska south to South America.
The distinguishing features of the Band-tailed Pigeon are its
yellow bill and legs, a white band just above the iridescent green
patch on the back of its neck—and its eponymous banded tail.
**VOICE** Often silent, but emits series of two-noted,
low-frequency *whooos* punctuated with a pause.
**NESTING** Flat, saucer-shaped, rather flimsy platform of
twigs, needles, and moss in a variety of trees; 1 egg;
1 brood; April–October.
**FEEDING** Forages on
the ground for grain,
seeds, fruit, acorns, and
pine nuts; hangs upside
down by its toes from
the branches of shrubs
and trees to eat dangling
nuts and flowers that are
otherwise out of reach.

**LARGE PIGEON**
This is North America's largest
pigeon, bigger than the Rock
Pigeon by about 10 percent.

**UNIFORMITY**
Unlike Rock Pigeons, Band-tailed Pigeons in
flocks have very uniform plumage.

**SIMILAR SPECIES**

**ROCK PIGEON**
see p.78
short
bill

gray back

**OCCURRENCE**
Breeds and winters in
temperate conifer rain forest
along the Pacific Coast, and in
mountain conifer and mixed-
species forests in the interior.
Lives in urban and rural areas
where there are evergreen trees
and access to grains, fruit, and
feeders. Some populations are
resident, others migratory.

| Length **13–16in (33–41cm)** | Wingspan **26in (66cm)** | Weight **12–13oz (350–375g)** |
|---|---|---|
| Social **Flocks** | Lifespan **Up to 18 years** | Status **Declining** |

| DATE SEEN | WHERE | NOTES |
|---|---|---|
| | | |
| | | |
| | | |
| | | |
| | | |

| Order **Columbiformes** | Family **Columbidae** | Species *Zenaida asiatica* |

# White-winged Dove ●

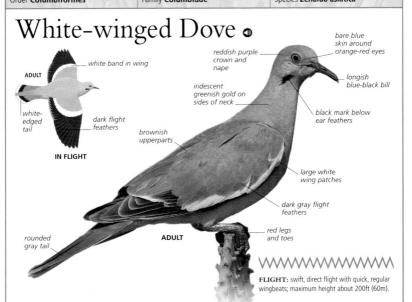

**ADULT**

white band in wing

**IN FLIGHT**

white-edged tail

dark flight feathers

bare blue skin around orange-red eyes

reddish purple crown and nape

iridescent greenish gold on sides of neck

longish blue-black bill

black mark below ear feathers

brownish upperparts

large white wing patches

dark gray flight feathers

rounded gray tail

**ADULT**

red legs and toes

**FLIGHT:** swift, direct flight with quick, regular wingbeats; maximum height about 200ft (60m).

As one of the larger gray-colored dove species in North America, the White-winged Dove is best identified in flight by the conspicuous white bands on its wings. When perched, the bright blue skin around its orange eyes and its longish, square tail with a white tip can be seen. This species has been expanding its population northward in recent decades, though not as rapidly as the Eurasian Collared-Dove. Increased farmland habitat and ornamental trees, both favorite roosting places, are the most likely cause. In common with many other doves, the nest is a somewhat flimsy structure, and eggs or nestlings frequently fall to their end if the nest is disturbed, or when there are high winds.

**VOICE** Distinctive, drawn-out cooing: *who-cooks-for-you*; also makes five-note variation from the nest: *la-coo-kla-coo-kla*.

**NESTING** Frail platform of twigs, moss, and grasses, on a sturdy branch in dense-canopied trees; 2 eggs; 2 broods; March–September.

**FEEDING** Forages for seeds, wild nuts, and fruit on the ground and in elevated locations; prefers corn, sorghum, wheat, and sunflower.

**DESERT DWELLER**
The White-winged Dove is much more at home in semiarid and desert areas than the Mourning Dove.

**SIMILAR SPECIES**

**MOURNING DOVE**
see p.81

smaller, rounder head

no white wing patch

longer tail

**OCCURRENCE**
Breeds and winters in dense, thorny woodlands dominated by mesquite and Texas ebony; deserts with cactus, palo verde, and other scrub plants; riverside woodlands, orchards, and residential areas. Formerly only abundant in the US in the Rio Grande Valley, it has now expanded north to Oklahoma.

| Length **11½in (29cm)** | Wingspan **19in (48cm)** | Weight **5oz (150g)** |
| Social **Solitary/Flocks** | Lifespan **Up to 21 years** | Status **Localized** |

| DATE SEEN | WHERE | NOTES |
| --- | --- | --- |
| | | |
| | | |
| | | |
| | | |
| | | |

| Order **Columbiformes** | Family **Columbidae** | Species *Zenaida macroura* |

# Mourning Dove 🔊

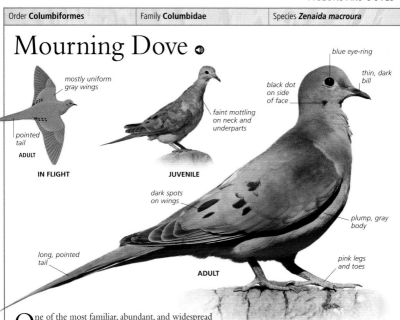

blue eye-ring

thin, dark bill

black dot on side of face

mostly uniform gray wings

faint mottling on neck and underparts

pointed tail

**ADULT**

**IN FLIGHT**

**JUVENILE**

dark spots on wings

plump, gray body

long, pointed tail

pink legs and toes

**ADULT**

Oue of the most familiar, abundant, and widespread of North American birds, the Mourning Dove is a long-tailed, plump, medium-sized dove with a small head. It has a grayish tan body with a pale, rosy breast and black spots on folded wings. While coveted by hunters—as many as 70 million are shot annually—the Mourning Dove is also well known to those who live on farms and in suburbia. Found all across North America, the species is divided into four subspecies—two of which occur in North America—the larger grayish brown *Z. m. carolinensis*, east of the Mississippi River, and the smaller, paler *Z. m. marginella* in the west.

**VOICE** Mellow, owl-like call: *hoO-Oo-oo, hoo-hoo-hoo.*

**NESTING** Flat, flimsy twig platform, mostly in trees, sometimes on the ground; 2 eggs; 2 broods; February–October.

**FEEDING** Forages mainly for seeds on the ground; obtains food quickly and digests it later at roost.

**FLIGHT:** swift, direct flight, with fairly quick wingbeats; twists and turns sometimes.

**FAMILIAR SIGHT**
The Mourning Dove is North America's most widespread member of this family.

**OCCURRENCE**
Breeds in a wide variety of habitats but shuns extensive forests; human-altered vegetation favored for feeding, including farmland and suburbia. Winters in small to medium sheltered woodland while feeding in grain fields; winters in southern Mexico and Central America.

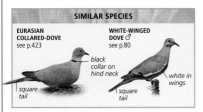

**SIMILAR SPECIES**

**EURASIAN COLLARED-DOVE** see p.423

**WHITE-WINGED DOVE ♂** see p.80

black collar on hind neck

square tail

white in wings

square tail

| Length **9–13½in (23–34cm)** | Wingspan **14½–17½in (37–45cm)** | Weight **3–6oz (85–175g)** |
| Social **Pairs/Winter flocks** | Lifespan **Up to 19 years** | Status **Secure** |

| DATE SEEN | WHERE | NOTES |
|---|---|---|
| | | |
| | | |
| | | |
| | | |
| | | |

# CUCKOOS

THE FAMILY CUCULIDAE includes typical cuckoos, anis, and roadrunners. Cuckoos favor forested areas, anis prefer more open bush country, and roadrunners are found in dry, bushy semidesert or desert regions. Cuckoos are mainly insectivorous, specializing in caterpillars from the ground or gleaned from foliage. Anis have a more varied diet. They are sociable, blackish, heavy-billed birds, found only in Florida and along the Gulf Coast but more widespread in Central America. Roadrunners are ground-feeders, rarely flying but able to run fast in pursuit of prey, which ranges from insects through small lizards to snakes (famously including rattlesnakes) and small rodents.

**PERCHED TO KILL**
After catching a lizard, the Greater Roadrunner bashes it repeatedly against a rock before gulping it down.

# NIGHTJARS

THE NIGHTJARS ARE active mostly around dusk and dawn, and so are not well known to many people, although their remarkable songs and calls may be more familiar. Common Nighthawks are easily seen and may even be spotted over suburban areas, but most nightjars are elusive species. Some inhabit scrub and bushy slopes and plains, while others are found in woodlands. They are medium-sized birds with long wings and wide tails. They have tiny legs and minute bills, but very wide mouths: they catch flying insects such as moths in the air, directly into the open gape. Their mouths are surrounded by bristles that help guide insects in when the birds are foraging.

**ELEGANT HUNTER**
This male Lesser Nighthawk soars through the air, hunting for insects, which it catches on the wing. Lesser Nighthawks are rare in the West.

**PART OF THE LITTER**
Not many bird species match the leaf litter of the forest floor as well as nightjars, as this Chuck-will's-widow shows. This species is rare in the West.

| Order **Cuculiformes** | Family **Cuculidae** | Species *Geococcyx californianus* |
|---|---|---|

# Greater Roadrunner

long, thick, powerful bill

large crest

**ADULT**

large, whitish crescent on wings

**ADULT**

light brown body

heavily streaked upperparts

dark brown, glossy green, and black streaks

**IN FLIGHT**

heavily streaked head, neck, and chest

long, dark tail with white-edged tip

unstreaked, lower belly

**FLIGHT:** weak flutter to high perches; open wing glide from elevated perch; prefers to run.

Unlike the other species of North American cuckoo, the Greater Roadrunner is a ground bird, but it can fly, despite preferring to run. Its speed enables it to overcome and chase prey on foot, especially lizards and small birds. Its generalized feeding habits allow this bird to take advantage of whatever food resources it comes across. This may be one of the main reasons roadrunners are expanding their range.

**VOICE** Cooing *coo-coo-coo-cooo-cooooo* series of 4–5 descending notes.

**NESTING** Shallow, loosely organized cup of twigs and branches, lined with grass, animal hair, and feathers; 3–5 eggs; 2 broods; April–September.

**FEEDING** Eats a wide variety of insects, small reptiles such as lizards, birds, and mammals; also eggs and carrion.

**DRINKING**
Roadrunners obtain much of their moisture from the food they eat, but will take full advantage of water whenever it is available.

**LOFTY ABODE**
This species nests off the ground, and can occasionally be seen occupying elevated perches.

### SIMILAR SPECIES

**PLAIN CHACHALACA**

darker, solid color

**RING-NECKED PHEASANT ♀**
see p.61

lighter brown overall

unstreaked upperparts

larger overall

no crest

plump body

**OCCURRENCE**
Widespread across southwestern US, from California to Louisiana, and north to Utah, Colorado, Kansas, and Arkansas; lives at low elevations in open brushy areas mixed with thorn scrub such as mesquite; also pinyon juniper shrubbery, and deserts and chaparral. Resident.

| Length **21in (53cm)** | Wingspan **23in (58cm)** | Weight **11oz (300g)** |
|---|---|---|
| Social **Solitary/Pairs** | Lifespan **Up to 6 years** | Status **Secure** |

| DATE SEEN | WHERE | NOTES |
|---|---|---|
| | | |
| | | |
| | | |
| | | |
| | | |

| Order **Cuculiformes** | Family **Cuculidae** | Species **Coccyzus americanus** |
| --- | --- | --- |

# Yellow-billed Cuckoo

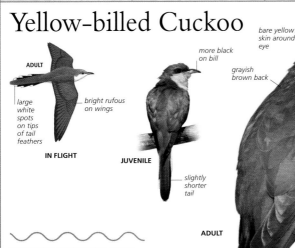

**ADULT**

large white spots on tips of tail feathers

bright rufous on wings

**IN FLIGHT**

**JUVENILE**

more black on bill

slightly shorter tail

**ADULT**

bare yellow skin around eye

grayish brown back

mostly yellow bill

rufous outer wing feathers

long tail

**FLIGHT:** flight is swift using long strokes to maintain level pattern.

The Yellow-billed Cuckoo is a shy, slow-moving bird, with a reputation for fairly odd behaviors, including its habit of calling more often on cloudy days. This tendency has earned it the nickname "rain crow" in some areas. In addition to raising young in its own nest, females occasionally lay eggs in the nests of more than a dozen other species, especially during years with abundant food. The host species may be chosen on the basis of how closely the color of its eggs matches those of the cuckoo. This brood parasitism is the rule in many species of Old World cuckoos, which is the origin of the word "cuckold."

**VOICE** Call a series of 10–12 low notes that slow down as it progresses, *ca ca ca ca coo coo coo cowl cowl cowl*.

**NESTING** Flimsy oval-shaped platform of small sticks and branches, often lined with leaves and strips of plants; 2–4 eggs; 1–2 broods; May–August.

**FEEDING** Mostly consumes insects such as grasshoppers, crickets, katydids, and caterpillars of several moth species; also eats seeds.

**RARE SIGHT**
Given the habitat they prefer and their skittish nature, a clear view of a Yellow-billed Cuckoo is rare.

**OCCURRENCE**
Has a wide range in the US. Found primarily in open forests with a mix of openings and thick understory cover, especially those near water. Winters in similar habitats in Central and South America.

**SIMILAR SPECIES**

**BLACK-BILLED CUCKOO**
see p.85

all-black bill

no rufous on wings

**MANGROVE CUCKOO**

black mask around eyes

buffy undertail and belly

| Length **10–12in (26–30cm)** | Wingspan **17–20in (43–51cm)** | Weight **2–2¼oz (55–65g)** |
| --- | --- | --- |
| Social **Small winter flocks** | Lifespan **Up to 4 years** | Status **Declining** |

| DATE SEEN | WHERE | NOTES |
| --- | --- | --- |
| | | |
| | | |
| | | |
| | | |
| | | |

| Order **Cuculiformes** | Family **Cuculidae** | Species *Coccyzus erythropthalmus* |

# Black-billed Cuckoo

long tail

small white spots on tips of tail feathers

long wings

**ADULT**

**IN FLIGHT**

bare red skin around eye

grayish brown back

**ADULT**

pale grayish white underparts

grayish toes

Although common, the Black-billed Cuckoo is usually difficult to spot because of its secretive nature and dense, leafy habitat. This species feeds mainly on spiny caterpillars, but the spines of these insects can become lodged in the cuckoo's stomach, obstructing digestion, so the bird periodically empties its stomach to clear any such blockage. The decline of this species is probably an indirect result of the chemical control of caterpillar outbreaks in forests throughout their range. During the breeding season, the birds call throughout the night, which leads some to believe erroneously that the cuckoo is nocturnal.

long tail

**VOICE** Series of 2–5 repeatedly whistled notes, *coo-coo-coo-coo*, with short breaks between series.
**NESTING** Shallow cup of sticks lined with moss, leaves, grass, and feathers; 2–4 eggs; 1 brood; May–July.
**FEEDING** Almost exclusively eats caterpillars, especially tent caterpillars and gypsy moths.

**FLIGHT:** flight is swift, direct, and graceful, with long, smooth wingbeats.

**SEARCHING FOR FOOD**
These cuckoos spend a lot of their time in trees as they search for their favorite hairy caterpillars.

### SIMILAR SPECIES

| YELLOW-BILLED CUCKOO see p.84 | MANGROVE CUCKOO specialized habitat |
|---|---|
| yellow bill | black mask around eyes |
| rufous outer wing feathers | buffy undertail and belly |

**OCCURRENCE**
Widespread northern and eastern North American species, lives in thickly wooded areas close to water, but can also be found in brushy forest edges and evergreen woods. Winters in South America in evergreen woodlands, scrub, and humid forests.

| Length **11–12in (28–31cm)** | Wingspan **16–19in (41–48cm)** | Weight **1⁹⁄₁₆–2oz (45–55g)** |
| Social **Solitary** | Lifespan **Up to 5 years** | Status **Declining** |

| DATE SEEN | WHERE | NOTES |
|---|---|---|
| | | |
| | | |
| | | |
| | | |
| | | |

| Order **Caprimulgiformes** | Family **Caprimulgidae** | Species ***Chordeiles minor*** |

# Common Nighthawk 🔊

**MALE**
pointed wings
white bars on outer wing feathers
narrow wings

**IN FLIGHT**
long wings

white throat
white wing patch
**MALE**
very small bill
large, dark eye
delicate, gray-black pattern overall

**FEMALE**
barring on gray underparts

**FLIGHT:** erratic flight with deep wingbeats interrupted by banking glides.

Common Nighthawks are easy to spot as they swoop over parking lots, city streets, and athletics fields during the warm summer months. They are more active at dawn and dusk than at night, pursuing insect prey up to 250ft (76m) in the air. The species once took the name Booming Nighthawk, a reference to the remarkable flight display of the male birds, during which they dive rapidly toward the ground, causing their feathers to vibrate and produce a characteristic "booming" sound.
**VOICE** Nasal *peeent*; also soft clucking noises from both sexes.
**NESTING** Nests on ground on rocks, wood, leaves, or sand, also on gravel-covered rooftops in urban areas; 2 eggs; 1 brood; May–July.
**FEEDING** Catches airborne insects, especially moths, mayflies, and beetles, also ants; predominantly active at dusk and dawn.

**A RARE SIGHT**
Common Nighthawks are seen in flight more often than other caprimulgids, but it is a rare treat to see one resting on a perch.

### SIMILAR SPECIES

**LESSER NIGHTHAWK** more buffy barring on underside of wings; see p.424

**COMMON PAURAQUE** longer, rounded tail with white patches
browner plumage
larger overall

**OCCURRENCE**
Wide variety of open habitats, such as cleared forests, fields, grassland, beaches, and sand dunes; also common in urban areas, including cities. The most common and widespread North American nighthawk, this species also occurs in Central and South America.

| Length **9–10in (23–26cm)** | Wingspan **22–24in (56–61cm)** | Weight **2⅞oz (80g)** |
| Social **Solitary/Flocks** | Lifespan **Up to 9 years** | Status **Declining** |

| DATE SEEN | WHERE | NOTES |
| --- | --- | --- |
| | | |
| | | |
| | | |
| | | |
| | | |

| Order **Caprimulgiformes** | Family **Caprimulgidae** | Species *Phalaenoptilus nuttallii* |

# Common Poorwill

**IN FLIGHT**

short rounded wings with tawny underparts

**ADULT**

short tail

large black eye

delicately mottled, brownish gray to pale gray plumage

very small bill

broad, white throat band

**ADULT**

grayish underparts, mottled dark gray and black

white-tipped outer tail feathers

tiny, dark legs and toes

This nocturnal bird is the smallest North American nightjar, with much shorter wings than its relatives, and a stubbier tail, but a comparatively large head. In 1946, scientists discovered that it was able to go into a state of torpor, similar to mammalian hibernation. During "hibernation" its body temperature is about 64°F (18°C) instead of the usual 106°F (41°C), and it may remain in this state for several weeks during cold weather when food is unavailable. This may account for its colloquial name, "sleeping one," among the Hopi of the Southwest. Males and females are similar in appearance, but the male has whitish corners to its tail, while the female's are more buffy.

**VOICE** Call low *purr-WHEEOO* or *pooor-WEELLUP*, whistled at night when perched in the open.

**NESTING** Eggs laid on the ground among rocks, sometimes under shrubs; 2 eggs; 2 broods; May–August.

**FEEDING** Jumps up from the ground and flies briefly to capture night-flying insects, such as moths and beetles.

**FLIGHT:** brief, erratic; with slow and deep wingbeats.

**GRAVEL ROADS**
The Common Poorwill uses gravel roads as a convenient place to jump at flying insects.

### SIMILAR SPECIES

**CHUCK-WILL'S-WIDOW**
see p.425

larger overall

browner upperparts

**EASTERN WHIP-POOR-WILL**
see p.425

large white patches on tail

larger bill

**OCCURRENCE**
Breeds from the western US southward into Mexico, in arid habitats with much bare ground and sparse vegetation, such as grasses, shrubs, and cacti. Winters in northern Mexico.

| Length **7½–8½in (19–21cm)** | Wingspan **15½–19in (40–48cm)** | Weight **1¼–2oz (35–55g)** |
| Social **Solitary** | Lifespan **Up to 3 years** | Status **Secure** |

| DATE SEEN | WHERE | NOTES |
|---|---|---|
| .................. | .......................................... | ............................................... |
| .................. | .......................................... | ............................................... |
| .................. | .......................................... | ............................................... |
| .................. | .......................................... | ............................................... |
| .................. | .......................................... | ............................................... |

| Order **Caprimulgiformes** | Family **Caprimulgidae** | Species *Antrostomus arizonae* |

# Mexican Whip-poor-will

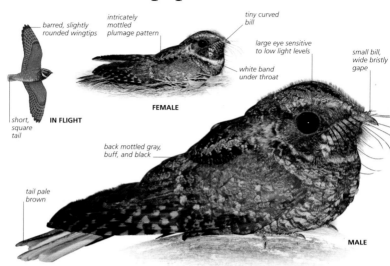

- barred, slightly rounded wingtips
- intricately mottled plumage pattern
- tiny curved bill
- large eye sensitive to low light levels
- small bill, wide bristly gape
- white band under throat

**IN FLIGHT**

- short, square tail

**FEMALE**

- back mottled gray, buff, and black
- tail pale brown

**MALE**

T his typical nightjar is active by night and rests during the day. However, seeking a Mexican Whip-poor-will in the leaf-litter of a wilderness forest is not easy. Best located on bright, moonlit nights, these birds may call more than 10,000 times in a single night. Although it is found in moderate numbers, local populations are limited by habitat, and increasingly warm conditions below 5,000ft (1,500m) may reduce the area of suitable forest. It has been recently separated from the easterly Eastern Whip-poor-will, based on vocal and genetic differences.

**VOICE** Vibrant, rippling rhythmic sequence, *WR-rrp-rra-wit*, quicker, deeper, less whistling than Eastern Whip-poor-will song.
**NESTING** Lays 2 eggs on forest floor; 2 broods; May–August.
**FEEDING** Catches large insects on the wing from tree perches or longer aerial forays.

**FLIGHT:** quick, acrobatic, using broad wings and long, fanned, and twisted tail.

**AERIAL HUNTER**
This bird captures insects in flight, swallowing them whole, at dusk or by moonlight.

| SIMILAR SPECIES | | |

**COMMON POORWILL**
see p.87
smaller, grayer

**EASTERN WHIP-POOR-WILL**
see p.425
nearly identical except for voice

**OCCURRENCE**
High elevation pine oak forests, pinyon junipers, and ponderosa pine forests with abundant insects; nests and rests by day in shady spots on the ground among dead leaves, but feeds by night in open spaces under trees and in clearings. Migrates south out of US in winter.

| Length **9–10in (22–27cm)** | Wingspan **17–20in (43–51cm)** | Weight **1¹⁄₁₆–2¹⁄₈oz (42–62g)** |
| Social **Solitary** | Lifespan **Up to 4 years** | Status **Secure** |

| DATE SEEN | WHERE | NOTES |
| --- | --- | --- |
| | | |
| | | |
| | | |
| | | |
| | | |

# SWIFTS

SWIFTS SPEND VIRTUALLY ALL their daylight hours as well as many night hours plying the skies. The most aerial birds in North America—if not the world—swifts eat, drink, court, mate, and even sleep on the wing. Swifts are some of the fastest and most acrobatic flyers of the bird world. Several species have been clocked at more than 100mph (160kph). They feed on insects caught in aerial pursuits. The family name, based on the Greek *apous*, which means "without feet," originates from the ancient belief that swifts had no feet and lived their entire lives in the air.

**ACROBATIC FLOCKS**
White-throated Swifts are usually seen in groups of a handful to hundreds of birds.

# HUMMINGBIRDS

FOUND ONLY IN THE Americas, hummingbirds are sometimes referred to as the crown jewels of the bird world. The first sight of a glittering hummingbird can be a life-changing experience. The amount of iridescence in their plumage varies from almost none to what seems like every feather. Most North American male hummingbirds have a colorful throat patch called a gorget, but females tend to lack this

**AGGRESSIVE MALES**
This male Ruby-throated Hummingbird defends his territory from a perch. This species is rare in the West.

gorgeous attribute. Because iridescent colors are structural and not pigment-based, a gorget can often appear blackish until seen at the correct angle toward the light. Hummingbirds are the only birds that can fly backward, an adaptation that allows them to move easily between flowers. Flying sideways, up, down, and hovering are also within hummingbirds' abilities, and all are achieved by their unique figure-eight, rapid wing strokes and reduced wing bone structure. Their long, thin bills allow them access to nectar in tubular flowers. Of the 14 species of hummingbirds in the West, about six are restricted to southwestern states. A couple of western species are restricted to California's coastal habitats, and one, the Rufous Hummingbird, breeds all the way north to Alaska.

**NECTAR FEEDERS**
All North American hummingbirds, such as this Black-chinned, subsist on nectar from wildflowers.

| Order **Apodiformes** | Family **Apodidae** | Species *Chaetura vauxi* |
|---|---|---|

# Vaux's Swift

ADULT
*pale throat and breast*
*short wings*
**IN FLIGHT**

ADULT
*sickle-shaped wings*
*very short bill*
*short tail*
*cylindrical body shape*
*spiny tail*

ADULT
*dark gray-brown back*
*paler rump and uppertail*
*black eyes*
*paler cheek patch*
*dark gray-brown wings*

This acrobatic and fast-flying bird is North America's smallest swift; it is slightly shorter than its eastern counterpart, the Chimney Swift. Its western range, small size, rapid and fluttering flight, and distinctive shape help distinguish this species from others. Vaux's Swifts are typically found foraging in flocks over mature forest and can be easily spotted on cold, cloudy days, often mixed with other swifts. Very large flocks are also sighted seemingly "pouring" into communal roost sites at dusk. It is fairly reliant on mature forest, and areas where this habitat has diminished have seen a corresponding decline in populations of Vaux's Swift. They may wander more widely in search of food in poor weather, even over towns.

**VOICE** High, insect-like chips and twittering in flight, often ending in buzzy trill.

**NESTING** Shallow cup of twigs, needles, and saliva attached to inside of hollow tree, rarely on chimneys; 4–6 eggs; 1 brood; June–September.

**FEEDING** Catches a wide variety of flying insects on the wing, including flies, moths, bees, beetles, and many others.

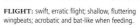

**FLIGHT:** swift, erratic flight; shallow, fluttering wingbeats; acrobatic and bat-like when feeding.

**AERIAL ACROBAT**
Vaux's Swifts rarely land, spending all day hawking insects and even mating in flight.

**SIMILAR SPECIES**

**BLACK SWIFT** see p.425
*larger overall*
*blackish body*
*longer, notched tail*

**CHIMNEY SWIFT** see p.425
*longer tail and wings*

**OCCURRENCE**
Occurs in North America from southeastern Alaska to California, where it breeds primarily in coniferous forests, nesting in large, hollow trunks; forages widely in many habitats. Resident population in Mexico, North American migrants move to Central America.

| Length **4¾in (12cm)** | Wingspan **12in (30cm)** | Weight **½–⅞oz (15–25g)** |
|---|---|---|
| Social **Migrant flocks** | Lifespan **Up to 7 years** | Status **Declining** |

| DATE SEEN | WHERE | NOTES |
|---|---|---|
| | | |
| | | |
| | | |
| | | |
| | | |

| Order **Apodiformes** | Family **Apodidae** | Species **Aeronautes saxatalis** |

# White-throated Swift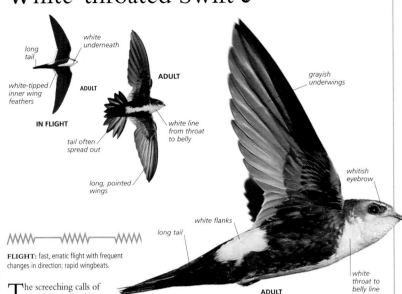

long tail

white underneath

**ADULT**

white-tipped inner wing feathers

**ADULT**

**IN FLIGHT**

tail often spread out

long, pointed wings

white line from throat to belly

grayish underwings

whitish eyebrow

white flanks

long tail

**FLIGHT:** fast, erratic flight with frequent changes in direction; rapid wingbeats.

white throat to belly line

**ADULT**

**ADULT**

The screeching calls of this black-and-white swift are a familiar sound in canyon country. Often seen racing around the cliffs in which they nest, White-throated Swifts are distinguished from other North American swifts by their black-and-white plumage and longer tail. This is also the only swift that winters in North America in large numbers. This species has become increasingly common in urban areas, as it has adapted to nesting in human structures that resemble its natural nest sites, such as bridges and quarries. As with other swifts, huge flocks of White-throated Swifts can be seen rushing into communal roosts at dusk, particularly outside the breeding season.

**VOICE** Drawn-out, descending, shrill twitter, *tee-tee-tee-ter-ter-ter-trr-trr-trr*, commonly given by flocks; occasionally gives two-note call in flight or a sharp single note.

**NESTING** Shallow cup of feathers and saliva in rock, wall, crevice, or human structure; 3–6 eggs; 1 brood; March–August.

**FEEDING** Forages on a variety of aerial insects.

**"AIR SAILOR"**
These swifts—the aeronauts—were named to emphasize their mastery of the air.

**SIMILAR SPECIES**

**VIOLET-GREEN SWALLOW** ♂
slower flight and wingbeats;
see p.282

greenish upper-parts

smaller overall

broader, shorter wings

**OCCURRENCE**
Breeds in western North America, from British Columbia to California, eastward to the Dakotas, and south to New Mexico. Prefers hilly and mountainous areas; forages over a wide variety of habitats and winters in extreme southwestern North America, in communal roosts in canyons.

| Length **6¾in (17cm)** | Wingspan **15in (38cm)** | Weight **1¹⁄₁₆–1⁹⁄₁₆oz (30–45g)** |
| Social **Flocks** | Lifespan **Unknown** | Status **Secure** |

| DATE SEEN | WHERE | | NOTES |
|-----------|-------|---|-------|
| .......... | .................... | | ........................... |
| .......... | .................... | | ........................... |
| .......... | .................... | | ........................... |
| .......... | .................... | | ........................... |
| .......... | .................... | | ........................... |

| Order **Apodiformes** | Family **Trochilidae** | Species **Archilochus alexandri** |

# Black-chinned Hummingbird

**MALE**

violet iridescence on lower part of throat

**IN FLIGHT**

notched tail

**IMMATURE (MALE)**

lighter gray-green crown

purple-and-black throat feathers

greenish upperparts

white tips to tail feathers

dusky flanks

whitish underparts

**FEMALE**

slightly curved, black bill

black throat

white collar below throat

dusky green sides and flanks

**MALE**

notched greenish tail with darker outer feathers

The Black-chinned Hummingbird is widespread across the western US, where it is found in a number of different environments. It readily accepts offerings of sugar water from birdfeeders. During courtship, the males perform a distinctive dive display comprising several broad arcs in addition to a short, back-and-forth "shuttle" display. The latter is accompanied by a droning noise produced by the bird's wings.

**VOICE** Call a soft, thick *chic*; fast, buzzy *tsi-tsi-tsi-tsi-tsi-tsi-tsi-tsi* is used to chase off other birds; song soft, warbling, very rarely heard.

**NESTING** Tiny cup of plant down, with leaves or lichen on the exterior, bound with spider's silk; usually built in a deciduous tree; 2 eggs; 1–2 broods; April–August.

**FEEDING** Drinks nectar from flowers; eats small insects and spiders, caught aerially or gleaned from foliage.

**FLIGHT:** rapid with very fast wingbeats; hovers at flowers and darts after insects.

**TAIL WAGGER**
Black-chinned Hummingbirds regularly wag their tails from side to side while feeding.

**SIMILAR SPECIES**

**RUBY-THROATED HUMMINGBIRD** ♀
see p.426

shorter bill

more rounded outer tail feathers

**COSTA'S HUMMINGBIRD** ♀
higher, metallic call notes;
see p.427

larger head

thicker neck

**OCCURRENCE**
Widespread in a variety of habitats, particularly scrub and woodlands close to rivers and streams, and irrigated urban areas; also found in drier habitats; forages away from breeding habitat where nectar sources are found. Winters along the Pacific Coast of Mexico.

| Length **3½in (9cm)** | Wingspan **4¾in (12cm)** | Weight **1/16–3/16oz (2–5g)** |
| Social **Solitary** | Lifespan **Up to 8 years** | Status **Secure** |

| DATE SEEN | WHERE | NOTES |
|---|---|---|
| | | |
| | | |
| | | |
| | | |

| Order **Apodiformes** | Family **Trochilidae** | Species **Calypte anna** |

# Anna's Hummingbird

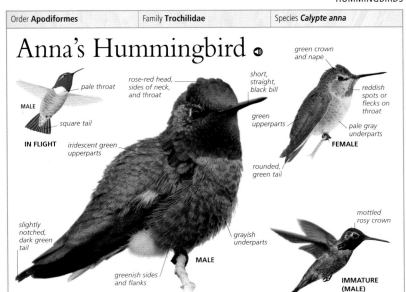

green crown and nape

pale throat

**MALE**

rose-red head, sides of neck, and throat

short, straight, black bill

green upperparts

reddish spots or flecks on throat

pale gray underparts

**FEMALE**

square tail

**IN FLIGHT**

iridescent green upperparts

rounded, green tail

slightly notched, dark green tail

grayish underparts

**MALE**

greenish sides and flanks

mottled rosy crown

**IMMATURE (MALE)**

The most common garden hummingbird along the Pacific Coast from British Columbia to Baja California, the iridescent rose-red helmet of a male Anna's Hummingbird is spectacular and distinctive. The females are rather drab by comparison. This adaptable hummingbird has expanded its range dramatically in the last century because of the availability of garden flowers and feeders. It previously bred only in areas of dense evergreen shrubs along the coast of southern California. The males perform an impressive diving display to court females.

**VOICE** Call a hard, sharp *tsit*, often doubled or given in series when perched; fast, buzzy chatter used to chase off other birds; song variable series of thin, high, buzzing, warbled notes.

**NESTING** Tiny cup of mostly plant down, with lichen on the exterior, bound with spider's silk, built in trees or shrubs; 2 eggs; 2 broods; December–July.

**FEEDING** Drinks nectar from flowers; eats small insects and spiders, caught aerially or gleaned from foliage.

**FLIGHT:** rapid flight with very fast wingbeats; hovers at flowers and darts after insects.

**VARIABLE THROAT**
Mature female Anna's Hummingbirds often show small iridescent patches on their throats.

**OCCURRENCE**
Primary breeding habitat is dense coastal shrubbery and open woodland; also human areas. Habitat during migration and in winter largely dependent on available nectar sources; range expands northward and eastward during this time. Some birds winter in northwestern Mexico; vagrant in the East.

| SIMILAR SPECIES | | |

**BLACK-CHINNED HUMMINGBIRD ♀**
see p.92

thinner neck

whiter underparts

**COSTA'S HUMMINGBIRD ♀**
see p.427

smaller overall

paler, cleaner underparts

| Length **4in (10cm)** | Wingspan **5in (13cm)** | Weight $^3/_{32}$–$^7/_{32}$**oz (3–6g)** |
| Social **Solitary** | Lifespan **Up to 8 years** | Status **Secure** |

| DATE SEEN | WHERE | NOTES |
| --- | --- | --- |
| | | |
| | | |
| | | |
| | | |
| | | |

93

| Order **Apodiformes** | Family **Trochilidae** | Species *Selasphorus platycercus* |
|---|---|---|

# Broad-tailed Hummingbird

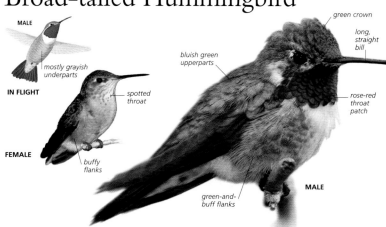

**MALE**

**IN FLIGHT**

mostly grayish underbody

**FEMALE**

spotted throat

buffy flanks

bluish green upperparts

green-and-buff flanks

green crown

long, straight bill

rose-red throat patch

**MALE**

The trilling sound generated by the male Broad-tailed Hummingbird's wings in flight is commonly heard in the alpine meadows of the Rocky Mountains and is likely a substitute for song during displays. Birds may arrive on their breeding grounds before the snow melts or flowers bloom, and they survive on insects and tree sap. During courtship, males perform spectacular dives, with their wings trilling loudly during the descent. They also have a buzzing display, bobbing back and forth in front of females.
**VOICE** Call a sharp *chik*; also short, buzzy warning call, *tssrr*; chase call variable, squeaky twittering.
**NESTING** Tiny cup of plant down, with lichen and leaves on exterior, bound with spider's silk, and built in trees; 1–2 eggs; 1–2 broods; April–August.
**FEEDING** Sucks nectar from flowers; insects and arthropods caught in air or on foliage.

**FLIGHT:** rapid flight with extremely fast wingbeats; hovers at flowers; darts after insects.

**LOUD APPROACH**
Whirring and trilling wings often announce the presence of a male Broad-tailed Hummingbird.

**RESTING AFTER FEEDING**
This male, perched on a twig, rests after an energy-draining bout of feeding.

**SIMILAR SPECIES**

**RUFOUS HUMMINGBIRD** ♀
lower pitched call;
see p.95

rufous flanks and under-tail

more graduated tail

**CALLIOPE HUMMINGBIRD** ♀
see p.97

shorter tail

**OCCURRENCE**
Inhabits a variety of mid- to high-elevation forest types; early migrants arrive in March in southern states and most leave by September; some individuals winter along the Gulf Coast. Winters mostly in fairly arid habitats in northeastern Mexico. Also breeds in northern Mexico.

| Length **4in (10cm)** | Wingspan **5in (13cm)** | Weight **³⁄₃₂–⁵⁄₃₂oz (3–4g)** |
|---|---|---|
| Social **Solitary** | Lifespan **Up to 12 years** | Status **Secure** |

| DATE SEEN | WHERE | NOTES |
|---|---|---|
| | | |
| | | |
| | | |
| | | |

| Order **Apodiformes** | Family **Trochilidae** | Species *Selasphorus rufus* |

# Rufous Hummingbird 🔊

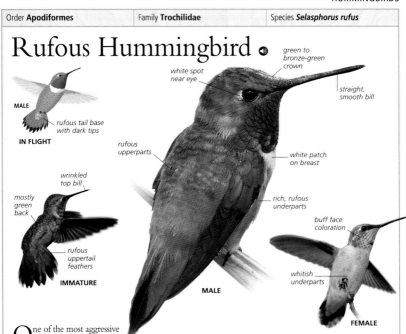

MALE

IN FLIGHT

rufous tail base
with dark tips

white spot
near eye

green to
bronze-green
crown

straight,
smooth bill

rufous
upperparts

white patch
on breast

wrinkled
top bill

mostly
green
back

rufous
uppertail
feathers

IMMATURE

rich, rufous
underparts

buff face
coloration

whitish
underparts

MALE

FEMALE

One of the most aggressive hummingbirds, the Rufous Hummingbird packs quite a punch, despite its small size; it often chases other hummingbirds away from nectar sources. This bird also breeds farther north than any other North American species of hummingbird and undertakes a lengthy migration. Males are recognizable by their overall fiery orange-rufous color, but females and immature birds are difficult to distinguish from Allen's Hummingbirds.

**VOICE** Call a hard *chuk*, sometimes in steady series or doubled; also short, buzzy warning call, *tssrr*; chase call a fast, raspy twitter, *tzzerr tichupy tichupy*.

**NESTING** Tiny cup of plant down, lichen, and other plant matter on exterior, bound with spider's silk, in shrubs or trees; 2 eggs; 1–2 broods; April–July.

**FEEDING** Drinks nectar from flowers and sap from trees; catches small insects and other arthropods in the air or gleans them off foliage.

**FLIGHT:** fast flight with extremely rapid wingbeats; hovers at flowers; darts after insects.

### SIMILAR SPECIES

**BROAD-TAILED HUMMINGBIRD** ♀
higher pitched call;
see p.94

dull pinkish
flanks

broad
tail

**ALLEN'S HUMMINGBIRD** ♂
see p.96

entirely
green
back

**FIERY MALE**
With temperaments matching their bold, flame-like color, males aggressively defend territories.

**OCCURRENCE**
Breeds in old-growth forest clearings, bushy country, as well as urban gardens; early migrants appear in March; most leave by August; it has become a regular winter inhabitant along the Gulf Coast and southern California; fall or winter vagrants are becoming more common in the East.

| Length **3½in (9cm)** | Wingspan **5in (13cm)** | Weight **³⁄₃₂–⁷⁄₃₂oz (3–6g)** |
| Social **Solitary** | Lifespan **Up to 12 years** | Status **Secure** |

| DATE SEEN | WHERE | | NOTES |
|-----------|-------|---|-------|
| .................. | .................. | | .................. |
| .................. | .................. | | .................. |
| .................. | .................. | | .................. |
| .................. | .................. | | .................. |
| .................. | .................. | | .................. |

| Order **Apodiformes** | Family **Trochilidae** | Species **Selasphorus sasin** |
|---|---|---|

# Allen's Hummingbird

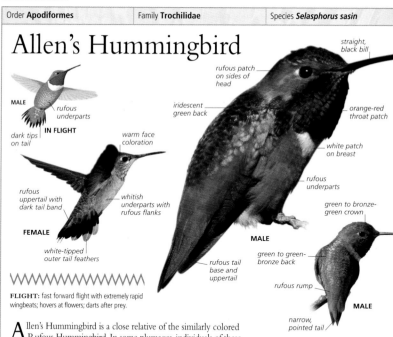

**MALE**

rufous underparts

dark tips on tail

**IN FLIGHT**

straight, black bill

rufous patch on sides of head

iridescent green back

orange-red throat patch

white patch on breast

rufous underparts

warm face coloration

rufous uppertail with dark tail band

whitish underparts with rufous flanks

**FEMALE**

white-tipped outer tail feathers

**MALE**

rufous tail base and uppertail

green to bronze-green crown

green to green-bronze back

rufous rump

**MALE**

narrow, pointed tail

**FLIGHT:** fast forward flight with extremely rapid wingbeats; hovers at flowers; darts after prey.

Allen's Hummingbird is a close relative of the similarly colored Rufous Hummingbird. In some plumages, individuals of these two species are hard, or even impossible, to tell apart. The range of this species is limited to the Pacific Coast and the adjacent interior of the western US from Oregon to California. Male Allen's Hummingbirds perform a spectacular flight display near females, which includes dives and a pendulum-like side-to-side motion, during which they make odd, buzzy, almost metallic sounds.

**VOICE** Call a hard *chuk*, in steady series or doubled; short, buzzy warning call, *tssrr*; chase call a fast, raspy twitter, *tzzerr tichupy tichupy*.

**NESTING** Tiny cup of plant matter and lichen, lined with plant down, bound with spider's silk, built in shrubs or trees; 2 eggs; 2 broods; February–July.

**FEEDING** Drinks nectar from a variety of flowers; catches small insects and spiders aerially or picks them off foliage.

**EARLY BREEDER**
Males may arrive on the California Coast and establish territories there as early as January.

**SIMILAR SPECIES**

**RUFOUS HUMMINGBIRD** ♂
see p.95

mostly rufous back

**CALLIOPE HUMMINGBIRD** ♀
softer call; see p.97

smaller overall

shorter tail

dull buffy flanks

**OCCURRENCE**
The subspecies *S. s. sasin* breeds in a narrow belt of fog-affected habitat along the US West Coast January– August; the second subspecies (*S. s. sedentarius*) is resident in dense shrubs on the Channel Islands of southern California and parts of the mainland; very rare east to Gulf Coast.

| Length **3½in (9cm)** | Wingspan **5in (13cm)** | Weight **¹⁄₁₆–⁵⁄₃₂oz (2–4g)** |
|---|---|---|
| Social **Solitary** | Lifespan **Up to 5 years** | Status **Secure** |

| DATE SEEN | WHERE | NOTES |
|---|---|---|
| | | |
| | | |
| | | |
| | | |
| | | |

| Order **Apodiformes** | Family **Trochilidae** | Species *Selasphorus calliope* |
|---|---|---|

# Calliope Hummingbird

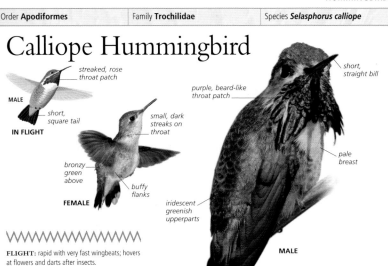

**MALE**
**IN FLIGHT**

streaked, rose throat patch

short, square tail

purple, beard-like throat patch

short, straight bill

small, dark streaks on throat

bronzy green above

buffy flanks

**FEMALE**

iridescent greenish upperparts

pale breast

**MALE**

**FLIGHT:** rapid with very fast wingbeats; hovers at flowers and darts after insects.

short tail

The Calliope Hummingbird is North America's smallest bird. Despite its diminutive size, it is just as territorial as other hummingbird species; the females even attack squirrels trying to rob their nests. The streaky, purplish throat patch of the males is unique, but the plainer females can be confused with other hummingbird species when their small size is not evident in a direct comparison. The male courtship display includes a number of J-shaped dives, which are accompanied by a high *tzzt-zing* at the bottom, in addition to a buzzing hover display in front of a female.

**VOICE** Relatively silent for a hummingbird; call a soft, high *chip*, sometimes doubled or repeated; series of high buzzes and chips used to chase off other birds.

**NESTING** Tiny cup of plant material and lichen, bound with spider's silk and lined with plant down, usually under an overhanging conifer branch; 2 eggs; 1 brood; May–August.

**FEEDING** Catches small insects aerially or gleans insects and spiders from foliage; also drinks nectar.

**ATTRACTED TO SAP**
The Calliope Hummingbird commonly feeds on sap and the insects attracted to it.

**MOUNTAIN GEM**
Like other hummingbirds, this mountain dweller hovers to take nectar from flowers.

**OCCURRENCE**
Present in western mountains primarily March–September; breeds mostly in coniferous mountain forests, meadows, and thickets; spring migrants found in a variety of lower elevation habitats; fall migrants are found at higher elevations; very rare in winter along the Gulf Coast.

### SIMILAR SPECIES

**BROAD-TAILED HUMMINGBIRD ♀**
sharper call note; see p.94

*larger overall*

longer, more graduated tail

**RUFOUS HUMMINGBIRD ♀**
harder call note; see p.95

more rufous flanks

longer, more graduated tail

| Length **3¼in (8cm)** | Wingspan **4¼in (10.5cm)** | Weight **1/16–5/32oz (2–4g)** |
|---|---|---|
| Social **Solitary** | Lifespan **Up to 12 years** | Status **Secure** |

| DATE SEEN | WHERE | NOTES |
|---|---|---|
| | | |
| | | |
| | | |
| | | |

# RAILS, CRANES, AND RELATIVES

THESE BIRDS OF THE marshes and WETLANDS include many distinctive groups. The Rallidae, or rail family, is a diverse group of small- to medium-sized marsh birds, represented in the US and Canada by four long-billed rails, three short-billed rails, two gallinules, and a coot. The cranes, or Gruidae, include very large to huge birds, superficially similar to storks and the largest of the herons and egrets. However, genetic and anatomical differences place cranes and the limpkin in a different order from storks, and herons and egrets.

## RAILS

Rails are mostly secretive, solitary, and inconspicuous in dense marsh vegetation, whereas coots and gallinules are seen on open water. Rails are all somewhat chicken-like birds with stubby tails and short, rounded wings, looking round-bodied from the side but very slender end-on. The rails of the genus *Rallus* have excellent camouflage, and are long-legged, long-toed, long-billed, and narrowbodied—the origin of the saying "as thin as a rail." The short-billed species are similar, but with shorter necks and stout, stubby bills. Both groups walk through wet marsh vegetation, though they can swim well. The gallinules, including the Common Gallinule and the Purple Gallinule, are more colorful than

rails. They have long, slender toes. The American Coot has broad lobes along the sides of its toes, making it a more proficient swimmer and diver in deeper water. None has a particularly specialized diet; they eat insects, small crabs, slugs, snails, and plant matter. Breeding pairs of rails keep in close contact in dense vegetation by calling out loudly.

**THIN AS A RAIL**
This marsh-dwelling Clapper Rail has a narrow body that enables it to slip easily through reedbeds.

## CRANES

The two North American species of cranes have long necks, small heads, and short bills. The long plumes on their inner wing feathers form a bustle, cloaking the tail on a standing crane, thereby giving them a different profile than any heron. Cranes fly with their necks straight out, rather than in the tight S-curve that is regularly seen in similar-sized herons. Cranes are long-distance migrants. The Whooping Crane, one of the world's rarest birds, is the tallest bird in North America, standing nearly 5ft (1.5m) high.

**CRANE RALLY**
Large numbers of Sandhill Cranes gather on feeding grounds in winter, groups arriving in V-formation.

| Order **Gruiformes** | Family **Rallidae** | Species ***Coturnicops noveboracensis*** |

# Yellow Rail

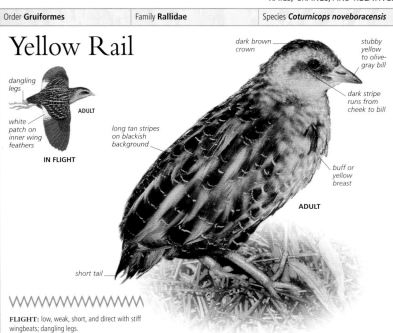

dark brown crown

stubby yellow to olive-gray bill

dark stripe runs from cheek to bill

buff or yellow breast

**ADULT**

dangling legs

**ADULT**

**IN FLIGHT**

white patch on inner wing feathers

long tan stripes on blackish background

short tail

**FLIGHT:** low, weak, short, and direct with stiff wingbeats; dangling legs.

Although widespread, the diminutive, secretive, nocturnal Yellow Rail is extremely difficult to observe in its dense, damp, grassy habitat, and is detected mainly by its voice. The Yellow Rail, whose Latin name of *noveboracensis* means "of New York" has a small head, almost no neck, a stubby bill, a plump, almost tail-less body, and short legs. The bill of the male turns yellow in the breeding season; for the rest of the year, it is olive-gray like the female's. Although the Yellow Rail tends to dart for cover when disturbed, when it does fly, it reveals a distinctive white patch on its inner wing.

**VOICE** Two clicking calls followed by three more given by males, usually at night, reminiscent of two pebbles being struck together; also descending cackles, quiet croaking, and soft clucking.

**NESTING** Small cup of grasses and sedges, on the ground or in a plant tuft above water, concealed by overhanging vegetation; 8–10 eggs; 1 brood; May–June.

**FEEDING** Plucks seeds, aquatic insects, various small crustaceans, and mollusks (primarily small freshwater snails) from vegetation or ground; forages on the marsh surface or in shallow water, hidden by grass.

**CURIOUS LISTENER**
Imitating the "tick" calls of the Yellow Rail is often an effective way to lure it out into the open.

**OCCURRENCE**
Breeds in brackish and freshwater marshes and wet sedge meadows in Canada and the north-central US; there is an isolated breeding population in Oregon. Winters predominantly in coastal marshes along the eastern seaboard.

**SIMILAR SPECIES**

**SORA** see p.101

black streaks on brown upperparts

gray underparts

| Length **7¼in (18.5cm)** | Wingspan **11in (28cm)** | Weight **1¾oz (50g)** |
| Social **Pairs** | Lifespan **Unknown** | Status **Endangered** |

| DATE SEEN | WHERE | NOTES |
|-----------|-------|-------|
| ............. | ................. | ................................ |
| ............. | ................. | ................................ |
| ............. | ................. | ................................ |
| ............. | ................. | ................................ |
| ............. | ................. | ................................ |

| Order **Gruiformes** | Family **Rallidae** | Species *Rallus limicola* |
|---|---|---|

# Virginia Rail

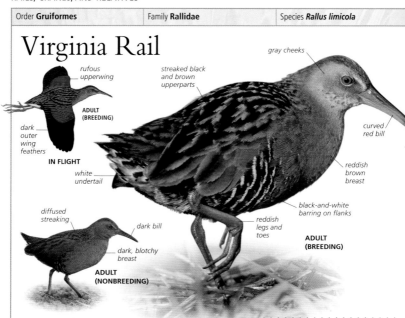

gray cheeks

rufous upperwing

streaked black and brown upperparts

**ADULT (BREEDING)**

dark outer wing feathers

**IN FLIGHT**

white undertail

curved red bill

reddish brown breast

black-and-white barring on flanks

reddish legs and toes

**ADULT (BREEDING)**

diffused streaking

dark bill

dark, blotchy breast

**ADULT (NONBREEDING)**

A smaller version of the King Rail, this freshwater marsh dweller is similar to its other relatives, more often heard than seen. Distributed in a wide range, the Virginia Rail spends most of its time in thick, reedy vegetation, which it pushes using its "rail thin" body and flexible vertebrae. Although it spends most of its life walking, it can swim and even dive to escape danger. The Virginia Rail is a partial migrant that leaves its northern breeding grounds in winter.

**VOICE** Series of pig-like grunting *oinks* that start loud and sharp, becoming steadily softer; also emits a series of double notes *ka-dik ka-dik*.

**NESTING** Substantial cup of plant material, concealed by bent-over stems; 5–12 eggs; 1–2 broods; April–July.

**FEEDING** Actively stalks prey or may wait and dive into water; primarily eats snails, insects, and spiders, but may also eat seeds.

**FLIGHT:** weak and struggling with outstretched neck and legs trailing behind.

**HARD TO SPOT**
The secretive Virginia Rail is difficult to spot in its reedy habitat.

**OCCURRENCE**
Breeds in freshwater habitats across North America, and is found throughout the year along the West Coast of the US. Other western populations move to central Mexico for the winter.

| SIMILAR SPECIES | | |
|---|---|---|

**CLAPPER RAIL** see p.428

**KING RAIL** see p.429

less gray face

larger overall

orange face

weak flank barring

dark undertail

yellow-orange bill

| Length **9½in (24cm)** | Wingspan **13in (33cm)** | Weight **3oz (85g)** |
|---|---|---|
| Social **Pairs** | Lifespan **Unknown** | Status **Secure** |

| DATE SEEN | WHERE | NOTES |
|---|---|---|
| | | |
| | | |
| | | |
| | | |
| | | |

| Order **Gruiformes** | Family **Rallidae** | Species **Porzana carolina** |

# Sora

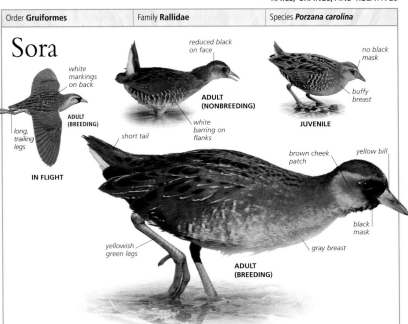

white markings on back

ADULT (BREEDING)

long, trailing legs

**IN FLIGHT**

reduced black on face

**ADULT (NONBREEDING)**

short tail

white barring on flanks

no black mask

buffy breast

**JUVENILE**

brown cheek patch

yellow bill

black mask

gray breast

yellowish green legs

**ADULT (BREEDING)**

Despite being the most widely distributed rail in North America, the Sora is rarely seen. It breeds in freshwater marshes and migrates hundreds of miles south in winter despite its weak and hesitant flight. It swims well, with a characteristic head-bobbing action. The Sora can be spotted walking at the edge of emergent vegetation—its yellow bill and black mask distinguish it from other rails.

**VOICE** Call a long, high, and loud, descending, horse-like whinny *ko-wee-hee-hee-hee-hee*; has an up-slurred whistle.

**NESTING** Loosely woven basket of marsh vegetation suspended above water or positioned in clumps of vegetation on the water's surface; 8–11 eggs; 1 brood; May–June.

**FEEDING** Rakes vegetation with feet or pulls with bill in search of seeds of wetland plants, insects, spiders, and snails.

**FLIGHT:** appears weak, yet strenuous; wingbeats hurried and constant.

**CHICKEN-LIKE WALK**
A rare sight, the Sora walks chicken-like through a marsh, its body in a low crouch.

### SIMILAR SPECIES

**YELLOW RAIL**
see p.99

buffy streaks

buffy breast

**VIRGINIA RAIL**
see p.100

longer bill

reddish legs

**OCCURRENCE**
Breeds in freshwater marshes with emergent vegetation across most of temperate North America; rarely in saltmarshes along the Atlantic Coast. Winters in freshwater, saltwater, and brackish marshes with spartina grass from the southern US to northern South America.

| Length **8½in (22cm)** | Wingspan **14in (36cm)** | Weight **2⅝oz (75g)** |
| Social **Solitary** | Lifespan **Unknown** | Status **Secure** |

| DATE SEEN | WHERE | NOTES |
| --- | --- | --- |
| | | |
| | | |
| | | |
| | | |
| | | |

| Order **Gruiformes** | Family **Rallidae** | Species **Gallinula galeata** |

# Common Gallinule 🔊

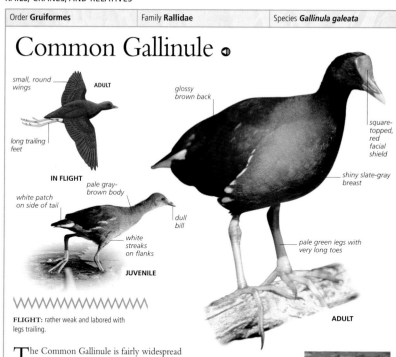

small, round wings

**ADULT**

glossy brown back

long trailing feet

**IN FLIGHT**

square-topped, red facial shield

shiny slate-gray breast

pale gray-brown body

white patch on side of tail

dull bill

white streaks on flanks

**JUVENILE**

pale green legs with very long toes

**ADULT**

**FLIGHT:** rather weak and labored with legs trailing.

The Common Gallinule is fairly widespread in southern Canada and the eastern US; its distribution is more scattered in the western states. It has similarities in behavior and habitat to both the true rails and the coots. Equally at home on land and water, its long toes allow it to walk easily over floating vegetation and soft mud. When walking or swimming, the Common Gallinule nervously jerks its short tail, revealing its white undertail feathers, and bobs its head.

**VOICE** A variety of rapid, raucous, cackling phrases and an explosive *krrooo*.

**NESTING** Bulky platform of aquatic vegetation with growing plants pulled over to conceal it, or close to water; 5–11 eggs, 1–3 broods; May–August, maybe year-round in Florida.

**FEEDING** Forages mainly on aquatic and terrestrial plants and aquatic vegetation; also eats snails, spiders, and insects.

**DUAL HABITAT**
A walker and a swimmer, the gallinule is equally at home on land and in water.

**OCCURRENCE**
Breeds in freshwater habitats in the eastern US and Canada; more localized in the West. Winters in warmer areas with open water, such as southern US, and Mexico. Also found in Central and South America.

**SIMILAR SPECIES**

**PURPLE GALLINULE** — blue frontal shield — bright yellow legs

**AMERICAN COOT** see p.103 — white bill — darker plumage

| Length **14in (36cm)** | Wingspan **21in (53cm)** | Weight **11oz (325g)** |
| Social **Pairs** | Lifespan **Up to 10 years** | Status **Secure** |

| DATE SEEN | WHERE | | NOTES |
|---|---|---|---|
| | | | |
| | | | |
| | | | |
| | | | |
| | | | |

| Order **Gruiformes** | Family **Rallidae** | Species *Fulica americana* |

# American Coot 🔊

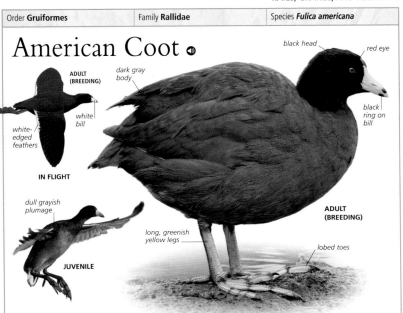

black head

red eye

**ADULT (BREEDING)**

dark gray body

white bill

black ring on bill

white-edged feathers

**IN FLIGHT**

dull grayish plumage

long, greenish yellow legs

**ADULT (BREEDING)**

lobed toes

**JUVENILE**

This duck-like species is the most abundant and widely distributed of North American rails. Its lobed toes make it well adapted to swimming and diving, but they are somewhat of an impediment on land. Its flight is clumsy; it becomes airborne with difficulty, running along the water surface before taking off. American Coots form large flocks on open water in winter, often associating with ducks—an unusual trait for a member of the rail family.

**VOICE** Various raucous clucks, grunts, and croaks and an explosive *keek*.

**NESTING** Bulky cup of plant material placed in aquatic vegetation on or near water; 5–15 eggs; 1–2 broods; April–July.

**FEEDING** Forages on or by diving under shallow water and on land; primarily herbivorous, but also eats snails, insects, spiders, tadpoles, fish, and even carrion.

**FLIGHT:** low and labored; runs for quite a long distance to takeoff.

**SWIMMING AWAY**
The red-headed, baldish looking American Coot chicks leave the nest a day after hatching.

**SIMILAR SPECIES**

**PURPLE GALLINULE**

red bill with yellow tip

bright yellow legs

**COMMON GALLINULE**
see p.102

white streaks on flanks

**OCCURRENCE**
Breeds in open water habitats west of the Appalachians and in Florida. Moves from the northern parts of its range in winter to the southeastern US, where open water persists; also migrates to western and southern Mexico.

| Length **15½in (40cm)** | Wingspan **24in (61cm)** | Weight **16oz (450g)** |
| Social **Flocks** | Lifespan **Up to 22 years** | Status **Secure** |

| DATE SEEN | WHERE | | NOTES |
| --- | --- | --- | --- |
| .................... | .................... | | .................... |
| .................... | .................... | | .................... |
| .................... | .................... | | .................... |
| .................... | .................... | | .................... |
| .................... | .................... | | .................... |

| Order **Gruiformes** | Family **Gruidae** | Species *Antigone canadensis* |

# Sandhill Crane 🔊

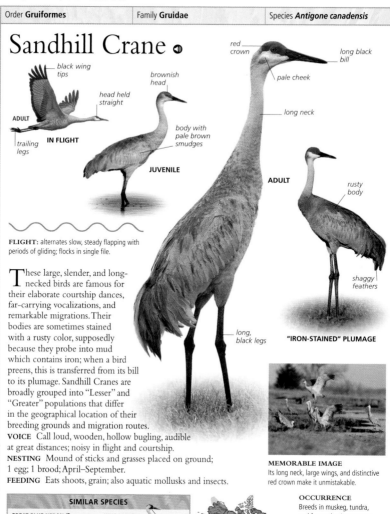

black wing tips

head held straight

**ADULT**

**IN FLIGHT**

trailing legs

brownish head

body with pale brown smudges

**JUVENILE**

red crown

long black bill

pale cheek

long neck

**ADULT**

rusty body

shaggy feathers

long, black legs

**"IRON-STAINED" PLUMAGE**

**FLIGHT:** alternates slow, steady flapping with periods of gliding; flocks in single file.

These large, slender, and long-necked birds are famous for their elaborate courtship dances, far-carrying vocalizations, and remarkable migrations. Their bodies are sometimes stained with a rusty color, supposedly because they probe into mud which contains iron; when a bird preens, this is transferred from its bill to its plumage. Sandhill Cranes are broadly grouped into "Lesser" and "Greater" populations that differ in the geographical location of their breeding grounds and migration routes.
**VOICE** Call loud, wooden, hollow bugling, audible at great distances; noisy in flight and courtship.
**NESTING** Mound of sticks and grasses placed on ground; 1 egg; 1 brood; April–September.
**FEEDING** Eats shoots, grain; also aquatic mollusks and insects.

**MEMORABLE IMAGE**
Its long neck, large wings, and distinctive red crown make it unmistakable.

**SIMILAR SPECIES**

**GREAT BLUE HERON** ◔ see p.183

dark crown

paler legs

**WHOOPING CRANE** see p.429

all-white plumage

red on face

larger overall

**OCCURRENCE**
Breeds in muskeg, tundra, and forest clearings across northwestern North America, east to Québec and the Great Lakes; large wintering and migratory flocks often densely packed, roosting in or near marshes. Winters south to northern Mexico.

| Length **2¾–4ft (0.8–1.2m)** | Wingspan **6–7½ft (1.8–2.3m)** | Weight **7¾–11lb (3.5–5kg)** |
| Social **Flocks** | Lifespan **Up to 25 years** | Status **Secure** |

| DATE SEEN | WHERE | NOTES |
|---|---|---|
| | | |

# SHOREBIRDS, GULLS, AUKS, AND RELATIVES

THE DIVERSE SHOREBIRD, gull, and auk families together form the order Charadriiformes. They are small to medium-sized, mostly migratory birds, associated with aquatic habitats. More than 100 species are found in North America.

**TYPICAL GULL**
Most large gulls, such as this Western Gull, have white heads and underparts with long wings and a bright sturdy bill.

## SHOREBIRDS
The various species popularly known as shorebirds belong to several different families. In North America there are the oystercatchers (Haematopodidae), the avocets and stilts (Recurvirostridae), the plovers (Charadriidae), and the sandpipers and phalaropes (Scolopacidae). They have long legs in proportion to their bodies, and a variety of bills, ranging from short to long, thin, thick, straight, down-curved and up-curved.

## GULLS
The more than 20 species of North American gulls in the subfamily Larinae all share similar stout body shapes, sturdy bills, and webbed toes. Nearly all are scavengers. Closely associated with coastal areas, few gulls venture far out to sea. Some species are seen around fishing ports and harbors, or inland, especially in urban areas and garbage dumps.

## TERNS
Terns are specialized long-billed predators that dive for fish. More slender and elegant than gulls, nearly all are immediately recognizable when breeding, because of their black caps and long, pointed bills. The related Black Skimmer also catches fish, but has a different bill.

## AUKS
Denizens of the northern oceans, these birds only come to land to breed. Most nest in colonies on sheer cliffs overlooking the ocean, but puffins excavate burrows in the ground, and some murrelets nest away from predators high up in treetops far inland.

**COLOR-CHANGE BILL**
The bright colors of a breeding Tufted Puffin's bill fade to more muted tones in winter, after the breeding season.

**ON THE MOVE**
Dunlins and other sandpipers gather in large, highly coordinated flocks on migration.

| Order **Charadriiformes** | Family **Recurvirostridae** | Species *Himantopus himantopus* |

# Black-necked Stilt

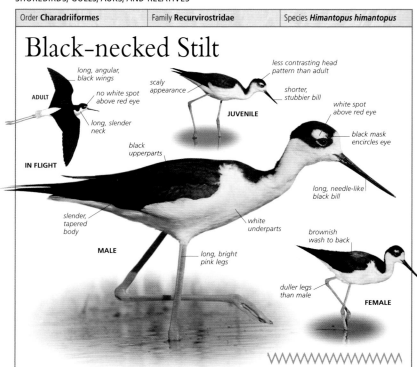

long, angular, black wings

**ADULT**

no white spot above red eye

long, slender neck

**IN FLIGHT**

scaly appearance

**JUVENILE**

less contrasting head pattern than adult

shorter, stubbier bill

white spot above red eye

black mask encircles eye

black upperparts

slender, tapered body

**MALE**

white underparts

long, needle-like black bill

brownish wash to back

long, bright pink legs

duller legs than male

**FEMALE**

This tall, slender, elegant, and black-and-white shorebird is a familiar sight at ponds and lagoons in the western and southern US. Even among the shorebirds, it is remarkably long-legged, at times almost grotesquely so: in flight, it often crosses its trailing feet as if for extra control and support. Breeding takes place in small colonies, with several pairs sharing the same site. In winter, these tall birds are often seen in small flocks of about 25 individuals. These groups feed quietly in sheltered areas, but they aggressively drive visitors away with their raucous calls, dog-like yips, and noisy communal protests. The increased use of pesticides and loss of wetland habitat could cause a decline in its numbers in the future. The US populations belong to the subspecies *mexicanus*.

**VOICE** Flight and alarm call a loud, continuous poodle-like *yip-yip-yip*, given in a long series when alarmed.

**NESTING** Simple scrape lined with grass in soft soil; 4 eggs; 1 brood; April–May.

**FEEDING** Walks slowly in shallow water, picking food off surface; diet includes tadpoles, shrimp, snails, flies, worms, clams, small fish, and frogs.

**FLIGHT:** direct, but somewhat awkward because of long, trailing legs; deep wingbeats.

**FRIENDLY BUNCH**
Black-necked Stilts are gregarious by nature, and often roost together in shallow water.

**OCCURRENCE**
Breeds around marshes, shallow grassy ponds, lake margins, and manmade waterbodies, such as reservoirs; uses similar habitats during migration and winter, as well as shallow lagoons, flooded fields, and mangrove swamps. Southern birds migrate locally only.

| Length **14–15½in (35–39cm)** | Wingspan **29–32in (73–81cm)** | Weight **4–8oz (125–225g)** |
| Social **Small flocks** | Lifespan **Up to 19 years** | Status **Secure** |

| DATE SEEN | WHERE | | NOTES |
|-----------|-------|--|-------|
| ..................... | ................................... | | ................................................. |
| ..................... | ................................... | | ................................................. |
| ..................... | ................................... | | ................................................. |
| ..................... | ................................... | | ................................................. |
| ..................... | ................................... | | ................................................. |

| Order **Charadriiformes** | Family **Recurvirostridae** | Species *Recurvirostra americana* |

# American Avocet

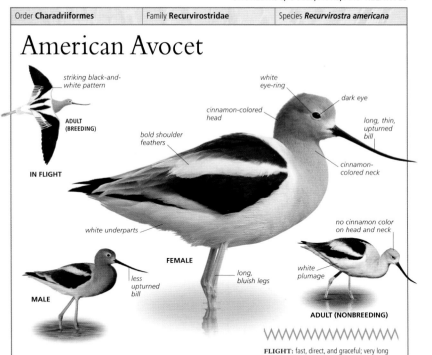

striking black-and-white pattern

**ADULT (BREEDING)**

**IN FLIGHT**

white eye-ring

dark eye

cinnamon-colored head

long, thin, upturned bill

bold shoulder feathers

cinnamon-colored neck

white underparts

**FEMALE**

less upturned bill

**MALE**

long, bluish legs

no cinnamon color on head and neck

white plumage

**ADULT (NONBREEDING)**

**FLIGHT:** fast, direct, and graceful; very long legs extend beyond tail.

With its long, thin, and upturned bill, this graceful, long-legged shorebird is unmistakable when foraging. When it takes off, its striking plumage pattern is clearly visible. It is the only one of the four avocet species in the world that changes plumage when breeding. Breeding birds have a cinnamon head and neck, and bold, patterns on their black-and-white wings and upperparts. The American Avocet forms large flocks during migration and in winter.

**VOICE** Flight call a variable melodic *kleet*, loud and repetitive, given when alarmed and by foraging birds.

**NESTING** Simple scrape in shallow depression; 4 eggs; 1 brood; May–June.

**FEEDING** Uses specialized bill to probe, scythe, or jab a variety of aquatic invertebrates, small fish, and seeds; walks steadily in belly-deep water to chase its prey.

**FORAGING FLOCK**
These birds walk through shallow water in flocks searching mainly for insects and crustaceans.

**TRICKY BALANCE**
During mating, the male supports himself with raised wings as the female extends her neck forward.

**OCCURRENCE**
Breeds in temporary wetlands, in dry to arid regions. In winter and migration, found in shallow water habitats, including ponds, reservoirs, fresh- and saltwater marshes, tidal mudflats, and lagoons. Each year, a flock of about 10,000 birds winters at Bolivar Flats, Texas. Regular East Coast visitor.

| Length **17–18½in (43–47cm)** | Wingspan **29–32in (74–81cm)** | Weight **10–12oz (275–350g)** |
| Social **Large flocks** | Lifespan **Up to 9 years** | Status **Secure** |

| DATE SEEN | WHERE | NOTES |
| --- | --- | --- |
| | | |
| | | |
| | | |
| | | |
| | | |

| Order **Charadriiformes** | Family **Haematopodidae** | Species *Haematopus bachmani* |
|---|---|---|

# Black Oystercatcher

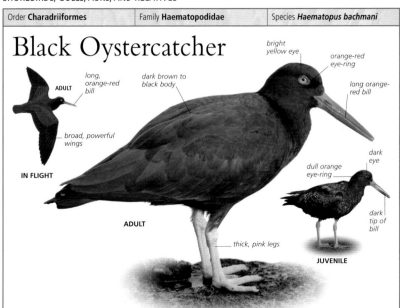

bright yellow eye

orange-red eye-ring

long orange-red bill

long, orange-red bill

**ADULT**

dark brown to black body

broad, powerful wings

**IN FLIGHT**

dark eye

dull orange eye-ring

dark tip of bill

**JUVENILE**

**ADULT**

thick, pink legs

This large, striking oystercatcher shares the typical round-bodied, hunch-backed, and squat-necked shape of other oystercatchers, as well as their typically thick legs and bill. But it is instantly recognizable because of its all-dark plumage, making the pale eyes and colorful bill all the more conspicuous. It is restricted to rocky coasts, where it feeds in pairs or family groups, using well-defined territories in summer. In winter, the birds gather in larger flocks where they are numerous, sometimes in hundreds, where mussels and barnacles are abundant. These are noisy, demonstrative birds, and always entertaining to watch.

**VOICE** Flight call a loud, whistled *wheeu*, with emphasis on first part of call; alarm call sharper *wheep*; courtship and posturing calls a series of whistles based on flight call, accelerating into descending piping calls.

**NESTING** Simple scrape just above high-tide line, often lined with broken shells and pebbles; 2–3 eggs; 1 brood; May–June.

**FEEDING** Feeds on slightly submerged shellfish beds; diet includes mollusks, particularly mussels and limpets; also eats a variety of crustaceans, such as crabs and barnacles; oysters are rarely consumed.

**FLIGHT:** strong, powerful flight with shallow wingbeats.

**BARNACLE LOVER**
The Black Oystercatcher can be spotted walking on top of exposed barnacle beds at low tide.

**SIMILAR SPECIES**

**AMERICAN OYSTERCATCHER** see p.429

black head

white underparts

**OCCURRENCE**
Feeds in the area between the high and low tide marks on rocky shores of western North America, from Alaska southward to Baja California. Breeds just above high-tide line on rocky headlands or sand, shell, and gravel beaches. In winter, also found on rocky jetties in southern part of range.

| Length **16½–18½in (42–47cm)** | Wingspan **30–34in (77–86cm)** | Weight **18–25oz (500–700g)** |
|---|---|---|
| Social **Pairs/Flocks** | Lifespan **10–15 years** | Status **Secure** |

| DATE SEEN | WHERE | NOTES |
|---|---|---|
| ..................... | ........................... | ........................... |
| ..................... | ........................... | ........................... |
| ..................... | ........................... | ........................... |
| ..................... | ........................... | ........................... |
| ..................... | ........................... | ........................... |

| Order **Charadriiformes** | Family **Charadriidae** | Species *Pluvialis squatarola* |

# Black-bellied Plover 🔊

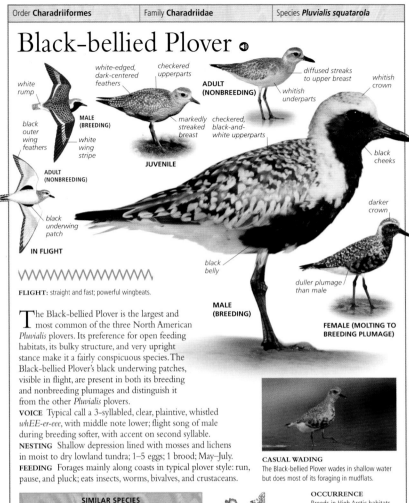

white rump

MALE (BREEDING)

black outer wing feathers

white wing stripe

white-edged, dark-centered feathers

checkered upperparts

**ADULT (NONBREEDING)**

markedly streaked breast

checkered, black-and-white upperparts

**JUVENILE**

diffused streaks to upper breast

whitish underparts

whitish crown

black cheeks

darker crown

**ADULT (NONBREEDING)**

black underwing patch

**IN FLIGHT**

black belly

black underwing patch

duller plumage than male

**MALE (BREEDING)**

**FEMALE (MOLTING TO BREEDING PLUMAGE)**

**FLIGHT:** straight and fast; powerful wingbeats.

The Black-bellied Plover is the largest and most common of the three North American *Pluvialis* plovers. Its preference for open feeding habitats, its bulky structure, and very upright stance make it a fairly conspicuous species. The Black-bellied Plover's black underwing patches, visible in flight in both its breeding and nonbreeding plumages and distinguish it from the other *Pluvialis* plovers.

**VOICE** Typical call a 3-syllabled, clear, plaintive, whistled *whEE-er-eee*, with middle note lower; flight song of male during breeding softer, with accent on second syllable.

**NESTING** Shallow depression lined with mosses and lichens in moist to dry lowland tundra; 1–5 eggs; 1 brood; May–July.

**FEEDING** Forages mainly along coasts in typical plover style: run, pause, and pluck; eats insects, worms, bivalves, and crustaceans.

**CASUAL WADING**
The Black-bellied Plover wades in shallow water but does most of its foraging in mudflats.

**OCCURRENCE**
Breeds in High Arctic habitats from western Russia across the Bering Sea to Alaska, and east to Baffin Island; winters primarily in coastal areas from southern Canada and US, south to southern South America. Found inland during migration. Migrates south all the way to South America.

**SIMILAR SPECIES**

AMERICAN GOLDEN-PLOVER ❋
see p.110

dingy, brownish upperparts

dark cap

MOUNTAIN PLOVER ❋
see p.430

sandy brown upperparts

white underparts

| Length **10½–12in (27–30cm)** | Wingspan **29–32in (73–81cm)** | Weight **5–9oz (150–250g)** |
| Social **Flocks** | Lifespan **Up to 12 years** | Status **Secure** |

| DATE SEEN | WHERE | | NOTES |
|---|---|---|---|
| | | | |
| | | | |
| | | | |
| | | | |
| | | | |

| Order **Charadriiformes** | Family **Charadriidae** | Species *Pluvialis dominica* |

# American Golden-Plover

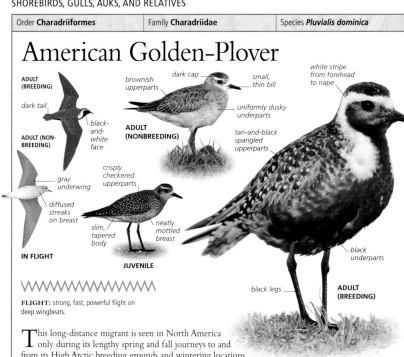

**ADULT (BREEDING)**
dark tail
black-and-white face

**ADULT (NON-BREEDING)**
gray underwing
diffused streaks on breast

**IN FLIGHT**

brownish upperparts
dark cap
small, thin bill

**ADULT (NONBREEDING)**
uniformly dusky underparts
tan-and-black spangled upperparts

crisply checkered upperparts
slim, tapered body
neatly mottled breast

**JUVENILE**

white stripe from forehead to nape

black underparts
black legs
**ADULT (BREEDING)**

**FLIGHT:** strong, fast, powerful flight on deep wingbeats.

This long-distance migrant is seen in North America only during its lengthy spring and fall journeys to and from its High Arctic breeding grounds and wintering locations in southern South America. An elegant, slender, yet large plover, it prefers inland grassy habitats and plowed fields to coastal mudflats. The American Golden-Plover's annual migration route includes a feeding stop at Labrador, then a 1,550–1,860 miles (2,500–3,000km) flight over the Atlantic Ocean to South America.
**VOICE** Flight call a whistled two-note *queE-dle*, or *klee-u*, with second note shorter and lower pitched; male flight song a strong, melodious whistled *kid-eek*, or *kid-EEp*.
**NESTING** Shallow depression lined with lichens in dry, open tundra; 4 eggs; 1 brood; May–July.
**FEEDING** Forages in run, pause, and pluck sequence on insects, mollusks, crustaceans, and worms; also berries and seeds.

**DISTRACTION TECHNIQUE**
This breeding American Golden-Plover is feigning an injury to its wing to draw predators away from its eggs or chicks in its nest.

| SIMILAR SPECIES | |
|---|---|
| **PACIFIC GOLDEN-PLOVER** ❀ see p.429 | **PACIFIC GOLDEN-PLOVER** ☾ see p.429 |
| longer legs / larger bill | checkered gold-and-black upperparts / pale golden wash |

**OCCURRENCE**
Breeds in Arctic tundra habitats. In migration, it occurs in prairies, tilled farmlands, golf courses, pastures, airports; also mudflats, shorelines, and beaches. In spring, seen in Texas and Great Plains; in fall, uncommon in northeast Maritimes and New England; scarce along the Pacific Coast.

| Length **9½–11in (24–28cm)** | Wingspan **23–28in (59–72cm)** | Weight **4–7oz (125–200g)** |
|---|---|---|
| Social **Solitary/Small flocks** | Lifespan **Unknown** | Status **Secure** |

| DATE SEEN | WHERE | | NOTES |
|---|---|---|---|
| | | | |
| | | | |
| | | | |
| | | | |
| | | | |

| Order **Charadriiformes** | Family **Charadriidae** | Species **Charadrius vociferus** |

# Killdeer 🔊

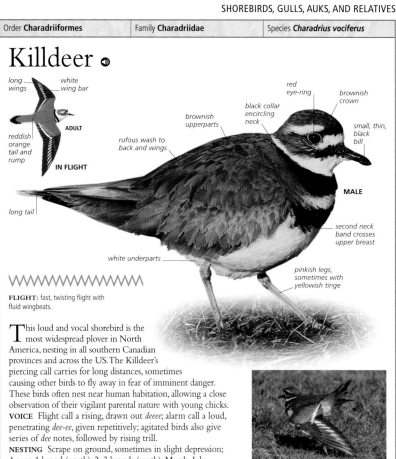

long wings

white wing bar

**ADULT**

reddish orange tail and rump

**IN FLIGHT**

rufous wash to back and wings

brownish upperparts

black collar encircling neck

red eye-ring

brownish crown

small, thin, black bill

**MALE**

long tail

second neck band crosses upper breast

white underparts

pinkish legs, sometimes with yellowish tinge

**FLIGHT:** fast, twisting flight with fluid wingbeats.

This loud and vocal shorebird is the most widespread plover in North America, nesting in all southern Canadian provinces and across the US. The Killdeer's piercing call carries for long distances, sometimes causing other birds to fly away in fear of imminent danger. These birds often nest near human habitation, allowing a close observation of their vigilant parental nature with young chicks.

**VOICE** Flight call a rising, drawn out *deeee*; alarm call a loud, penetrating *dee-ee*, given repetitively; agitated birds also give series of *dee* notes, followed by rising trill.

**NESTING** Scrape on ground, sometimes in slight depression; 4 eggs; 1 brood (north), 2–3 broods (south); March–July.

**FEEDING** Forages in typical plover style: run, pause, and pick; eats a variety of invertebrates such as worms, snails, grasshoppers, and beetles; also small vertebrates and seeds.

**CLEVER MANEUVER**
The Killdeer lures intruders away from its nest with a "broken wing" display.

### SIMILAR SPECIES

**SEMIPALMATED PLOVER** ❄
see p.112

single dark neckband

orange-yellow legs

smaller overall

**WILSON'S PLOVER**
see p.430

single, black collar

pinkish legs

short tail

**OCCURRENCE**
Widespread across Canada and the US, the Killdeer occurs in a wide variety of habitats. These include shorelines, mudflats, lake and river edges, sparsely grassy fields and pastures, golf courses, roadsides, parking lots, flat rooftops, driveways, and other terrestrial habitats.

| Length **9–10in (23–26cm)** | Wingspan **23–25in (58–63cm)** | Weight **2¼–3⅛ oz (65–90g)** |
| Social **Small flocks** | Lifespan **Up to 10 years** | Status **Declining** |

| DATE SEEN | WHERE | NOTES |
|-----------|-------|-------|
| | | |
| | | |
| | | |
| | | |
| | | |

| Order **Charadriiformes** | Family **Charadriidae** | Species ***Charadrius semipalmatus*** |

# Semipalmated Plover 🔊

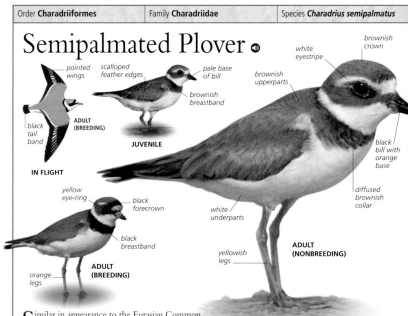

**pointed wings**

**scalloped feather edges**

**pale base of bill**

**white eyestripe**

**brownish crown**

**brownish upperparts**

**brownish breastband**

**ADULT (BREEDING)**

**JUVENILE**

**black tail band**

**IN FLIGHT**

**black bill with orange base**

**diffused brownish collar**

**yellow eye-ring**

**black forecrown**

**black breastband**

**white underparts**

**yellowish legs**

**ADULT (NONBREEDING)**

**orange legs**

**ADULT (BREEDING)**

Similar in appearance to the Eurasian Common Ringed Plover, the Semipalmated Plover is a small shorebird with a tapered shape. It is a familiar sight in a wide variety of habitats during migration and in winter, when these birds gather in loose flocks. A casual walk down a sandy beach between fall and spring might awaken up to 100 Semipalmated Plovers, sleeping in slight depressions in the sand, though flocks of up to 1,000 birds may also be encountered.

**VOICE** Flight call a whistled, abrupt double note, *chu-WEEp*, with soft emphasis on second syllable; courtship display song is a version of flight call followed by rough *r-r-r-r-r-r-r*, ending with a slurred, descending *yelp*.

**NESTING** Simple scrape on bare or slightly vegetated ground in Arctic tundra; 3–4 eggs; 1 brood; May–June.

**FEEDING** Forages in typical plover style: run, pause, and pluck; eats aquatic mollusks, crustaceans, flies, beetles, and spiders.

**FLIGHT:** straight, fast; with fluttering wingbeats.

**BY SIGHT AND FEEL**
Semipalmated Plovers locate prey by sight or through the sensitive soles of their toes.

## SIMILAR SPECIES

**WILSON'S PLOVER** see p.430

*heavier, dark bill*

**COMMON RINGED PLOVER** see p.470

*wider breastband*

**pinkish legs**

**OCCURRENCE**
Breeding habitat is Arctic or subarctic tundra, well-drained gravel, shale, or other sparsely vegetated ground. During migration, mudflats, saltwater marshes, lake edges, tidal areas, and flooded fields. During winter, coastal or near coastal habitats.

| Length **6¾–7½in (17–19cm)** | Wingspan **17–20½in (43–52cm)** | Weight **1¹⁄₁₆–2½oz (30–70g)** |
| Social **Solitary/Flocks** | Lifespan **Up to 6 years** | Status **Secure** |

| DATE SEEN | WHERE | NOTES |
|-----------|-------|-------|
| | | |
| | | |
| | | |
| | | |
| | | |

| Order **Charadriiformes** | Family **Charadriidae** | Species **Charadrius melodus** |

# Piping Plover

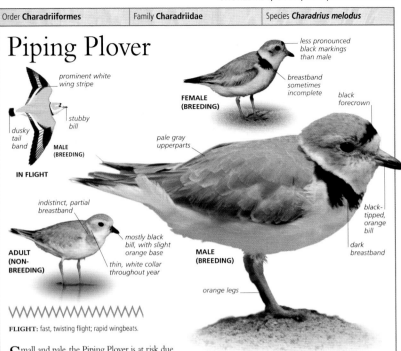

less pronounced black markings than male

**FEMALE (BREEDING)**

breastband sometimes incomplete

black forecrown

prominent white wing stripe

stubby bill

dusky tail band

**MALE (BREEDING)**

**IN FLIGHT**

pale gray upperparts

black-tipped, orange bill

dark breastband

indistinct, partial breastband

mostly black bill, with slight orange base

**ADULT (NON-BREEDING)**

thin, white collar throughout year

**MALE (BREEDING)**

orange legs

**FLIGHT:** fast, twisting flight; rapid wingbeats.

Small and pale, the Piping Plover is at risk due to eroding coastlines, human disturbance, and predation by foxes, raccoons, and cats. With its pale gray back, it is well camouflaged along beaches or in dunes, but conservation measures, such as fencing off nesting beaches and control of predators, are necessary to restore populations. Two subspecies of the Piping Plover are recognized; one nests on the Atlantic Coast, and the other inland.

**VOICE** Clear, whistled *peep* call in flight; quiet *peep-lo* during courtship and contact; high-pitched *pipe-pipe-pipe* song.
**NESTING** Shallow scrape in sand, gravel, dunes, or salt flats; 4 eggs; 1 brood; April–May.
**FEEDING** Typical run, pause, and pluck plover feeding style; diet includes marine worms, insects, and mollusks.

**VULNERABLE NESTS**
The fragile nature of their preferred nesting sites has led to this species becoming endangered.

**OCCURRENCE**
Found along beaches, in saline sandflats, and adjacent mudflats; during winter, found exclusively along the Atlantic and Gulf Coasts, sandflats, and mudflats. Inland subspecies nests on sand or gravel beaches adjacent to large lakes, rivers, and saline lakes.

**SIMILAR SPECIES**

**SEMIPALMATED PLOVER** ✽
see p.112

dark, brown upperparts

**SNOWY PLOVER** ✽
see p.114

black bill

narrow, white collar

darker legs

| Length **6½–7in (17–18cm)** | Wingspan **18–18½in (45–47cm)** | Weight **1⅝–2⅜oz (45–65g)** |
| Social **Small flocks** | Lifespan **Up to 11 years** | Status **Endangered** |

| DATE SEEN | WHERE | NOTES |
| --- | --- | --- |
| | | |
| | | |
| | | |
| | | |

| Order **Charadriiformes** | Family **Charadriidae** | Species *Charadrius nivosus* |
| --- | --- | --- |

# Snowy Plover

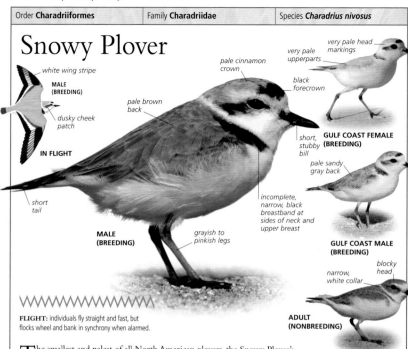

*white wing stripe*

**MALE (BREEDING)**

*pale cinnamon crown*

*very pale upperparts*

*very pale head markings*

*black forecrown*

**GULF COAST FEMALE (BREEDING)**

*pale brown back*

*dusky cheek patch*

**IN FLIGHT**

*short, stubby bill*

*pale sandy gray back*

*short tail*

**MALE (BREEDING)**

*grayish to pinkish legs*

*incomplete, narrow, black breastband at sides of neck and upper breast*

**GULF COAST MALE (BREEDING)**

*blocky head*

*narrow, white collar*

**ADULT (NONBREEDING)**

**FLIGHT:** individuals fly straight and fast, but flocks wheel and bank in synchrony when alarmed.

The smallest and palest of all North American plovers, the Snowy Plover's cryptic coloration blends in so well with its beach and dune habitat that it often remains unnoticed. This bird often runs faster and covers longer distances than other beach plovers, sprinting along the sand for extended spurts, like sanderlings. Nests are frequently destroyed by weather, disturbance, or predators, but the birds readily construct new nests, even up to six times in the face of regular losses. Nevertheless, habitat destruction has resulted in shrinking populations, and the species is designated as threatened along the Pacific Coast.
**VOICE** Repeated *tow-heet*; *purrt* and single *churr*; typically silent when not breeding, tinkling *ti* at roosts or before flight.
**NESTING** Shallow scrape in sand; 2–3 eggs; 2–3 broods; March–June.
**FEEDING** Feeds in run, pause, and pluck style on terrestrial and aquatic invertebrates, such as snails and clams.

**TRULY SNOWY**
The Snowy Plover breeds in sandy areas that are as pale as snow.

**OCCURRENCE**
Breeds on open beach and dune habitats on the Pacific and Gulf Coasts, and inland on brackish lakes in the Great Basin and southern Great Plains region. Coastal birds are only partially migratory, but most inland birds winter at the coast.

### SIMILAR SPECIES

| **SEMIPALMATED PLOVER** ♀ see p.112 | **PIPING PLOVER** ♂ see p.113 |
| --- | --- |
| *brown breastband* | *orange legs* |
| *plumper overall* | |

| Length **6–6½in (15–17cm)** | Wingspan **16–18in (41–46cm)** | Weight **1¼–2⅛oz (35–60g)** |
| --- | --- | --- |
| Social **Large flocks** | Lifespan **Up to 4 years** | Status **Endangered** |

| DATE SEEN | WHERE | NOTES |
| --- | --- | --- |
| | | |
| | | |
| | | |
| | | |
| | | |

| Order **Charadriiformes** | Family **Scolopacidae** | Species **Numenius phaeopus** |
|---|---|---|

# Whimbrel

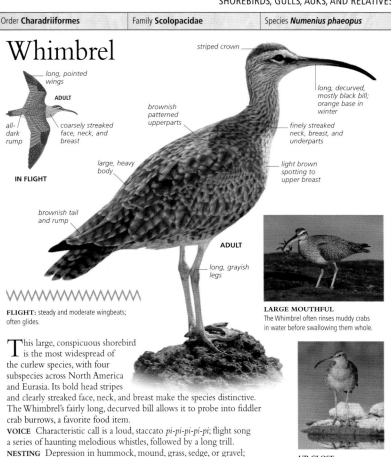

striped crown

long, pointed wings

**ADULT**

all-dark rump

coarsely streaked face, neck, and breast

**IN FLIGHT**

brownish patterned upperparts

large, heavy body

brownish tail and rump

long, decurved, mostly black bill; orange base in winter

finely streaked neck, breast, and underparts

light brown spotting to upper breast

**ADULT**

long, grayish legs

**FLIGHT:** steady and moderate wingbeats; often glides.

This large, conspicuous shorebird is the most widespread of the curlew species, with four subspecies across North America and Eurasia. Its bold head stripes and clearly streaked face, neck, and breast make the species distinctive. The Whimbrel's fairly long, decurved bill allows it to probe into fiddler crab burrows, a favorite food item.

**VOICE** Characteristic call is a loud, staccato *pi-pi-pi-pi-pi*; flight song a series of haunting melodious whistles, followed by a long trill.

**NESTING** Depression in hummock, mound, grass, sedge, or gravel; 4 eggs; 1 brood; May–August.

**FEEDING** Probes for crabs, in addition to worms, mollusks, and fish; also eats insects and berries.

**LARGE MOUTHFUL**
The Whimbrel often rinses muddy crabs in water before swallowing them whole.

**UP CLOSE**
A close look at the Whimbrel shows this bird's beautiful, fine patterning.

**OCCURRENCE**
Several populations breed in northern, subarctic, and low-Arctic regions of North America; during migration and in winter, found mostly in coastal marshes, tidal creeks, flats, and mangroves; also at inland Salton Sea, California. Winters along rocky coasts in South America.

**SIMILAR SPECIES**

**BRISTLE-THIGHED CURLEW**
see p.430

pale rump

more spotted

longer, slightly curved bill

**LONG-BILLED CURLEW**
see p.116

larger overall

long, decurved bill

| Length **15½–16½in (39–42cm)** | Wingspan **30–35in (76–89cm)** | Weight **11–18oz (300–500g)** |
|---|---|---|
| Social **Flocks** | Lifespan **Up to 19 years** | Status **Secure** |

| DATE SEEN | WHERE | NOTES |
|---|---|---|
| | | |
| | | |
| | | |
| | | |
| | | |

| Order **Charadriiformes** | Family **Scolopacidae** | Species **Numenius americanus** |
|---|---|---|

# Long-billed Curlew

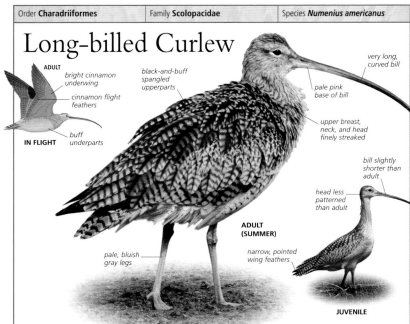

**ADULT**

bright cinnamon underwing

cinnamon flight feathers

**IN FLIGHT** buff underparts

black-and-buff spangled upperparts

very long, curved bill

pale pink base of bill

upper breast, neck, and head finely streaked

bill slightly shorter than adult

head less patterned than adult

**ADULT (SUMMER)**

pale, bluish gray legs

narrow, pointed wing feathers

**JUVENILE**

The Long-billed Curlew has the southernmost breeding range and northernmost wintering range of the four North American curlews. It is also one of nine species of birds that are endemic to the grasslands of the Great Plains. Its large size and tame behavior on its wintering grounds in North America add to its mystique. The curvature of its bill is adapted to probe for food in soft mud and sand.

**VOICE** Flight call a 2-note *cur-LUoo*, often accompanied by rapid *qui-pi-pi-pi-pi*; flight song consists of haunting whistles, trills *werr-EEEer.*

**NESTING** Shallow depression in sparsely vegetated prairie habitat; 4 eggs; 1 brood; April–May.

**FEEDING** Picks insects on the surface or probes in soft mud for insects, crustaceans, mollusks, and worms; also eats fish.

**FLIGHT:** graceful and strong series of flaps alternating with a glide.

**APTLY NAMED**
The Long-billed Curlew is the longest-billed shorebird in North America.

### SIMILAR SPECIES

**MARBLED GODWIT** see p.117

straight bill

more rounded body shape

darker, grayish legs

**WHIMBREL** smaller; see p.115

streaks on face, neck, and breast

brownish upperparts

**OCCURRENCE**
Breeds in prairies, short grass and mixed-grass habitats of the Great Basin and Great Plains. Winters in wet pastures, marshes, beaches, and tidal mudflats primarily of California, Texas, and Mexico, with some stragglers occurring in Florida. Generally not a "shorebird" found along shores.

| Length **20–26in (51–65cm)** | Wingspan **30–39in (75–100cm)** | Weight **16–28oz (450–800g)** |
|---|---|---|
| Social **Solitary/Winter flocks** | Lifespan **At least 8 years** | Status **Vulnerable** |

| DATE SEEN | WHERE | NOTES |
|---|---|---|
| | | |
| | | |
| | | |
| | | |
| | | |

| Order **Charadriiformes** | Family **Scolopacidae** | Species *Limosa fedoa* |

# Marbled Godwit

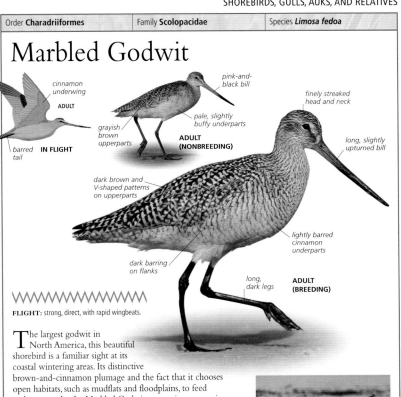

cinnamon underwing

**ADULT**

barred tail   **IN FLIGHT**

pink-and-black bill

grayish brown upperparts

pale, slightly buffy underparts

**ADULT (NONBREEDING)**

finely streaked head and neck

long, slightly upturned bill

dark brown and V-shaped patterns on upperparts

lightly barred cinnamon underparts

dark barring on flanks

long, dark legs

**ADULT (BREEDING)**

**FLIGHT:** strong, direct, with rapid wingbeats.

The largest godwit in North America, this beautiful shorebird is a familiar sight at its coastal wintering areas. Its distinctive brown-and-cinnamon plumage and the fact that it chooses open habitats, such as mudflats and floodplains, to feed and roost, make the Marbled Godwit a conspicuous species. A monogamous bird, the Marbled Godwit is also long-lived—the oldest bird recorded was 29 years old.

**VOICE** Call a nasal *ah-ahk*, and single *ahk*; breeding call, *goddWhit*, *wik-wik*; other calls include *rack-a, karatica, ratica, ratica*.

**NESTING** Depression in short grass in Alaska; also nests on vegetation in water; 4 eggs; 1 brood; May–July.

**FEEDING** Probes mudflats, beaches, short grass for insects, especially grasshoppers; also crustaceans, mollusks, and small fish.

**EASILY RECOGNIZED**
Its large size and buffy to cinnamon color make this godwit a very distinctive shorebird.

### SIMILAR SPECIES

**HUDSONIAN GODWIT**
white rump;
see p.431
black barring overall

**BLACK-TAILED GODWIT**
see p.470
smaller overall

deep orange neck and breast

**OCCURRENCE**
Breeds in the grassy marshes of the Great Plains. During migration and in winter, prefers sandy beaches and coastal mudflats with adjoining meadows or savannas in California and the Gulf of Mexico. Also seen on inland wetlands and along lake shores.

| Length **16½–19in (42–48cm)** | Wingspan **28–32in (70–81cm)** | Weight **10–16oz (275–450g)** |
| Social **Winter flocks** | Lifespan **Up to 29 years** | Status **Secure** |

| DATE SEEN | WHERE | | NOTES |
| --- | --- | --- | --- |
| | | | |
| | | | |
| | | | |
| | | | |
| | | | |

| Order **Charadriiformes** | Family **Scolopacidae** | Species *Arenaria interpres* |
| --- | --- | --- |

# Ruddy Turnstone

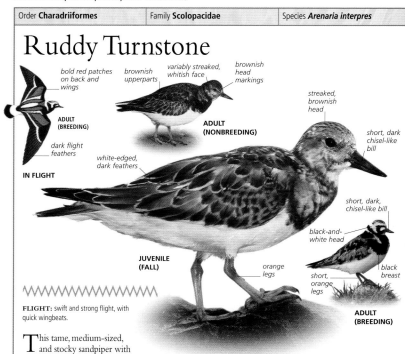

bold red patches on back and wings

brownish upperparts

variably streaked, whitish face

brownish head markings

streaked, brownish head

**ADULT (BREEDING)**

**ADULT (NONBREEDING)**

short, dark chisel-like bill

dark flight feathers

**IN FLIGHT**

white-edged, dark feathers

short, dark, chisel-like bill

black-and-white head

**JUVENILE (FALL)**

orange legs

short, orange legs

black breast

**FLIGHT:** swift and strong flight, with quick wingbeats.

**ADULT (BREEDING)**

This tame, medium-sized, and stocky sandpiper with a chisel-shaped bill is a common visitor along the shorelines of North and South America. On its High Arctic breeding grounds, it is bold and aggressive and is able to drive off predators as large as the Glaucous Gull and Parasitic Jaeger. The Ruddy Turnstone was given its name because of its reddish back color and because of its habit of flipping and overturning items like mollusk shells and pebbles, or digging in the sand and looking for small crustaceans and other marine invertebrates. Two subspecies live in Arctic North America: *A. i. interpres* in northeastern Canada and *A. i. morinellas* elsewhere in Canada and Alaska.

**VOICE** Rapid chatter on breeding ground: *TTT-wooo TTT-woooRTTititititit*; flight call a low, rapid *kut-a-kut*.

**NESTING** Simple scrape lined with lichens and grasses in dry, open areas; 4 eggs; 1 brood; June.

**FEEDING** Forages along shoreline for crustaceans, insects, including beetles, spiders; also eats plants.

**WINTER GATHERINGS**
Ruddy Turnstones often congregate in large winter flocks on rocky shorelines.

**SIMILAR SPECIES**

**BLACK TURNSTONE**
see p.119
darker overall

no rust color in plumage

duller legs

**OCCURRENCE**
Breeds in High Arctic: wide-open, barren, and grassy habitats and rocky coasts, usually near water. In winter, on sandy or gravel beaches and rocky shorelines, from northern California to South America, and from northern Massachusetts south along Atlantic and Gulf Coasts.

| Length **8–10½in (20–27cm)** | Wingspan **20–22½in (51–57cm)** | Weight **3½–7oz (100–200g)** |
| --- | --- | --- |
| Social **Flocks** | Lifespan **Up to 7 years** | Status **Secure** |

| DATE SEEN | WHERE | | NOTES |
| --- | --- | --- | --- |
| | | | |
| | | | |
| | | | |
| | | | |
| | | | |

| Order **Charadriiformes** | Family **Scolopacidae** | Species *Arenaria melanocephala* |
|---|---|---|

# Black Turnstone

dark chocolate-brown head and breast

short, blackish, chisel-like bill

stocky, pointed wings

white patch on back

brownish upperparts, with scattered black feathers

black tail band

**ADULT (NONBREEDING)**

**IN FLIGHT**

black head and breast with white flecking

white patch

blackish back

**ADULT (NONBREEDING)**

pale edges to some feathers

white belly

yellowish legs

darker legs

**ADULT (BREEDING)**

The Black Turnstone is found along the entire North American Pacific coastline in winter, from Kodiak Island, Alaska, to the Gulf of California. Highly dependent on rocky shorelines, the zebra-like but cryptic plumage of this species blends in well, and it becomes almost invisible when it forages or roosts on dark, rocky surfaces. Although the Black Turnstone flips stones and beach litter in search of food, it uses its chisel-like bill to pry loose or crack tougher prey, particularly mussels and barnacles. On its breeding grounds, this species is a vocal and aggressive defender of the nesting community, even physically attacking predators such as jaegers.

**VOICE** Flight call a *breerp*, often continued as rapid chattering; variety of trills, purrs, and a *tu-whit* call.

**NESTING** Hollow depression in tundra; 4 eggs; 1 brood; May–June.

**FEEDING** Eats invertebrates such as mussels, barnacles, limpets, snails, and crabs, also seeds, small bird eggs, and carrion.

**FLIGHT:** swift and direct, with strong, shallow wingbeats.

**CRACKING IT**
Black Turnstones use their chisel-shaped bills to break open barnacles on rocks.

**SIMILAR SPECIES**

**RUDDY TURNSTONE** see p.118
black-and-white head

orange-red legs

**OCCURRENCE**
Breeds in tundra of western Alaska; also inland along rivers and lakes. It is strictly coastal during migration and winter where it is found in the tidal zone of rocky shorelines, on sand and gravel beaches, mudflats, and rocky jetties of the West Coast, south to Baja, California.

| Length **8½–10½in (22–27cm)** | Wingspan **20–22½in (51–57cm)** | Weight **3⅛–6oz (90–175g)** |
|---|---|---|
| Social **Flocks** | Lifespan **At least 4 years** | Status **Secure** |

| DATE SEEN | WHERE | NOTES |
|---|---|---|
| ......... | ......... | ......... |
| ......... | ......... | ......... |
| ......... | ......... | ......... |
| ......... | ......... | ......... |
| ......... | ......... | ......... |

| Order **Charadriiformes** | Family **Scolopacidae** | Species *Calidris canutus* |

# Red Knot

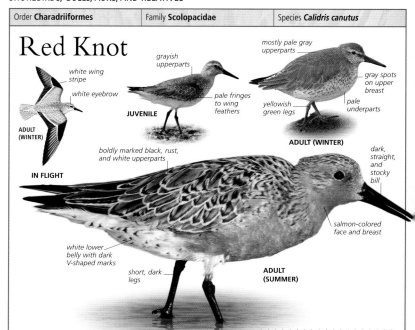

**ADULT (WINTER)**

white wing stripe

white eyebrow

grayish upperparts

pale fringes to wing feathers

**JUVENILE**

**IN FLIGHT**

mostly pale gray upperparts

gray spots on upper breast

yellowish green legs

pale underparts

**ADULT (WINTER)**

boldly marked black, rust, and white upperparts

dark, straight, and stocky bill

salmon-colored face and breast

white lower belly with dark V-shaped marks

short, dark legs

**ADULT (SUMMER)**

A substantial, plump sandpiper, the Red Knot is the largest North American shorebird in the genus *Calidris*. There are two North American subspecies—*C. c. rufa* and *C. c. roselaari*. Noted for its extraordinary long-distance migration, *C. c. rufa* flies about 9,300 miles (15,000km) between its High Arctic breeding grounds and wintering area in South America, especially in Tierra del Fuego, at the tip of South America. Recent declines have occurred in this population, attributed to over-harvesting of horseshoe crab eggs—its critical food source. With the population of *C. c. rufa* having declined from more than 100,000 birds in the mid-1980s to below 15,000 today, the Red Knot is now listed as endangered in New Jersey, and faces possible extinction.

**VOICE** Flight call a soft *kuEEt* or *kuup*; display song *eerie por-meeee por-meeee*, followed by *por-por por-por*.

**NESTING** Simple scrape in grassy or barren tundra, often lined; 4 eggs; 1 brood; June.

**FEEDING** Probes mud or sand for insects, plant material, small mollusks, crustaceans, especially small snails, worms, and other invertebrates.

**FLIGHT:** powerful, swift, direct flight with rapid wingbeats.

**STAGING AREAS**
Red Knots form dense flocks during migration and on their wintering grounds.

**OCCURRENCE**
Breeds in flat, barren tundra in High Arctic islands and peninsulas. Mostly coastal during migration and winter, preferring sandbars, beaches, and tidal flats, where it congregates in huge flocks.

| SIMILAR SPECIES | |
|---|---|
| **BLACK-BELLIED PLOVER** see p.109 | *large, dark eye* |
| *longer, dark legs* | |

| Length **9–10in (23–25cm)** | Wingspan **23–24in (58–61cm)** | Weight **3⅜–8oz (95–225g)** |
|---|---|---|
| Social **Large flocks** | Lifespan **Unknown** | Status **Declining** |

| DATE SEEN | WHERE | NOTES |
|---|---|---|
| | | |
| | | |
| | | |
| | | |
| | | |

| Order **Charadriiformes** | Family **Scolopacidae** | Species *Calidris virgata* |
|---|---|---|

# Surfbird

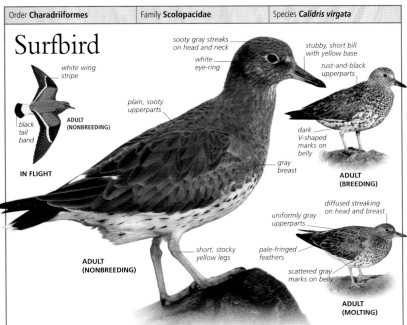

sooty gray streaks on head and neck

white eye-ring

white wing stripe

**ADULT (NONBREEDING)**

plain, sooty upperparts

black tail band

**IN FLIGHT**

stubby, short bill with yellow base

rust-and-black upperparts

dark V-shaped marks on belly

gray breast

**ADULT (BREEDING)**

gray breast

short, stocky yellow legs

**ADULT (NONBREEDING)**

uniformly gray upperparts

pale-fringed feathers

diffused streaking on head and breast

scattered gray marks on belly

**ADULT (MOLTING)**

The chunky, stubby-billed Surfbird has a dual lifestyle—it breeds in the high mountain tundra of Alaska and then migrates to the rocky Pacific Coasts of both North and South America. Some individuals migrate as far as southern Chile, a round trip of about 19,000 miles (30,500km) each year. This remarkable wintering range is among the largest of all North American shorebirds. The extent of the rust color on the upperparts of breeding Surfbirds is variable.

**VOICE** Flight call a soft *whiff-if-if*; feeding flocks soft, chattering *whiks*; display call *kree, kree…ki-drr ki-drr*, and *quoy quoy quoy*.

**NESTING** Shallow lined depression on vegetated or bare ground; 4 eggs; 1 brood; May–June.

**FEEDING** Eats mainly insects, especially beetles; also aquatic mollusks and crustaceans, such as mussels and barnacles.

**FLIGHT:** swift and direct, with strong, powerful wingbeats.

**COASTAL PROXIMITY**
Except when breeding, Surfbirds spend their lives along rocky intertidal shores.

**OCCURRENCE**
Breeds in low to high-elevation steep, rocky slopes of ridges and mountains; the rest of the year it spends exclusively on rocky Pacific coastlines, typically within 6½ft (2m) of the high-tide line (the narrowest range of all North American shorebirds).

**SIMILAR SPECIES**

**PURPLE SANDPIPER** ❋

purplish gray upperparts

**ROCK SANDPIPER**
see p.431

darker feathers on back

longer bill

longer, slightly curved bill

short, yellow-orange legs

| Length **9½–10½in (24–27cm)** | Wingspan **25–27in (63–68cm)** | Weight **4–8oz (125–225g)** |
|---|---|---|
| Social **Small flocks** | Lifespan **Unknown** | Status **Secure** |

| DATE SEEN | WHERE | NOTES |
|---|---|---|
| | | |
| | | |
| | | |
| | | |
| | | |

| Order **Charadriiformes** | Family **Scolopacidae** | Species ***Calidris himantopus*** |
| --- | --- | --- |

# Stilt Sandpiper

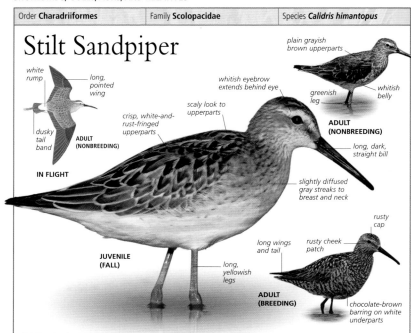

**IN FLIGHT**

white rump

long, pointed wing

dusky tail band

**ADULT (NONBREEDING)**

crisp, white-and-rust-fringed upperparts

scaly look to upperparts

whitish eyebrow extends behind eye

plain grayish brown upperparts

greenish leg

whitish belly

**ADULT (NONBREEDING)**

long, dark, straight bill

slightly diffused gray streaks to breast and neck

**JUVENILE (FALL)**

long, yellowish legs

long wings and tail

rusty cheek patch

rusty cap

**ADULT (BREEDING)**

chocolate-brown barring on white underparts

The slender Stilt Sandpiper is uncommon and unique to North America, where it breeds in several small areas of northern tundra. It favors shallow, freshwater habitats, where it feeds in a distinctive style, walking slowly through belly-deep water with its neck outstretched and bill pointed downward. It either picks at the surface, or submerges itself, keeping its tail raised up all the while. During migration it forms dense, rapidly moving flocks that sometimes include other sandpiper species.

**VOICE** Flight or alarm call low, muffled *chuf*; also *krrit* and sharp *kew-it*; display call *xxree-xxree-xxree-xxree-ee-haw, ee-haw*.

**NESTING** Shallow depression on raised knolls or ridges in tundra; 4 eggs; 1 brood; June.

**FEEDING** Eats mostly adult and larval insects; also some snails, mollusks, and seeds.

**FLIGHT:** fast and direct, with rapid beats of its long wings.

### SIMILAR SPECIES

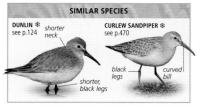

**DUNLIN** ❀ see p.124

shorter neck

shorter, black legs

**CURLEW SANDPIPER** ❀ see p.470

black legs

curved bill

**PALE BELOW**
Wading through shallow water, this Stilt Sandpiper displays its whitish underparts.

**OCCURRENCE**
Breeds in moist to wet coastal tundra on well-drained, raised knolls or ridges in Alaska, Yukon, and northwestern territories and Hudson Bay. During migration and in winter, prefers freshwater habitats, such as flooded fields, marsh pools, reservoirs, and sheltered lagoons to tidal mudflats.

| Length **8–9in (20–23cm)** | Wingspan **17–18½in (43–47cm)** | Weight **1¾–2⅛oz (50–60g)** |
| --- | --- | --- |
| Social **Pairs/Flocks** | Lifespan **At least 3 years** | Status **Secure** |

| DATE SEEN | WHERE | NOTES |
| --- | --- | --- |
| | | |
| | | |
| | | |
| | | |
| | | |

| Order **Charadriiformes** | Family **Scolopacidae** | Species *Calidris alba* |

# Sanderling

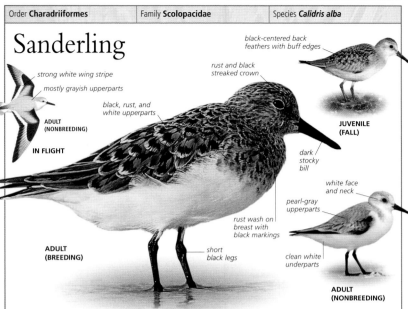

strong white wing stripe

mostly grayish upperparts

black, rust, and white upperparts

**ADULT (NONBREEDING)**

**IN FLIGHT**

black-centered back feathers with buff edges

rust and black streaked crown

**JUVENILE (FALL)**

dark stocky bill

white face and neck

pearl-gray upperparts

rust wash on breast with black markings

**ADULT (BREEDING)**

short black legs

clean white underparts

**ADULT (NONBREEDING)**

The Sanderling is probably the best-known shorebird in the world. It breeds in some of the most remote, High Arctic habitats, from Greenland to Siberia, but occupies just about every temperate and tropical shoreline in the Americas when not breeding. Indeed, its wintering range spans both American coasts, from Canada to Argentina. Feeding in flocks, it is a common sight in winter on sandy beaches. In many places, though, the bird is declining rapidly—pollution of the sea and shore, and the disturbance caused by people using beaches for various recreational purposes are the main causes.

**VOICE** Flight call squeaky *pweet*, threat call *sew-sew-sew*; display song harsh, buzzy notes and chattering *cher-cher-cher*.

**NESTING** Small, shallow depression on dry, stony ground; 4 eggs; 1–3 broods; June–July.

**FEEDING** Probes along the surf-line in sand for insects, small crustaceans, small mollusks, and worms.

**FLIGHT:** rapid, free-form; birds in flocks twisting and turning as if they were one.

**CHASING THE WAVES**
The Sanderling scampers after retreating waves to pick up any small creatures stranded by the sea.

**SIMILAR SPECIES**

**SEMIPALMATED SANDPIPER** ☼ see p.112

less contrasting upperparts

paler throat and breast

**WESTERN SANDPIPER** see p.130

prominent eyebrow

tapering bill

**OCCURRENCE**
Breeds in barren High Arctic coastal tundra of northernmost Canada, including the islands, north to Ellesmere Island. During winter months and on migration, found along all North American coastlines, but especially sandy beaches; inland migrants found along lake and river edges.

| Length **7½–8in (19–20cm)** | Wingspan **16–18in (41–46cm)** | Weight **1³⁄₁₆–3½oz (40–100g)** |
| Social **Small flocks** | Lifespan **Up to 10 years** | Status **Declining** |

| DATE SEEN | WHERE | NOTES |
|---|---|---|
| | | |
| | | |
| | | |
| | | |
| | | |

| Order **Charadriiformes** | Family **Scolopacidae** | Species *Calidris alpina* |

# Dunlin

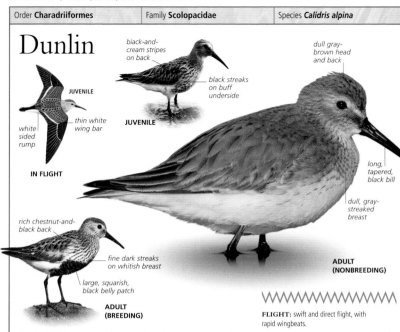

black-and-cream stripes on back

JUVENILE

black streaks on buff underside

**JUVENILE**

dull gray-brown head and back

white sided rump

thin white wing bar

**IN FLIGHT**

long, tapered, black bill

dull, gray-streaked breast

**ADULT (NONBREEDING)**

rich chestnut-and-black back

fine dark streaks on whitish breast

large, squarish, black belly patch

**ADULT (BREEDING)**

**FLIGHT:** swift and direct flight, with rapid wingbeats.

The Dunlin is one of the most abundant and widespread of North America's shorebirds, but of the ten recognized subspecies, only three breed in North America: *C. a. arcticola*, *C. a. pacifica*, and *C. a. hudsonia*. The Dunlin is unmistakable in its striking, red-backed, black-bellied breeding plumage. In winter it sports much drabber colors, but more than makes up for this by gathering in spectacular flocks of many thousands of birds on its favorite coastal mudflats.

**VOICE** Call accented trill, *drurr-drurr*, that rises slightly, then descends; flight call *jeeezp*; song *wrraah-wrraah*.

**NESTING** Simple cup lined with grasses, leaves, and lichens in moist to wet tundra; 4 eggs; 1 brood; June–July.

**FEEDING** Probes for marine, freshwater, terrestrial invertebrates: clams, worms, insect larvae, crustaceans; also plants and small fish.

**OLD RED BACK**
The Dunlin was once known as the Red-backed Sandpiper because of its distinct breeding plumage.

### SIMILAR SPECIES

**STILT SANDPIPER** ❊
see p.122

longer, thinner neck

yellowish green legs

**CURLEW SANDPIPER** ❊
see p.470

less streaking on chest

longer legs

**OCCURRENCE**
Breeds in Arctic and subarctic moist, wet tundra, often near ponds, with drier islands for nest sites. In migration and winter, prefers coastal areas with extensive mudflats and sandy beaches; also feeds in flooded fields and seasonal inland wetlands.

| Length **6½–8½in (16–22cm)** | Wingspan **12½–17½in (32–44cm)** | Weight **1⁹⁄₁₆–2¼oz (45–65g)** |
| Social **Large flocks** | Lifespan **Up to 24 years** | Status **Declining** |

| DATE SEEN | WHERE | NOTES |
|---|---|---|
| | | |
| | | |
| | | |
| | | |
| | | |

| Order **Charadriiformes** | Family **Scolopacidae** | Species *Calidris bairdii* |

# Baird's Sandpiper

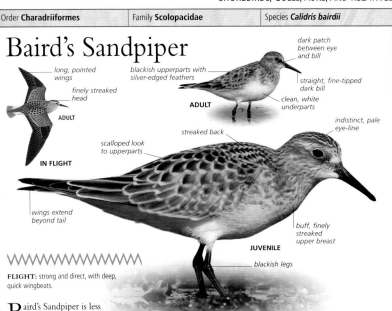

long, pointed wings

finely streaked head

**ADULT**

**IN FLIGHT**

blackish upperparts with silver-edged feathers

**ADULT**

dark patch between eye and bill

straight, fine-tipped dark bill

clean, white underparts

indistinct, pale eye-line

streaked back

scalloped look to upperparts

wings extend beyond tail

buff, finely streaked upper breast

**JUVENILE**

blackish legs

**FLIGHT:** strong and direct, with deep, quick wingbeats.

Baird's Sandpiper is less well known than the other North American *Calidris* sandpipers. It was described in 1861, later than its relatives, by the famous North American ornithologist Elliott Cowes, a former surgeon in the US Army, in honor of Spencer Fullerton Baird. Both men were founding members of the AOU (the American Ornithologists' Union). From its High Arctic, tundra habitat, Baird's Sandpiper moves across North America and the western US, into South America, and all the way to Tierra del Fuego, a remarkable biannual journey of 6,000–9,000 miles (9,700–14,500km).

**VOICE** Flight call a low, dry *preep*; song on Arctic breeding ground: *brraay, bray, bray*, followed by *hee-aaw, hee-aaw, hee-aaw*.

**NESTING** Shallow depression in coastal or upland tundra; 4 eggs; 1 brood; June.

**FEEDING** Picks and probes for insects and larvae; also spiders and pond crustaceans.

**FEEDING IN FLOCKS**
Flocks of this sandpiper rush about in search of food in shallow water and muddy areas.

## SIMILAR SPECIES

**WHITE-RUMPED SANDPIPER**
see p.127

prominent, white eyebrow

slightly bulkier body

**PECTORAL SANDPIPER**
larger; see p.128

yellowish legs

streaked breast-band

**OCCURRENCE**
Breeds in tundra habitats of High Arctic Alaska and Canada. During migration and winter, inland freshwater habitats: lake and river margins, wet pastures, rice fields; also tidal flats at coastal locations. In winter, common in the high Andes of South America, and sometimes all the way to Tierra del Fuego.

| Length 5¾–7¼in (14.5–18.5cm) | Wingspan **16–18½in (41–47cm)** | Weight **1¹⁄₁₆–2oz (30–55g)** |
| Social **Flocks** | Lifespan **Unknown** | Status **Secure** |

| DATE SEEN | WHERE | NOTES |
|---|---|---|
| | | |
| | | |
| | | |
| | | |
| | | |

125

| Order **Charadriiformes** | Family **Scolopacidae** | Species *Calidris minutilla* |

# Least Sandpiper

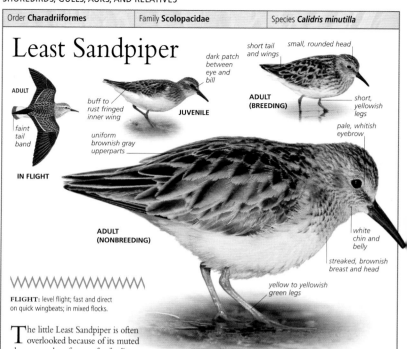

**ADULT**

**IN FLIGHT**

faint tail band

buff to rust fringed inner wing

uniform brownish gray upperparts

**JUVENILE**

dark patch between eye and bill

short tail and wings — small, rounded head

**ADULT (BREEDING)**

short, yellowish legs

pale, whitish eyebrow

**ADULT (NONBREEDING)**

white chin and belly

streaked, brownish breast and head

yellow to yellowish green legs

**FLIGHT:** level flight; fast and direct on quick wingbeats; in mixed flocks.

The little Least Sandpiper is often overlooked because of its muted plumage and preference for feeding unobtrusively near vegetative cover. With its brown or brownish gray plumage, the Least Sandpiper virtually disappears in the landscape when feeding crouched down on wet margins of water bodies. The bird is often found in small to medium flocks, members of which typically are nervous when foraging, and frequently burst into flight, only to alight a short way off.
**VOICE** Its flight call, *kreeeep*, rises in pitch, often repeated two-syllable *kree-eep*; display call trilled *b-reeee, b-reeee, b-reeee*.
**NESTING** Depression in open, subarctic habitat near water; 4 eggs; 1 brood; May–June.
**FEEDING** Forages for variety of small terrestrial and aquatic prey, especially sand fleas, mollusks, and flies.

**FLOCK IN FLIGHT**
The narrow pointed wings of the Least Sandpiper allow it to fly fast and level.

**SIMILAR SPECIES**

**SEMIPALMATED SANDPIPER** ✿
see p.129

grayer overall

whiter throat

larger overall

**PECTORAL SANDPIPER**
see p.128

larger overall

heavier bill

**OCCURRENCE**
Breeds in wet low-Arctic areas from Alaska and the Yukon to Québec and Newfoundland. During migration and in winter, uses muddy areas such as lake shores, riverbanks, flooded fields, and tidal flats. Winters from southern North America south to Peru and Brazil.

| Length **4¾in (12cm)** | Wingspan **13–14in (33–35cm)** | Weight **⁵⁄₁₆–1oz (9–27g)** |
| Social **Flocks** | Lifespan **Up to 16 years** | Status **Declining** |

| DATE SEEN | WHERE | | NOTES |
|---|---|---|---|
| | | | |
| | | | |
| | | | |
| | | | |
| | | | |

| Order **Charadriiformes** | Family **Scolopacidae** | Species **Calidris fuscicollis** |

# White-rumped Sandpiper

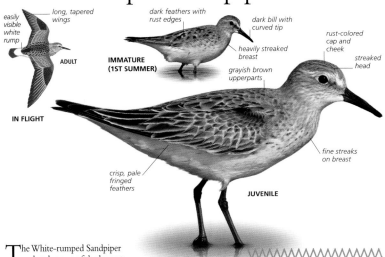

easily visible white rump

long, tapered wings

**ADULT**

**IN FLIGHT**

dark feathers with rust edges

**IMMATURE (1ST SUMMER)**

dark bill with curved tip

heavily streaked breast

grayish brown upperparts

rust-colored cap and cheek

streaked head

fine streaks on breast

crisp, pale fringed feathers

**JUVENILE**

The White-rumped Sandpiper undertakes one of the longest migrations of any bird in the Western Hemisphere. From its High Arctic breeding grounds in Alaska and Canada, it migrates in several long jumps to extreme southern South America—about 9,000–12,000 miles (14,500–19,300km), twice a year. Almost the entire population migrates through the central US in spring, with several stopovers, which are critical to the success of its journey. While associating with other shorebird species during migration and winter, it can be overlooked in the crowd. Its insect-like call and white rump aid identification.

**VOICE** Call a very high-pitched, insect-like *tzeet*; flight song an insect-like, high-pitched, rattling buzz, interspersed with grunts.

**NESTING** Shallow depression in usually wet but well-vegetated tundra; 4 eggs; 1 brood; June.

**FEEDING** Picks and probes for insects, spiders, earthworms, and marine worms; also some plant matter.

**FLIGHT:** fast, strong, and direct flight with deep wingbeats.

**WING POWER**
Long narrow wings enable this species to migrate to and from the Arctic and Tierra del Fuego.

**OCCURRENCE**
Breeds in wet but well-vegetated tundra, usually near ponds, lakes, or streams. In migration and winter, grassy areas: flooded fields, grassy lake margins, rivers, ponds, grassy margins of tidal mudflats, and roadside ditches. On wintering grounds, often associates with Baird's Sandpiper.

| SIMILAR SPECIES | | |

**SEMIPALMATED SANDPIPER** see p.129

slightly rufous crown

**BAIRD'S SANDPIPER** see p.125

no white rump

more distinct streaks on breast

| Length **6–6¾in (15–17cm)** | Wingspan **16–18in (41–46cm)** | Weight **⅞–1¾oz (25–50g)** |
| Social **Flocks** | Lifespan **Unknown** | Status **Secure** |

| DATE SEEN | WHERE | NOTES |
| --- | --- | --- |
| | | |
| | | |
| | | |
| | | |
| | | |

| Order **Charadriiformes** | Family **Scolopacidae** | Species *Calidris melanotos* |

# Pectoral Sandpiper

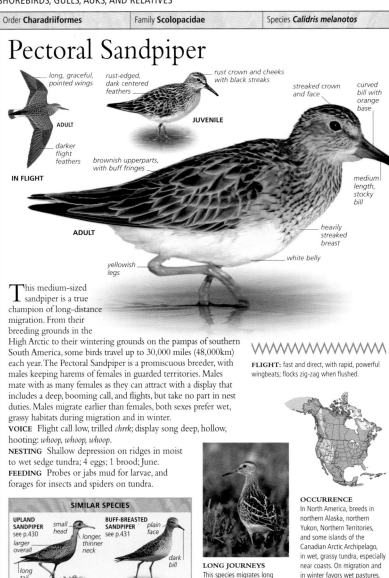

long, graceful, pointed wings

**ADULT**

darker flight feathers

**IN FLIGHT**

rust-edged, dark centered feathers

brownish upperparts, with buff fringes

rust crown and cheeks with black streaks

**JUVENILE**

streaked crown and face

curved bill with orange base

medium length, stocky bill

heavily streaked breast

white belly

**ADULT**

yellowish legs

This medium-sized sandpiper is a true champion of long-distance migration. From their breeding grounds in the High Arctic to their wintering grounds on the pampas of southern South America, some birds travel up to 30,000 miles (48,000km) each year. The Pectoral Sandpiper is a promiscuous breeder, with males keeping harems of females in guarded territories. Males mate with as many females as they can attract with a display that includes a deep, booming call, and flights, but take no part in nest duties. Males migrate earlier than females, both sexes prefer wet, grassy habitats during migration and in winter.

**VOICE** Flight call low, trilled *chrrk*; display song deep, hollow, hooting: *whoop, whoop, whoop*.

**NESTING** Shallow depression on ridges in moist to wet sedge tundra; 4 eggs; 1 brood; June.

**FEEDING** Probes or jabs mud for larvae, and forages for insects and spiders on tundra.

**FLIGHT:** fast and direct, with rapid, powerful wingbeats; flocks zig-zag when flushed.

**OCCURRENCE**
In North America, breeds in northern Alaska, northern Yukon, Northern Territories, and some islands of the Canadian Arctic Archipelago, in wet, grassy tundra, especially near coasts. On migration and in winter favors wet pastures, the grassy margins of ponds and lakes, and saltmarshes.

### SIMILAR SPECIES

**UPLAND SANDPIPER** see p.430
small head
larger overall
long tail
longer, thinner neck

**BUFF-BREASTED SANDPIPER** see p.431
plain face
dark bill

**LONG JOURNEYS**
This species migrates long distances to arrive in southern South America for the winter.

| Length **7½–9in (19–23cm)** | Wingspan **16½–19½in (42–49cm)** | Weight **1¾–4oz (50–125g)** |
| --- | --- | --- |
| Social **Migrant flocks** | Lifespan **Up to 4½ years** | Status **Secure** |

| DATE SEEN | WHERE | NOTES |
| --- | --- | --- |
| | | |
| | | |
| | | |
| | | |

| Order **Charadriiformes** | Family **Scolopacidae** | Species **Calidris pusilla** |

# Semipalmated Sandpiper

crisp, pale fringed feathers

white eyebrow

short bill with blunt tip

**SUMMER**

pale grayish black legs

pale wing stripe along flight feathers

dark-centered back feathers with buff fringes

slightly paler grayish nape

streaked black and rust crown

**JUVENILE**

**IN FLIGHT**

short, dark bill

wing tips extend to tail tip

**ADULT (SUMMER)**

lightly streaked breast

This is the most abundant of the so-called "peep" *Calidris* sandpipers, especially in the eastern US. Flocks of up to 300,000 birds gather on migration staging areas. As a species, though, it can be hard to identify, because of plumage variation between juveniles and breeding adults, and a bill that varies markedly in size and shape from west to east. Semipalmated sandpipers from northeasterly breeding grounds may fly nonstop to their South American wintering grounds in the fall.

**VOICE** Flight call *chrrk* or higher, sharper *chit*; display song monotonous, droning trill, often repeated for minutes at a time.
**NESTING** Shallow, lined scrape in short grass habitat; 4 eggs; 1 brood; May–June.
**FEEDING** Probes mud for aquatic and terrestrial invertebrates such as mollusks, worms, and spiders.

**FLIGHT:** fast and direct on narrow, pointed, wings; flies in large flocks in winter.

**SLEEPING TOGETHER**
Semipalmated Sandpipers form large feeding or resting flocks on migration and in winter.

**OCCURRENCE**
Breeds in Arctic and subarctic tundra habitats near water; in Alaska, on outer coastal plain. Migrants occur in shallow fresh- or saltwater and open muddy areas with little vegetation, such as intertidal flats or lake shores. Winters in Central and South America, south to Brazil and Peru.

**SIMILAR SPECIES**

**SANDERLING**
see p.123
*more contrasting upperparts*

*darker breast*

**WESTERN SANDPIPER** ❋
see p.130
*usually longer legs*

*puffier head*

*usually more pointed bill*

**LEAST SANDPIPER** ❋
see p.126

*yellowish legs*

*smaller overall*

| Length **5¼–6in (13.5–15cm)** | Wingspan **13½–15in (34–38cm)** | Weight **½–1⁷⁄₁₆oz (14–40g)** |
| Social **Large flocks** | Lifespan **Up to 12 years** | Status **Secure** |

| DATE SEEN | WHERE | NOTES |
|---|---|---|
| ............... | ............... | ............... |
| ............... | ............... | ............... |
| ............... | ............... | ............... |
| ............... | ............... | ............... |
| ............... | ............... | ............... |

| Order **Charadriiformes** | Family **Scolopacidae** | Species *Calidris mauri* |
|---|---|---|

# Western Sandpiper

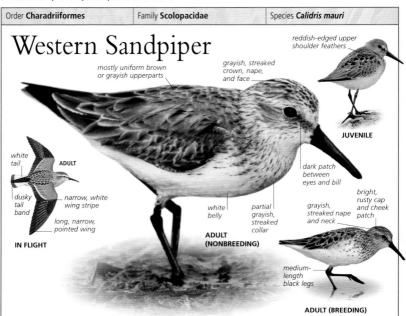

reddish-edged upper shoulder feathers

mostly uniform brown or grayish upperparts

grayish, streaked crown, nape, and face

**JUVENILE**

white tail

**ADULT**

dusky tail band

narrow, white wing stripe

long, narrow, pointed wing

**IN FLIGHT**

white belly

partial grayish, streaked collar

**ADULT (NONBREEDING)**

dark patch between eyes and bill

bright, rusty cap and cheek patch

grayish, streaked nape and neck

medium-length black legs

**ADULT (BREEDING)**

Despite its restricted breeding range in western Alaska, the Western Sandpiper is one of the most common shorebirds in the Western Hemisphere. During its spring migration spectacularly large flocks are seen at several Pacific Coast locations. At the Copper River Delta in Alaska, for instance, more than four million Western Sandpipers stop on their way to their tundra breeding grounds to fatten up and refuel for the last hop northward. Many of these migrate over relatively short distances to winter along US coastlines, so the timing of their molt in fall is earlier than that of the similar Semipalmated Sandpiper, which migrates later in winter.

**VOICE** Flight call loud *chir-eep*; flushed birds make *sirp* call, or *chir-ir-ip*; song *tweer, tweer, tweer,* followed by descending trill.

**NESTING** Shallow depression on drained Arctic and subarctic tundra; 4 eggs; 1 brood; May–June.

**FEEDING** Probes mud for insect larvae, crustaceans, and worms.

**FLIGHT:** direct, rapid flight on narrow, pointed wings; in large flocks.

**FORAGING FOR FOOD**
The Western Sandpiper feels for hidden prey with the touch-sensitive tip of its bill.

| SIMILAR SPECIES | | |
|---|---|---|
| **SEMIPALMATED SANDPIPER** ☼ see p.129 | **DUNLIN** ❄ see p.124 | *longer, downcurved bill* |
| | smaller, more rounded head | dusky head and neck |
| slightly shorter legs | smaller, more blunt-tipped bill | |

**OCCURRENCE**
Breeds in wet sedge, grassy habitats with well-drained microhabitats; in migration and in winter, prefers shallow freshwater or saltwater habitats with open muddy or sandy areas and little vegetation, such as intertidal mudflats and lake shores. Winters along both coasts.

| Length **5½–6½in (14–16cm)** | Wingspan **14–15in (35–38cm)** | Weight **¹¹⁄₁₆–1¼oz (19–35g)** |
|---|---|---|
| Social **Flocks** | Lifespan **Up to 9 years** | Status **Secure** |

| DATE SEEN | WHERE | NOTES |
|---|---|---|
| | | |
| | | |
| | | |
| | | |

| Order **Charadriiformes** | Family **Scolopacidae** | Species *Limnodromus griseus* |

# Short-billed Dowitcher

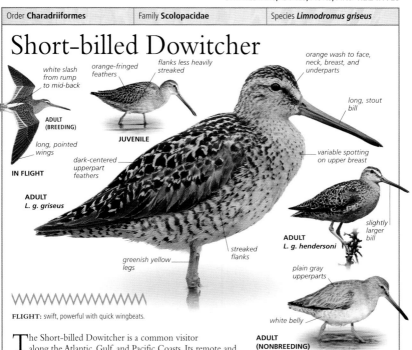

white slash from rump to mid-back

orange-fringed feathers

flanks less heavily streaked

orange wash to face, neck, breast, and underparts

long, stout bill

**ADULT (BREEDING)**

**JUVENILE**

long, pointed wings

**IN FLIGHT**

dark-centered upperpart feathers

**ADULT**
*L. g. griseus*

variable spotting on upper breast

slightly larger bill

**ADULT**
*L. g. hendersoni*

plain gray upperparts

greenish yellow legs

streaked flanks

white belly

**ADULT (NONBREEDING)**

**FLIGHT:** swift, powerful with quick wingbeats.

The Short-billed Dowitcher is a common visitor along the Atlantic, Gulf, and Pacific Coasts. Its remote and bug-infested breeding areas in northern bogs have hindered the study of its breeding behavior until recent years. There are three subspecies (*L. g. griseus*, *L. g. hendersoni*, and *L. g. caurinus*), which differ in plumage, size, and respective breeding areas. Recent knowledge about shape and structure has helped ornithologists distinguish the Short-billed from the Long-billed Dowitcher.

**VOICE** Flight call low, plaintive *tu-tu-tu*, 3–4 notes; flight song *tu-tu*, *tu-tu*, *toodle-ee*, *tu-tu*, ending with low *anh-anh-anh*.

**NESTING** Simple depression, typically in sedge hummock; 4 eggs; 1 brood; May–June.

**FEEDING** Probes in "sewing machine" feeding style with water up to belly for aquatic mollusks, crustaceans, and insects.

**ORANGE UNDERPARTS**
In complete breeding plumage, the Short-billed Dowitcher is orange, even in late afternoon light.

**SIMILAR SPECIES**

**WILSON'S SNIPE** ♂
see p.133

shorter legs

**LONG-BILLED DOWITCHER**
see p.132

slightly thicker neck

slightly longer legs

**OCCURRENCE**
Breeds mostly in sedge meadows or bogs with interspersed spruce and tamaracks between subarctic tundra and boreal forest. Migrates south to Central and South America, preferring coastal mudflats, saltmarshes or adjacent freshwater pools.

| Length **9–10in (23–25cm)** | Wingspan **18–20in (46–51cm)** | Weight **2½–5½oz (70–155g)** |
| Social **Pairs/Flocks** | Lifespan **Up to 20 years** | Status **Secure (p)** |

| DATE SEEN | WHERE | | NOTES |
|---|---|---|---|
| | | | |
| | | | |
| | | | |
| | | | |
| | | | |

| Order **Charadriiformes** | Family **Scolopacidae** | Species *Limnodromus scolopaceus* |
|---|---|---|

# Long-billed Dowitcher

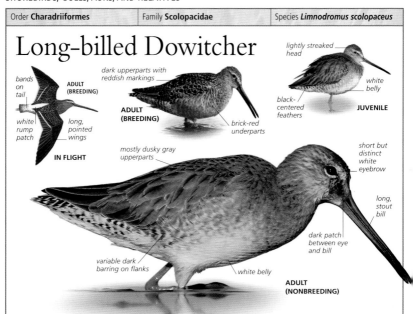

**ADULT (BREEDING)**

bands on tail

white rump patch

long, pointed wings

**IN FLIGHT**

dark upperparts with reddish markings

**ADULT (BREEDING)**

brick-red underparts

lightly streaked head

white belly

black-centered feathers

**JUVENILE**

short but distinct white eyebrow

mostly dusky gray upperparts

long, stout bill

dark patch between eye and bill

variable dark barring on flanks

white belly

**ADULT (NONBREEDING)**

It was not until 1950 that, after museum and field studies, scientists recognized two separate species of dowitcher in North America. The Long-billed Dowitcher is usually slightly larger, longer-legged, and heavier in the chest and neck than the Short-billed Dowitcher. The breeding ranges of the two species are separate, but their migration and en route stop-over areas overlap. The Long-billed Dowitcher is usually found in freshwater wetlands, and in the fall most of its population occurs west of the Mississippi River.

**VOICE** Flight and alarm call sharp, whistled *keek*, given singly or in series when agitated; song buzzy *pipipipipipi-chi-drrr*.

**NESTING** Deep sedge or grass-lined depression in sedge or grass; 4 eggs; 1 brood; May–June.

**FEEDING** Probes wet ground with "sewing-machine" motion for spiders, snails, worms, insects, and seeds.

**FLIGHT:** swift, direct flier with fast, powerful wingbeats.

**TOUCHY FEELY**
Sensitive touch-receptors at the tip of the bird's bill enable it to feel in the mud for food.

**OCCURRENCE**
Breeds in wet, grassy meadows or coastal sedge tundra near freshwater pools. Migrates to Mexico and Central America, south to Panama, where found in freshwater habitats, including ponds, flooded fields, lake shores, also sheltered lagoons, saltmarsh pools, and tidal mudflats.

**SIMILAR SPECIES**

**WILSON'S SNIPE** see p.133

pale, central crown stripe

shorter legs

**SHORT-BILLED DOWITCHER** see p.131

slightly smaller overall

orangish underparts

| Length **9½–10in (24–26cm)** | Wingspan **18–20½in (46–52cm)** | Weight **3–4oz (85–125g)** |
|---|---|---|
| Social **Pairs/Flocks** | Lifespan **Unknown** | Status **Vulnerable** |

| DATE SEEN | WHERE | NOTES |
|---|---|---|
| | | |
| | | |
| | | |
| | | |
| | | |

| Order **Charadriiformes** | Family **Scolopacidae** | Species *Gallinago delicata* |

# Wilson's Snipe

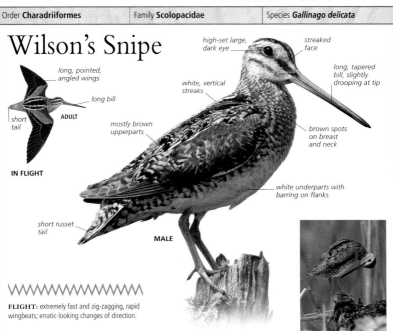

high-set large, dark eye

streaked face

long, tapered bill, slightly drooping at tip

white, vertical streaks

brown spots on breast and neck

mostly brown upperparts

white underparts with barring on flanks

long, pointed, angled wings

long bill

short tail

**ADULT**

**IN FLIGHT**

short russet tail

**MALE**

**FLIGHT:** extremely fast and zig-zagging, rapid wingbeats; erratic-looking changes of direction.

This secretive and well camouflaged member of the sandpiper family has an unsettled taxonomic history. On its breeding grounds Wilson's Snipe produces rather eerie sounds during its aerial, mainly nocturnal, display flights. The birds fly up silently from the ground, then, from about 330ft (100m) up, they descend quickly, with their tail feathers spread, producing a unique, loud and vibrating sound through modified feathers. The North American populations belong to subspecies *delicata*.

**VOICE** Alarm and overhead flight call raspy *kraitsch*; perched and low flying breeding birds give repetitive, monotonous *kup-kup-kup-kup* in alarm or aggression; distinctive whistling sound during territorial displays.

**NESTING** Elaborate woven nest lined with fine grass on ground, sedge, or moss; 4 eggs; 1 brood; May–June.

**FEEDING** Forages in mud or shallow water; probes deep into subsoil; diet includes mostly insect larvae, but also crustaceans, earthworms, and mollusks.

**RUSSET TAIL**
Wilson's Snipe's russet-colored tail is usually hard to see, but it is evident on this preening bird.

| SIMILAR SPECIES | | |
|---|---|---|
| **AMERICAN WOODCOCK** see p.470 | **SHORT-BILLED DOWITCHER** see p.131 | **LONG-BILLED DOWITCHER** see p.132 |

plump body

buffy orange underparts

smaller eye

orange tint to breast

no white streaks on back

longer legs

**OCCURRENCE**
Widespread from Alaska to Québec and Labrador south of the tundra zone; breeds in a variety of wetlands, including marshes, bogs, and open areas with rich soil. Winters farther south, where it prefers damp areas with vegetative cover, such as marshes, wet fields, and other bodies of water.

| Length **10–11in (25–28cm)** | Wingspan **17–19in (43–48cm)** | Weight **2⅞–5oz (80–150g)** |
| Social **Solitary** | Lifespan **Up to 10 years** | Status **Secure** |

| DATE SEEN | WHERE | NOTES |
|---|---|---|
| | | |
| | | |
| | | |
| | | |
| | | |

| Order **Charadriiformes** | Family **Scolopacidae** | Species *Actitis macularius* |

# Spotted Sandpiper

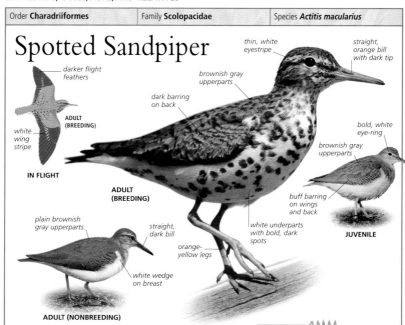

thin, white eyestripe

straight, orange bill with dark tip

brownish gray upperparts

dark barring on back

darker flight feathers

**ADULT (BREEDING)**

white wing stripe

white wing stripe

**IN FLIGHT**

**ADULT (BREEDING)**

bold, white eye-ring

brownish gray upperparts

buff barring on wings and back

white underparts with bold, dark spots

**JUVENILE**

plain brownish gray upperparts

straight, dark bill

orange-yellow legs

white wedge on breast

**ADULT (NONBREEDING)**

O ne of only two species of the genus *Actitis*, from the Latin meaning "a coastal inhabitant," this small, short-legged sandpiper is the most widespread shorebird in North America. It is characterized by its quick walking pace, its habit of constantly teetering and bobbing its tail, and its unique style of flying low over water with stiff wingbeats. These birds have an unusual mating behavior, in which the females take on an aggressive role, defending territories and mating with three or more males per season.

**VOICE** Call a clear, ringing note *tee-tee-tee-tee*; flight song a monotonous *cree-cree-cree*.

**NESTING** Nest cup shaded by or scrape built under herbaceous vegetation; 3 eggs; 1–3 broods; May–June.

**FEEDING** Eats many items, including adult and larval insects, mollusks, small crabs, and worms.

**FLIGHT:** mostly shallow, rapidly, stiffly fluttering wingbeats, usually low above water.

**BEHAVIORAL QUIRKS**
This sandpiper "teeters," raising and lowering its tail while walking along the water's edge.

**OCCURRENCE**
Breeds across North America in a wide variety of grassy, brushy, forested habitats near water, but not High Arctic tundra. During migration and in winter found in habitats near freshwater, including lake shores, rivers, streams, beaches, sewage ponds, ditches, seawalls, sometimes estuaries.

### SIMILAR SPECIES

**SOLITARY SANDPIPER** ☾
see p.135
more slender body

longer legs

streaked breast

**COMMON SANDPIPER**
see p.470
longer tail

more grayish green legs

| Length **7¼–8in (18.5–20cm)** | Wingspan **15–16in (38–41cm)** | Weight **1⁹⁄₁₆–1¾oz (45–50g)** |
| Social **Small flocks** | Lifespan **Up to 12 years** | Status **Secure** |

| DATE SEEN | WHERE | NOTES |
|-----------|-------|-------|
| ............... | ............................... | ........................................... |
| ............... | ............................... | ........................................... |
| ............... | ............................... | ........................................... |
| ............... | ............................... | ........................................... |
| ............... | ............................... | ........................................... |

| Order **Charadriiformes** | Family **Scolopacidae** | Species *Tringa solitaria* |

# Solitary Sandpiper

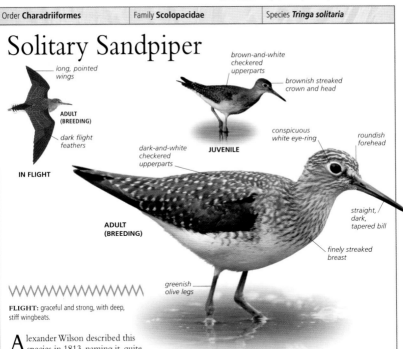

long, pointed wings

**ADULT (BREEDING)**

dark flight feathers

**IN FLIGHT**

brown-and-white checkered upperparts

brownish streaked crown and head

**JUVENILE**

dark-and-white checkered upperparts

conspicuous white eye-ring

roundish forehead

straight, dark, tapered bill

finely streaked breast

**ADULT (BREEDING)**

greenish olive legs

**FLIGHT:** graceful and strong, with deep, stiff wingbeats.

Alexander Wilson described this species in 1813, naming it, quite appropriately, "Solitary." This sandpiper seldom associates with other shorebirds as it moves nervously along margins of wetlands. When feeding, the Solitary Sandpiper constantly bobs its head like the Spotted Sandpiper. When disturbed, the Solitary Sandpiper often flies directly upward, and when landing, it keeps its wings upright briefly, flashing the white underneath, before carefully folding them to its body.

**VOICE** Flight and alarm call a high-pitched *weet-weet-weet* or *pit*; display song a *pit-pit-pit-pit; kik-kik-kik*.

**NESTING** Abandoned nests in trees (a unique behavior for a North American shorebird); 4 eggs; 1 brood; May–June.

**FEEDING** Eats insects, small crustaceans, snails, and small frogs.

**LONE RANGER**
This sandpiper is indeed solitary and is found in quiet, sheltered habitats and along river shores.

### SIMILAR SPECIES

**LESSER YELLOWLEGS** ♀
see p.136

slimmer body

yellow-orange legs

**SPOTTED SANDPIPER**
see p.134

bulkier body

shorter bill

shorter legs

**OCCURRENCE**
Breeds primarily in bogs in northern forests; in winter and during migration, occurs in sheltered pools or muddy areas near forests. Winters from Mexico down to South America, sometimes in tiny pools at high altitude in the Andes; also riverbanks, streams, rain pools, and ditches.

| Length **7½–9in (19–23cm)** | Wingspan **22–23in (56–59cm)** | Weight **1¹⁄₁₆–2¼oz (30–65g)** |
| Social **Solitary/Small flocks** | Lifespan **Unknown** | Status **Secure** |

| DATE SEEN | WHERE | NOTES |
| --- | --- | --- |
| | | |
| | | |
| | | |
| | | |
| | | |

| Order **Charadriiformes** | Family **Scolopacidae** | Species ***Tringa flavipes*** |

# Lesser Yellowlegs

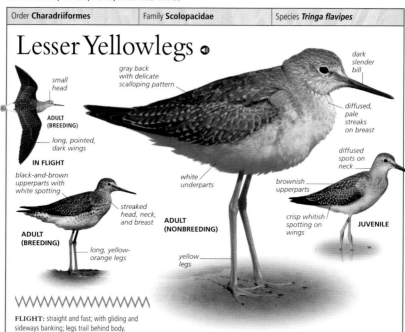

dark slender bill

diffused, pale streaks on breast

gray back with delicate scalloping pattern

small head

**ADULT (BREEDING)**

long, pointed, dark wings

**IN FLIGHT**

black-and-brown upperparts with white spotting

streaked head, neck, and breast

white underparts

**ADULT (NONBREEDING)**

yellow legs

diffused spots on neck

brownish upperparts

crisp whitish spotting on wings

**JUVENILE**

**ADULT (BREEDING)**

long, yellow-orange legs

**FLIGHT:** straight and fast; with gliding and sideways banking; legs trail behind body.

With its smaller head, thinner bill, and smoother body shape, the Lesser Yellowlegs has a more elegant profile than the Greater Yellowlegs. It prefers smaller, freshwater, or brackish pools to open saltwater habitats, and it walks quickly and methodically while feeding. Although this species is a solitary feeder, it is often seen in small to large loose flocks in migration and winter.

**VOICE** Low, whistled *tu*, or *tu-tu* call; series of *tu* or *cuw* notes when agitated; display song a *pill-e-wee, pill-e-wee, pill-e-wee*.

**NESTING** Depression in ground or moss, lined with grass and leaves; 4 eggs; 1 brood; May–June.

**FEEDING** Eats a wide variety of aquatic and terrestrial insects, mollusks, and crustaceans, especially flies and beetles; also seeds.

**READY TO FLY**
This Lesser Yellowlegs raises its wings before takeoff.

**SIMILAR SPECIES**

**GREATER YELLOWLEGS**
see p.138

larger and heavier

longer, thicker bill

**SOLITARY SANDPIPER**
see p.135

shorter, greenish yellow legs

more defined breast streaks

**OCCURRENCE**
Breeds in northerly forest with clearings, and where forest meets tundra. In migration and in winter, uses wide variety of shallow wetlands, including flooded pastures and agricultural fields, swamps, lake and river shores, tidal creeks, and brackish mudflats. Winters from Mexico to Argentina.

| Length **9–10in (23–25cm)** | Wingspan **23–25in (58–64cm)** | Weight **2–3⅜oz (55–95g)** |
| Social **Flocks** | Lifespan **Unknown** | Status **Secure** |

| DATE SEEN | WHERE | NOTES |
|-----------|-------|-------|
|           |       |       |
|           |       |       |
|           |       |       |
|           |       |       |
|           |       |       |

| Order **Charadriiformes** | Family **Scolopacidae** | Species *Tringa semipalmata* |
|---|---|---|

# Willet 🔊

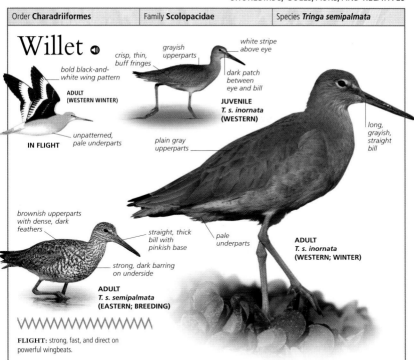

bold black-and-white wing pattern

**ADULT (WESTERN WINTER)**

grayish upperparts

crisp, thin, buff fringes

white stripe above eye

dark patch between eye and bill

**JUVENILE T. s. inornata (WESTERN)**

long, grayish, straight bill

**IN FLIGHT** unpatterned, pale underparts

plain gray upperparts

**ADULT T. s. inornata (WESTERN; WINTER)**

pale underparts

brownish upperparts with dense, dark feathers

straight, thick bill with pinkish base

strong, dark barring on underside

**ADULT T. s. semipalmata (EASTERN; BREEDING)**

**FLIGHT:** strong, fast, and direct on powerful wingbeats.

The two distinct subspecies of the Willet, Eastern (*T. s. semipalmata*) and Western (*T. s. inornata*), differ in breeding habit, plumage coloration, vocalizations, and migratory habits. The Eastern Willet leaves North America from September to March; whereas the Western Willet winters along southern North American shorelines south to South America.

**VOICE** Flight call a loud *kyah-yah*; alarm call a sharp, repeated *kleep*; song an urgent, rapid *pill-will-willet*.
**NESTING** Depression in vegetated dunes, wetlands, prairies, or saltmarshes; 4 eggs; 1 brood; April–June.
**FEEDING** Picks, probes, or swishes for crustaceans, such as fiddler and mole, crab, aquatic insects, marine worms, small mollusks, and fish.

**EXPOSED PERCH**
Willets display on exposed perches at breeding grounds.

**OCCURRENCE**
Eastern subspecies breeds in coastal saltwater habitats: saltmarshes, barrier islands, beaches, mangroves; winters in similar habitats. Western subspecies breeds near sparsely vegetated prairie wetlands or adjacent semiarid grasslands; winters in coastal regions.

**SIMILAR SPECIES**

**GREATER YELLOWLEGS** see p.138

longer neck

yellowish orange legs

**WANDERING TATTLER** 🔵1ST🔵 see p.432

stockier body

yellowish legs

| Length **12½–16½in (32–42cm)** | Wingspan **21½–28½in (54–72cm)** | Weight **7–12oz (200–350g)** |
|---|---|---|
| Social **Flocks** | Lifespan **Up to 10 years** | Status **Secure** |

| DATE SEEN | WHERE | NOTES |
|---|---|---|
| | | |
| | | |
| | | |
| | | |
| | | |

| Order **Charadriiformes** | Family **Scolopacidae** | Species ***Tringa melanoleuca*** |

# Greater Yellowlegs 🔊

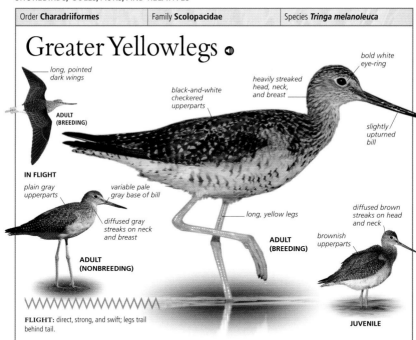

long, pointed dark wings

**ADULT (BREEDING)**

**IN FLIGHT**

heavily streaked head, neck, and breast

bold white eye-ring

black-and-white checkered upperparts

slightly upturned bill

plain gray upperparts

variable pale gray base of bill

diffused gray streaks on neck and breast

**ADULT (NONBREEDING)**

long, yellow legs

**ADULT (BREEDING)**

diffused brown streaks on head and neck

brownish upperparts

**JUVENILE**

**FLIGHT:** direct, strong, and swift; legs trail behind tail.

This fairly large shorebird often runs frantically in many directions while pursuing small prey. It is one of the first northbound shorebird migrants in the spring, and one of the first to return south in late June or early July. Its plumage, a mixture of brown, black, and white checkered upperparts, and streaked underparts, is more streaked during the breeding season.
**VOICE** Call a loud, penetrating *tew-tew-tew*; agitated birds make repetitive *keu* notes; song a continuous *too-whee*.
**NESTING** Simple scrape in moss or peat, usually close to water; 4 eggs; 1 brood; May–June.
**FEEDING** Picks water surface and mud for small aquatic and terrestrial crustaceans and worms; also eats small fish, frogs, seeds, and berries.

**EFFECTIVE METHOD**
The Greater Yellowlegs often catches its prey by sweeping its bill sideways through water.

### SIMILAR SPECIES

**LESSER YELLOWLEGS** see p.136

less angular body contours

thinner, more pointed bill

**WILLET** see p.137 lacks checkered upperparts

heavier, thicker bill

**OCCURRENCE**
Breeds in openings in northerly forests with bogs and wet meadows, a habitat called muskegs. In migration and winter, uses a wide variety of shallow water habitats, including freshwater and saltwater marshes, reservoirs, and tidal mudflats.

| Length **11½–13in (29–33cm)** | Wingspan **28–29in (70–74cm)** | Weight **4–8oz (125–225g)** |
| Social **Solitary/Flocks** | Lifespan **Unknown** | Status **Secure** |

| DATE SEEN | WHERE | NOTES |
|---|---|---|
| | | |
| | | |
| | | |
| | | |
| | | |

| Order **Charadriiformes** | Family **Scolopacidae** | Species ***Phalaropus tricolor*** |

# Wilson's Phalarope

**FEMALE (BREEDING)**
reddish brown markings on sides of back

**IN FLIGHT**
grayish brown wings

plain gray upperparts

yellowish legs

**JUVENILE (MOLTING TO 1ST WINTER)**
gray and reddish brown back

largely white face

white cheek

white underparts

black stripe from bill to nape

plain gray-and-black upperparts

paler head markings

**MALE**

white eyebrow

fairly long straight bill

rust neck and throat

**FEMALE (BREEDING)**

A truly American phalarope, Wilson's is the largest of the three phalarope species. Unlike its two relatives, it does not breed in the Arctic, but in the shallow wetlands of western North America, and winters mainly in continental habitats of Bolivia and Argentina instead of in the ocean. This species can be found employing the feeding technique of spinning in shallow water to churn up adult and larval insects, or running in various directions on muddy wetland edges with its head held low to the ground while chasing and picking up insects. This bird is quite tolerant of humans on its breeding grounds, but this attitude changes immediately before migration, as it has gained weight and its movement is sluggish.

**VOICE** Flight call a low, nasal *werpf*; also higher, repetitive *emf, emf, emf, emf,* or *luk, luk, luk.*

**NESTING** Simple scrape lined with grass; 4 eggs; 1 brood; May–June.

**FEEDING** Eats brine shrimp, various insects, and insect larvae.

**FLIGHT:** fast and direct with quick wingbeats.

**ODD ONE OUT**
Unlike its two essentially oceanic relatives, Wilson's Phalarope is also found in freshwater habitats.

**OCCURRENCE**
Breeds in shallow, grassy wetlands of interior North America; during migration and winter, occurs in salty lakes and saline ponds as well as inland waterbodies. In winter, tens of thousands can be seen in the middle of Titicaca Lake in Bolivia.

**SIMILAR SPECIES**

**LESSER YELLOWLEGS**
see p.136
darker, spotted back

**RED-NECKED PHALAROPE** ♀
see p.140
streaked head and neck
black cheek patch
shorter bill

| Length **8½–9½in (22–24cm)** | Wingspan **15½–17in (39–43cm)** | Weight **1¼–3oz (35–85g)** |
| Social **Large flocks** | Lifespan **Up to 10 years** | Status **Secure** |

| DATE SEEN | WHERE | NOTES |
|-----------|-------|-------|
|  |  |  |
|  |  |  |
|  |  |  |
|  |  |  |
|  |  |  |

| Order **Charadriiformes** | Family **Scolopacidae** | Species ***Phalaropus lobatus*** |
|---|---|---|

# Red-necked Phalarope

pointed wings

narrow, white
wing stripe

dark cap and
cheek patch

dark upperparts
with buff stripes

dark gray
crown and
face

black back with
dull, white lines

**JUVENILE**

white
throat

**FEMALE
(BREEDING)**

**IN FLIGHT**

**JUVENILE (WORN PLUMAGE)**

dark upperparts
with buff or rust
feather edges

needle-like
dark bill

rust neck
and upper
breast

**FEMALE
(BREEDING)**

white underparts
with dusky
streaked flanks

This aquatic sandpiper spends much of its life in deep ocean
waters feeding on tiny plankton; each year, after nine months
at sea, it comes to nest in the Arctic. Its Latin name *lobatus* reflects
the morphology of its toes, which are webbed (lobed). Both the
Red-necked Phalarope and the Red Phalarope are oceanic birds
that are found in large flocks or "rafts" far from shore. However,
both species are occasionally found swimming inland, in
freshwater habitats. Like the other two phalaropes, the
Red-necked has a fascinating and unusual reversal of typical
sex roles. The female is more brightly colored and slightly larger
than the male; she will also pursue the male, compete savagely
for him, and will migrate shortly after laying her eggs.
**VOICE** Flight call a hard, squeaky *pwit* or *kit*; on breeding
grounds, vocalizations include variations of flight call notes.
**NESTING** Depression in wet sedge or grass; 3–4 eggs;
1–2 broods; May–June.
**FEEDING** Eats plankton; also insects, brine shrimp, and mollusks.

**FLIGHT:** fast and direct, with rapid wingbeats.

**SINGLE FATHER**
Male phalaropes perform all nesting and rearing
duties after the female lays the eggs.

### SIMILAR SPECIES

**WILSON'S PHALAROPE** ♀
see p.139

paler
face

larger
overall

**RED PHALAROPE** ♀ *slightly
thicker bill*
see p.432

larger head
and thicker
neck

**OCCURRENCE**
Breeds in wet tundra, on
raised ridges, or hummocks,
but during migration and
in winter, occurs far out
at sea and away from
shores, although sometimes
found in freshwater habitats.

| Length **7–7½in (18–19cm)** | Wingspan **12½–16in (32–41cm)** | Weight **1¹⁄₁₆–1⁹⁄₁₆oz (30–45g)** |
|---|---|---|
| Social **Flocks** | Lifespan **Unknown** | Status **Declining** |

| DATE SEEN | WHERE | NOTES |
|---|---|---|
| | | |
| | | |
| | | |
| | | |
| | | |

| Order **Charadriiformes** | Family **Stercorariidae** | Species *Stercorarius pomarinus* |

# Pomarine Jaeger

prominent white "flash" in feathers

**ADULT (BREEDING; PALE FORM)**

all-dark body

deep, barrel breast

blackish cap

pale based, thick bill

**JUVENILE (FALL; DARK FORM)**

gray-brown back

cream cheeks

white wing flash

barred flanks

**ADULT (NONBREEDING; PALE FORM)**

dusky breastband

**ADULT (DARK FORM)**

dark overall

blunt tail spike

**IN FLIGHT**

twisted, spoon-like central tail feathers

dusky breast-band

**ADULT (BREEDING; PALE FORM)**

The intimidating Pomarine Jaeger uses its size and strength to overpower larger seabirds, such as gulls and shearwaters, in order to steal their food. Thought to be nomadic during the breeding season, it only nests opportunistically, when populations of lemmings are at their peak to provide food for its young. Although larger and more powerful than the Parasitic Jaeger, the Pomarine Jaeger is not as acrobatic in the air and is readily driven away from breeding territories by the more dynamic Parasitic Jaeger. Interestingly, research suggests that the Pomarine Jaeger is actually more closely related to the large skuas—such as the Great and South Polar Skuas—than to other jaegers.

**VOICE** Nasal *cow-cow-cow* and various sharp, low whistles.

**NESTING** Shallow unlined depression on a rise or hummock in open tundra; 2 eggs; 1 brood; June–August.

**FEEDING** Hunts lemmings and other rodents; eats fish or scavenges refuse from fishing boats during nonbreeding season; often steals fish from other seabirds, such as gulls.

**FLIGHT:** powerful, deep, quick wingbeats, with glides; rapid twists and turns in pursuit of prey.

**OCCURRENCE**
Breeds on open tundra in the Canadian Arctic. Migrates north in spring and south in fall, along coasts and also far offshore. Most often seen when brought close to land by gales. Storm-driven birds very occasionally found inland. More commonly seen on West Coast than East Coast; winters far out at sea.

### SIMILAR SPECIES

**PARASITIC JAEGER**
see p.142

white "necklace"

gray breastband

**LONG-TAILED JAEGER** ☼
see p.143

extremely long tail

pale breast

**OBVIOUS FEATURE**
The twisted, spoon-like central tail feathers are clearly visible when the Pomarine Jaeger flies.

| Length **17–20in (43–51cm)** | Wingspan **4ft (1.2m)** | Weight **23–26oz (650–750g)** |
| Social **Solitary** | Lifespan **Unknown** | Status **Secure** |

| DATE SEEN | WHERE | NOTES |
| --- | --- | --- |
| .......... | .......... | .......... |
| .......... | .......... | .......... |
| .......... | .......... | .......... |
| .......... | .......... | .......... |
| .......... | .......... | .......... |

| Order **Charadriiformes** | Family **Stercorariidae** | Species ***Stercorarius parasiticus*** |

# Parasitic Jaeger

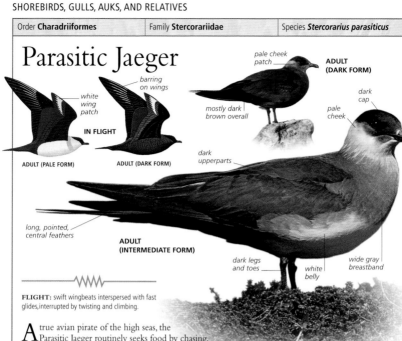

pale cheek patch

**ADULT (DARK FORM)**

barring on wings

white wing patch

**IN FLIGHT**

mostly dark brown overall

dark upperparts

dark cap

pale cheek

**ADULT (PALE FORM)**   **ADULT (DARK FORM)**

dark upperparts

long, pointed, central feathers

**ADULT (INTERMEDIATE FORM)**

dark legs and toes

white belly

wide gray breastband

**FLIGHT:** swift wingbeats interspersed with fast glides, interrupted by twisting and climbing.

A true avian pirate of the high seas, the Parasitic Jaeger routinely seeks food by chasing, bullying, and forcing other seabirds to drop or regurgitate fish or other food they have caught. Unlike most jaegers, the Parasitic Jaeger is adaptable in its feeding habits so that it can forage and raise its young under a wide range of environmental conditions. Breeding on the Arctic tundra, it migrates to offshore areas during the nonbreeding season.

**VOICE** Variety of terrier-like yelps and soft squeals, often during interactions with other jaegers or predators, usually around nesting territories.

**NESTING** Shallow unlined depression on a rise or hummock in open tundra; 2 eggs; 1 brood; May–August.

**FEEDING** Steals fish and other aquatic prey from gulls and terns; catches small birds, eats eggs, or hunts small rodents on breeding grounds.

**PARASITIC PIRATE**
This Parasitic Jaeger is harrying a gull by pecking at it, to make it disgorge its hard-won meal.

**SIMILAR SPECIES**

**POMARINE JAEGER** see p.141

two long, central, twisted tail feathers

heavy hooked bill

**LONG-TAILED JAEGER** see p.143

black cap

longer pointed tail

**OCCURRENCE**
Breeds on tundra in northern Canada and Alaska (breeds farther south than other jaegers); during migration and in winter, uses both nearshore and offshore waters; rarely found inland in the US outside the breeding season.

| Length **16–18½in (41–47cm)** | Wingspan **3ft 3in–3½ ft (1–1.1m)** | Weight **13–18oz (375–500g)** |
| Social **Solitary/Small flocks** | Lifespan **Up to 18 years** | Status **Secure** |

| DATE SEEN | WHERE | | NOTES |
|---|---|---|---|
| | | | |
| | | | |
| | | | |
| | | | |
| | | | |

| Order **Charadriiformes** | Family **Stercorariidae** | Species *Stercorarius longicaudus* |
|---|---|---|

# Long-tailed Jaeger

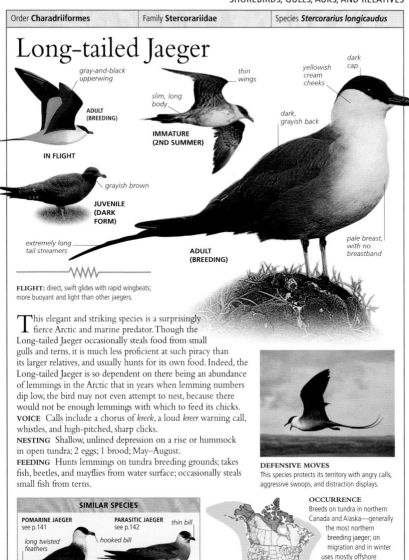

gray-and-black upperwing

thin wings

yellowish cream cheeks

dark cap

slim, long body

**ADULT (BREEDING)**

**IN FLIGHT**

**IMMATURE (2ND SUMMER)**

dark, grayish back

grayish brown

**JUVENILE (DARK FORM)**

dark, grayish back

extremely long tail streamers

**ADULT (BREEDING)**

pale breast, with no breastband

**FLIGHT:** direct, swift glides with rapid wingbeats; more buoyant and light than other jaegers.

This elegant and striking species is a surprisingly fierce Arctic and marine predator. Though the Long-tailed Jaeger occasionally steals food from small gulls and terns, it is much less proficient at such piracy than its larger relatives, and usually hunts for its own food. Indeed, the Long-tailed Jaeger is so dependent on there being an abundance of lemmings in the Arctic that in years when lemming numbers dip low, the bird may not even attempt to nest, because there would not be enough lemmings with which to feed its chicks.
**VOICE** Calls include a chorus of *kreek*, a loud *kreer* warning call, whistles, and high-pitched, sharp clicks.
**NESTING** Shallow, unlined depression on a rise or hummock in open tundra; 2 eggs; 1 brood; May–August.
**FEEDING** Hunts lemmings on tundra breeding grounds; takes fish, beetles, and mayflies from water surface; occasionally steals small fish from terns.

**DEFENSIVE MOVES**
This species protects its territory with angry calls, aggressive swoops, and distraction displays.

**SIMILAR SPECIES**

**POMARINE JAEGER** see p.141

long twisted feathers

**PARASITIC JAEGER** see p.142

thin bill

hooked bill

shorter tail

**OCCURRENCE**
Breeds on tundra in northern Canada and Alaska—generally the most northern breeding jaeger; on migration and in winter uses mostly offshore waters; very rarely seen inland in winter.

| Length **19–21in (48–53cm)** | Wingspan **3½ft (1.1m)** | Weight **10–11oz (275–300g)** |
|---|---|---|
| Social **Solitary/Flocks** | Lifespan **Up to 8 years** | Status **Secure** |

| DATE SEEN | WHERE | NOTES |
|---|---|---|
| | | |
| | | |
| | | |
| | | |
| | | |

| Order **Charadriiformes** | Family **Alcidae** | Species *Uria aalge* |
| --- | --- | --- |

# Common Murre

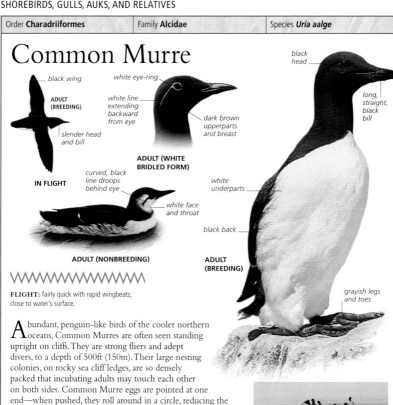

*black head*

*black wing*

**ADULT (BREEDING)**

*slender head and bill*

**IN FLIGHT**

*white eye-ring*

*white line extending backward from eye*

*dark brown upperparts and breast*

**ADULT (WHITE BRIDLED FORM)**

*long, straight, black bill*

*curved, black line droops behind eye*

*white face and throat*

**ADULT (NONBREEDING)**

*white underparts*

*black back*

**ADULT (BREEDING)**

*grayish legs and toes*

**FLIGHT:** fairly quick with rapid wingbeats; close to water's surface.

Abundant, penguin-like birds of the cooler northern oceans, Common Murres are often seen standing upright on cliffs. They are strong fliers and adept divers, to a depth of 500ft (150m). Their large nesting colonies, on rocky sea cliff ledges, are so densely packed that incubating adults may touch each other on both sides. Common Murre eggs are pointed at one end—when pushed, they roll around in a circle, reducing the risk of rolling off the nesting ledge. It has been suggested that unique egg markings may help adults recognize their own eggs.
**VOICE** Low-pitched, descending call given from cliffs or water, reminiscent of trumpeting elephant.
**NESTING** Directly on bare rock near shore, on wide cliff ledge, or large crevice; 1 egg; 1 brood; May–July.
**FEEDING** Pursues small schooling fish, such as herring, sand lance, and haddock; also crustaceans, marine worms, and squid.

**BREEDING COLONY**
Crowded together, Common Murres are not territorial but will defend a personal space.

**SIMILAR SPECIES**

**THICK-BILLED MURRE**
see p.433

*thick, pale line between eye and bill*

**RAZORBILL** ✿

*bill with white bar near tip*

**OCCURRENCE**
Breeds close to rocky shorelines, nesting on coastal cliff ledges or flat rocks on top of sea stacks on both East and West Coasts. Found farther offshore during nonbreeding season, spending extended periods on the open ocean and in large bays. Winters at sea.

| Length **17½in (44cm)** | Wingspan **26in (65cm)** | Weight **35oz (1,000g)** |
| --- | --- | --- |
| Social **Colonies** | Lifespan **At least 40 years** | Status **Localized** |

| DATE SEEN | WHERE | NOTES |
| --- | --- | --- |
| | | |
| | | |
| | | |
| | | |

| Order **Charadriiformes** | Family **Alcidae** | Species **Cepphus columba** |
| --- | --- | --- |

# Pigeon Guillemot

oval, snowy white upperwing patch

**ADULT**

**IN FLIGHT**

toes and legs trail in flight

dusky neck and face

dusky crown

black upperparts

**JUVENILE**

**ADULT (BREEDING)**

broad, rounded wings

dark bar across white wing patch

stocky, round body

dark rump

bright red-orange legs and toes

The Pigeon Guillemot, a North Pacific seabird, is found along rocky shores in small colonies or isolated pairs. This auk nests in burrows or under rocks, often on small islands that provide protection from land-bound predators. The male excavates a burrow, or chooses an abandoned burrow or crevice, to build a nest. During the breeding season, the bird's striking red-orange legs and mouth lining are used in courtship displays to attract a mate.

**VOICE** Excited, squeaky whistles, and twitters; nesting birds give a weak whistle *peeeee*.

**NESTING** Shallow scrape in burrow or crevice; 2 eggs; 1 brood; May–August.

**FEEDING** Feeds near shore; dives to seabed, then uses bill to forage for small rock eels, sculpin, crabs, shrimp, marine worms, and mollusks; carries food for chicks in bill.

**FLIGHT:** flies close to water surface with very rapid, fluttering wingbeats.

**VULNERABLE TO PREDATORS**
Predatory gulls can kill adult Pigeon Guillemots and sometimes eat their chicks and eggs.

## SIMILAR SPECIES

**BLACK GUILLEMOT** ☾ see p.433

mottled white upperparts

**MARBLED MURRELET** see p.146

dark crown

gray neck

white underparts

**OCCURRENCE**
Breeds on rocky islands, coastlines, and cliffs where it is less accessible to predators. At sea, it generally remains close to rocky coasts, except in the Bering Sea, where it is found farther out along the edges of the pack ice. In winter, some populations are forced south by sea ice.

| Length **13½in (34cm)** | Wingspan **23in (58cm)** | Weight **18oz (500g)** |
| --- | --- | --- |
| Social **Colonies** | Lifespan **Up to 14 years** | Status **Localized** |

| DATE SEEN | WHERE | NOTES |
| --- | --- | --- |
| | | |
| | | |
| | | |
| | | |

| Order **Charadriiformes** | Family **Alcidae** | Species *Brachyramphus marmoratus* |

# Marbled Murrelet

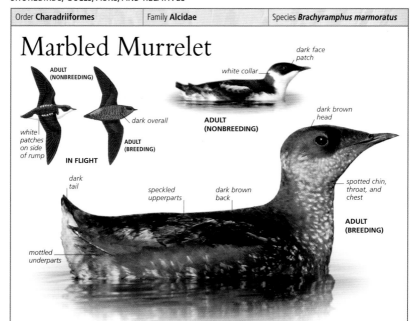

**ADULT (NONBREEDING)**

white patches on side of rump

**IN FLIGHT**

dark overall

**ADULT (BREEDING)**

dark face patch

white collar

**ADULT (NONBREEDING)**

dark brown head

dark tail

speckled upperparts

dark brown back

spotted chin, throat, and chest

**ADULT (BREEDING)**

mottled underparts

The breeding habits of the Marbled Murrelet, a bird of both sea and forest, remained a mystery until 1974, when the first nest was discovered high in a douglas fir in a California park. Unlike most auks and their relatives, which have black and white breeding plumage, the Marbled Murrelet's breeding plumage is brown, to camouflage the bird on its nest in the branches of trees or, in places, on the ground. Ornithologists are eager to learn more about this secretive seabird, even as its numbers decline because of clear-cutting of old-growth conifer forests, where it nests, entanglement of the bird in fishing gear, and oil pollution out at sea, where it feeds.

**VOICE** Flight call series of high-pitched, squealing, slightly descending *kleeer* notes.

**NESTING** In northern part of its range, on island mountainsides; in the South, on tree limbs in old-growth forests; 1 egg; 1 brood; April–September.

**FEEDING** Short dives to catch small fish and crustaceans in shallow offshore waters, "flying" underwater; feeds at night, in pairs.

**FLIGHT:** straight, fast, and low over water, with extremely rapid wingbeats.

**RUNNING ON WATER**
The Marbled Murrelet flaps its wings energetically and runs across the surface to become airborne.

**SIMILAR SPECIES**

**KITTLITZ'S MURRELET**
see p.433

white above eyes

white undertail

**OCCURRENCE**
Relies on marine and forested habitats for both feeding and breeding, on Pacific Coasts from Alaska to California; at sea, usually found near coast, in relatively shallow waters. In the breeding season, travels back and forth between the sea and inland breeding grounds.

| Length **10in (26cm)** | Wingspan **16in (41cm)** | Weight **8oz (225g)** |
| Social **Pairs/Small groups** | Lifespan **Unknown** | Status **Vulnerable** |

| DATE SEEN | WHERE | NOTES |
| --- | --- | --- |
| | | |
| | | |
| | | |
| | | |

| Order **Charadriiformes** | Family **Alcidae** | Species *Synthliboramphus antiquus* |

# Ancient Murrelet

lacks distinctive white plumes behind eyes

lacks black throat

**ADULT (NONBREEDING)**

**ADULT (BREEDING)**

white underwing

**IN FLIGHT**

white underparts with gray sides

uniform gray upperparts

distinctive white plumes behind eyes

black face and throat

pale bill tip

distinctive white collar on side of neck

**ADULT (BREEDING)**

Of the six murrelets that occur regularly in North America, this little species is the most numerous. Like its close relatives, Scripps's Murrelet and Craveri's Murrelet, the Ancient Murrelet usually raises two chicks, and takes them out to sea when they are just a few days old, usually under the cover of darkness. The Ancient Murrelet can also leap straight out of the sea and into flight. White eyebrow-like plumes on the head, combined with a shawl-like gray back, give the bird its supposedly "ancient" appearance.

**VOICE** Short, high-pitched trills and rattles given by nesting birds while perched in trees.

**NESTING** Burrow in soft soil, often among forest tree roots; 2 eggs; 1 brood; June–August.

**FEEDING** Dives for prey in groups, often at the same time, driving schools of small fish to the surface; euphansiid shrimps, which are about 1in (2.5cm) long, are its primary diet.

**FLIGHT:** flies fast, low, and straight with rapid wingbeats; capable of quick takeoff from water.

**GROUP FEEDER**
The Ancient Murrelet flies low to the water in flocks on the lookout for food.

**OCCURRENCE**
Lives in the north Pacific, and Bering Sea. Concentrates where food is abundant—most often in straits, sounds, and coastal waters—where it often feeds quite close to shore. Nests on coastal islands, mainly on forest floors but also where there is proper cover and sufficient peaty soil to dig burrows.

**SIMILAR SPECIES**

**SCRIPPS'S MURRELET**
see p.433

lacks white head plumes

gray back

white throat

**CRAVERI'S MURRELET**
see p.434

dark in front of eye

white throat

| Length **10in (26cm)** | Wingspan **17in (43cm)** | Weight **7oz (200g)** |
| Social **Colonies** | Lifespan **At least 4 years** | Status **Localized** |

| DATE SEEN | WHERE | NOTES |
|---|---|---|
| | | |
| | | |
| | | |
| | | |
| | | |

| Order **Charadriiformes** | Family **Alcidae** | Species *Ptychoramphus aleuticus* |

# Cassin's Auklet

white patch

rounded wing tips

**ADULT (NONBREEDING)**

dark underwing with pale stripe

**IN FLIGHT**

whitish belly

pale gray underparts

**ADULT (NONBREEDING)**

sooty overall

pale eyes

thin, white eyebrow

short, thick, gray bill

pale patch at base of bill

**ADULT (BREEDING)**

This secretive little seabird usually nests in an underground burrow, which can take a breeding pair many weeks to scratch out. Parent birds fish by day, returning to the nest in the safety of darkness to avoid gulls and other predators. Nestlings encourage regurgitation by nibbling at a white spot at the base of the parent's lower mandible. Uniquely for a member of the alcid family, Cassin's Auklet has been known to raise more than one brood in a season.

**VOICE** Hoarse, rhythmic night calls in colonies; squeals and peeps when in burrow; silent at sea.

**NESTING** On offshore islands, in crevices or burrows; 1 egg; 1–2 broods; March–September.

**FEEDING** Dives and swims underwater using wings to pursue small crustaceans, fish, and squid.

**FLIGHT:** low over the surface of the sea, with rapid wingbeats.

**RUNNING ON WATER**
After a long run and some energetic wing beating, Cassin's Auklet eventually takes off from the water.

**SIMILAR SPECIES**

**MARBLED MURRELET (BREEDING)**
see p.146

paler head

reddish brown upperparts

**KITTLITZ'S MURRELET (BREEDING)**
lacks white stripe on underwing; see p.433

mottled brown-and-white feathers

**OCCURRENCE**
Pacific distribution; breeds on cliffs, grassy plains, or slopes on coastal islands. During the nonbreeding season, northern birds found in deep waters beyond the continental shelf, where upwelling currents bring food from the depths. Southern birds remain near their colonies year-round.

| Length **9in (23cm)** | Wingspan **15in (38cm)** | Weight **6oz (175g)** |
| Social **Colonies** | Lifespan **At least 6 years** | Status **Localized** |

| DATE SEEN | WHERE | NOTES |
| --- | --- | --- |
| | | |
| | | |
| | | |
| | | |
| | | |

| Order **Charadriiformes** | Family **Alcidae** | Species *Cerorhinca monocerata* |

# Rhinoceros Auklet

*dark wings*

**ADULT (NONBREEDING)**

*white belly*

**IN FLIGHT**

*lacks facial plumes*

*smaller bill*

**ADULT (NONBREEDING)**

*horny structure at base of upper bill*

*dark upperparts*

*thin, white plumes curving back*

**ADULT (BREEDING)**

This robust bird is closely related to puffins, and is the only auk with a prominent "horn" on top of its bill; it is this structure that gives the bird its common name. The Rhinoceros Auklet forages closer to shore than its puffin relatives, and usually returns to its nesting colonies at night. This trusting seabird often allows boats to approach very closely. It became locally extinct, but reestablished its population on California's Farallon Islands in the 1970s when non-native rabbits that were competing for nesting burrows were removed. When fishing, it carries its catch in its bill, rather than in a throat pouch like other auks.

**VOICE** Adults give series of low, mooing calls, as well as short barks and groans.

**NESTING** Cup of moss or twigs on islands, under vegetation, in crevice or long, soil burrow; 1 egg; 1 brood; April–September.

**FEEDING** Forages underwater during breeding season, looks for small schooling fish for nestlings; also eats crustaceans; powerful diver and swimmer.

**FLIGHT:** swift, direct with quick wingbeats; takeoff appears labored.

**SUBMARINE-LIKE**
Its body nearly submerged and its head looking behind, this Rhinoceros Auklet is ready to dive.

**OCCURRENCE**
Throughout temperate North Pacific waters, generally south of puffin habitat. Typically lives far out at sea, but may feed near shore where currents concentrate food; usually forages and returns to nesting colonies by night.

**SIMILAR SPECIES**

**PARAKEET AUKLET** ♂
see p.434

*paler breast*

| Length **15in (38cm)** | Wingspan **22in (56cm)** | Weight **16oz (450g)** |
| Social **Colonies** | Lifespan **Unknown** | Status **Localized** |

| DATE SEEN | WHERE | NOTES |
|---|---|---|
| | | |
| | | |
| | | |
| | | |
| | | |

| Order **Charadriiformes** | Family **Alcidae** | Species *Fratercula cirrhata* |

# Tufted Puffin

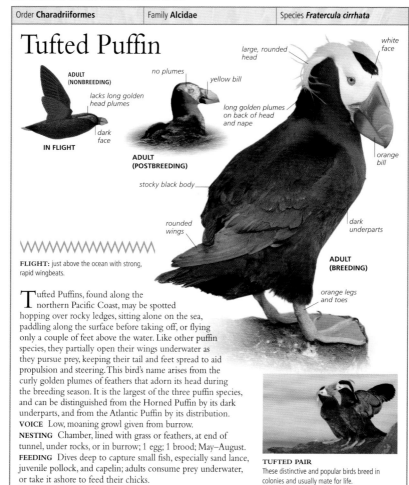

white face

large, rounded head

**ADULT (NONBREEDING)**

lacks long golden head plumes

dark face

**IN FLIGHT**

no plumes

yellow bill

long golden plumes on back of head and nape

**ADULT (POSTBREEDING)**

orange bill

stocky black body

rounded wings

dark underparts

**FLIGHT:** just above the ocean with strong, rapid wingbeats.

**ADULT (BREEDING)**

orange legs and toes

Tufted Puffins, found along the northern Pacific Coast, may be spotted hopping over rocky ledges, sitting alone on the sea, paddling along the surface before taking off, or flying only a couple of feet above the water. Like other puffin species, they partially open their wings underwater as they pursue prey, keeping their tail and feet spread to aid propulsion and steering. This bird's name arises from the curly golden plumes of feathers that adorn its head during the breeding season. It is the largest of the three puffin species, and can be distinguished from the Horned Puffin by its dark underparts, and from the Atlantic Puffin by its distribution.

**VOICE** Low, moaning growl given from burrow.

**NESTING** Chamber, lined with grass or feathers, at end of tunnel, under rocks, or in burrow; 1 egg; 1 brood; May–August.

**FEEDING** Dives deep to capture small fish, especially sand lance, juvenile pollock, and capelin; adults consume prey underwater, or take it ashore to feed their chicks.

**TUFTED PAIR**
These distinctive and popular birds breed in colonies and usually mate for life.

### SIMILAR SPECIES

**RHINOCEROS AUKLET (NONBREEDING)**
see p.149

darker face

smaller bill

**RHINOCEROS AUKLET (BREEDING)**
see p.149

no white on face

slimmer build

**OCCURRENCE**
Breeds on rocky islands, and coastal cliffs of the North Pacific, especially treeless offshore islands with sea cliffs or grassy slopes; elevation may help them take flight. Found over unusually wide geographic and climatic range. Winters at sea, usually over deep waters of the central North Pacific.

| Length **15in (38cm)** | Wingspan **25in (64cm)** | Weight **27oz (775g)** |
| Social **Colonies** | Lifespan **Up to 30 years** | Status **Localized** |

| DATE SEEN | WHERE | NOTES |
|---|---|---|
| | | |
| | | |
| | | |
| | | |

| Order **Charadriiformes** | Family **Laridae** | Species *Rissa tridactyla* |

# Black-legged Kittiwake

greenish yellow bill

white head

pale gray back feathers

**ADULT**

black legs and toes

pale outer wing feathers

black "M" pattern in wings

pale gray upperparts

black tip to tail

**ADULT**

black bill

**JUVENILE**

**IN FLIGHT**

black wing tip

dark neck collar

dark wing bar

**JUVENILE**

A kittiwake nesting colony is an impressive sight, with sometimes thousands of birds lined up along steep cliff ledges overlooking the sea. The ledges are often so narrow that the birds' tails stick out over the edge. Kittiwakes have sharper claws than other gulls, probably to give them a better grip on their ledges. In the late 20th century, the Black-legged Kittiwake population expanded greatly in the Canadian maritime provinces, with numbers doubling in the Gulf of St. Lawrence.

**VOICE** Repeated, nasal *kit-ti-wake, kit-ti-wake* call; vocal near nesting cliffs; usually silent in winter.

**NESTING** Mound of mud and vegetation on narrow cliff ledge; 1–3 eggs; 1 brood; April–August.

**FEEDING** Snatches small marine fish and invertebrates from the surface, or dives just below the water's surface; feeds in flocks.

**FLIGHT:** very stiff-winged; rapid, shallow wingbeats; overall more buoyant than most gulls.

**LIVING ON THE EDGE**
Young and adult kittiwakes pack together tightly on their precariously narrow cliff ledges.

### SIMILAR SPECIES

**RING-BILLED GULL**
see p.156

heavier, dark-marked bill

white spots in outer wing feathers

**RED-LEGGED KITTIWAKE**
see p.435

darker shoulder feathers

red legs

gray underwings

**OCCURRENCE**
Rarely seen far from the ocean; common in summer around sea cliffs, with ledges suitable for nesting, and nearby offshore waters; winters at sea; most likely to be seen from land during and after storms; strays have appeared throughout the interior.

| Length **15–16in (38–41cm)** | Wingspan **3ft 1in–4ft (0.95m–1.2m)** | Weight **11–18oz (300–500g)** |
| Social **Colonies** | Lifespan **Up to 26 years** | Status **Secure** |

| DATE SEEN | WHERE | | NOTES |
|-----------|-------|--|-------|
| | | | |
| | | | |
| | | | |
| | | | |

| Order **Charadriiformes** | Family **Laridae** | Species *Chroicocephalus philadelphia* |

# Bonaparte's Gull

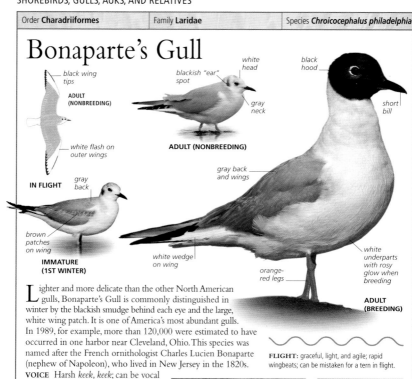

black wing tips

**ADULT (NONBREEDING)**

white flash on outer wings

**IN FLIGHT**

gray back

brown patches on wing

**IMMATURE (1ST WINTER)**

white wedge on wing

white head

blackish "ear" spot

gray neck

**ADULT (NONBREEDING)**

gray back and wings

black hood

short bill

gray back and wings

white underparts with rosy glow when breeding

orange-red legs

**ADULT (BREEDING)**

Lighter and more delicate than the other North American gulls, Bonaparte's Gull is commonly distinguished in winter by the blackish smudge behind each eye and the large, white wing patch. It is one of America's most abundant gulls. In 1989, for example, more than 120,000 were estimated to have occurred in one harbor near Cleveland, Ohio. This species was named after the French ornithologist Charles Lucien Bonaparte (nephew of Napoleon), who lived in New Jersey in the 1820s.

**VOICE** Harsh *keek, keek*; can be vocal in feeding flocks, *kew, kew, kew.*

**NESTING** Stick nest of twigs, branches, tree bark, lined with mosses or lichens; usually in conifers 5–20ft (1.5–6m) above ground; also in rushes over water; 1–4 eggs; 1 brood; May–July.

**FEEDING** Catches insects in flight on breeding grounds; picks crustaceans, mollusks, and small fish from water's surface; also plunge-dives.

**FLIGHT:** graceful, light, and agile; rapid wingbeats; can be mistaken for a tern in flight.

**TERN-LIKE GULL**
Bonaparte's Gulls are very social and, flying in flocks, these pale, delicate birds look like terns.

**WHITE UNDERWINGS**
In all plumages, Bonaparte's Gulls have white underwings, unlike other similar small gulls.

**OCCURRENCE**
During breeding season, found in northern forest zone, in lakes, ponds, or bogs; on migration, may be found anywhere where there is water: ponds, lakes, sewage pools, or rivers. Winters on Great Lakes and along the coast; often found in large numbers at coastal inlets.

**SIMILAR SPECIES**

**BLACK-HEADED GULL**

dark outer wing feathers

larger overall

**LITTLE GULL**

smaller overall

red bill

uniform gray upperwing

| Length **11–12in (28–30cm)** | Wingspan **35in–3ft 3in (90–100cm)** | Weight **6–8oz (175–225g)** |
| Social **Flocks** | Lifespan **Up to 18 years** | Status **Secure** |

| DATE SEEN | WHERE | NOTES |
|---|---|---|
| | | |
| | | |
| | | |
| | | |

| Order **Charadriiformes** | Family **Laridae** | Species *Leucophaeus pipixcan* |

# Franklin's Gull

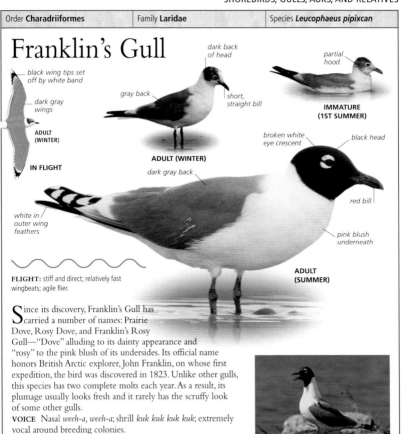

black wing tips set off by white band

dark gray wings

**ADULT (WINTER)**

**IN FLIGHT**

dark back of head

gray back

short, straight bill

**ADULT (WINTER)**

dark gray back

partial hood

**IMMATURE (1ST SUMMER)**

broken white eye crescent

black head

red bill

white in outer wing feathers

pink blush underneath

**ADULT (SUMMER)**

**FLIGHT:** stiff and direct; relatively fast wingbeats; agile flier.

Since its discovery, Franklin's Gull has carried a number of names: Prairie Dove, Rosy Dove, and Franklin's Rosy Gull—"Dove" alluding to its dainty appearance and "rosy" to the pink blush of its undersides. Its official name honors British Arctic explorer, John Franklin, on whose first expedition the bird was discovered in 1823. Unlike other gulls, this species has two complete molts each year. As a result, its plumage usually looks fresh and it rarely has the scruffy look of some other gulls.

**VOICE** Nasal *weeh-a, weeh-a*; shrill *kuk kuk kuk kuk*; extremely vocal around breeding colonies.

**NESTING** Floating mass of bulrushes or other plants; material added as nest sinks; 2–4 eggs; 1 brood; April–July.

**FEEDING** Feeds mainly on earthworms and insects during breeding and some seeds, taken while walking or flying; opportunistic feeder during migration and winter.

**PROMINENT EYES**
In all plumages, Franklin's Gull has much more prominent white eye-crescents than similar species.

**SIMILAR SPECIES**

**LAUGHING GULL** see p.470
longer, drooped bill
longer legs

**LAUGHING GULL ♂ ❄** see p.470
longer legs
longer, drooped bill

smaller eye-crescents

**OCCURRENCE**
In summer, a bird of the high prairies; always nests over water. On migration often found in agricultural areas; large numbers frequent plowed fields or follow plows. Winters mainly along the Pacific Coast of South America.

| Length **12½–14in (32–36cm)** | Wingspan **33in–3ft 1in (85–95cm)** | Weight **8–11oz (225–325g)** |
| Social **Colonial** | Lifespan **At least 10 years** | Status **Declining** |

| DATE SEEN | WHERE | | NOTES |
|---|---|---|---|
| | | | |
| | | | |
| | | | |
| | | | |
| | | | |

| Order **Charadriiformes** | Family **Laridae** | Species *Larus heermanni* |

# Heermann's Gull

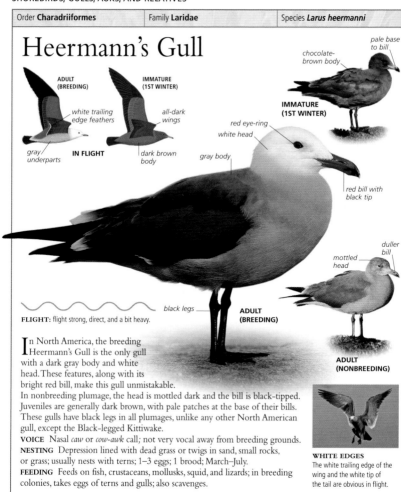

**ADULT (BREEDING)**

**IMMATURE (1ST WINTER)**

*white trailing edge feathers*

*all-dark wings*

**IN FLIGHT**

*gray underparts*

*dark brown body*

*red eye-ring*

*white head*

*gray body*

**IMMATURE (1ST WINTER)**

*pale base to bill*

*chocolate-brown body*

*red bill with black tip*

*duller bill*

*mottled head*

**ADULT (NONBREEDING)**

*black legs*

**ADULT (BREEDING)**

**FLIGHT:** flight strong, direct, and a bit heavy.

In North America, the breeding Heermann's Gull is the only gull with a dark gray body and white head. These features, along with its bright red bill, make this gull unmistakable. In nonbreeding plumage, the head is mottled dark and the bill is black-tipped. Juveniles are generally dark brown, with pale patches at the base of their bills. These gulls have black legs in all plumages, unlike any other North American gull, except the Black-legged Kittiwake.

**VOICE** Nasal *caw* or *cow-awk* call; not very vocal away from breeding grounds.
**NESTING** Depression lined with dead grass or twigs in sand, small rocks, or grass; usually nests with terns; 1–3 eggs; 1 brood; March–July.
**FEEDING** Feeds on fish, crustaceans, mollusks, squid, and lizards; in breeding colonies, takes eggs of terns and gulls; also scavenges.

**WHITE EDGES**
The white trailing edge of the wing and the white tip of the tail are obvious in flight.

**OCCURRENCE**
A truly western North American gull, it nests on islands off Baja California; more than 90 percent of the world's population nests on Isla Raza; occasionally in California; after breeding spreads north along coast to British Columbia, uncommon north of Monterey; rare inland and accidental elsewhere.

### SIMILAR SPECIES

**POMARINE JAEGER (DARK FORM)**
see p.141

*dark bill*

*white flash in outer wing*

**PARASITIC JAEGER (DARK FORM)**
see p.142

*white flash in outer wing feathers*

| Length **18–21in (46–53cm)** | Wingspan **4¼ft (1.3m)** | Weight **13–23oz (375–650g)** |
| Social **Colonies** | Lifespan **Up to 13 years** | Status **Secure** |

| DATE SEEN | WHERE | NOTES |
| --- | --- | --- |
| | | |
| | | |
| | | |
| | | |

| Order **Charadriiformes** | Family **Laridae** | Species *Larus canus* |

# Mew Gull

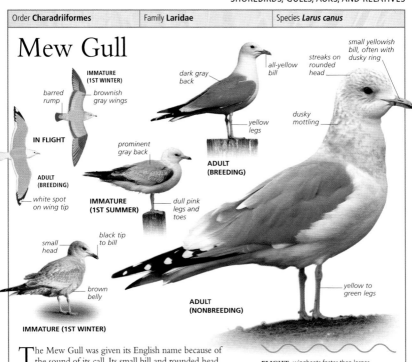

IMMATURE (1ST WINTER)
- barred rump
- brownish gray wings

IN FLIGHT

ADULT (BREEDING)
- white spot on wing tip

dark gray back

all-yellow bill

streaks on rounded head

small yellowish bill, often with dusky ring

dusky mottling

prominent gray back

yellow legs

ADULT (BREEDING)

IMMATURE (1ST SUMMER)
- dull pink legs and toes

small head

black tip to bill

brown belly

ADULT (NONBREEDING)

yellow to green legs

IMMATURE (1ST WINTER)

The Mew Gull was given its English name because of the sound of its call. Its small bill and rounded head give it a rather dove-like profile. It can be confused with the widespread Ring-billed Gull, which it resembles in all plumages. Some taxonomists split the Mew Gull into four species—the European "Common Gull" (*L. c. canus*), the northeastern Asian species (*L. c. heinei*), the "Kamchatka Gull" (*L. c. kamtschatschensis*), and the North American "Short-billed Gull" (*L. c. brachyrhynchus*).
**VOICE** Shrill mewing calls; higher pitched than other gulls.
**NESTING** Platform of mainly dry vegetation in trees or on ground; 1–5 eggs; 1 brood; May–August.
**FEEDING** Eats aquatic crustaceans and mollusks, insects, fish, bird eggs, chicks; scavenges trash and steals food from other birds.

**FLIGHT:** wingbeats faster than larger, similar-looking gulls.

**PLAIN YELLOW BILL**
Although back color and bill size vary in different forms, all adult Mew Gulls have plain yellowish bills.

**OCCURRENCE**
Breeds in Alaska, except extreme north and northwest Canada, south along coast to British Columbia; winters along the Pacific Coast south to Baja California and inland on major river systems. Casual to accidental across the continent to Atlantic Coast.

**SIMILAR SPECIES**

RING-BILLED GULL
see p.156
- paler back
- smaller white spots in wing tips

RING-BILLED GULL ♀
see p.156
- dark mark on bill
- flatter head
- paler back
- larger bill

| Length **15–16in (38–41cm)** | Wingspan **3ft 3in–4ft (1–1.2m)** | Weight **13–18oz (375–500g)** |
| Social **Pairs/Colonies** | Lifespan **Up to 24 years** | Status **Secure** |

| DATE SEEN | WHERE | | NOTES |
|---|---|---|---|
| | | | |
| | | | |
| | | | |
| | | | |
| | | | |

| Order **Charadriiformes** | Family **Laridae** | Species *Larus delawarensis* |

# Ring-billed Gull 🔊

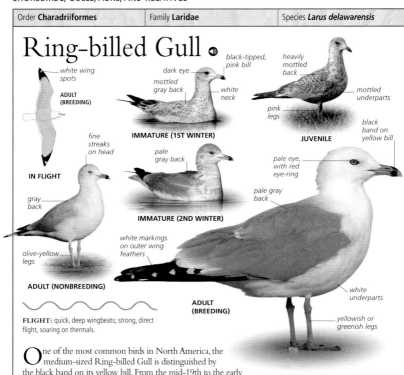

**ADULT (BREEDING)** — white wing spots

**IN FLIGHT** — fine streaks on head

**ADULT (NONBREEDING)** — gray back, olive-yellow legs, white markings on outer wing feathers

**IMMATURE (1ST WINTER)** — dark eye, mottled gray back, white neck, black-tipped pink bill

**IMMATURE (2ND WINTER)** — pale gray back, pale eye with red eye-ring, pale gray back

**JUVENILE** — heavily mottled back, mottled underparts, pink legs, black band on yellow bill

**ADULT (BREEDING)** — white underparts, yellowish or greenish legs

**FLIGHT:** quick, deep wingbeats; strong, direct flight, soaring on thermals.

One of the most common birds in North America, the medium-sized Ring-billed Gull is distinguished by the black band on its yellow bill. From the mid-19th to the early 20th century, population numbers crashed because of hunting and habitat loss. Protection allowed the species to make a spectacular comeback, and in the 1990s, there were an estimated 3–4 million birds. It can often be seen scavenging in parking lots at malls.
**VOICE** Call a slightly nasal and whiny *kee-ow* or *meee-ow*; series of 4–6 *kyaw* notes, higher pitched than Herring Gull.
**NESTING** Shallow cup of plant matter on ground in open areas, usually near low vegetation; 1–5 eggs; 1 brood; April–August.
**FEEDING** Picks food while walking; also dips and plunges in water; eats small fish, insects, grain, small rodents; also scavenges.

**BLACK WING MARKING**
The sharply demarcated black wing tips are prominent from both above and below.

**SIMILAR SPECIES**

**MEW GULL** see p.155 — darker mantle, round head, small bill

**MEW GULL 1ST** see p.155 — round head, less distinct streaks, small bill

**OCCURRENCE**
Breeds in freshwater habitats in the interior of the continent. In winter, switches to mostly saltwater areas and along both the East and West Coasts; also along major river systems and reservoirs. Found year-round near the southern Great Lakes.

| Length **17–21½in (43–54cm)** | Wingspan **4–5ft (1.2–1.5m)** | Weight **11–25oz (300–700g)** |
| Social **Colonies** | Lifespan **Up to 32 years** | Status **Secure** |

| DATE SEEN | WHERE | NOTES |
|---|---|---|
| | | |

| Order **Charadriiformes** | Family **Laridae** | Species *Larus occidentalis* |

# Western Gull

black wing tip with white edges

**ADULT**
*L.o.wymani*
**(BREEDING)**

dark gray wings

**IN FLIGHT**

broad, white trailing edge feathers

white head

orange eye-ring

large, yellow bill with red spot

slate-gray mantle

uniform brown back

**JUVENILE**

brownish gray mantle

**IMMATURE (1ST WINTER)**

dusky head

dark gray mantle

**IMMATURE (2ND WINTER)**

pinkish legs

**ADULT**
*L. o. wymani*
**(BREEDING)**

paler gray back

**ADULT**
*L. o. occidentalis*

The Western Gull is the only dark-backed gull found regularly within its normal range and habitat. However, identification is complicated because of two subspecies: the paler *occidentalis* in the North, and the darker *wymani* in the South. Western Gulls interbreed with Glaucous-winged Gulls, producing confusing hybrids. The total population of these gulls is small, and the small number of nesting colonies makes conservation a concern.

**VOICE** Shrill, repeated *heyaa…heyaa…heyaa* similar to Herring Gull, but lower in pitch, harsher; very vocal at breeding sites.
**NESTING** Scrape filled with vegetation, usually next to bush or rock; 3–4 eggs; 1 brood; April–August.
**FEEDING** Eats crabs, squid, insects, fish, bird eggs, and chicks; also eats sea lion pups; scavenges.

**FLIGHT:** strong, slow with heavy wingbeats; also commonly soars.

**DARK UNDERWINGS**
The undersides of the outer wing feathers are much darker in this bird than in similar species.

**SIMILAR SPECIES**

**YELLOW-FOOTED GULL**
see p.436

darker back

yellow legs

**SLATY-BACKED GULL**
see p.470

thinner bill

**OCCURRENCE**
Nests on offshore islands along West Coast; about one-third of the total population breeds on Southeast Farallon Island, west of San Francisco; nonbreeders and wintering birds occur along the coast and in major bays and estuaries southward to Baja California; very rare inland or far offshore.

| Length **22–26in (56–66cm)** | Wingspan **4¼–4½ft (1.3–1.4m)** | Weight **1¾–2¾lb (0.8–1.2kg)** |
| Social **Colonies** | Lifespan **Up to 28 years** | Status **Vulnerable** |

| DATE SEEN | WHERE | NOTES |
| --- | --- | --- |
| | | |
| | | |
| | | |
| | | |
| | | |

| Order **Charadriiformes** | Family **Laridae** | Species *Larus californicus* |

# California Gull 🔊

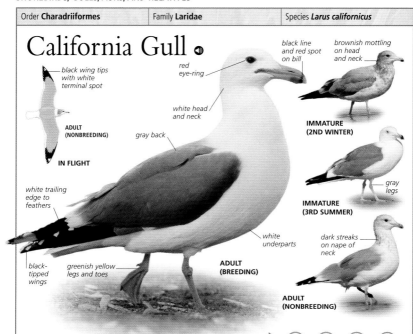

**black wing tips with white terminal spot**

**ADULT (NONBREEDING)**

**IN FLIGHT**

**red eye-ring**

**black line and red spot on bill**

**brownish mottling on head and neck**

**white head and neck**

**gray back**

**IMMATURE (2ND WINTER)**

**white trailing edge to feathers**

**gray legs**

**IMMATURE (3RD SUMMER)**

**white underparts**

**dark streaks on nape of neck**

**black-tipped wings**

**greenish yellow legs and toes**

**ADULT (BREEDING)**

**ADULT (NONBREEDING)**

Slightly smaller than the Herring Gull, the medium-sized California Gull has a darker back and longer wings. In breeding plumage, it can also be distinguished by the black and red coloration on its bill and its greenish yellow legs. In winter and on young birds, dark streaks are prominent on the nape of the neck. A common interior gull, it is honored by a large, gilded statue in Salt Lake City that commemorates the birds' rescue of the settlers' crops from a plague of grasshoppers in 1848.

**VOICE** Call a repeated *kee-yah, kee-yah, kee-yah*.

**NESTING** Shallow scrape, lined with feathers, bones, and vegetation, usually on islands; 2–3 eggs; 1 brood; May–July.

**FEEDING** Forages around lakes for insects, mollusks; hovers over cherry trees dislodging fruit with its wings.

**FLIGHT:** strong and direct, but somewhat stiff, with deep wingbeats.

**AGGRESSIVE POSTURE**
This California Gull is displaying signs of aggression—possibly against another bird.

### SIMILAR SPECIES

**HERRING GULL** ✿
see p.159

*paler back*

*pink legs*

*larger body*

**HERRING GULL** ❄
see p.159

*heavy streaking on head*

*paler back*

**OCCURRENCE**
Breeds at scattered locations across interior western Canada and the US. Some of the largest colonies are on the highly saline Mono Lake and the Great Salt Lake; winters along the Pacific Coast from British Columbia to Mexico; strays increasingly reported in the East.

| Length **17½–20in (45–51cm)** | Wingspan **4–4½ft (1.2–1.4m)** | Weight **18–35oz (0.5–1kg)** |
| Social **Colonies** | Lifespan **Up to 30 years** | Status **Secure** |

| DATE SEEN | WHERE | NOTES |
|-----------|-------|-------|
| | | |
| | | |
| | | |
| | | |
| | | |

| Order **Charadriiformes** | Family **Laridae** | Species *Larus argentatus* |

# Herring Gull 🔊

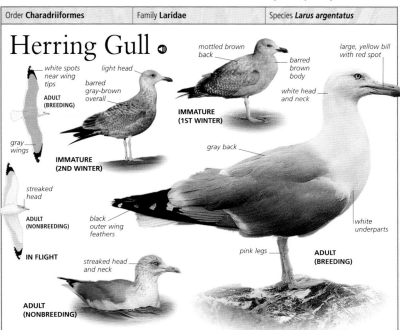

white spots near wing tips

**ADULT (BREEDING)**

light head

barred gray-brown overall

mottled brown back

barred brown body

white head and neck

large, yellow bill with red spot

gray wings

**IMMATURE (2ND WINTER)**

**IMMATURE (1ST WINTER)**

gray back

streaked head

**ADULT (NONBREEDING)**

black outer wing feathers

white underparts

**IN FLIGHT**

streaked head and neck

**ADULT (BREEDING)**

pink legs

**ADULT (NONBREEDING)**

The Herring Gull is the archetypal, large "white-headed" gull to which nearly all other gulls are compared. When people mention "seagulls" they usually refer to the Herring Gull, but this term is misleading because the Herring Gull, like most other gulls, does not commonly go far out to sea—it is a bird of near-shore waters, coasts, lakes, rivers, and inland waterways. Now very common, the Herring Gull was nearly wiped out in the late 19th and early 20th century by plumage hunters and egg collectors.

**VOICE** Typical call a high-pitched, shrill, repeated *heyaa… heyaa…heyaa…heyaa*; vocal throughout the year.

**NESTING** Shallow bowl on ground lined with feathers, vegetation, detritus; 2–4 eggs; 1 brood; April–August.

**FEEDING** Eats fish, crustaceans, mollusks, worms; eggs and chicks of other seabirds; scavenges carrion, garbage; steals from other birds.

**FLIGHT:** steady, regular, slow wingbeats; also commonly soars and glides.

**MASTER SCAVENGER**
A common sight near any water body, the Herring Gull is an expert scavenger of carrion and trash.

### SIMILAR SPECIES

**RING-BILLED GULL** see p.156
smaller overall

black ring on bill

yellow-green legs

**CALIFORNIA GULL** see p.158

black-and-red spot on bill

greenish legs

**OCCURRENCE**
Found throughout North America along coasts and inland on lakes, rivers, and reservoirs; also frequents garbage dumps. Breeds in northeastern US and across Canada. Migrates southward across much of the continent to winter in coastal areas and along lakes and major rivers.

| Length **22–26in (56–66cm)** | Wingspan **4–5ft (1.2–1.5m)** | Weight **28–42oz (800–1,200g)** |
| Social **Colonies** | Lifespan **At least 35 years** | Status **Secure** |

| DATE SEEN | WHERE | NOTES |
| --- | --- | --- |
| | | |
| | | |
| | | |
| | | |
| | | |

| Order **Charadriiformes** | Family **Laridae** | Species *Larus glaucescens* |

# Glaucous-winged Gull

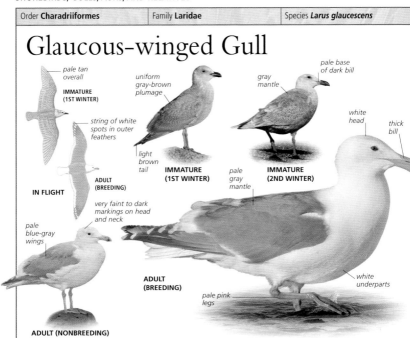

**IMMATURE (1ST WINTER)**
pale tan overall

string of white spots in outer feathers

**IN FLIGHT**

**ADULT (BREEDING)**
light brown tail

**IMMATURE (1ST WINTER)**
uniform gray-brown plumage

pale gray mantle

**IMMATURE (2ND WINTER)**
gray mantle

pale base of dark bill

white head
thick bill

very faint to dark markings on head and neck

pale blue-gray wings

**ADULT (BREEDING)**
pale pink legs

white underparts

**ADULT (NONBREEDING)**

The Glaucous-winged Gull, the most common large gull on the north Pacific Coast, is found around towns and cities, even nesting on the roofs of shorefront buildings. This species commonly interbreeds with Western Gulls in the southern part of its range, and with Herring and Glaucous Gulls in the North, producing intermediate birds that are more difficult to identify.
**VOICE** Call a slow, deep *aah-aah-aah*; many types of calls heard around colonies; voice lower pitched than Herring Gull.
**NESTING** Scrape surrounded by ring of torn up grass or other vegetation; forms colonies usually on small, low islands; 2–3 eggs; 1 brood; May–August.
**FEEDING** Snatches fish, aquatic mollusks, and crustaceans while walking, swimming, or diving; also scavenges carrion and trash.

**FLIGHT:** strong and graceful; shallow wingbeats; also soars.

**PALE WINGS**
The Glaucous-winged Gull is named for its delicate, pale, bluish gray wings.

**SIMILAR SPECIES**

**GLAUCOUS GULL** ❉ see p.161
larger and paler body

white wing tips

**ICELAND GULL**
smaller bill

rounder head

**OCCURRENCE**
Breeds along coast of northwest Oregon northward to the Bering Sea coast of Alaska; winters within its breeding range and southward, to Gulf of California; primarily a coastal and offshore gull (farther offshore in winter); it is very rare inland and accidental to central US.

| Length **23–24in (58–62cm)** | Wingspan **4½–5ft (1.4–1.5m)** | Weight **2–2¾lb (0.9–1.3kg)** |
| Social **Colonies** | Lifespan **Up to 32 years** | Status **Secure** |

| DATE SEEN | WHERE | NOTES |
| --- | --- | --- |
| | | |
| | | |
| | | |
| | | |

| Order **Charadriiformes** | Family **Laridae** | Species *Larus hyperboreus* |
|---|---|---|

# Glaucous Gull

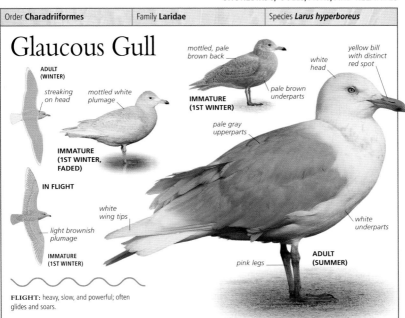

ADULT (WINTER)

*streaking on head*

*mottled white plumage*

IMMATURE (1ST WINTER, FADED)

IN FLIGHT

*white wing tips*

*light brownish plumage*

IMMATURE (1ST WINTER)

*mottled, pale brown back*

IMMATURE (1ST WINTER)

*white head*

*pale brown underparts*

*pale gray upperparts*

*yellow bill with distinct red spot*

*white underparts*

ADULT (SUMMER)

*pink legs*

**FLIGHT:** heavy, slow, and powerful; often glides and soars.

The Glaucous Gull is the largest of the "white-winged" gulls. Its large, pale shape is immediately apparent in a group of gulls as it appears like a large white spectre among its smaller, darker cousins. In the southern part of its US winter range, pale immatures are encountered more frequently than adults. In the Arctic, successful pairs of Glaucous Gulls maintain the bonds with their mates for years, often returning to the same nest site year after year.

**VOICE** Similar to that of the Herring Gull, but slightly harsher and deeper; hoarse, nasal *ku-ku-ku*.

**NESTING** Shallow cup lined with vegetation on ground, at edge of tundra pools, on cliffs and ledges and islands; 1–3 eggs; 1 brood; May–July.

**FEEDING** Eats fish, crustaceans, mollusks; also eggs and chicks of waterfowl, small seabirds, and small mammals.

**NORTHERN VISITOR**
This large gull is an uncommon visitor over most of North America during the winter months.

**SIMILAR SPECIES**

GLAUCOUS-WINGED GULL see p.160

*dusky wing tips*

ICELAND GULL

*much smaller bill*

*much smaller overall*

**OCCURRENCE**
Breeds along the High Arctic Coast, rarely inland; winters along northern Atlantic and Pacific Coasts and the Great Lakes; frequently seen at Niagara Falls. Strays, usually immatures, can occur inland anywhere where concentrations of gulls are found, such as trash dumps.

| Length **26–30in (65–75cm)** | Wingspan **5–6ft (1.5–1.8m)** | Weight **2¾–6lb (1.2–2.7kg)** |
|---|---|---|
| Social **Colonies** | Lifespan **Up to 21 years** | Status **Secure** |

| DATE SEEN | WHERE | NOTES |
|---|---|---|
| | | |
| | | |
| | | |
| | | |
| | | |

| Order **Charadriiformes** | Family **Laridae** | Species *Hydroprogne caspia* |

# Caspian Tern

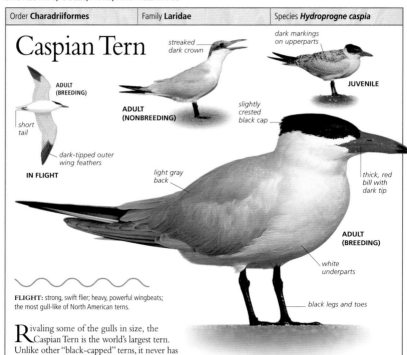

ADULT
(BREEDING)

*streaked dark crown*

*dark markings on upperparts*

JUVENILE

ADULT
(NONBREEDING)

*slightly crested black cap*

*short tail*

*dark-tipped outer wing feathers*

IN FLIGHT

*light gray back*

*slightly crested black cap*

*thick, red bill with dark tip*

ADULT
(BREEDING)

*white underparts*

**FLIGHT:** strong, swift flier; heavy, powerful wingbeats; the most gull-like of North American terns.

*black legs and toes*

Rivaling some of the gulls in size, the Caspian Tern is the world's largest tern. Unlike other "black-capped" terns, it never has a completely white forehead, even in winter. In nonbreeding plumage the cap is very heavily streaked. The Caspian Tern is known for its predatory habits, stealing prey from other seabirds, as well as snatching eggs from, and hunting the chicks of, other gulls and terns. It is aggressive in defending its nesting territory, giving hoarse alarm calls and rhythmically opening and closing its bill in a threatening display to intruders.

**VOICE** Hoarse, deep *kraaa, kraaa*; also barks at intruders; male's wings vibrate loudly in courtship flight.

**NESTING** Shallow scrape on ground; 2–3 eggs; 1 brood; May–August.

**FEEDING** Plunges into water to snatch fish, barnacles, and snails.

**AGGRESSIVE BIRDS**
The Caspian Tern is one of the most aggressive terns, though actual physical contact is rare.

**SIMILAR SPECIES**

**ELEGANT TERN**
see p.438

*smaller overall*

**ROYAL TERN**
see p.437

*thin, orange-yellow bill*

*thinner, orange bill*

*slender build*

**OCCURRENCE**
Found in a variety of aquatic habitats, freshwater and marine; rare offshore; breeds on interior lakes, saltmarsh, and on coastal barrier islands; winters on and near the coast. May be seen on marshes and wetlands during migration.

| Length **18½–21½in (47–54cm)** | Wingspan **4¼–5ft (1.3–1.5m)** | Weight **19–27oz (525–775g)** |
| Social **Colonies/Pairs** | Lifespan **Up to 30 years** | Status **Secure** |

| DATE SEEN | WHERE | | NOTES |
|---|---|---|---|
| | | | |
| | | | |
| | | | |
| | | | |
| | | | |

| Order **Charadriiformes** | Family **Laridae** | Species *Chlidonias niger* |

# Black Tern

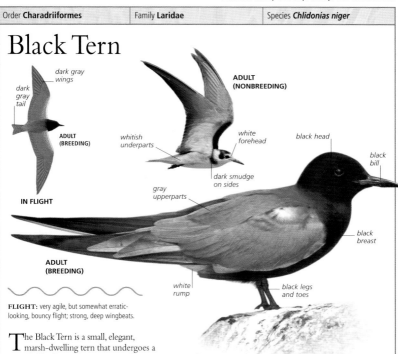

dark gray wings

dark gray tail

**ADULT (BREEDING)**

**ADULT (NONBREEDING)**

whitish underparts

white forehead

black head

black bill

**IN FLIGHT**

dark smudge on sides

gray upperparts

black breast

**ADULT (BREEDING)**

white rump

black legs and toes

**FLIGHT:** very agile, but somewhat erratic-looking, bouncy flight; strong, deep wingbeats.

The Black Tern is a small, elegant, marsh-dwelling tern that undergoes a remarkable change in appearance from summer to winter—more so than any other regularly occurring North American tern. The Black Tern's breeding plumage can cause the bird to be confused with the closely related White-winged Tern, which is an accidental visitor to North America. The Black Tern's nonbreeding plumage is much paler than its breeding plumage—the head turns white with irregular black streaks, and the neck, breast, and belly become whitish gray.

**VOICE** Call nasal and harsh *krik*, *kip*, or *kik*; most vocal during breeding, but calls throughout the year.

**NESTING** Shallow cup on top of floating mass of vegetation, sometimes on top of muskrat lodges; usually 3 eggs; 1 brood; May–August.

**FEEDING** Picks prey off water's surface or vegetation; rarely plunge dives; in summer, feeds on mainly insects, caught from the air or ground, also freshwater fish; in winter, eats mainly small sea fish.

**FLOATING NEST**
A floating nest is a dry place to lay eggs and raise chicks in a watery environment.

**SIMILAR SPECIES**

SOOTY TERN ◐

white spots on back

much larger overall

**OCCURRENCE**
Freshwater marshes in summer, but nonbreeding plumaged birds—probably young—occasionally seen along the coast. During migration, can be found almost anywhere near water. Winters in the marine coastal waters of Central and South America.

| Length **9–10in (23–26cm)** | Wingspan **25–35in (63–88cm)** | Weight **1¾–2½oz (50–70g)** |
| Social **Colonies** | Lifespan **Up to 9 years** | Status **Vulnerable** |

| DATE SEEN | WHERE | NOTES |
|-----------|-------|-------|
| | | |
| | | |
| | | |
| | | |
| | | |

| Order **Charadriiformes** | Family **Laridae** | Species **Sterna hirundo** |

# Common Tern 🔊

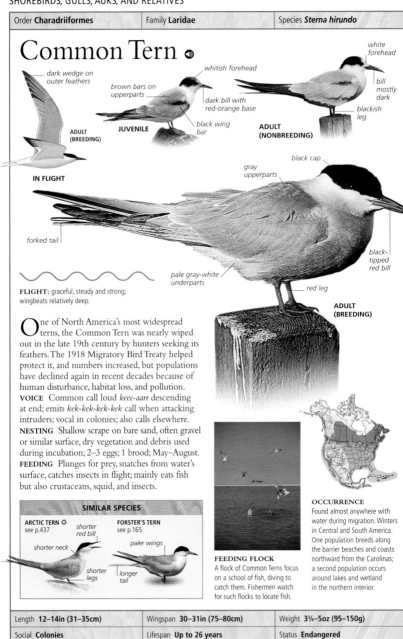

dark wedge on outer featbers

brown bars on upperparts

whitish forehead

dark bill with red-orange base

black wing bar

**JUVENILE**

white forehead

bill mostly dark

blackish leg

**ADULT (NONBREEDING)**

**ADULT (BREEDING)**

**IN FLIGHT**

forked tail

black cap

gray upperparts

pale gray-white underparts

red leg

black-tipped red bill

**ADULT (BREEDING)**

**FLIGHT:** graceful, steady and strong; wingbeats relatively deep.

One of North America's most widespread terns, the Common Tern was nearly wiped out in the late 19th century by hunters seeking its feathers. The 1918 Migratory Bird Treaty helped protect it, and numbers increased, but populations have declined again in recent decades because of human disturbance, habitat loss, and pollution.
**VOICE** Common call loud *keee-aarr* descending at end; emits *kek-kek-kek-kek* call when attacking intruders; vocal in colonies; also calls elsewhere.
**NESTING** Shallow scrape on bare sand, often gravel or similar surface, dry vegetation and debris used during incubation; 2–3 eggs; 1 brood; May–August.
**FEEDING** Plunges for prey, snatches from water's surface, catches insects in flight; mainly eats fish but also crustaceans, squid, and insects.

### SIMILAR SPECIES

**ARCTIC TERN** ☼
see p.437

shorter red bill

shorter neck

shorter legs

**FORSTER'S TERN**
see p.165

paler wings

longer tail

**FEEDING FLOCK**
A flock of Common Terns focus on a school of fish, diving to catch them. Fishermen watch for such flocks to locate fish.

**OCCURRENCE**
Found almost anywhere with water during migration. Winters in Central and South America. One population breeds along the barrier beaches and coasts northward from the Carolinas; a second population occurs around lakes and wetland in the northern interior.

| Length **12–14in (31–35cm)** | Wingspan **30–31in (75–80cm)** | Weight **3⅜–5oz (95–150g)** |
| Social **Colonies** | Lifespan **Up to 26 years** | Status **Endangered** |

| DATE SEEN | WHERE | NOTES |
|-----------|-------|-------|
| | | |
| | | |
| | | |
| | | |
| | | |

| Order **Charadriiformes** | Family **Laridae** | Species *Sterna forsteri* |

# Forster's Tern

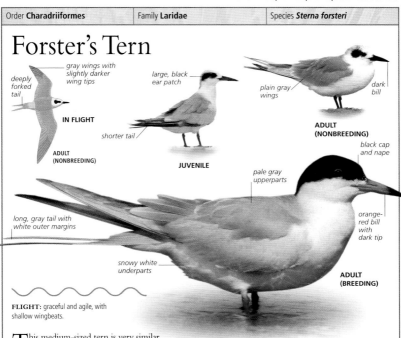

deeply forked tail

gray wings with slightly darker wing tips

**IN FLIGHT**

**ADULT (NONBREEDING)**

large, black ear patch

shorter tail

**JUVENILE**

plain gray wings

dark bill

**ADULT (NONBREEDING)**

black cap and nape

pale gray upperparts

long, gray tail with white outer margins

snowy white underparts

orange-red bill with dark tip

**ADULT (BREEDING)**

**FLIGHT:** graceful and agile, with shallow wingbeats.

This medium-sized tern is very similar in appearance to the Common Tern. The features that differentiate it from the Common Tern are its lighter outer wing feathers and longer tail. Early naturalists could not tell the two species apart until 1834 when English botanist Thomas Nuttall made the distinction. He named this tern after Johann Reinhold Forster, a naturalist who accompanied the English explorer Captain Cook on his epic second voyage (1772–75).
**VOICE** Harsh, descending *kyerr*; more nasal than Common Tern.
**NESTING** Shallow scrape in mud or sand, but occasionally nests on top of muskrat lodge or on old grebe nest; sometimes constructs raft of floating vegetation; 2–3 eggs; 1 brood; May–August.
**FEEDING** Catches fish and crustaceans with shallow plunge-diving, often only head submerges; also catches insects in flight.

**BLACK EARS**
With its black ear patch, Forster's Tern is more distinctive in nonbreeding than breeding plumage.

**SIMILAR SPECIES**

**COMMON TERN** see p.164
shorter tail
redder bill

**ARCTIC TERN** see p.437
shorter neck
shorter red bill
shorter legs

**OCCURRENCE**
Breeds in northeastern Mexico, in freshwater and saltwater marshes with large stretches of open water. Winters on both coasts and across southern US states, unlike the Common Tern, which primarily winters in South America.

| Length **13–14in (33–36cm)** | Wingspan **29–32in (73–82cm)** | Weight **4–7oz (125–190g)** |
| Social **Colonies** | Lifespan **Up to 16 years** | Status **Secure** |

| DATE SEEN | WHERE | NOTES |
|-----------|-------|-------|
| | | |
| | | |
| | | |
| | | |
| | | |

# LOONS

WORLDWIDE THERE ARE only five species of loons, comprising a single genus (*Gavia*), a single family (the Gaviidae), and a single order (the Gaviiformes). The five species are limited to the Northern Hemisphere, where they are found in both northern North America and northern Eurasia. One feature of loons is that their legs are positioned so far to the rear of their body that they must shuffle on their bellies when they go from water to land. Not surprisingly, therefore, loons are almost entirely aquatic birds. In summer they are found on rivers, lakes, and ponds, where they nest close to the water's edge. After breeding, they occur along coasts, often after flying hundreds of miles away from their freshwater breeding grounds. Excellent swimmers and divers, loons are unusual among birds in that their bones are less hollow than those of other groups. Consequently, they can expel air from their lungs and compress their body feathers until they slowly sink beneath the surface. They can remain submerged like this for several minutes. A loon's wings are relatively small in proportion to its body weight. This means that they have to run a long way across the surface of the water, flapping energetically, before they can get airborne. Once in the air, they keep on flapping, and can fly at up to 60mph (95kmh).

**WIDESPREAD**
The Common Loon has the widest range of any loon in North America.

**PROVIDING FOR THE FUTURE**
A Red-throated Loon gives a fish to its chick to gulp down headfirst and whole.

---

# TUBENOSES

THE NAME "TUBENOSES" IS given to several families of seabirds with tubular nostrils, which help get rid of excess salt and may enhance their sense of smell. Tubenoses are all members of the order Procellariiformes.

## STORM-PETRELS
The smallest tubenoses in North American waters, the storm-petrels (families Oceanitidae, Hydrobatidae) are also the most agile fliers. They often patter or "dance" as they fly low over the surface of the ocean in search of small fish, squid, and crustaceans. Storm-petrels spend most of their lives flying over the open sea, only visiting land in the breeding season, when they form huge colonies.

## SHEARWATERS AND PETRELS
Shearwaters and gadfly petrels (family Procellariidae) are smaller than their larger cousins, albatrosses (family Diomedeidae). Like albatrosses, they are excellent gliders, but their lighter weight and proportionately shorter wings mean that they use more powered flight. They range over all the world's oceans. With its far more numerous islands, the Pacific Ocean is home to a greater variety of these seabirds than the Atlantic. During and after storms are the best times to look for these birds from land, as this is when they have been drifting away from the deep sea because of wind and waves.

**FLAP AND GLIDE**
Shearwaters alternate stiff-winged flapping with gliding just over the ocean's surface.

| Order **Gaviiformes** | Family **Gaviidae** | Species *Gavia stellata* |

# Red-throated Loon

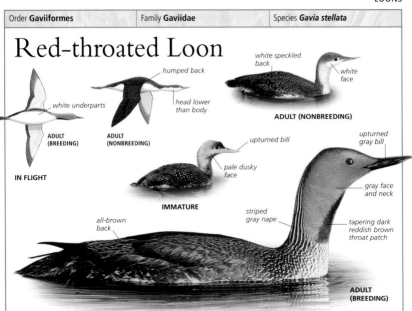

white speckled back

white face

**ADULT (NONBREEDING)**

humped back

head lower than body

white underparts

**ADULT (BREEDING)**

**ADULT (NONBREEDING)**

**IN FLIGHT**

upturned bill

pale dusky face

**IMMATURE**

all-brown back

upturned gray bill

gray face and neck

striped gray nape

tapering dark reddish brown throat patch

**ADULT (BREEDING)**

Even when seen from a distance, this elegant loon is almost unmistakable, with a pale, slim body, upward-tilted head, and a thin, upturned bill. Unlike other Loons, the Red-throated Loon can leap straight into the air from both land and water, although most of the time it needs a "runway." The Red-throated Loon has an elaborate breeding ritual—side by side, a pair of birds races upright across the surface of water. Downy chicks climb onto the parents back only when very young.

**VOICE** High gull-like or even cat-like wail and low goose-like growl; vocal on breeding grounds, otherwise silent.

**NESTING** Scrape with mud and vegetation added during incubation, placed at water's edge in coastal and lake bays, shallow ponds, often at high altitudes; 2 eggs; 1 brood; April–July.

**FEEDING** Mainly eats fish; also spiders, crustaceans, and mollusks; flies long distances from shallow ponds when food is scarce.

**FLIGHT:** very direct; fast, with constant wingbeats; head held lower than other loons.

**TAKING OFF**
While this bird is using the water's surface to takeoff, it can leap directly into flight from water or land.

| | SIMILAR SPECIES | |
| --- | --- | --- |
| **YELLOW-BILLED LOON** ✷ | **RED-NECKED GREBE** ✷ see p.74 | |

massive, light-colored bill

larger overall

darker back

smaller overall

yellow in bill

**OCCURRENCE**
Lives in open areas within northern boreal forest, muskeg, and tundra; in Canadian Arctic Archipelago, sometimes in areas almost devoid of vegetation. Winters on the Great Lakes, and both coasts southward to Florida and northern Mexico.

| Length **24–27in (61–69cm)** | Wingspan **3½ft (1.1m)** | Weight **3¼lb (1.5kg)** |
| --- | --- | --- |
| Social **Solitary/Loose flocks** | Lifespan **Up to 23 years** | Status **Declining** |

| DATE SEEN | WHERE | NOTES |
| --- | --- | --- |
| | | |
| | | |
| | | |
| | | |
| | | |

| Order **Gaviiformes** | Family **Gaviidae** | Species **Gavia pacifica** |
|---|---|---|

# Pacific Loon

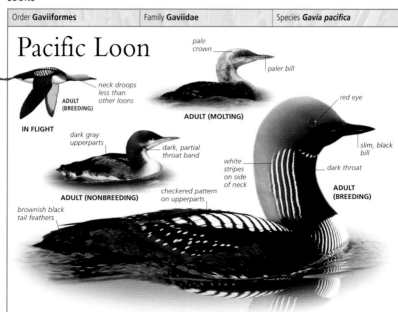

*pale crown*

*paler bill*

**ADULT (MOLTING)**

*neck droops less than other loons*

**ADULT (BREEDING)**

**IN FLIGHT**

*red eye*

*dark gray upperparts*

*dark, partial throat band*

*white stripes on side of neck*

*slim, black bill*

*dark throat*

**ADULT (NONBREEDING)**

*checkered pattern on upperparts*

**ADULT (BREEDING)**

*brownish black tail feathers*

Although the Pacific Loon's breeding range is about a third of that of the Common Loon, it is believed to be the most abundant loon species in North America. It shares its habitat in northern Alaska with the nearly identical, but slightly larger and darker Arctic Loon. It is a conspicuous migrant along the Pacific Coast in spring, but disappears to its remote breeding grounds in summer. The Pacific Loon is an expert diver and swimmer, capable of remaining underwater for sustained periods of time, usually in pursuit of fish. However, on its terrestrial nesting site, its chicks are vulnerable to a number of mammalian predators.
**VOICE** Deep barking *kowk*; high-pitched wail, croaks, and growls when breeding; makes a yelping noise when diving.
**NESTING** Simple scrape in flat area close to water, vegetation and mud added during incubation; 1–2 eggs; June–July.
**FEEDING** Eats fish, aquatic insects, and mollusks in breeding lake or nearby waters; may dip or dive, depending on the depth.

**FLIGHT:** swift and direct with constant wingbeats; humped back, but head in line with body.

**LEVEL GROUND**
As loons cannot takeoff from land, nest sites need to be on flat land close to the water.

**SIMILAR SPECIES**

ARCTIC LOON ☼

*darker nape*

*bolder black-and-white stripes on neck*

ARCTIC LOON ❄

*heavier bill*

*brownish neck and head*

**OCCURRENCE**
Breeds across Arctic and subarctic North America, from Alaska and northern Canadian provinces to Hudson Bay and on some islands of the Canadian Arctic; in tundra lakes and muskeg. Winters on Pacific Coast, with small numbers in Great Lakes and along Atlantic Coast from Québec to Florida. Vagrant elsewhere.

| Length **23–29in (58–74cm)** | Wingspan **2¾–4¼ft (0.9–1.3m)** | Weight **2½–5½lb (1–2.5kg)** |
|---|---|---|
| Social **Flocks** | Lifespan **Up to 25 years** | Status **Secure** |

| DATE SEEN | WHERE | NOTES |
|---|---|---|
| | | |
| | | |
| | | |
| | | |

| Order **Gaviiformes** | Family **Gaviidae** | Species *Gavia immer* |
|---|---|---|

# Common Loon 🔊

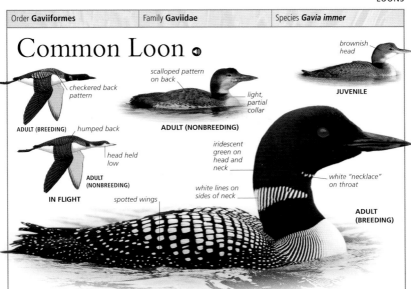

brownish head

**JUVENILE**

checkered back pattern

**ADULT (BREEDING)** humped back

scalloped pattern on back

light, partial collar

**ADULT (NONBREEDING)**

head held low

**ADULT (NONBREEDING)**

**IN FLIGHT** spotted wings

iridescent green on head and neck

white "necklace" on throat

white lines on sides of neck

**ADULT (BREEDING)**

The Common Loon has the largest range of all loons in North America and is the only species to nest in a few of the northern states. It is slightly smaller than the Yellow-billed Loon but larger than the other three loons. It can remain underwater for well over 10 minutes, although it usually stays submerged for 40 seconds to 2 minutes while fishing, or a few more minutes if it is being pursued. Evidence shows that, occasionally, it interbreeds with its closest relative, the Yellow-billed Loon, in addition to the Arctic and Pacific Loons.
**VOICE** Most recognized call a 3–10 note falsetto yodel, rising, then fading; other calls similar in quality.
**NESTING** Simple scrape in large mound of vegetation, a few feet from open water; 2 eggs; 1 brood; April–June.
**FEEDING** Feeds primarily on fish underwater; also eats crustaceans, mollusks, amphibians, leeches, insects, and aquatic plants.

**FLIGHT:** fast, direct, with constant wingbeats; head and neck held just above belly.

**COZY RIDE**
Downy Common Loon chicks climb up the backs of male and female adults for a safe ride.

**BATHING RITUAL**
Common Loons often shake their wings after bathing.

**OCCURRENCE**
Breeds across North America, Canada, and south to northern US. Winters on large ice-free lakes in Canada and the US, and along the Pacific and Atlantic Coasts, south to Baja California and Florida. In the Old World breeds only in Iceland.

**SIMILAR SPECIES**

**YELLOW-BILLED LOON**

large, whitish or yellow bill

larger, checkered back pattern

**RED-NECKED GREBE** ✳
see p.74

much smaller overall

yellowish bill

brownish gray cheeks

| Length **26–36in (66–91cm)** | Wingspan **4¼–5ft (1.3–1.5m)** | Weight **4½–18lb (2–8kg)** |
|---|---|---|
| Social **Family groups** | Lifespan **Up to 30 years** | Status **Vulnerable** |

| DATE SEEN | WHERE | NOTES |
|---|---|---|
| | | |
| | | |
| | | |
| | | |
| | | |

| Order **Procellariiformes** | Family **Hydrobatidae** | Species *Hydrobates furcatus* |

# Fork-tailed Storm-Petrel

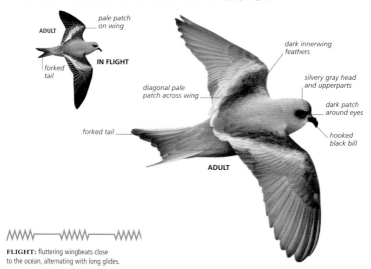

**ADULT**

pale patch on wing

**IN FLIGHT**

forked tail

dark innerwing feathers

silvery gray head and upperparts

diagonal pale patch across wing

dark patch around eyes

forked tail

hooked black bill

**ADULT**

**FLIGHT:** fluttering wingbeats close to the ocean, alternating with long glides.

The Fork-tailed Storm-Petrel is one of the most distinctive of all storm-petrels in North American waters, with its ghostly silvery-gray plumage, and forked tail. It is the most northerly breeding storm-petrel in the North Pacific, nesting all the way north to the Aleutian Islands. It incubates its eggs at lower temperatures than other petrels do, and its chicks can be left alone between feeding for a longer time—apparently an adaptation to northern conditions. Its chicks can also lower their body temperature, thereby conserving energy.

**VOICE** Silent at sea; various purring sounds at colonies.
**NESTING** Underground burrow on offshore island; 1 egg; 1 brood; March–November.
**FEEDING** Plucks shrimps, squids, and small fish from the surface of the ocean.

**AERIAL SURVEY**
Flying low over the ocean, the Fork-tailed Storm-Petrel looks out for fish below.

**SIMILAR SPECIES**

**LEACH'S STORM-PETREL**
see p.171

white rump patch

dark brown overall

**ASHY STORM-PETREL**
see p.439

slightly smaller

brown overall

**OCCURRENCE**
Breeds in colonies on rocky islands along the Pacific Coasts of North America. Most common in the Aleutian Islands of Alaska, but nests as far south as northern California. Winters at sea in the North Pacific.

| Length **8in (20cm)** | Wingspan **18in (46cm)** | Weight **2oz (55g)** |
| Social **Colonies** | Lifespan **At least 14 years** | Status **Secure** |

| DATE SEEN | WHERE | | NOTES |
|---|---|---|---|
| | | | |
| | | | |
| | | | |
| | | | |
| | | | |

| Order **Procellariiformes** | Family **Hydrobatidae** | Species *Hydrobates leucorhous* |

# Leach's Storm-Petrel

long, angled wings

**ADULT**

**IN FLIGHT**

white rump with thin, dark line down center

brown bar across blackish wings

**ADULT**

forked tail

dark sooty black underwings

dark smudge beside eye

**ADULT**

dark sooty brown underparts

**FLIGHT:** buoyant, deep wingbeats low over ocean's surface, interrupted by twists and turns.

L each's Storm-Petrel is widespread in both the Atlantic and Pacific Oceans, unlike most other storm-petrels. It breeds in colonies on islands off the coasts, coming to land at night and feeding offshore during the day, often many miles from the colony. This wide-ranging storm-petrel has both geographical and individual variation; most populations show a white rump, but others have a dark rump that is the same color as the rest of the body. Leach's Storm-Petrel and the very similar, endangered, Townsend's Storm-Petrel *(H. socorroensis)* were thought to be a single species until they were split in 2016. The latter is identified only by its breeding location and smaller size.
**VOICE** At nesting sites, often from burrows, calls are long series of soft purring and chattering sounds.
**NESTING** Underground burrow on island free of predators such as rats; 1 egg; 1 brood; May–November.
**FEEDING** Gleans small crustaceans and small fish from the water's surface while in flight.

**BALANCING ACT**
Leach's Storm-Petrels will occasionally balance themselves with their toes while foraging.

### SIMILAR SPECIES

**BAND-RUMPED STORM-PETREL**
white of rump extends toward belly
tail not notched

**BLACK STORM-PETREL**
see p.439
dark rump

**OCCURRENCE**
Breeds on islands in the Pacific Ocean from Alaska and the Aleutian Islands south to California; in the Atlantic Ocean, from Newfoundland to Maine. After breeding, it wanders widely on both oceans, keeping well out of sight of land.

| Length  **7–8½in (18–22cm)** | Wingspan  **17½–19in (45–48cm)** | Weight  **1⁹⁄₁₆–1¾oz (45–50g)** |
| Social  **Colonies** | Lifespan  **Up to 36 years** | Status  **Secure** |

| DATE SEEN | WHERE | | NOTES |
|-----------|-------|--|-------|
| | | | |
| | | | |
| | | | |
| | | | |
| | | | |

| Order **Procellariiformes** | Family **Procellariidae** | Species *Fulmarus glacialis* |
|---|---|---|

# Northern Fulmar

white patch on wing

**ADULT**

**IN FLIGHT**

paddle-like wings

gray back

white head

**ADULT (ATLANTIC FORM)**

small dark patch in front of eye

thick, yellow bill

white underparts

short, rounded, gray tail

**ADULT (LIGHT PACIFIC FORM)**

dark gray overall

**FLIGHT:** snappy wingbeats and long glides near the surface of the ocean.

**ADULT (DARK PACIFIC FORM)**

Possessing paddle-shaped wings and distinctive color patterns ranging from almost all-white to all-gray, the latter mostly in the Pacific, the Northern Fulmar is among the most common seabirds in places like the Bering Sea. It breeds at high latitudes, then disperses south to offshore waters along both coasts of the continent. It can regularly be seen in large mixed flocks containing albatrosses, shearwaters, and small petrels. Fulmars often follow boats, eager to pounce on the offal thrown overboard by fishermen.

**VOICE** Mostly silent at sea; occasionally utters cackles and grunts.
**NESTING** Scrape in rock or soil on edge of cliff; 1 egg; 1 brood; May–October.
**FEEDING** Picks fish and offal from the surface of the ocean; also dives underwater to catch fish.

**FEEDING FRENZY**
Large numbers of Northern Fulmars compete for the offal discarded by fishing trawlers.

**SIMILAR SPECIES**

| SOOTY SHEARWATER see p.174 | GREAT SHEARWATER |
|---|---|
| more slender wings | dark bill | more slender wings | dark cap |
| dark overall | | | white collar |

**OCCURRENCE**
Breeds on remote, high, coastal cliffs in Alaska and northern Canada; winters at sea in offshore Pacific and Atlantic waters, farther north than most other seabirds. Breeds in Europe, northward to Greenland, Svalbard; also parts of Russia.

| Length **17½–19½in (45–50cm)** | Wingspan **3¼–3½ft (1–1.1m)** | Weight **16–35oz (0.45–1kg)** |
|---|---|---|
| Social **Flocks** | Lifespan **Up to 50 years** | Status **Secure** |

| DATE SEEN | WHERE | NOTES |
|---|---|---|
| | | |
| | | |
| | | |
| | | |
| | | |

| Order **Procellariiformes** | Family **Procellariidae** | Species ***Ardenna tenuirostris*** |
| --- | --- | --- |

# Short-tailed Shearwater

thin wing

**ADULT**

dark underwing
with central
paler line

**IN FLIGHT**

dark cap contrasts
with paler cheeks
and white throat

rounded
crown

dark sooty
brown overall

"bulb"
at tip

dark,
short
bill

rounded
crown

**ADULT**

Short-tailed Shearwaters are abundant off the Alaskan Coast in the summer, where they have been seen in gigantic groups numbering perhaps in the millions. The total world population may be about 50 million. The Short-tailed Shearwater spends most of its life at sea, and its migration route follows a huge figure 8 around the North Pacific. Field identification is difficult, as they look very similar to Sooty Shearwaters. However, the Short-tailed Shearwater has some distinguishing features. It is more compact overall, with a rounder crown, shorter bill, a dark head contrasting with a paler throat and breast, and more uniform underwings, that may include a pale part extending onto the outer wing feathers.

**VOICE** Silent at sea; varied, agitated vocalizations when feeding.
**NESTING** Burrow dug in peat; 1 egg; 1 brood; September–April.
**FEEDING** Dives and picks at surface for small schooling fish, squid, octopus, and crustaceans.

**FLIGHT:** rapid, stiff wingbeats interspersed with glides; will arch up high in strong winds.

**DARK BIRD**
A rounded head, short bill, pale throat, and dark underwings identify this bird.

**SIMILAR SPECIES**

**NORTHERN FULMAR (DARK FORM)**
see p.172

pale bill

wing more rounded

**SOOTY SHEARWATER**
see p.174

sooty brown

silvery underwings

**OCCURRENCE**
Breeds on islands off eastern Australia from New South Wales to Tasmania; migrates north to spend its winter (US summer) in the Gulf of Alaska and the Bering Sea, where it is common; during spring migration (US fall and early winter) it passes along the West Coast of North America.

| Length **17in (43cm)** | Wingspan **3ft 3in (1m)** | Weight **19oz (550g)** |
| --- | --- | --- |
| Social **Large flocks** | Lifespan **Unknown** | Status **Secure** |

| DATE SEEN | WHERE | NOTES |
| --- | --- | --- |
| | | |
| | | |
| | | |
| | | |
| | | |

| Order **Procellariiformes** | Family **Procellariidae** | Species **Ardenna grisea** |
|---|---|---|

# Sooty Shearwater

silvery white patch along underwing

**ADULT**

all-dark underparts

**IN FLIGHT**

long, slender wings

**ADULT**

**ADULT**

all-dark upperparts

sooty head

long, hooked bill

**FLIGHT:** rapid, stiff wingbeats, interspersed with glides; arcs up highly in strong winds.

Sooty Shearwaters are extremely long-distance migrants, with both Atlantic and Pacific populations undergoing lengthy circular migrations. Pacific birds in particular travel as far as 300 miles (480km) per day and an extraordinary 45,000 miles (72,500km) or more per year. Huge flocks of this species are often seen off the coast of California. It is fairly easy to identify off the East Coast of the US, as it is the only all-dark shearwater found there.

**VOICE** Silent at sea; occasionally gives varied, agitated vocalizations when feeding, very loud calls at breeding colonies.
**NESTING** In burrow or rocky crevice; 1 egg; 1 brood; October–May.
**FEEDING** Dives and picks at surface for small schooling fish and mollusks such as squid.

**HUGE FLOCKS**
Sooty Shearwaters are often found in "rafts" numbering many thousands of birds.

**TUBENOSE**
Shearwaters are tubenoses, so-called for the salt-excreting tubes on their bills.

### SIMILAR SPECIES

**SHORT-TAILED SHEARWATER** see p.173

dark upperparts

**GREAT SHEARWATER**

dark cap

white tail band

shorter bill

pale throat

white collar

**OCCURRENCE**
Sooty Shearwaters breed on islands in the southern ocean and nearby waters, some colonies numbering thousands of pairs. Postbreeding movements take them north into the Pacific and Atlantic Ocean, on 8-shaped migrations.

| Length **18in (46cm)** | Wingspan **3ft 3in (1m)** | Weight **27oz (775g)** |
|---|---|---|
| Social **Flocks** | Lifespan **Unknown** | Status **Secure** |

| DATE SEEN | WHERE | NOTES |
|---|---|---|
| | | |
| | | |
| | | |
| | | |
| | | |

# FRIGATEBIRDS, GANNETS, CORMORANTS, AND ANHINGAS

## FRIGATEBIRDS
Frigatebirds are large seabirds characterized by very long, angular wings, lengthy, deeply forked tails, and extended, sturdy, and sharply hooked bills. Although they feed over the ocean, catching flying fish or forcing other birds to disgorge food, frigatebirds have neither fully webbed feet nor thoroughly waterproof plumage, so they rarely settle on water.

## GANNETS AND BOOBIES
Gannets, and the related boobies of the tropics, have pointed bills, long wings, and fully webbed toes. Their eyes face well forward and air sacs beneath the skin of the head and neck provide protection when they dive headlong from the air to catch fish. They breed in large colonies—gannets on cliffs and islands, and boobies also in trees.

## CORMORANTS AND ANHINGAS
The birds in this group also have four fully webbed toes. Their long, angular wings resemble those of gannets but are less pointed. Cormorants, which

have slightly hooked bills, comprise both marine and freshwater species. Anhingas, or darters, are also known as "snakebirds," which describes them well as they swim with their bodies submerged and heads raised. Their heads are barely wider than their necks, and their bills are long and pointed, giving them a snake-like appearance.

**WING SPREADING**
For this Neotropic Cormorant grooming includes spreading its wings to dry them in the sun. Neotropic Cormorants are rare in the West.

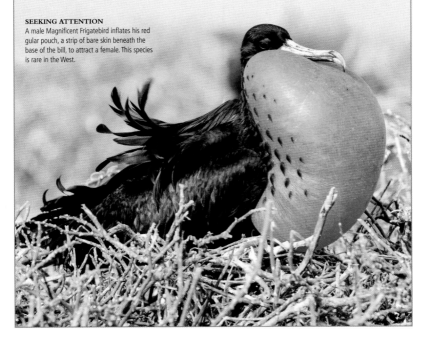

**SEEKING ATTENTION**
A male Magnificent Frigatebird inflates his red gular pouch, a strip of bare skin beneath the base of the bill, to attract a female. This species is rare in the West.

| Order **Suliformes** | Family **Phalacrocoracidae** | Species *Phalacrocorax penicillatus* |

# Brandt's Cormorant

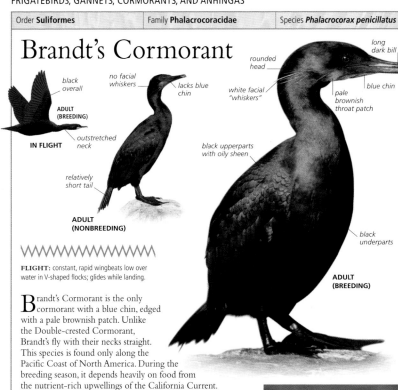

**ADULT (BREEDING)**

**IN FLIGHT**

black overall

outstretched neck

no facial whiskers

lacks blue chin

relatively short tail

**ADULT (NONBREEDING)**

long dark bill

rounded head

white facial "whiskers"

blue chin

pale brownish throat patch

black upperparts with oily sheen

black underparts

**ADULT (BREEDING)**

**FLIGHT:** constant, rapid wingbeats low over water in V-shaped flocks; glides while landing.

Brandt's Cormorant is the only cormorant with a blue chin, edged with a pale brownish patch. Unlike the Double-crested Cormorant, Brandt's fly with their necks straight. This species is found only along the Pacific Coast of North America. During the breeding season, it depends heavily on food from the nutrient-rich upwellings of the California Current. Named after a German who was the director of the zoological museum in St. Petersburg, Russia, this species is at risk from commercial fishing, pollution, and recreational disturbance.

**VOICE** Emits croaks, growls, gargles and coughing sounds.

**NESTING** Circular, drum-shaped nest of grass, moss, weeds, seaweed, sticks, and trash, on gentle slopes of islands or ledges on cliffs; 1–6 eggs; 1 brood; April–August.

**FEEDING** Dives and chases after surface- and bottom-dwelling fish; grasps fish in bill, crushes it, and swallows it head-first.

**DRYING OUT**
Like all cormorants, this species stretches its wings to drain its soggy feathers after diving for fish.

### SIMILAR SPECIES

**DOUBLE-CRESTED CORMORANT**
see p.177

lighter colored overall

large yellow or orange throat pouch

**PELAGIC CORMORANT**
see p.178

slender neck

very thin bill

**OCCURRENCE**
Breeding colonies are found on offshore or near-shore islands or on mainland promontories on the Pacific Coast of North America; occasionally found in inshore lagoons; winters in sheltered inlets and other protected waters or on open ocean within 1 mile (1.6km) of land.

| Length **28–31in (70–79cm)** | Wingspan **3½ft (1.1m)** | Weight **3–6lb (1.4–2.7kg)** |
| Social **Flocks/Colonies** | Lifespan **Up to 18 years** | Status **Secure** |

| DATE SEEN | WHERE | NOTES |
|-----------|-------|-------|
| | | |
| | | |
| | | |
| | | |
| | | |

| Order **Suliformes** | Family **Phalacrocoracidae** | Species *Phalacrocorax auritus* |

# Double-crested Cormorant

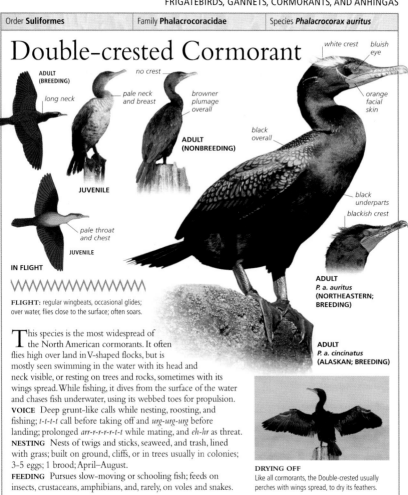

white crest

bluish eye

orange facial skin

**ADULT (BREEDING)**

long neck

no crest

pale neck and breast

browner plumage overall

black overall

**ADULT (NONBREEDING)**

**JUVENILE**

black underparts

blackish crest

pale throat and chest

**JUVENILE**

**IN FLIGHT**

**FLIGHT:** regular wingbeats, occasional glides; over water, flies close to the surface; often soars.

**ADULT**
*P. a. auritus*
**(NORTHEASTERN; BREEDING)**

**ADULT**
*P. a. cincinatus*
**(ALASKAN; BREEDING)**

This species is the most widespread of the North American cormorants. It often flies high over land in V-shaped flocks, but is mostly seen swimming in the water with its head and neck visible, or resting on trees and rocks, sometimes with its wings spread. While fishing, it dives from the surface of the water and chases fish underwater, using its webbed toes for propulsion.
**VOICE** Deep grunt-like calls while nesting, roosting, and fishing; *t-t-t-t* call before taking off and *urg-urg-urg* before landing; prolonged *arr-r-r-r-r-t-t* while mating, and *eh-hr* as threat.
**NESTING** Nests of twigs and sticks, seaweed, and trash, lined with grass; built on ground, cliffs, or in trees usually in colonies; 3-5 eggs; 1 brood; April–August.
**FEEDING** Pursues slow–moving or schooling fish; feeds on insects, crustaceans, amphibians, and, rarely, on voles and snakes.

**DRYING OFF**
Like all cormorants, the Double-crested usually perches with wings spread, to dry its feathers.

**SIMILAR SPECIES**

**BRANDT'S CORMORANT** see p.176

throat pouch paler and less visible

**NEOTROPIC CORMORANT** see p.440

shorter body

longer tail

**OCCURRENCE**
Breeds in a wide range of aquatic habitats, including ponds, artificial and natural lakes, slow-moving rivers, estuaries, lagoons, and seashores; winters on coastlines and sandbars in coastal inlets; roosts near catfish farms in some areas.

| Length **28–35in (70–90cm)** | Wingspan **3½–4ft (1.1–1.2m)** | Weight **2¾–5½lb (1.2–2.5kg)** |
| Social **Flocks** | Lifespan **Up to 18 years** | Status **Secure** |

| DATE SEEN | WHERE | NOTES |
|---|---|---|
| | | |
| | | |
| | | |
| | | |
| | | |

| Order **Suliformes** | Family **Phalacrocoracidae** | Species *Phalacrocorax pelagicus* |

# Pelagic Cormorant

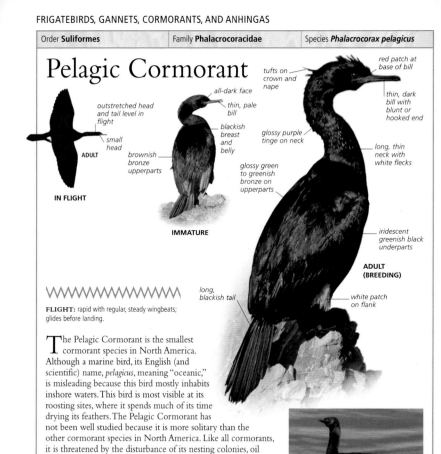

**IN FLIGHT**

outstretched head and tail level in flight

small head

**ADULT**

red patch at base of bill

tufts on crown and nape

all-dark face

thin, pale bill

thin, dark bill with blunt or hooked end

blackish breast and belly

glossy purple tinge on neck

brownish bronze upperparts

**IMMATURE**

glossy green to greenish bronze on upperparts

long, thin neck with white flecks

iridescent greenish black underparts

**ADULT (BREEDING)**

long, blackish tail

white patch on flank

〜〜〜〜〜〜〜〜〜〜〜〜〜〜

**FLIGHT:** rapid with regular, steady wingbeats; glides before landing.

The Pelagic Cormorant is the smallest cormorant species in North America. Although a marine bird, its English (and scientific) name, *pelagicus*, meaning "oceanic," is misleading because this bird mostly inhabits inshore waters. This bird is most visible at its roosting sites, where it spends much of its time drying its feathers. The Pelagic Cormorant has not been well studied because it is more solitary than the other cormorant species in North America. Like all cormorants, it is threatened by the disturbance of its nesting colonies, oil spills, entanglement in fishing nets, and pollution.

**VOICE** Female 2-note call *igh-ugh*, similar to ticking grandfather clock; male call note *purring* or *arr-arr-arr;* both utter croaks, hisses, and low groans.

**NESTING** Saucer-shaped nest of grass, seaweed, sticks, feathers, and marine debris, cemented to cliff face with guano; 3–5 eggs; 1 brood; May–October.

**FEEDING** Dives from water's surface for any medium-sized fish, and also invertebrates, such as shrimps, worms, and hermit crabs.

**SITTING LOW**
Pelagic Cormorants sit low in the water with only their head, neck, and back visible.

**SIMILAR SPECIES**

**BRANDT'S CORMORANT** see p.176

thicker neck

shorter tail

round head

larger overall

**OCCURRENCE**
Found in rocky habitat on outer coast, shallow bays, inlets, estuaries, harbors, and lagoons; nesting colonies found on steep cliffs on forested and grassy islands, and on rocky promontories along the shoreline; also seen on built structures such as wharf pilings, bridges, and harbor buoys.

| Length **20–30in (51–76cm)** | Wingspan **3¼–4ft (1–1.2m)** | Weight **2¾–5¼lb (1.3–2.4kg)** |
| Social **Solitary/Pairs** | Lifespan **Up to 17 years** | Status **Secure** |

| DATE SEEN | WHERE | NOTES |
| --- | --- | --- |
| | | |
| | | |
| | | |
| | | |

# PELICANS, HERONS, IBISES, AND RELATIVES

THESE RELATED WATERBIRDS exploit a diversity of water and waterside habitats in different ways, from plunge-diving in the ocean to wading at the edge of mangroves and freshwater swamps, from scooping up fish to stealthy and patient hunting from overhanging branches.

## PELICANS
Pelicans are large fish-eating birds, bulky but buoyant on water. Brown Pelicans dive head first to catch fish, while White Pelicans work together to herd fish into shallow bays, and scoop them up in flexible pouches beneath their long bills.

## HERONS, EGRETS, AND BITTERNS
These waterside birds have long toes, which enable them to walk on wet mud and wade among reed stems. Their long toes also aid their balance as they lean forward in search of fish and when catching prey in their long, pointed bills. Herons and egrets have slender, feathered necks with a distinct kink that gives a lightning forward thrust when catching prey. Most herons and egrets make bulky nests in treetop colonies, whereas bitterns nest on the ground in marshes. Unlike storks and cranes, they all fly with their heads withdrawn into their shoulders.

**EVER ALERT**
The Green Heron catches fish by waiting and watching patiently until prey is near.

## IBISES AND SPOONBILL
Ibises and the related spoonbill are long-legged, waterside or dry-land birds. Ibises have long, decurved bills that are adapted to picking insects, worms, small mollusks, and crustaceans from wet mud. Spoonbills have a unique flat, spatula-shaped bill that they sweep from side to side in shallow water to catch aquatic prey.

**WATER BIRD**
Webbed toes help the Brown Pelican negotiate water with ease, while strong wings allow easy takeoffs.

| Order **Pelecaniformes** | Family **Pelecanidae** | Species *Pelecanus erythrorhynchos* |

# American White Pelican

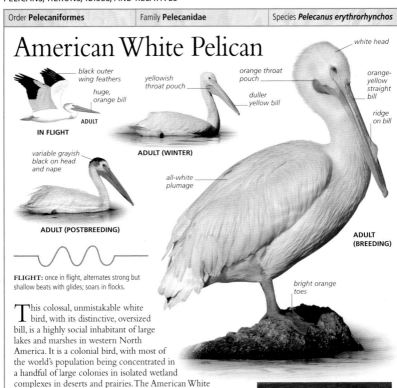

black outer wing feathers

huge, orange bill

**ADULT**

**IN FLIGHT**

yellowish throat pouch

duller yellow bill

**ADULT (WINTER)**

variable grayish black on head and nape

all-white plumage

**ADULT (POSTBREEDING)**

white head

orange throat pouch

orange-yellow straight bill

ridge on bill

**ADULT (BREEDING)**

bright orange toes

**FLIGHT:** once in flight, alternates strong but shallow beats with glides; soars in flocks.

This colossal, unmistakable white bird, with its distinctive, oversized bill, is a highly social inhabitant of large lakes and marshes in western North America. It is a colonial bird, with most of the world's population being concentrated in a handful of large colonies in isolated wetland complexes in deserts and prairies. The American White Pelican forms foraging flocks, which beat their wings in coordinated movements to drive fish into shallow water, where they can be caught more easily.

**VOICE** Usually silent except around nesting colonies; around the nest, young and adults exchange various grunts and hisses.

**NESTING** Depression in the ground, both sexes incubate; 1–2 eggs; 1 brood; April–August.

**FEEDING** Mainly gulps down small fish, occasionally eats small amphibians, and crayfish.

**LARGE COLONIES**
The White Pelican is highly social and is usually seen feeding or roosting in large groups.

**SIMILAR SPECIES**

**WOOD STORK** see p.470

bare head

long thin legs

**BROWN PELICAN** see p.181

gray bill

curved bill

dark underparts

**OCCURRENCE**
Breeds on islands in freshwater lakes in south-central Canada, intermontane areas of the western US, and in coastal northeastern Mexico; an early spring migrant, often returning to breeding grounds in early March. Winters in coastal regions from California and Texas to Mexico and Central America.

| Length  4¼–5½ft (1.3–1.7m) | Wingspan  7¾–9½ft (2.4–2.9m) | Weight  12–20lb (5.5–9kg) |
| Social  **Colonies** | Lifespan  **Up to 26 years** | Status  **Vulnerable** |

| DATE SEEN | WHERE | NOTES |
| --- | --- | --- |
| | | |
| | | |
| | | |
| | | |
| | | |

| Order **Pelecaniformes** | Family **Pelecanidae** | Species *Pelecanus occidentalis* |

# Brown Pelican

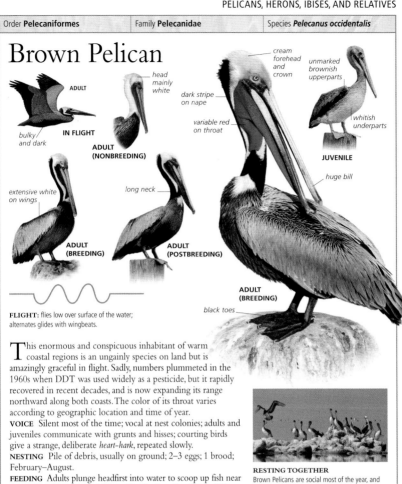

**ADULT**

**IN FLIGHT**

bulky and dark

head mainly white

**ADULT (NONBREEDING)**

dark stripe on nape

variable red on throat

cream forehead and crown

unmarked brownish upperparts

whitish underparts

**JUVENILE**

huge bill

extensive white on wings

**ADULT (BREEDING)**

long neck

**ADULT (POSTBREEDING)**

**ADULT (BREEDING)**

black toes

**ADULT (BREEDING)**

**FLIGHT:** flies low over surface of the water; alternates glides with wingbeats.

This enormous and conspicuous inhabitant of warm coastal regions is an ungainly species on land but is amazingly graceful in flight. Sadly, numbers plummeted in the 1960s when DDT was used widely as a pesticide, but it rapidly recovered in recent decades, and is now expanding its range northward along both coasts. The color of its throat varies according to geographic location and time of year.

**VOICE** Silent most of the time; vocal at nest colonies; adults and juveniles communicate with grunts and hisses; courting birds give a strange, deliberate *heart-hark*, repeated slowly.

**NESTING** Pile of debris, usually on ground; 2–3 eggs; 1 brood; February–August.

**FEEDING** Adults plunge headfirst into water to scoop up fish near the surface; does not herd fish, unlike the American White Pelican.

**RESTING TOGETHER**
Brown Pelicans are social most of the year, and can often be seen roosting in groups.

### SIMILAR SPECIES

**BLACK-FOOTED ALBATROSS** see p.438

short bill

long, pointed wings

**AMERICAN WHITE PELICAN** see p.180

white plumage

orange bill

**OCCURRENCE**
Found in and around warm coastal waters, flying above the water's surface over the cresting waves; small numbers breed in the interior US; individuals and small flocks can be found around docks and marinas.

| Length **4–4¼ft (1.2–1.3m)** | Wingspan **6½–7ft (2–2.1m)** | Weight **4–8¾lb (1.8–4kg)** |
| Social **Colonies** | Lifespan **Up to 10 years** | Status **Secure** |

| DATE SEEN | WHERE | NOTES |
| --- | --- | --- |
| | | |
| | | |
| | | |
| | | |

| Order **Pelecaniformes** | Family **Ardeidae** | Species ***Botaurus lentiginosus*** |

# American Bittern

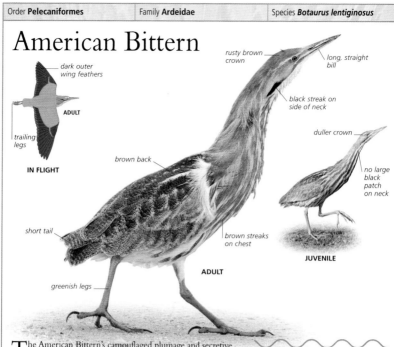

*dark outer wing feathers*

**ADULT**

*trailing legs*

**IN FLIGHT**

*rusty brown crown*

*long, straight bill*

*black streak on side of neck*

*duller crown*

*no large black patch on neck*

*brown back*

**JUVENILE**

*short tail*

*brown streaks on chest*

**ADULT**

*greenish legs*

The American Bittern's camouflaged plumage and secretive behavior help it to blend into the thick vegetation of its freshwater wetland habitat. It is heard much more often than it is seen; its call is unmistakable and has given rise to many evocative colloquial names, such as "thunder pumper."

**FLIGHT:** steady, deep, slightly stiff wingbeats; usually flies relatively low and direct.

**VOICE** Deep, resonant *pump-er-unk, pump-er-unk*; calls mainly at dawn, dusk, and nighttime, but also during the day in the early mating season.

**NESTING** Platform or mound constructed of available marsh vegetation, usually over shallow water; 2–7 eggs; 1 brood; April–August.

**FEEDING** Stands still or moves slowly, then strikes downward with bill to catch prey; eats fish, insects, crustaceans, snakes, amphibians, and small mammals.

**LOOKING UP**
Bitterns are secretive birds, but can occasionally be found walking slowly through reeds.

**OCCURRENCE**
Breeds in heavily vegetated freshwater wetlands across the northern US and southern Canada; also occasionally in estuarine wetlands; winters in southern and coastal wetlands where temperatures stay above freezing; can appear in any wetland habitat during migration.

**SIMILAR SPECIES**

**LEAST BITTERN**
see p.439
*black back*
*smaller overall*
*yellowish legs*

**BLACK-CROWNED NIGHT-HERON** ☾
see p.188
*white spots*
*thicker bill*

| Length **23½–31in (60–80cm)** | Wingspan **3½–4¼ft (1.1–1.3m)** | Weight **13–20oz (375–575g)** |
| Social **Solitary** | Lifespan **At least 8 years** | Status **Declining** |

| DATE SEEN | WHERE | | NOTES |
| --- | --- | --- | --- |
| | | | |
| | | | |
| | | | |
| | | | |
| | | | |

| Order **Pelecaniformes** | Family **Ardeidae** | Species *Ardea herodias* |

# Great Blue Heron 🔊

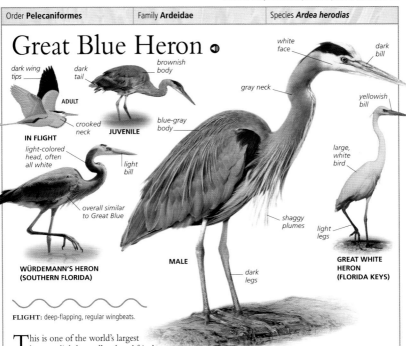

**white face**

**dark bill**

**gray neck**

**yellowish bill**

**dark wing tips**

**dark tail**

**brownish body**

**ADULT**

**crooked neck**

**blue-gray body**

**JUVENILE**

**IN FLIGHT**

**light-colored head, often all white**

**light bill**

**overall similar to Great Blue**

**large, white bird**

**shaggy plumes**

**light legs**

**WÜRDEMANN'S HERON (SOUTHERN FLORIDA)**

**MALE**

**dark legs**

**GREAT WHITE HERON (FLORIDA KEYS)**

**FLIGHT:** deep-flapping, regular wingbeats.

This is one of the world's largest herons, slightly smaller than Africa's Goliath Heron but of similar stature to the more closely related Gray Heron of Eurasia and Cocoi Heron of South America. The Great Blue Heron is a common inhabitant of a variety of North American waterbodies, from marshes to swamps, as well as along sea coasts. Its majestic, deliberate flight is wonderful to behold.

**VOICE** Mostly silent; gives a loud, barking squawk or *crank* in breeding colonies or when disturbed.

**NESTING** Nest of twigs and branches; usually in colonies, but also singly; in trees, often over water, but also over ground; 2–4 eggs; 1–2 broods; February–August.

**FEEDING** Catches prey with quick jab of bill; primarily fish.

**LOFTY ABODE**
Great Blue Herons nest in small colonies in trees, and often roost in them.

### SIMILAR SPECIES

**TRICOLORED HERON**
see p.471
smaller overall

**dark bill**

**white underparts**

**LITTLE BLUE HERON**
smaller overall;
see p.471

**greenish legs**

**darker overall**

**OCCURRENCE**
Across southern Canada and the US in wetlands, such as marshes, lake edges, and along rivers and swamps; also in marine habitats, especially tidal grass flats. The Great White Heron is common in mangroves in the Florida Keys; also West Indies and Yucatán.

| Length 2¾–4¼ft (0.9–1.3m) | Wingspan 5¼–6½ft (1.6–2m) | Weight 4¾–5½lb (2.1–2.5kg) |
| Social **Solitary/Flocks** | Lifespan **Up to 20 years** | Status **Secure** |

| DATE SEEN | WHERE | NOTES |
| --- | --- | --- |
| | | |
| | | |
| | | |
| | | |
| | | |

| Order **Pelecaniformes** | Family **Ardeidae** | Species ***Ardea alba*** |

# Great Egret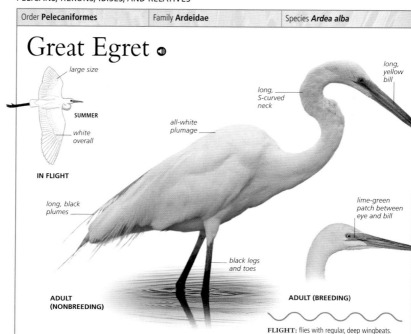

large size

**SUMMER**

white overall

**IN FLIGHT**

long, S-curved neck

long, yellow bill

all-white plumage

long, black plumes

lime-green patch between eye and bill

black legs and toes

**ADULT (NONBREEDING)**

**ADULT (BREEDING)**

**FLIGHT:** flies with regular, deep wingbeats.

This large white heron is found on every continent except Antarctica. When feeding, the Great Egret would apparently rather forage alone than in flocks—it maintains space around itself, and will defend a territory of 10ft (3m) in diameter from other wading birds. This territory "moves" with the bird as it feeds. In years of scarce food supplies, a chick may kill a sibling, permitting the survival of at least one bird.

**VOICE** Largely vocal during courtship and breeding; otherwise, *kraak* or *cuk-cuk-cuk* when disturbed or in a combative encounter.

**NESTING** Nest of twigs in trees, over land or water; 2–4 eggs; 1 brood; March–July.

**FEEDING** Catches prey with quick thrust of bill; feeds on aquatic prey, primarily fish, also crustaceans.

**TREE PERCHES**
Great Egrets nest in trees and regularly perch in them when not feeding.

### SIMILAR SPECIES

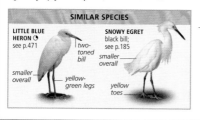

**LITTLE BLUE HERON** ♀
see p.471

two-toned bill

smaller overall

yellow-green legs

**SNOWY EGRET**
black bill;
see p.185

smaller overall

yellow toes

**OCCURRENCE**
Breeds in trees over water or on islands; forages in almost all types of freshwater and marine wetlands from marshes and ponds to rivers. Migratory over much of its North American range; more southerly populations resident. Distance migrated depends on severity of winter.

| Length **3¼ft (1m)** | Wingspan **6ft (1.8m)** | Weight **1¾–3¼ft (0.8–1.5kg)** |
| Social **Solitary** | Lifespan **Up to 25 years** | Status **Secure** |

| DATE SEEN | WHERE | NOTES |
|---|---|---|
| | | |
| | | |
| | | |
| | | |

| Order **Pelecaniformes** | Family **Ardeidae** | Species *Egretta thula* |

# Snowy Egret

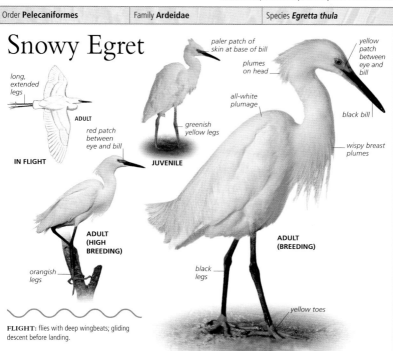

long, extended legs

**ADULT**

**IN FLIGHT**

paler patch of skin at base of bill

plumes on head

all-white plumage

red patch between eye and bill

greenish yellow legs

**JUVENILE**

yellow patch between eye and bill

black bill

wispy breast plumes

**ADULT (HIGH BREEDING)**

orangish legs

**ADULT (BREEDING)**

black legs

yellow toes

**FLIGHT:** flies with deep wingbeats; gliding descent before landing.

A New World species, the Snowy Egret is similar to an Old Word species, the Little Egret. It is very adaptable in estuarine and freshwater habitats. When foraging, it uses a wide variety of behaviors, including wing-flicking, foot-stirring, and foot-probing to get its prey moving, making it easier to capture.

**VOICE** High-pitched *Aargaarg* when flushed; low-pitched *Arg* and *Raah* aggressive calls; *Aarg* call during attacks and pursuits.

**NESTING** Small sticks, branches, and rushes over water or on land; also on ground, in shrubs, mangroves, and other trees; 3–5 eggs; 1 brood; March–August.

**FEEDING** Feeds on aquatic prey, from invertebrates, such as insects, shrimp, and prawns, to small fish, amphibians, and snakes.

**WIDESPREAD SPECIES**
Snowy Egrets feed in a wide variety of wetland habitats, using different foraging techniques.

**SIMILAR SPECIES**

**GREAT EGRET** see p.184

yellow bill

black legs and toes

**LITTLE BLUE HERON** see p.471

black legs and toes

**OCCURRENCE**
Found in a wide variety of wetlands throughout North and South America: from mangroves in Florida to marshlands in New England and the western US. Highly adaptable and widely found. Sites of breeding colonies may change from year to year within a set range.

| Length **24in (62cm)** | Wingspan **3½ft (1.1m)** | Weight **12oz (350g)** |
| Social **Solitary** | Lifespan **Up to 22 years** | Status **Declining** |

| DATE SEEN | WHERE | NOTES |
|-----------|-------|-------|
| ........... | ........... | ........... |
| ........... | ........... | ........... |
| ........... | ........... | ........... |
| ........... | ........... | ........... |
| ........... | ........... | ........... |

| Order **Pelecaniformes** | Family **Ardeidae** | Species ***Bubulcus ibis*** |
|---|---|---|

# Cattle Egret

rich buff on back

**ADULT (BREEDING)**

**IN FLIGHT**

all-white body

yellow bill

**ADULT (NONBREEDING)**

rich buff crown

yellow bill, reddish in spring

short neck

white body and wings

rich buff on breast in spring

**ADULT (BREEDING)**

looks all-white in flight at long range

dark legs and toes

**ADULT (BREEDING)**

yellow legs and toes

**FLIGHT:** flies with regular wingbeats; neck crooked and legs extended.

Unlike most other herons, the Cattle Egret is a grassland species that rarely wades in water, and is most likely to be seen in association with livestock, feeding on the insects disturbed by their feet. It is thought to have originated in the savannas of Africa and is now found worldwide. It was first seen in Florida in 1941, but expanded rapidly and has now bred in more than 40 US states.

**VOICE** Generally silent; vocal at the nest: *rick-rack* common.

**NESTING** Nest of branches or plants placed in trees over ground; also in trees or shrubs over water; 2–5 eggs; 1 brood; March–October.

**FEEDING** Eats in groups, consumes insects, spiders as well as larger animals such as frogs; insects stirred up in grasslands by cattle.

**VOCAL BREEDERS**
This bird almost never calls away from a breeding colony, but is vocal near its nests.

### SIMILAR SPECIES

**GREAT EGRET**
see p.184

much larger

long bill

black legs and toes

**SNOWY EGRET**
see p.185

black bill

yellow toes

**OCCURRENCE**
Since the 1940s, it has expanded to many habitats in much of North America, primarily in grasslands and prairies, but also wetland areas. In tropical regions, the Cattle Egrets flock around the cattle feeding in shallow wetlands.

| Length **20in (51cm)** | Wingspan **31in (78cm)** | Weight **13oz (375g)** |
|---|---|---|
| Social **Colonies** | Lifespan **Up to 17 years** | Status **Secure** |

| DATE SEEN | WHERE | NOTES |
|---|---|---|
| .................... | .................... | .................... |
| .................... | .................... | .................... |
| .................... | .................... | .................... |
| .................... | .................... | .................... |
| .................... | .................... | .................... |

Order **Pelecaniformes** | Family **Ardeidae** | Species *Butorides virescens*

# Green Heron 🔊

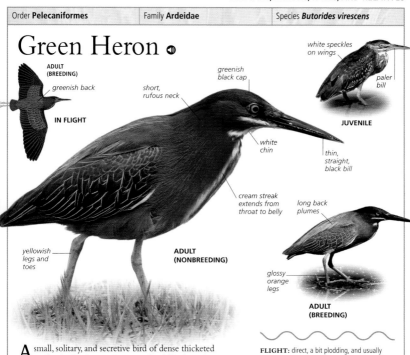

**ADULT (BREEDING)**

greenish back

**IN FLIGHT**

greenish black cap

short, rufous neck

white chin

cream streak extends from throat to belly

yellowish legs and toes

**ADULT (NONBREEDING)**

white speckles on wings

paler bill

**JUVENILE**

thin, straight, black bill

long back plumes

glossy orange legs

**ADULT (BREEDING)**

A small, solitary, and secretive bird of dense thicketed wetlands, the Green Heron can be difficult to observe. This dark, crested heron is most often seen flying away from a perceived threat, emitting a loud squawk. While the Green Heron of North and Central America has now been recognized as a separate species, it was earlier grouped with what is now the Striated Heron (*B. striata*), which is found in the tropics and subtropics throughout the world.

**VOICE** Squawking *keow* when flying from disturbance.
**NESTING** Nest of twigs often in bushes or trees, often over water but also on land; 1–2 broods; 3–5 eggs; March–July.
**FEEDING** Stands quietly on the shore or in shallow water and strikes quickly; mainly fish, but also frogs, insects, and spiders.

**FLIGHT:** direct, a bit plodding, and usually over short distances.

**READY TO STRIKE**
Green Herons usually catch their prey by lunging forward and downward with their whole body.

**SIMILAR SPECIES**

**BLACK-CROWNED NIGHT-HERON** 🔊
see p.188
larger overall

**YELLOW-CROWNED NIGHT-HERON** 🔊
see p.471
thicker bill
larger overall

**OCCURRENCE**
An inhabitant of swampy thickets, but occasionally dry land close to water across much of North America, but missing in the plains, the Rocky Mountains, and the western deserts that do not provide appropriate wetlands. Winters in coastal wetlands.

Length **14½–15½ in (37–39cm)** | Wingspan **25–27in (63–68cm)** | Weight **7–9oz (200–250g)**
Social **Solitary/Pairs/Small flocks** | Lifespan **Up to 10 years** | Status **Secure**

| DATE SEEN | WHERE | NOTES |
|---|---|---|
| | | |
| | | |
| | | |
| | | |
| | | |

| Order **Pelecaniformes** | Family **Ardeidae** | Species *Nycticorax nycticorax* |

# Black-crowned Night-Heron

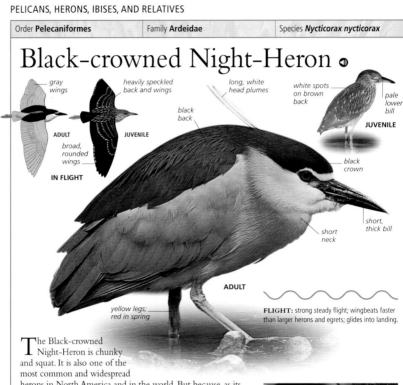

gray wings

heavily speckled back and wings

long, white head plumes

white spots on brown back

pale lower bill

**JUVENILE**

black back

**ADULT**          **JUVENILE**

broad, rounded wings

**IN FLIGHT**

black crown

short, thick bill

short neck

**ADULT**

yellow legs; red in spring

**FLIGHT:** strong steady flight; wingbeats faster than larger herons and egrets; glides into landing.

The Black-crowned Night-Heron is chunky and squat. It is also one of the most common and widespread herons in North America and in the world. But because, as its name suggests, it is mainly active at twilight and at night, many people have never seen one. However, its distinctive barking call can be heard at night—even at the center of large cities.

**VOICE** Loud, distinctive *quark* or *wok*, often given in flight and around colonies.

**NESTING** Large stick nests built usually 20–40ft (6–12m) up in trees; 3–5 eggs; 1 brood; November–August.

**FEEDING** Feeds primarily on aquatic animals, such as fish, crustaceans, insects, and mollusks; also eggs and chicks of colonial birds, such as egrets, ibises, and terns.

**LONG PLUMES**
In breeding plumage, the plumes of the male of this species are longer than the female's.

**SIMILAR SPECIES**

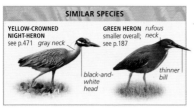

**YELLOW-CROWNED NIGHT-HERON**
see p.471   gray neck

black-and-white head

**GREEN HERON** *rufous neck*
smaller overall;
see p.187

thinner bill

**OCCURRENCE**
Widespread; can be found wherever there are waterbodies, such as lakes, ponds, streams; generally absent from higher elevations. Colonies often on islands or in marshes; colony sites may be used for decades. In winter, found in areas where water remains open.

| Length **23–26in (58–65cm)** | Wingspan **3½–4ft (1.1–1.2m)** | Weight **1½–2½lb (0.7–1kg)** |
| Social **Colonies** | Lifespan **Up to 21 years** | Status **Secure** |

| DATE SEEN | WHERE | NOTES |
|---|---|---|
| | | |
| | | |
| | | |
| | | |
| | | |

| Order **Pelecaniformes** | Family **Threskiornithidae** | Species *Plegadis chihi* |

# White-faced Ibis

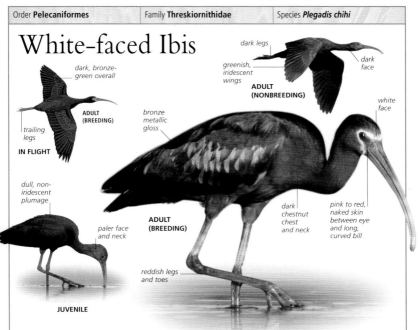

dark, bronze-green overall

**ADULT (BREEDING)**

trailing legs

**IN FLIGHT**

dark legs

greenish, iridescent wings

**ADULT (NONBREEDING)**

dark face

white face

bronze metallic gloss

dull, non-iridescent plumage

paler face and neck

**ADULT (BREEDING)**

dark chestnut chest and neck

pink to red, naked skin between eye and long, curved bill

reddish legs and toes

**JUVENILE**

The White-faced Ibis is not only the most widespread member of its family in North America but also the only ibis found commonly in its range. Very similar to the closely related Glossy Ibis, it is separable in winter only by its reddish eye and the absence of a thin blue line around the face, though the two are only likely to be seen together in the Louisiana area.

**VOICE** Generally silent; soft calls at the nest, including feeding calls, vocalizations after mating, and greeting calls to mates and chicks; outside breeding, a raucous *khah* or *krah*.

**NESTING** Flat or columnar nest lined with plant matter, such as cattail, or bulrush in low trees or shrubs over shallow water, or on ground on small islands; 2–5 eggs; 1 brood; May–July.

**FEEDING** Captures prey below soil by probing with bill; eats aquatic prey such as crayfish, small fish, and frogs.

**FLIGHT:** strong and direct, with rapid wingbeats, alternating with glides; soars on thermals.

**LARGE FLOCKS**
The White-faced Ibis is social, feeding and traveling in flocks, which can be large.

**OCCURRENCE**
Found in freshwater wetlands, especially in flooded fields, marshes, and lake edges with cattails and bulrushes. Although birds may disperse farther east after breeding, they are, for the most part, restricted to the western part of the United States, and in Central and South America.

| SIMILAR SPECIES | |
|---|---|
| **GLOSSY IBIS** see p.471 | **BLACK-CROWNED NIGHT-HERON** ◐ see p.188 |

less white on face

darker legs

brown, streaked body

thick, straight bill

| Length **23in (59cm)** | Wingspan **36in (92cm)** | Weight **22oz (625g)** |
| Social **Flocks/Colonies** | Lifespan **Up to 14 years** | Status **Secure** |

| DATE SEEN | WHERE | NOTES |
|---|---|---|
| | | |
| | | |
| | | |
| | | |
| | | |

# NEW WORLD VULTURES

NEW WORLD VULTURES are not related to Old World vultures, although they look somewhat similar, having long, broad wings with "fingered" tips. Their heads and necks are more or less bare, which helps prevent meat and bacteria from collecting in their feathers when they feed on carcasses. Their bills are large and hooked, to tear flesh, but their feet are unspecialized, with short claws, and not used for capturing prey. All the birds in this group have exceptional eyesight and find their food by sight while soaring high over open ground. The Turkey Vulture, a common sight in many areas, also has a keen sense of smell and can even find dead animals inside woodland. The largest species in this group is the California Condor, a scavenger that was recently on the verge of extinction, before conservation efforts turned things around.

**WEAK TOOL**
In spite of its sharp bill, the Turkey Vulture cannot always break the skin of carcasses.

# HAWKS, EAGLES, AND RELATIVES

THESE DIURNAL BIRDS OF prey include several loosely related groups. All have hooked bills and large eyes, but their shapes and lifestyles are varied.

### OSPREY
The sole member of the Pandionidae family, the Osprey catches fish in a headlong dive from a hover. It has long, curved claws and toes equipped with sharp scales to give extra grip.

### HAWKS, KITES, AND EAGLES
The Accipitridae family covers a range of raptors with much variation in shape, size, and habitat. Graceful, long-winged kites and harriers are medium-sized birds that feed in open spaces or over marshes. Huge, powerful eagles of mountains and open country have long, broad wings and feathered legs. "Sea-eagles" such as the Bald Eagle have massive bills and long wings but very short tails and bare legs. Sea-eagles feed on fish as well as birds, mammals, and carrion. Bird-eating hawks (in the genus *Accipiter*) have rounded wings and slender tails and long claws for catching prey with their feet. Other hawks (in the genus *Buteo*) are more like small eagles, with small but powerful bills. Some are more widespread than eagles, and are found in a broader range of habitats.

**DOUBLE SHOT**
With lots of fish running in a tight school, this Osprey has the strength and skill to catch two with one dive.

| Order **Cathartiformes** | Family **Cathartidae** | Species **Cathartes aura** |
| --- | --- | --- |

# Turkey Vulture

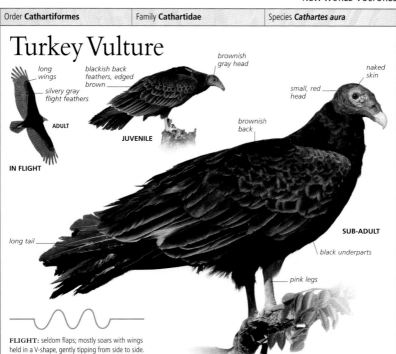

brownish gray head

long wings

blackish back feathers, edged brown

silvery gray flight feathers

**ADULT**

**JUVENILE**

naked skin

small, red head

brownish back

**IN FLIGHT**

long tail

**SUB-ADULT**

black underparts

pink legs

**FLIGHT:** seldom flaps; mostly soars with wings held in a V-shape, gently tipping from side to side.

The most widely distributed vulture in North America, the Turkey Vulture is found in most of the US and has expanded its range into southern Canada. It possesses a better sense of smell than the Black Vulture, which often follows it and displaces it from carcasses. The Turkey Vulture's habit of defecating down its legs, which it shares with the Wood Stork, may serve to cool it or to kill bacteria with its ammonia content.

**VOICE** Silent, but will hiss at intruders; also grunts.

**NESTING** Dark recesses, such as under large rocks or stumps, on rocky ledges in caves, and crevices, in mammal burrows and hollow logs, and abandoned buildings; 1–3 eggs; 1 brood; March–August.

**FEEDING** Feeds on a wide range of wild and domestic carrion, mostly mammals, but also birds, reptiles, amphibians, and fish; occasionally takes live prey such as nestlings or trapped birds.

**SOAKING UP THE SUN**
Turkey Vultures often spread their wings to sun themselves and increase their body temperature.

**SIMILAR SPECIES**

**BLACK VULTURE** see p.440

shorter tail

all-black body

**OCCURRENCE**
Generally forages and migrates over mixed farmland and forest; prefers to nest in forested or partly forested hillsides; roosts in large trees on rocky outcrops, and on power line transmission towers; some winter in urban areas and near landfills. Also widespread in the Caribbean, and in Central and South America.

| Length **25–32in (64–81cm)** | Wingspan **5½–6ft (1.7–1.8m)** | Weight **4½lb (2kg)** |
| --- | --- | --- |
| Social **Flocks** | Lifespan **At least 17 years** | Status **Secure** |

| DATE SEEN | WHERE | NOTES |
| --- | --- | --- |
| | | |
| | | |
| | | |
| | | |
| | | |

| Order **Accipitriformes** | Family **Pandionidae** | Species **Pandion haliaetus** |
|---|---|---|

# Osprey 🔊

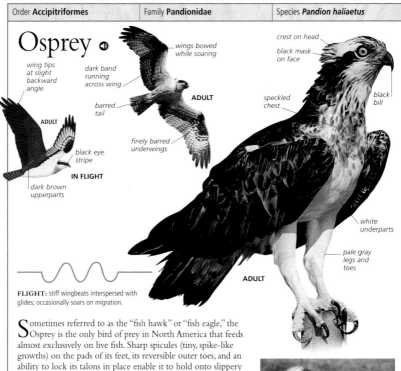

wing tips at slight backward angle

dark band running across wing

wings bowed while soaring

barred tail

**ADULT**

crest on head

black mask on face

speckled chest

black bill

**ADULT**

black eye stripe

finely barred underwings

**IN FLIGHT**

dark brown upperparts

white underparts

pale gray legs and toes

**ADULT**

**FLIGHT:** stiff wingbeats interspersed with glides; occasionally soars on migration.

Sometimes referred to as the "fish hawk" or "fish eagle," the Osprey is the only bird of prey in North America that feeds almost exclusively on live fish. Sharp spicules (tiny, spike-like growths) on the pads of its feet, its reversible outer toes, and an ability to lock its talons in place enable it to hold onto slippery fish. Some populations declined between the 1950s and 1980s due to the use of dangerous pesticides. However, the ban on use of these chemicals, along with availability of artificial nest sites and a tolerance of nearby human activity has allowed the Osprey to return to its former numbers. It is Nova Scotia's official bird.

**VOICE** Slow, whistled notes, falling in pitch: *tiooop, tioooop, tiooop;* also screams by displaying male.

**NESTING** Twig nest on tree, cliff, rock pinnacles, boulders, ground; 1–4 eggs; 1 brood; March–August.

**FEEDING** Dives to catch fish up to top 3ft (90cm) of water.

**IMPROVING AERODYNAMICS**
Once caught, a fish is held with its head pointing forward reducing drag as the bird flies.

## SIMILAR SPECIES

**BALD EAGLE (2ND YEAR)** see p.199

**GOLDEN EAGLE** see p.194

dark brown head

no crook in wings during flight

paler tail

brown, feathered legs

**OCCURRENCE**
Breeds in a wide variety of habitats: northern forests, near shallow reservoirs, along freshwater rivers and large lakes, estuaries and saltmarshes, coastal deserts and desert saltflat lagoons. Migrates through and winters in similar habitats.

| Length **21–23in (53–58cm)** | Wingspan **5–6ft (1.5–1.8m)** | Weight **3–4½lb (1.4–2kg)** |
|---|---|---|
| Social **Solitary/Pairs** | Lifespan **Up to 25 years** | Status **Secure** |

| DATE SEEN | WHERE | NOTES |
|---|---|---|
| .................. | .................. | .................. |
| .................. | .................. | .................. |
| .................. | .................. | .................. |
| .................. | .................. | .................. |
| .................. | .................. | .................. |

| Order **Accipitriformes** | Family **Accipitridae** | Species ***Elanus leucurus*** |

# White-tailed Kite

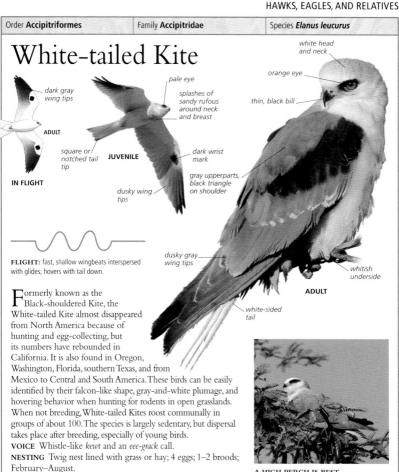

white head and neck

orange eye

thin, black bill

dark gray wing tips

**ADULT**

pale eye

splashes of sandy rufous around neck and breast

square or notched tail tip

**JUVENILE**

**IN FLIGHT**

dark wrist mark

dusky wing tips

gray upperparts, black triangle on shoulder

dusky gray wing tips

**FLIGHT:** fast, shallow wingbeats interspersed with glides; hovers with tail down.

white-sided tail

whitish underside

**ADULT**

Formerly known as the Black-shouldered Kite, the White-tailed Kite almost disappeared from North America because of hunting and egg-collecting, but its numbers have rebounded in California. It is also found in Oregon, Washington, Florida, southern Texas, and from Mexico to Central and South America. These birds can be easily identified by their falcon-like shape, gray-and-white plumage, and hovering behavior when hunting for rodents in open grasslands. When not breeding, White-tailed Kites roost communally in groups of about 100. The species is largely sedentary, but dispersal takes place after breeding, especially of young birds.

**VOICE** Whistle-like *kewt* and an *eee-grack* call.

**NESTING** Twig nest lined with grass or hay; 4 eggs; 1–2 broods; February–August.

**FEEDING** Captures rodents such as voles and field mice; also birds, lizards, and insects from a hovering position.

**A HIGH PERCH IS BEST**
The White-tailed Kite likes to perch high up in trees as possible.

**SIMILAR SPECIES**

**MISSISSIPPI KITE** see p.441

darker body

deep red eyes

**NORTHERN HARRIER** ♂ see p.195

dark grayish wings

marked underparts

**OCCURRENCE**
Limited range in the US, breeds and winters in a restricted range; found in open grassland areas, and over large agricultural fields, as well as in rough wetlands with low, reedy, or brushy growth, open oak woodland and light savanna woods. Especially fond of damp, riverside areas.

| Length **13–15in (33–38cm)** | Wingspan **3ft 3in–3½ft (1–1.1m)** | Weight **11–12oz (300–350g)** |
| Social **Colonies** | Lifespan **Up to 6 years** | Status **Secure** |

| DATE SEEN | WHERE | NOTES |
|-----------|-------|-------|
| | | |
| | | |
| | | |
| | | |
| | | |

| Order **Accipitriformes** | Family **Accipitridae** | Species *Aquila chrysaetos* |
|---|---|---|

# Golden Eagle

holds wings in distinctive "V"

**long, narrow white wing patches**

**IMMATURE**  **ADULT**

brown overall

dark brown underparts

black tail band  **IN FLIGHT**

flat, broad head merges into heavy bill

golden feathers on long neck

large, powerful bill

**ADULT**

heavy feathering on legs

pale head

dark plumage with variable white

white tail feathers

**FLIGHT:** slow, steady wingbeats; most often seen gliding or soaring.

**JUVENILE**

Perhaps the most formidable of all North American birds of prey, the Golden Eagle is found mostly in the western part of the continent. It defends large territories ranging from 8 to 12 square miles (20–30 square kilometers), containing up to 14 nests. Although it appears sluggish, it is amazingly swift and agile, and employs a variety of hunting techniques to catch specific prey. Shot and poisoned by ranchers and trappers, it is unfortunately also faced with dwindling habitat and food sources because of human development.

**VOICE** Mostly silent, but breeding adults yelp and mew.

**NESTING** Large pile of sticks and vegetation on cliffs, in trees, and on manmade structures; 1–3 eggs; 1 brood; April–August.

**FEEDING** Eats mammals, such as hares, rabbits, ground squirrels, prairie dogs, marmots, foxes, and coyotes; also birds.

**POWER AND STRENGTH**
The Golden Eagle symbolizes all birds of prey, with its sharp talons, hooked bill, and large size.

## SIMILAR SPECIES

**BALD EAGLE ⓘ** see p.199
white head and neck

some pale wing feathers

**FERRUGINOUS HAWK ⓘ (DARK FORM)** see p.204

no golden tinge

smaller overall

**OCCURRENCE**
In North America occurs mostly in grasslands, wetlands, and rocky areas; breeds south to Mexico, in open and semi-open habitats from sea level to 12,000ft (3,500m) including tundra, shrublands, grasslands, coniferous forests, farmland, areas close to streams or rivers; winters in open habitat.

| Length **28–33in (70–84cm)** | Wingspan **6–7¼ft (1.8–2.2m)** | Weight **6½–13lb (3–6kg)** |
|---|---|---|
| Social **Solitary/Pairs** | Lifespan **Up to 39 years** | Status **Declining (p)** |

| DATE SEEN | WHERE | NOTES |
|---|---|---|
| | | |
| | | |
| | | |
| | | |

| Order **Accipitriformes** | Family **Accipitridae** | Species *Circus hudsonius* |
|---|---|---|

# Northern Harrier

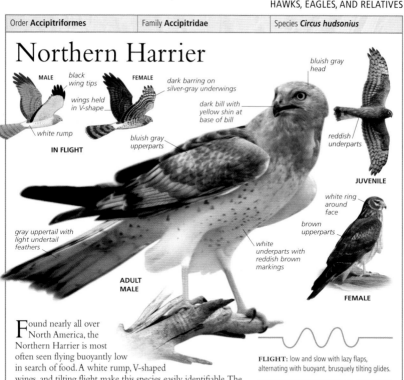

**MALE** black wing tips

wings held in V-shape

white rump

**IN FLIGHT**

**FEMALE** dark barring on silver-gray underwings

bluish gray upperparts

bluish gray head

dark bill with yellow shin at base of bill

reddish underparts

**JUVENILE**

white ring around face

brown upperparts

**FEMALE**

gray uppertail with light undertail feathers

white underparts with reddish brown markings

**ADULT MALE**

Found nearly all over North America, the Northern Harrier is most often seen flying buoyantly low in search of food. A white rump, V-shaped wings, and tilting flight make this species easily identifiable. The blue-gray males are quite different to the dark-brown females. The bird's most recognizable characteristic is its owl-like face, which contains stiff feathers to help channel in sounds from prey. Northern Harriers are highly migratory throughout their range.

**VOICE** Call given by both sexes in rapid succession at nest: *kek* becomes more high-pitched when intruders are spotted.

**NESTING** Platform of sticks on ground in open, wet field; 4–6 eggs; 1 brood; April–September.

**FEEDING** Mostly hunts rodents, such as mice and muskrats; also birds, frogs, reptiles; occasionally takes larger prey such as rabbits.

**FLIGHT:** low and slow with lazy flaps, alternating with buoyant, brusquely tilting glides.

**WATERY DWELLING**
To avoid predators, Northern Harriers prefer to raise their young on wet sites in tall, dense vegetation.

**SIMILAR SPECIES**

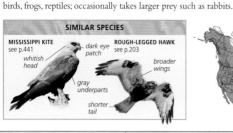

**MISSISSIPPI KITE** see p.441

whitish head

gray underparts

dark eye patch

**ROUGH-LEGGED HAWK** see p.203

broader wings

shorter tail

**OCCURRENCE**
Breeds in a variety of open wetlands: marshes, meadows, pastures, fallow fields across most of North America; winters in open habitats like deserts, coastal sand dunes, cropland, grasslands, marshy, and riverside areas.

| Length **18–20in (46–51cm)** | Wingspan **3½–4ft (1.1m–1.2m)** | Weight **11–26oz (300–750g)** |
|---|---|---|
| Social **Solitary/Pairs/Colonies** | Lifespan **Up to 16 years** | Status **Secure** |

| DATE SEEN | WHERE | NOTES |
|---|---|---|
| | | |
| | | |
| | | |
| | | |
| | | |

| Order **Accipitriformes** | Family **Accipitridae** | Species *Accipiter striatus* |

# Sharp-shinned Hawk

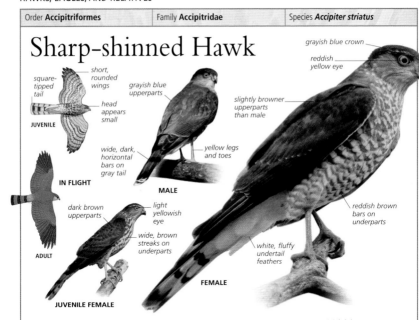

grayish blue crown

reddish yellow eye

square-tipped tail

short, rounded wings

head appears small

**JUVENILE**

grayish blue upperparts

slightly browner upperparts than male

slightly browner upperparts than male

wide, dark, horizontal bars on gray tail

yellow legs and toes

**IN FLIGHT**

**MALE**

dark brown upperparts

light yellowish eye

wide, brown streaks on underparts

**ADULT**

reddish brown bars on underparts

white, fluffy undertail feathers

**FEMALE**

**JUVENILE FEMALE**

This small and swift hawk is quite adept at capturing birds, occasionally even taking species larger than itself. The Sharp-shinned Hawk's short, rounded wings and long tail allow it to make abrupt turns and lightning-fast dashes in thick woods and dense shrubby terrain. With needle-like talons, long, spindle-thin legs, and long toes, this hawk is well adapted to snatching birds in flight. The prey is plucked before being consumed or fed to the nestlings.

**VOICE** High-pitched, repeated *kiu kiu kiu* call; sometimes makes squealing sound when disturbed at nest.

**NESTING** Sturdy nest of sticks lined with twigs or pieces of bark; sometimes an old crow or squirrel nest; 3–4 eggs; 1 brood; March–June.

**FEEDING** Catches small birds, such as sparrows and wood warblers, on the wing, or takes them unaware while perched.

**FLIGHT:** rapid, direct, and strong; nimble enough to maneuver in dense forest; soars during migration.

**HUNTING BIRDS**
A Sharp-shinned Hawk pauses on the ground with a freshly captured sparrow in its talons.

### SIMILAR SPECIES

**MERLIN**
see p.238

light eye-stripe

long pointed wings

**COOPER'S HAWK**
see p.197

larger overall

rounded tip of tail

**OCCURRENCE**
Deep coniferous forests and mixed hardwood–conifer woodlands across North America from the tree limit in northern Canada to the Gulf states. During fall migration sometimes seen in flocks of hundreds of individuals. Winters in Central America from Guatemala to Panama.

| Length **11in (28cm)** | Wingspan **23in (58cm)** | Weight **3½–6oz (100–175g)** |
| Social **Solitary/Flocks** | Lifespan **At least 10 years** | Status **Secure** |

| DATE SEEN | WHERE | NOTES |
|---|---|---|
| | | |
| | | |
| | | |
| | | |
| | | |

| Order **Accipitriformes** | Family **Accipitridae** | Species *Accipiter cooperii* |

# Cooper's Hawk 🔊

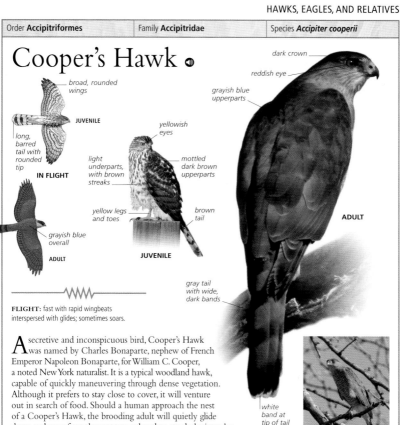

broad, rounded wings

**JUVENILE**

long, barred tail with rounded tip

**IN FLIGHT**

dark crown

reddish eye

grayish blue upperparts

yellowish eyes

light underparts, with brown streaks

mottled dark brown upperparts

yellow legs and toes

brown tail

**JUVENILE**

grayish blue overall

**ADULT**

**ADULT**

gray tail with wide, dark bands

**FLIGHT:** fast with rapid wingbeats interspersed with glides; sometimes soars.

A secretive and inconspicuous bird, Cooper's Hawk was named by Charles Bonaparte, nephew of French Emperor Napoleon Bonaparte, for William C. Cooper, a noted New York naturalist. It is a typical woodland hawk, capable of quickly maneuvering through dense vegetation. Although it prefers to stay close to cover, it will venture out in search of food. Should a human approach the nest of a Cooper's Hawk, the brooding adult will quietly glide down and away from the nest tree rather than attack the intruder.

white band at tip of tail

**VOICE** Most common call a staccato *ca-ca-ca-ca*; other vocalizations include as many as 40 different calls.

**NESTING** Medium-sized, stick nest, usually in a large deciduous tree; 4–5 eggs; 1 brood; April–May.

**FEEDING** Catches birds, such as robins and blackbirds; larger females can capture grouse; also eats chipmunks, small squirrels, and even bats.

**DENSE BARRING**
This hawk has characteristic fine, reddish brown, horizontal barring on its undersides.

**OCCURRENCE**
Breeds in woodlands across southern Canada and most of the US, south to Mexico. Prefers mature deciduous forests and also conifers in winter. Winters mostly in the US south through Central America.

**SIMILAR SPECIES**

**NORTHERN HARRIER ♀**
see p.195

larger overall

whitish underparts

square-tipped tail

**SHARP-SHINNED HAWK**
see p.196

much smaller head

| Length **15½–17½in (40–45cm)** | Wingspan **28–34in (70–86cm)** | Weight **13–19oz (375–525g)** |
| Social **Solitary/Pairs** | Lifespan **At least 10 years** | Status **Secure** |

| DATE SEEN | WHERE | NOTES |
| --- | --- | --- |
| | | |
| | | |
| | | |
| | | |
| | | |

| Order **Accipitriformes** | Family **Accipitridae** | Species **_Accipiter gentilis_** |
|---|---|---|

# Northern Goshawk

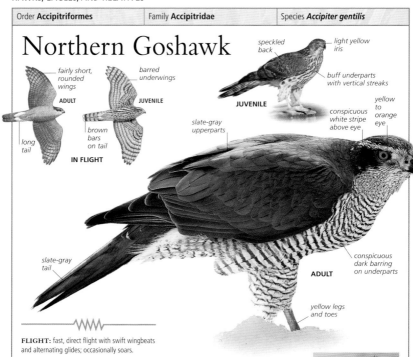

speckled back

light yellow iris

buff underparts with vertical streaks

**JUVENILE**

fairly short, rounded wings

**ADULT**

barred underwings

**JUVENILE**

conspicuous white stripe above eye

yellow to orange eye

slate-gray upperparts

brown bars on tail

long tail

**IN FLIGHT**

slate-gray upperparts

slate-gray tail

conspicuous dark barring on underparts

**ADULT**

yellow legs and toes

**FLIGHT:** fast, direct flight with swift wingbeats and alternating glides; occasionally soars.

The powerful and agile Northern Goshawk is secretive by nature and not easily observed, even in regions where it is common. It has few natural enemies, but will defend its territories, nests, and young fiercely, by repeatedly diving and screaming at intruders that get too close. Spring hikers and turkey-hunters occasionally discover Northern Goshawks by wandering into their territory and being driven off by the angry occupants.
**VOICE** Loud, high-pitched *gek-gek-gek* when agitated.
**NESTING** Large stick structures lined with bark and plant matter in the mid- to lower region of trees; 1–3 eggs; 1 brood; May–June.
**FEEDING** Sits and waits on perch before diving rapidly; preys on birds as large as grouse and pheasants; also mammals, including hares and squirrels.

**OCCASIONAL SOARER**
A juvenile Northern Goshawk takes advantage of a thermal, soaring over its territory.

**OCCURRENCE**
Breeds in deep deciduous, coniferous, and mixed woodlands in northern North America, from the tundra–taiga border south to California, northern Mexico, and Pennsylvania in the eastern US, absent from east-central US. The Northern Goshawk is widespread in northern Eurasia.

**SIMILAR SPECIES**

**GYRFALCON (GRAY FORM)**
see p.446

longer, pointed wings

**COOPER'S HAWK**
see p.197

no streaks on underparts

streaked underparts

brownish upperparts

| Length **21in (53cm)** | Wingspan **3½ft (1.1m)** | Weight **2–3lb (0.9–1.4kg)** |
|---|---|---|
| Social **Solitary/Pairs** | Lifespan **Up to 20 years** | Status **Secure** |

| DATE SEEN | WHERE | NOTES |
|---|---|---|
| | | |
| | | |
| | | |
| | | |
| | | |

| Order **Accipitriformes** | Family **Accipitridae** | Species *Haliaeetus leucocephalus* |

# Bald Eagle 🔊

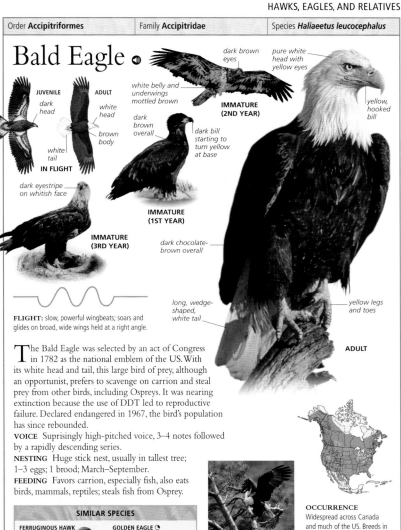

dark brown eyes

pure white head with yellow eyes

**IMMATURE (2ND YEAR)**

white belly and underwings mottled brown

yellow, hooked bill

dark brown overall

dark bill starting to turn yellow at base

**JUVENILE**

dark head

**ADULT**

white head

brown body

white tail

**IN FLIGHT**

dark eyestripe on whitish face

**IMMATURE (1ST YEAR)**

**IMMATURE (3RD YEAR)**

dark chocolate-brown overall

**FLIGHT:** slow, powerful wingbeats; soars and glides on broad, wide wings held at a right angle.

long, wedge-shaped, white tail

yellow legs and toes

**ADULT**

The Bald Eagle was selected by an act of Congress in 1782 as the national emblem of the US. With its white head and tail, this large bird of prey, although an opportunist, prefers to scavenge on carrion and steal prey from other birds, including Ospreys. It was nearing extinction because the use of DDT led to reproductive failure. Declared endangered in 1967, the bird's population has since rebounded.

**VOICE** Suprisingly high-pitched voice, 3–4 notes followed by a rapidly descending series.

**NESTING** Huge stick nest, usually in tallest tree; 1–3 eggs; 1 brood; March–September.

**FEEDING** Favors carrion, especially fish, also eats birds, mammals, reptiles; steals fish from Osprey.

**SUBSTANTIAL ABODE**
Bald eagles make the largest stick nest of all raptors; it can weigh up to two tons.

**OCCURRENCE**
Widespread across Canada and much of the US. Breeds in forested areas near water; also shoreline areas ranging from undeveloped to relatively well-developed with marked human activity; winters along major river systems and in coastal areas and occasionally even in arid regions of southwest US.

## SIMILAR SPECIES

**FERRUGINOUS HAWK**
dark head;
see p.204

**GOLDEN EAGLE** ♂
white in flight feathers; see p.194

whitish underparts

feathered legs

| Length **28–38in (71–96cm)** | Wingspan **6½ft (2m)** | Weight **6½–14lb (3–6.5kg)** |
| Social **Solitary/Pairs** | Lifespan **Up to 28 years** | Status **Secure** |

| DATE SEEN | WHERE | NOTES |
|-----------|-------|-------|
| | | |
| | | |
| | | |
| | | |
| | | |

| Order **Accipitriformes** | Family **Accipitridae** | Species **_Buteo lineatus_** |
|---|---|---|

# Red-shouldered Hawk 🔊

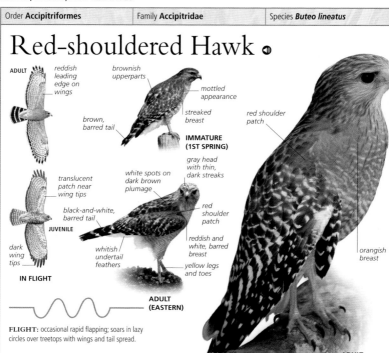

**ADULT**
reddish leading edge on wings

brownish upperparts

mottled appearance

streaked breast

red shoulder patch

brown, barred tail

**IMMATURE (1ST SPRING)**

gray head with thin, dark streaks

red shoulder patch

translucent patch near wing tips

white spots on dark brown plumage

reddish and white, barred breast

**JUVENILE**

black-and-white, barred tail

dark wing tips

whitish undertail feathers

yellow legs and toes

**IN FLIGHT**

**ADULT (EASTERN)**

orangish breast

**ADULT
_B. l. elegans_
(WESTERN)**

**FLIGHT:** occasional rapid flapping; soars in lazy circles over treetops with wings and tail spread.

The Red-shouldered Hawk has a remarkable distribution, with widespread populations in the East, Northeast, and Midwest, then in the West, from Oregon to Baja California, despite a geographical gap of 1,000 miles (1,600km) between the two regions. Eastern birds are divided into four subspecies; western populations belong to the subspecies _B. l. elegans_. The red shoulder patches are not always evident, but the striped tail and translucent "windows" in the wings are easily identifiable.
**VOICE** Call a whistled _kee-aah_, accented on first syllable, descending on second.
**NESTING** Platform of sticks, dried leaves, bark, moss, and lichens in trees not far from water; 3–4 eggs; 1 brood; March–July.
**FEEDING** Catches mice, chipmunks, and voles; also snakes, toads, frogs, crayfish, and small birds.

**SIMILAR SPECIES**

**BROAD-WINGED HAWK** 🔊
see p.442
chunkier body
shorter legs

**RED-TAILED HAWK** 🔊
see p.202
no white tail bands

no red on "shoulder"
slightly larger overall

**CHESTNUT WING**
When seen from below, the reddish forewing of this adult hawk is clearly visible.

**OCCURRENCE**
Eastern populations breed in woodlands and forest, deciduous or mixed, whereas those in the West occur in oak woodlands and eucalyptus groves. In Florida, this species also lives in mangroves. Northeastern birds migrate to Mexico.

| Length **17–24in (43–61cm)** | Wingspan **3–3½ft (0.9–1.1m)** | Weight **17–27oz (475–775g)** |
|---|---|---|
| Social **Solitary/Flocks** | Lifespan **Up to 18 years** | Status **Secure** |

| DATE SEEN | WHERE | NOTES |
|---|---|---|
| | | |
| | | |
| | | |
| | | |
| | | |

| Order **Accipitriformes** | Family **Accipitridae** | Species *Buteo swainsoni* |
|---|---|---|

# Swainson's Hawk

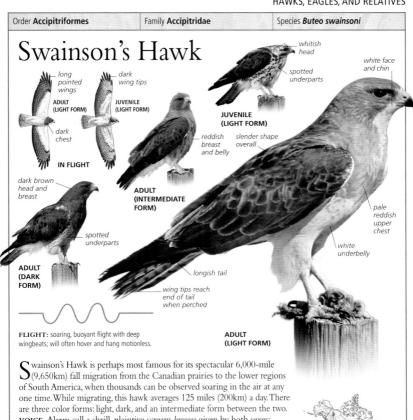

long pointed wings

**ADULT (LIGHT FORM)**

dark wing tips

**JUVENILE (LIGHT FORM)**

dark chest

**IN FLIGHT**

whitish head

spotted underparts

**JUVENILE (LIGHT FORM)**

white face and chin

reddish breast and belly

slender shape overall

**ADULT (INTERMEDIATE FORM)**

dark brown head and breast

spotted underparts

**ADULT (DARK FORM)**

pale reddish upper chest

white underbelly

longish tail

wing tips reach end of tail when perched

**FLIGHT:** soaring, buoyant flight with deep wingbeats; will often hover and hang motionless.

**ADULT (LIGHT FORM)**

Swainson's Hawk is perhaps most famous for its spectacular 6,000-mile (9,650km) fall migration from the Canadian prairies to the lower regions of South America, when thousands can be observed soaring in the air at any one time. While migrating, this hawk averages 125 miles (200km) a day. There are three color forms: light, dark, and an intermediate form between the two.

**VOICE** Alarm call a shrill, plaintive scream *kreeeee* given by both sexes; high-pitched *keeeoooo* fading at the end.

**NESTING** Bulky, flimsy pile of sticks or various debris, in solitary tree or on utility poles; 1–4 eggs; 1 brood; April–July.

**FEEDING** Eats ground squirrels, pocket gophers, mice, voles, bats, rabbits; also snakes, lizards, songbirds.

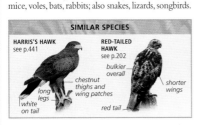

**SIMILAR SPECIES**

**HARRIS'S HAWK** see p.441

chestnut thighs and wing patches

long legs

white on tail

**RED-TAILED HAWK** see p.202

bulkier overall

shorter wings

red tail

**ON THE LOOKOUT**
This slim, elegant species will perch before diving for its prey.

**OCCURRENCE**
Breeds in scattered trees along streams; found in areas of open woodland, sparse shrubland, grasslands, and agricultural land; winters in native Argentinian grassland, and in harvested fields where grasshoppers are found abundantly.

| Length **19–22in (48–56cm)** | Wingspan **4½ft (1.4m)** | Weight **1½–3lb (0.7–1.4kg)** |
|---|---|---|
| Social **Solitary/Pairs/Flocks** | Lifespan **Up to 19 years** | Status **Declining (p)** |

| DATE SEEN | WHERE | | NOTES |
|---|---|---|---|
| | | | |
| | | | |
| | | | |
| | | | |
| | | | |

| Order **Accipitriformes** | Family **Accipitridae** | Species **Buteo jamaicensis** |

# Red-tailed Hawk 🔊

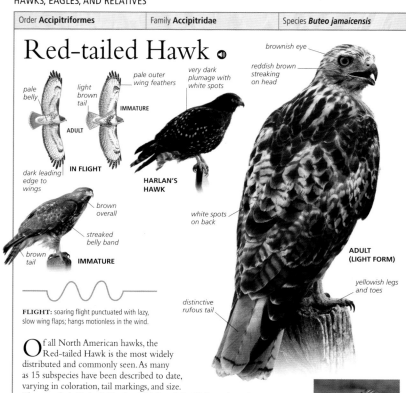

pale belly

light brown tail

pale outer wing feathers

very dark plumage with white spots

brownish eye

reddish brown streaking on head

**IMMATURE**

**ADULT**

**IN FLIGHT**

dark leading edge to wings

**HARLAN'S HAWK**

brown overall

streaked belly band

brown tail

**IMMATURE**

white spots on back

**ADULT (LIGHT FORM)**

yellowish legs and toes

distinctive rufous tail

**FLIGHT:** soaring flight punctuated with lazy, slow wing flaps; hangs motionless in the wind.

Of all North American hawks, the Red-tailed Hawk is the most widely distributed and commonly seen. As many as 15 subspecies have been described to date, varying in coloration, tail markings, and size. The very dark Harlan's Hawk, which breeds in Alaska and northwestern Canada, is considered a subspecies of the Red-tailed Hawk. While it occasionally stoops on prey, the Red-tailed Hawk usually adopts a sit-and-wait approach.

**VOICE** Call *kee-eee-arrr* that rises then descends over a period of 2–3 seconds.

**NESTING** Large platform of sticks, twigs on top of tall tree, cliff, building, ledge, or billboard; 2 eggs; 1 brood; February–September.

**FEEDING** Captures small mammals, such as voles, mice, rats; birds including pheasant, quail; small reptiles; carrion also eaten.

**FLYING HIGH**
A Red-tailed Hawk soaring over an open field is a common sight; this bird is an immature.

**OCCURRENCE**
Breeds, forages in open areas in wide range of habitats and altitudes: scrub desert, grasslands, agricultural fields and pastures, coniferous and deciduous woodland, and tropical rain forest. Prefers areas with tall perch sites; can be found in suburban woodlots.

**SIMILAR SPECIES**

**FERRUGINOUS HAWK (LIGHT FORM)**
see p.204

larger bill

larger overall

mostly white underparts

**ROUGH-LEGGED HAWK (DARK FORM)**
see p.203

dark band on white tail

| Length  18–26in (46–65cm) | Wingspan  3½–4¼ft (1.1–1.3m) | Weight  1½–3¼lb  (0.7–1.5kg) |
| Social  **Solitary/Pairs** | Lifespan  **Up to 21 years** | Status  **Secure** |

| DATE SEEN | WHERE | | NOTES |
| --- | --- | --- | --- |
| | | | |
| | | | |
| | | | |
| | | | |

| Order **Accipitriformes** | Family **Accipitridae** | Species **Buteo lagopus** |

# Rough-legged Hawk

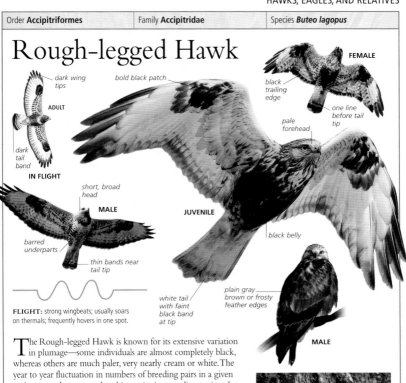

**FEMALE**

dark wing tips

bold black patch

black trailing edge

**ADULT**

pale forehead

one line before tail tip

dark tail band

**IN FLIGHT**

short, broad head

**MALE**

**JUVENILE**

black belly

barred underparts

thin bands near tail tip

plain gray brown or frosty feather edges

**FLIGHT:** strong wingbeats; usually soars on thermals; frequently hovers in one spot.

white tail with faint black band at tip

**MALE**

The Rough-legged Hawk is known for its extensive variation in plumage—some individuals are almost completely black, whereas others are much paler, very nearly cream or white. The year to year fluctuation in numbers of breeding pairs in a given region strongly suggests that this species is nomadic, moving about as a response to the availability of its rodent prey.

**VOICE** Wintering birds silent; breeding birds utter loud, cat-like mewing or thin whistles, slurred downward when alarmed.

**NESTING** Bulky mass of sticks, lined with grasses, sedges, feathers and fur from prey, constructed on cliff ledge; 2–6 eggs; 1 brood; April–August.

**FEEDING** Hovers in one spot over fields in search of prey; lemmings and voles in spring and summer; mice and shrews in winters; variety of birds, ground squirrels, and rabbits year-round.

**ABUNDANT FOOD SUPPLY**
When small mammals are abundant, these hawks produce large broods on cliff ledges in the tundra.

**SIMILAR SPECIES**

**NORTHERN HARRIER** ♀
see p.195

reddish underparts

**FERRUGINOUS HAWK**
see p.204

reddish upperparts

white underparts

longer wings

**OCCURRENCE**
Breeds in rough, open country with low crags and cliffs, in high subarctic and Arctic regions; found on the edge of extensive forest or forest clearings, and in treeless tundra, uplands, and alpine habitats. Winters in open areas with fields, marshes, and rough grasslands.

| Length **19–20in (48–51cm)** | Wingspan **4¼–4½ft (1.3–1.4m)** | Weight **1½–3lb (0.7–1.4kg)** |
| Social **Solitary** | Lifespan **Up to 18 years** | Status **Secure** |

| DATE SEEN | WHERE | NOTES |
|---|---|---|
| | | |
| | | |
| | | |
| | | |
| | | |

| Order **Accipitriformes** | Family **Accipitridae** | Species ***Buteo regalis*** |
|---|---|---|

# Ferruginous Hawk

**ADULT (LIGHT FORM)**

dark chocolate brown

brown and white contrast on wings

relatively long pointed wings

white undertail

large bill

**ADULT (DARK FORM)**

**ADULT (LIGHT FORM)**

**IN FLIGHT**

dark brown overall

**JUVENILE (DARK FORM)**

reddish tinge to tail

all-white underparts

**ADULT (LIGHT FORM)**

dark spots on belly

**JUVENILE (LIGHT FORM)**

fully feathered legs

This inhabitant of open country is the largest North American hawk. Its Latin name *regalis* means kingly, and its English name refers to its rusty coloring. It is a versatile nester: it builds its stick nests on cliffs or nearly level ground, trees, and manmade structures like farm buildings. Regrettably, its preference for prairie dogs, which are declining because of habitat loss, shooting, and pesticide use, threatens Ferruginous Hawk populations.

**VOICE** Screaming *Kree-aa* or *kaah, kaah* during courtship; quieter, lower pitched, longer alarm call.

**NESTING** Large stick nest of old sagebrush stems, sticks, and various debris, lined with bark strips; 2–4 eggs; March–August.

**FEEDING** Hunts mainly rabbits, hares, ground squirrels, and prairie dogs; rarely fledgling birds, amphibians, and reptiles.

**FLIGHT:** slow, deep wingbeats alternating with lazy glides; soars high with thermals.

**PERCHED HUNTER**
The Ferruginous Hawk usually hunts from a perch such as a rock or a branch.

**OCCURRENCE**
In western North America, breeds in low-elevation grasslands interrupted by cliffs or isolated trees for nesting; winters across southwestern US and Mexico in open terrain ranging from grassland to desert.

**SIMILAR SPECIES**

**RED-TAILED HAWK, (LIGHT FORM)** see p.202

**ROUGH-LEGGED HAWK** see p.203

smaller bill

smaller bill

smaller overall

dark rufous tail

white tail with dark band

| Length **22–27in (56–69cm)** | Wingspan **4¼–4½ft (1.3–1.4m)** | Weight **2½–4½lb (1–2kg)** |
|---|---|---|
| Social **Solitary/Pairs** | Lifespan **Up to 20 years** | Status **Secure** |

| DATE SEEN | WHERE | NOTES |
|---|---|---|
| | | |
| | | |
| | | |
| | | |
| | | |

# OWLS

OWLS HAVE FASCINATED humans throughout history, partly because of their nocturnal habits and eerie cries. They are placed in the order Strigiformes, and two families are represented in North America: the Barn Owl is classified in Tytonidae, other North American owl species are in the Strigidae. Most owls are active primarily at night and have developed adaptations for living in low-light environments. Their large eyes are sensitive enough to see in the dark, and face forward to maximize binocular vision. Since the eyes are fixed in their sockets, a flexible neck helps owls turn

**OWL AT TWILIGHT**
The best time to see the nocturnal Barn Owl is often at dawn or dusk.

their heads almost 180° toward a direction of interest. Ears are offset on each side of the head to help identify the source of a sound. A few species have "ear" tufts but they are for visual effect only and are unrelated to hearing. Many owls have serrations on the forward edges of their flight feathers to cushion airflow, so their

**BIG HORNS**
The "ear" tufts of the Great Horned Owl are taller than those of other "tufted" owls.

flight is silent while stalking prey. All North American owls are predatory to some degree and they inhabit most areas of the continent. The Burrowing Owl is unique in that it hunts during the day and nests underground.

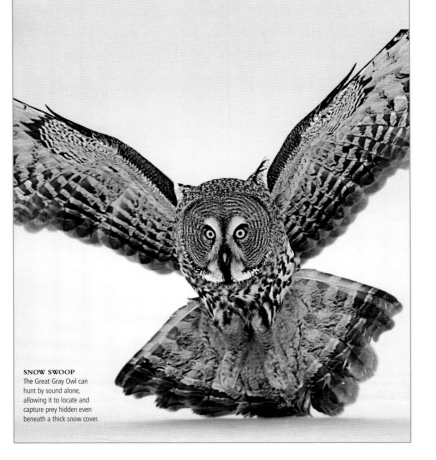

**SNOW SWOOP**
The Great Gray Owl can hunt by sound alone, allowing it to locate and capture prey hidden even beneath a thick snow cover.

| Order **Strigiformes** | Family **Tytonidae** | Species *Tyto alba* |

# Barn Owl 🔊

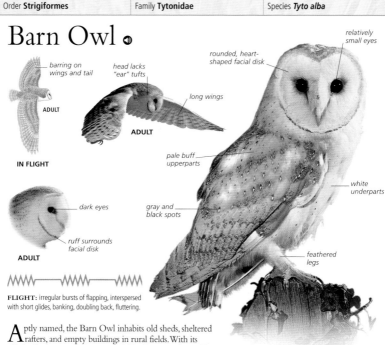

relatively small eyes

rounded, heart-shaped facial disk

barring on wings and tail

**ADULT**

head lacks "ear" tufts

long wings

**ADULT**

**IN FLIGHT**

pale buff upperparts

white underparts

dark eyes

ruff surrounds facial disk

**ADULT**

gray and black spots

feathered legs

**FLIGHT:** irregular bursts of flapping, interspersed with short glides, banking, doubling back, fluttering.

Aptly named, the Barn Owl inhabits old sheds, sheltered rafters, and empty buildings in rural fields. With its affinity for human settlement, and 32 subspecies, this owl has an extensive range covering every continent except Antarctica. Although widespread, the Barn Owl is secretive. Primarily nocturnal, it can fly undetected until its screeching call pierces the air. The Barn Owl is endangered in several Midwestern states as a result of modern farming practices, which have decimated prey populations and reduced the number of barns for nesting.

**VOICE** Typical call loud, raspy, screeching shriek, *shkreee,* often given in flight; also clicking sounds associated with courtship.

**NESTING** Unlined cavity in tree, cave, building, hay bale, or nest box; 5–7 eggs; 1–2 broods; March–September.

**FEEDING** Hunts on the wing for small rodents such as mice; research reveals it can detect the slightest rustle made by prey even in total darkness.

**NOCTURNAL HUNTER**
The Barn Owl hunts at night for small rodents, but may be seen before sunset feeding its young.

**OCCURRENCE**
In North America breeds from northwestern and northeastern US south to Mexico. Resident in all except very north of range. Prefers open habitats, such as desert, grassland, and fields, wherever prey and suitable nest sites are available. Generally not found in mountain or heavily forested areas.

**SIMILAR SPECIES**

**SNOWY OWL**
see p.210
black markings on female and juvenile

**SHORT-EARED OWL**
see p.217
dark patches on outer wing

dark barring on underparts

| Length **12½–15½in (32–40cm)** | Wingspan **3ft 3in (100cm)** | Weight **14–25oz (400–700g)** |
| Social **Solitary** | Lifespan **Up to 8 years** | Status **Declining** |

| DATE SEEN | WHERE | NOTES |
|-----------|-------|-------|
| | | |
| | | |
| | | |
| | | |
| | | |

| Order **Strigiformes** | Family **Strigidae** | Species *Psiloscops flammeolus* |
|---|---|---|

# Flammulated Owl

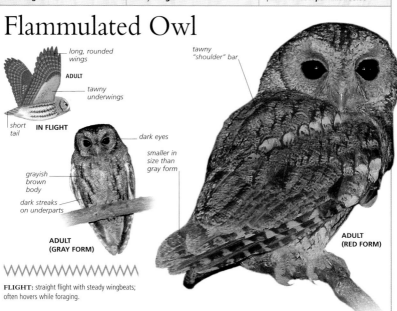

long, rounded wings

**ADULT**

tawny underwings

short tail  **IN FLIGHT**

tawny "shoulder" bar

dark eyes

smaller in size than gray form

grayish brown body

dark streaks on underparts

**ADULT (GRAY FORM)**

**ADULT (RED FORM)**

**FLIGHT:** straight flight with steady wingbeats; often hovers while foraging.

The tiny Flammulated Owl nests in dry mountain pine forests from British Columbia south to Mexico. From most of its range, birds move south to Mexico and Central America in winter. Its dark, watery-looking eyes distinguish it from other species of small North American owls. Entirely nocturnal, it is heard more often than seen. A resting Flammulated Owl blends well with the colors of pine bark: like some other owls, it has "red" and "gray" forms, both beautifully patterned for camouflage. This species breeds in loose groups, perhaps reflecting a patchiness in habitat quality.

**VOICE** Series of soft low-frequency toots, often difficult to locate, can continue for hours; barks and screams when disturbed at nest site.

**NESTING** Cavity in tree, woodpecker hole, nest box; 3–4 eggs; 1–2 broods; May–August.

**FEEDING** Hunts from stationary perch, from which it flies to capture insects—mostly moths and beetles—from branches, foliage, or ground.

**BLENDING IN**
If this owl peeks out of a tree-hole, its plumage blends in remarkably well with the bark.

**OCCURRENCE**
Breeds in semiarid mountain forests, especially ponderosa and yellow pine, open wooded areas at middle elevations with scattered clearings, older trees, and groves of saplings. Winters in habitat similar to breeding season, primarily in southern Mexico, Guatemala, and El Salvador.

**SIMILAR SPECIES**

**WESTERN SCREECH-OWL** see p.208
yellow eyes

**NORTHERN SAW-WHET OWL** see p.219
yellow eyes

different streaking

| Length **6–6¾in (15–17cm)** | Wingspan **16in (41cm)** | Weight **1⁹⁄₁₆–2¼oz (45–65g)** |
|---|---|---|
| Social **Solitary** | Lifespan **Up to 8 years** | Status **Secure** |

| DATE SEEN | WHERE | NOTES |
|---|---|---|
| | | |
| | | |
| | | |
| | | |
| | | |

| Order **Strigiformes** | Family **Strigidae** | Species *Megascops kennicottii* |

# Western Screech-Owl 🔊

dark gray bars on rounded wings

**ADULT**

yellow eyes

small "ear" tufts

short tail **IN FLIGHT**

gray to brown upperparts

streaked underparts

**ADULT**

feathered legs and toes

The Western Screech-Owl is tolerant of human presence, and lives in a wide variety of wooded areas, including suburban habitats. Because of its nocturnal habits, the Western Screech-Owl is heard more often than it is seen; its "bouncing ball" call, sometimes repeated for hours, is a familiar sound in much of western North America. This species exhibits significant differences in plumage color and size (six subspecies in North America), depending on its geographical location.
**VOICE** Series of toots accelerating and descending in pitch; also occasional trills, barks, chirps; female higher pitched.
**NESTING** Hole in a tree, nest box, woodpecker cavity; 2–5 eggs; 1 brood; March–July.
**FEEDING** Sits quietly under canopy waiting to spot small prey below, then pounces; eats small birds and mammals, insects, crayfish, and worms.

**FLIGHT:** straight, steady flight, seldom over long distances; rarely hovers or glides.

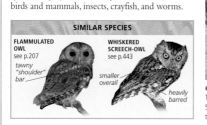

**SIMILAR SPECIES**

**FLAMMULATED OWL** see p.207
tawny "shoulder" bar

**WHISKERED SCREECH-OWL** see p.443
smaller overall
heavily barred

**GOOD CAMOUFLAGE**
This roosting Western Screech-Owl blends in with the bark color of a tree.

**OCCURRENCE**
Breeds from British Columbia southward to Baja California and continental Mexico. Favors riverside and mixed deciduous woodlands, but uses many types of woodlands, parks, and gardens in residential areas; most common at lower elevations. Nonmigratory.

| Length **7½–10in (19–25cm)** | Wingspan **21–22in (53–56cm)** | Weight **3½–11oz (100–300g)** |
| Social **Family groups** | Lifespan **Up to 13 years** | Status **Secure** |

| DATE SEEN | WHERE | NOTES |
|---|---|---|
| | | |
| | | |
| | | |
| | | |
| | | |

| Order **Strigiformes** | Family **Strigidae** | Species ***Bubo virginianus*** |

# Great Horned Owl

**ADULT**

long, broad wing

dark arc on wing

large "ears"

yellow eye

rusty facial disk

**IN FLIGHT**

white throat and chin

mottled, barred, brownish and gray upperparts

barred underparts

**ADULT**

**ADULT**

**FLIGHT:** fairly slow with heavy wingbeats alternating with short glides; swoops when hunting.

heavy barring of underparts

barring on undertail

The Great Horned Owl is perhaps the archetypal owl. Large and adaptable, it is resident from Alaska to Tierra del Fuego. With such a big range, geographical variation occurs; at least 13 subspecies have been described. The southernmost populations—*B. v. magellanicus*, from Peru to Patagonia—are often considered a distinct species. The Great Horned Owl's deep hoots are easily recognized, and can often be heard in movie soundtracks. The bird is the top predator in its food chain, often killing and eating other owls, and even skunks. An early breeder, it starts hooting in the middle of winter, and often lays its eggs in January.

**VOICE** Series of hoots *whoo-hoo-oo-o*; also screams, barks, and hisses; female higher pitched.

**NESTING** Old stick nest, in tree, exposed cavity, cliff, human structure, or on the ground; 1–5 eggs; 1 brood; January–April.

**FEEDING** Hunts mammals, reptiles, amphibians, birds, and insects; mostly nocturnal.

### SIMILAR SPECIES

**RED-TAILED HAWK** diurnal; see p.202

smaller head

**GREAT GRAY OWL** see p.215

no tufts

large, round head

long, red tail

**RECYCLING**
The Great Horned Owl breeds in old stick nests constructed by other large birds, like crows.

**OCCURRENCE**
In North America, found in nearly every type of habitat except Arctic tundra. Prefers fragmented landscapes: desert, swamp, prairie, woodland, and urban areas. Rare only in the Appalachian Mountains in the East and in the Sonoran and Mohave Deserts in the West.

| Length **18–25in (46–63cm)** | Wingspan **3–5ft (0.9–1.6m)** | Weight **1⅛–5½lb (0.9–2.5kg)** |
| Social **Solitary** | Lifespan **Up to 28 years** | Status **Secure** |

| DATE SEEN | WHERE | NOTES |
| --- | --- | --- |
| | | |
| | | |
| | | |
| | | |

| Order **Strigiformes** | Family **Strigidae** | Species ***Bubo scandiacus*** |
|---|---|---|

# Snowy Owl

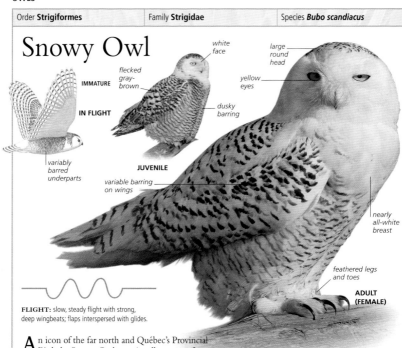

*white face*

*large round head*

*yellow eyes*

**IMMATURE**

*flecked gray-brown*

**IN FLIGHT**

*dusky barring*

*variably barred underparts*

**JUVENILE**

*variable barring on wings*

*nearly all-white breast*

*feathered legs and toes*

**ADULT (FEMALE)**

**FLIGHT:** slow, steady flight with strong, deep wingbeats; flaps interspersed with glides.

An icon of the far north and Québec's Provincial Bird, the Snowy Owl occasionally appears far to the south of its usual range, making an eyecatching addition to the local landscape. This is a bird of the open tundra, where it hunts from headlands or hummocks and nests on the ground. In such a harsh environment, the Snowy Owl largely depends on lemmings for prey. It is fiercely territorial, and will valiantly defend its young in the nest even against larger animals, such as the Arctic Fox.

**VOICE** Deep hoots, doubled or given in a short series, usually by male; also rattles, whistles, and hisses.

**NESTING** Scrape in ground vegetation or dirt, with no lining; 3–12 eggs; 1 brood; May–September.

**FEEDING** Mostly hunts lemmings, but takes whatever other small mammals, birds, and occasionally fish it can find.

**SNOWY MALE**
Some adult males show no barring at all and have pure white plumage.

| SIMILAR SPECIES | | |
|---|---|---|

**BARN OWL** see p.206

*golden brown*

*black eyes*

**SHORT-EARED OWL** see p.217

*mottled brown markings*

*larger overall*

**OCCURRENCE**
Breeds in the tundra of Eurasia and northern North America, north to Ellesmere Island; North American birds winter south to the Great Plains. In some years, many North American birds winter south of their normal range, including in dunes, marshes, and airfields, as far south as Florida and California.

| Length **20–27in (51–68cm)** | Wingspan **4¼–5¼ft (1.3–1.6m)** | Weight **3½–6½lb (1.6–2.9kg)** |
|---|---|---|
| Social **Solitary** | Lifespan **Up to 9 years** | Status **Vulnerable** |

| DATE SEEN | WHERE | NOTES |
|---|---|---|
| | | |
| | | |
| | | |
| | | |

| Order **Strigiformes** | Family **Strigidae** | Species *Surnia ulula* |

# Northern Hawk Owl

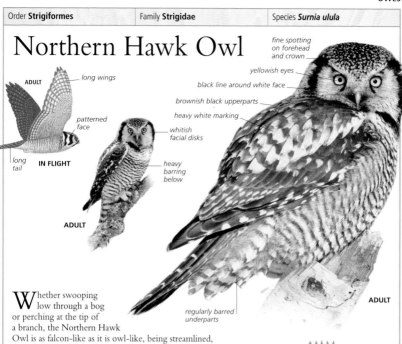

fine spotting on forehead and crown

yellowish eyes

black line around white face

brownish black upperparts

heavy white marking

whitish facial disks

**ADULT**

long wings

**IN FLIGHT**

patterned face

long tail

heavy barring below

**ADULT**

regularly barred underparts

**ADULT**

Whether swooping low through a bog or perching at the tip of a branch, the Northern Hawk Owl is as falcon-like as it is owl-like, being streamlined, a powerful flier, and an active daytime hunter. It is patchily distributed across the northern North American forests, far from most human settlements, so it is seldom seen—and is not well studied—on its breeding grounds. In winter the bird is somewhat nomadic and is occasionally seen south of its breeding range for a few days or weeks in southern Canada and the northern US.

**VOICE** Ascending, whistled, drawn-out trill; also chirps, screeches, and yelps.
**NESTING** Cavities, hollows, broken-off branches, old stick nests, nest boxes; 3–13 eggs; 1 brood; April–August.
**FEEDING** Swoops like a falcon, from an elevated perch, to pounce on prey; preys mainly on rodents in summer, and on grouse and ptarmigan in winter.

**FLIGHT:** powerful, deep wingbeats; glides; highly maneuverable, occasionally soars.

**KEEN-EYED OWL**
The Northern Hawk Owl hunts mainly by sight, swooping down on prey from a high perch.

**OCCURRENCE**
Breeds across the forests of northern Canada, from Alaska to Québec and Newfoundland, in sparse woodland or mixed conifer forest with swamps, bogs, burned areas, or storm damage. In winter occasionally moves south to southern Canada, Great Lakes region and New England.

**SIMILAR SPECIES**

**MERLIN** see p.238 — small head, smaller overall, buffy orange underneath

**GREAT HORNED OWL** see p.209 — "ear" tufts, chunky shape, much larger overall

| Length **14–17½in (36–44cm)** | Wingspan **31in (80cm)** | Weight **11–12oz (300–350g)** |
| Social **Family groups** | Lifespan **Up to 10 years** | Status **Secure** |

| DATE SEEN | WHERE | | NOTES |
| --- | --- | --- | --- |
| | | | |
| | | | |
| | | | |
| | | | |
| | | | |

| Order **Strigiformes** | Family **Strigidae** | Species **Glaucidium gnoma** |

# Northern Pygmy-Owl

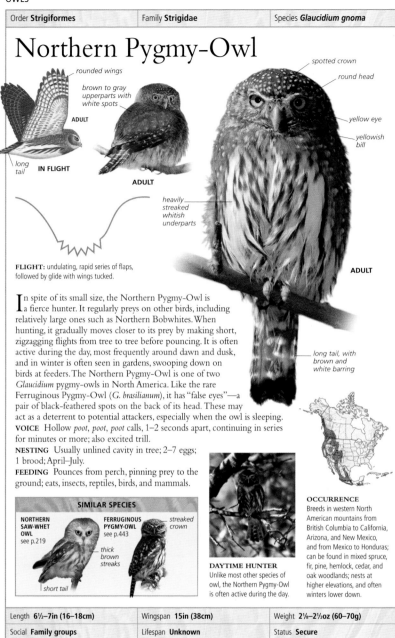

rounded wings

spotted crown

round head

brown to gray
upperparts with
white spots

**ADULT**

yellow eye

yellowish
bill

long
tail **IN FLIGHT**

**ADULT**

heavily
streaked
whitish
underparts

**FLIGHT:** undulating, rapid series of flaps,
followed by glide with wings tucked.

**ADULT**

long tail, with
brown and
white barring

In spite of its small size, the Northern Pygmy-Owl is
a fierce hunter. It regularly preys on other birds, including
relatively large ones such as Northern Bobwhites. When
hunting, it gradually moves closer to its prey by making short,
zigzagging flights from tree to tree before pouncing. It is often
active during the day, most frequently around dawn and dusk,
and in winter is often seen in gardens, swooping down on
birds at feeders. The Northern Pygmy-Owl is one of two
*Glaucidium* pygmy-owls in North America. Like the rare
Ferruginous Pygmy-Owl (*G. brasilianum*), it has "false eyes"—a
pair of black-feathered spots on the back of its head. These may
act as a deterrent to potential attackers, especially when the owl is sleeping.
**VOICE** Hollow *poot*, *poot*, *poot* calls, 1–2 seconds apart, continuing in series
for minutes or more; also excited trill.
**NESTING** Usually unlined cavity in tree; 2–7 eggs;
1 brood; April–July.
**FEEDING** Pounces from perch, pinning prey to the
ground; eats, insects, reptiles, birds, and mammals.

| SIMILAR SPECIES | | |

**NORTHERN
SAW-WHET
OWL**
see p.219

**FERRUGINOUS
PYGMY-OWL**
see p.443

streaked
crown

thick
brown
streaks

short tail

**DAYTIME HUNTER**
Unlike most other species of
owl, the Northern Pygmy-Owl
is often active during the day.

**OCCURRENCE**
Breeds in western North
American mountains from
British Columbia to California,
Arizona, and New Mexico,
and from Mexico to Honduras;
can be found in mixed spruce,
fir, pine, hemlock, cedar, and
oak woodlands; nests at
higher elevations, and often
winters lower down.

| Length  6½–7in (16–18cm) | Wingspan  **15in (38cm)** | Weight  **2⅛–2½oz (60–70g)** |
| Social  **Family groups** | Lifespan  **Unknown** | Status  **Secure** |

| DATE SEEN | WHERE | NOTES |
| --- | --- | --- |
| | | |
| | | |
| | | |
| | | |
| | | |

| Order **Strigiformes** | Family **Strigidae** | Species *Athene cunicularia* |

# Burrowing Owl

short, rounded wings

**ADULT**

brown ear feathers

**IN FLIGHT**

short tail

white streaking on forehead and crown

chest spotted with white

brown upperparts with white spotting

**ADULT**

short tail

yellow eyes

white contrasting with dark brown band below

white spots

brown streaks on lower belly

**ADULT**

short tail

long, feathered legs

~~~~~~~

**FLIGHT:** buoyant, often undulating; close to ground; sometimes hovers while hunting.

The Burrowing Owl is unique among North American owls in nesting underground. Usually it uses the abandoned burrows of prairie dogs, ground squirrels, armadillos, badgers, and other mammals. Where such burrows are scarce, however—in built-up areas of Florida, notably—it excavates its own burrow, digging out the soil with its bill and scraping it away with its feet. Usually it nests in loose colonies, too. Active by day or night, the Burrowing Owl hunts prey on foot or on the wing. Populations of the bird in southern areas of North America tend to stay there year-round, but those farther north move south to Mexico for the winter.

**VOICE** *Coo-cooo*, or *ha-haaa*, with accent on second syllable; also clucks, chatters, warbles, and screams.

**NESTING** Cavity lined with grass, feathers, sometimes animal dung, at end of burrow; 8–10 eggs; 1 brood; March–August.

**FEEDING** Walks, hops, runs, hovers, or flies from perch to capture mainly insects, and occasionally small mammals, birds, reptiles, and amphibians.

**ON THE ALERT**
A Burrowing Owl keeps watch from the entrance of its burrow, which can be 10ft (3m) long.

**SIMILAR SPECIES**

SHORT-EARED OWL
see p.217
larger overall

streaked below

**OCCURRENCE**
Breeds in Florida, the western US, and southwestern Canada, in a wide range of open, well-drained habitats not prone to flooding, including pastures, plains, deserts, grasslands, and steppes, but also developed area, up to about 6,500ft (2,000m). Partial migrant.

| Length **7½–10in (19–25cm)** | Wingspan **21½in (55cm)** | Weight **5oz (150g)** |
| Social **Loose colonies** | Lifespan **Up to 9 years** | Status **Declining** |

| DATE SEEN | WHERE | NOTES |
| --- | --- | --- |
| | | |
| | | |
| | | |
| | | |
| | | |

213

| Order **Strigiformes** | Family **Strigidae** | Species ***Strix varia*** |
|---|---|---|

# Barred Owl 🔊

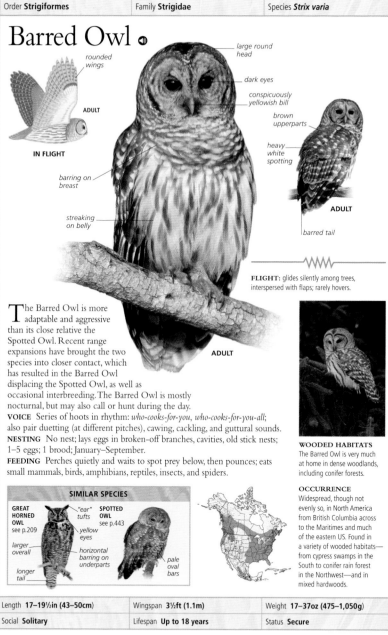

rounded wings

**ADULT**

**IN FLIGHT**

barring on breast

streaking on belly

large round head

dark eyes

conspicuously yellowish bill

brown upperparts

heavy white spotting

**ADULT**

barred tail

**ADULT**

~~~〰️~~~

**FLIGHT:** glides silently among trees, interspersed with flaps; rarely hovers.

The Barred Owl is more adaptable and aggressive than its close relative the Spotted Owl. Recent range expansions have brought the two species into closer contact, which has resulted in the Barred Owl displacing the Spotted Owl, as well as occasional interbreeding. The Barred Owl is mostly nocturnal, but may also call or hunt during the day.

**VOICE** Series of hoots in rhythm: *who-cooks-for-you, who-cooks-for-you-all;* also pair duetting (at different pitches), cawing, cackling, and guttural sounds.

**NESTING** No nest; lays eggs in broken-off branches, cavities, old stick nests; 1–5 eggs; 1 brood; January–September.

**FEEDING** Perches quietly and waits to spot prey below, then pounces; eats small mammals, birds, amphibians, reptiles, insects, and spiders.

**WOODED HABITATS**
The Barred Owl is very much at home in dense woodlands, including conifer forests.

**OCCURRENCE**
Widespread, though not evenly so, in North America from British Columbia across to the Maritimes and much of the eastern US. Found in a variety of wooded habitats—from cypress swamps in the South to conifer rain forest in the Northwest—and in mixed hardwoods.

### SIMILAR SPECIES

| GREAT HORNED OWL see p.209 | "ear" tufts | SPOTTED OWL see p.443 |
|---|---|---|
| larger overall | yellow eyes | |
| longer tail | horizontal barring on underparts | pale oval bars |

| Length **17–19½in (43–50cm)** | Wingspan **3½ft (1.1m)** | Weight **17–37oz (475–1,050g)** |
|---|---|---|
| Social **Solitary** | Lifespan **Up to 18 years** | Status **Secure** |

| DATE SEEN | WHERE | NOTES |
|---|---|---|
| | | |
| | | |
| | | |
| | | |

| Order **Strigiformes** | Family **Strigidae** | Species **Strix nebulosa** |
|---|---|---|

# Great Gray Owl

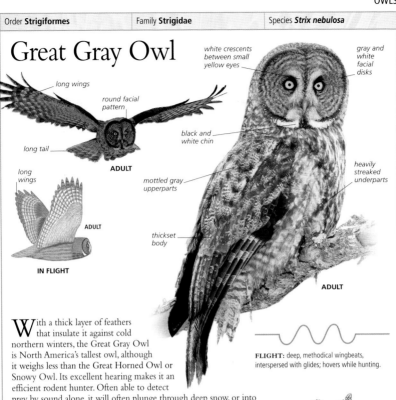

white crescents between small yellow eyes

gray and white facial disks

long wings

round facial pattern

black and white chin

long tail

heavily streaked underparts

**ADULT**

long wings

mottled gray upperparts

**ADULT**

thickset body

**IN FLIGHT**

**ADULT**

With a thick layer of feathers that insulate it against cold northern winters, the Great Gray Owl is North America's tallest owl, although it weighs less than the Great Horned Owl or Snowy Owl. Its excellent hearing makes it an efficient rodent hunter. Often able to detect prey by sound alone, it will often plunge through deep snow, or into a burrow, to snatch unseen prey. This bird is primarily nocturnal, but may also hunt by daylight, usually at dawn or dusk.

**FLIGHT:** deep, methodical wingbeats, interspersed with glides; hovers while hunting.

**VOICE** Slow series of deep hoots, evenly spaced; also variety of hisses and chattering noises around nest site.

**NESTING** Reuses old eagle or hawk nests, broken-off trees; 2–5 eggs; 1 brood; March–July.

**FEEDING** Eats rodents and other small mammals; waits to pounce from perch or hunts in flight.

**MAKESHIFT NEST**
The Great Gray Owl often utilizes hollow snags as nesting sites, besides reusing deserted nests.

**OCCURRENCE**
In North America, resident across northern forests from Alaska to Québec, south to Montana and Wyoming. Also resident in Eurasia from Scandinavia to the Russian Far East. Found in taiga, and muskeg (peat bogs), in fir, spruce, and pine forests.

**SIMILAR SPECIES**

| GREAT HORNED OWL see p.209 | "ear" tufts | BARRED OWL see p.214 | dark eyes |
|---|---|---|---|

barring on breast

barring on belly

| Length **24–33in (61–84cm)** | Wingspan **4½ft (1.4m)** | Weight **1½–3¾lb (0.7–1.7kg)** |
|---|---|---|
| Social **Solitary** | Lifespan **Up to 14 years** | Status **Secure** |

| DATE SEEN | WHERE | | NOTES |
|---|---|---|---|
| | | | |
| | | | |
| | | | |
| | | | |
| | | | |

| Order **Strigiformes** | Family **Strigidae** | Species *Asio otus* |
|---|---|---|

# Long-eared Owl

conspicuous "ear" tufts

dark eye-ring

yellow eye

black bill

tan patch on outer wing

long "ear" tufts

rusty face disks

dark wrist patch

gray tips

**IN FLIGHT**

slender body

mottled upperwings

finely streaked underparts

**ADULT**

**ADULT**

**FLIGHT:** quick, deep wingbeats and long glides; often hovers while hunting.

Although widely distributed across Eurasia and North America, the Long-eared Owl is seldom seen, being secretive and nocturnal. By day it roosts high up and out of sight in thick cover. Only at nightfall does it fly out to hunt on the wing over open areas, patrolling for small mammals. Its wing feathers, like those of many other owls, have sound-suppressing structures that allow it to fly almost silently.

**VOICE** Evenly spaced *hooo* notes, continuously repeated, about 3 seconds apart, typically 10–50 per series, sometimes more; barks when alarmed.

**NESTING** Old stick nests of ravens, crows, magpies, and hawks; 2–7 eggs; 1 brood; March–July.

**FEEDING** Preys mainly on mice and other small rodents, occasionally small birds.

**OWL ON THE WING**
In flight this bird's "ear" tufts are flattened back and not visible, but the face and underwing markings are clearly revealed.

### SIMILAR SPECIES

**GREAT HORNED OWL** see p.209

much larger overall

tufts farther apart

horizontal barring on underparts

**SHORT-EARED OWL** see p.217

patterned buffy above

pale below

larger overall

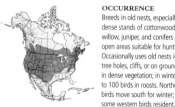

**OCCURRENCE**
Breeds in old nests, especially in dense stands of cottonwood, willow, juniper, and conifers near open areas suitable for hunting. Occasionally uses old nests in tree holes, cliffs, or on ground in dense vegetation; in winter, up to 100 birds in roosts. Northern birds move south for winter; some western birds resident.

| Length **14–15½in (35–40cm)** | Wingspan **34–39in (86–98cm)** | Weight **8–15oz (225–425g)** |
|---|---|---|
| Social **Solitary/Winter flocks** | Lifespan **Up to 27 years** | Status **Secure** |

| DATE SEEN | WHERE | NOTES |
|---|---|---|
| | | |
| | | |
| | | |
| | | |
| | | |

| Order **Strigiformes** | Family **Strigidae** | Species *Asio flammeus* |

# Short-eared Owl

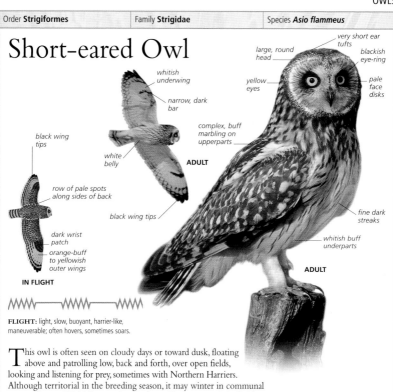

very short ear tufts

large, round head

blackish eye-ring

whitish underwing

yellow eyes

pale face disks

narrow, dark bar

complex, buff marbling on upperparts

black wing tips

white belly

**ADULT**

row of pale spots along sides of back

black wing tips

fine dark streaks

dark wrist patch

whitish buff underparts

orange-buff to yellowish outer wings

**ADULT**

**IN FLIGHT**

**FLIGHT:** light, slow, buoyant, harrier-like, maneuverable; often hovers, sometimes soars.

This owl is often seen on cloudy days or toward dusk, floating above and patrolling low, back and forth, over open fields, looking and listening for prey, sometimes with Northern Harriers. Although territorial in the breeding season, it may winter in communal roosts of up to 200 birds, occasionally alongside Long-eared Owls. About 10 subspecies are widely distributed across five continents and numerous island groups, including the Greater Antilles, Galápagos, the Falklands and Hawaii. Unlike other North American owls, the Short-eared Owl builds its own nest.

**VOICE** Usually silent; male courtship call a rapid *hoo hoo hoo*, often given during display flights; about 16 notes in 3 seconds; also barking, *chee-oww*.

**NESTING** Scrape lined with grass and feathers on ground; 4–7 eggs; 1–2 broods; March–June.

**FEEDING** Eats small mammals and some birds.

### SIMILAR SPECIES

**NORTHERN HARRIER**
see p.195

gray upperparts

whitish underparts

long tail

**LONG-EARED OWL**
see p.216

"ear" tufts

rusty face disks

**LOOKOUT POST**
Perched on a branch, a Short-eared Owl keeps a wary eye on any intruder on its territory.

**OCCURRENCE**
Breeds in open areas, including prairie, grasslands, tundra, fields, and marshes across northern North America, from Alaska, the Yukon, and British Columbia to Québec, and Newfoundland, south to the western and central prairies, and east to New England. Northern populations move south in winter.

| Length **13½–16in (34–41cm)** | Wingspan **2¾–3½ft (0.9–1.1m)** | Weight **11–13oz (325–375g)** |
| Social **Solitary/Winter flocks** | Lifespan **Up to 13 years** | Status **Vulnerable** |

| DATE SEEN | WHERE | NOTES |
| --- | --- | --- |
| | | |
| | | |
| | | |
| | | |
| | | |

| Order **Strigiformes** | Family **Strigidae** | Species ***Aegolius funereus*** |

# Boreal Owl

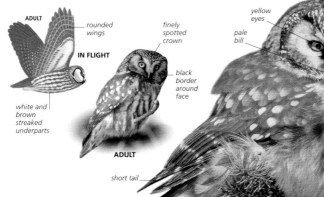

usually flat-topped head, with fine white spots

yellow eyes

pale bill

**ADULT**

*rounded wings*

**IN FLIGHT**

*finely spotted crown*

*black border around face*

*white and brown streaked underparts*

**ADULT**

*short tail*

**FLIGHT:** quick, strong wingbeats; adept at maneuvering; glides down to attack prey.

**ADULT**

The female Boreal Owl is bigger than the male. Males will mate with two or three females in years when voles and other small rodents are abundant. The Boreal Owl roosts on an inconspicuous perch by day and hunts at night, detecting its prey by sound. In the US it is elusive and rarely seen, as it breeds at high elevations in isolated western mountain ranges. White spotting on the crown, a grayish bill, and a black facial disk distinguish the Boreal Owl from the Northern Saw-whet Owl.

**VOICE** Prolonged series of whistles, usually increasing in volume and intensity toward the end; also screeches and hisses; can be heard from afar.

**NESTING** Natural and woodpecker-built tree cavities, also nest boxes; 3–6 eggs; 1 brood; March–July.

**FEEDING** Mainly eats small mammals, occasionally birds and insects; pounces from elevated perch; sometimes stores prey.

**DAYTIME ROOSTING**
The Boreal Owl roosts in dense vegetation by day, even when the branches are laden with snow.

### SIMILAR SPECIES

**NORTHERN PYGMY-OWL**
see p.212
*black streaks on belly*
*longer tail*

**NORTHERN SAW-WHET OWL**
see p.219
*lacks dark frame to facial disk*
*dark bill*

**OCCURRENCE**
Breeds in northern forests from Alaska to Newfoundland and Québec, south into the Rockies to Colorado and New Mexico. Largely sedentary, but irregular movements take place south of the breeding range, southward to New England and New York. In the Old World it is called Tengmalm's Owl.

| Length **8½–11in (21–28cm)** | Wingspan **21½–24in (54–62cm)** | Weight **3⅜–8oz (90–225g)** |
| Social **Solitary** | Lifespan **Up to 11 years** | Status **Secure** |

| DATE SEEN | WHERE | | NOTES |
|---|---|---|---|
| | | | |
| | | | |
| | | | |
| | | | |
| | | | |

| Order **Strigiformes** | Family **Strigidae** | Species *Aegolius acadicus* |

# Northern Saw-whet Owl

**ADULT**

rounded wings

thin white streaks on forehead and crown

whitish eyebrows

white patch between eyes

yellow eyes

dark bill

chestnut-brown upperparts with white spots

short tail

**IN FLIGHT**

brown streaks

**ADULT**

**ADULT**

**FLIGHT:** swift and direct; low to ground with quick wingbeats; swoops up to perch.

unmarked white undertail feathers

One of the most secretive yet common and widespread owls in North America, the Northern Saw-whet Owl is much more often heard than seen. Strictly nocturnal, it is concealed as it sleeps by day in thick vegetation, usually in conifers. Although the same site may be used for months if it remains undisturbed, it is never an easy bird to locate and, like most owls, it is elusive, even though it sometimes roosts in large garden trees. When it is discovered, the Northern Saw-whet Owl "freezes," and relies on its camouflage rather than flying off. At night it watches intently from a perch, before swooping down to snatch its prey.

**VOICE** Series of rapid whistled notes, on constant pitch; can continue for minutes on end; also whines and squeaks.

**NESTING** Unlined cavity in tree, usually old woodpecker hole or nest box; 4–7 eggs; 1 brood; March–July.

**FEEDING** Hunts from elevated perch; eats small mammals, including mice and voles; also eats insects and small birds.

**RARE SIGHT**
Despite being abundant in its range, this shy species is seldom seen.

| SIMILAR SPECIES | | |
|---|---|---|

**ELF OWL**
see p.443
gray back
smaller overall

**BOREAL OWL**
see p.218
darker face
spotted crown
black facial border

**OCCURRENCE**
Breeds from Alaska and British Columbia to Maritimes; in West, south to Mexico; in East, south to Appalachians; coniferous and mixed deciduous forests, swampy forests, wooded wetlands, bogs. Winters in southern to central states, in open woodlands, pine plantations, and shrubby areas.

| Length **7–8½in (18–21cm)** | Wingspan **16½–19in (42–48cm)** | Weight **3½oz (100g)** |
| Social **Solitary** | Lifespan **Up to 10 years** | Status **Secure** |

| DATE SEEN | WHERE | NOTES |
|---|---|---|
| | | |
| | | |
| | | |
| | | |
| | | |

# KINGFISHERS

KINGFISHERS ARE primarily a tropical family (Alcedinidae) that apparently originated in the Australasian region. Three species are found in North America, but only one, the Belted Kingfisher, is widespread. Like most species of kingfishers, these birds are large-headed and large-billed but have comparatively short legs and toes. Although North American kingfishers lack the array of bright blues, greens, and reds associated with their tropical and European counterparts, they are striking birds, distinguished by chestnut-colored chest bands and white underparts. While they also eat frogs and crayfish, North American species are primarily fish-eaters. After catching a fish, they routinely stun their prey by beating it against a perch before turning the fish around so that it can be eaten head first. Smaller species such as the Green Kingfisher are shy and not often seen.

**FISH DINNER**
A female Belted Kingfisher uses its large bill to catch and hold slippery prey.

# WOODPECKERS

WOODPECKERS ARE FOUND throughout North America except in the tundra. They are adapted to gripping upright tree trunks, using the tail as a support or prop. Most woodpeckers have two toes facing forward and two facing backward, to give an extra strong grip on a rounded branch. Unlike nuthatches, they do not perch upside-down but they can cling to the underside of angled branches. They have striking plumage patterns with simple, bold colors. Many proclaim their territory by instrumental, rather than vocal, means, hammering the bill against a hard surface to give a brief but rapid "drumroll." The bill is also used for chipping into bark and excavating deep nestholes in solid wood. Sapsuckers also make rows or rings of small holes on tree trunks, allowing sap to ooze freely: they feed on the sap and also on the insects that are attracted to it. Several species, especially the flickers, also feed on the ground, probing inside ant nests for larvae, with catching them with their long, sticky tongues.

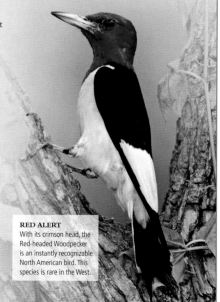

**RED ALERT**
With its crimson head, the Red-headed Woodpecker is an instantly recognizable North American bird. This species is rare in the West.

| Order **Coraciiformes** | Family **Alcedinidae** | Species ***Megaceryle alcyon*** |

# Belted Kingfisher 🔊

**MALE** large head

single blue breastband

barred tail

**IN FLIGHT**

bluish gray head with shaggy crest

white collar

bluish slate upperparts

white belly

**MALE**

prominent crest

long, thick, powerful bill

chestnut band across breast

chestnut flanks

**FEMALE**

double crest

white collar

single dark breastband

**IMMATURE MALE**

**FLIGHT:** strongly flaps its wings and then glides after two or three beats; frequently hovers.

Its stocky body, double-pointed crest, large head, and contrasting white collar distinguish the Belted Kingfisher from other species in its range. This kingfisher's loud and far-carrying rattles are heard more often than the bird is seen. Interestingly, it is one of the few birds in North America in which the female is more colorful than the male. The Belted Kingfisher can be found in a large variety of aquatic habitats, both coastal and inland, vigorously defending its territory all year round.

**VOICE** Harsh mechanical rattle given in flight or from a perch; sometimes emits screams or trill-like warble during breeding.

**NESTING** Unlined chamber in subterranean burrow 3–6ft (1–2m) deep, excavated in earthen bank usually over water, but sometimes in ditches, sand, or gravel pits; 6–7 eggs; 1 brood; March–July.

**FEEDING** Plunge-dives from branches or wires to catch a wide variety of fish near the surface, including sticklebacks and trout; also takes crustaceans, such as crayfish.

**SIMILAR SPECIES**

RINGED KINGFISHER ♂
see p.444

larger overall

chestnut belly

**CATCH OF THE DAY**
The female's chestnut belly band and flanks are clearly visible here as she perches with her catch.

**OCCURRENCE**
Breeds and winters around clear, open waters of streams, rivers, lakes, estuaries, and protected marine shorelines, where perches are available and prey is visible. Avoids water with emergent vegetation. Northern populations migrate south to Mexico, Central America, and the West Indies.

| Length **11–14in (28–35cm)** | Wingspan **19–23in (48–58cm)** | Weight **5–6oz (150–175g)** |
| Social **Solitary** | Lifespan **Unknown** | Status **Secure** |

| DATE SEEN | WHERE | NOTES |
|-----------|-------|-------|
| | | |
| | | |
| | | |
| | | |

| Order **Piciformes** | Family **Picidae** | Species ***Melanerpes lewis*** |

# Lewis's Woodpecker

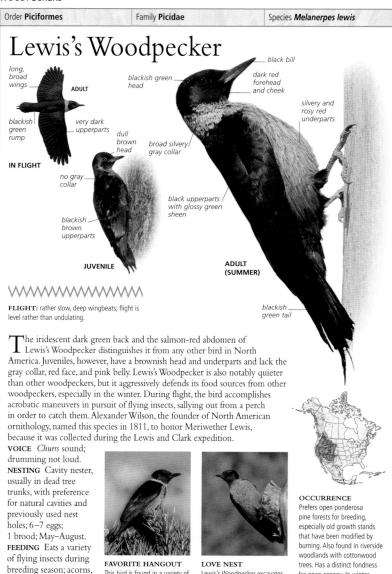

long, broad wings
**ADULT**

blackish green head

black bill

dark red forehead and cheek

silvery and rosy red underparts

blackish green rump

very dark upperparts

dull brown head

broad silvery gray collar

**IN FLIGHT**

no gray collar

black upperparts with glossy green sheen

blackish brown upperparts

**JUVENILE**

**ADULT (SUMMER)**

blackish green tail

**FLIGHT:** rather slow, deep wingbeats; flight is level rather than undulating.

The iridescent dark green back and the salmon-red abdomen of Lewis's Woodpecker distinguishes it from any other bird in North America. Juveniles, however, have a brownish head and underparts and lack the gray collar, red face, and pink belly. Lewis's Woodpecker is also notably quieter than other woodpeckers, but it aggressively defends its food sources from other woodpeckers, especially in the winter. During flight, the bird accomplishes acrobatic maneuvers in pursuit of flying insects, sallying out from a perch in order to catch them. Alexander Wilson, the founder of North American ornithology, named this species in 1811, to honor Meriwether Lewis, because it was collected during the Lewis and Clark expedition.

**VOICE** *Churrs* sound; drumming not loud.
**NESTING** Cavity nester, usually in dead tree trunks, with preference for natural cavities and previously used nest holes; 6–7 eggs; 1 brood; May–August.
**FEEDING** Eats a variety of flying insects during breeding season; acorns, other nuts, and fruit, at other times.

**FAVORITE HANGOUT**
This bird is found in a variety of habitats, but is most common in ponderosa pine forests.

**LOVE NEST**
Lewis's Woodpecker excavates cavities in dead trees for nesting purposes.

**OCCURRENCE**
Prefers open ponderosa pine forests for breeding, especially old growth stands that have been modified by burning. Also found in riverside woodlands with cottonwood trees. Has a distinct fondness for open canopy. In winter, favors oak woodlands and nut and fruit orchards.

| Length **10–11in (25–28cm)** | Wingspan **19–20in (48–51cm)** | Weight **3¼–5oz (90–150g)** |
| Social **Solitary** | Lifespan **Unknown** | Status **Localized** |

| DATE SEEN | WHERE | | NOTES |
|---|---|---|---|
| | | | |
| | | | |
| | | | |
| | | | |

| Order **Piciformes** | Family **Picidae** | Species *Melanerpes formicivorus* |

# Acorn Woodpecker

red crown
white brow
white eye-ring
glossy black back
white underparts with black streaks
**MALE**

**MALE**
red crown
white wing patch
**IN FLIGHT**
black wing feathers

black crown
white, finely streaked underparts
**FEMALE**

**FLIGHT:** typical woodpecker undulations with short periods of wingbeats then closing of wings.

Unlike most other North American woodpeckers, the Acorn Woodpecker stores its food in trees for its winter supply. A very loud and highly social species, family members cooperate to gather acorns. The birds prefer old forests because these tend to produce more acorns and the wood is softer, making it easier to excavate cavities and store the acorns. This makes the species highly dependent on oak trees. They adopt areas where there is more than one species of oak, so that if one species fails to produce, another might yield acorns.

**VOICE** Primary year-round call a loud *waka-waka-waka*, repeated often; drumming accelerates toward the end.

**NESTING** Cavities in trunks or limbs of dead trees; 4–6 eggs; April–June.

**FEEDING** Feeds mainly on acorns; fruit and insects also eaten.

### SIMILAR SPECIES

**WHITE-HEADED WOODPECKER**
see p.233
white face
black back

**TREE CAVITIES**
A nest site may contain several cavities for breeding, typically in a large tree.

**STORING FOOD**
An obsessive acorn storer, it drills holes in oaks and accumulates large numbers of acorns.

**OCCURRENCE**
Occurs in western US and Mexico, south to Nicaragua. Primarily uses oak and pine oak woodlands as its breeding and wintering habitat. Also found in urban parks and suburban areas where oak trees are present. Will use areas with other kinds of trees as long as oak trees also occur in the vicinity.

| Length **7–9in (17.5–23cm)** | Wingspan **14–17in (36–43cm)** | Weight **2¼–3oz (65–85g)** |
| Social **Family groups** | Lifespan **Up to 16 years** | Status **Secure** |

| DATE SEEN | WHERE | NOTES |
| --- | --- | --- |
| | | |
| | | |
| | | |
| | | |
| | | |

| Order **Piciformes** | Family **Picidae** | Species *Sphyrapicus thyroideus* |
|---|---|---|

# Williamson's Sapsucker

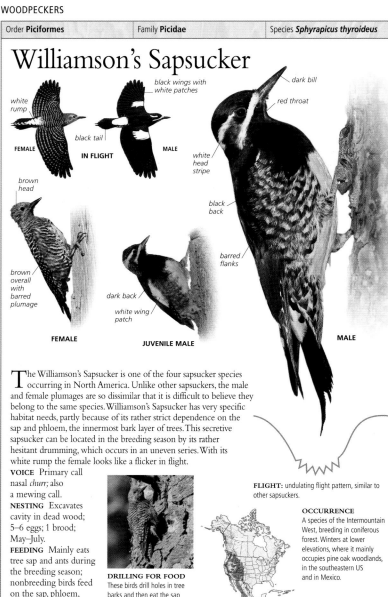

white rump

**FEMALE**

black wings with white patches

black tail

**MALE**

**IN FLIGHT**

dark bill

red throat

white head stripe

black back

barred flanks

**MALE**

brown head

brown overall with barred plumage

**FEMALE**

dark back

white wing patch

**JUVENILE MALE**

The Williamson's Sapsucker is one of the four sapsucker species occurring in North America. Unlike other sapsuckers, the male and female plumages are so dissimilar that it is difficult to believe they belong to the same species. Williamson's Sapsucker has very specific habitat needs, partly because of its rather strict dependence on the sap and phloem, the innermost bark layer of trees. This secretive sapsucker can be located in the breeding season by its rather hesitant drumming, which occurs in an uneven series. With its white rump the female looks like a flicker in flight.

**VOICE** Primary call nasal *churr*; also a mewing call.
**NESTING** Excavates cavity in dead wood; 5–6 eggs; 1 brood; May–July.
**FEEDING** Mainly eats tree sap and ants during the breeding season; nonbreeding birds feed on the sap, phloem, and fruit of trees.

**DRILLING FOR FOOD**
These birds drill holes in tree barks and then eat the sap and insects that emerge.

**FLIGHT:** undulating flight pattern, similar to other sapsuckers.

**OCCURRENCE**
A species of the Intermountain West, breeding in coniferous forest. Winters at lower elevations, where it mainly occupies pine oak woodlands, in the southeastern US and in Mexico.

| Length **9in (23cm)** | Wingspan **17in (43cm)** | Weight **1¾ oz (50g)** |
|---|---|---|
| Social **Pairs** | Lifespan **Unknown** | Status **Declining** |

| DATE SEEN | WHERE | NOTES |
|---|---|---|
| | | |
| | | |
| | | |
| | | |
| | | |

| Order **Piciformes** | Family **Picidae** | Species *Sphyrapicus varius* |

# Yellow-bellied Sapsucker 🔊

**MALE**

**IN FLIGHT**

white patch on inner wing

red forehead

red throat

pale yellow to breast and belly

black-and-white patterned face

white rump

dark brown fore-head

no red on throat

white throat

black-and-white barring on back

**JUVENILE**     **FEMALE**     **MALE**

The Yellow-bellied Sapsucker, with its red, black, and white coloring and soft yellow wash on its underparts, is a striking bird. Like its relatives, the Red-breasted Sapsucker and the Red-naped Sapsucker, it drills holes in trees to drink sap. It was only in 1983 that the sapsuckers were allocated to four separate species. This is one of the only two North American woodpeckers that are completely migratory, with females moving farther south than males. The other species is the Red-naped Sapsucker, its western relative.

**VOICE** Primary call a mewing *wheer-wheer-wheer*.

**NESTING** Cavities in dead trees; 5–6 eggs; 1 brood; May–June.

**FEEDING** Drinks sap; eats ants and other small insects; feeds on the inner bark of trees, also a variety of fruit.

**FLIGHT:** typical woodpecker, undulating flight pattern with intermittent flapping and gliding.

**STRIKING SPECIES**
The Yellow-bellied Sapsucker's white rump and black-and-white forked tail are clearly evident here.

**SIMILAR SPECIES**

**WILLIAMSON'S SAPSUCKER ♀**
see p.224

brown head

more extensive barring on back

**RED-NAPED SAPSUCKER**
see p.226

red patch on forehead

two rows of white bars on back

**OCCURRENCE**
Breeds in eastern Alaska, Canada, and south to the Appalachians. Prefers either deciduous forests or mixed deciduous-coniferous forests; preferably young forests. In winter, it is found in open wooded areas in southeastern states, Caribbean islands, and Central America.

| Length **8–9in (20–23cm)** | Wingspan **16–18in (41–46cm)** | Weight **1¾ oz (50g)** |
| Social **Solitary/Pairs** | Lifespan **Up to 7 years** | Status **Secure** |

| DATE SEEN | WHERE | NOTES |
|---|---|---|
| | | |
| | | |
| | | |
| | | |

| Order **Piciformes** | Family **Picidae** | Species *Sphyrapicus nuchalis* |

# Red-naped Sapsucker

**ADULT**

white rump

**IN FLIGHT**

red throat patch

black and white bars on tail

red forehead and crown

red patch on nape

extensive red on throat

white stripe on face

red patch on back of head

whitish chin

black-and-white barring on back

white patches on wings

**FEMALE**

**MALE**

The Red-naped Sapsucker is closely related to the Red-breasted Sapsucker and the Yellow-bellied Sapsucker. Indeed, where these three species overlap geographically, they occasionally interbreed, and birds with intermediate plumages can sometimes be seen. Like the other sapsuckers, this bird drills concentric rings in trees, and extends its specialized tongue into the wound to reach the sap.

**VOICE** Mewing *wheer-wheer-wheer*, virtually identical to that of the Red-breasted and Yellow-bellied sapsuckers.

**NESTING** Cavity nester; 4–5 eggs; 1 brood; May–August.

**FEEDING** Feeds on sap and seeds; fruit and other vegetable matter; also insects and spiders.

**FLIGHT:** typical woodpecker, undulating flight pattern, with intermittent flapping and gliding.

**ASPEN DWELLER**
The Red-naped Sapsucker excavates its nest cavities in live aspens.

| SIMILAR SPECIES | | |
|---|---|---|
| **YELLOW-BELLIED SAPSUCKER** see p.225 — less red on throat / no red on nape | **RED-BREASTED SAPSUCKER** see p.227 — all-red head / red breast | |

**OCCURRENCE**
Breeds in coniferous forest, intermixed with aspen, in the Rocky Mountains from western Canada south to California; also riverside woodlands. Winter habitats include forests, open woodlands, parks, and orchards in the Southwest. North American populations migrate south to Mexico.

| Length **8–9in (20–23cm)** | Wingspan **17in (43cm)** | Weight **2⅛ oz (60g)** |
| Social **Solitary/Migrant flocks** | Lifespan **Up to 3 years** | Status **Localized** |

| DATE SEEN | WHERE | NOTES |
|---|---|---|
| | | |
| | | |
| | | |
| | | |
| | | |

| Order **Piciformes** | Family **Picidae** | Species *Sphyrapicus ruber* |

# Red-breasted Sapsucker

**IN FLIGHT**

white rump

yellowish spots on back

**MALE (S. r. ruber)**

duller head

red head

thick bill

large white patch on wing

red breast

deep red head

heavy white markings on upperparts

black back with white feathers

pale yellowish belly

**ADULT (S. r. ruber)**

**ADULT (S. r. daggetti)**

**ADULT (S. r. daggetti)**

**FLIGHT:** undulating flight pattern with intermittent flapping and gliding.

A part from its distinctive red head and breast, the Red-breasted Sapsucker resembles other sapsuckers—so much so that the closely related Red-breasted, Red-naped, and Yellow-bellied Sapsuckers were once all considered to belong to the same species. Like its relatives, the Red-breasted Sapsucker drills holes in tree trunks to extract sap. Other birds, and mammals, such as squirrels and bats, obtain food from these holes. The northern subspecies, *S. r. ruber*, occurs from Alaska to Oregon, and has a back lightly marked with gold spots and a more brightly colored head. Its southern counterpart, *S. r. daggetti*, has a back more heavily marked with white.
**VOICE** Call reminiscent of a mewing cat; normally does not vocalize outside the breeding season.
**NESTING** Excavates cavity in deciduous trees such as aspen and willow, but will also nest in conifers if deciduous trees are not available; 4–5 eggs; 1 brood; May–July.
**FEEDING** Mainly drills for sap from a number of plants; also eats the insects that have become trapped in the sap.

**RED-HEADED DRILLER**
Red-breasted Sapsuckers drill holes in trees to drink sap and eat the insects attracted to it.

**OCCURRENCE**
Breeds in a wide range of habitats, including coniferous forests, but may also select deciduous forests and habitats along rivers. Prefers areas with dead trees. A partial migrant, it winters within its breeding range, but also moves south, as far as northern Baja California.

**SIMILAR SPECIES**

**RED-NAPED SAPSUCKER**
see p.226

red crown

more white on back

| Length **8–9in (20–23cm)** | Wingspan **15–16in (38–41cm)** | Weight **2oz (55g)** |
| Social **Solitary** | Lifespan **2–3 years** | Status **Localized** |

| DATE SEEN | WHERE | NOTES |
|---|---|---|
| | | |
| | | |
| | | |
| | | |

| Order **Piciformes** | Family **Picidae** | Species *Picoides dorsalis* |
|---|---|---|

# American Three-toed Woodpecker

black-and-white barred back

**MALE**

**IN FLIGHT**

large yellow patch

black head

long, straight bill

black bars on flanks

black-and-white streaked crown

white breast

**FEMALE**

**MALE**

This subspecies, formerly a separate species, breeds farther north than any other North American woodpecker, including its close relative, the Black-backed Woodpecker. It resembles the Black-backed Woodpecker in terms of size and head markings, and because they are the only two North American woodpeckers with three toes on each foot. The population of this woodpecker is decreasing as a result of habitat loss. This bird and its relative require mature forests with old or dead trees.

**VOICE** Call notes *queep*, *quip*, or *pik*; generally quiet, likened to the Yellow-bellied Sapsucker.

**NESTING** Excavates cavity mainly in dead or dying wood, sometimes in live wood; 4 eggs; 1 brood; May–July.

**FEEDING** Flakes off bark and eats insects underneath, mainly the larvae of bark beetles.

slightly forked tail

black tail, with white outer tail feathers

**FLIGHT:** undulating flight with rapid wingbeats typical of other woodpeckers.

**COLOR VARIATION**
The streaks on this species' back are highly variable; some populations have nearly all-white backs.

### SIMILAR SPECIES

**BLACK-BACKED WOODPECKER**
shorter call;
see p.229

solid black back

**OCCURRENCE**
Breeds in mature northern coniferous forests from Alaska to eastern Canada and south through the Rockies. Since it is largely nonmigratory, this is also the winter habitat for most populations, although it is found in more open areas in winter.

| Length **8–9in (20–23cm)** | Wingspan **15in (38cm)** | Weight **2¼–2½oz (65–70g)** |
|---|---|---|
| Social **Solitary/Pairs** | Lifespan **Unknown** | Status **Vulnerable** |

| DATE SEEN | WHERE | NOTES |
|---|---|---|
| | | |
| | | |
| | | |
| | | |
| | | |

| Order **Piciformes** | Family **Picidae** | Species ***Picoides arcticus*** |

# Black-backed Woodpecker

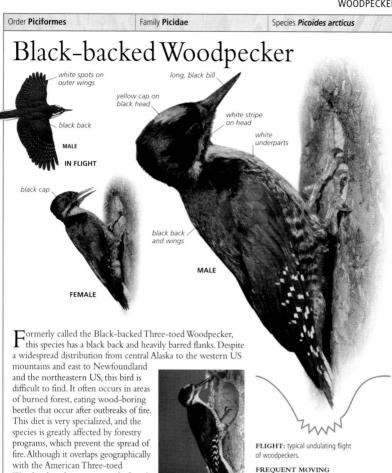

white spots on outer wings

long, black bill

yellow cap on black head

black back

**MALE**

**IN FLIGHT**

white stripe on head

white underparts

black cap

black back and wings

**MALE**

**FEMALE**

Formerly called the Black-backed Three-toed Woodpecker, this species has a black back and heavily barred flanks. Despite a widespread distribution from central Alaska to the western US mountains and east to Newfoundland and the northeastern US, this bird is difficult to find. It often occurs in areas of burned forest, eating wood-boring beetles that occur after outbreaks of fire. This diet is very specialized, and the species is greatly affected by forestry programs, which prevent the spread of fire. Although it overlaps geographically with the American Three-toed Woodpecker, the two are rarely found together in the same locality.

**VOICE** Main call a single *pik*.
**NESTING** Cavity excavated in tree; 3–4 eggs; 1 brood; May–July.
**FEEDING** Eats beetles, especially larvae of wood-boring beetles, by flaking off bark.

**FLIGHT:** typical undulating flight of woodpeckers.

**FREQUENT MOVING**
This bird excavates a new nest cavity each year, rarely returning in subsequent years.

**SIMILAR SPECIES**

AMERICAN THREE-TOED WOODPECKER see p.228

black-and-white barred upperparts

**OCCURRENCE**
Inhabitant of northern and mountain coniferous forests that require fire for renewal. Breeding occurs soon after sites are burned as new colonies are attracted to the habitat. In Michigan's Upper Peninsula, the bird uses trees similar to those in its northern habitat.

| Length **9–9½in (23–24cm)** | Wingspan **15–16in (38–41cm)** | Weight **2½oz (70g)** |
| Social **Pairs** | Lifespan **Unknown** | Status **Secure** |

| DATE SEEN | WHERE | NOTES |
|---|---|---|
| | | |
| | | |
| | | |
| | | |
| | | |

| Order **Piciformes** | Family **Picidae** | Species **Dryobates pubescens** |

# Downy Woodpecker 🔊

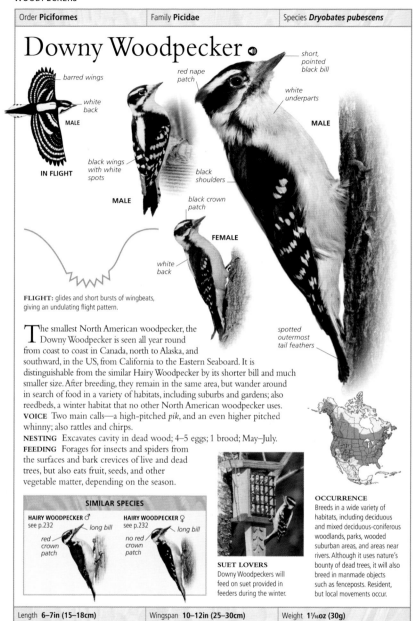

barred wings

white back

**MALE**

red nape patch

short, pointed black bill

white underparts

**MALE**

**IN FLIGHT**

black wings with white spots

**MALE**

black shoulders

black crown patch

**FEMALE**

white back

white back

**FLIGHT:** glides and short bursts of wingbeats, giving an undulating flight pattern.

spotted outermost tail feathers

The smallest North American woodpecker, the Downy Woodpecker is seen all year round from coast to coast in Canada, north to Alaska, and southward, in the US, from California to the Eastern Seaboard. It is distinguishable from the similar Hairy Woodpecker by its shorter bill and much smaller size. After breeding, they remain in the same area, but wander around in search of food in a variety of habitats, including suburbs and gardens; also reedbeds, a winter habitat that no other North American woodpecker uses.

**VOICE** Two main calls—a high-pitched *pik*, and an even higher pitched whinny; also rattles and chirps.

**NESTING** Excavates cavity in dead wood; 4–5 eggs; 1 brood; May–July.

**FEEDING** Forages for insects and spiders from the surfaces and bark crevices of live and dead trees, but also eats fruit, seeds, and other vegetable matter, depending on the season.

### SIMILAR SPECIES

**HAIRY WOODPECKER ♂**
see p.232
long bill
red crown patch

**HAIRY WOODPECKER ♀**
see p.232
long bill
no red crown patch

**SUET LOVERS**
Downy Woodpeckers will feed on suet provided in feeders during the winter.

**OCCURRENCE**
Breeds in a wide variety of habitats, including deciduous and mixed deciduous-coniferous woodlands, parks, wooded suburban areas, and areas near rivers. Although it uses nature's bounty of dead trees, it will also breed in manmade objects such as fenceposts. Resident, but local movements occur.

| Length **6–7in (15–18cm)** | Wingspan **10–12in (25–30cm)** | Weight **1¹⁄₁₆oz (30g)** |
| Social **Solitary/Flocks** | Lifespan **Up to 11 years** | Status **Secure** |

| DATE SEEN | WHERE | NOTES |
| --- | --- | --- |
| | | |
| | | |
| | | |
| | | |
| | | |

| Order **Piciformes** | Family **Picidae** | Species ***Dryobates scalaris*** |

# Ladder-backed Woodpecker

**MALE**

**IN FLIGHT**

*barred wings*

*buffy forehead patch*

*black crown*

*red crown*

*straight, black bill*

*fine streaking*

**FEMALE**

*barred back*

**MALE**

*black-and-white bars on back*

**MALE**

*white-barred outer tail feathers*

A bird of the southwestern US and Mexico, the Ladder-backed Woodpecker has conspicuous, zebra-like black-and-white barring on its back, and a wide black-and-white striped facial pattern. The male, like many other North American woodpeckers, has a red crown. This nonmigratory species can be seen year-round in its range. The Ladder-backed Woodpecker occasionally hybridizes with its closest relative, the Nuttall's Woodpecker. Desert cacti are used both as a place to breed and as a food source.

**VOICE** Two main calls: short *peek* call, and rattle- or whinny-like call of many notes; call descends at end.

**NESTING** Excavates cavity in dead or dying wood; 4–5 eggs; 1 brood; May–July.

**FEEDING** Males forage lower and on the ground, probing for insects, sometimes around cactus roots; females forage higher, gleaning insects from bark; also feeds on fruit of cactus.

**FLIGHT:** undulating and swift.

### SIMILAR SPECIES

**NUTTALL'S WOODPECKER ♂**
see p.445

*red on rear of crown*

**TREE GRUB**
This male Ladder-backed Woodpecker has just extracted a beetle larva from a tree trunk.

**OCCURRENCE**
Breeds in arid scrub, montane shrubbery, wooded canyons, and pine oak woodlands. In southern Arizona, the bird is seen in grasslands, but in Colorado it is found in piñon juniper woodlands. Nonmigratory species. Occurs south to Nicaragua.

| Length **7¼in (18.5cm)** | Wingspan **11–12in (28–30cm)** | Weight **1¹⁄₁₆–1¼oz (30–35g)** |
| Social **Unknown** | Lifespan **Up to 4 years** | Status **Secure** |

| DATE SEEN | WHERE | NOTES |
| --- | --- | --- |
| | | |
| | | |
| | | |
| | | |

| Order **Piciformes** | Family **Picidae** | Species *Dryobates villosus* |

# Hairy Woodpecker 🔊

**MALE**
- white back
- IN FLIGHT

- red patch on back of head
- no red patch on back of head
- black nape
- **MALE**
- **FEMALE**

- long, black bill
- black-and-white cheek stripes
- white underparts
- black upperparts
- black wing feathers with white barring
- black tail, with white outer feathers

L ike its smaller relative, the Downy Woodpecker, the Hairy Woodpecker is widespread in North America, breeding and wintering from coast to coast in the US and Canada. While in many respects the two species look quite similar, the Hairy Woodpecker has a larger and thicker bill and is about twice as large as the Downy Woodpecker. The Hairy Woodpecker is a bird of forests, where it uses live tree trunks both as nesting sites and as places to forage.

**VOICE** Call a bold, grating, sharp *Peek,* similar to that of the Downy Woodpecker, but lower in pitch, and louder. Drumming a rather loud, even series of taps.

**NESTING** Excavates cavity in live trees; 4 eggs; 1 brood; May–July.

**FEEDING** Eats mainly insects and their larvae; also nuts and seeds.

**FLIGHT:** undulating; short glides alternating with wingbeats.

**HOME SWEET HOME**
The Hairy Woodpecker is generally found in forests and prefers mature woodland areas, using both deciduous and coniferous trees.

**OCCURRENCE**
Breeds primarily in forests, both deciduous and coniferous, but also in more open woodlands, swamps, suburban parks, and wooded areas. Resident in North America all year round, though in the far north of its range it may move south for the winter.

### SIMILAR SPECIES

**DOWNY WOODPECKER ♂**
see p.230
- shorter bill
- black markings on outer wing feathers

**DOWNY WOODPECKER ♀**
see p.230
- shorter bill
- black markings on outer wing feathers

| Length **9–9½in (23–24cm)** | Wingspan **15–16in (38–41cm)** | Weight **2½oz (70g)** |
| Social **Solitary/Winter flocks** | Lifespan **At least 16 years** | Status **Secure** |

| DATE SEEN | WHERE | NOTES |
| --- | --- | --- |
| | | |
| | | |
| | | |
| | | |
| | | |

| Order **Piciformes** | Family **Picidae** | Species ***Dryobates albolarvatus*** |
|---|---|---|

# White-headed Woodpecker

**MALE** — conspicuous white wing patches

white head

**IN FLIGHT** — white head

red patch on nape

white head

pale yellowish wash to face

**MALE**

variable red to pinkish patch

lacks red patch

black body

duller/ black body

large white wing patch

**JUVENILE**

**FEMALE**

With its white head, black body, and white wing patches, the White-headed Woodpecker of western North America is striking; its plumage pattern is unique among North American woodpeckers. While it is common in some areas of its geographically restricted range, its population is vulnerable, especially in the Northwest, because of forest fragmentation. Ponderosa pine seeds are basic to its diet, and poor pine crops may result in low breeding success. In winter, males and females tend to forage separately, and females feed lower in trees.

**VOICE** Most common call 2–3 note sharp *peek-it* or *pitit*.

**NESTING** Excavates nest in dead trees and snags; 4–5 eggs; 1 brood; May–July.

**FEEDING** Eats arthropods, including ants, beetles, and spiders; also berries, and seeds, particularly pine seeds.

**FLIGHT:** undulating flight pattern typical of woodpeckers.

### SIMILAR SPECIES

**ACORN WOODPECKER** see p.223

white forehead patch

red crown

**PARENTING CHORES**
This bird is carrying food back to the nest to feed its young.

**OCCURRENCE**
A strictly western North American bird, occurs from British Columbia to California in mountain pine forests, especially with ponderosa pines. Habitat specialist, but many birds move to lower elevations in winter, can be seen in deserts of Montana, Wyoming, and California.

| Length **9–9½in (23–24cm)** | Wingspan **16–17in (41–43cm)** | Weight **2oz (55g)** |
|---|---|---|
| Social **Solitary** | Lifespan **Unknown** | Status **Localized** |

| DATE SEEN | WHERE | NOTES |
|---|---|---|
| | | |
| | | |
| | | |
| | | |
| | | |

| Order **Piciformes** | Family **Picidae** | Species **Colaptes auratus** |
|---|---|---|

# Northern Flicker 🔊

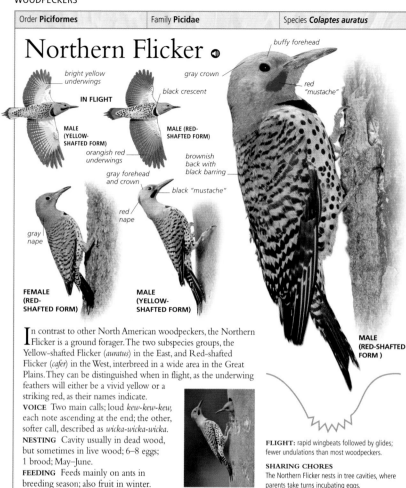

buffy forehead

gray crown

black crescent

red "mustache"

**IN FLIGHT**

bright yellow underwings

**MALE (YELLOW-SHAFTED FORM)**

**MALE (RED-SHAFTED FORM)**

orangish red underwings

brownish back with black barring

gray forehead and crown

black "mustache"

red nape

gray nape

**FEMALE (RED-SHAFTED FORM)**

**MALE (YELLOW-SHAFTED FORM)**

**MALE (RED-SHAFTED FORM )**

In contrast to other North American woodpeckers, the Northern Flicker is a ground forager. The two subspecies groups, the Yellow-shafted Flicker (*auratus*) in the East, and Red-shafted Flicker (*cafer*) in the West, interbreed in a wide area in the Great Plains. They can be distinguished when in flight, as the underwing feathers will either be a vivid yellow or a striking red, as their names indicate.

**VOICE** Two main calls; loud *kew-kew-kew*, each note ascending at the end; the other, softer call, described as *wicka-wicka-wicka*.

**NESTING** Cavity usually in dead wood, but sometimes in live wood; 6–8 eggs; 1 brood; May–June.

**FEEDING** Feeds mainly on ants in breeding season; also fruit in winter.

**FLIGHT:** rapid wingbeats followed by glides; fewer undulations than most woodpeckers.

**SHARING CHORES**
The Northern Flicker nests in tree cavities, where parents take turns incubating eggs.

**SIMILAR SPECIES**

**GILDED FLICKER**
see p.446

cinnamon crown

paler brown back

**FEET ON THE GROUND**
Unlike other woodpeckers, flickers can be found foraging for ants on the ground.

**OCCURRENCE**
A common species found in woodland in every part of the US, the southern half of Canada, and north into Alaska. During breeding season, prefers open woodlands and forest edge; also suburbs. Little is known about this bird's winter habitat.

| Length **12–13in (31–33cm)** | Wingspan **19–21in (48–53cm)** | Weight **4oz (125g)** |
|---|---|---|
| Social **Solitary** | Lifespan **9 years** | Status **Secure** |

| DATE SEEN | WHERE | NOTES |
|---|---|---|
| | | |
| | | |
| | | |
| | | |
| | | |

| Order **Piciformes** | Family **Picidae** | Species *Dryocopus pileatus* |

# Pileated Woodpecker ◀

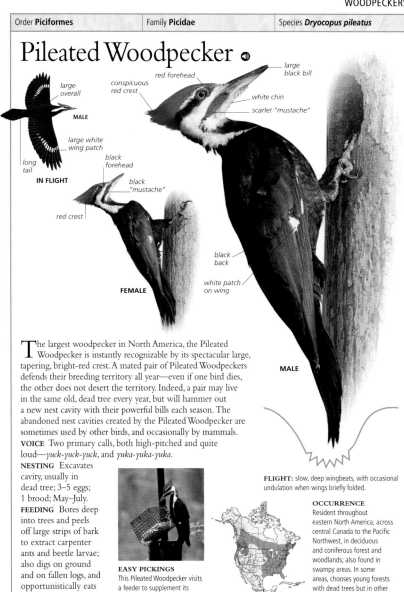

**MALE**

large overall

**IN FLIGHT**

large white wing patch

long tail

red forehead

conspicuous red crest

black forehead

black "mustache"

red crest

**FEMALE**

large black bill

white chin

scarlet "mustache"

black back

white patch on wing

**MALE**

The largest woodpecker in North America, the Pileated Woodpecker is instantly recognizable by its spectacular large, tapering, bright-red crest. A mated pair of Pileated Woodpeckers defends their breeding territory all year—even if one bird dies, the other does not desert the territory. Indeed, a pair may live in the same old, dead tree every year, but will hammer out a new nest cavity with their powerful bills each season. The abandoned nest cavities created by the Pileated Woodpecker are sometimes used by other birds, and occasionally by mammals.

**VOICE** Two primary calls, both high-pitched and quite loud—*yuck-yuck-yuck*, and *yuka-yuka-yuka*.

**NESTING** Excavates cavity, usually in dead tree; 3–5 eggs; 1 brood; May–July.

**FEEDING** Bores deep into trees and peels off large strips of bark to extract carpenter ants and beetle larvae; also digs on ground and on fallen logs, and opportunistically eats fruit and nuts.

**EASY PICKINGS**
This Pileated Woodpecker visits a feeder to supplement its natural diet.

**FLIGHT:** slow, deep wingbeats, with occasional undulation when wings briefly folded.

**OCCURRENCE**
Resident throughout eastern North America, across central Canada to the Pacific Northwest, in deciduous and coniferous forest and woodlands; also found in swampy areas. In some areas, chooses young forests with dead trees but in other places, old-growth forests.

| Length **16–18in (41–46cm)** | Wingspan **26–30in (66–76cm)** | Weight **10oz (275g)** |
| Social **Pairs** | Lifespan **Up to 9 years** | Status **Secure** |

| DATE SEEN | WHERE | NOTES |
|-----------|-------|-------|
| | | |
| | | |
| | | |
| | | |
| | | |

# FALCONS

FALCONS INCLUDE birds that catch insects on the wing, others that hover to search for prey below, and yet others that are more dramatic aerial hunters. Some use high-speed "stoops" from above, seizing birds up to their own size, while larger species such as the Gyrfalcon can kill prey much heavier than themselves. They are distinguished from bird-eating hawks in the genus *Accipiter* by their dark eyes and their hunting styles: both use their toes to catch prey, but while falcons kill primarily with their bills, hawks kill with their toes. Falcons' bills are equipped with a notch or "tooth" on the upper mandible. Unlike hawks and eagles, falcons do not build nests, but some use old nests of other birds.

**PRECISION LANDING**
A Peregrine Falcon swoops down to settle on the branch, thrusting out its toes to absorb the shock of landing.

# NEW WORLD FLYCATCHERS

BIRDS POPULARLY known as "flycatchers" occur in many parts of the world; however several different families of songbirds have this name. With the exception of some Old World species that stray into Alaska, the North American flycatchers are members of a single family—the Tyrant Flycatchers (Tyrannidae). With about 400 species, this is the largest bird family in the New World. These birds are uniform in appearance, with only a hint of the diversity in the family that is found in Central and South America. Most are drab-colored, olive-green or gray birds, sometimes with yellow underparts. The Vermilion Flycatcher is a striking exception, as is the gray and salmon-pink Scissor-tailed Flycatcher, which also has elongated outer tail feathers. Members of the genus *Empidonax* include some of the most difficult birds to identify in North America; they are best distinguished by their songs. Typical flycatcher feeding behavior is to sit on a branch or exposed perch, then sally to catch flying insects. Tyrannid flycatchers are found across North America, except in Arctic regions. Most are found in wooded habitats, though others prefer woodland edges and deserts. Nearly all flycatchers are long-distance migrants and spend the northern winter in Central and South America.

**BIG MOUTHS**
Young Dusky Flycatchers display the wide bills that help them catch flying insects as adults.

| Order **Falconiformes** | Family **Falconidae** | Species *Falco sparverius* |

# American Kestrel 🔊

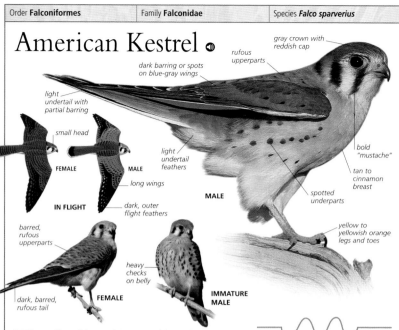

gray crown with reddish cap

rufous upperparts

dark barring or spots on blue-gray wings

light undertail with partial barring

small head

light undertail feathers

**FEMALE**

**MALE**

long wings

**IN FLIGHT**

dark, outer flight feathers

bold "mustache"

tan to cinnamon breast

spotted underparts

**MALE**

yellow to yellowish orange legs and toes

barred, rufous upperparts

heavy checks on belly

dark, barred, rufous tail

**FEMALE**

**IMMATURE MALE**

The smallest of the North American falcons, the American Kestrel features long pointed wings, a "tooth and notch" bill structure, and the dark brown eyes typical of falcons, though kestrels have shorter toes than other falcons. This may be because of the fact that kestrels often dive into long grass to capture insects and small mammals, which would be more difficult with long, thin toes. Male and female American Kestrels show differences in plumage, and also in size.

**VOICE** Common call a high-pitched *killy-killy-killy*.

**NESTING** Natural cavities, crevices, holes in dead trees, woodpeckers' holes, crevices in barns, manmade nest boxes if constructed and located properly; 4–5 eggs; 1 brood; April–June.

**FEEDING** Plunges for grasshoppers and crickets in spring and summer; small birds and mice in fall and winter; lizards and snakes.

**FLIGHT:** delicate and almost moth-like; may hover in one place for long, searching for prey.

**HIGH FLIER**
A male American Kestrel hovers over a field, its sharp eyes scanning the ground for insects and rodents.

### SIMILAR SPECIES

**MERLIN**
see p.238

no distinct stripes on head

**SHARP-SHINNED HAWK** ⊙
see p.196

brownish upperparts

darker belly

longer toes

**OCCURRENCE**
From near the northern tree line in Alaska and Canada south, east, and west throughout most of North America. Also occurs in Central and South America. Habitat ranges from semi-open tree groves to grasslands, cultivated and fallow farmland, and open desert.

| Length **9in (23cm)** | Wingspan **22in (56cm)** | Weight **3½–4oz (100–125g)** |
| Social **Family groups** | Lifespan **10–15 years** | Status **Vulnerable** |

| DATE SEEN | WHERE | NOTES |
|---|---|---|
| | | |
| | | |
| | | |
| | | |
| | | |

| Order **Falconiformes** | Family **Falconidae** | Species **Falco columbarius** |
| --- | --- | --- |

# Merlin

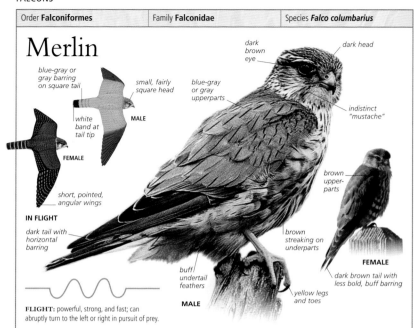

dark brown eye

dark head

blue-gray or gray barring on square tail

small, fairly square head

blue-gray or gray upperparts

indistinct "mustache"

white band at tail tip

**MALE**

**FEMALE**

short, pointed, angular wings

brown upperparts

**IN FLIGHT**

dark tail with horizontal barring

brown streaking on underparts

**FEMALE**

dark brown tail with less bold, buff barring

buff undertail feathers

**MALE**

yellow legs and toes

**FLIGHT:** powerful, strong, and fast; can abruptly turn to the left or right in pursuit of prey.

Merlins are small, fast-flying falcons that were formerly known as "pigeon hawks," because their shape and flight are similar to those strong fliers. Merlins can overtake and capture a wide variety of prey. They can turn on a dime, and use their long, thin toes, typical of falcons, to pluck birds from the air after launching a direct attack. Males are smaller than females, and different in color. Both males and females show geographical color variations.

**VOICE** Male call a high-pitched *ki-ki-ki-ki*; female call a low-pitched *kek-ek-ek-ek-ek*.

**NESTING** Small scrapes on ground in open country, or abandoned nests of other species, such as crows, in forested areas; 4–6 eggs; 1 brood; April–June.

**FEEDING** Catches small birds in midair, and occasionally birds as large as doves; also feeds on small mammals, including bats.

**ABOUT TO ROUSE**
An adult female Merlin sits on a moss-covered rock, about to "rouse," or fluff out and shake her feathers.

**SIMILAR SPECIES**

**AMERICAN KESTREL**
see p.237

**SHARP-SHINNED HAWK**
see p.196

rounder wings

barred underparts

cinnamon flanks

tan breast

longer tail

**OCCURRENCE**
In North America breeds throughout Alaska and Canada. Highly migratory, winters throughout the US south to northern South America. Merlins can be seen hunting along coastlines, over marshlands and open fields, and in desert areas.

| Length **10in (25cm)** | Wingspan **24in (61cm)** | Weight **5–7oz (150–200g)** |
| --- | --- | --- |
| Social **Pairs/Family groups** | Lifespan **10–15 years** | Status **Secure** |

| DATE SEEN | WHERE | NOTES |
| --- | --- | --- |
| | | |
| | | |
| | | |
| | | |
| | | |

| Order **Falconiformes** | Family **Falconidae** | Species *Falco peregrinus* |

# Peregrine Falcon 🔊

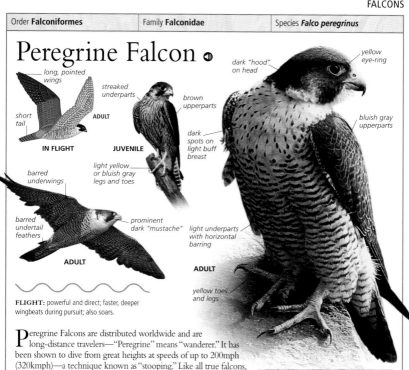

*long, pointed wings*

*short tail*

**IN FLIGHT**

*streaked underparts*

**ADULT**

**JUVENILE**

*brown upperparts*

*dark spots on light buff breast*

*light yellow or bluish gray legs and toes*

*barred underwings*

*barred undertail feathers*

*prominent dark "mustache"*

**ADULT**

*light underparts with horizontal barring*

**ADULT**

*dark "hood" on head*

*yellow eye-ring*

*bluish gray upperparts*

*yellow toes and legs*

**FLIGHT:** powerful and direct; faster, deeper wingbeats during pursuit; also soars.

Peregrine Falcons are distributed worldwide and are long-distance travelers—"Peregrine" means "wanderer." It has been shown to dive from great heights at speeds of up to 200mph (320kmph)—a technique known as "stooping." Like all true falcons, this species has a pointed "tooth" on its upper bill and a "notch" on the lower one, and it instinctively bites the neck of captured prey to kill it. From the 1950s to the 1980s, its breeding ability was reduced by the insecticide DDT, which resulted in thin eggshells that could easily be crushed by the parent. Peregrines were then bred in captivity, and later released into the wild. Their status is now secure.

**VOICE** Sharp *hek-hek-hek* when alarmed.

**NESTING** Shallow scrape on cliff or building (nest sites are used year after year); 2–5 eggs; 1 brood; March–June.

**FEEDING** Dives on prey—birds of various sizes in flight; now feeds on pigeons in cities.

**PARENTAL CARE**
An adult Peregrine gently feeds a hatchling bits of meat; the remaining egg is likely to hatch soon.

### SIMILAR SPECIES

**GYRFALCON**
see p.446
*larger and stockier*
*longer tail*

*less defined "hood"*
*light sandy brown upperparts*

**PRAIRIE FALCON**
see p.240

*lighter head color*

**OCCURRENCE**
A variety of habitats across northern North America, ranging from open valleys to cities with tall buildings. Peregrines prefer to inhabit cliffs along sea coasts, in addition to inland mountain ranges, but also occur in open country such as scrubland and saltmarshes.

| Length **16in (41cm)** | Wingspan **3¼–3½ft (1–1.1m)** | Weight **22–35oz (620–1,000g)** |
| Social **Solitary/Pairs** | Lifespan **15–20 years** | Status **Secure** |

| DATE SEEN | WHERE | NOTES |
|-----------|-------|-------|
| | | |
| | | |
| | | |
| | | |
| | | |

| Order **Falconiformes** | Family **Falconidae** | Species *Falco mexicanus* |

# Prairie Falcon

yellow eye-ring

yellow patch of skin near bill

light head and "mustache"

white cheek

long, pointed wings

**ADULT**

light, sandy brown upperparts with incomplete barring

longish tail

distinctive, triangle-shaped patch on wingpit feathers

**IN FLIGHT**

light underparts with brown spots

**ADULT**

yellow legs and toes

light undertail feathers

Prairie Falcons are light-colored, buoyant residents of the arid regions of North America. They blend in well with their surroundings (cliff faces and dry grass), where they are invisible to their prey. Prairie Falcons chase their prey close to the ground and do not often dive or "stoop" on prey from a great height. Ground squirrels are important prey items in some areas, and breeding is often linked with the squirrels' emergence. The sexes are very similar in coloration, though juveniles have a streaked rather than spotted breast. The underwing pattern with almost black feathers in the "wingpits" is distinctive; no other North American falcon shows this mark.

**VOICE** Repeated shrill *kik-kik-kik-kik-kik*.

**NESTING** Slight, shallow scrapes, almost always located on high cliff ledges or bluffs; 3–6 eggs; 1 brood; March–July.

**FEEDING** Feeds on small to medium-sized birds and small mammals, such as ground squirrels.

**FLIGHT:** fast flight; capable of soaring and diving; usually chases prey low above the ground.

**STRIKING MUSTACHE**
An inquisitive Prairie Falcon stares at the camera. The white cheek is obvious from this angle.

**SIMILAR SPECIES**

**MERLIN**
see p.238

smaller overall

heavily streaked underparts

**PEREGRINE FALCON** ○
see p.239

darker head

streaked underparts

yellow or bluish gray legs and toes

**OCCURRENCE**
Interior North America, from central British Columbia east to western North Dakota and south to southern California, and Mexico, Arizona, northern Texas. Found in open plains, prairies, and grasslands, dotted with buttes or cliffs. A partial migrant, it moves east of its breeding range in winter.

| Length **16in (41cm)** | Wingspan **3¼ft (1m)** | Weight **22–30oz (625–850g)** |
| Social **Solitary/Pairs** | Lifespan **10–20 years** | Status **Localized** |

| DATE SEEN | WHERE | NOTES |
| --- | --- | --- |
| | | |
| | | |
| | | |
| | | |

| Order **Passeriformes** | Family **Tyrannidae** | Species **Myiarchus cinerascens** |

# Ash-throated Flycatcher

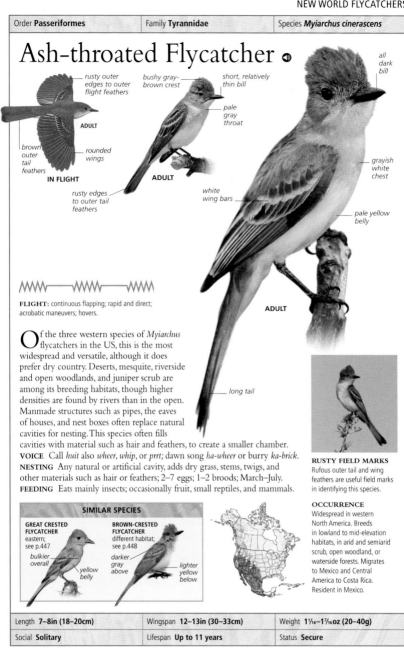

rusty outer edges to outer flight feathers

bushy gray-brown crest

short, relatively thin bill

all dark bill

**ADULT**

pale gray throat

brown outer tail feathers

rounded wings

**IN FLIGHT**

**ADULT**

grayish white chest

rusty edges to outer tail feathers

white wing bars

pale yellow belly

white wing bars

**ADULT**

**FLIGHT:** continuous flapping; rapid and direct; acrobatic maneuvers; hovers.

long tail

Of the three western species of *Myiarchus* flycatchers in the US, this is the most widespread and versatile, although it does prefer dry country. Deserts, mesquite, riverside and open woodlands, and juniper scrub are among its breeding habitats, though higher densities are found by rivers than in the open. Manmade structures such as pipes, the eaves of houses, and nest boxes often replace natural cavities for nesting. This species often fills cavities with material such as hair and feathers, to create a smaller chamber.

**VOICE** Call *huit* also *wheer, whip,* or *prrt;* dawn song *ha-wheer* or burry *ka-brick.*
**NESTING** Any natural or artificial cavity, adds dry grass, stems, twigs, and other materials such as hair or feathers; 2–7 eggs; 1–2 broods; March–July.
**FEEDING** Eats mainly insects; occasionally fruit, small reptiles, and mammals.

**RUSTY FIELD MARKS**
Rufous outer tail and wing feathers are useful field marks in identifying this species.

**OCCURRENCE**
Widespread in western North America. Breeds in lowland to mid-elevation habitats, in arid and semiarid scrub, open woodland, or waterside forests. Migrates to Mexico and Central America to Costa Rica. Resident in Mexico.

## SIMILAR SPECIES

**GREAT CRESTED FLYCATCHER** eastern; see p.447

bulkier overall

yellow belly

**BROWN-CRESTED FLYCATCHER** different habitat; see p.448

darker gray above

lighter yellow below

| Length **7–8in (18–20cm)** | Wingspan **12–13in (30–33cm)** | Weight **1¹/₁₆–1⁷/₁₆oz (20–40g)** |
| Social **Solitary** | Lifespan **Up to 11 years** | Status **Secure** |

| DATE SEEN | WHERE | NOTES |
|---|---|---|
| | | |
| | | |
| | | |
| | | |
| | | |

241

| Order **Passeriformes** | Family **Tyrannidae** | Species **Tyrannus vociferans** |

# Cassin's Kingbird

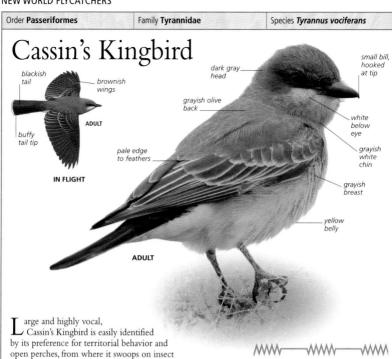

blackish tail

brownish wings

**ADULT**

buffy tail tip

**IN FLIGHT**

pale edge to feathers

**ADULT**

dark gray head

grayish olive back

small bill, hooked at tip

white below eye

grayish white chin

grayish breast

yellow belly

L arge and highly vocal, Cassin's Kingbird is easily identified by its preference for territorial behavior and open perches, from where it swoops on insect prey. Courting birds impress each other in a display in which they hover in unison over a favorite perch. Cassin's Kingbird overlaps in range with the Western Kingbird, although there appears to be minimal competition between the two species. However, the nesting success of Cassin's Kingbird's is lower in areas where both birds occur.

**FLIGHT:** direct, strong; males engage in "tumble flight"—fly up, stall, twist, pitch, tumble down.

**VOICE** Calls *ch-tuur* and low, nasal *chi-beer* or *chi-queer;* dawn song 1–2 rasping sounds followed by a prolonged *keecyur.*

**NESTING** Large, bulky open cup of twigs and rootlets; on branch high in deciduous tree; 3–5 eggs; 1 brood; April–August.

**FEEDING** Mainly insectivorous; feeds on beetles, bees, wasps, ants, flies, aphids, and grasshoppers; also eats fruit.

**SIMILAR SPECIES**

**TROPICAL KINGBIRD**
thick-billed;
see p.448

paler breast

**WESTERN KINGBIRD**
see p.243

paler breast

darker wing

**HIGH ALERT**
This gray-breasted Cassin's
Kingbird is perched and alert
in mature riverside woodland.

**OCCURRENCE**
Breeds in California, and
the interior West in waterside
woodland, piñon pine, juniper
forests, grassland, desert
scrub, rural, and suburban
habitats. US population
winters south to Mexico
and Guatemala, overlapping
with resident population.

| Length **8–9in (20–23cm)** | Wingspan **16in (41cm)** | Weight **1⁹⁄₁₆oz (45g)** |
| Social **Solitary** | Lifespan **Unknown** | Status **Secure** |

| DATE SEEN | WHERE | NOTES |
|-----------|-------|-------|
| | | |
| | | |
| | | |
| | | |
| | | |

| Order **Passeriformes** | Family **Tyrannidae** | Species *Tyrannus verticalis* |

# Western Kingbird 🔊

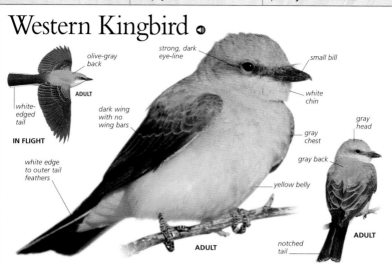

**IN FLIGHT**

olive-gray back

**ADULT**

white-edged tail

strong, dark eye-line

small bill

white chin

dark wing with no wing bars

gray head

gray chest

gray back

white edge to outer tail feathers

yellow belly

**ADULT**

notched tail

**ADULT**

A conspicuous summer breeder in the US, the Western Kingbird occurs in open habitats in much of western North America. The white outer edges on its outer tail feathers distinguish it from other kingbirds. Its population has expanded eastward over the last 100 years. A large, loosely defined territory is defended against other kingbirds when breeding begins in spring; a smaller core area is defended as the season progresses.

**VOICE** Calls include *whit*, *pwee-t*, and chatter; song, regularly repeated sharp *kip* notes and high-pitched notes.

**NESTING** Open, bulky cup of grass, rootlets, and twigs in tree, shrub, utility pole; 2–7 eggs; 1 brood; April–July.

**FEEDING** Feeds on a wide variety of insects; also berries and fruit.

**FLIGHT:** agile, fast, direct, flapping flight; flies to catch insects; hovers to pick bugs on vegetation.

**FENCE POST**
A favorite place for the Western Kingbird to perch, and look around, is on fenceposts.

**QUENCHING THIRST**
A juvenile Western Kingbird drinks at the edge of a shallow pool of water.

**SIMILAR SPECIES**

**TROPICAL KINGBIRD** see p.448

**CASSIN'S KINGBIRD** see p.242

heavier bill

paler wings

olive-yellow chest

gray tip to tail

**OCCURRENCE**
Widespread in southwestern Canada and the western US, in open habitats, such as grasslands, prairie, desert shrub, pastures, and cropland, near elevated perches; particularly near water. Winters in similar habitats and in tropical forest and shrubbery from Mexico to Costa Rica.

| Length **8–9in (20–23cm)** | Wingspan **15–16in (38–41cm)** | Weight **1¼–1⁹⁄₁₆oz (35–45g)** |
|---|---|---|
| Social **Solitary** | Lifespan **Up to 6 years** | Status **Secure** |

| DATE SEEN | WHERE | NOTES |
|---|---|---|
| | | |
| | | |
| | | |
| | | |
| | | |

| Order **Passeriformes** | Family **Tyrannidae** | Species *Tyrannus tyrannus* |

# Eastern Kingbird 🔊

**ADULT**

dark eyes

dark crown and cheeks, almost black

faint gray "necklace"

white throat and underparts

relatively short, thick bill

**IN FLIGHT**

white-tipped tail

white throat

pale edges to wing feathers

**ADULT**

slate-gray back

white belly

black legs and toes

**ADULT**

white undertail feathers

black tail with white tip

black tail with white tip

The Eastern Kingbird is a tame and widely distributed bird. It is a highly territorial species and is known for its aggressive behavior toward potential predators, particularly crows and hawks, which it pursues relentlessly. It is able to identify and remove the eggs of the Brown-headed Cowbird when they are laid in its nest. The Eastern Kingbird is generally monogamous and pairs will return to the same territory in subsequent years. This species winters in tropical South America, where it forages for fruit in the treetops of evergreen forests.

**VOICE** Principal call is loud, metallic *chatter-zeer*; song rapid, electric *kdik-kdik-kdik-pika-pika-pika-kzeeeer*.

**NESTING** Open cup of twigs, roots, stems in hawthorn, elm, stump, fence, or post; 2–5 eggs; 1 brood; May–August.

**FEEDING** Catches flying insects from elevated perch or gleans insects from foliage; eats berries and fruit, except in spring.

**FLIGHT:** strong, direct, and very agile with vigorous, rapid wingbeats; hovers and sails.

**WHITE-TIPPED**
The white-tipped tails of these two Eastern Kingbirds are conspicuous as they sit on a budding twig.

**SIMILAR SPECIES**

**THICK-BILLED KINGBIRD**
see p.448

dark mask

thicker bill

yellowish belly

**GRAY KINGBIRD**

larger bill

gray crown and back

no white on tail

**OCCURRENCE**
Breeds across much of North America in a variety of open habitats, including urban areas, parks, golf courses, fields with scattered shrubs, beaver ponds, and along forest edges. Long-distance migrant; winters in South America, south to Argentina.

| Length **7–9in (18–23cm)** | Wingspan **13–15in (33–38cm)** | Weight **1¹⁄₁₆–2oz (30–55g)** |
| Social **Solitary/Pairs** | Lifespan **Up to 7 years** | Status **Secure** |

| DATE SEEN | WHERE | NOTES |
|---|---|---|
| | | |
| | | |
| | | |
| | | |

| Order **Passeriformes** | Family **Tyrannidae** | Species ***Contopus cooperi*** |

# Olive-sided Flycatcher 🔊

short tail

**ADULT (SUMMER)**

pointed wings

**IN FLIGHT**

large, dark head

lower base of bill often dull orange

brownish gray back

dull white throat

brownish olive flanks

white belly

**ADULT (SUMMER)**

**FLIGHT:** fast and direct, with deep, rapid wingbeats; turns sharply to chase prey.

The Olive-sided Flycatcher is identified by its distinctive song, relatively large size, and contrasting belly and flank colors, which make its underside appear like a vest with the buttons undone. Both members of a breeding pair are known to aggressively defend their territory. This flycatcher undertakes a long journey from northern parts of North America to winter in Panama and the Andes.

**VOICE** Call an evenly spaced *pip-pip-pip*; song a loud 3-note whistle: *quick-THREE-BEERS* or *whip-WEE-DEER*.

**NESTING** Open cup of twigs, rootlets, lichens; 2–5 eggs; 1 brood; May–August.

**FEEDING** Sits and waits for prey to fly past its perch before swooping after it; eats flying insects, such as bees, wasps, and flying ants.

**BUILDING THE NEST**
The female Olive-sided Flycatcher usually constructs the nest on her own.

**EXPOSED PERCH**
This species can often be found singing from an exposed twig emerging from the canopy.

**OCCURRENCE**
Breeds in mountainous, northern coniferous forests at edges or openings around ponds, bogs, meadows where standing dead trees occur. Also found in post-fire forests with abundant stumps. Winters in forest edges with tall trees and stumps.

**SIMILAR SPECIES**

**EASTERN PHOEBE** see p.450

lacks "vest"

**WESTERN WOOD-PEWEE** see p.246

lacks "vest"

longer tail

| Length **7–8in (18–20cm)** | Wingspan **13in (33cm)** | Weight **1¹⁄₁₆–1¼oz (30–35g)** |
| Social **Solitary** | Lifespan **Up to 7 years** | Status **Declining** |

| DATE SEEN | WHERE | | NOTES |
|---|---|---|---|
| | | | |
| | | | |
| | | | |
| | | | |
| | | | |

| Order **Passeriformes** | Family **Tyrannidae** | Species *Contopus sordidulus* |
|---|---|---|

# Western Wood-Pewee 🔊

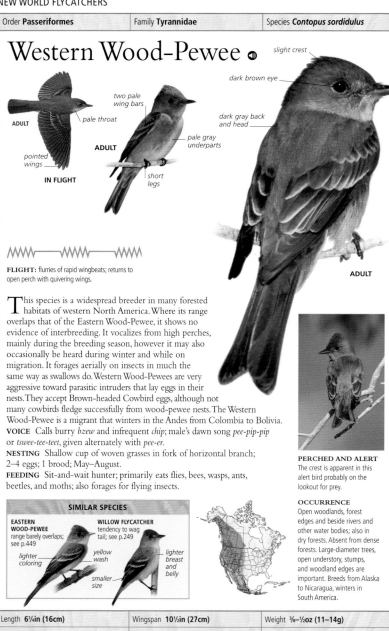

slight crest

dark brown eye

dark gray back and head

pale gray underparts

two pale wing bars

pale throat

**ADULT**

pointed wings

**IN FLIGHT**

**ADULT**

short legs

**ADULT**

**FLIGHT:** flurries of rapid wingbeats; returns to open perch with quivering wings.

This species is a widespread breeder in many forested habitats of western North America. Where its range overlaps that of the Eastern Wood-Pewee, it shows no evidence of interbreeding. It vocalizes from high perches, mainly during the breeding season, however it may also occasionally be heard during winter and while on migration. It forages aerially on insects in much the same way as swallows do. Western Wood-Pewees are very aggressive toward parasitic intruders that lay eggs in their nests. They accept Brown-headed Cowbird eggs, although not many cowbirds fledge successfully from wood-pewee nests. The Western Wood-Pewee is a migrant that winters in the Andes from Colombia to Bolivia.

**VOICE** Calls burry *bzew* and infrequent *chip*; male's dawn song *pee-pip-pip* or *tswee-tee-teet*, given alternately with *pee-er*.

**NESTING** Shallow cup of woven grasses in fork of horizontal branch; 2–4 eggs; 1 brood; May–August.

**FEEDING** Sit-and-wait hunter; primarily eats flies, bees, wasps, ants, beetles, and moths; also forages for flying insects.

**PERCHED AND ALERT**
The crest is apparent in this alert bird probably on the lookout for prey.

**OCCURRENCE**
Open woodlands, forest edges and beside rivers and other water bodies; also in dry forests. Absent from dense forests. Large-diameter trees, open understory, stumps, and woodland edges are important. Breeds from Alaska to Nicaragua, winters in South America.

### SIMILAR SPECIES

**EASTERN WOOD-PEWEE**
range barely overlaps; see p.449

lighter coloring

**WILLOW FLYCATCHER**
tendency to wag tail; see p.249

yellow wash

lighter breast and belly

smaller size

| Length **6¼in (16cm)** | Wingspan **10½in (27cm)** | Weight **⅜–½oz (11–14g)** |
|---|---|---|
| Social **Solitary** | Lifespan **Up to 6 years** | Status **Declining** |

| DATE SEEN | WHERE | NOTES |
|---|---|---|
| | | |
| | | |
| | | |
| | | |

| Order **Passeriformes** | Family **Tyrannidae** | Species ***Empidonax flaviventris*** |

# Yellow-bellied Flycatcher

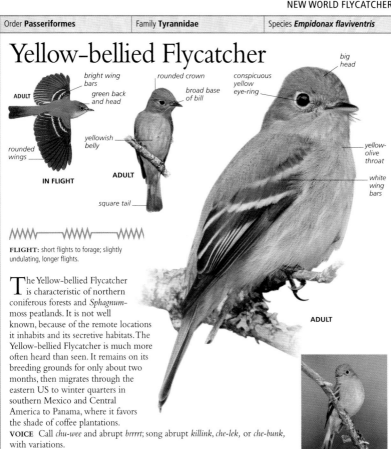

ADULT

bright wing bars

green back and head

rounded crown

broad base of bill

conspicuous yellow eye-ring

big head

rounded wings

yellowish belly

**IN FLIGHT**

**ADULT**

square tail

yellow-olive throat

white wing bars

**ADULT**

**FLIGHT:** short flights to forage; slightly undulating, longer flights.

The Yellow-bellied Flycatcher is characteristic of northern coniferous forests and *Sphagnum*-moss peatlands. It is not well known, because of the remote locations it inhabits and its secretive habitats. The Yellow-bellied Flycatcher is much more often heard than seen. It remains on its breeding grounds for only about two months, then migrates through the eastern US to winter quarters in southern Mexico and Central America to Panama, where it favors the shade of coffee plantations.

**VOICE** Call *chu-wee* and abrupt *brrrrt*; song abrupt *killink, che-lek,* or *che-bunk,* with variations.

**NESTING** Cup of moss, twigs, and needles on or near ground, often in a bog; 3–5 eggs; 1 brood; June–July.

**FEEDING** Catches insects in the air or gleans mosquitoes, midges, and flies from foliage; sometimes eats berries and seeds.

**YELLOW BELLY**
A frontal view clearly shows this species' field mark.

**OCCURRENCE**
Breeds from Alaska to Québec, Newfoundland, and the northeast US (New England) in boreal forests and bogs dominated by spruce trees. Winters in Mexico and Central America to Panama, in lowland forests, second-growth, and riverside habitats.

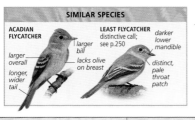

**SIMILAR SPECIES**

**ACADIAN FLYCATCHER**

larger overall

longer, wider tail

larger bill

lacks olive on breast

**LEAST FLYCATCHER** distinctive call; see p.250

darker lower mandible

distinct, pale throat patch

| Length **5½in (14cm)** | Wingspan **8in (20cm)** | Weight **⁹⁄₃₂–½oz (8–15g)** |
| Social **Solitary** | Lifespan **At least 4 years** | Status **Secure** |

| DATE SEEN | WHERE | NOTES |
|---|---|---|
| | | |
| | | |
| | | |
| | | |
| | | |

| Order **Passeriformes** | Family **Tyrannidae** | Species *Empidonax alnorum* |
|---|---|---|

# Alder Flycatcher 🔊

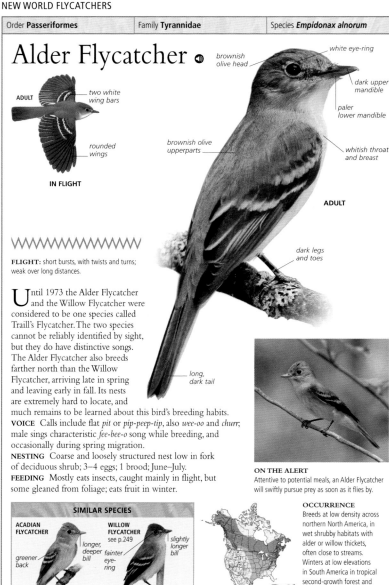

*brownish olive head*

*white eye-ring*

*dark upper mandible*

*paler lower mandible*

*whitish throat and breast*

**ADULT**

*two white wing bars*

*rounded wings*

**IN FLIGHT**

*brownish olive upperparts*

**ADULT**

*dark legs and toes*

**FLIGHT:** short bursts, with twists and turns; weak over long distances.

Until 1973 the Alder Flycatcher and the Willow Flycatcher were considered to be one species called Traill's Flycatcher. The two species cannot be reliably identified by sight, but they do have distinctive songs. The Alder Flycatcher also breeds farther north than the Willow Flycatcher, arriving late in spring and leaving early in fall. Its nests are extremely hard to locate, and much remains to be learned about this bird's breeding habits.

*long, dark tail*

**VOICE** Calls include flat *pit* or *pip-peep-tip*, also *wee-oo* and *churr*; male sings characteristic *fee-bee-o* song while breeding, and occasionally during spring migration.

**NESTING** Coarse and loosely structured nest low in fork of deciduous shrub; 3–4 eggs; 1 brood; June–July.

**FEEDING** Mostly eats insects, caught mainly in flight, but some gleaned from foliage; eats fruit in winter.

**ON THE ALERT**
Attentive to potential meals, an Alder Flycatcher will swiftly pursue prey as soon as it flies by.

**SIMILAR SPECIES**

**ACADIAN FLYCATCHER**

*greener back*

*longer, deeper bill*

**WILLOW FLYCATCHER**
see p.249

*fainter eye-ring*

*slightly longer bill*

**OCCURRENCE**
Breeds at low density across northern North America, in wet shrubby habitats with alder or willow thickets, often close to streams. Winters at low elevations in South America in tropical second-growth forest and forest edges.

| Length **5¾in (14.5cm)** | Wingspan **8½in (22cm)** | Weight **½oz (14g)** |
|---|---|---|
| Social **Solitary** | Lifespan **At least 3 years** | Status **Secure** |

| DATE SEEN | WHERE | NOTES |
|---|---|---|
| | | |
| | | |
| | | |
| | | |

| Order **Passeriformes** | Family **Tyrannidae** | Species *Empidonax traillii* |

# Willow Flycatcher 🔊

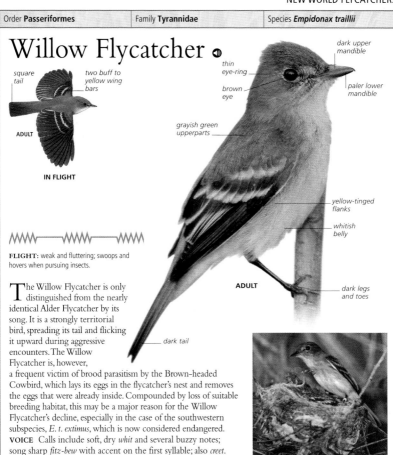

**square tail**

**two buff to yellow wing bars**

**ADULT**

**IN FLIGHT**

**thin eye-ring**

**brown eye**

**grayish green upperparts**

**dark upper mandible**

**paler lower mandible**

**yellow-tinged flanks**

**whitish belly**

**ADULT**

**dark legs and toes**

**dark tail**

**FLIGHT:** weak and fluttering; swoops and hovers when pursuing insects.

The Willow Flycatcher is only distinguished from the nearly identical Alder Flycatcher by its song. It is a strongly territorial bird, spreading its tail and flicking it upward during aggressive encounters. The Willow Flycatcher is, however, a frequent victim of brood parasitism by the Brown-headed Cowbird, which lays its eggs in the flycatcher's nest and removes the eggs that were already inside. Compounded by loss of suitable breeding habitat, this may be a major reason for the Willow Flycatcher's decline, especially in the case of the southwestern subspecies, *E. t. extimus*, which is now considered endangered.

**VOICE** Calls include soft, dry *whit* and several buzzy notes; song sharp *fitz-bew* with accent on the first syllable; also *creet*.

**NESTING** Rather loose and untidy cup in base of shrub near water; 3–4 eggs; 1 brood; May–August.

**FEEDING** Eats insects, mostly caught in flight; eats fruit in winter.

**UNEVEN WORKLOAD**
Although both parents feed their young, the female Willow Flycatcher does so the most.

### SIMILAR SPECIES

**ALDER FLYCATCHER**
different song;
see p.248

**bolder wing bars**

**LEAST FLYCATCHER**
see p.250

**larger head**

**bold white eye-ring**

**OCCURRENCE**
Breeds from southern Canada to eastern and southwestern US, mainly in willow thickets and other moist shrubby areas along watercourses. On winter grounds, it favors lighter woodland, shrubby clearings, and brush near water in coastal areas.

| Length **5–6¾in (13–17cm)** | Wingspan **7½–9½in (19–24cm)** | Weight **⅜–⁹⁄₁₆oz (11–16g)** |
| Social **Solitary** | Lifespan **Up to 11 years** | Status **Declining** |

| DATE SEEN | WHERE | NOTES |
|---|---|---|
| | | |
| | | |
| | | |
| | | |
| | | |

| Order **Passeriformes** | Family **Tyrannidae** | Species *Empidonax minimus* |

# Least Flycatcher

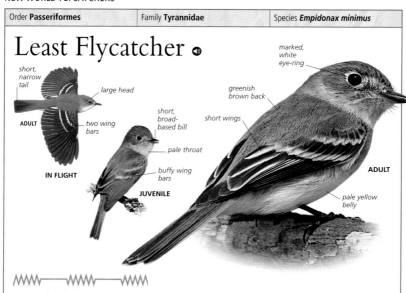

short, narrow tail

large head

**ADULT**

two wing bars

**IN FLIGHT**

short, broad-based bill

pale throat

buffy wing bars

**JUVENILE**

marked, white eye-ring

greenish brown back

short wings

**ADULT**

pale yellow belly

**FLIGHT:** direct, short forays with rapid wingbeats to catch prey; sometimes hovers briefly.

The smallest eastern member of the *Empidonax* genus is a solitary bird and is very aggressive toward intruders encroaching upon its breeding territory, including other species of flycatchers. This combative behavior reduces the likelihood of acting as unwitting host parents to eggs laid by the Brown-headed Cowbird. The Least Flycatcher is very active, and frequently flicks its wings and tail upward. Common in the eastern US in mixed and deciduous woodland, especially at the edges, it spends a short time—up to only two months—on its northern breeding grounds before migrating south. Adults molt in winter, while young molt before and during fall migration.
**VOICE** Call soft, short *whit*; song frequent, persistent, characteristic *tchebeck*, sings during spring migration and breeding season.
**NESTING** Compact cup of tightly woven bark strips and plant fibers in fork of deciduous tree; 3–5 eggs; 1 brood; May–July.
**FEEDING** Feeds principally on insects, such as flies, midges, beetles, ants, butterflies, and larvae; occasionally eats berries and seeds.

**YELLOW TINGE**
The subtle yellow tinge to its underparts and white undertail feathers are evident here.

**OCCURRENCE**
Breeds in coniferous and mixed deciduous forests across North America, east of Rockies to East Coast; occasionally in conifer groves or wooded wetlands, often near openings or edges. Winters in Central America in varied habitat from second-growth evergreen woodland to arid scrub.

| SIMILAR SPECIES | | |
|---|---|---|
| **WILLOW FLYCATCHER** see p.249 | **ALDER FLYCATCHER** see p.248 | |

larger body

longer bill

larger overall

wider tail

| Length **5¼in (13.5cm)** | Wingspan **7¾in (19.5cm)** | Weight **⁹⁄₃₂–⁷⁄₁₆oz (8–13g)** |
|---|---|---|
| Social **Solitary** | Lifespan **Up to 6 years** | Status **Secure** |

| DATE SEEN | WHERE | NOTES |
|---|---|---|
| | | |
| | | |
| | | |
| | | |
| | | |

| Order **Passeriformes** | Family **Tyrannidae** | Species *Empidonax hammondii* |

# Hammond's Flycatcher

*gray head*

*notched tail*

*tear-shaped spot behind eye*

*small, dark bill*

*olive back*

**ADULT**

*grayish white throat and upper breast*

*olive breast and flanks*

*two white wing bars*

**IN FLIGHT**

**ADULT**

*yellow tinge to lower belly*

**FLIGHT:** short, direct flights to pursue prey; occasionally hovers.

*notched tail*

A small, gray bird of mature coniferous forests in western North America, the Hammond's Flycatcher is generally silent on its wintering grounds, but starts performing its distinctive song shortly after arriving on its breeding grounds. In the breeding season, males are competitive and aggressive, and are known to lock together in mid-air to resolve their territorial squabbles. Since this species is dependent on mature old-growth forest, logging is thought to be adversely affecting its numbers.

**VOICE** Calls *peek* or *wheep*; song of 3 elements—dry, brisk *se-put*, low, burry *tsurrt*, or *greep*, and drawn-out *chu-lup*.

**NESTING** Compact open cup of plant fibers and fine grass saddled on large branch; 3–4 eggs; 1 brood; May–August.

**FEEDING** Sit-and-wait predator; pursues flying insects from perch.

**DISTINCTIVE EYE-RING**
Hammond's Flycatcher's white tear-shaped spot behind the eye is only visible in good lighting.

### SIMILAR SPECIES

**DUSKY FLYCATCHER**
distinctive "whit" call;
see p.253

*mouse gray overall*

*wider, longer bill*

**GRAY FLYCATCHER**
wags tail;
see p.252

*smaller body*

*paler overall*

**OCCURRENCE**
Breeds in mature coniferous and mixed woodland from Alaska to California. Also found in the Rockies and the Great Basin. Inhabits mainly firs or conifers, but also occurs in aspen and other broadleaf mixed forests. Winters in oak pine forests and dry shrubbery in Mexico and Central America.

| Length **5–6in (12.5–15cm)** | Wingspan **9in (22cm)** | Weight **⁹⁄₃₂–⁷⁄₁₆oz (8–12g)** |
| Social **Solitary** | Lifespan **Up to 7 years** | Status **Secure** |

| DATE SEEN | WHERE | | NOTES |
|---|---|---|---|
| | | | |
| | | | |
| | | | |
| | | | |
| | | | |

| Order **Passeriformes** | Family **Tyrannidae** | Species ***Empidonax wrightii*** |

# Gray Flycatcher

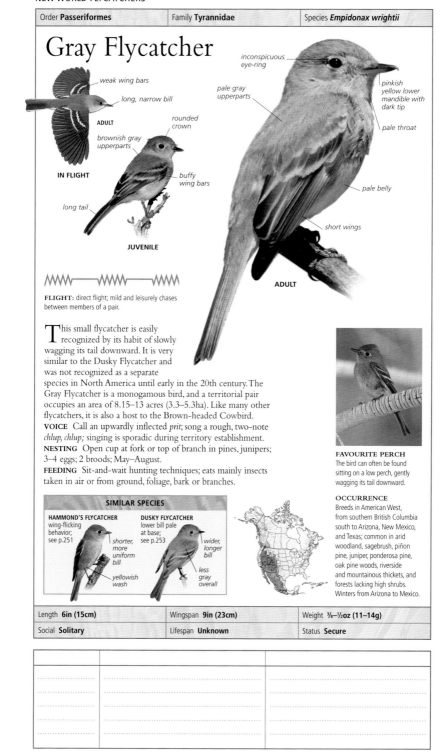

inconspicuous eye-ring

pale gray upperparts

pinkish yellow lower mandible with dark tip

pale throat

weak wing bars

long, narrow bill

**ADULT**

rounded crown

brownish gray upperparts

**IN FLIGHT**

buffy wing bars

long tail

**JUVENILE**

pale belly

short wings

**ADULT**

**FLIGHT:** direct flight; mild and leisurely chases between members of a pair.

This small flycatcher is easily recognized by its habit of slowly wagging its tail downward. It is very similar to the Dusky Flycatcher and was not recognized as a separate species in North America until early in the 20th century. The Gray Flycatcher is a monogamous bird, and a territorial pair occupies an area of 8.15–13 acres (3.3–5.3ha). Like many other flycatchers, it is also a host to the Brown-headed Cowbird.

**VOICE** Call an upwardly inflected *prit;* song a rough, two-note *chlup, chlup;* singing is sporadic during territory establishment.

**NESTING** Open cup at fork or top of branch in pines, junipers; 3–4 eggs; 2 broods; May–August.

**FEEDING** Sit-and-wait hunting techniques; eats mainly insects taken in air or from ground, foliage, bark or branches.

**FAVOURITE PERCH**
The bird can often be found sitting on a low perch, gently wagging its tail downward.

**OCCURRENCE**
Breeds in American West, from southern British Columbia south to Arizona, New Mexico, and Texas; common in arid woodland, sagebrush, piñon pine, juniper, ponderosa pine, oak pine woods, riverside and mountainous thickets, and forests lacking high shrubs. Winters from Arizona to Mexico.

| SIMILAR SPECIES | | |
|---|---|---|
| **HAMMOND'S FLYCATCHER** wing-flicking behavior; see p.251 | **DUSKY FLYCATCHER** lower bill pale at base; see p.253 | |

shorter, more uniform bill

yellowish wash

wider, longer bill

less gray overall

| Length **6in (15cm)** | Wingspan **9in (23cm)** | Weight **⅜–½oz (11–14g)** |
|---|---|---|
| Social **Solitary** | Lifespan **Unknown** | Status **Secure** |

| Order **Passeriformes** | Family **Tyrannidae** | Species *Empidonax oberholseri* |

# Dusky Flycatcher

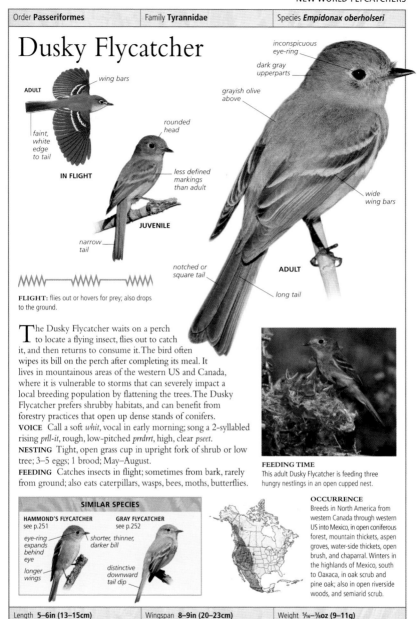

inconspicuous eye-ring

dark gray upperparts

grayish olive above

**ADULT**

wing bars

faint, white edge to tail

**IN FLIGHT**

rounded head

less defined markings than adult

**JUVENILE**

narrow tail

notched or square tail

wide wing bars

**ADULT**

long tail

**FLIGHT:** flies out or hovers for prey; also drops to the ground.

The Dusky Flycatcher waits on a perch to locate a flying insect, flies out to catch it, and then returns to consume it. The bird often wipes its bill on the perch after completing its meal. It lives in mountainous areas of the western US and Canada, where it is vulnerable to storms that can severely impact a local breeding population by flattening the trees. The Dusky Flycatcher prefers shrubby habitats, and can benefit from forestry practices that open up dense stands of conifers.

**VOICE** Call a soft *whit*, vocal in early morning; song a 2-syllabled rising *prll-it*, rough, low-pitched *prrdrrt*, high, clear *pseet*.

**NESTING** Tight, open grass cup in upright fork of shrub or low tree; 3–5 eggs; 1 brood; May–August.

**FEEDING** Catches insects in flight; sometimes from bark, rarely from ground; also eats caterpillars, wasps, bees, moths, butterflies.

**FEEDING TIME**
This adult Dusky Flycatcher is feeding three hungry nestlings in an open cupped nest.

### SIMILAR SPECIES

**HAMMOND'S FLYCATCHER**
see p.251

eye-ring expands behind eye

longer wings

**GRAY FLYCATCHER**
see p.252

shorter, thinner, darker bill

distinctive downward tail dip

**OCCURRENCE**
Breeds in North America from western Canada through western US into Mexico, in open coniferous forest, mountain thickets, aspen groves, water-side thickets, open brush, and chaparral. Winters in the highlands of Mexico, south to Oaxaca, in oak scrub and pine oak; also in open riverside woods, and semiarid scrub.

| Length **5–6in (13–15cm)** | Wingspan **8–9in (20–23cm)** | Weight **⁵⁄₁₆–³⁄₈oz (9–11g)** |
| Social **Solitary** | Lifespan **Up to 8 years** | Status **Secure** |

| Order **Passeriformes** | Family **Tyrannidae** | Species *Empidonax difficilis* |
|---|---|---|

# Pacific-slope Flycatcher

**ADULT**

**IN FLIGHT**

*yellow-washed throat*

*rounded wings*

slight crest

*conspicuous eye-ring*

*olive back and head*

*yellow-orange lower mandible*

*brown-washed breast*

*yellowish belly*

**ADULT**

**FLIGHT:** sallies forth from a perch to hawk or glean insects.

The Pacific-slope Flycatcher is almost identical to the Cordilleran Flycatcher—both were formerly considered to be one species called the Western Flycatcher. Differences in song led researchers to find genetic and behavioral differences between the two species. A population of Pacific-slope Flycatchers found on the Channel Islands off California may also be a distinct species, larger than mainland forms. The Pacific-slope Flycatcher is a short-distance migrant that winters in Mexico. The female is active during nest-building and incubation, but the male provides food for nestlings.

**VOICE** Call *chrrip, seet, zeet*; song 3 squeaky, repeated syllables *ps-SEET, ptsick, seet*, or *TSEE-wee, pttuck, tseep*.

**NESTING** Open cup, often with shelter above, in fork of tree or shelf on bank or bridge; 2–4 eggs; 2 broods; April–July.

**FEEDING** Feeds on insects caught in air or gleaned from foliage: beetles, wasps, bees, flies, moths, caterpillars, spiders; rarely berries.

**DISTINCT MARKINGS**
The Pacific-slope Flycatcher has distinct buffy wing bars and a streaked breast and belly.

**SIMILAR SPECIES**

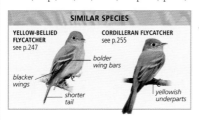

YELLOW-BELLIED FLYCATCHER
see p.247

*blacker wings*

*shorter tail*

CORDILLERAN FLYCATCHER
see p.255

*bolder wing bars*

*yellowish underparts*

**OCCURRENCE**
Breeds to west of mountains from northern British Columbia to southern California in humid coastal coniferous forest, pine oak forest, and dense second-growth forest. Resides in well-shaded woods, along stream bottoms, and steep-walled ravines.

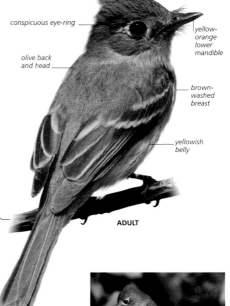

| Length **6–7in (15–17.5cm)** | Wingspan **8–9in (20–23cm)** | Weight **9/32–7/16oz (8–12g)** |
|---|---|---|
| Social **Solitary** | Lifespan **Up to 6 years** | Status **Declining** |

| DATE SEEN | WHERE | NOTES |
|---|---|---|
| | | |
| | | |
| | | |
| | | |
| | | |

| Order **Passeriformes** | Family **Tyrannidae** | Species *Empidonax occidentalis* |

# Cordilleran Flycatcher

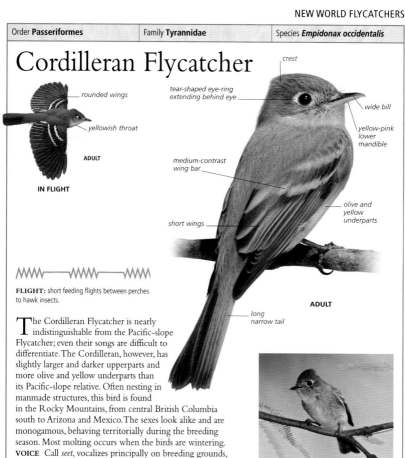

crest

tear-shaped eye-ring extending behind eye

wide bill

yellow-pink lower mandible

rounded wings

yellowish throat

**ADULT**

**IN FLIGHT**

medium-contrast wing bar

olive and yellow underparts

short wings

**ADULT**

long narrow tail

**FLIGHT:** short feeding flights between perches to hawk insects.

The Cordilleran Flycatcher is nearly indistinguishable from the Pacific-slope Flycatcher; even their songs are difficult to differentiate. The Cordilleran, however, has slightly larger and darker upperparts and more olive and yellow underparts than its Pacific-slope relative. Often nesting in manmade structures, this bird is found in the Rocky Mountains, from central British Columbia south to Arizona and Mexico. The sexes look alike and are monogamous, behaving territorially during the breeding season. Most molting occurs when the birds are wintering.

**VOICE** Call *seet*, vocalizes principally on breeding grounds, with occasional calls at other times; song *ps-SEET, ptsick, seet*.

**NESTING** Cup on rocky outcrop, in natural cavity or root mass; 2–5 eggs; 2 broods; April–July.

**FEEDING** Feeds on insects; waits on perch to fly out for hunt.

**CRESTED**
The Cordilleran Flycatcher shows a more marked crest than the Pacific-slope species.

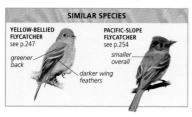

**SIMILAR SPECIES**

YELLOW-BELLIED FLYCATCHER
see p.247

greener back

PACIFIC-SLOPE FLYCATCHER
see p.254

smaller overall

darker wing feathers

**OCCURRENCE**
Breeds in cool, arid, relatively dense forests of pine, fir, and spruce, at mid- to high elevation, often associated with watercourses and openings. Winters in the mountains of Mexico.

| Length **6–7in (15–17.5cm)** | Wingspan **9in (23cm)** | Weight **³⁄₈–⁷⁄₁₆oz (11–13g)** |
| Social **Solitary** | Lifespan **Unknown** | Status **Secure** |

| DATE SEEN | WHERE | NOTES |
|-----------|-------|-------|
|           |       |       |
|           |       |       |
|           |       |       |
|           |       |       |
|           |       |       |

| Order **Passeriformes** | Family **Tyrannidae** | Species *Sayornis nigricans* |
|---|---|---|

# Black Phoebe

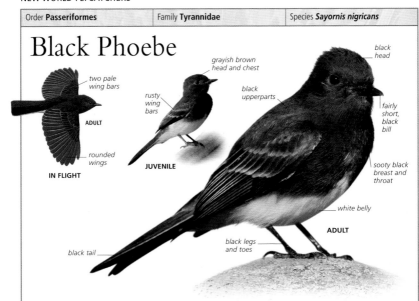

two pale wing bars

**ADULT**

rounded wings

**IN FLIGHT**

grayish brown head and chest

rusty wing bars

**JUVENILE**

black upperparts

black head

fairly short, black bill

sooty black breast and throat

white belly

**ADULT**

black legs and toes

black tail

N orth America's only black-and-white flycatcher, the distinctive Black Phoebe is found in the southwestern part of the continent, where it is a year-round resident. This area is the northernmost part of the bird's range, which extends southward to Argentina. This species is commonly found close to water, where it conducts most of its foraging. It has even been known to dive into ponds to capture minnows—an unusual foraging method for a flycatcher. In the breeding season the male shows his mate potential nest sites by hovering in front of a likely spot, with the female deciding where the nest will eventually be.

**VOICE** Simple *tsip* call; also *tweedle-deedle-eek* during courting or when chasing rivals; song a *tee-hee, tee-hoo* or *sisee, sitseu.*

**NESTING** Open cup of mud mixed with grass, cemented to wall, or under bridge, cliff, or eave; 2–5 eggs; 2–3 broods; March–June.

**FEEDING** Mainly catches flying insects, but will also pick insects from ground; occasionally dives for small fish; also eats berries.

**FLIGHT:** direct with steady wingbeats; hovers while foraging; vertical zig-zag courting display.

**PERCHED AND ALERT**
The Black Phoebe perches in an upright position, with its tail dipping and fanning.

**SIMILAR SPECIES**

**SAY'S PHOEBE**
see p.257
paler upperparts

cinnamon belly

**EASTERN KINGBIRD**
see p.244
charcoal-gray upperparts

white breast and throat

**OCCURRENCE**
In the US, breeds and winters in Oregon, California, Nevada, Utah, Colorado, Arizona, New Mexico, and Texas, in areas close to water, such as coastal cliffs, banks of rivers, streams, lakes, and ponds. Also seen at fountains and cattle troughs. Forages in open areas over water or grassland.

| Length **6in (15.5cm)** | Wingspan **11in (28cm)** | Weight **½–¹¹⁄₁₆oz (15–20g)** |
|---|---|---|
| Social **Solitary** | Lifespan **Up to 8 years** | Status **Secure** |

| DATE SEEN | WHERE | NOTES |
|---|---|---|
| | | |
| | | |
| | | |
| | | |
| | | |

| Order **Passeriformes** | Family **Tyrannidae** | Species *Sayornis saya* |

# Say's Phoebe

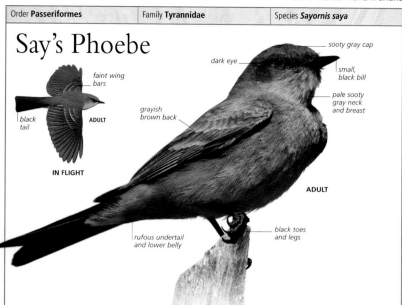

sooty gray cap

dark eye

small, black bill

pale sooty gray neck and breast

faint wing bars

grayish brown back

**ADULT**

black tail

**IN FLIGHT**

**ADULT**

black toes and legs

rufous undertail and lower belly

Say's Phoebe breeds farther north than any other New World flycatcher. Although it is a bird of open country, it is not particularly shy around people, and from early spring to late fall is a common sight on ranches and farms. Its contrasting dark cap is conspicuous even at a distance as it perches on bushes, boulders, or power lines, often wagging its tail. Shortly after a pair is formed on the breeding grounds, the male will hover in front of potential nest sites, in a manner similar to the Black Phoebe. The pair bond among Say's Phoebes is relatively weak, though, and does not last through the summer.

**VOICE** Call a *pee-ee* or *pee-ur*; also a whistled *churr-eep*, which may be integrated with a chatter; primary song a *pit-see-eur* and *pit-eet*.

**NESTING** Shallow cup of twigs, moss, or stems on ledge or in rocky crevice; 3–7 eggs; 1–2 broods; April–July.

**FEEDING** Catches insects in flight, such as beetles, wasps, grasshoppers, and crickets; also eats berries.

**FLIGHT:** direct, with regular wingbeats; chases may be erratic; hovers while foraging.

**HOVERING MALE**
Say's Phoebes characteristically hover in the breeding season.

### SIMILAR SPECIES

**VERMILLION FLYCATCHER ♀**
see p.450

pale eyebrow

white throat

faintly streaked breast

**CASSIN'S KINGBIRD**
see p.242

gray-olive upperparts

yellow belly

**OCCURRENCE**
Breeds in dry, open, or semi-open country, such as desert canyons, sagebrush ranch, and agricultural areas; also breeds in tundra in Alaska; avoids watercourses. Birds in the southwestern US are resident year-round, but those breeding farther north fly south for the winter.

| Length **7in (17.5cm)** | Wingspan **13in (33cm)** | Weight **¹¹⁄₁₆oz (20g)** |
| Social **Solitary** | Lifespan **At least 3–4 years** | Status **Secure** |

| DATE SEEN | WHERE | NOTES |
|---|---|---|
| | | |
| | | |
| | | |
| | | |

# SHRIKES AND VIREOS

## SHRIKES

Two of the thirty species of shrikes (Laniidae) occur in Canada and the United States. The Loggerhead Shrike is truly North American, but the other North American species, the Northern (or Gray) Shrike, is also widespread in Europe and western Asia. Shrikes have a strongly hooked bill, almost like a bird of prey. In fact, shrikes capture not only insects, but also birds, rodents, and lizards, which they impale on a thorn in a shrub (a larder). Shrikes pounce down on their prey from high

**KEEN SONGSTER**
The White-eyed Vireo sings almost continuously, even on the hottest of summer days.

perches in trees or on fenceposts, catching it on or near the ground. Many shrike species are declining.

## VIREOS

Vireos are a family of songbirds restricted to the New World, with about 15 species occurring in the United States and Canada. Their classification has long been problematic—traditionally they were associated with warblers, but recent molecular studies suggest that they are actually related to crow-like birds. Vireo plumage is drab, often predominantly greenish or grayish above and whitish below, augmented by eye-rings, ("spectacles,") eyestripes, and wing bars. Most vireos have a preference for broadleaved habitats, where they move about deliberately, hopping and climbing as they slowly forage for their prey. They are mainly insect-eaters. Most species are mid- to long-distance migrants, retreating to warmer climes in winter, when insects are dormant. Vireos are most often detected by the male's loud and clear territorial song, which is repetitive and persistent.

**SEPARATE SPECIES**
The Blue-headed Vireo is one of three species, formerly known as just one species, the Solitary Vireo.

# JAYS AND CROWS

ALTHOUGH JAYS AND crows belong to a highly diverse family, the Corvidae, most members share some important characteristics. They are remarkably social, some species even breed cooperatively, but at the same time they can be quiet and stealthy. Always opportunistic, corvids use strong bills and toes to obtain a varied, omnivorous diet. Ornithologists have shown that ravens, magpies, and crows are among the most intelligent birds. They exhibit self-awareness when looking into mirrors, can make tools, and successfully tackle difficult counting and problem-solving. As a rule, most corvid plumage comes in shades of blue, black, and white. The plumage of adult corvids does not vary by season. Corvidae are part of an ancient bird lineage (Corvoidea) that originated in Australasia. Crows and jays were among the birds most affected by the spread of West Nile virus in the early 2000s, but most populations seem to have recovered quickly.

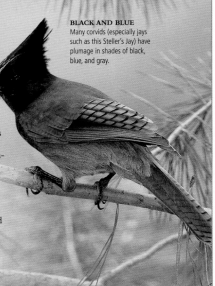

**BLACK AND BLUE**
Many corvids (especially jays such as this Steller's Jay) have plumage in shades of black, blue, and gray.

| Order **Passeriformes** | Family **Laniidae** | Species *Lanius ludovicianus* |

# Loggerhead Shrike 🔊

**ADULT**

white flash in wings

white edges to tail

**IN FLIGHT**

gray crown

black "mask"

hooked bill

black wings

pale undertail feathers

**JUVENILE**

unstreaked, gray underparts

**ADULT**

rounded tail

**FLIGHT:** fast with rapid wingbeats, sometimes interspersed with glides; swoops from perches.

Although a songbird, the Loggerhead Shrike behaves like a small bird of prey and has a hooked bill and strong, sharp, curved claws. It sits atop posts or tall trees, swooping down to catch prey on the ground. It has the unusual habit of then impaling its prey on thorns, barbed wire, or sharp twigs, which is the reason for the nickname "butcher bird." Unfortunately, the Loggerhead Shrike is declining, principally because of human alteration of its habitat.

**VOICE** Quiet warbles, trills, and harsh notes; song harsh notes singly or in series: *chaa chaa chaa*.

**NESTING** Open cup of vegetation, placed in thorny tree; 5 eggs; 1 brood; March–June.

**FEEDING** Kills large insects and small vertebrates—rodents, birds, reptiles—with powerful bill.

**GEARED FOR HUNTING**
The Loggerhead Shrike perches upright on tall shrubs or small trees, where it scans for prey.

### SIMILAR SPECIES

**NORTHERN SHRIKE** see p.260
smaller bill
lighter upperparts

**NORTHERN MOCKINGBIRD** see p.324
darker upperparts
longer tail

**OCCURRENCE**
Found in semi-open country with scattered perches, but its distribution is erratic, occurring in relatively high densities in certain areas, but absent from seemingly suitable habitat. Occurs in congested residential areas in some regions (south Florida), but generally favors fairly remote habitats.

| Length **9in (23cm)** | Wingspan **12in (31cm)** | Weight **1¼–2⅛oz (35–60g)** |
| Social **Solitary** | Lifespan **Unknown** | Status **Declining** |

| DATE SEEN | WHERE | NOTES |
|---|---|---|
| | | |
| | | |
| | | |
| | | |
| | | |

| Order **Passeriformes** | Family **Laniidae** | Species *Lanius borealis* |

# Northern Shrike

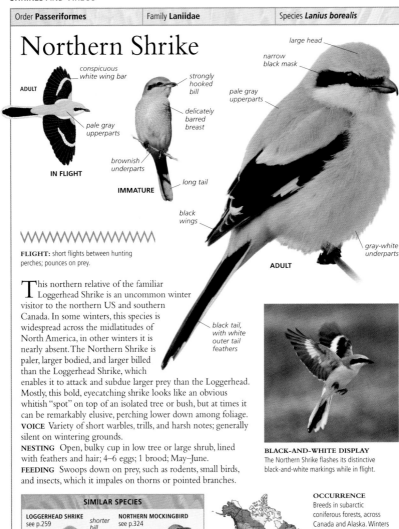

large head

narrow black mask

pale gray upperparts

**ADULT**

conspicuous white wing bar

**ADULT**

strongly hooked bill

delicately barred breast

pale gray upperparts

brownish underparts

**IN FLIGHT**

long tail

**IMMATURE**

black wings

gray-white underparts

**ADULT**

black tail, with white outer tail feathers

**FLIGHT:** short flights between hunting perches; pounces on prey.

This northern relative of the familiar Loggerhead Shrike is an uncommon winter visitor to the northern US and southern Canada. In some winters, this species is widespread across the midlatitudes of North America, in other winters it is nearly absent. The Northern Shrike is paler, larger bodied, and larger billed than the Loggerhead Shrike, which enables it to attack and subdue larger prey than the Loggerhead. Mostly, this bold, eyecatching shrike looks like an obvious whitish "spot" on top of an isolated tree or bush, but at times it can be remarkably elusive, perching lower down among foliage.

**VOICE** Variety of short warbles, trills, and harsh notes; generally silent on wintering grounds.

**NESTING** Open, bulky cup in low tree or large shrub, lined with feathers and hair; 4–6 eggs; 1 brood; May–June.

**FEEDING** Swoops down on prey, such as rodents, small birds, and insects, which it impales on thorns or pointed branches.

**BLACK-AND-WHITE DISPLAY**
The Northern Shrike flashes its distinctive black-and-white markings while in flight.

### SIMILAR SPECIES

**LOGGERHEAD SHRIKE**
see p.259

shorter bill

darker, smaller overall

**NORTHERN MOCKINGBIRD**
see p.324

straight, white-edged tail

thin bill

less black in wings

**OCCURRENCE**
Breeds in subarctic coniferous forests, across Canada and Alaska. Winters in more southerly open country with sufficient perches. Avoids built-up and residential districts, but spends much time perching on fenceposts and roadside signs.

| Length **10in (25cm)** | Wingspan **14in (35cm)** | Weight **1¾–2⅝oz (50–75g)** |
| Social **Solitary** | Lifespan **Unknown** | Status **Vulnerable** |

| DATE SEEN | WHERE | NOTES |
|---|---|---|
| | | |
| | | |
| | | |
| | | |
| | | |

| Order **Passeriformes** | Family **Vireonidae** | Species **Vireo bellii** |
|---|---|---|

# Bell's Vireo

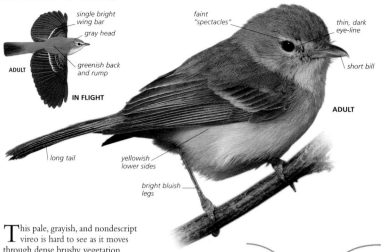

single bright wing bar

gray head

greenish back and rump

**ADULT**

**IN FLIGHT**

faint "spectacles"

thin, dark eye-line

short bill

**ADULT**

long tail

yellowish lower sides

bright bluish legs

This pale, grayish, and nondescript vireo is hard to see as it moves through dense brushy vegetation searching for food. Its most distinctive feature is a long tail, which it flicks as it moves. In the arid western parts of its range, in northern Mexico and Arizona, Bell's Vireo is usually found close to rivers or streams. The Eastern subspecies (*V. b. bellii*) is distinctly brighter in plumage than the three western subspecies, one of which, the Least Bell's Vireo (*V. b. pusillus*) of southern California, is endangered.

**VOICE** Call high, raspy, and nasal; males highly vocal and sing all day long during the breeding season; song quite fast for a vireo.

**NESTING** Deep, rounded cup constructed of coarse materials, lined with fine grasses and hair, and bound with spider webs, in dense shrubbery woven to twigs by the rim; 3–5 eggs; 2 broods; April–May.

**FEEDING** Actively gleans its insect and spider prey from leaves and twigs, hopping from branch to branch in brushy vegetation.

**FLIGHT:** slightly undulating flight with rapid wingbeats followed by short glides.

**TAIL FLICKING**
Unlike other vireos, Bell's Vireo is known for flicking its long tail as it sings.

**SIMILAR SPECIES**

**WARBLING VIREO** see p.268

white eyebrow

no wing bar

**PHILADELPHIA VIREO** see p.267

greenish upperparts

**OCCURRENCE**
Fairly common breeder in the bushy habitats of the central US, and the riverside thickets of the southwestern US, southward into northern Mexico. Winters along the Pacific slopes of Mexico.

| Length **4¾in (12cm)** | Wingspan **7in (18cm)** | Weight **⁵⁄₁₆oz (9g)** |
|---|---|---|
| Social **Solitary** | Lifespan **Up to 8 years** | Status **Vulnerable** |

| DATE SEEN | WHERE | NOTES |
|---|---|---|
| | | |
| | | |
| | | |
| | | |
| | | |

| Order **Passeriformes** | Family **Vireonidae** | Species ***Vireo vicinior*** |
|---|---|---|

# Gray Vireo

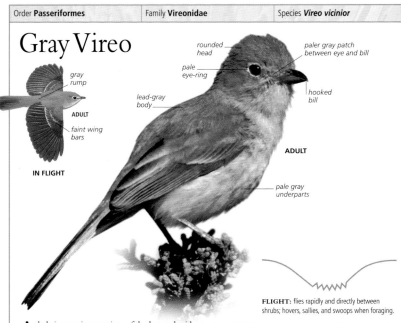

gray rump

**ADULT**

faint wing bars

**IN FLIGHT**

rounded head

pale eye-ring

lead-gray body

paler gray patch between eye and bill

hooked bill

**ADULT**

pale gray underparts

**FLIGHT:** flies rapidly and directly between shrubs; hovers, sallies, and swoops when foraging.

A drab, inconspicuous vireo of the hot and arid southwestern US, the Gray Vireo is reminiscent of a miniature shrike in terms of posture and shape. Found mainly in dense, shrubby vegetation such as pinyon and juniper, it is most often detected by its distinctive voice. In its restricted habitat, it can be confused with other small, gray birds such as gnatcatchers, titmice, and the Bushtit.

**VOICE** Varied calls, include trills and chatters; song given by male, harsh three- to four-note phrase.

**NESTING** Cup of dry plant materials and spider webs, suspended from twigs by rim, fairly low in shrub or tree, lined with fine fibers; 3–4 eggs; 1 brood; April–May.

**FEEDING** Gleans insects and spiders from leaves, twigs, and branches; also catches flies in flight; in winter, primarily eats fruit.

**PERCHED SINGER**
From the top of a shrub, a male sings to declare his ownership of the surrounding territory.

**UNCOMMON BIRD**
The Gray Vireo is an uncommon little bird and can be difficult to spot in its scrubby habitat.

**OCCURRENCE**
Breeds in the hot and arid, shrubby scrublands of the southwestern US, in parts of Nevada, Colorado, Utah, Arizona, New Mexico, and Texas; short-distance migrant. Winters largely in Mexico, in similarly arid areas.

**SIMILAR SPECIES**

**GRAY FLYCATCHER** see p.252

white-edged tail

pale lower bill with dark tip

**JUNIPER TITMOUSE** see p.291

crested head

no eye-ring

| Length **5½in (14cm)** | Wingspan **8in (20cm)** | Weight **⁷⁄₁₆oz (13g)** |
|---|---|---|
| Social **Solitary/Pairs** | Lifespan **Up to 5 years** | Status **Localized** |

| DATE SEEN | WHERE | NOTES |
|---|---|---|
| | | |
| | | |
| | | |
| | | |
| | | |

| Order **Passeriformes** | Family **Vireonidae** | Species *Vireo huttoni* |

# Hutton's Vireo

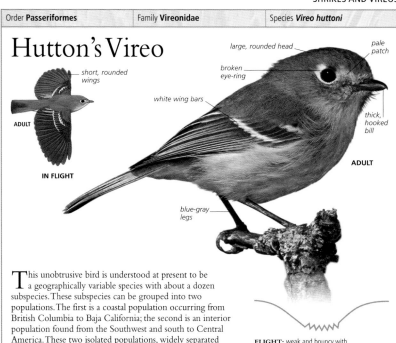

large, rounded head

pale patch

broken eye-ring

short, rounded wings

white wing bars

thick, hooked bill

**ADULT**

**IN FLIGHT**

**ADULT**

blue-gray legs

This unobtrusive bird is understood at present to be a geographically variable species with about a dozen subspecies. These subspecies can be grouped into two populations. The first is a coastal population occurring from British Columbia to Baja California; the second is an interior population found from the Southwest and south to Central America. These two isolated populations, widely separated by desert, may actually represent different species. Very similar in appearance to the Ruby-crowned Kinglet with which it flocks in winter, Hutton's Vireo is distinguishable by its larger size and thicker bill. Unlike other vireos, this bird is largely nonmigratory.

**VOICE** Varied calls include harsh mewing and nasal, raspy *spit*; male's song a repetition of a simple phrase.
**NESTING** Deep cup constructed from plant and animal fibers, lined with finer materials, often incorporating lichens, suspended from twigs by the rim; 3–5 eggs; 1–2 broods; February–May.
**FEEDING** Hops diligently from branch to branch searching for caterpillars, spiders, and flies; also eats berries; gleans from leaves usually while perched, but occasionally sallies or hovers.

**FLIGHT:** weak and bouncy with rapid wingbeats.

**FOLLOW THE SONG**
This kinglet-sized vireo is easily overlooked and is often detected by its song.

### SIMILAR SPECIES

**PACIFIC-SLOPE FLYCATCHER**
see p.254

unbroken eye-ring

long tail

wide, flat bill

**RUBY-CROWNED KINGLET** ♂
see p.310

thin bill

smaller overall

**OCCURRENCE**
Year-round resident in mixed evergreen forests; particularly common in live oak woods. Breeds in mixed oak pine woodlands along the Pacific Coast from British Columbia southward to northern Baja California, and from southwest California and New Mexico to Mexico and Guatemala.

| Length **5in (13cm)** | Wingspan **8in (20cm)** | Weight **⅜oz (11g)** |
| Social **Solitary/Pairs** | Lifespan **Up to 13 years** | Status **Secure** |

| DATE SEEN | WHERE | NOTES |
|---|---|---|
| | | |
| | | |
| | | |
| | | |

| Order **Passeriformes** | Family **Vireonidae** | Species *Vireo cassinii* |

# Cassin's Vireo

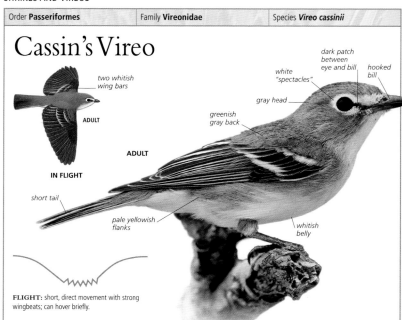

two whitish wing bars

**ADULT**
**IN FLIGHT**

**ADULT**

white "spectacles"

dark patch between eye and bill

hooked bill

gray head

greenish gray back

short tail

pale yellowish flanks

whitish belly

**FLIGHT:** short, direct movement with strong wingbeats; can hover briefly.

Cassin's Vireo is similar to the closely related Plumbeous and Blue-headed Vireos in appearance and song. It is conspicuous and vocal throughout its breeding grounds in the far west of the US and north into southwest Canada. In winter, virtually the entire population migrates to Mexico. Cassin's Vireo was named in honor of John Cassin, who published the first comprehensive study of North American birds in 1865.

**VOICE** Call a harsh, scolding chatter; male's song a broken series of whistles, which ascend then descend; lower in tone than Blue-headed Vireo and higher than the Plumbeous.
**NESTING** Cup of fibers, lined with fine plant down; suspended from twigs; 2–5 eggs; 1–2 broods; April–July.
**FEEDING** Picks insects and spiders from leaves and twigs as it hops from branch to branch; occasionally sallies out or hovers.

**TIRELESS SINGER**
Cassin's Vireo is well known for its loud and incessant singing throughout the spring and into the summer.

**SIMILAR SPECIES**

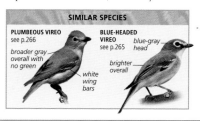

**PLUMBEOUS VIREO**
see p.266
broader gray overall with no green
white wing bars

**BLUE-HEADED VIREO**
see p.265
blue-gray head
brighter overall

**OCCURRENCE**
Breeds in coniferous and mixed forests in the hills and mountains of British Columbia, Alberta, and, in the US, the Pacific Northwest through to southern California. Winters in western Mexico.

| Length **5½in (14cm)** | Wingspan **9½in (24cm)** | Weight **9/16oz (16g)** |
| Social **Solitary/Pairs** | Lifespan **Unknown** | Status **Secure** |

| DATE SEEN | WHERE | NOTES |
|---|---|---|
| | | |
| | | |
| | | |
| | | |
| | | |

| Order **Passeriformes** | Family **Vireonidae** | Species **Vireo solitarius** |

# Blue-headed Vireo

two wing
bars

greenish
back

**ADULT**

**IN FLIGHT**

gray
head

looks "big-
headed"

conspicuous white
"spectacles"

contrasting
white throat

**ADULT**

white belly

bright greenish
flanks

relatively
short tail

Closely related to the Cassin's Vireo and Plumbeous Vireo, the fairly common Blue-headed Vireo is the brightest and most colorful of the three. Its blue-gray, helmeted head, adorned with striking white "spectacles" around its dark eyes also helps to distinguish it from other vireos in its range. This stocky and slow moving bird is heard more often than it is seen in its forest breeding habitat. However, during migration it can be more conspicuous and is the first vireo to return in spring.
**VOICE** Call a harsh, scolding chatter; male's song a series of rich, sweet, high phrases of two to six notes slurred together.
**NESTING** Shallow, rounded cup loosely constructed of animal and plant fibers, lined with finer material and suspended from twigs by the rim; 3–5 eggs; 2 broods; May–July.
**FEEDING** Gleans insects from branches and leaves, usually high in shrubs and trees; often makes short sallies after prey.

**FLIGHT:** slow, heavy, undulating flight with a series of deep wingbeats followed by short pauses.

**SPECTACLED VIREO**
Its rather thick head with conspicuous "spectacles" and gray color are distinctive field marks.

### SIMILAR SPECIES

**BLACK-CAPPED VIREO**
see p.450

smaller
overall

**CASSIN'S VIREO**
see p.264

thin bill

duller
overall

**OCCURRENCE**
Breeds in large tracts of undisturbed coniferous and mixed forests with a rich understory, largely across eastern North America. It winters in woodlands across the southeastern US from Virginia to Texas, as well as in Mexico and northern Central America to Costa Rica.

| Length 5½in (14in) | Wingspan 9½in (24cm) | Weight %₆oz (16g) |
| Social **Solitary/Pairs** | Lifespan **Up to 7 years** | Status **Secure** |

| DATE SEEN | WHERE | NOTES |
| --- | --- | --- |
| | | |
| | | |
| | | |
| | | |

| Order **Passeriformes** | Family **Vireonidae** | Species ***Vireo plumbeus*** |
|---|---|---|

# Plumbeous Vireo

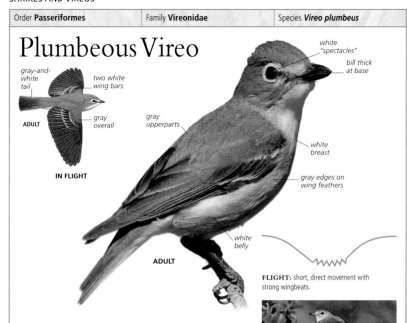

white "spectacles"

bill thick at base

gray-and-white tail

two white wing bars

gray overall

**ADULT**

**IN FLIGHT**

gray upperparts

white breast

white belly

gray edges on wing feathers

**ADULT**

**FLIGHT:** short, direct movement with strong wingbeats.

This gray-and-white bird, with its conspicuous white "spectacles" and wing bars was recognized as a distinct species only in 1997. In that year, the bird formerly known as "Solitary Vireo" was split into three vireo species—Cassin's, Blue-headed, and Plumbeous—based on genetic, plumage, and voice differences. The range of the Plumbeous Vireo has been expanding west since the 1940s and it can now be found alongside the greenish-toned Cassin's Vireo.

**VOICE** Call a harsh scold; male song a series of rough, slurred, two- or three-note phrases.

**NESTING** Loose, round cup of fibers, bound with spider webs, lined with fine material, suspended by rim from twigs; 3–5 eggs; 1 brood; April–June.

**FEEDING** Plucks insects from leaves or twigs, slowly hopping through foliage; often sallies to catch prey.

**NEST COVER**
This species tends to build its nest at the end of a branch and may cover it with lichens.

**BIG VOICE**
Like other vireos, the male Plumbeous Vireo will often sing continuously.

**OCCURRENCE**
Breeds largely in mountainous coniferous forests of the interior West US south through Mexico to Honduras and El Salvador. Winters mostly on the Pacific Slope of Mexico. Central American birds are nonmigratory.

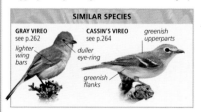

### SIMILAR SPECIES

**GRAY VIREO** see p.262

lighter wing bars

**CASSIN'S VIREO** see p.264

duller eye-ring

greenish flanks

greenish upperparts

| Length **5¾in (14.5cm)** | Wingspan **10in (25cm)** | Weight **⅝oz (18g)** |
|---|---|---|
| Social **Solitary** | Lifespan **Unknown** | Status **Secure** |

| DATE SEEN | WHERE | NOTES |
|---|---|---|
| | | |
| | | |
| | | |
| | | |

| Order **Passeriformes** | Family **Vireonidae** | Species **Vireo philadelphicus** |

# Philadelphia Vireo

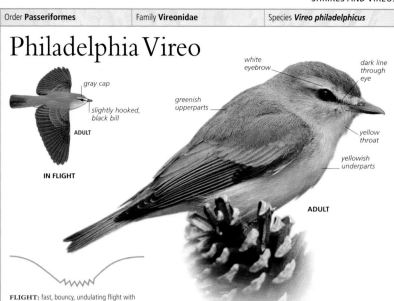

gray cap

slightly hooked, black bill

**ADULT**

**IN FLIGHT**

white eyebrow

greenish upperparts

dark line through eye

yellow throat

yellowish underparts

**ADULT**

**FLIGHT:** fast, bouncy, undulating flight with strong wingbeats.

Despite being widespread, the Philadelphia Vireo remains rather poorly studied. It shares its breeding habitat with the similar looking, but larger and more numerous, Red-eyed Vireo, and, interestingly, it modifies its behavior to avoid competition. It is the most northerly breeding vireo, with its southernmost breeding range barely reaching the US. Its scientific and English names derive from the fact that the bird was first discovered near Philadelphia in the mid-19th century.

**VOICE** Song a series of two and four note phrases, remarkably similar to the song of the Red-eyed Vireo.

**NESTING** Rounded cup of plant fibers bound by spider webs, hanging between forked twigs that narrows at the rim; 3–5 eggs; 1–2 broods; June–August.

**FEEDING** Gleans caterpillars, bees, flies, and bugs from leaves; usually forages high in trees, moving with short hops and flights.

**DISTINGUISHED APPEARANCE**
The Philadelphia Vireo's gentle expression and pudgy appearance help separate it from its neighbor, the Red-eyed Vireo.

**SIMILAR SPECIES**

**BELL'S VIREO**
see p.261

faint wing bar

longer tail

**WARBLING VIREO**
see p.268

plainer face

less yellow below

**OCCURRENCE**
Breeds in deciduous woodlands, mixed woodlands, and woodland edges, in a wide belt across Canada, reaching the Great Lakes and northern New England. The Philadelphia Vireo winters from Mexico to Panama and northern Colombia.

| Length **5¼in (13.5cm)** | Wingspan **8in (20cm)** | Weight **⁷⁄₁₆oz (12g)** |
| Social **Solitary/Pairs** | Lifespan **Up to 8 years** | Status **Secure** |

| DATE SEEN | WHERE | | NOTES |
|---|---|---|---|
| | | | |
| | | | |
| | | | |
| | | | |
| | | | |

| Order **Passeriformes** | Family **Vireonidae** | Species **Vireo gilvus** |
|---|---|---|

# Warbling Vireo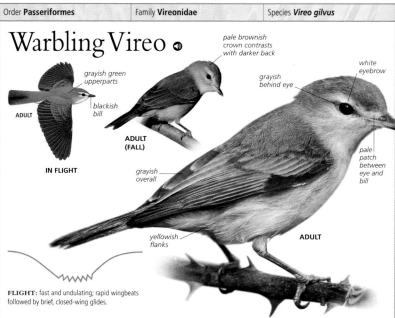

pale brownish crown contrasts with darker back

grayish green upperparts

blackish bill

**ADULT**

**ADULT (FALL)**

grayish behind eye

white eyebrow

grayish overall

**IN FLIGHT**

pale patch between eye and bill

yellowish flanks

**ADULT**

**FLIGHT:** fast and undulating; rapid wingbeats followed by brief, closed-wing glides.

Widely distributed across North America, this rather drab vireo is better known for its cheerful warbling song than for its plumage, and coincidentally, its thin bill and longish tail give this rather active vireo a somewhat warbler-like appearance. Eastern and western Warbling Vireos are quite different and may in fact be separate species. Eastern birds are heavier and have a larger bill. Out of all the vireos, the Warbling Vireo is most likely to breed in human developments, such as city parks, suburbs, and orchards.

**VOICE** Harsh, raspy scold call; male's persistent song a high, rapid, and highly variable warble.

**NESTING** Rough cup placed high in a deciduous tree, hung from the rim between forked twigs; 3–5 eggs; 2 broods; March–July.

**FEEDING** Gleans a variety of insects, including grasshoppers, aphids, and beetles from leaves; eats fruit in winter.

**PLAIN-LOOKING SONGSTER**
The Warbling Vireo makes up for its plain appearance with its colorful voice, full of rounded notes and melodious warbles.

### SIMILAR SPECIES

**BELL'S VIREO**
see p.261

faint wing bar

longer tail

**PHILADELPHIA VIREO**
see p.267

no wing bar

dark line extends to bill

shorter bill

yellow on breast and throat

**OCCURRENCE**
Extensive distribution across most of temperate North America, from Alaska to western, central, and eastern North America. Breeds in deciduous and mixed forests, particularly near water. Winters in southern Mexico and Central America.

| Length 5½in (14cm) | Wingspan 8½in (21cm) | Weight 7⁄16oz (12g) |
|---|---|---|
| Social **Solitary/Pairs** | Lifespan **Up to 13 years** | Status **Secure** |

| DATE SEEN | WHERE | NOTES |
|---|---|---|
| | | |
| | | |
| | | |
| | | |

| Order **Passeriformes** | Family **Vireonidae** | Species *Vireo olivaceus* |

# Red-eyed Vireo 🔊

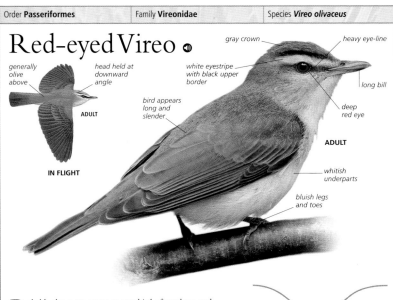

gray crown

heavy eye-line

generally olive above

head held at downward angle

white eyestripe with black upper border

long bill

bird appears long and slender

deep red eye

**ADULT**

**ADULT**

**IN FLIGHT**

whitish underparts

bluish legs and toes

Probably the most common songbird of northern and eastern North America, the Red-eyed Vireo is perhaps the quintessential North American vireo, although it is heard far more often than it is seen. It sings persistently and monotonously all day long and late into the season, long after other species have stopped singing. It generally stays high in the canopy of the deciduous and mixed woodlands where it breeds. The entire population migrates to central South America in winter. To reach their Amazonian winter habitats, Red-eyed Vireos migrate in fall (August–October) through Central America, Caribbean Islands, and northern South America to Ecuador, Peru, and Brazil.

**VOICE** Nasal mewing call; male song consists of slurred three-note phrases.
**NESTING** Open cup nest hanging on horizontal fork of tree branch; built with plant fibers bound with spider's web; exterior is sometimes decorated with lichen; 3–5 eggs; 1 brood; May–July.
**FEEDING** Gleans insects from leaves, hopping methodically in the canopy and sub-canopy of deciduous trees; during fall and winter, primarily feeds on fruit.

**FLIGHT:** fast, strong, and undulating with the body angled upward.

**HOPPING BIRD**
The Red-eyed Vireo's primary form of locomotion is hopping; at ground level and in trees.

**OCCURRENCE**
Breeds across North America from the Yukon and British Columbia east to the Canadian maritimes, and from Washington to eastern and southeastern US. Inhabits the canopy of deciduous forests and pine hardwood forests.

**SIMILAR SPECIES**

**BLACK-WHISKERED VIREO**

faint black "mustache"

duller green upperparts

**BROWN EYES**
Immature Red-eyed Vireos have brown eyes, but those of the adult birds are red.

| Length **6in (15cm)** | Wingspan **10in (25cm)** | Weight **⅝oz (17g)** |
| Social **Solitary/Pairs** | Lifespan **Up to 10 years** | Status **Secure** |

| DATE SEEN | WHERE | NOTES |
|---|---|---|
| | | |
| | | |
| | | |
| | | |
| | | |

| Order **Passeriformes** | Family **Corvidae** | Species **Perisoreus canadensis** |

# Canada Jay

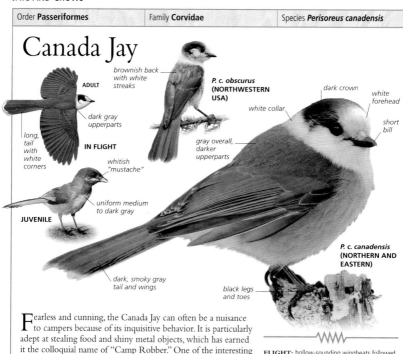

brownish back with white streaks

**ADULT**

*P. c. obscurus*
**(NORTHWESTERN USA)**

dark crown

white forehead

white collar

short bill

dark gray upperparts

long tail with white corners

**IN FLIGHT**

gray overall, darker upperparts

whitish "mustache"

uniform medium to dark gray

**JUVENILE**

*P. c. canadensis*
**(NORTHERN AND EASTERN)**

dark, smoky gray tail and wings

black legs and toes

Fearless and cunning, the Canada Jay can often be a nuisance to campers because of its inquisitive behavior. It is particularly adept at stealing food and shiny metal objects, which has earned it the colloquial name of "Camp Robber." One of the interesting aspects of its behavior is the way it stores food for later use by sticking it to trees with its viscous saliva. This is thought to be one of the reasons that enable it to survive the long northern winters. Canada Jays can often gather in noisy groups of three to six birds in order to investigate intruders encroaching upon their territory.

**VOICE** Mostly silent, but also produces variety of odd clucks and screeches; sometimes Blue Jay-like *jay!* and eerie whistles, including bisyllabic *whee-oo* or *ew*.

**NESTING** Bulky platform of sticks with cocoons on south side of coniferous tree; 2–5 eggs; 1 brood; February–May.

**FEEDING** Forages for insects and berries; also raids birds' nests.

**FLIGHT:** hollow-sounding wingbeats followed by slow, seemingly awkward, rocking glides.

**BUILT FOR COLD**
The Canada Jay's short extremities and dense, fluffy plumage are perfect for long, harsh winters.

### SIMILAR SPECIES

**CLARK'S NUTCRACKER** see p.274

white wing patch

longer bill

**NORTHERN MOCKINGBIRD** see p.324

no dark crown

white wing patch

longer tail

**OCCURRENCE**
Northern forests, especially lichen-festooned areas with firs and spruce. Found in coniferous forests across northern North America from Alaska to Newfoundland, the Maritimes, and northern New York and New England; south to western mountains; an isolated population in the Black Hills.

| Length **10–11½in (25–29cm)** | Wingspan **18in (46cm)** | Weight **2⅛–2⅞oz (60–80g)** |
| Social **Family groups** | Lifespan **Up to 10 years** | Status **Secure** |

| DATE SEEN | WHERE | | NOTES |
| --- | --- | --- | --- |
| | | | |
| | | | |
| | | | |
| | | | |
| | | | |

| Order **Passeriformes** | Family **Corvidae** | Species *Gymnorhinus cyanocephalus* |

# Pinyon Jay

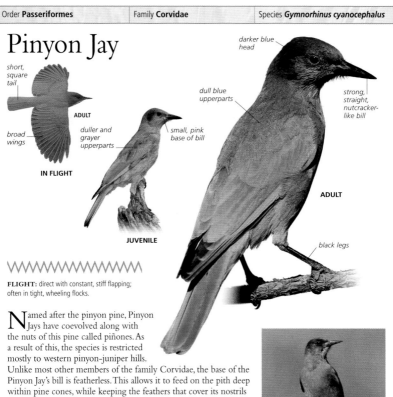

darker blue head

short, square tail

dull blue upperparts

strong, straight, nutcracker-like bill

**ADULT**

broad wings

duller and grayer upperparts

small, pink base of bill

**IN FLIGHT**

**ADULT**

**JUVENILE**

black legs

**FLIGHT:** direct with constant, stiff flapping; often in tight, wheeling flocks.

Named after the pinyon pine, Pinyon Jays have coevolved along with the nuts of this pine called piñones. As a result of this, the species is restricted mostly to western pinyon-juniper hills. Unlike most other members of the family Corvidae, the base of the Pinyon Jay's bill is featherless. This allows it to feed on the pith deep within pine cones, while keeping the feathers that cover its nostrils clean. Pinyon Jays form long-term partnerships, and nest in colonies that sometimes number in the hundreds.

**VOICE** Far-carrying, upslurred *howah, howah, howah* in flight.
**NESTING** Well-insulated, three layered cup on south side of tree or shrub; 3–5 eggs; 1–2 broods; February–May, sometimes also in fall if pine cones are plentiful.
**FEEDING** Feeds on piñones, other nuts, fruit, and insects; will also raid nests for eggs and hawk for insects.

**PINE SPECIALIST**
Pinyon Jays specialize in eating pine nuts from ponderosas and their namesake pinyons.

**SIMILAR SPECIES**

**CALIFORNIA SCRUB-JAY** see p.451
white eyebrow
longer tail

**CLARK'S NUTCRACKER** see p.274
gray in plumage
paler underparts and throat

**OCCURRENCE**
Nomadic, seeking out ripe seeds in pinyon juniper scrub on the foothills and plateaus of the western states, from Montana to New Mexico and California; less common in drier, open pine with juniper understory; flocks may descend to lower elevations in the fall and winter.

| Length **10–11in (25–28cm)** | Wingspan **19in (48cm)** | Weight **3½oz (100g)** |
| Social **Colonies** | Lifespan **Up to 15 years** | Status **Vulnerable** |

| DATE SEEN | WHERE | | NOTES |
| --- | --- | --- | --- |
| | | | |
| | | | |
| | | | |
| | | | |
| | | | |

| Order **Passeriformes** | Family **Corvidae** | Species **Cyanocitta stelleri** |
|---|---|---|

# Steller's Jay 🔊

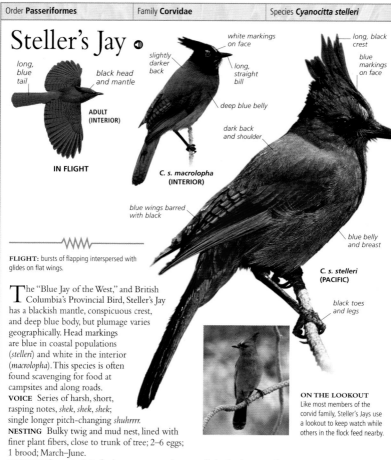

long, blue tail

black head and mantle

**ADULT (INTERIOR)**

**IN FLIGHT**

white markings on face

slightly darker back

long, straight bill

deep blue belly

dark back and shoulder

**C. s. macrolopha (INTERIOR)**

blue wings barred with black

long, black crest

blue markings on face

blue belly and breast

**C. s. stelleri (PACIFIC)**

black toes and legs

**FLIGHT:** bursts of flapping interspersed with glides on flat wings.

The "Blue Jay of the West," and British Columbia's Provincial Bird, Steller's Jay has a blackish mantle, conspicuous crest, and deep blue body, but plumage varies geographically. Head markings are blue in coastal populations (*stelleri*) and white in the interior (*macrolopha*). This species is often found scavenging for food at campsites and along roads.

**VOICE** Series of harsh, short, rasping notes, *shek, shek, shek*; single longer pitch-changing *shuhrrrr*.

**NESTING** Bulky twig and mud nest, lined with finer plant fibers, close to trunk of tree; 2–6 eggs; 1 brood; March–June.

**FEEDING** Opportunistic feeder, eats acorns, pine nuts, fruit; also insects and spiders; small vertebrates such as lizards and rodents; also raids birds' nests.

**ON THE LOOKOUT**
Like most members of the corvid family, Steller's Jays use a lookout to keep watch while others in the flock feed nearby.

**SIMILAR SPECIES**

**BLUE JAY** see p.451
short blue crest
grayish white below

**CALIFORNIA SCRUB-JAY** see p.451
white eyebrow
whitish below

**OCCURRENCE**
Found mainly in montane coniferous and mixed forests; but also in adjacent broad-leafed habitats; and occasionally, in winter, makes sudden migrations to lower elevations, east onto the Great Plains. Interbreeds locally with the Blue Jay where their ranges meet at the foot of the Rockies.

| Length **11–12½in (28–32cm)** | Wingspan **19in (48cm)** | Weight **3½–5oz (100–150g)** |
|---|---|---|
| Social **Small flocks** | Lifespan **Up to 15 years** | Status **Secure** |

| DATE SEEN | WHERE | NOTES |
|---|---|---|
| | | |
| | | |
| | | |
| | | |
| | | |

Order **Passeriformes** | Family **Corvidae** | Species ***Aphelocoma woodhouseii***

# Woodhouse's Scrub-Jay

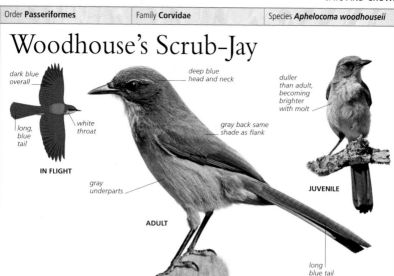

dark blue overall

deep blue head and neck

white throat

long, blue tail

**IN FLIGHT**

gray underparts

**ADULT**

gray back same shade as flank

duller than adult, becoming brighter with molt

**JUVENILE**

long blue tail

W estern Scrub-Jays were considered a single species until 2016, but the duller, less strongly patterned birds found in pinyon pines from Oregon and Idaho to Mexico are now considered a separate species, Woodhouse's Scrub-Jay. There is a little overlap with the California Scrub-Jay, which prefers oaks, in eastern California and western Nevada. The straighter bill of Woodhouse's Scrub-Jay is adapted to pick seeds from between the open scales of pine cones. It is a slightly duller, "dustier" bird than the California species, plainer gray beneath, and lacks the crest of a Blue Jay or Steller's Jay.

**VOICE** A nasal, buzzy *chairrp* and soft *weep*; quiet, bubbly song and many other notes; bill-rattling sounds.

**NESTING** Low nest in a piñon pine, well hidden in foliage; 1–5 eggs; 1 brood; March–June.

**FEEDING** Eats insects and fruit in summer, and nuts, seeds, and juniper berries at other times; takes seeds from ripe open pine cones.

**FLIGHT:** slow, labored, with flappy beats between glides, short swoops to perch.

**FORAGER OF BERRIES**
Scrub-jays are great berry-eaters in the fall and winter, foraging in low thickets.

### SIMILAR SPECIES

**CALIFORNIA SCRUB-JAY** see p.451

gray back

white flank

**PINYON JAY** see p.271

uniformly blue-gray

**OCCURRENCE**
From Oregon and Idaho south to Mexico, a bird of oak and pinyon or pinyon juniper woodland, sometimes found in mahogany, cactus or oak scrub, roadside belts, suburban parks, and golf courses.

| Length **11–12in (27–31cm)** | Wingspan **15in (39cm)** | Weight **2.8oz (80g)** |
|---|---|---|
| Social **Small groups** | Lifespan **8–9 years** | Status **Secure** |

| DATE SEEN | WHERE | NOTES |
|---|---|---|
| | | |
| | | |
| | | |
| | | |

| Order **Passeriformes** | Family **Corvidae** | Species *Nucifraga columbiana* |
|---|---|---|

# Clark's Nutcracker

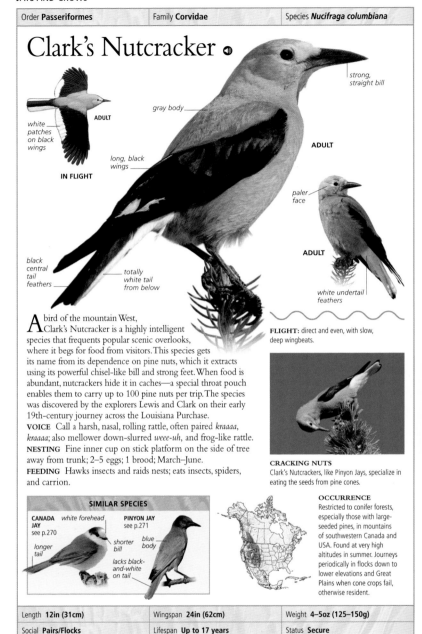

strong, straight bill

gray body

ADULT

white patches on black wings

long, black wings

**IN FLIGHT**

ADULT

paler face

ADULT

black central tail feathers

totally white tail from below

white undertail feathers

A bird of the mountain West, Clark's Nutcracker is a highly intelligent species that frequents popular scenic overlooks, where it begs for food from visitors. This species gets its name from its dependence on pine nuts, which it extracts using its powerful chisel-like bill and strong feet. When food is abundant, nutcrackers hide it in caches—a special throat pouch enables them to carry up to 100 pine nuts per trip. The species was discovered by the explorers Lewis and Clark on their early 19th-century journey across the Louisiana Purchase.

**VOICE** Call a harsh, nasal, rolling rattle, often paired *kraaaa, kraaaa*; also mellower down-slurred *weee-uh*, and frog-like rattle.

**NESTING** Fine inner cup on stick platform on the side of tree away from trunk; 2–5 eggs; 1 brood; March–June.

**FEEDING** Hawks insects and raids nests; eats insects, spiders, and carrion.

**FLIGHT:** direct and even, with slow, deep wingbeats.

**CRACKING NUTS**
Clark's Nutcrackers, like Pinyon Jays, specialize in eating the seeds from pine cones.

### SIMILAR SPECIES

**CANADA JAY** see p.270

white forehead

longer tail

**PINYON JAY** see p.271

shorter bill

blue body

lacks black-and-white on tail

**OCCURRENCE**
Restricted to conifer forests, especially those with large-seeded pines, in mountains of southwestern Canada and USA. Found at very high altitudes in summer. Journeys periodically in flocks down to lower elevations and Great Plains when cone crops fail, otherwise resident.

| Length **12in (31cm)** | Wingspan **24in (62cm)** | Weight **4–5oz (125–150g)** |
|---|---|---|
| Social **Pairs/Flocks** | Lifespan **Up to 17 years** | Status **Secure** |

| DATE SEEN | WHERE | NOTES |
|---|---|---|
| .................. | .................................. | .................................. |
| .................. | .................................. | .................................. |
| .................. | .................................. | .................................. |
| .................. | .................................. | .................................. |

| Order **Passeriformes** | Family **Corvidae** | Species *Pica hudsonia* |

# Black-billed Magpie 🔊

large white patches on outer wings

black back and head

thick black bill

white shoulders

**ADULT**

black breast

blue-green iridescence to wings and tail

**IN FLIGHT**

**ADULT**

white belly

long black tail

Loud, flashy, and conspicuous, the Black-billed Magpie is abundant in the northwestern quarter of the continent, from Alaska to interior US. It has adapted to suburbia, confidently strutting across front lawns locally. Until recently, it was considered the same species as the Eurasian Magpie (*P. pica*), and even though they look nearly identical, scientific evidence points instead to a close relationship with the other North American magpie, the Yellow-billed Magpie. Its long tail enables it to make rapid changes in direction in flight. The male uses his tail to display while courting a female. Why the Black-billed Magpie does not occur widely in eastern North America is a biological mystery.

**VOICE** Common call a questioning, nasal *ehnk*; also raspy *shenk, shenk, shenk*, usually in series.

**NESTING** Large, domed, often made of thorny sticks; 5–8 eggs; 1 brood; March–June.

**FEEDING** Omnivorous; forages on ground, mainly for insects, worms, seeds, and carrion; even picks ticks from mammals.

**FLIGHT:** direct, with slow, steady, and often shallow wingbeats; occasional shallow glides.

**IRIDESCENT SHEEN**
In bright sunlight, beautiful iridescent blues, greens, golds, and purples appear on the wings and tail.

**SIMILAR SPECIES**

YELLOW-BILLED MAGPIE
see p.451

yellow bill

yellow patch around eye

**OCCURRENCE**
Found in open habitats, foothills, and plains of the western US and Canada; nests in streamside vegetation; persecution has made it wary and restricted to wilderness in some areas, but in others it has adapted to suburbs of towns and cities.

| Length **17–19½in (43–50cm)** | Wingspan **25in (63cm)** | Weight **6–7oz (175–200g)** |
| Social **Small flocks** | Lifespan **Up to 15 years** | Status **Secure** |

| DATE SEEN | WHERE | NOTES |
|-----------|-------|-------|
| | | |
| | | |
| | | |
| | | |
| | | |

| Order **Passeriformes** | Family **Corvidae** | Species ***Corvus brachyrhynchos*** |
|---|---|---|

# American Crow

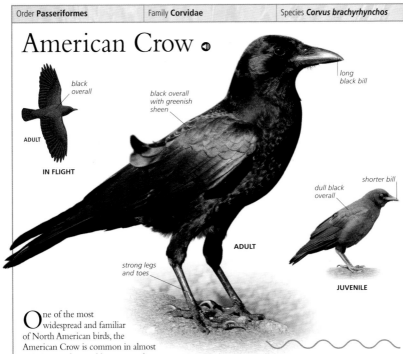

black overall

**ADULT**

**IN FLIGHT**

black overall
with greenish
sheen

long
black bill

shorter bill

dull black
overall

**ADULT**

strong legs
and toes

**JUVENILE**

One of the most widespread and familiar of North American birds, the American Crow is common in almost all habitats—from wilderness to urban centers. Like most birds with large ranges, there is substantial geographical variation in this species. Birds are black across the whole continent, but size and bill shape vary from region to region. Birds from western Canada and western USA (*C. b. hesperis*) are on average smaller and have a lower pitched voice; birds from southern Florida (*C. b. pascuus*) are more solitary and more wary.

**VOICE** Call a loud, familiar *caw!*; juveniles' call higher pitched.

**NESTING** Stick base with finer inner cup; 3–7 eggs; 1 brood; April–June.

**FEEDING** Feeds omnivorously on fruit, carrion, garbage, insects, spiders; raids nests.

**FLIGHT:** direct and level with slow, steady flapping; does not soar.

**LOOKING AROUND**
Extremely inquisitive, American Crows are always on the lookout for food or something of interest.

**OCCURRENCE**
Often seen converging at dusk toward favored roosting areas; most numerous in relatively open areas with large and widely spaced trees; has become abundant in some cities; a partial migrant, some populations are more migratory than others.

### SIMILAR SPECIES

**FISH CROW**
higher, more
nasal call

slightly
smaller
overall

smaller
head

**CHIHUAHUAN
RAVEN**
see p.452

larger
overall

larger
bill

wedge-
shaped tail

| Length **15½–19½in (39–49cm)** | Wingspan **3ft (1m)** | Weight **15–22oz (425–625g)** |
|---|---|---|
| Social **Social** | Lifespan **Up to 15 years** | Status **Secure** |

| DATE SEEN | WHERE | NOTES |
|---|---|---|
| .................... | .................... | .................... |
| .................... | .................... | .................... |
| .................... | .................... | .................... |
| .................... | .................... | .................... |
| .................... | .................... | .................... |

| Order **Passeriformes** | Family **Corvidae** | Species **Corvus corax** |

# Common Raven

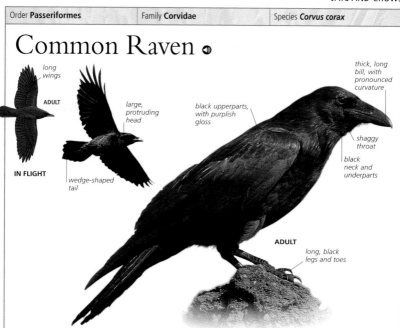

long wings

**ADULT**

thick, long bill, with pronounced curvature

large, protruding head

black upperparts, with purplish gloss

shaggy throat

**IN FLIGHT**

black neck and underparts

wedge-shaped tail

**ADULT**

long, black legs and toes

The Common Raven, twice the size of the American Crow, is a bird of Viking legend, literature, scientific wonder, and the Yukon Official Bird. Its Latin name, *Corvus corax*, means "crow of crows." Ravens are perhaps the most intelligent of all birds: they learn quickly, adapt to new circumstances with remarkable mental agility, and communicate with each other through an array of vocal and motional behaviors. They are master problem solvers and deceivers, tricking each other with ingenious methods.

**VOICE** Varied and numerous vocalizations, including hoarse, rolling *krruuk*, twangy peals, guttural clicks, resonant *bonks*.
**NESTING** Platform of sticks with fine inner material on trees, cliffs, or manmade structure; 4–5 eggs; 1 brood; March–June.
**FEEDING** Feeds omnivorously on carrion, small crustaceans, fish, rodents, fruit, grain, and garbage; also raids nests.

**FLIGHT:** slow, steady, powerful, direct; can also be quite acrobatic; commonly soars.

**SHARING INFORMATION**
Ravens in flocks can communicate information about food sources.

### SIMILAR SPECIES

**AMERICAN CROW** lacks shaggy throat feathers; see p.276

smaller bill

**CHIHUAHUAN RAVEN** see p.452

much smaller overall

lacks wedge-shaped tail

slightly smaller overall

**OCCURRENCE**
Found in almost every kind of habitat, including tundra, mountains, northern forest, woodlands, prairies, arid regions, coasts, and around human settlements; has recently recolonized areas at southern edge of range, from which it was once expelled by humans.

| Length **23½–27in (60–69cm)** | Wingspan **4½ft (1.4m)** | Weight **2½–3¼lb (1–1.5kg)** |
| Social **Solitary/Pairs/Small flocks** | Lifespan **Up to 15 years** | Status **Secure** |

| DATE SEEN | WHERE | NOTES |
|---|---|---|
| | | |
| | | |
| | | |
| | | |
| | | |

# SWALLOWS

SWALLOWS ARE A COSMOPOLITAN family of birds with species found nearly everywhere, except in the polar regions and some of the largest deserts, although during migration they fly over some of the world's harshest deserts, including the Sahara and Atacama. Most species have relatively short, notched tails but some have elongated outer tail feathers. Among these latter species, females appear to prefer males with the longest tails as mates. The Bank Swallow and the Barn Swallow, which are also found across Eurasia, are the most widespread. All North American swallows are migratory, and most of them winter in Central and South America, where they feed on flying insects that occur year-round. They are all superb fliers, and skilled at aerial pursuit and capture of flying insects. They are sometimes confused with swifts, which belong to a different family and order, and have a different style of flight. Swallows have relatively shorter, broader wings and less stiff wingbeats.

**SURFACE SKIMMER**
This Tree Swallow flies low over freshwater to catch insects as they emerge into the air.

# CHICKADEES AND TITMICE

CHICKADEES AND TITMICE may be some of the most well-known and widespread birds in North America. Once considered to be in the same genus, recent genetic studies have placed titmice and chickadees in different genera.

## CHICKADEES
Chickadees are readily distinguished from titmice by their smooth-looking, dark caps and black bibs. Some chickadees are frequent visitors to backyards. The name "chickadee" is derived from the common calls of several species. Highly social outside the breeding season and generally tolerant of people, these energetic little birds form flocks in winter. Some species, such as the Black-capped Chickadee, can lower their body temperature to survive the cold, but others, like the similar-looking Carolina Chickadee, have a high winter mortality rate. Most species eat a combination of insects and plant material.

## TITMICE
Titmice are distinguished from chickadees by their crests; most, like the familiar Tufted Titmouse, also have plain throats. Like chickadees, titmice are highly territorial and insectivorous during the breeding season, then become gregarious seed-eaters afterward. At that time they often form mixed-species flocks with other small birds, like kinglets, as they move through woodlands searching for food. Titmice are nonmigratory.

**TAME BIRDS**
Black-capped Chickadees have distinctive black-and-white markings and are often very tame.

| Order **Passeriformes** | Family **Alaudidae** | Species *Eremophila alpestris* |

# Horned Lark 🔊

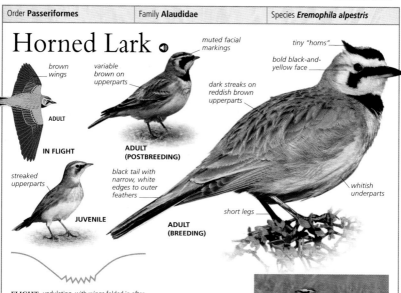

muted facial markings

tiny "horns"

brown wings

variable brown on upperparts

**ADULT**

bold black-and-yellow face

dark streaks on reddish brown upperparts

**IN FLIGHT**

**ADULT (POSTBREEDING)**

whitish underparts

streaked upperparts

black tail with narrow, white edges to outer feathers

short legs

**JUVENILE**

**ADULT (BREEDING)**

**FLIGHT:** undulating, with wings folded in after every few beats.

The Horned Lark is a bird of open country, especially places with extensive bare ground. The species is characteristic of arid, alpine, and Arctic regions; in these areas, it flourishes in the bleakest of habitats imaginable, from sun-scorched, arid lakeshores in the Great Basin, to windswept tundra north of the timberline. In some places, the only breeding bird species are the Horned Lark and the equally resilient Common Raven. In Europe and Asia, this species is known as the Shorelark.

**VOICE** Flight call a sharp *sweet* or *soo-weet*; song, either in flight or from the ground, pleasant, musical tinkling series, followed by *sweet… swit… sweet… s'sweea'weea'witta'swit*.

**NESTING** In depression in bare ground, somewhat sheltered by grass or low shrubs, lined with plant matter; 2–5 eggs; 1–3 broods; March–July.

**FEEDING** Survives exclusively on seeds of grasses and sedges in winter; eats mostly insects in summer.

**GROUND FORAGER**
With its short legs bent under its body, an adult looks for insects and seeds.

**OCCURRENCE**
Breeds widely, in any sort of open, even barren habitat with extensive bare ground, especially shortgrass prairies and deserts. Winters wherever there are snow-free openings, including along beaches and roads. Winters from southern Canada southward to Florida and Mexico.

### SIMILAR SPECIES

**SPRAGUE'S PIPIT**
see p.459

shorter tail

shorter wings

**EURASIAN SKYLARK**
see p.452

streaked crest

streaked overall

**VERY VOCAL**
The Horned Lark is a highly vocal bird, singing from the air, the ground, or low shrubs.

| Length **7in (18cm)** | Wingspan **12in (30cm)** | Weight **1¹⁄₁₆oz (30g)** |
| Social **Winter flocks** | Lifespan **Up to 8 years** | Status **Secure** |

| DATE SEEN | WHERE | NOTES |
|---|---|---|
| | | |
| | | |
| | | |
| | | |
| | | |

| Order **Passeriformes** | Family **Hirundinidae** | Species *Riparia riparia* |
| --- | --- | --- |

# Bank Swallow

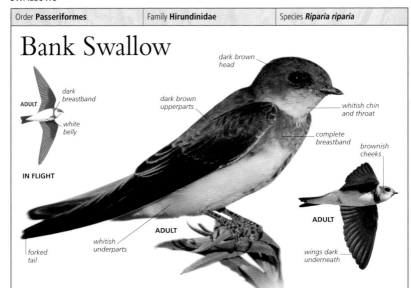

**ADULT**
dark breastband
white belly

**IN FLIGHT**

dark brown head

dark brown upperparts

whitish chin and throat

complete breastband

brownish cheeks

**ADULT**
wings dark underneath

**ADULT**

forked tail

whitish underparts

The Bank Swallow, known in the UK as the Sand Martin, is the slimmest and smallest of North American swallows. As its scientific name *riparia* (meaning "riverbanks") and common names suggest, the Bank Swallow nests in the banks and bluffs of rivers, streams, and lakes. It also favors sand and gravel quarries in the East. It is widely distributed across North America, breeding from south of the tundra–taiga line south to the central US. Nesting colonies can range from as few as 10 pairs to as many as 2,000, which are quite busy and noisy when all the birds are calling or coming in to simultaneously feed the young.

**VOICE** Call a soft *brrrrr* or *breee* often issued in pairs; song a harsh twittering or continuous chatter.

**NESTING** Both sexes excavate burrows in sandy banks containing a flat platform of grass, feathers, and twigs; 2–6 eggs; 1 brood; April–August.

**FEEDING** Catches insects, such as flies, moths, dragonflies, and bees in flight, but occasionally skims aquatic insects or their larvae off the water or terrestrial insects from the ground.

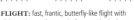

**FLIGHT:** fast, frantic, butterfly-like flight with glides, twists, and turns; shallow, rapid wingbeats.

**WAITING FOR MOM OR DAD**
Hungry youngsters still expect to be fed, even when they're ready to fledge.

**OCCURRENCE**
Widespread in North America. Breeds in lowland habitats associated with rivers, streams, lakes, reservoirs, and coasts, as well as in sand and gravel quarries. Often prefers manmade sites; winters in grasslands, open farm habitat, and freshwater areas in South America, south to Chile and Argentina.

**SIMILAR SPECIES**

**TREE SWALLOW** ☾
larger; gray-brown upperparts with greenish tinge; see p.281

incomplete breastband

**NORTHERN ROUGH-WINGED SWALLOW**
larger overall; see p.283

uniformly colored upperparts

| Length **4¾–5½in (12–14cm)** | Wingspan **10–11in (25–28cm)** | Weight **⅜–¹¹⁄₁₆oz (10–19g)** |
| --- | --- | --- |
| Social **Colonies** | Lifespan **Up to 9 years** | Status **Secure** |

| DATE SEEN | WHERE | NOTES |
| --- | --- | --- |
| | | |
| | | |
| | | |
| | | |

| Order **Passeriformes** | Family **Hirundinidae** | Species *Tachycineta bicolor* |

# Tree Swallow 🔊

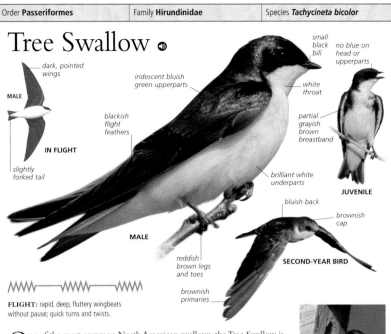

dark, pointed wings

**MALE**

iridescent bluish green upperparts

small black bill

no blue on head or upperparts

white throat

blackish flight feathers

**IN FLIGHT**

slightly forked tail

partial grayish brown breastband

**JUVENILE**

brilliant white underparts

bluish back

brownish cap

**MALE**

reddish brown legs and toes

**SECOND-YEAR BIRD**

brownish primaries

**FLIGHT:** rapid, deep, fluttery wingbeats without pause; quick turns and twists.

One of the most common North American swallows, the Tree Swallow is found from coast to coast in the northern two-thirds of the continent all the way north to Alaska. As its Latin name *bicolor* suggests, it is a two-toned bird, with iridescent bluish green upperparts and white underparts. Juveniles can be confused with the smaller Bank Swallow, which has a more complete breastband. The Tree Swallow lives in a variety of habitats, but its hole-nesting habit makes it dependent on crevices in old trees, abandoned woodpecker cavities, and on artificial "housing" such as nest boxes. The size of the population fluctuates according to the availability of nesting sites.

**VOICE** Ranges from variable high, chirping notes to chatters and soft trills; also complex high and clear 2-note whistle phrases.

**NESTING** Layer of fine plant matter in abandoned woodpecker hole or nest box, lined with feathers; 4–6 eggs; 1 brood; May–July.

**FEEDING** Swoops after flying insects from dawn to dusk; also takes bayberries.

**KEEPING LOOKOUT**
This species uses artificial nest boxes, which the males defend as soon as they arrive.

**OCCURRENCE**
Typically breeds close to water in open habitat, such as fields, marshes, lakes, and swamps, especially those with standing dead wood for cavity-nesting. Winters in roosts of hundreds of thousands of birds in marshes, in the southern US, and from Mexico to Panama; also Cuba.

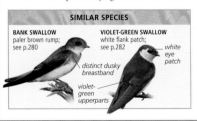

**SIMILAR SPECIES**

**BANK SWALLOW**
paler brown rump;
see p.280

distinct dusky breastband

**VIOLET-GREEN SWALLOW**
white flank patch;
see p.282

white eye patch

violet-green upperparts

| Length **5–6in (13–15cm)** | Wingspan **12–14in (30–35cm)** | Weight ⅝–⅞oz (17–25g) |
| Social **Large flocks** | Lifespan **Up to 11 years** | Status **Secure** |

| DATE SEEN | WHERE | NOTES |
|-----------|-------|-------|
| | | |
| | | |
| | | |
| | | |
| | | |

| Order **Passeriformes** | Family **Hirundinidae** | Species *Tachycineta thalassina* |

# Violet-green Swallow

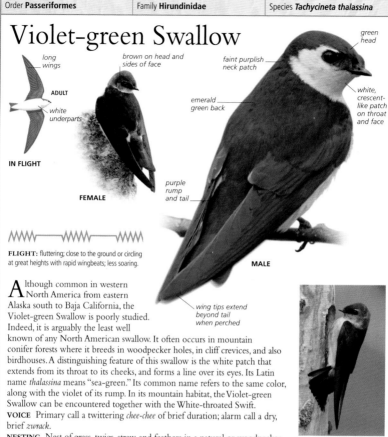

long wings

**ADULT**

white underparts

**IN FLIGHT**

brown on head and sides of face

**FEMALE**

faint purplish neck patch

emerald green back

purple rump and tail

green head

white, crescent-like patch on throat and face

**FLIGHT:** fluttering; close to the ground or circling at great heights with rapid wingbeats; less soaring.

wing tips extend beyond tail when perched

**MALE**

Although common in western North America from eastern Alaska south to Baja California, the Violet-green Swallow is poorly studied. Indeed, it is arguably the least well known of any North American swallow. It often occurs in mountain conifer forests where it breeds in woodpecker holes, in cliff crevices, and also birdhouses. A distinguishing feature of this swallow is the white patch that extends from its throat to its cheeks, and forms a line over its eyes. Its Latin name *thalassina* means "sea-green." Its common name refers to the same color, along with the violet of its rump. In its mountain habitat, the Violet-green Swallow can be encountered together with the White-throated Swift.

**VOICE** Primary call a twittering *chee-chee* of brief duration; alarm call a dry, brief *zwrack*.

**NESTING** Nest of grass, twigs, straw, and feathers in a natural or woodpecker cavity in a tree, also cliff or nesting box; 4–6 eggs; 2 broods; March–August.

**FEEDING** Catches flying insects, such as bees, wasps, moths, and flies; usually at higher levels than other species of swallows.

**AT THE NEST HOLE**
The female of this species can be distinguished from the male by her darker face.

**OCCURRENCE**
In the western US and Canada, breeds in coniferous, and mixed woodlands, especially ponderosa and monterey pine and quaking aspen; also wooded canyons. Frequents waterways during migration; prefers high elevations in general. Breeds in Mexico, winters south to Costa Rica.

### SIMILAR SPECIES

**WHITE-THROATED SWIFT** see p.91

white sides of rump

**TREE SWALLOW ♂** see p.281
iridescent greenish blue upperparts
blackish brown crown

| Length **5in (13cm)** | Wingspan **11in (28cm)** | Weight **½oz (14g)** |
| Social **Solitary/Colonies** | Lifespan **Unknown** | Status **Secure** |

| DATE SEEN | WHERE | NOTES |
|---|---|---|
| | | |
| | | |
| | | |
| | | |
| | | |

| Order **Passeriformes** | Family **Hirundinidae** | Species *Stelgidopteryx serripennis* |

# Northern Rough-winged Swallow 🔊

dark brown overall

black eye

light crescent from cheek to crown

brown head

square tail

**ADULT**

**JUVENILE**

tan-buffy wing bars

dark face

pale underparts

pale brown breast

pale, grayish brown belly

**ADULT**

**IN FLIGHT**

long, brown wings

square tail

Given the name *serripennis*—"saw feather"—by Audubon in 1888, and characterized by the stiff barbs on the leading edges of its outer wing feathers, this species is otherwise somewhat drab in color and aspect. The Northern Rough-winged Swallow has a broad distribution in North America, across southern Canada and throughout the US. This brown-backed, dusky-throated swallow can be spotted hunting insects over water. In size and habit, the Northern Rough-winged Swallow shares many similarities with the Bank Swallow, including breeding habits and color, but the latter's notched tail and smaller size help tell them apart.

**VOICE** Steady repetition of short, rapid *brrrt* notes inflected upward; sometimes a buzzy *jee-jee-jee* or high-pitched *brzzzzzt*.

**NESTING** Loose cup of twigs and straw in a cavity or burrow in a bank, such as road cuts; 4–7 eggs; 1 brood; May–July.

**FEEDING** Captures flying insects, including flies, wasps, bees, damselflies, and beetles in the air; more likely to feed over water and at lower altitudes than other swallows.

**FLIGHT:** slow, deliberate wingbeats; short to long glides; long, straight flight, ends in steep climb.

**BROWN BIRD**
This swallow is brownish above, pale grayish below, with a brown smudge on the sides of its neck.

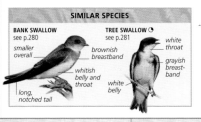

**SIMILAR SPECIES**

**BANK SWALLOW**
see p.280

smaller overall

brownish breastband

whitish belly and throat

long, notched tail

**TREE SWALLOW** ☾
see p.281

white throat

grayish breast-band

white belly

**OCCURRENCE**
In North America widespread from coast to coast. Nests at a wide variety of altitudes, prefers exposed banks of clay, sand, or gravel such as gorges, shale banks, and gravel pits. Forages along watercourses where aerial insects are plentiful. Breeds south to Costa Rica. Winters in Central America.

| Length **4¾–6in (12–15cm)** | Wingspan **11–12in (28–30cm)** | Weight **⅜–⅝oz (10–18g)** |
| Social **Solitary** | Lifespan **Unknown** | Status **Secure** |

| DATE SEEN | WHERE | | NOTES |
|---|---|---|---|
| | | | |
| | | | |
| | | | |
| | | | |
| | | | |

| Order **Passeriformes** | Family **Hirundinidae** | Species ***Progne subis*** |
|---|---|---|

# Purple Martin

large, peaked head

wings lighter in color than in male

**FEMALE**

pale collar

bluish gray upperparts

black bill

blue-black upperparts

whitish gray underparts

**FEMALE**

blue-black underparts

**MALE**

**IN FLIGHT**

**MALE**

long, forked black tail

long, dark wings

**FLIGHT:** direct, powerful flight with deep wingbeats; soars and glides when foraging.

The Purple Martin, the largest species of North American swallow, is one of the most popular of all backyard birds. Thousands of people have become devoted to the Purple Martin populations in their local areas: in the eastern half of the continent, especially, the Purple Martin now depends almost entirely on specially built "apartment-style" birdhouses for nest sites. In the West, this glossy-blue swallow is a more localized bird, although common in some areas. Here, it nests principally in old woodpecker holes.

**VOICE** Alarm call a *zwrack* or *zweet*; other calls are a variety of rolling, bubbling sounds; song a series of gurgles, chortles, and croaking phrases.

**NESTING** Loose mat of vegetation and mud in birdhouse compartments, rarely in natural cavities; 4 eggs; 1 brood; April–August.

**FEEDING** Captures flying insects at 150–500ft (45–150m) in the air; sometimes gleans insects from foliage or the ground.

**FLOCK TOGETHER**
Purple Martins are social birds: they breed in colonies and roost in flocks.

**OCCURRENCE**
In North America, eastern birds found almost exclusively in towns and cities where nest boxes are provided; western populations occur in more rural areas such as mountain and coastal forests where woodpecker holes are abundant; also uses saguaro cactus for nesting in the Southwest. Winters in Brazil.

| Length **7–8in (18–20cm)** | Wingspan **15–16in (38–41cm)** | Weight **1⁷⁄₁₆–2¹⁄₈oz (40–60g)** |
|---|---|---|
| Social **Large flocks/Colonies** | Lifespan **Up to 13 years** | Status **Secure** |

| DATE SEEN | WHERE | NOTES |
|---|---|---|
| | | |
| | | |
| | | |
| | | |
| | | |

| Order **Passeriformes** | Family **Hirundinidae** | Species *Hirundo rustica* |
| --- | --- | --- |

# Barn Swallow

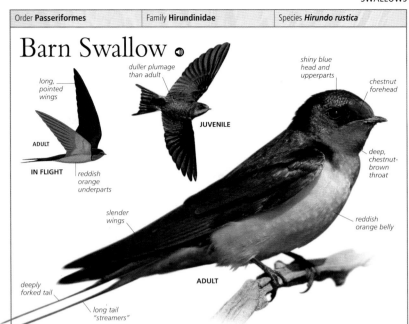

duller plumage than adult

long, pointed wings

**JUVENILE**

shiny blue head and upperparts

chestnut forehead

**ADULT**

**IN FLIGHT**

reddish orange underparts

deep, chestnut-brown throat

slender wings

reddish orange belly

deeply forked tail

long tail "streamers"

**ADULT**

The most widely distributed and abundant swallow in the world, the Barn Swallow is found just about everywhere in North America south of the Arctic timberline. Originally a cave-nester before Europeans settlers came to the New World, the Barn Swallow readily adapted to nesting under the eaves of houses, under bridges, and inside buildings such as barns. It is now rare to find this elegant swallow breeding in a natural site. Steely blue upperparts, reddish underparts, and a deeply forked tail identify the Barn Swallow. North American breeders have deep, reddish orange underparts, but birds from Eurasia are white-bellied.

**VOICE** High-pitched, squeaky *chee-chee* call; song a long series of chatty, pleasant churrs, squeaks, chitterings, and buzzes.

**NESTING** Deep cup of mud and grass-stems attached to vertical surfaces or on ledges; 4–6 eggs; 1–2 broods; May–September.

**FEEDING** Snatches flying insects, such as flies, mosquitoes, wasps, and beetles in the air at lower altitudes than other swallows; sometimes eats wild berries and seeds.

**FLIGHT:** bursts of straight flight; close to the ground; weaves left and right, with sharp turns.

**WELL PROTECTED**
Whether in a barn or other structure, this swallow's nest is totally protected from wind and rain.

**OCCURRENCE**
Breeds across North America; south to central Mexico. Prefers agricultural regions and towns. Winters near sugarcane fields, grain fields, and marshes, south in South America as far as Patagonia. Hundreds of thousands winter in marshes of northern Argentina.

**SIMILAR SPECIES**

TREE SWALLOW ♂
see p.281
lacks forked tail and dark breast band

white under-parts

| Length **6–7½in (15–19cm)** | Wingspan **11½–13in (29–33cm)** | Weight **⅝–¹¹⁄₁₆oz (17–20g)** |
| --- | --- | --- |
| Social **Small colonies/Flocks** | Lifespan **Up to 8 years** | Status **Secure** |

| DATE SEEN | WHERE | NOTES |
| --- | --- | --- |
| | | |
| | | |
| | | |
| | | |
| | | |

| Order **Passeriformes** | Family **Hirundinidae** | Species **Petrochelidon pyrrhonata** |
|---|---|---|

# Cliff Swallow 🔊

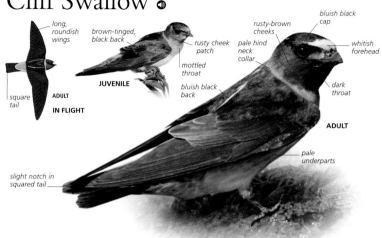

long, roundish wings

brown-tinged, black back

rusty cheek patch

mottled throat

**JUVENILE**

bluish black back

**ADULT**

square tail

**IN FLIGHT**

rusty-brown cheeks

pale hind neck collar

bluish black cap

whitish forehead

dark throat

**ADULT**

pale underparts

slight notch in squared tail

The Cliff Swallow is one of North America's most social land birds, sometimes nesting in colonies of more than 3,500 pairs, especially in the western US. It is more locally distributed in the East. It can be distinguished from other North American swallows by its square tail and orange rump, but it resembles its close relative, the Cave Swallow, in color, pattern, and in affixing its mud nests to the sides of highway culverts, bridges, and buildings. The considerable increase in such structures has allowed the species to expand its range from the West to breed almost everywhere except in dense forests and desert habitats.
**VOICE** Gives *purr* and *churr* calls when alarmed; song a low, squeaky, 6-second twitter given in flight and near nests.
**NESTING** Domed nests of mud pellets on cave walls, buildings, culverts, bridges, and dams; 3–5 eggs; 1–2 broods; April–August.
**FEEDING** Catches flying insects (often swarming varieties) while on the wing; sometimes forages on the ground; ingests grit to aid digestion.

**FLIGHT:** strong, fast wingbeats; glides more often but less acrobatically than other swallows.

**GATHERING MUD**
The Cliff Swallow gathers wet mud from puddles, pond edges, and streamsides to build its nest.

**SIMILAR SPECIES**

**CAVE SWALLOW** see p.452

brighter orange cheek

paler overall

**INDIVIDUAL HOMES**
In a Cliff Swallow colony, each nest has a single opening.

**OCCURRENCE**
Breeds in North America from Alaska to Mexico. Prefers walls, culverts, buildings, cliffs, and undersides of piers on which to affix mud nests. Migrates to South America, where hundreds of thousands winter in the marshes of northern Argentina.

| Length **5in (13cm)** | Wingspan **11–12in (28–30cm)** | Weight **¹¹⁄₁₆–1¼oz (20–35g)** |
|---|---|---|
| Social **Colonies** | Lifespan **Up to 11 years** | Status **Secure** |

| DATE SEEN | WHERE | NOTES |
|---|---|---|
| ................. | ..................... | ........................... |
| ................. | ..................... | ........................... |
| ................. | ..................... | ........................... |
| ................. | ..................... | ........................... |
| ................. | ..................... | ........................... |

| Order **Passeriformes** | Family **Paridae** | Species *Poecile atricapillus* |

# Black-capped Chickadee

**IN FLIGHT**

white on wings and tail

black-and-white head

ADULT

grayish brown upperparts

white edges on wing feathers

white edges on outer tail feathers

faded buff flanks

bright white cheeks

short black bill

black cap and bib

ADULT

The Black-capped Chickadee, the State Bird of Maine and Massachusetts, is the most widespread chickadee in North America, equally at home in the cold far north and in warm Appalachian valleys. To cope with the harsh winters in the northern parts of its range, this species can decrease its body temperature, entering a controlled hypothermia to conserve energy. There is variation in appearance depending on geographical location, northern birds being slightly larger and possessing brighter white wing edgings than southern birds. Although it is largely nonmigratory, winter chickadee flocks occasionally travel south of their traditional range.

**VOICE** Raspy *tsick-a-dee-dee-dee* call; song loud, clear whistle *bee-bee* or *bee-bee-be*, first note higher in pitch.

**NESTING** Cavity in rotting tree stump, lined with hair, fur, feathers, plant fibers; 6–8 eggs; 1 brood; April–June.

**FEEDING** Forages for insects and their eggs, and spiders in trees and bushes; mainly seeds in winter; may take seeds from an outstretched hand.

**FLIGHT:** swift and undulating, with fast wingbeats.

**ROUGH-EDGED BIB**
The Black-capped Chickadee has a less well-defined lower bib margin than the Carolina Chickadee.

### SIMILAR SPECIES

**CAROLINA CHICKADEE**
see p.453
lacks white wing edges

no white tail edges

**MEXICAN CHICKADEE**
see p.453

large bib extends to upper breast

**OCCURRENCE**
Variety of wooded habitats, from vast forests in the far north to small woodlands in urban parks and suburbs. In years of poor seed crops in northern parts of the range, large numbers migrate southward as far as the Carolina Chickadee's range.

| Length 5¼in (13.5cm) | Wingspan 8½in (22cm) | Weight ⅜oz (11g) |
| Social **Mixed flocks** | Lifespan **Up to 12 years** | Status **Secure** |

| DATE SEEN | WHERE | NOTES |
|-----------|-------|-------|
| | | |
| | | |
| | | |
| | | |
| | | |

| Order **Passeriformes** | Family **Paridae** | Species ***Poecile gambeli*** |

# Mountain Chickadee

**ADULT (EASTERN)**
black crown
black bib
buff-tinged flanks

**IN FLIGHT**

conspicuous white eyebrow
**ADULT (THE ROCKIES)**

faint white eyebrow
white cheeks
dull gray upperparts

grayish tinged flanks

**ADULT (CALIFORNIA)**

**FLIGHT:** bouncy, with fast wingbeats; interrupted by brief glides.

The Mountain Chickadee is aptly named as it is found at high elevations, up to 12,000ft (3,600m). Like other chickadees, it stores pine and spruce seeds. Social groups defend their winter territories and food resources, and migrate to lower elevations when seeds are scarce. Birds in the Rocky Mountains have a conspicuous white eyebrow and buff-tinged flanks; those in the mountains of California have grayish flanks and a fainter eyebrow.

**VOICE** Call raspy *tsick-jee-jee*; whistle song of descending notes *bee-bee-bay*.
**NESTING** Natural tree cavity or old woodpecker hole, lined with moss and fur; 7–9 eggs; 1–2 broods; May–June.
**FEEDING** Forages high in trees for insects and spiders; eats seeds and berries; stores seeds in fall in preparation for winter.

**VARIABLE EYEBROW**
The white eyebrow is evident, but it may become duller in worn spring and summer plumage.

**TYPICAL PERCH**
The species spends much of its time perched in conifer trees, where it feeds.

**OCCURRENCE**
High elevations, preferring coniferous forests. May even be seen higher than the limit of tree growth. Some birds, especially the young, move down to the foothills and valleys in winter and may visit feeders. Some also wander away from the mountains and out onto the Great Plains.

**SIMILAR SPECIES**

**BLACK-CAPPED CHICKADEE** see p.287 — no white eyebrow
**MEXICAN CHICKADEE** see p.453 — no white eyebrow, larger black bib

| Length **5¼in (13.5cm)** | Wingspan **8½in (22cm)** | Weight **⅜oz (11g)** |
| Social **Winter flocks** | Lifespan **Up to 10 years** | Status **Secure** |

| DATE SEEN | WHERE | NOTES |
| --- | --- | --- |
| | | |

| Order **Passeriformes** | Family **Paridae** | Species *Poecile rufescens* |

# Chestnut-backed Chickadee 🔊

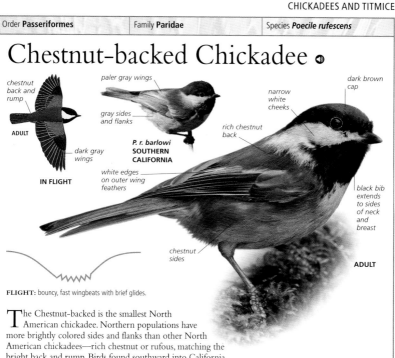

chestnut back and rump

**ADULT**

paler gray wings

gray sides and flanks

dark gray wings

*P. r. barlowi*
**SOUTHERN
CALIFORNIA**

**IN FLIGHT**

white edges on outer wing feathers

narrow white cheeks

rich chestnut back

dark brown cap

black bib extends to sides of neck and breast

chestnut sides

**ADULT**

**FLIGHT:** bouncy, fast wingbeats with brief glides.

The Chestnut-backed is the smallest North American chickadee. Northern populations have more brightly colored sides and flanks than other North American chickadees—rich chestnut or rufous, matching the bright back and rump. Birds found southward into California (subspecies *barlowi*) have paler and less extensive rufous underparts. Further south still, in southern California, the sides and flanks are dull olive-brown or gray. The Chestnut-backed Chickadee may nest in loose colonies, unlike any other chickadee species.

**VOICE** A fast, high-pitched *sic-zee-zee, seet-seet-seet*, sharp *chek-chek*, crisp *twit-twit-twit*, and many variations; no whistled song.

**NESTING** Excavates hole, or uses natural cavity or old woodpecker hole; lined with moss, hair, fur; 5–8 eggs; 1 brood; April–June.

**FEEDING** Forages high in conifers for caterpillars and other insects; eats seeds and berries in winter.

**A DASH OF WHITE**
Bright white edges on the wing feathers are often a conspicuous field mark of this species.

**SIMILAR SPECIES**

**BOREAL CHICKADEE**
see p.290

grayish brown back

gray cheeks

rich brown flanks and belly

**DARK CAP**
In good light, this chickadee's brown cap is apparent; in poor light, the cap may look black.

**OCCURRENCE**
Year-round resident in humid coniferous forests of western Canada and the Pacific Northwest; in drier mixed and deciduous woodlands, and even in urban and suburban habitats south of San Francisco. Northern coastal populations have one of the most specialized habitats of North American chickadees.

| Length **4¾in (12cm)** | Wingspan **7½in (19cm)** | Weight **⅜oz (10g)** |
| Social **Flocks** | Lifespan **Up to 9 years** | Status **Secure** |

| DATE SEEN | WHERE | NOTES |
|-----------|-------|-------|
| | | |
| | | |
| | | |
| | | |

| Order **Passeriformes** | Family **Paridae** | Species *Poecile hudsonicus* |
| --- | --- | --- |

# Boreal Chickadee

**ADULT**

**IN FLIGHT**

gray tail

gray cheeks

gray wings

grayish brown back

brown cap

black bib

rich brown flanks and belly

**ADULT**

**FLIGHT:** bouncy, fast wingbeats with brief glides.

The Boreal Chickadee was previously known by other names, including Hudsonian Chickadee, referring to its northern range, and Brown-capped Chickadee. In the past, this species made large, irregular journeys south of its breeding range during winters of food shortage, but this pattern of invasions has not occurred in recent decades. Its back color is an interesting example of geographic variation—grayish in the West and brown in the central and eastern portions of its range.
**VOICE** Call a low-pitched, buzzy, a rather slow *tsee-day-day*; also a high-pitched trill, *dididididididi*; no whistled song.
**NESTING** Cavity lined with fur, hair, plant down; in natural, excavated, or old woodpecker hole; 4–9 eggs; 1 brood; May–June.
**FEEDING** Gleans insects, conifer seeds; hoards larvae and seeds in bark crevices in fall in preparation for winter.

**IDENTIFICATION TIP**
A brown back or flank helps distinguish a Boreal Chickadee from a Black-capped Chickadee.

### SIMILAR SPECIES

**CHESTNUT-BACKED CHICKADEE** *narrow, white cheeks*
see p.289

chestnut sides

**ACROBATIC FORAGER**
This acrobatic feeder is able to cling on to conifer needles as it searches for insects and spiders.

**OCCURRENCE**
Found across the vast northern spruce-fir forests from Alaska to Newfoundland, and from the treeline at the tundra south to the northeastern and northwestern states. The southern edge of the range appears to be retracting, for unknown reasons.

| Length **5½in (14cm)** | Wingspan **8½in (21cm)** | Weight **⅜oz (10g)** |
| --- | --- | --- |
| Social **Flocks** | Lifespan **Up to 5 years** | Status **Secure** |

| DATE SEEN | WHERE | NOTES |
| --- | --- | --- |
| | | |
| | | |
| | | |
| | | |
| | | |

| Order **Passeriformes** | Family **Paridae** | Species **Baeolophus ridgwayi** |

# Juniper Titmouse

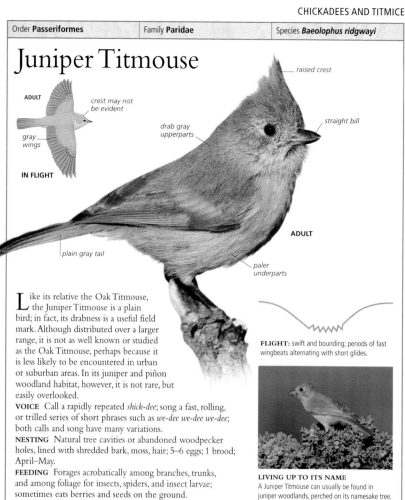

**ADULT**

crest may not be evident

gray wings

**IN FLIGHT**

raised crest

drab gray upperparts

straight bill

**ADULT**

plain gray tail

paler underparts

L ike its relative the Oak Titmouse, the Juniper Titmouse is a plain bird; in fact, its drabness is a useful field mark. Although distributed over a larger range, it is not as well known or studied as the Oak Titmouse, perhaps because it is less likely to be encountered in urban or suburban areas. In its juniper and piñon woodland habitat, however, it is not rare, but easily overlooked.

**VOICE** Call a rapidly repeated *shick-dee*; song a fast, rolling, or trilled series of short phrases such as *we-dee we-dee we-dee*; both calls and song have many variations.

**NESTING** Natural tree cavities or abandoned woodpecker holes, lined with shredded bark, moss, hair; 5–6 eggs; 1 brood; April–May.

**FEEDING** Forages acrobatically among branches, trunks, and among foliage for insects, spiders, and insect larvae; sometimes eats berries and seeds on the ground.

**FLIGHT:** swift and bounding; periods of fast wingbeats alternating with short glides.

**LIVING UP TO ITS NAME**
A Juniper Titmouse can usually be found in juniper woodlands, perched on its namesake tree.

### SIMILAR SPECIES

**GRAY VIREO**
see p.262

lacks crest

**OAK TITMOUSE**
see p.453

slightly darker overall

**OCCURRENCE**
Year-round resident of dry juniper and piñon juniper woodlands of the West. Inhabits moderate elevations, up to 8,000ft (2,400m) in the southern portions of the range. Its population is irregularly and locally distributed, although it may be more common in its habitat than is generally recognised.

| Length 5¾in (14.5cm) | Wingspan **9in (23cm)** | Weight ⅝oz (17g) |
| Social **Family groups** | Lifespan **Up to 8 years** | Status **Secure** |

| DATE SEEN | WHERE | NOTES |
| --- | --- | --- |
| | | |
| | | |
| | | |
| | | |
| | | |

| Order **Passeriformes** | Family **Remizidae** | Species **Auriparus flaviceps** |
| --- | --- | --- |

# Verdin 🔊

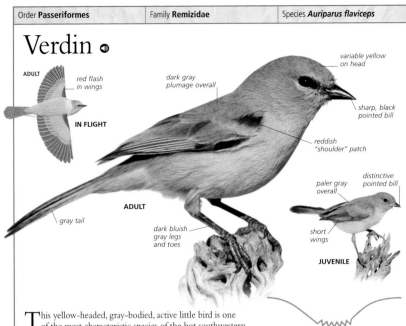

**ADULT**

red flash in wings

**IN FLIGHT**

variable yellow on head

dark gray plumage overall

sharp, black pointed bill

reddish "shoulder" patch

**ADULT**

gray tail

dark bluish gray legs and toes

distinctive pointed bill

paler gray overall

short wings

**JUVENILE**

This yellow-headed, gray-bodied, active little bird is one of the most characteristic species of the hot southwestern deserts. The Verdin is constantly on the move, flitting from shrub to shrub, inspecting flowers and cobwebs, and flying short distances across clearings. In behavior and habitat preferences, Verdins resemble chickadees, bushtits, or perhaps even wrens. The species is the only American representative of a bird family that is otherwise restricted to Eurasia, the Penduline Tits, or Remizidae, an interesting biological puzzle.
**VOICE** Call a bright, simple *beep*, made frequently as the bird forages, all day long and throughout the year.
**NESTING** Large-sized sphere with side entrance, made of twigs and leaves in thorny shrub; 4–5 eggs; 1–2 broods; April–July.
**FEEDING** Gleans small insects from leaves and flowers; also drinks nectar from flowers, and sometimes visits hummingbird feeders.

**FLIGHT:** weak, floppy, undulating; Verdins forage in shrubbery, sometimes fly across clearings.

**NECTAR FEEDER**
The Verdin will often drink nectar from tubular flowers, particularly in winter.

## SIMILAR SPECIES

**LUCY'S WARBLER** ♀
see p.466
chestnut rump

longer, thinner bill

**LUCY'S WARBLER** ♂
see p.466
gray face

chestnut rump

**OCCURRENCE**
Permanent resident in thorny vegetation of southwestern and Mexican deserts at low elevations, also in tamarisks in dry creek beds, and shrubs at the edge of desert oases. Many birds wander out into even sparser desert habitats.

| Length **4½in (11.5cm)** | Wingspan **6½in (16cm)** | Weight **³⁄₁₆–¼oz (5–7g)** |
| --- | --- | --- |
| Social **Solitary** | Lifespan **Up to 5 years** | Status **Secure** |

| DATE SEEN | WHERE | NOTES |
| --- | --- | --- |
| | | |
| | | |
| | | |
| | | |

| Order **Passeriformes** | Family **Aegithalidae** | Species *Psaltriparus minimus* |

# Bushtit

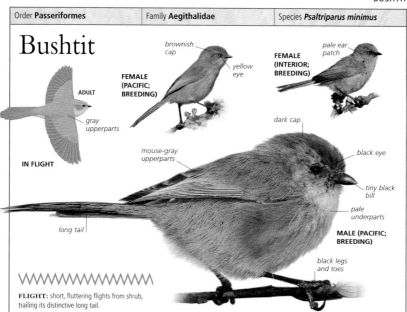

**ADULT**

gray upperparts

**IN FLIGHT**

brownish cap

yellow eye

**FEMALE (PACIFIC; BREEDING)**

**FEMALE (INTERIOR; BREEDING)**

pale ear patch

dark cap

mouse-gray upperparts

black eye

tiny black bill

pale underparts

long tail

**MALE (PACIFIC; BREEDING)**

black legs and toes

**FLIGHT:** short, fluttering flights from shrub, trailing its distinctive long tail.

The Bushtit is most often found roaming the foothills and valleys of the western US, in flocks that usually number just a handful, but occasionally total many hundreds. This little bird is constantly on the move, foraging busily in the foliage of shrubs and small trees. One moment a flock is there; the next, it has moved on. Even during the breeding season, when most other perching birds become territorial, the Bushtit retains something of its social nature—raising the young is often a communal affair, with both siblings and single adults helping in the rearing of a pair's chicks.

**VOICE** Basic call a 2–3-part soft lisp, *ps psss pit*, interspersed with hard *spit* and *spick* notes, like little sparks.

**NESTING** Enormous pendant structure of cobwebs and leaves, hung from branch; 4–10 eggs; 2 broods; April–July.

**FEEDING** Gleans spiders and insects from vegetation; acrobatic while feeding, often hangs upside-down.

**FORAGING**
Constantly aflutter, the Bushtit flits through foliage, looking for insects and other small arthropods.

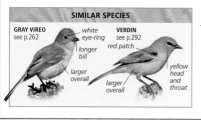

| SIMILAR SPECIES | | |
| --- | --- | --- |

**GRAY VIREO**
see p.262

white eye-ring

longer bill

larger overall

**VERDIN**
see p.292

red patch

yellow head and throat

larger overall

**OCCURRENCE**
Away from the coast, common in open woodlands and areas of shrubs, mainly on hillsides in summer, some birds move down to low-elevation valleys in the fall. Coastal populations commonly seen in cities and gardens as well as on hillsides, occur in native and non-native plant communities.

| Length **4½in (11.5cm)** | Wingspan **6in (15.5cm)** | Weight **³⁄₁₆–¹⁄₃₂oz (4.5–6g)** |
| Social **Flocks** | Lifespan **Up to 8 years** | Status **Secure** |

| DATE SEEN | WHERE | NOTES |
| --- | --- | --- |
| | | |
| | | |
| | | |
| | | |
| | | |

# NUTHATCHES

COMMON WOODLAND BIRDS, nuthatches are easily recognized by their distinctive shape and characteristic feeding techniques, and often located by loud squeaky calls. They are tree dwellers, feeding around branches and nesting in small tree holes. Nuthatches are quite plump-bodied, short-tailed but large-headed birds, with strong, pointed bills and short legs, strong toes, and arched claws. Unlike woodpeckers and creepers, which mostly climb in an upward direction, they do not need to use the tail as a prop when exploring a tree's bark. These birds rely solely on their strong and secure grip to hop and shuffle in all directions, frequently hanging upside down. They feed on spiders and also probe for insects and their larvae in the cracks of tree bark. They also eat seeds and nuts, which they may wedge into a crevice and break open with noisy taps of the bill—hence, the name "nuthatch."

**ACROBATIC POSE**
Downward-facing nuthatches such as this White-breasted Nuthatch, often lift their heads in a characteristic pose.

# WRENS

WITH ONE EXCEPTION, the Eurasian Winter Wren, wrens are small American songbirds. They are sharp-billed birds with short- or medium-length tails that are frequently cocked. Wrens are intricately patterned, mostly with dark bars and streaks, and pale spots on buff and rusty backgrounds. Their family name, *Troglodytidae*, derives from a Greek word for "cave-dweller"—while they do not really inhabit caves, the description is apt as some North American species, such as the Winter and Pacific Wrens, forage deep inside thick cover of all kinds, from scrub to upturned tree roots and overgrown stumps, or in dense growth inside ditches. Marsh Wrens are found in marshes and Sedge Wrens in sedge meadows. Wrens are often best located by their calls, which are fairly loud for such small birds. There are some species that sing precisely synchronized duets.

**COCKED TAIL**
As they sing, Winter Wrens often hold their tails upward in a near-vertical position.

| Order **Passeriformes** | Family **Sittidae** | Species *Sitta canadensis* |

# Red-breasted Nuthatch 🔊

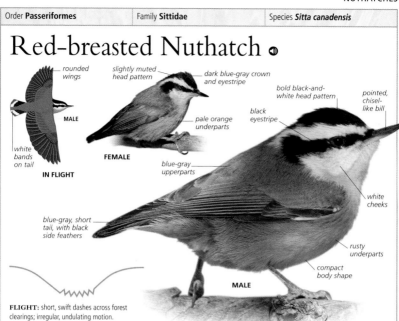

rounded wings

MALE

slightly muted head pattern

dark blue-gray crown and eyestripe

FEMALE

pale orange underparts

blue-gray upperparts

white bands on tail

IN FLIGHT

bold black-and-white head pattern

black eyestripe

pointed, chisel-like bill

white cheeks

rusty underparts

compact body shape

blue-gray, short tail, with black side feathers

MALE

**FLIGHT:** short, swift dashes across forest clearings; irregular, undulating motion.

This inquisitive nuthatch, with its distinctive black eyestripe, breeds in conifer forests across North America. The bird inhabits mountains in the West; in the East, it is found in lowlands and hills. However, sometimes it breeds in conifer groves away from its core range. Each fall, birds move from their main breeding grounds, but the extent of this exodus varies from year to year, depending on population cycles and food availability.
**VOICE** Call a one-note tooting sound, often repeated, with strong nasal yet musical quality: *aaank, enk, ink*, rather like a horn.
**NESTING** Excavates cavity in pine tree; nest of grass lined with feathers, with sticky pine resin applied to entrance; 5–7 eggs, 1 brood; May–July.
**FEEDING** Probes bark for beetle grubs; also eats insect larvae found on conifer needles; seeds in winter.

**TASTY GRUB**
This nuthatch has just extracted its dinner from the bark of a tree, a favorite foraging habitat.

### SIMILAR SPECIES

**BROWN-HEADED NUTHATCH**

brown nape

slightly smaller overall

pale gray

**WHITE-BREASTED NUTHATCH**
see p.296

larger overall

lacks black eye-stripe

white belly

chestnut undertail

**OCCURRENCE**
Found year-round in coniferous and mixed hardwood forests. During breeding season, absent from southeastern pine forests, except in the Appalachians. In the West, shares its habitat with Pygmy Nuthatch, but ranges to higher elevations.

| Length **4¼in (11cm)** | Wingspan **8½in (22cm)** | Weight **⅜–⁷⁄₁₆oz (10–13g)** |
| Social **Solitary/Pairs** | Lifespan **Up to 7 years** | Status **Secure** |

| DATE SEEN | WHERE | NOTES |
|---|---|---|
| | | |
| | | |
| | | |
| | | |

| Order **Passeriformes** | Family **Sittidae** | Species *Sitta carolinensis* |

# White-breasted Nuthatch 🔊

white flashes on tail

**MALE**

**IN FLIGHT**

rounded wings

blue-gray upperparts

short tail

chestnut undertail and lower belly

**MALE**

long, strong claws

black crown and nape

white face

conspicuous black eye

long, pointed, chisel-like bill

white throat

narrower, black band on nape

gray crown

dull gray upperparts

whitish underparts

whitish gray underparts

**FEMALE**

**FLIGHT:** weak, with quick wingbeats followed by glide; often short, from tree to tree.

The amiable White-breasted Nuthatch inhabits woodlands across the US and southern Canada, but often visits birdfeeders in winter. The largest of our nuthatches, it spends more time probing furrows and crevices on trunks and boughs than other nuthatches do. It walks irregularly on trees: forward, backward, upside-down, or horizontally. Of the 11 subspecies in its Canada-to-Mexico range, five occur in Canada and in the US. They differ in call notes and, to a lesser extent, in plumage.
**VOICE** Calls vary geographically: eastern birds nasal *yank yank*; interior birds stuttering *st't't't't'*; Pacific slope birds tremulous *yiiiirk*; song of all populations a mellow *tu tu tu tu*, like a flicker, but softer.
**NESTING** Tree cavity, once used by woodpeckers, lined with grass and hair, adds mud to cavity opening; 5–9 eggs, 1 brood; April–June.
**FEEDING** Scours bark methodically for insects such as beetle larvae.

**UNUSUAL DESCENT**
Nuthatches are unusual in that they routinely descend branches and trunks head-first.

**OCCURRENCE**
More liberal than other nuthatches in use of forest types; overlaps with the smaller species in coniferous forest ranges, but also common in broadleaf deciduous or mixed forests; weakly migratory: little movement in most falls, but moderate departures from breeding grounds in some years.

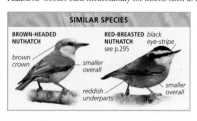

**SIMILAR SPECIES**

**BROWN-HEADED NUTHATCH**

brown crown

smaller overall

**RED-BREASTED NUTHATCH**
see p.295

black eye-stripe

reddish underparts

smaller overall

| Length **5¾in (14.5cm)** | Wingspan **11in (28cm)** | Weight **¹¹/₁₆–⅞oz (19–25g)** |
| Social **Solitary/Pairs** | Lifespan **Up to 9 years** | Status **Secure** |

| DATE SEEN | WHERE | | NOTES |
|---|---|---|---|
| | | | |
| | | | |
| | | | |
| | | | |
| | | | |

| Order **Passeriformes** | Family **Sittidae** | Species *Sitta pygmaea* |

# Pygmy Nuthatch

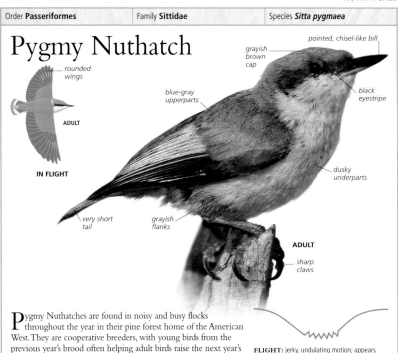

*rounded wings*

**ADULT**

**IN FLIGHT**

*blue-gray upperparts*

*grayish brown cap*

*pointed, chisel-like bill*

*black eyestripe*

*dusky underparts*

*very short tail*

*grayish flanks*

**ADULT**

*sharp claws*

Pygmy Nuthatches are found in noisy and busy flocks throughout the year in their pine forest home of the American West. They are cooperative breeders, with young birds from the previous year's brood often helping adult birds raise the next year's young. They have a particular preference for ponderosa and jeffery pines and are often absent from mountain ranges that lack their favorite trees. Pygmy Nuthatches are heard more often than they are seen, probably because they like to stick to the treetops.

**VOICE** Highly vocal species; calls piercing *peep* and *pip* notes, given singly or in frenzied series; in series, call resembles vocalizations of some Red Crossbills; calls of birds in flocks are somewhat bell-like.

**NESTING** Excavates cavity in pine tree; nest is a mass of plant material and feathers; 5–9 eggs; 1–2 broods; April–July.

**FEEDING** Forages on pine trees; mainly eats insects, caterpillars, moths, and grubs.

**FLIGHT:** jerky, undulating motion; appears bobtailed and rotund in flight.

**SQUEEZING OUT OF A NEST**
All nuthatches nest in tree cavities, which they wholly or partially excavate themselves.

### SIMILAR SPECIES

**WHITE-BREASTED NUTHATCH**
see p.296

*black crown*

*white face*

**PINE FORAGER**
A Pygmy Nuthatch hangs upside down, carrying a tiny piece of food.

**OCCURRENCE**
Patchily distributed in pine forests of western North America, from British Columbia south to California, Arizona, New Mexico, and Texas; also in Mexico. Most numerous in dry mountain forests up to 650ft (2,000m), but in California ranges down to sea level. Generally patchy distribution.

| Length **4¼in (11cm)** | Wingspan **8in (20cm)** | Weight **⅜oz (11g)** |
| Social **Small flocks** | Lifespan **Up to 2 years** | Status **Secure** |

| DATE SEEN | WHERE | NOTES |
| --- | --- | --- |
| | | |
| | | |
| | | |
| | | |

| Order **Passeriformes** | Family **Certhiidae** | Species **Certhia americana** |
| --- | --- | --- |

# Brown Creeper 🔊

**IN FLIGHT**

- buff wing bars
- ADULT
- rusty rump and uppertail feathers
- rounded wings

- thin, downward-curving bill
- whitish streak above eye
- finely streaked crown
- mottled brown above
- pale streaks on brown background
- white chin, throat, and breast
- rusty tint to belly and undertail
- long, forked tail

**ADULT (SUMMER)**

**FLIGHT:** short, floppy flights from one tree to another; also capable of sustained migration.

Although distinctive, widespread, and fairly common, the Brown Creeper is one of the most understated of the forest birds, with its soft vocalizations and cryptic plumage. As it forages, it hops up a tree trunk, then flies down to another tree, starts again from near the ground, hops up, and so on. These birds have adapted to habitat changes in the Northeast and their numbers have increased in regenerating forests. Mid- and southwestern populations, by contrast, have declined because forest cutting has reduced their breeding habitat. The Brown Creeper is a partial migrant—some individuals move south in the fall, and head north in the spring; others remain close to their breeding grounds.

**VOICE** High-pitched and easily overlooked call a buzzy *zwisss*, flight call an abrupt *tswit*; song a wheezy jumble of thin whistles and short buzzes.

**NESTING** Unique hammock-shaped nest, behind piece of peeling bark; 5–6 eggs, 1 brood; May–July.

**FEEDING** Probes bark for insects, especially larvae, eggs, pupae, and aphids.

### SIMILAR SPECIES

**PYGMY NUTHATCH**
see p.297
- blue-gray upperparts
- smaller overall
- straight bill
- smaller overall

**BROWN-HEADED NUTHATCH**
- blue-gray upperparts
- shorter tail

**STRONG TAIL**
The Brown Creeper uses its forked tail to prop it against the trunk of this tree.

**OCCURRENCE**
The only North American creeper, it breeds in a variety of forests, particularly fairly moist coniferous or mixed hardwood forests, also large stands with snags and standing dead trees. In winter it is seen in small groves without coniferous trees; also in residential districts or suburbs.

| Length **5¼in (13.5cm)** | Wingspan **8in (20cm)** | Weight **¼–⅜oz (7–10g)** |
| --- | --- | --- |
| Social **Solitary** | Lifespan **Up to 4 years** | Status **Declining** |

| DATE SEEN | WHERE | NOTES |
| --- | --- | --- |
| | | |
| | | |
| | | |
| | | |
| | | |

| Order **Passeriformes** | Family **Troglodytidae** | Species *Salpinctes obsoletus* |

# Rock Wren

faint eyestripe

rusty rump

**ADULT**

grayish brown upperparts

bright buff feather tips

**IN FLIGHT**

thin, brown streaks

pale lemon-yellow belly

**ADULT**

black-and-white barring on undertail

pale buff lower flanks

**FLIGHT:** straight, with fast wingbeats; sometimes glides from high perch.

An inhabitant of various rocky landscapes—it often sings from the edge of a high precipice—the Rock Wren's voice, while not particularly loud, carries surprisingly far through the dry air of the West. It is perpetually busy running, fluttering, and darting in and out of crevices in search of food. A well-known behavioral quirk of the Rock Wren is to bob and sway conspicuously when a human approaches. However, its oddest habit is to "pave" the area in front of its nest entrance with a walkway of pebbles—the purpose of this is unknown.
**VOICE** Call a sharp *ch'keer*, varied series of warbles, trills, chatters, and repeated musical phrases such as *chuwee chuwee, teedee teedee*, reminiscent of a mockingbird or a thrasher.
**NESTING** Cup of various grasses lined with soft materials, in rock crevice or under overhang; 4–8 eggs; 1–2 broods; April–August.
**FEEDING** Probes in rock crevices on ground and in dirt banks for a variety of insects and spiders.

**A CHANGE OF SCENERY**
Rock Wrens occasionally venture out into open grasslands and perch on manmade structures, well away from their usual surroundings.

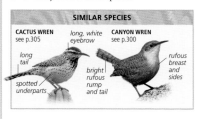

**SIMILAR SPECIES**

**CACTUS WREN**
see p.305

long tail

spotted underparts

long, white eyebrow

**CANYON WREN**
see p.300

bright rufous rump and tail

rufous breast and sides

**OCCURRENCE**
Inhabits arid country with rocky cliffs and canyons, as well as manmade quarries and gravel piles; a wide variety of elevations from hot, low deserts to windswept mountain tops as high as 10,000ft (3,000m). Northern birds migrate to southern states for winter.

| Length **6in (15cm)** | Wingspan **9in (23cm)** | Weight **⅝oz (17g)** |
| Social **Solitary/Pairs** | Lifespan **Unknown** | Status **Secure** |

| DATE SEEN | WHERE | | NOTES |
|---|---|---|---|
| | | | |
| | | | |
| | | | |
| | | | |
| | | | |

| Order **Passeriformes** | Family **Troglodytidae** | Species ***Catherpes mexicanus*** |

# Canyon Wren

grayish cap and cheeks

long bill

thinly barred rufous tail

small black-and-white spots on back and wings

white throat

bright rufous rump

long, curved bill

**ADULT**

round wings

**ADULT**

rufous underparts barred with black and brown

**IN FLIGHT**

The Canyon Wren's loud, clear whistles echo across canyons in the West, but the singer usually stays out of sight, remaining high among the crevices of its cliffside home. When it can be observed, the most striking aspect of its behavior is its extraordinary ability to walk up, down, and sideways on vertical rock walls. This remarkable agility is achieved through its strong toes and long claws; these features enable Canyon Wrens to find a grip in the tiniest of depressions and fissures in the rock.

**VOICE** Series of 10–15 loud, ringing whistles, descending in pitch, gradually slowing, and ending with several thin buzzes.

**NESTING** Cup of sticks lined with soft material such as plant down, in crevice or hole; 4–6 eggs; 1–2 broods; April–August.

**FEEDING** Uses extremely long bill to probe crevices for insects and spiders; can flatten itself by spreading legs to enter low overhangs.

**FLIGHT:** steady, straight, and fluttery; broad, rounded wings let it glide to a lower perch.

**BLENDING IN**
Except for the white throat, the Canyon Wren's plumage matches its rocky habitat.

**CLIFF-HOPPER**
This bird can half-fly and half-hop up steep cliffs by flapping its broad wings for extra lift.

### SIMILAR SPECIES

**CACTUS WREN** see p.305

brown cap

longer tail

buffy underparts

black breast spots

**ROCK WREN** see p.299

dull gray upperparts

pale gray underparts

**OCCURRENCE**
Maintains year-round territory on rocky hillsides, outcroppings, and vertical rock-walled canyons through much of the west of the continent and southward to Mexico. Sometimes nests in holes in stone buildings, old sheds, and other structures, apparently unconcerned by nearby human activity.

| Length **5¾in (14.5cm)** | Wingspan **7½in (19cm)** | Weight **⅜oz (11g)** |
| Social **Solitary/Pairs** | Lifespan **Unknown** | Status **Secure** |

| DATE SEEN | WHERE | NOTES |
| --- | --- | --- |
| | | |
| | | |
| | | |
| | | |

| Order **Passeriformes** | Family **Troglodytidae** | Species *Troglodytes aedon* |

# House Wren 🔊

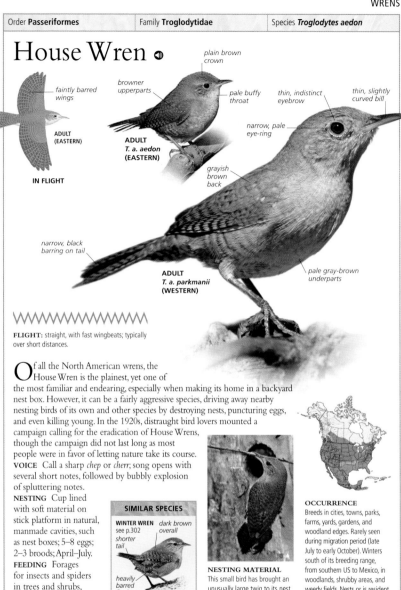

faintly barred wings

**ADULT (EASTERN)**

**IN FLIGHT**

plain brown crown

browner upperparts

pale buffy throat

**ADULT T. a. aedon (EASTERN)**

grayish brown back

thin, indistinct eyebrow

thin, slightly curved bill

narrow, pale eye-ring

narrow, black barring on tail

**ADULT T. a. parkmanii (WESTERN)**

pale gray-brown underparts

**FLIGHT:** straight, with fast wingbeats; typically over short distances.

Of all the North American wrens, the House Wren is the plainest, yet one of the most familiar and endearing, especially when making its home in a backyard nest box. However, it can be a fairly aggressive species, driving away nearby nesting birds of its own and other species by destroying nests, puncturing eggs, and even killing young. In the 1920s, distraught bird lovers mounted a campaign calling for the eradication of House Wrens, though the campaign did not last long as most people were in favor of letting nature take its course.

**VOICE** Call a sharp *chep* or *cherr*; song opens with several short notes, followed by bubbly explosion of spluttering notes.

**NESTING** Cup lined with soft material on stick platform in natural, manmade cavities, such as nest boxes; 5–8 eggs; 2–3 broods; April–July.

**FEEDING** Forages for insects and spiders in trees and shrubs, gardens, and yards.

**SIMILAR SPECIES**

WINTER WREN see p.302

dark brown overall

shorter tail

heavily barred flanks

**NESTING MATERIAL**
This small bird has brought an unusually large twig to its nest inside an old woodpecker hole.

**OCCURRENCE**
Breeds in cities, towns, parks, farms, yards, gardens, and woodland edges. Rarely seen during migration period (late July to early October). Winters south of its breeding range, from southern US to Mexico, in woodlands, shrubby areas, and weedy fields. Nests or is resident as far south as Tierra del Fuego.

| Length **4½in (11.5cm)** | Wingspan **6in (15cm)** | Weight **⅜oz (11g)** |
| Social **Solitary** | Lifespan **Up to 9 years** | Status **Secure** |

| DATE SEEN | WHERE | NOTES |
|-----------|-------|-------|
| | | |
| | | |
| | | |
| | | |
| | | |

| Order **Passeriformes** | Family **Troglodytidae** | Species **Troglodytes hiemalis** |
| --- | --- | --- |

# Winter Wren 🔊

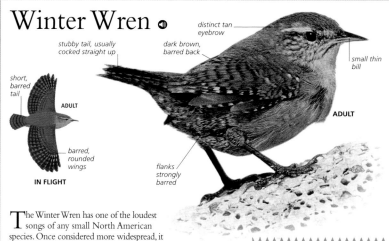

distinct tan eyebrow

stubby tail, usually cocked straight up

dark brown, barred back

small thin bill

short, barred tail

**ADULT**

**ADULT**

barred, rounded wings

flanks strongly barred

**IN FLIGHT**

The Winter Wren has one of the loudest songs of any small North American species. Once considered more widespread, it has recently been split from the Pacific Wren, which occupies much of the western fringe of the continent. It is a bird of low undergrowth and tangled roots, often foraging in the upturned roots and broken branches of fallen trees, appearing mouse-like as it creeps amid the shadows. It frequently appears in full view, gives a few harsh, scolding calls, then dives back out of sight into the low cover. It can survive periods of intense cold and even snow cover by finding insects and spiders, in crevices in bark and soil-encrusted roots. Several Winter Wrens may roost together in small cavities for warmth.

**VOICE** Call a double *chek-chek* or *chimp-chimp*; song a loud, extremely long, complex series of warbles, trills, and single notes.

**NESTING** Well-hidden in a cavity near ground with dead wood and crevices; nest a messy mound lined with feathers; 4–7 eggs; 1–2 broods; April–July.

**FEEDING** Forages for insects in low, dense undergrowth, often in wet areas along streams; sometimes thrusts its head into water to capture prey.

**FLIGHT:** fast and direct, with rapid beats of its short, broad wings.

**VOCAL VIRTUOSO**
The Winter Wren is a skulker, but in the breeding season singing males show up on lower perches.

**NERVOUS REACTION**
When alarmed, this wren cocks its tail almost vertically, before escaping into a mossy thicket.

**OCCURRENCE**
Breeds in northern and mountain forests dominated by evergreen trees with a dense understory, fallen trees, and banks of streams. In the Appalachians, breeds in treeless areas with grass near cliffs. Northernmost birds migrate south to winter in woodlands, brush piles, tangles, and secluded spots.

| SIMILAR SPECIES | SUBSPECIES |
| --- | --- |

**HOUSE WREN**
see p.301
pale brown back

long tail

plain, unbarred flanks

*T. pacificus*
(Pacific Wren)
warm brown back

barred primaries

| Length **4in (10cm)** | Wingspan **5½in (14cm)** | Weight **⁵⁄₁₆oz (9g)** |
| --- | --- | --- |
| Social **Solitary/Family groups** | Lifespan **At least 4 years** | Status **Secure** |

| DATE SEEN | WHERE | NOTES |
| --- | --- | --- |
| | | |
| | | |
| | | |
| | | |
| | | |

| Order **Passeriformes** | Family **Troglodytidae** | Species *Cistothorus palustris* |

# Marsh Wren

**ADULT**

boldly striped black-and-white back

rusty rump

plain, rusty wing patches

**IN FLIGHT**

barred tail feathers

heavily streaked, black-and-white back

rusty flanks and uppertail feathers

whitish eyebrow

brown forehead and cap

dull whitish, buff underparts

long bill

**ADULT**

**FLIGHT:** straight, with rapid wingbeats over short distances, from one reed patch to another.

The Marsh Wren, a common resident of saltwater and freshwater marshes, is known for singing loudly through both day and night. The males perform fluttery, aerial courtship flights while singing, and are polygamous, mating with two or more females. Like the Sedge Wren, the male builds several dummy nests before his mate constructs one herself. The Marsh Wren nests in taller vegetation than the Sedge Wren and over deeper water. Eastern and Western Marsh Wrens differ in voice and behavior, and some ornithologists classify them as separate species.

**VOICE** Calls a low *chek* and a raspy *churr*; song a loud *chuk chuk chuk*, then fast *tih-tih-tih-rih-tih-tih*, an enthusiastic singer.

**NESTING** Oblong structure with side entrance, woven of reeds and lined with soft materials; 4–5 eggs; 2 broods; March–July.

**FEEDING** Forages acrobatically for insects, such as mosquitoes, dragonflies, and beetles, within dense clusters of cattails and reeds.

**DELICATELY PERCHED**
This wren perches on vertical reeds and often holds itself up by spreading its legs across two stalks.

**SIMILAR SPECIES**

**SEDGE WREN** see p.454

streaked cap

barred wings

buffy underparts

**HOUSE WREN** see p.301

plain back

grayish brown underparts

**OCCURRENCE**
Breeds from Canada down to the mountains of western US as well as the central and northeastern US states. Inhabits freshwater and saltwater marshes with tall vegetation, above water, sometimes more than 3ft (1m) deep. It is irregularly distributed in its range. Winters in grassy marshes.

| Length **5in (13cm)** | Wingspan **6in (15cm)** | Weight **⅜oz (11g)** |
| Social **Loose colonies** | Lifespan **Unknown** | Status **Localized** |

| DATE SEEN | WHERE | NOTES |
|-----------|-------|-------|
| | | |
| | | |
| | | |
| | | |
| | | |

| Order **Passeriformes** | Family **Troglodytidae** | Species ***Thryomanes bewickii*** |

# Bewick's Wren

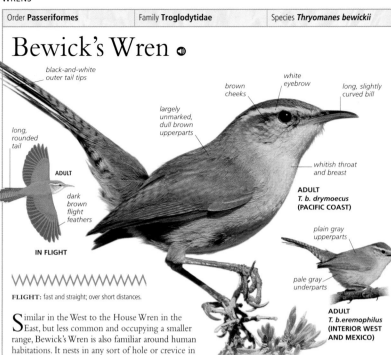

black-and-white
outer tail tips

white
eyebrow

brown
cheeks

long, slightly
curved bill

largely
unmarked,
dull brown
upperparts

long,
rounded
tail

**ADULT**

whitish throat
and breast

dark
brown
flight
feathers

**ADULT**
*T. b. drymoecus*
**(PACIFIC COAST)**

plain gray
upperparts

**IN FLIGHT**

pale gray
underparts

**ADULT**
*T. b.eremophilus*
**(INTERIOR WEST
AND MEXICO)**

**FLIGHT:** fast and straight; over short distances.

Similar in the West to the House Wren in the East, but less common and occupying a smaller range, Bewick's Wren is also familiar around human habitations. It nests in any sort of hole or crevice in barns, houses, abandoned machinery, woodpiles, and even trash heaps in farms and towns. Bewick's Wren has undergone large-scale changes in geographic distribution: in the 19th century its range expanded northward to the eastern and midwestern US, but it gradually disappeared from those regions in the 20th century. It has been suggested that the more aggressive House Wren slowly replaced Bewick's Wren in these areas.

**VOICE** Loud, complex, and varied mixture of cheeps, buzzes, and clear notes; vocalizations differ according to geographic location; also mimics other birds.

**NESTING** Cup of sticks lined with leaves, and other soft materials, in natural or manmade cavity, including nest boxes; 5–10 eggs; 2 broods; March–June.

**FEEDING** Forages for insects in brush, shrubs, crannies of buildings, and leaf litter on ground.

**TALENTED MIMIC**
Bewick's is sometimes known as the "Mocking Wren," because it can imitate other species' songs.

**OCCURRENCE**
Year-round resident in brushy areas, open woodlands, and around human structures; from southern British Columbia southward to Baja California, east to Arkansas, and as far south as Oaxaca in Mexico. May withdraw slightly southward from northernmost portions of its range in winter.

| SIMILAR SPECIES | | |

**CAROLINA WREN**
see p.454

rufous
upperparts

buffy
underparts

**TYPICAL POSTURE**
Bewick's Wren may often be spotted with its distinctive tail cocked vertically.

| Length **5in (13cm)** | Wingspan **7in (18cm)** | Weight **⅜oz (11g)** |
| Social **Solitary/Pairs** | Lifespan **At least 8 years** | Status **Secure** |

| DATE SEEN | WHERE | | NOTES |
|-----------|-------|--|-------|
| | | | |
| | | | |
| | | | |
| | | | |
| | | | |

| Order **Passeriformes** | Family **Troglodytidae** | Species ***Campylorhynchus brunneicapillus*** |
|---|---|---|

# Cactus Wren 🔊

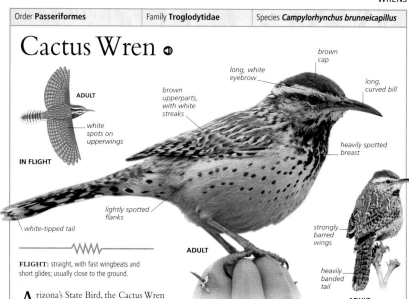

**ADULT**

white spots on upperwings

**IN FLIGHT**

brown cap

long, white eyebrow

long, curved bill

brown upperparts, with white streaks

heavily spotted breast

lightly spotted flanks

white-tipped tail

**FLIGHT:** straight, with fast wingbeats and short glides; usually close to the ground.

**ADULT**

strongly barred wings

heavily banded tail

**ADULT**

Arizona's State Bird, the Cactus Wren is the largest and among the most brightly colored of the North American wrens. Unfortunately, its population has been declining as its habitat is destroyed by agricultural development and wildfires. Its distinctively pale and weakly spotted subspecies, the "San Diego," is especially susceptible to loss of habitat. The Cactus Wren is known for building large, ball-shaped nests, often in cacti, which act as superbly effective deterrents to predators.
**VOICE** Call a loud *chack*; song a grating *kchar kchar kchar kchar*, with a harsh cluck-like quality; sings repeatedly from top of cactus or shrub, especially in the morning.
**NESTING** Bulky globular mass of woven grasses and stems with entrance hole on side; 3–5 eggs; 1–2 broods; March–August.
**FEEDING** Plucks insects and spiders from ground or shrubs.

**SAFE HOUSE**
The large globular nests that Cactus Wrens build contain a small passage that leads to the nest chamber.

**NEST CONSTRUCTION**
Strongly woven with pieces of plant matter, the nest protects the young from the hot sun.

**OCCURRENCE**
Occupies deserts and arid hillsides dominated by cacti and thorny shrubs in the Southwest. Also suburbs where artificial plantings provide nest sites. The "San Diego" subspecies (*sandiegensis*) is found in sagebrush along the coast of southern California and northwestern Baja California.

**SIMILAR SPECIES**

**ROCK WREN**
see p.299
dull brown upperparts
smaller overall

**SAGE THRASHER**
see p.323
grayish brown upperparts
streaked underparts

| Length **8½in (22cm)** | Wingspan **11in (28cm)** | Weight **1¼oz (35g)** |
|---|---|---|
| Social **Family groups** | Lifespan **Up to 7 years** | Status **Declining** |

| DATE SEEN | WHERE | NOTES |
|---|---|---|
| | | |
| | | |
| | | |
| | | |
| | | |

| Order **Passeriformes** | Family **Polioptilidae** | Species **Polioptila caerulea** |
|---|---|---|

# Blue-gray Gnatcatcher 🔊

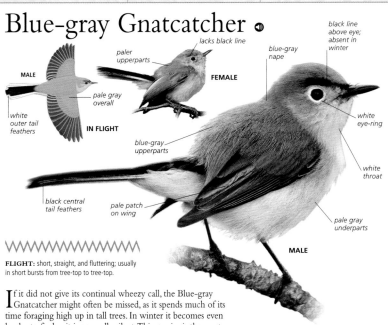

MALE

pale gray overall

white outer tail feathers

**IN FLIGHT**

paler upperparts

lacks black line

**FEMALE**

blue-gray nape

black line above eye; absent in winter

white eye-ring

white throat

blue-gray upperparts

black central tail feathers

pale patch on wing

white throat

pale gray underparts

**MALE**

**FLIGHT:** short, straight, and fluttering; usually in short bursts from tree-top to tree-top.

If it did not give its continual wheezy call, the Blue-gray Gnatcatcher might often be missed, as it spends much of its time foraging high up in tall trees. In winter it becomes even harder to find as it is generally silent. This species is the most northern of the North American gnatcatchers and is also the only one to migrate. It can exhibit aggressive behavior and is capable of driving off considerably larger birds than itself. The range of the Blue-gray Gnatcatcher appears to be expanding and populations are increasing.

**VOICE** Call soft, irregular *zhee, zhee*, uttered constantly while foraging; song soft combination of short notes and nasal wheezes.

**NESTING** Cup of plant fibers, spider webs, mosses; usually high on branch; lined with soft plant material; 4–5 eggs; 1–2 broods; April–June.

**FEEDING** Forages for small insects and spiders by acrobatically flitting from twig to twig, while twitching long tail.

**LISTEN CLOSELY**
The rather faint complex song is best heard when the bird is singing from a low perch.

### SIMILAR SPECIES

**BLACK-TAILED GNATCATCHER**
see p.307

black cap

tail white only at tip

**TENNESSEE WARBLER**
see p.390

no eye-ring

greenish upperparts

short tail

white underparts

**OCCURRENCE**
In eastern North America, breeds in deciduous or pine woodlands; in the West, in scrubby habitats, often near water. Winters in brushy habitats in southern US, Mexico, and Central America. Also breeds in Mexico, Belize, and the Bahamas.

| Length **4¼in (11cm)** | Wingspan **6in (15cm)** | Weight **⁷⁄₃₂oz (6g)** |
|---|---|---|
| Social **Solitary/Flocks** | Lifespan **At least 4 years** | Status **Secure** |

| DATE SEEN | WHERE | NOTES |
|---|---|---|
| | | |
| | | |
| | | |
| | | |

| Order **Passeriformes** | Family **Polioptilidae** | Species *Polioptila melanura* |

# Black-tailed Gnatcatcher

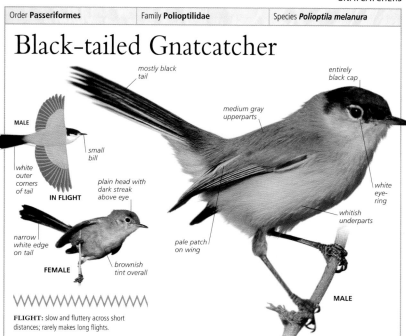

mostly black tail

entirely black cap

medium gray upperparts

**MALE**

small bill

white outer corners of tail

**IN FLIGHT**

plain head with dark streak above eye

white eye-ring

whitish underparts

narrow white edge on tail

pale patch on wing

**FEMALE**

brownish tint overall

**MALE**

**FLIGHT:** slow and fluttery across short distances; rarely makes long flights.

Few birds favor the hot, low-elevation desert of the Southwest as much as the Black-tailed Gnatcatcher. This tiny species spends most of its time flitting about among shrubs and foliage, perpetually flicking its tail from side to side. It is monogamous, and after pairs have established a nesting territory, they defend it aggressively throughout the year.

**VOICE** Various scolding notes *zhee-zhee-zhee*, *chih-chih-chih*, and *chee-chee-chee*; song, rarely heard, soft *tse-dee-dee-dee*.

**NESTING** Cup of plant fibers and spider webs, placed in shrub usually close to the ground; often lined with fine fibers; 3–4 eggs; 2 broods; April–July.

**FEEDING** Forages for insects, such as beetles and moths, among branches and leaves of shrubs; occasionally eats fruit and seeds.

**BREEDING CAP**
The male Black-tailed Gnatcatcher sports a black cap in the breeding season.

### SIMILAR SPECIES

**BLUE-GRAY GNATCATCHER**
see p.306

blue-tinted upperparts

white throat

**VIRGINIA'S WARBLER**
see p.393

pale gray upperparts

yellow undertail feathers

dark reddish cap

**OCCURRENCE**
Resident in hot, low-elevation southwestern deserts in thorny scrub, acacia, mesquite, saguaro, creosote bush, saltbush, and other shrubs. Mostly found in dry riverbeds, but also in brushy groves along waterways. Range extends south into Mexico.

| Length **4½in (11.5cm)** | Wingspan **5½in (14cm)** | Weight **⁷⁄₃₂oz (6g)** |
| Social **Solitary/Pairs** | Lifespan **Unknown** | Status **Localized** |

| DATE SEEN | WHERE | NOTES |
| --- | --- | --- |
| | | |
| | | |
| | | |
| | | |

| Order **Passeriformes** | Family **Cinclidae** | Species *Cinclus mexicanus* |
| --- | --- | --- |

# American Dipper

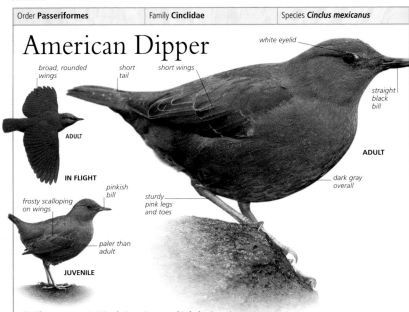

broad, rounded wings

short tail

short wings

white eyelid

straight black bill

**ADULT**

**IN FLIGHT**

**ADULT**

dark gray overall

pinkish bill

frosty scalloping on wings

sturdy pink legs and toes

paler than adult

**JUVENILE**

The most aquatic North American songbird, the American Dipper is at home in the cold, rushing streams of the American West. It is known for its feeding technique of plunging into streams for insect larvae under stones or in the streambed. When not foraging, it watches from a rock or log, bobbing up and down, constantly flashing its nictitating membrane (the transparent third eyelid that protects the eye when the bird is underwater). Susceptible to changes in water chemistry and turbulence, which alter the abundance of its main food, caddisfly larvae, this bird has been proposed as an indicator for stream quality.
**VOICE** Call a harsh *bzzt*, given singly or in rapid series; song a loud, disorganized series of pleasing warbles, whistles, and trills.
**NESTING** Domed nest with side entrance, placed underneath bridge or behind waterfall; 4–5 eggs; 1–2 broods; March–August.
**FEEDING** Forages for insects and insect larvae, especially caddisflies; sometimes eats small fish and fish eggs.

**FLIGHT:** low over water, twisting and turning with the stream with rapid, buzzy wingbeats.

**BOBBING MOTION**
The American Dipper often pauses on rocks in streams, where it bobs up and down.

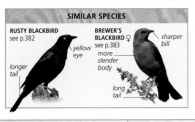

**SIMILAR SPECIES**

**RUSTY BLACKBIRD** see p.382

yellow eye

longer tail

**BREWER'S BLACKBIRD ♀** see p.383

more slender body

sharper bill

long tail

**OCCURRENCE**
Found from Alaska, the Yukon, and British Columbia, south to California, Arizona, New Mexico, Mexico, and Panama. On Pacific slope, breeds down to sea level; in interior West, breeds mainly in mountains and foothills; retreats to lower elevations in winter.

| Length **7½in (19cm)** | Wingspan **11in (28cm)** | Weight **1¾–2¼oz (50–65g)** |
| --- | --- | --- |
| Social **Solitary** | Lifespan **Up to 7 years** | Status **Secure** |

| DATE SEEN | WHERE | NOTES |
| --- | --- | --- |
| | | |
| | | |
| | | |
| | | |

| Order **Passeriformes** | Family **Regulidae** | Species *Regulus satrapa* |

# Golden-crowned Kinglet 🔊

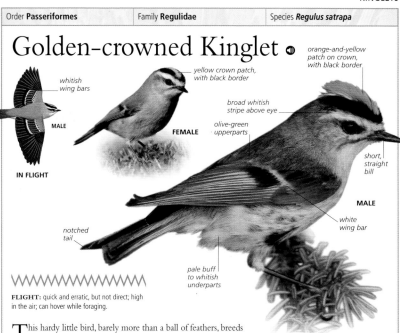

whitish wing bars

**MALE**

**IN FLIGHT**

yellow crown patch, with black border

**FEMALE**

orange-and-yellow patch on crown, with black border

broad whitish stripe above eye

olive-green upperparts

short, straight bill

**MALE**

white wing bar

notched tail

pale buff to whitish underparts

**FLIGHT:** quick and erratic, but not direct; high in the air; can hover while foraging.

This hardy little bird, barely more than a ball of feathers, breeds in northern and mountainous coniferous forests in North America. Other unconnected populations are resident in high-elevation forests of Mexico and Guatemala. Planting of spruce trees in parts of the US Midwest has allowed this species to increase its range in recent years to Ohio, Indiana, Illinois, and Pennsylvania.

**VOICE** Call a thin, high-pitched and thread-like *tsee* or *see see*; song a series of high-pitched ascending notes for 2 seconds; complex song *tsee-tsee-tsee-tsee-teet-leetle*, followed by brief trill.

**NESTING** Deep, cup-shaped nest with rims arching inward, made of moss, lichen, and bark, and lined with finer strips of the same; 8–9 eggs; 1–2 broods; May–August.

**FEEDING** Gleans flies, beetles, mites, spiders, and their eggs from tips of branches, under bark, tufts of conifer needles; eats seeds, and persimmon fruit.

**EXPANDING RANGE**
This bird has expanded its range southward following spruce forestation.

### SIMILAR SPECIES

**RUBY-CROWNED KINGLET**
see p.310

white eye-ring

no eye-stripe

olive underparts

**HIGHER VOICE**
The Golden-crowned has a higher pitched and less musical song than the Ruby-crowned.

**OCCURRENCE**
Breeds in remote northern and subalpine spruce or fir forests, mixed coniferous–deciduous forests, single-species stands, and pine plantations; winters in a wide variety of habitats—coniferous and deciduous forests, pine groves, low-lying hardwood forests, swamps, and urban and suburban habitats.

| Length 3¼–4¼in (8–11cm) | Wingspan 5½–7in (14–18cm) | Weight ⁵⁄₃₂–⁹⁄₃₂oz (4–8g) |
| Social **Solitary/Pairs** | Lifespan **Up to 5 years** | Status **Secure** |

| DATE SEEN | WHERE | | NOTES |
|---|---|---|---|
| | | | |
| | | | |
| | | | |
| | | | |
| | | | |

| Order **Passeriformes** | Family **Regulidae** | Species *Regulus calendula* |
|---|---|---|

# Ruby-crowned Kinglet 🔊

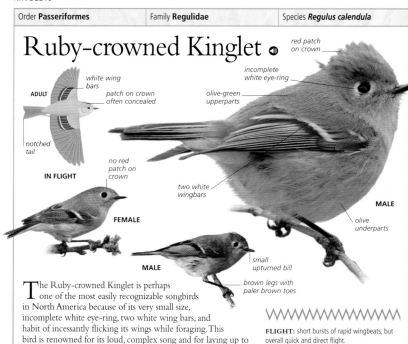

red patch
on crown

**ADULT**

white wing
bars

patch on crown
often concealed

incomplete
white eye-ring

olive-green
upperparts

notched
tail

**IN FLIGHT**

no red
patch on
crown

two white
wingbars

**FEMALE**

**MALE**

**MALE**

small
upturned bill

brown legs with
paler brown toes

olive
underparts

The Ruby-crowned Kinglet is perhaps one of the most easily recognizable songbirds in North America because of its very small size, incomplete white eye-ring, two white wing bars, and habit of incessantly flicking its wings while foraging. This bird is renowned for its loud, complex song and for laying up to 12 eggs in a clutch—probably the highest of any North American songbird. Despite local declines resulting from logging and forest fires, the Ruby-crowned Kinglet is common across the continent. It will sometimes be found in mixed-species flocks in winter, together with nuthatches and titmice.

**VOICE** Call a low, husky *jidit*; song, remarkably loud for such a small bird, begins with 2–3 high, clear notes *tee* or *zee* followed by 5–6 lower *tu* or *turr* notes, and ends with ringing galloping notes *tee-da-leet, tee-da-leet, tee-da-leet*.

**NESTING** Globular or elongated nest hanging from or on large branch with an enclosed or open cup, made of mosses, feathers, lichens, spider's silk, bark, hair, and fur; 5–12 eggs; 1 brood; May–October.

**FEEDING** Gleans a wide variety of insects, spiders, and their eggs among the leaves on the outer tips of higher, smaller branches; eats fruit and seeds; often hovers to catch prey.

〰〰〰〰〰〰〰〰〰〰〰〰

**FLIGHT:** short bursts of rapid wingbeats, but overall quick and direct flight.

**CONCEALED COLOR**
This bird's red patch is often concealed unless the bird is agitated or excited.

**OCCURRENCE**
Within the northern forest zone, breeds near water in black spruce and tamarack forests, muskegs, forests with mixed conifers and northern hardwoods; in the mountainous West, spruce-fir, lodgepole pine, and douglas fir forests. Winters in a broad range of forests, thickets, and borders.

**SIMILAR SPECIES**

**HUTTON'S VIREO**
see p.263

larger
head

stouter
bill

heavier
overall

**ALWAYS FLICKING**
Ruby-crowned Kinglets are easily identified by their habit of constantly flicking their wings.

| Length **3½–4¼in (9–11cm)** | Wingspan **6–7in (15–18cm)** | Weight **³⁄₁₆–³⁄₈oz (5–10g)** |
|---|---|---|
| Social **Winter flocks** | Lifespan **Up to 5 years** | Status **Secure** |

| DATE SEEN | WHERE | | NOTES |
|---|---|---|---|
| .................... | ....................... | | ............................................ |
| .................... | ....................... | | ............................................ |
| .................... | ....................... | | ............................................ |
| .................... | ....................... | | ............................................ |
| .................... | ....................... | | ............................................ |

# THRUSHES AND CHATS

THRUSHES, CHATS (Wheatears and Bluethroats), and their relatives are small- to medium-sized birds. Many are forest species but feed mostly on the ground, while others such as the Mountain Bluebird and Northern Wheatear are birds of open countryside. Many thrushes have a plain, brown upperside and spotted underside, but make up for lack of color with their beautiful, flute-like songs. Some, however, are brightly colored and strongly patterned: the Varied Thrush is one of the most distinctive of all thrushes and the American Robin is one of the most familiar birds. The smaller bluebirds are renowned for their bright blues while the Townsend's Solitaire is a much grayer species.

**GROUND BIRDS**
Though they perch to sing, thrushes, including this Varied Thrush, spend a lot of their time on or near the ground.

# THRASHERS

THE FAMILY NAME for thrashers, mockingbirds, and catbirds, Mimidae, is derived from the Latin for "to imitate," or mimic. Perhaps no other word better describes the dozen or so thrashers of North America. They are well known for their ability to mimic the songs of other species and incorporate phrases into their own complex song sequences. In appearance, they are superficially thrush-like but thrashers are more elongated and have long, more or less curved bills, long legs, and long tails. While mockingbirds may be bold, brash, and conspicuous—they are often found on open perches—thrashers are more reclusive, tending to forage deep within thickets or low vegetation, hopping on their strong feet, and digging into the leaf layer to find food with their bills. Only one species of thrasher, the Brown Thrasher, is found in the eastern US.

**DISTINCTIVE BILL**
Like other thrashers, the Long-billed Thrasher is characterized by its slender, curved bill, long, thin legs, and long, rounded tail. This species is rare in the West.

| Order **Passeriformes** | Family **Turdidae** | Species *Sialia mexicana* |
|---|---|---|

# Western Bluebird 🔊

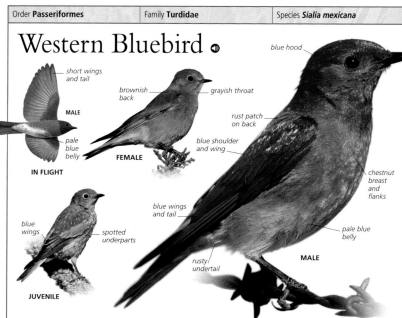

*short wings and tail*

**MALE**

*pale blue belly*

**IN FLIGHT**

*brownish back*

*grayish throat*

**FEMALE**

*blue hood*

*rust patch on back*

*blue shoulder and wing*

*chestnut breast and flanks*

*blue wings and tail*

*pale blue belly*

*rusty undertail*

**MALE**

*blue wings*

*spotted underparts*

**JUVENILE**

Very similar to its close relative, the Eastern Bluebird, but with a distribution restricted to the western part of the continent, the male Western Bluebird is endowed with a spectacular plumage—brilliant blue upperparts and deep chestnut-orange underparts. Unlike the Eastern Bluebird, the Western Bluebird has a brown back and a complete blue hood. Females and juveniles are harder to distinguish, but their ranges are quite different.
**VOICE** Vocalizations similar to those of the Eastern Bluebird; calls soft *few, few* or *fewrr-fewrr*; song a pleasant, soft series of churring notes, all strung together, often given at dawn.
**NESTING** Shallow cup of dry grass and feathers in natural tree cavity or old woodpecker cavity; 4–6 eggs; 1–2 broods; March–July.
**FEEDING** Feeds mainly on insects in breeding season; eats berries, such as juniper, in winter.

**FLIGHT:** slow and easy-looking, with shallow wingbeats.

### SIMILAR SPECIES

**EASTERN BLUEBIRD** ♀
see p.456

*orange throat, breast, and sides*

*white belly*

**MOUNTAIN BLUEBIRD** ♀
see p.313

*gray-brown head*

*blue wings and tail*

**PERCHED MALE**
The Western Bluebird hunts from low perches, from where it takes insects from the ground or air.

**OCCURRENCE**
During breeding season, open woodlands (coniferous and deciduous) and forest edges. In winter, moves to lower elevations and occupies open and semi-open areas, such as piñon juniper forests and deserts. Partial migrant; northern birds move south where southern breeders reside.

| Length **6–7in (15–18cm)** | Wingspan **11½–13in (29–33cm)** | Weight **⅞–1¹⁄₁₆ oz (25–30g)** |
|---|---|---|
| Social **Winter flocks** | Lifespan **Up to 7 years** | Status **Secure** |

| DATE SEEN | WHERE | NOTES |
|---|---|---|
| | | |
| | | |
| | | |
| | | |
| | | |

| Order **Passeriformes** | Family **Turdidae** | Species *Sialia currucoides* |

# Mountain Bluebird 🔊

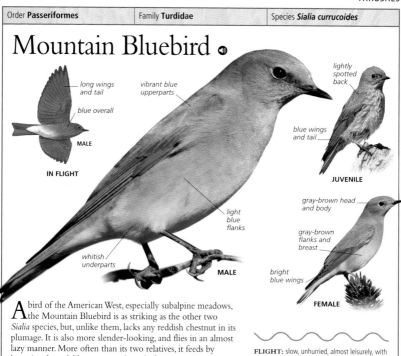

long wings and tail

blue overall

**MALE**

**IN FLIGHT**

vibrant blue upperparts

light blue flanks

whitish underparts

**MALE**

lightly spotted back

blue wings and tail

**JUVENILE**

gray-brown head and body

gray-brown flanks and breast

bright blue wings

**FEMALE**

A bird of the American West, especially subalpine meadows, the Mountain Bluebird is as striking as the other two *Sialia* species, but, unlike them, lacks any reddish chestnut in its plumage. It is also more slender-looking, and flies in an almost lazy manner. More often than its two relatives, it feeds by hovering, kestrel-like, over meadows, before pouncing on insects. Males guard their mates from pair-bond time to egg-hatching time.
**VOICE** Calls rolled, soft churring; one song, loud but infrequent, similar to the American Robin's song—*sing-song cheerily cheer-up cheerio*; the other, soft and repetitive whistle.
**NESTING** Cavity nest of grass, weeds, and bark; 5–6 eggs; 2 broods; May–July.
**FEEDING** Insects, including crickets, grasshoppers, bees, and caterpillars, dominate its diet year-round; also berries.

**FLIGHT:** slow, unhurried, almost leisurely, with shallow wingbeats.

**BERRY LOVER**
Berries are an important part of the bird's diet along with insects and caterpillars.

**OCCURRENCE**
Breeds in western North America, in grassland or open canyons with scattered trees, or alpine parklands. In winter, prefers open habitats and avoids dry areas. Winter habitat includes juniper forests and ponderosa pine in the south of its territory.

**SIMILAR SPECIES**

**EASTERN BLUEBIRD** ♀ see p.456
brownish back
white belly

**WESTERN BLUEBIRD** ♀ see p.312
grayish throat
pale orange on breast and flanks

**TOWNSEND'S SOLITAIRE** see p.314
white eye-ring
gray overall
longer tail

| Length **6–8in (15–20cm)** | Wingspan **11–12½in (28–32cm)** | Weight **1¹⁄₁₆oz (30g)** |
| Social **Flocks** | Lifespan **At least 5 years** | Status **Secure** |

| DATE SEEN | WHERE | NOTES |
|---|---|---|
| | | |

| Order **Passeriformes** | Family **Turdidae** | Species *Myadestes townsendi* |

# Townsend's Solitaire 🔊

**ADULT**

IN FLIGHT
- dark gray outer flight feathers
- wide, buff bands on flight feathers
- long tail
- short head

**ADULT**
- plain gray
- upright posture
- black legs and toes

large, black eye
white eye-ring
gray upperparts and head
short, black bill
paler underparts
**ADULT**
pale chestnut-tan patches

**JUVENILE**
- spotted back
- heavily spotted breast
- long tail

long, dark tail with white outer feathers

The rather shy Townsend's Solitaire inhabits most of western North America, especially high-elevation coniferous forests of the Sierras and Rockies. Its drab gray plumage, with a chestnut-tan wing pattern, remains the same throughout the year, and the sexes look alike. From a perch high on a branch, Townsend's Solitaire darts after flying insects and snaps its bill shut after catching its prey, unlike other thrushes.

**VOICE** Calls are single-note, high-pitched whistles; sings all year, but especially when establishing territories; main song robin-like, full of rolled or trilled sounds, interspersed with squeaky notes.

**NESTING** Cup of pine needles, dry grass, weed stems, and bark on ground or under overhang; 4 eggs; 1–2 broods; May–August.

**FEEDING** Forages for a wide variety of insects and spiders during breeding season; feeds on fruit and berries after breeding, particularly junipers.

**FLIGHT:** unhurried motion, usually over short distances, with slow, steady wingbeats.

**JUNIPER LOVER**
Solitaires love the berry-like cones of junipers, which they eat to supplement their winter diet.

**SIMILAR SPECIES**

**MOUNTAIN BLUEBIRD** ♀
see p.313
- dull bluish back
- blue in wings and tail
- short tail

**GRAY PLUMAGE**
Townsend's Solitaire is a drab gray overall, but has a conspicuous white eye-ring.

**OCCURRENCE**
During breeding season, found in open conifer forests along steep slopes or areas with landslides; during winter, at lower elevations, in open woodlands where junipers are abundant. Partial-migrant northern populations move south in winter, as far as central Mexico.

| Length **8–8½in (20–22cm)** | Wingspan **13–14½in (33–37cm)** | Weight **1¹⁄₁₆–1¼oz (30–35g)** |
| Social **Solitary** | Lifespan **Up to 5 years** | Status **Secure** |

| DATE SEEN | WHERE | NOTES |
|-----------|-------|-------|
| | | |
| | | |
| | | |
| | | |
| | | |

| Order **Passeriformes** | Family **Turdidae** | Species *Catharus fuscescens* |

# Veery 🔊

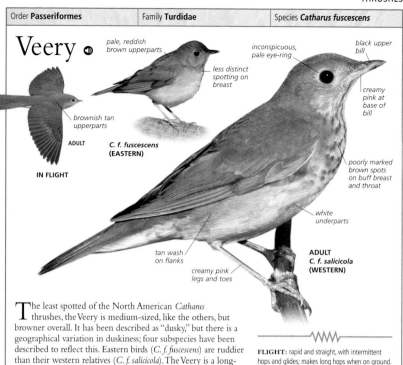

pale, reddish brown upperparts

brownish tan upperparts

**ADULT**

**IN FLIGHT**

*C. f. fuscescens* (EASTERN)

less distinct spotting on breast

inconspicuous, pale eye-ring

black upper bill

creamy pink at base of bill

poorly marked brown spots on buff breast and throat

white underparts

tan wash on flanks

creamy pink legs and toes

**ADULT** *C. f. salicicola* (WESTERN)

The least spotted of the North American *Catharus* thrushes, the Veery is medium-sized, like the others, but browner overall. It has been described as "dusky," but there is a geographical variation in duskiness; four subspecies have been described to reflect this. Eastern birds (*C. f. fuscescens*) are ruddier than their western relatives (*C. f. salicicola*). The Veery is a long-distance migrant, spending the northern winter months in Venezuela, Colombia, the Guianas, and Brazil in a variety of tropical habitats.

**VOICE** A series of descending *da-vee-ur, vee-ur, veer, veer,* somewhat bitonal, sounding like the name Veery; call a rather soft *veer*.

**NESTING** Cup of dead leaves, bark, weed stems, and moss on or near ground; 4 eggs; 1–2 broods; May–July.

**FEEDING** Forages on the ground for insects, spiders, snails; eats fruit and berries after breeding.

**FLIGHT:** rapid and straight, with intermittent hops and glides; makes long hops when on ground.

**DAMP DWELLINGS**
The Veery breeds in damp habitats, such as moist wooded areas or in trees near or in swamps.

### SIMILAR SPECIES

**GRAY-CHEEKED THRUSH** see p.456
gray face
bold black-brown breast spots

**BICKNELL'S THRUSH**
bold brown breast spots
grayish brown upperparts

**SWAINSON'S THRUSH** see p.316
buffy-colored face
bold brown-black breast spots

**OCCURRENCE**
In summer, mainly found in damp deciduous forests, but in some places habitat near rivers preferred. In winter, choice of habitat flexible; found in tropical broadleaf evergreen forest, on forest edges, in open woodlands, and in second-growth areas regenerating after fires or clearing.

| Length **7in (18cm)** | Wingspan **11–11½in (28–29cm)** | Weight **1¹⁄₁₆–2oz (28–54g)** |
| Social **Pairs** | Lifespan **Up to 10 years** | Status **Declining** |

| DATE SEEN | WHERE | NOTES |
|---|---|---|
| | | |
| | | |
| | | |
| | | |
| | | |

| Order **Passeriformes** | Family **Turdidae** | Species *Catharus ustulatus* |
|---|---|---|

# Swainson's Thrush

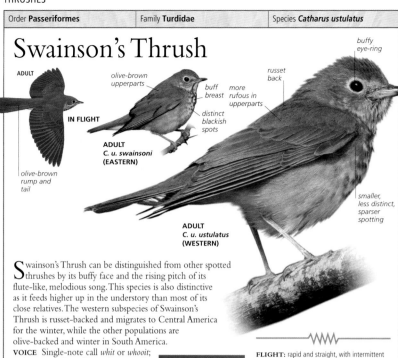

**ADULT**

**IN FLIGHT**

olive-brown
rump and
tail

olive-brown
upperparts

buff
breast

distinct
blackish
spots

more
rufous in
upperparts

**ADULT**
**C. u. swainsoni**
**(EASTERN)**

buffy
eye-ring

russet
back

smaller,
less distinct,
sparser
spotting

**ADULT**
**C. u. ustulatus**
**(WESTERN)**

Swainson's Thrush can be distinguished from other spotted thrushes by its buffy face and the rising pitch of its flute-like, melodious song. This species is also distinctive as it feeds higher up in the understory than most of its close relatives. The western subspecies of Swainson's Thrush is russet-backed and migrates to Central America for the winter, while the other populations are olive-backed and winter in South America.

**VOICE** Single-note call *whit* or *whooit*; main song delivered by males, several phrases, each one spiraling upward; flute-like song is given during breeding and migration.

**NESTING** Open cup of twigs, moss, dead leaves, bark, and mud, on branches near trunks of small trees or in shrubs; 3–4 eggs; 1–2 broods; April–July.

**FEEDING** Forages in the air, using fly-catching methods to capture a wide range of insects during breeding season; berries during migration and in winter.

**FLIGHT:** rapid and straight, with intermittent flaps and glides.

**DISTINCTIVE SONG**
This bird's song distinguishes it from other thrushes.

**TREE DWELLER**
Shy and retiring, Swainson's Thrush feeds higher in trees more than other *Catharus* thrushes.

**SIMILAR SPECIES**

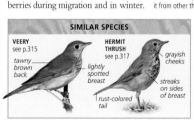

**VEERY**
see p.315

tawny
brown
back

**HERMIT**
**THRUSH**
see p.317

lightly
spotted
breast

rust-colored
tail

grayish
cheeks

streaks
on sides
of breast

**OCCURRENCE**
Breeds mainly in coniferous forests, especially spruce and fir, except in California, where it prefers deciduous riverside woodlands and damp meadows with shrubbery. During spring and fall migrations, dense understory preferred. Winter habitat is mainly old growth forest.

| Length **6½–7½in (16–19cm)** | Wingspan **11½–12in (29–31cm)** | Weight **⅞–1⁹⁄₁₆ oz (25–45g)** |
|---|---|---|
| Social **Pairs/Flocks** | Lifespan **Up to 11 years** | Status **Declining** |

| DATE SEEN | WHERE | NOTES |
|---|---|---|
| | | |
| | | |
| | | |
| | | |
| | | |

| Order **Passeriformes** | Family **Turdidae** | Species *Catharus guttatus* |
| --- | --- | --- |

# Hermit Thrush 🔊

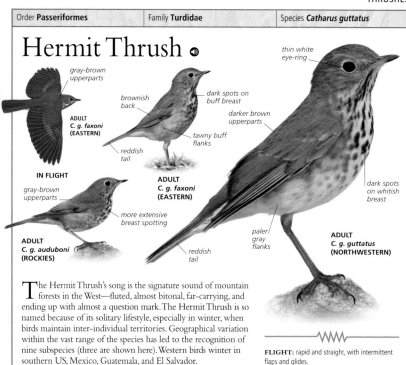

gray-brown
upperparts

**ADULT**
**C. g. faxoni**
**(EASTERN)**

**IN FLIGHT**

thin white
eye-ring

brownish
back

dark spots on
buff breast

darker brown
upperparts

tawny buff
flanks

reddish
tail

**ADULT**
**C. g. faxoni**
**(EASTERN)**

gray-brown
upperparts

more extensive
breast spotting

**ADULT**
**C. g. auduboni**
**(ROCKIES)**

reddish
tail

dark spots
on whitish
breast

paler
gray
flanks

**ADULT**
**C. g. guttatus**
**(NORTHWESTERN)**

The Hermit Thrush's song is the signature sound of mountain
forests in the West—fluted, almost bitonal, far-carrying, and
ending up with almost a question mark. The Hermit Thrush is so
named because of its solitary lifestyle, especially in winter, when
birds maintain inter-individual territories. Geographical variation
within the vast range of the species has led to the recognition of
nine subspecies (three are shown here). Western birds winter in
southern US, Mexico, Guatemala, and El Salvador.

**FLIGHT:** rapid and straight, with intermittent
flaps and glides.

**VOICE** Calls *tchek*, soft, dry; song
flute-like, ethereal, falling, repetitive,
and varied; several phrases delivered
on a different pitch.
**NESTING** Cup of grasses, mosses,
twigs, leaves, mud, hair, on ground
or in low tree branches; 4 eggs;
1–2 broods; May–July.
**FEEDING** Mainly forages on ground
for insects, larvae, earthworms, and
snails; in winter, also eats fruit.

**URBAN VISITOR**
This thrush is frequently seen in wooded areas
in urban and suburban parks.

**OCCURRENCE**
Occurs in coniferous forests
and mixed conifer–deciduous
woodlands; prefers to nest
along the edges of a forest
interior, like a bog. During
migration, found in many
wooded habitats. Found
in forest and other open
woodlands during winter.

| SIMILAR SPECIES | | |
| --- | --- | --- |
| **VEERY**<br>see p.315<br>tawny<br>brown<br>back<br>lightly<br>spotted<br>breast | **BICKNELL'S THRUSH**<br>olive-<br>brown<br>back<br>yellow<br>base of<br>bill | **SWAINSON'S THRUSH**<br>see p.316<br>olive-brown<br>upperparts |

| Length **6–7in (15–18cm)** | Wingspan **10–11in (25–28cm)** | Weight **⅞–1¹⁄₁₆ oz (25–30g)** |
| --- | --- | --- |
| Social **Solitary** | Lifespan **Up to 9 years** | Status **Secure** |

| DATE SEEN | WHERE | | NOTES |
| --- | --- | --- | --- |
| | | | |
| | | | |
| | | | |
| | | | |

| Order **Passeriformes** | Family **Turdidae** | Species **Turdus migratorius** |
|---|---|---|

# American Robin 🔊

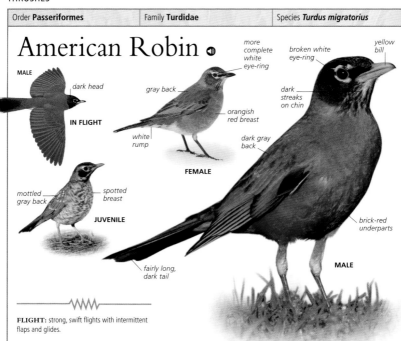

**MALE**

**dark head**

**IN FLIGHT**

more complete white eye-ring

**gray back**

**orangish red breast**

**FEMALE**

white rump

broken white eye-ring

yellow bill

dark streaks on chin

dark gray back

**MALE**

brick-red underparts

mottled gray back

spotted breast

**JUVENILE**

fairly long, dark tail

**FLIGHT:** strong, swift flights with intermittent flaps and glides.

The American Robin, the largest and most abundant of the North American thrushes, is probably also the most familiar bird across the entire continent, its presence on suburban lawns is a clear sign of spring. Unlike other species, it has adapted and prospered in human-altered habitats. It breeds in the entire US and Canada, winters across the US, and migrates out of most of Canada in the fall. The decision to migrate is largely governed by changes in the availability of food. As the breeding season approaches, it is the males that sing first, either late in winter or early spring. The bird's brick-red breast—more vivid in males than in females—is its most distinguishing feature.
**VOICE** Calls a high pitch *tjip* and a multi-note, throaty *tjuj-tjuk*; primary song a melodious *cheer-up, cheer-up, cheer-wee*, one of the first birds to be heard during dawn chorus, and one of the last to cease singing in the evening.
**NESTING** Substantial cup of grass, weeds, twigs, strengthened with mud, in trees or shrub, in fork of tree, or on branch on tree; 4 eggs; 2–3 broods; April–July.
**FEEDING** Forages in leaf litter, mainly for earthworms and small insects; mostly consumes fruit in the winter season.

**SEASONAL DIET**
Robins are particularly dependent on the availability of fruit during the winter months.

**OCCURRENCE**
Breeding habitat a mix of forest, woodland, suburban gardens, lawns, municipal parks, and farms. A partial migrant; found in woodlands with berry-bearing trees. Nonmigrating populations' winter habitat is similar to breeding habitat. Reaches Guatemala in winter.

**SIMILAR SPECIES**

**VARIED THRUSH** see p.319

orange eyebrow

bluish gray upperparts

wide black "necklace"

| Length **8–11in (20–28cm)** | Wingspan **12–16in (30–41cm)** | Weight **2⅝oz (75g)** |
|---|---|---|
| Social **Flocks** | Lifespan **Up to 13 years** | Status **Secure** |

| DATE SEEN | WHERE | NOTES |
|---|---|---|
| | | |
| | | |
| | | |
| | | |

| Order **Passeriformes** | Family **Turdidae** | Species *Ixoreus naevius* |

# Varied Thrush 🔊

orange
eyebrow

black
cheeks

brownish gray
upperparts

orange breast
and throat with
distinct spotting

white double
underwing bar

bluish gray
upperparts

**MALE**

rusty orange
patches

**FEMALE**

black
breastband

**IN FLIGHT**

**MALE**

rusty orange
breast, faintly
spotted on
flanks

white
undertail
feathers

The voice of the old-growth forests of southern Alaska and British Columbia, the Varied Thrush is also the most beautiful of the North American thrushes. Its song is so haunting and ethereal that to hear it can give the listener goosebumps. To see the bird is another matter, as it is often rather shy, except when bringing food to its nestlings. The Varied Thrush's orange and black head, deep bluish black back, and its two rusty wing bars are an unmistakable combination of markings.

**VOICE** Song is a single note that rises or falls in tone; repeats its song after about 10 seconds; sings for long periods of time from one perch, then moves to another to start anew.

**NESTING** Bulky cup of twigs, dead leaves, pieces of bark, stems of grass and weeds, lined with fine grass stems, mainly in conifer trees, against trunk; 3–4 eggs; 1–2 broods; April–August.

**FEEDING** Feeds on insects and caterpillars while breeding; fruit and berries in winter.

**FLIGHT:** rapid wingbeats; fast and direct.

**SUMMER DIET**
During its breeding season, this thrush forages for insects, often outside the forest interior.

**SIMILAR SPECIES**

AMERICAN
ROBIN
see p.318

dark
back

yellow
bill

brick-
red
breast

**FOREST DWELLER**
The Varied Thrush is often difficult to find because it inhabits dark forests.

**OCCURRENCE**
Breeds from Alaska south to Montana; prefers moist coniferous forests throughout breeding range; likely to be found in mature forests. Winters south of its breeding range; habitat varies between ravines and thickets to suburban lawns. Habitat in migration much like winter choices.

| Length **7–10in (18–25cm)** | Wingspan **13–15in (33–38cm)** | Weight **2¼–3½oz (65–100g)** |
| Social **Solitary/Flocks** | Lifespan **At least 5 years** | Status **Declining** |

| DATE SEEN | WHERE | NOTES |
| --- | --- | --- |
| | | |
| | | |
| | | |
| | | |
| | | |

| Order **Passeriformes** | Family **Mimidae** | Species **Dumetella carolinensis** |

# Gray Catbird

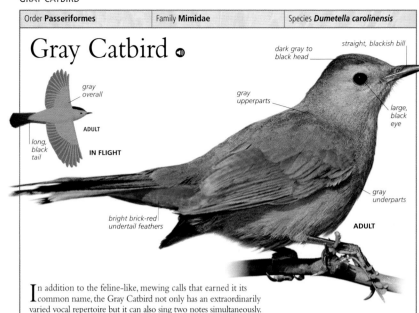

gray
overall

**ADULT**

long,
black
tail

**IN FLIGHT**

dark gray to
black head

gray
upperparts

straight, blackish bill

large,
black
eye

gray
underparts

bright brick-red
undertail feathers

**ADULT**

In addition to the feline-like, mewing calls that earned it its common name, the Gray Catbird not only has an extraordinarily varied vocal repertoire but it can also sing two notes simultaneously. It has been reported to imitate the vocalizations of more than 40 bird species, at least one frog species, and several sounds produced by machines and electronic devices. Despite their shy, retiring nature, Gray Catbirds tolerate human presence and will rest in shrubs in suburban and urban lots. Another fascinating skill is the Gray Catbird's ability to recognize and remove eggs of the brood parasite, the Brown-headed Cowbird.

**VOICE** *Mew* call, like a young kitten; song a long, complex series of unhurried, often grouped notes, sometimes interspersed with whistles and squeaks.

**NESTING** Large, untidy cup of woven twigs, grass, and hair lined with finer material; 3–4 eggs; 1–2 broods; May–August.

**FEEDING** Feeds on a wide variety of berries and insects, usually whatever is most abundant in season.

**FLIGHT:** short flights between habitat patches with constant, medium-speed wingbeats.

**ANGLED ATTITUDE**
Between bouts of feeding, a Gray Catbird often rests with its body and tail at a 50-degree angle.

**LARGE BLACK EYES**
Peering from the foliage, a Gray Catbird investigates its surroundings.

**OCCURRENCE**
Breeds in mixed young to mid-aged forests with abundant undergrowth, from British Columbia east to Maritimes and Newfoundland, and in the US diagonally west-east from Washington State to New Mexico, east to the Gulf Coast, north to New England. Northern population migratory.

**SIMILAR SPECIES**

**NORTHERN MOCKINGBIRD**
see p.324
white wing
patch

longer
tail
edged
in white

**CRISSAL THRASHER**
see p.458
brown-gray
overall

lighter gray

longer,
curved bill

| Length **8–9½in (20–24cm)** | Wingspan **10–12in (25–30cm)** | Weight **1¼–2⅛oz (35–60g)** |
| Social **Solitary/Pairs** | Lifespan **Up to 11 years** | Status **Secure** |

| DATE SEEN | WHERE | NOTES |
|-----------|-------|-------|
| | | |
| | | |
| | | |
| | | |
| | | |

| Order **Passeriformes** | Family **Mimidae** | Species *Toxostoma curvirostre* |

# Curve-billed Thrasher

curved bill

orange eye

whitish throat

light, dusty gray back

**ADULT**

dusty gray-brown spots on whitish buff underparts

**ADULT**

brownish gray legs and toes

long, dark tail

**ADULT**

long, curved bill

whitish corners to tail

**IN FLIGHT**

long, dark gray tail

**FLIGHT:** rapid and quite erratic, usually between patches of habitat.

Several species of North American thrashers would equally deserve the English name of "curve-billed," including California, Long-billed, Crissal, and LeConte's, but *curvirostre* was described by the English ornithologist William Swainson back in 1827, years before these other species. So, following a general rule in giving birds a common name, "Curve-billed" stuck. The arid-country-loving Curve-billed is somewhat unkempt looking, with a thick bill and powerful legs. Less of a mimic than other thrashers, it is nevertheless quite vocal, and its two-note *twit-twit* call is a characteristic sound of the southwestern semideserts.

**VOICE** Two-note *qwit-qweet*; song a series of clear, warbled whistles broken into distinct phrases; some mimicry of other species' calls.

**NESTING** Bulky, rather messy-looking cup of thorny sticks, in cactus or shrub, lined with grass, feathers, and hair; 3–5 eggs; 2 broods; February–July.

**FEEDING** Forages on ground and in leaf litter for insects and snails; eats fruit and berries in the fall.

**DISTINCTIVE JUVENILE**
Juvenile birds show less spotting on their underparts and paler eyes than the adults.

**OCCURRENCE**
In the US, the Curve-billed Thrasher inhabits open, scrubby, arid to semiarid areas, where it is often found along edges between brush and clearings. Its Mexican range extends south to Veracruz and Oaxaca. It is largely resident throughout its US and Mexican range.

### SIMILAR SPECIES

**LONG-BILLED THRASHER**
see p.457

brown back and head

black streaks on white underparts

**BENDIRE'S THRASHER**
see p.457

yellow eye

smaller overall

lighter gray tail

| Length **10–13in (25–33cm)** | Wingspan **12–15in (30–38cm)** | Weight **2⅛–2⅞oz (60–80g)** |
| Social **Pairs** | Lifespan **Up to 11 years** | Status **Localized** |

| DATE SEEN | WHERE | NOTES |
|---|---|---|
| | | |
| | | |
| | | |
| | | |
| | | |

| Order **Passeriformes** | Family **Mimidae** | Species *Toxostoma rufum* |

# Brown Thrasher 🔊

fairly straight, dark bill

bright yellow eye

grayish cheeks

indistinct "mustache"

rufous wings and upperparts

reddish brown upperparts

dark streaking on pale underparts

**ADULT**

long tail with pale outer tips

**IN FLIGHT**

two pale wing bars

long tail, paler than back

**ADULT**

The Brown Thrasher is usually difficult to view clearly because it keeps to dense underbrush. Like most other thrashers, this species prefers running or hopping to flying. When nesting, it can recognize and remove the eggs of brood parasites like the Brown-headed Cowbird. The current population decline is most likely the result of fragmentation of large, wooded habitats into patches, which lack the forest interior habitat this species needs.

**FLIGHT:** slow and heavy with deep wingbeats; below treetops, especially in and around ground.

**VOICE** Calls varied, including rasping sounds; song a long series of musical notes, sometimes imitating other species; repeats phrase twice before moving onto the next one.

**NESTING** Bulky cup of twigs, close to ground, lined with leaves, grass, bark; 3–5 eggs; 1 brood; April–July.

**FEEDING** Mainly insects (especially beetles) and worms gathered from leaf litter on the forest floor; will peck at cultivated grains, nuts, berries, and fruit.

**STREAKED BREAST**
Displaying its heavily-streaked underparts, this Brown Thrasher is perched and ready to sing.

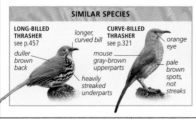

### SIMILAR SPECIES

**LONG-BILLED THRASHER**
see p.457

longer, curved bill

duller brown back

heavily streaked underparts

**CURVE-BILLED THRASHER**
see p.321

orange eye

mouse gray-brown upperparts

pale brown spots, not streaks

**OCCURRENCE**
Widespread across central and eastern North America, from Canada to Texas and Florida, in a variety of densely wooded habitats, particularly those with thick undergrowth, but will use woodland edges, hedges, and riverside trees. A partial migrant, it winters in the southern part of its range.

| Length **10–12in (25–30cm)** | Wingspan **11–14in (28–36cm)** | Weight **2⅛–2⅞oz (60–80g)** |
| Social **Solitary/Flocks** | Lifespan **Up to 13 years** | Status **Declining** |

| DATE SEEN | WHERE | NOTES |
| --- | --- | --- |
| | | |
| | | |
| | | |
| | | |
| | | |

| Order **Passeriformes** | Family **Mimidae** | Species **Oreoscoptes montanus** |

# Sage Thrasher 🔊

**ADULT**

thin, white wing bars

gray overall

white corners on wedge-shaped tail

**IN FLIGHT**

pale yellowish eye

whitish ring around back of cheek

dusky, brownish gray upperparts

short, straight bill

thin "mustache"

thin, brown streaking on off-white throat, breast, and belly

**ADULT**

**FLIGHT:** prefers to run; may dart low between patches of habitat using short, rapid wingbeats.

This plain-colored little bird is the smallest of the North American thrashers. Together with several other members of this group, the Sage Thrasher recognizes and removes the eggs of brood parasites, especially those of the Brown-headed Cowbird. Unfortunately, it may also be the least studied of the thrasher group, perhaps because the dense nature of its habitat makes study difficult. The English name, "Sage Thrasher," truly describes this bird's western habitat.

**VOICE** Song varies in duration: low, repeated, very musical notes or phrases that may blend together in a melodious song.

**NESTING** Large cup with stick frame lined with grass, horse hair, sheep's wool, and fur; 3–6 eggs; 1-2 broods; April–July.

**FEEDING** Eats insects, especially ants and beetles, on the ground; will also consume berries when seasonally available.

**JUICY MEAL**
This thrasher forages mostly on or near the ground; it feeds on insects and berries.

**SHOW-OFF TENDENCIES**
Males attract mates and defend their territory with raised wings, in a fluttering display.

### SIMILAR SPECIES

**LONG-BILLED THRASHER** see p.457
dull brown back

long, curved bill

dark streaks on white underparts

**CURVE-BILLED THRASHER** see p.321
orange eye
more gray on back
pale gray spots

**OCCURRENCE**
Very closely associated with sagebrush habitat in low-elevation, semiarid valleys of the western US. Winters from southwestern US to Baja California and continental Mexico, southwards to Sonora and Coahuila.

| Length **8–9in (20–23cm)** | Wingspan **10–13in (25–33cm)** | Weight **1⁷⁄₁₆–1¾oz (40–50g)** |
| Social **Solitary/Pairs** | Lifespan **Unknown** | Status **Localized** |

| DATE SEEN | WHERE | NOTES |
| --- | --- | --- |
| | | |
| | | |
| | | |
| | | |
| | | |

| Order **Passeriformes** | Family **Mimidae** | Species *Mimus polyglottos* |
| --- | --- | --- |

# Northern Mockingbird 🔊

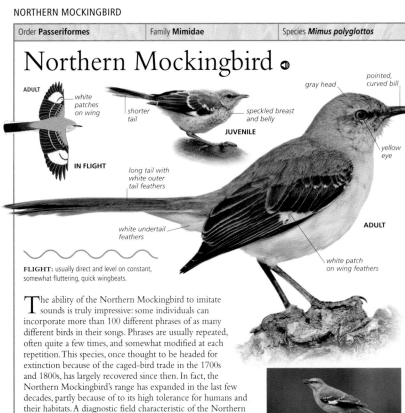

**ADULT**
white patches on wing

**IN FLIGHT**

shorter tail

gray head

pointed, curved bill

speckled breast and belly

**JUVENILE**

yellow eye

**ADULT**

long tail with white outer tail feathers

white undertail feathers

white patch on wing feathers

**FLIGHT:** usually direct and level on constant, somewhat fluttering, quick wingbeats.

The ability of the Northern Mockingbird to imitate sounds is truly impressive: some individuals can incorporate more than 100 different phrases of as many different birds in their songs. Phrases are usually repeated, often quite a few times, and somewhat modified at each repetition. This species, once thought to be headed for extinction because of the caged-bird trade in the 1700s and 1800s, has largely recovered since then. In fact, the Northern Mockingbird's range has expanded in the last few decades, partly because of to its high tolerance for humans and their habitats. A diagnostic field characteristic of the Northern Mockingbird is its tendency to "wing flash," showing its white outer wing feather patches when holding its wings overhead.

**VOICE** Long, complex repertoire often imitating other birds, non-bird noises, and the sounds of mechanical devices.

**NESTING** Bulky cup of twigs, lined, in shrub or tree; 3–5 eggs; 1–3 broods; March–August.

**FEEDING** Eats a wide variety of fruit, berries, and insects, including ants, beetles, and grasshoppers.

**BERRY PICKER**
Northern Mockingbirds love berries, and make good use of them during the fall.

**SIMILAR SPECIES**

**LOGGERHEAD SHRIKE** ♂
see p.259
brown mask
black wings
whiter sides to tail

**CLARK'S NUTCRACKER**
see p.274
white patch low on wing
darker gray belly

**OCCURRENCE**
Widespread in the US from coast to coast, primarily along edges of disturbed habitats, including young forests and especially suburban and urban areas with shrubs or hedges.

| Length **8½–10in (22–25cm)** | Wingspan **13–15in (33–38cm)** | Weight **1⁹⁄₁₆–2oz (45–55g)** |
| --- | --- | --- |
| Social **Pairs** | Lifespan **Up to 20 years** | Status **Secure** |

| DATE SEEN | WHERE | NOTES |
| --- | --- | --- |
| | | |
| | | |
| | | |
| | | |
| | | |

| Order **Passeriformes** | Family **Sturnidae** | Species *Acridotheres tristis* |
|---|---|---|

# Common Myna

**bold white wing band**

**yellow bill and face patch**

**black, hooded head**

**pinkish gray body**

**dark face**

**JUVENILE**

**IN FLIGHT**

**crest can be raised**

**white tail tip**

**ADULT**

**ADULT**

**white undertail**

**yellow legs**

**FLIGHT:** fast, swooping, with flurries of wingbeats and short glides.

This stocky, noisy bird of the starling family is native to southern Asia but has been introduced, deliberately or accidentally, into many other countries. In the US, it is found in Florida (since 1980s) and in Hawaii, where it was introduced to control pests in 1865. It now competes with more sensitive and specialized native species for food and nest sites. Other species nest in tree holes, but the Common Myna is typically more aggressive and assertive; it frequently preys on small nestlings, causing considerable conservation concern. Almost everywhere it is an adaptable and successful species. The Common Myna is easily recognized by its dark brown body, black head, and yellow eye patch; in flight, the wings flash large white patches.

**VOICE** Many croaks, chirping and clicking notes, loud, fluty whistles, and a screech in alarm.

**NESTING** Requires a hole or cavity in a tree or wall for the nest, and often evicts other birds; 4–6 eggs; 1–2 broods; March–August.

**FEEDING** Very varied, diet includes insects—especially grasshoppers and crickets—mostly picked from the ground, other small invertebrates, reptiles, seeds, and fruit.

**FIGHTING FOR FOOD**
Although usually found in pairs or families, Mynas often gather to squabble noisily over scraps of food.

**OCCURRENCE**
Established in Florida, found in grasslands, parks, open woodland, and on bushy slopes, roosting communally in dense trees.

| Length **9in (23cm)** | Wingspan **15in (39cm)** | Weight **3oz (125g)** |
|---|---|---|
| Social **Small groups, especially at roost** | Lifespan **5 years** | Status **Secure** |

| DATE SEEN | WHERE | NOTES |
|---|---|---|
| | | |
| | | |
| | | |
| | | |
| | | |

| Order **Passeriformes** | Family **Sturnidae** | Species *Sturnus vulgaris* |
|---|---|---|

# European Starling 🔊

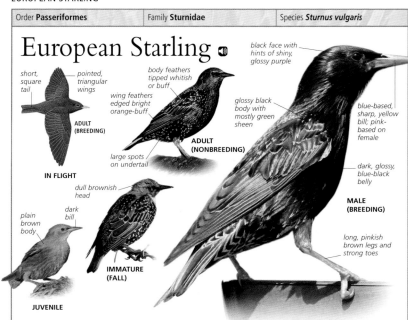

short, square tail

pointed, triangular wings

**ADULT (BREEDING)**

**IN FLIGHT**

wing feathers edged bright orange-buff

body feathers tipped whitish or buff

large spots on undertail

**ADULT (NONBREEDING)**

black face with hints of shiny, glossy purple

glossy black body with mostly green sheen

blue-based, sharp, yellow bill; pink-based on female

dark, glossy, blue-black belly

**MALE (BREEDING)**

long, pinkish brown legs and strong toes

dull brownish head

plain brown body

dark bill

**IMMATURE (FALL)**

**JUVENILE**

This distinctive non-native species is perhaps the most successful bird in North America—and probably the most maligned. In the 1890s, 100 European Starlings were released in New York City's Central Park; these were the ancestors of the many millions of birds that now live all across the US. This adaptable and aggressive bird competes with native species for nest sites, and the starling usually wins—even against larger species such as the Northern Flicker.

**VOICE** Highly varied; gives whooshing *ssssheer*, often in flight; also whistled *wheeeooo*; song an elaborate pulsing series with slurred whistles and clicking notes; imitates other species' vocalizations.

**NESTING** Natural or artificial cavity of any sort; 4–6 eggs; 1–2 broods; March–July.

**FEEDING** Omnivorous; picks at anything that might be edible; insects and berries are common food items; also visits birdfeeders and trash cans; often feeds on grubs in lawns.

**FLIGHT:** individuals fly in direct, buzzy manner; flocks bunch up tightly in flight.

**INSECT EATER**
Despite its parents' omnivorous diet, the nestlings are fed almost exclusively on insects and larvae.

### SIMILAR SPECIES

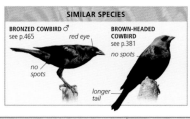

**BRONZED COWBIRD** ♂
see p.465

red eye

no spots

**BROWN-HEADED COWBIRD**
see p.381

no spots

longer tail

**OCCURRENCE**
In North America from southern Canada to the US–Mexico border; also Puerto Rico and other Caribbean islands. Common to abundant in cities, towns, and farmlands; also occurs in relatively "wild" settings far from human habitation. Forms flocks at all times, huge in winter.

| Length **8½in (21cm)** | Wingspan **16in (41cm)** | Weight **2⅝– 3⅜oz (75–95g)** |
|---|---|---|
| Social **Colonies** | Lifespan **Up to 17 years** | Status **Secure** |

| DATE SEEN | WHERE | NOTES |
|---|---|---|
| | | |
| | | |
| | | |
| | | |
| | | |

| Order **Passeriformes** | Family **Bombycillidae** | Species *Bombycilla garrulus* |
|---|---|---|

# Bohemian Waxwing

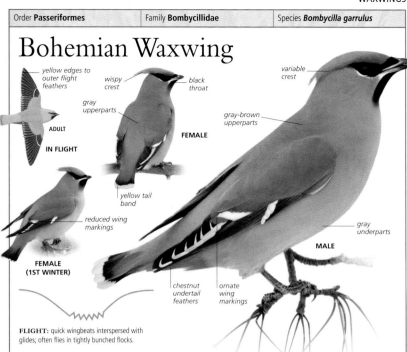

yellow edges to outer flight feathers

wispy crest

gray upperparts

**ADULT**

**IN FLIGHT**

black throat

variable crest

gray-brown upperparts

**FEMALE**

reduced wing markings

yellow tail band

**FEMALE (1ST WINTER)**

chestnut undertail feathers

ornate wing markings

gray underparts

**MALE**

**FLIGHT:** quick wingbeats interspersed with glides; often flies in tightly bunched flocks.

The Bohemian Waxwing is the wilder and rarer of the two waxwing species in North America. It breeds mainly in Alaska and western Canada. The species is migratory, but the extent of its wintertime movement is notoriously variable, depending on the availability of wild fruits. In most winters, relatively few Bohemian Waxwings visit the lower 48 states, but in special "irruption" years, tens of thousands may reach as far south as Colorado.
**VOICE** Call actually a dull trill, but effect of hundreds of birds calling together is remarkable and sounds like a high-pitched chorus; flocks vocalize constantly.
**NESTING** Dishevelled cup of sticks and grasses, placed in tree; 4–6 eggs; number of broods unknown; June–July.
**FEEDING** Catches insects on the wing in summer; flocks devour berries of native and exotic trees and shrubs throughout the year.

**STRIKING TAIL**
The Bohemian Waxwing's yellow tail band and chestnut undertail are evident here.

**OCCURRENCE**
Breeds in subarctic coniferous forest, favoring disturbed areas such as beaver ponds and logging sites. Flocks gather at forest edges, hedges, and residential areas in winter. Hundreds or thousands of birds appear in an area, then disappear once food is depleted.

| SIMILAR SPECIES | | |
|---|---|---|
| **CEDAR WAXWING** see p.328 <br> plainer wing markings | **CEDAR WAXWING** ♂ see p.328 <br> warmer tones overall <br> unmarked wings | smaller overall |

see p.328

| Length **8½in (21cm)** | Wingspan **14½in (37cm)** | Weight **1⁹⁄₁₆–2½oz (45–70g)** |
|---|---|---|
| Social **Flocks** | Lifespan **Up to 12 years** | Status **Localized** |

| DATE SEEN | WHERE | NOTES |
|---|---|---|
| | | |
| | | |
| | | |
| | | |

| Order **Passeriformes** | Family **Bombycillidae** | Species *Bombycilla cedrorum* |

# Cedar Waxwing

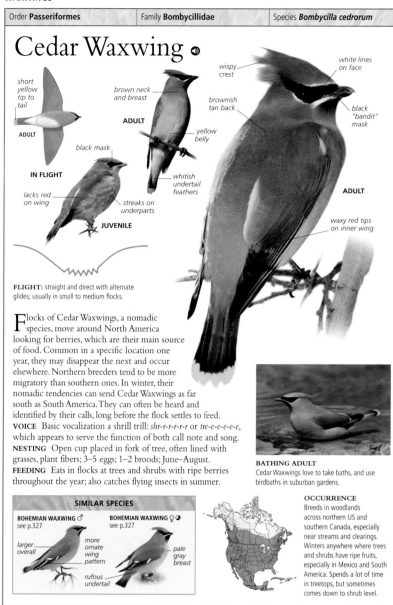

short yellow tip to tail

**ADULT**

**ADULT** — **IN FLIGHT**

brown neck and breast

**ADULT**

yellow belly

black mask

**JUVENILE**

lacks red on wing

streaks on underparts

whitish undertail feathers

wispy crest

brownish tan back

white lines on face

black "bandit" mask

**ADULT**

waxy red tips on inner wing

**FLIGHT:** straight and direct with alternate glides; usually in small to medium flocks.

Flocks of Cedar Waxwings, a nomadic species, move around North America looking for berries, which are their main source of food. Common in a specific location one year, they may disappear the next and occur elsewhere. Northern breeders tend to be more migratory than southern ones. In winter, their nomadic tendencies can send Cedar Waxwings as far south as South America. They can often be heard and identified by their calls, long before the flock settles to feed.

**VOICE** Basic vocalization a shrill trill: *shr-r-r-r-r-r* or *tre-e-e-e-e-e*, which appears to serve the function of both call note and song.

**NESTING** Open cup placed in fork of tree, often lined with grasses, plant fibers; 3–5 eggs; 1–2 broods; June–August.

**FEEDING** Eats in flocks at trees and shrubs with ripe berries throughout the year; also catches flying insects in summer.

**BATHING ADULT**
Cedar Waxwings love to take baths, and use birdbaths in suburban gardens.

**SIMILAR SPECIES**

**BOHEMIAN WAXWING ♂**
see p.327

larger overall

**BOHEMIAN WAXWING ♀**
see p.327

more ornate wing pattern

rufous undertail

pale gray breast

**OCCURRENCE**
Breeds in woodlands across northern US and southern Canada, especially near streams and clearings. Winters anywhere where trees and shrubs have ripe fruits, especially in Mexico and South America. Spends a lot of time in treetops, but sometimes comes down to shrub level.

| Length **7½in (19cm)** | Wingspan **12in (30cm)** | Weight **1¹⁄₁₆–1¼oz (30–35g)** |
| Social **Flocks** | Lifespan **Up to 7 years** | Status **Secure** |

| DATE SEEN | WHERE | NOTES |
|-----------|-------|-------|
| | | |
| | | |
| | | |
| | | |
| | | |

# OLD WORLD SPARROWS

THESE SMALL, SHORT-LEGGED, short-billed, principally seed-eating birds were introduced to North America from Europe and Asia, and their name has carried over to many unrelated New World species. House and Tree Sparrows are small and finch-like, but always unstreaked below. Male and female House Sparrows differ in appearance, while Tree Sparrows of both sexes are more like the male House Sparrow, with pale cheeks and a black bib. House Sparrows are familiar urban and suburban birds, always associated with buildings, parks, or farmsteads.

**MATCHED MARKINGS**
Unlike House Sparrows, which have marked sexual dimorphism, both sexes of the Eurasian Tree Sparrow are alike, with brown caps, black bibs, and black cheek spots.

**FEEDING FRENZY**
House Sparrows feed their chicks on caterpillars, visiting the nest scores of times each day.

# WAGTAILS AND PIPITS

THERE ARE FOUR SPECIES of these ground-living birds in North America, although two are rarely seen as they breed in remote parts of Alaska. All are slim and long-tailed, with the wagtails typically bobbing their tails up and down. The pipits are dull, brown birds, although more streaked than wagtails. They inhabit open, treeless country, walking rather than hopping on the ground. They are more likely to be seen in their widespread wintering areas than in their remote breeding range.

**COUNTRY-LOVERS**
Pipits, such as this American Pipit, live in open country, including beaches, dunes, and tundra.

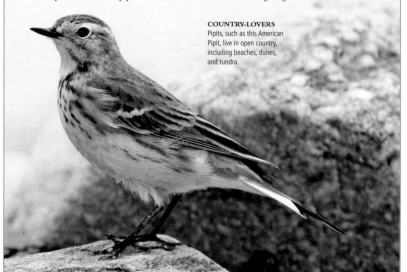

| Order **Passeriformes** | Family **Passeridae** | Species *Passer domesticus* |

# House Sparrow 🔊

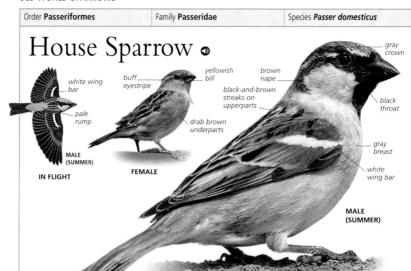

**IN FLIGHT**

white wing bar

pale rump

**MALE (SUMMER)**

buff eyestripe

yellowish bill

drab brown underparts

**FEMALE**

brown nape

black-and-brown streaks on upperparts

gray crown

black throat

gray breast

white wing bar

**MALE (SUMMER)**

This is the familiar "sparrow" of towns, cities, suburbs, and farms. The House Sparrow is not one of the American Sparrows—family Passerellidae—more commonly known in North America; rather it is a member of the Eurasian family, Passeridae. It was first introduced in Brooklyn, New York, in 1850. From this modest beginning, and with the help of several other introductions up until the late 1860s, this hardy and aggressive bird eventually spread right through the North American continent. In a little more than 150 years, the House Sparrow has evolved and shows the same sort of geographic variation as some widespread native birds. It is pale in the arid Southwest, and darker in wetter regions.
**VOICE** Variety of calls, including a *cheery chirp*, a dull *jurv* and a rough *jigga*; song consists of *chirp* notes repeated endlessly.
**NESTING** Untidy mass of dried vegetable material in either natural or artificial cavities; 3–5 eggs; 2–3 broods; April–August.
**FEEDING** Mostly seeds; sometimes gleans insects and fruit.

**FLIGHT:** fast and bouncing, with rapid wingbeats; short wings and tail give it a portly profile.

**APTLY NAMED**
This sparrow is seen near human structures—roofs, outbuildings, loading docks, curbs, and streetlights.

**SIMILAR SPECIES**

**DICKCISSEL ♀**
see p.469

pale bill

pale throat

yellowish highlights

**DICKCISSEL ♂ ✳**
see p.469

black and tan streaks

pale bill

**OCCURRENCE**
Flourishes in the downtown sections of cities and anywhere near human habitations, including agricultural outbuildings in remote areas of the continent. Also found in Mexico, Central and South America, the West Indies, Eurasia, southern Africa, Australia, and New Zealand.

| Length **6in (15.5cm)** | Wingspan **9½in (24cm)** | Weight **⅝–1¹⁄₁₆oz (18–30g)** |
| Social **Flocks** | Lifespan **Up to 7 years** | Status **Declining** |

| DATE SEEN | WHERE | NOTES |
|-----------|-------|-------|
| | | |
| | | |
| | | |
| | | |
| | | |

| Order **Passeriformes** | Family **Motacillidae** | Species **Anthus rubescens** |

# American Pipit

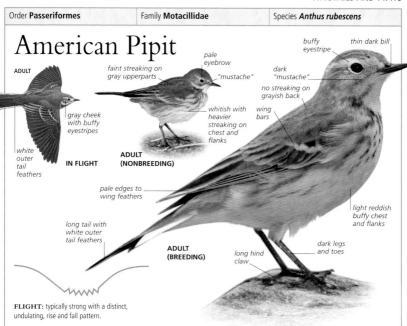

**ADULT**

pale
eyebrow

faint streaking on
gray upperparts

"mustache"

buffy
eyestripe

thin dark bill

dark
"mustache"

no streaking on
grayish back

wing
bars

**ADULT
(NONBREEDING)**

whitish with
heavier
streaking on
chest and
flanks

gray cheek
with buffy
eyestripes

**IN FLIGHT**

white
outer
tail
feathers

pale edges to
wing feathers

long tail with
white outer
tail feathers

light reddish
buffy chest
and flanks

**ADULT
(BREEDING)**

long hind
claw

dark legs
and toes

**FLIGHT:** typically strong with a distinct,
undulating, rise and fall pattern.

The American Pipit is divided into four subspecies, three of
which breed in North America, and the fourth in Siberia.
In nonbreeding plumage, the American Pipit is a drab-looking,
brownish gray bird that forages for insects along waterways and
lakeshores, or in cultivated fields with short stems. In the breeding
season, molting transforms it into a beauty—with gray upperparts
and reddish underparts. American Pipits are known for pumping
their tails up and down. When breeding, males display by rising
into the air, then flying down with wings open and singing. Its
migration takes the American Pipit as far south as Guatemala.
**VOICE** Alarm call a *tzeeep*; song repeated *tzwee-tzooo* from the air.
**NESTING** Cup in shallow depression on ground, outer frame of
grass, lined with fine grass and hair; 4–6 eggs; 1 brood; June–July.
**FEEDING** Picks insects; also eats seeds during migration.

**WINTER DRAB**
Foraging in short vegetation, this bird is almost
the same color as its surroundings.

### SIMILAR SPECIES

**HORNED LARK** ♂
see p.279

less white
on tail
edge

**SPRAGUE'S PIPIT**
see p.459

heavy streaking
on back

less streaking
on throat
and chest

pale
cheeks
and
throat

pale legs

**OCCURRENCE**
Breeds in Arctic tundra in the
North, and alpine tundra in
the Rockies; also breeds on
treeless mountaintops in
Maine and New Hampshire.
Winters in open coastal areas
and harvested agricultural
fields across the US. Some
North American migrants
fly to Asia for the winter.

| Length **6–8in (15–20cm)** | Wingspan **10–11in (25–28cm)** | Weight **¹¹⁄₁₆oz (20g)** |
| Social **Flocks** | Lifespan **Up to 6 years** | Status **Secure** |

| DATE SEEN | WHERE | NOTES |
| --- | --- | --- |
| | | |
| | | |
| | | |
| | | |
| | | |

# FINCHES

FINCHES IN THE FAMILY Fringillidae comprise a family of seed-eating birds, of which 16 species can be found in North America. They vary in size and shape from the small and fragile-looking redpolls to the robust and chunky Evening Grosbeak. Finch colors range from whitish with some pink (redpolls) to gold (American Goldfinch), bright red (crossbills), and yellow, white, and black (Evening Grosbeak). However, irrespective of body shape, size, and color, all have conical bills with razor-sharp edges. Finches do not crush seeds. Instead, they cut open the hard hull, then seize the seed inside with their tongue and swallow it. The bills of conifer-loving crossbills are crossed at the tip, a unique arrangement that permits them to open tough-hulled pine cones. Roughly 50 percent of crossbills are "left-billed" and 50 percent "right-billed"—lefties are right-footed, and vice versa. Most finches are social. Although they breed in pairs, after nesting finches form flocks, some of which are huge. Most finch populations fluctuate in size, synchronized with seed production and abundance. All finches are vocal, calling constantly while flying, and singing in the spring. Calls are usually sharp, somewhat metallic sounds, although the American Goldfinch's tinkling calls are sweeter. Songs can be quite musical, clear-sounding melodies, like that of the Cassin's Finch. Finches make open cup-shaped nests of grasses and lichens, in trees or shrubs, and are remarkably adept at hiding them.

**NOT REALLY PURPLE**
The inaccurately named Purple Finch actually has a lovely wine-red color.

**CROSSBILL**
Perched on a pine tree branch, a female Red Crossbill grinds a seed in her bill to break open the hull and reach the fat-rich kernel inside.

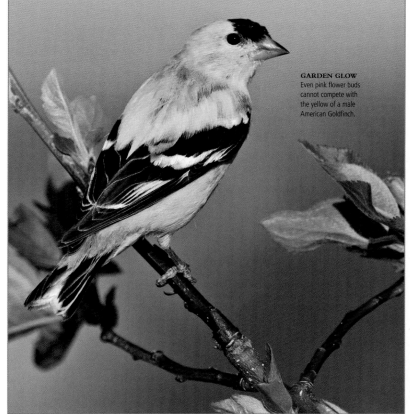

**GARDEN GLOW**
Even pink flower buds cannot compete with the yellow of a male American Goldfinch.

| Order **Passeriformes** | Family **Fringillidae** | Species *Coccothraustes vespertinus* |

# Evening Grosbeak

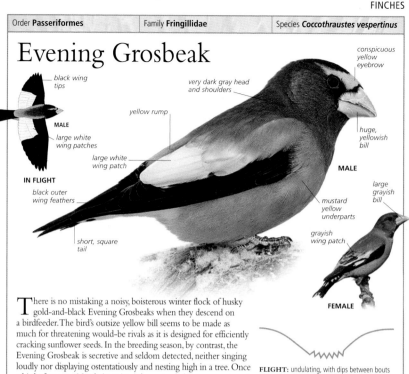

conspicuous yellow eyebrow

black wing tips

**MALE**

large white wing patches

**IN FLIGHT**

very dark gray head and shoulders

yellow rump

large white wing patch

black outer wing feathers

short, square tail

huge, yellowish bill

**MALE**

mustard yellow underparts

grayish wing patch

large grayish bill

**FEMALE**

There is no mistaking a noisy, boisterous winter flock of husky gold-and-black Evening Grosbeaks when they descend on a birdfeeder. The bird's outsize yellow bill seems to be made as much for threatening would-be rivals as it is designed for efficiently cracking sunflower seeds. In the breeding season, by contrast, the Evening Grosbeak is secretive and seldom detected, neither singing loudly nor displaying ostentatiously and nesting high in a tree. Once a bird of western North America, it has extended its range eastward in the past 200 years, and now breeds as far as Newfoundland. This may be a result of the planting of ornamental box elder, which carries its abundant seeds winter-long, ensuring a ready food supply for the bird.

**VOICE** Call descending *feeew*; also buzzy notes and beeping chatter.
**NESTING** Loose, grass-lined twig cup, usually on conifer branch; 3–4 eggs; 1–2 broods; May–July.
**FEEDING** Eats seeds of pines and other conifers; also maple and box elder seeds; also insects and their larvae, particularly spruce budworms, which are actually tortricid moths.

**FLIGHT:** undulating, with dips between bouts of wingbeats, may hover briefly.

**SIMILAR SPECIES**

**PINE GROSBEAK** ♀ see p.334 — stubby bill, wing bars, gray underparts

**BALTIMORE ORIOLE** ♀ see p.465 — mottled head, slender aspect, pale orange underparts

**CAPABLE BILL** This bird's extremely robust bill can deal with all kinds of winter fruit and seeds.

**OCCURRENCE** Breeds in mixed conifer and spruce forests from the Rocky Mountain region to eastern Canada, and in western mountain ranges south to Mexico. Winters in coniferous or deciduous woodlands, often in suburban locations; may move south from northern range, depending on food supply.

| Length **6½–7in (16–18cm)** | Wingspan **12–14in (30–36cm)** | Weight **2–2½oz (55–70g)** |
| Social **Flocks** | Lifespan **Up to 15 years** | Status **Secure** |

| DATE SEEN | WHERE | NOTES |
|---|---|---|
| | | |

| Order **Passeriformes** | Family **Fringillidae** | Species **Pinicola enucleator** |

# Pine Grosbeak

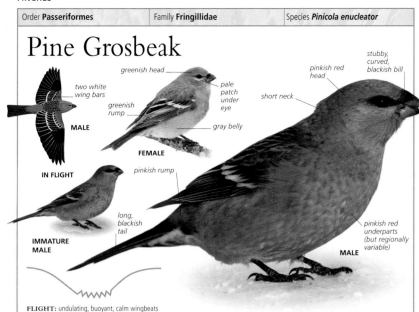

two white wing bars

**MALE**

greenish head

greenish rump

**FEMALE**

pale patch under eye

gray belly

**IN FLIGHT**

pinkish rump

long, blackish tail

**IMMATURE MALE**

pinkish red head

short neck

stubby, curved, blackish bill

pinkish red underparts (but regionally variable)

**MALE**

**FLIGHT:** undulating, buoyant, calm wingbeats interrupted by glides.

The largest member of the family Fringillidae in North America, and easily distinguished by the male's unmistakable thick, stubby bill, the Pine Grosbeak is a resident of boreal forests across Canada and Alaska and some mountain ranges in the western US. In winter, northern birds occasionally move south into the northern US. Because of extensive color variation of individual plumages, the age and sex of given individuals are not always easily determined.
**VOICE** Contact calls of eastern birds *tee-tew*, or *tee-tee-tew*; western forms give more complex *tweedle*; warbling song.
**NESTING** Well-hidden, open cup nest usually in spruce or larch trees; 2–5 eggs, 1 brood; June–July.
**FEEDING** Eats spruce buds, maple seeds, and mountain ash berries throughout the year; consumes insects in summer.

**FRUIT LOVER**
This species can often be seen hanging from branches, gorging on ripe fruit.

**SIMILAR SPECIES**

**RED CROSSBILL**
see p.340

brownish back

**WHITE-WINGED CROSSBILL**
see p.341

mandibles crossed

mandibles crossed

white bars on wing

**OCCURRENCE**
Found in the boreal zone from Alaska to Newfoundland in Canada, and in California, the Southwest, and the Rockies in the US. Occurs in open, northern coniferous forests in summer, usually near freshwater. Winters throughout its breeding range, but may move southward to southern Canada and the northeastern US.

| Length **8–10in (20–25cm)** | Wingspan **13in (33cm)** | Weight **2–2½oz (55–70g)** |
| Social **Flocks** | Lifespan **Up to 10 years** | Status **Secure** |

| DATE SEEN | WHERE | NOTES |
|---|---|---|
| | | |
| | | |
| | | |
| | | |
| | | |

| Order **Passeriformes** | Family **Fringillidae** | Species *Leucosticte tephrocotis* |

# Gray-crowned Rosy-Finch

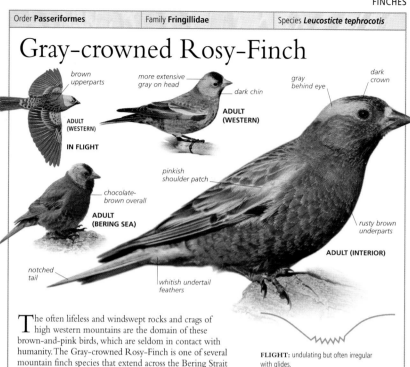

brown
upperparts

ADULT
(WESTERN)

IN FLIGHT

more extensive
gray on head

dark chin

ADULT
(WESTERN)

gray
behind eye

dark
crown

pinkish
shoulder patch

chocolate-
brown overall

ADULT
(BERING SEA)

rusty brown
underparts

ADULT (INTERIOR)

notched
tail

whitish undertail
feathers

The often lifeless and windswept rocks and crags of high western mountains are the domain of these brown-and-pink birds, which are seldom in contact with humanity. The Gray-crowned Rosy-Finch is one of several mountain finch species that extend across the Bering Strait into eastern Asia. Geographically variable in size and coloration, with exceptionally large forms occurring on the Pribilof and Aleutian Islands, the Gray-crowned Rosy-Finch is the most abundant of the North American rosy-finches.

**VOICE** High-pitched *peew*, given singly or in short series; song repetitive series of *twee* notes.

**NESTING** Bulky assemblage of grasses, lichens, and twigs in cracks or under rock overhangs; 3–5 eggs; 1–2 broods; May–June.

**FEEDING** Feeds on the ground on a variety of seeds, with insects and their larvae comprising a larger part of the diet in summer.

**FLIGHT:** undulating but often irregular with glides.

**ROCK LOVER**
This dark rusty-brown species watches its surroundings from a rocky perch near an icy field.

| SIMILAR SPECIES | | |
|---|---|---|
| **BLACK ROSY-FINCH** see p.459 | **BROWN-CAPPED ROSY-FINCH** see p.460 | |

darker
cheeks

rosy underparts

**OCCURRENCE**
Most widely distributed of the three North American rosy-finch species, occurring from Alaska south to the Rockies; breeds in alpine habitats like rocky screes above snow line and Arctic tundra; in winter also occurs at lower elevations; sometimes at feeders.

| Length **5½–8½in (14–21cm)** | Wingspan **13in (33cm)** | Weight **⅞–2⅛oz (25–60g)** |
| Social **Flocks** | Lifespan **Unknown** | Status **Localized** |

| DATE SEEN | WHERE | NOTES |
|---|---|---|
| | | |
| | | |
| | | |
| | | |
| | | |

| Order **Passeriformes** | Family **Fringillidae** | Species *Haemorhous mexicanus* |

# House Finch 🔊

brown cap

grayish streaks all over

red face

**MALE (BREEDING)**

brown upperparts

usually brick-red bib and head

**FEMALE**

**IN FLIGHT**

pinkish head

pale brown streaking

streaked belly

**MALE (NONBREEDING)**

brown streaked undertail feathers

long tail feathers

**MALE (BREEDING)**

**FLIGHT:** bouncy, undulating flight typical of finches; usually flies above treetop level.

Historically, the House Finch was a western bird, and was first reported in the eastern side of the US on Long Island, New York in 1941. These birds are said to have originated from the illegal bird trade. The population of the eastern birds started expanding in the 1960s, so much so that by the late 1990s, their population had expanded westward to link up with the original western population. The male House Finch is distinguished from the Purple and Cassin's Finches by its brown streaked underparts, while the females have plainer faces and generally blurrier streaking.

**VOICE** Call note *queet*; varied jumble of notes, often starting with husky notes to whistled and burry notes, and ending with a long *wheeerr*.

**NESTING** Females build nests from grass stems, thin twigs, and thin weeds in trees and on manmade structures; 1–6 eggs; 2–3 broods; March–August.

**FEEDING** Eats, almost exclusively, vegetable matter, such as buds, fruit, and seeds; readily comes to feeders.

**RED IN THE FACE**
The breeding male House-Finch can be identified by its stunning brick-red plumage.

**OCCURRENCE**
Found in urban, suburban, and settled areas; in the West also in wilder areas, such as savannas, desert grasslands, and chaparral, particularly near people; in the East almost exclusively in settled areas, including the centers of large cities. Resident, some birds move after breeding.

| SIMILAR SPECIES | | |
| --- | --- | --- |
| **PURPLE FINCH** see p.337 | **CASSIN'S FINCH** see p.338 | |

pinkish neck

reddish head

whitish underparts

white underparts

| Length **5–6in (12.5–15cm)** | Wingspan **8–10in (20–25cm)** | Weight **⁹⁄₁₆–1oz (16–27g)** |
| --- | --- | --- |
| Social **Flocks** | Lifespan **Up to 12 years** | Status **Secure** |

| DATE SEEN | WHERE | NOTES |
| --- | --- | --- |
| | | |
| | | |
| | | |
| | | |
| | | |

| Order **Passeriformes** | Family **Fringillidae** | Species *Haemorhous purpureus* |

# Purple Finch 🔊

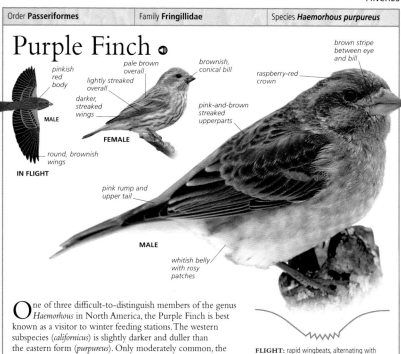

**MALE**

pinkish red body

lightly streaked overall

darker, streaked wings

round, brownish wings

**IN FLIGHT**

pale brown overall

**FEMALE**

brownish, conical bill

pink-and-brown streaked upperparts

brown stripe between eye and bill

raspberry-red crown

pink rump and upper tail

**MALE**

whitish belly with rosy patches

One of three difficult-to-distinguish members of the genus *Haemorhous* in North America, the Purple Finch is best known as a visitor to winter feeding stations. The western subspecies (*californicus*) is slightly darker and duller than the eastern form (*purpureus*). Only moderately common, the raspberry-red males pose less of an identification challenge than the brown-streaked females. Even on their breeding grounds in open and mixed coniferous forest, Purple Finches are more often heard than seen.

**VOICE** Flight call single, rough *pikh*; songs rich series of notes, up and down in pitch.
**NESTING** Cup of sticks and grasses on a conifer branch; 4 eggs; 2 broods; May–July.
**FEEDING** Eats buds, seeds, flowers of deciduous trees; insects and caterpillars in summer; also seeds and berries.

**FLIGHT:** rapid wingbeats, alternating with downward glides.

**RASPBERRY TINTED**
On a lichen-covered branch this male's delicate coloring is quite striking.

**OCCURRENCE**
Resident from Baja California north along the Pacific Coast and the Cascade Mountains to Yukon Territory. Breeds in northern mixed conifer and hardwood forests in the East, where it is partially migratory, moves as far south as the Gulf Coast.

| SIMILAR SPECIES |
|---|

**HOUSE FINCH ♀** western; see p.336 — *thinner streaks*

**CASSIN'S FINCH ♀** see p.338 — *more marked facial patterning*

**RED-WINGED BLACKBIRD ♀** see p.380 — *larger overall*, *heavily streaked*, *darker overall*

| Length 4¾–6in (12–15cm) | Wingspan 8½–10in (22–26cm) | Weight ¹¹⁄₁₆–1¹⁄₁₆oz (20–30g) |
| Social **Flocks** | Lifespan **Unknown** | Status **Declining** |

| DATE SEEN | WHERE | NOTES |
|---|---|---|
| | | |

| Order **Passeriformes** | Family **Fringillidae** | Species *Haemorhous cassinii* |

# Cassin's Finch 🔊

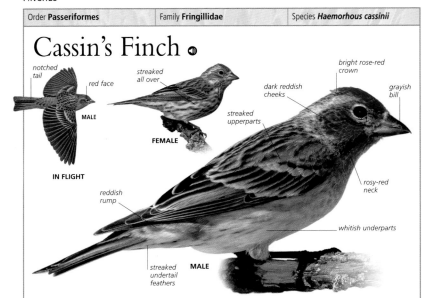

notched tail

red face

**MALE**

streaked all over

**FEMALE**

streaked upperparts

bright rose-red crown

dark reddish cheeks

grayish bill

rosy-red neck

whitish underparts

**IN FLIGHT**

reddish rump

streaked undertail feathers

**MALE**

Named after the 19th-century ornithologist John Cassin, this finch has a rich, melodious song that incorporates phrases from the songs of several different Rocky Mountain species. From below, the male Cassin's Finch resembles a sparrow, but when it alights on a tree stump, its full, purple-red plumage is immediately evident. This species closely resembles the other two species in the genus *Haemorhous*, the Purple and House Finches, whose ranges it overlaps, so it may take time and practice to be certain of this species' identity in the field. The female Cassin's Finch is not distinctive—it resembles a generic fledgling or a sparrow.

**VOICE** Call *tee-uhh* or *piddlit*; song rich and warbling; may include high-frequency whistles and imitations of other species.
**NESTING** Open cup on lateral branch of conifer, also in aspen or sagebrush; 4–5 eggs; 1 brood; May–July.
**FEEDING** Eats berries, pine seeds, aspen buds, insects, larvae; feeds mainly on ground but frequents feeding stations in winter.

**FLIGHT:** rapid wingbeats, then a glide, in a regular sequence.

**ARBOREAL FINCH**
Cassin's Finch likes to perch on an elevated twig or branch, often in coniferous forests.

### SIMILAR SPECIES

**PURPLE FINCH**
see p.337

shorter, less pointed bill

pinkish neck

**HOUSE FINCH**
see p.336

reddish orange bib and head

**OCCURRENCE**
Found in coniferous forests in mountains of western US; may occur in sagebrush juniper plains or open areas with ponderosa or lodgepole pine. Migratory both toward lower elevations and southward. Winters throughout its breeding range.

| Length **5½–6½in (14–16cm)** | Wingspan **10–10½in (25–27cm)** | Weight **⅞–1¼oz (25–35g)** |
| Social **Flocks** | Lifespan **Up to 10 years** | Status **Secure** |

| DATE SEEN | WHERE | NOTES |
|-----------|-------|-------|
| | | |
| | | |
| | | |
| | | |
| | | |

| Order **Passeriformes** | Family **Fringillidae** | Species *Acanthis flammea* |

# Common Redpoll

ruby-red cap

small, pointed yellow bill

red cap

**MALE**

**MALE (BREEDING)**

rosy-red breast

**IN FLIGHT**

wing bars

reddish cap

**FEMALE**

streaked underparts

black streaks on rosy-red breast

**MALE (NONBREEDING)**

pale wing bars

notched tail

pale wing bar

**JUVENILE**

Every other year, spruce, birch, and other trees in the northern forest zone fail to produce a good crop of seeds, forcing the Common Redpoll to look for food farther south than usual—as far south as the northern US states. The Common Redpoll is oddly tame around people and is easily attracted to winter feeders. The degree of whiteness in its plumage varies greatly among individuals, related to sex and age. The taxonomy of the Common Redpoll includes three subspecies around the world, and there are suggestions that some may be distinct species.

**VOICE** Flight call dry *zit-zit-zit-zit* and rattling *chirr*; also high *too-ee* call while perched; song series of rapid trills.

**NESTING** Cup of small twigs in spruces, larches, willows, alders; 4–6 eggs; 1–2 broods; May–June.

**FEEDING** Feeds on small seeds from conifers, sedge, birch, willow, alder; also insects and spiders.

**FLIGHT:** deeply undulating, with dips between bouts of wingbeats.

---

#### SIMILAR SPECIES

| | |
|---|---|
| **PINE SISKIN** see p.342 | **HOARY REDPOLL** see p.460 |

red cap

brownish upperparts

yellow on tail

two wing bars

pale overall

whitish underparts

**FRIENDLY FLOCK**
Common Redpolls are only weakly territorial, sometimes even nesting close together.

**OCCURRENCE**
Mainly in extreme northern North America from Alaska to Québec and Labrador, in low forest, subarctic, and shrubby tundra habitats. More southern winter appearances typically occur every other year, rarely south of northern US, from the Dakotas east to New York and New England.

| Length **4¾–5½in (12–14cm)** | Wingspan **6½–6¾in (16–17cm)** | Weight **⅜–¹¹⁄₁₆oz (11–19g)** |
|---|---|---|
| Social **Flocks** | Lifespan **Up to 10 years** | Status **Secure** |

| DATE SEEN | WHERE | NOTES |
|---|---|---|
| | | |
| | | |
| | | |
| | | |
| | | |

| Order **Passeriformes** | Family **Fringillidae** | Species *Loxia curvirostra* |
|---|---|---|

# Red Crossbill

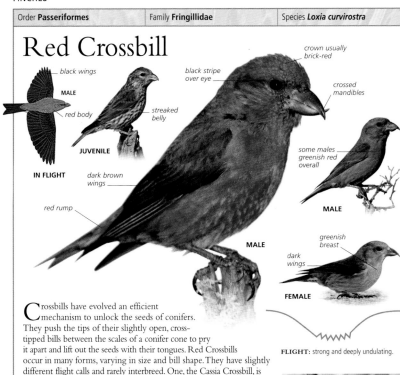

black wings

**MALE**

red body

*black stripe over eye*

*crown usually brick-red*

*crossed mandibles*

**JUVENILE**

*streaked belly*

**IN FLIGHT**

*dark brown wings*

*red rump*

*some males greenish red overall*

**MALE**

**MALE**

*greenish breast*

*dark wings*

**FEMALE**

Crossbills have evolved an efficient mechanism to unlock the seeds of conifers. They push the tips of their slightly open, cross-tipped bills between the scales of a conifer cone to pry it apart and lift out the seeds with their tongues. Red Crossbills occur in many forms, varying in size and bill shape. They have slightly different flight calls and rarely interbreed. One, the Cassia Crossbill, is treated as a separate species, *Loxia sinesciuris*. Other forms are nomadic, but this species remains in a tiny part of Idaho all year, feeding on lodgepole pine. It is nearly impossible to identify the different forms of the Red Crossbill other than by voice or DNA.

**VOICE** Common call *jit* repeated 2–5 times; song complex, continuous warbling of notes, whistles, and buzzes.

**NESTING** Cup nest on lateral conifer branch; 3–5 eggs; 2 broods; can breed year-round.

**FEEDING** Feeds on pine seeds; also insects and larvae, particularly aphids; also other seeds.

**FLIGHT:** strong and deeply undulating.

**PROCESSING SEEDS**
The Red Crossbill manipulates seeds with its tongue before swallowing them.

| SIMILAR SPECIES | | OCCURRENCE |
|---|---|---|

**SIMILAR SPECIES**

**WHITE-WINGED CROSSBILL**
see p.341

*conspicuous wing bars*

**SCARLET TANAGER**

*vivid red plumage*

*no black stripe*

*pinker plumage*

**OCCURRENCE**
Range covers coniferous or mixed-coniferous and deciduous forests from Newfoundland to British Columbia and southern Alaska; also mountain forests in the Rockies, south to Mexico; irregular movements, depending on the availability of pine cones.

| Length **5–6¾in (13–17cm)** | Wingspan **10–10½in (25–27cm)** | Weight **⅞–1¼oz (25–35g)** |
|---|---|---|
| Social **Flocks** | Lifespan **Up to 10 years** | Status **Secure** |

| DATE SEEN | WHERE | NOTES |
|---|---|---|
| | | |
| | | |
| | | |
| | | |
| | | |

| Order **Passeriformes** | Family **Fringillidae** | Species *Loxia leucoptera* |

# White-winged Crossbill

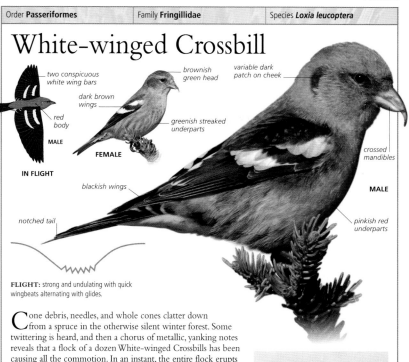

two conspicuous
white wing bars

dark brown
wings

red
body

**MALE**

**IN FLIGHT**

brownish
green head

greenish streaked
underparts

**FEMALE**

variable dark
patch on cheek

crossed
mandibles

**MALE**

blackish wings

notched tail

pinkish red
underparts

**FLIGHT:** strong and undulating with quick
wingbeats alternating with glides.

Cone debris, needles, and whole cones clatter down
from a spruce in the otherwise silent winter forest. Some
twittering is heard, and then a chorus of metallic, yanking notes
reveals that a flock of a dozen White-winged Crossbills has been
causing all the commotion. In an instant, the entire flock erupts
into the air, calling loudly in flight, only to disappear completely
in the distance. Few other creatures of the northern forests go
about their business with such determined energy, and no others
accent a winter woodland with hot pink and magenta—the
colors of the White-winged Crossbill's head and breast.
**VOICE** Calls are sharp, chattering *plik*, or deeper *tyoop*,
repeated in series of 3–7 notes; song melodious trilling.
**NESTING** Open cup nest, usually high on end of a spruce
branch; 3–5 eggs; 2 broods; July, January–February.
**FEEDING** Eats seeds from small-coned conifers; spruces,
firs, larches; feeds on insects when available.

**EATING SNOW**
The White-winged Crossbill frequently eats snow
to provide essential moisture.

| SIMILAR SPECIES | | |
|---|---|---|
| **PINE GROSBEAK**<br>see p.334 | **RED CROSSBILL**<br>see p.340 | |
| blunt bill | no wing<br>bars | |
| longer<br>tail | | redder<br>plumage |

**OCCURRENCE**
Nomadic; most common
in the spruce zone of
Alaska and Canada but
has bred as far south as
Colorado in the West; in
the East, from Québec and
Newfoundland southward to
New York and New England.

| Length **5½–6in (14–15cm)** | Wingspan **10–10½in (26–27cm)** | Weight **¹¹⁄₁₆–1¹⁄₁₆oz (20–30g)** |
| Social **Flocks** | Lifespan **Up to 10 years** | Status **Secure** |

| DATE SEEN | WHERE | NOTES |
|---|---|---|
| | | |
| | | |
| | | |
| | | |
| | | |

| Order **Passeriformes** | Family **Fringillidae** | Species **Spinus pinus** |
|---|---|---|

# Pine Siskin 🔊

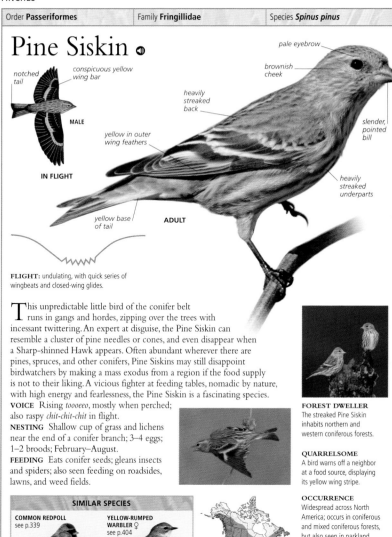

**MALE**

notched tail

conspicuous yellow wing bar

**IN FLIGHT**

yellow in outer wing feathers

yellow base of tail

**ADULT**

pale eyebrow

brownish cheek

heavily streaked back

slender, pointed bill

heavily streaked underparts

**FLIGHT:** undulating, with quick series of wingbeats and closed-wing glides.

This unpredictable little bird of the conifer belt runs in gangs and hordes, zipping over the trees with incessant twittering. An expert at disguise, the Pine Siskin can resemble a cluster of pine needles or cones, and even disappear when a Sharp-shinned Hawk appears. Often abundant wherever there are pines, spruces, and other conifers, Pine Siskins may still disappoint birdwatchers by making a mass exodus from a region if the food supply is not to their liking. A vicious fighter at feeding tables, nomadic by nature, with high energy and fearlessness, the Pine Siskin is a fascinating species.

**VOICE** Rising *toooeeo*, mostly when perched; also raspy *chit-chit-chit* in flight.

**NESTING** Shallow cup of grass and lichens near the end of a conifer branch; 3–4 eggs; 1–2 broods; February–August.

**FEEDING** Eats conifer seeds; gleans insects and spiders; also seen feeding on roadsides, lawns, and weed fields.

**FOREST DWELLER**
The streaked Pine Siskin inhabits northern and western coniferous forests.

**QUARRELSOME**
A bird warns off a neighbor at a food source, displaying its yellow wing stripe.

**OCCURRENCE**
Widespread across North America; occurs in coniferous and mixed coniferous forests, but also seen in parkland and suburbs. In some winters may appear south of regular breeding range to Missouri and Tennessee, also Mexico. Prefers open areas to continuous forest.

### SIMILAR SPECIES

**COMMON REDPOLL**
see p.339

tiny, pale bill

heavier streaking

**YELLOW-RUMPED WARBLER** ♀
see p.404

yellow rump

yellow patches

| Length **4¼–5½in (11–14cm)** | Wingspan **7–9in (18–23cm)** | Weight **⁷⁄₁₆–⅝oz (12–18g)** |
|---|---|---|
| Social **Flocks** | Lifespan **Up to 10 years** | Status **Secure** |

| DATE SEEN | WHERE | NOTES |
|---|---|---|
| | | |
| | | |
| | | |
| | | |

| Order **Passeriformes** | Family **Fringillidae** | Species *Spinus psaltria* |

# Lesser Goldfinch 🔊

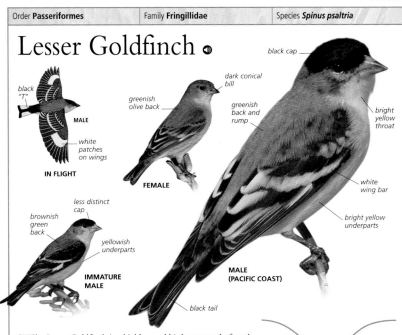

black cap

black "T"

**MALE**

white patches on wings

**IN FLIGHT**

dark conical bill

greenish olive back

greenish back and rump

bright yellow throat

**FEMALE**

less distinct cap

brownish green back

yellowish underparts

**IMMATURE MALE**

white wing bar

bright yellow underparts

**MALE (PACIFIC COAST)**

black tail

The Lesser Goldfinch is a highly vocal bird, commonly found in gardens, suburbs, and farmlands, in addition to its natural habitats of open fields and scrub. Single birds and small flocks are often seen zooming around and flying overhead, calling noisily or singing in flight. The male has a brighter yellow breast and belly than the female. It also has a black cap, unlike the female, and its nape and back color varies from black in Texas and Mexico, to green along the Pacific Coast.

**VOICE** Call descending *peeyee* and 2-note *tee-eee*, with second note higher; also rapid *dididit*; song warbles and trills.

**NESTING** Well-concealed cup, 10–30ft (3–9m) up in densely foliaged trees; 4 eggs; 1 brood; April–September.

**FEEDING** Eats a range of weed seeds; also eats insects, especially aphids, when available.

**FLIGHT:** undulating with dips; similar to other goldfinches.

**GREENISH BACK**
A western version of the American Goldfinch, the male Lesser Goldfinch is also greenish above.

**SIMILAR SPECIES**

**AMERICAN GOLDFINCH** see p.344
all yellow
black forehead
white rump

**LAWRENCE'S GOLDFINCH** see p.460
gray back
yellow breast
yellow wing bars

**OCCURRENCE**
This western species is not picky in its choice of habitat, which includes deciduous and coniferous woodlands, thickets, desert oases, parks and gardens; occurs from California to Texas in the breeding season and south to Mexico in winter.

| Length 3½–4¼in (9–11cm) | Wingspan 6–6¾in (15–17cm) | Weight ⅜oz (10g) |
| Social **Flocks** | Lifespan **Up to 6 years** | Status **Secure** |

| DATE SEEN | WHERE | NOTES |
|-----------|-------|-------|
| | | |
| | | |
| | | |
| | | |
| | | |

| Order **Passeriformes** | Family **Fringillidae** | Species *Spinus tristis* |
|---|---|---|

# American Goldfinch

**MALE (BREEDING)**

**IN FLIGHT**

bright yellow back

tan back

brownish bill

yellow throat and collar

pale tan underparts

**MALE (NONBREEDING)**

brownish olive back

pinkish bill

**FEMALE (BREEDING)**

black forehead and crown

black tail

white rump

white wing bar

brownish overall

dull yellow throat

**FEMALE (NONBREEDING)**

short conical pinkish bill

bright yellow underparts

pinkish legs and toes

**MALE (BREEDING)**

The male American Goldfinch is a spectacular summer sight. Goldfinches reveal their presence before they are seen by their tinkling, bell-like calls. If there are weeds in seed around, goldfinches will find them and feed energetically on the manna. This all-American species is the State Bird of Washington State.

**VOICE** Loud, rising, quizzical *pter-yee?* by males; 3–5-note *tit-tse-tew-tew* by both sexes, usually in flight; song complex, warbling, tinkling, and melodious.

**NESTING** Neat open cup of grass, shaded by leaves, in a tree or tall shrub; 4–5 eggs; 1–2 broods; June–September.

**FEEDING** Feed mainly on seeds from annuals; also birch and alder; some insects; love sunflower and thistle seed, whether on flower heads or at feeders.

**FLIGHT:** deeply undulating; wingbeats alternating with closed-wing dips.

### SIMILAR SPECIES

**LESSER GOLDFINCH**
see p.343

greenish back

conspicuous wing bars

**LAWRENCE'S GOLDFINCH**
see p.460

yellow wing bars

yellow breast

black face

**WILSON'S WARBLER**
see p.410

black cap

black face

yellow face

**OCCURRENCE**
In low shrubs, deciduous woodlands, farmlands, orchards, suburbs, and gardens across much of North America, from southern Canada to California and Georgia; in winter south to northern Mexico and Florida; winter habitats similar to those used at other times.

| Length **4¼–5in (11–13cm)** | Wingspan **7–9in (18–23cm)** | Weight **⅜–¹¹⁄₁₆oz (11–20g)** |
|---|---|---|
| Social **Small flocks** | Lifespan **Up to 11 years** | Status **Secure** |

| DATE SEEN | WHERE | NOTES |
|---|---|---|
| | | |
| | | |
| | | |
| | | |
| | | |

# LONGSPURS AND SNOW BUNTING

FOUR SPECIES OF longspurs, the Snow Bunting, and McKay's Bunting all generally forage on bare or open ground, from tundra and mountain tops to open prairies, often in flocks. Their short, blackish legs help give longspurs a long, low shape on the ground. Their calls provide useful clues for identification as they fly. Snow Buntings have distinctive white bands on their wings.

**CHANGING COLORS**
Snow Buntings are well camouflaged against exposed rocks and snow throughout the year. Brown edges on the feathers in winter wear off, so they become pristine black and white in spring.

# NEW WORLD SPARROWS

NEW WORLD SPARROWS are more akin to Old World buntings than other sparrows, but, as with robins, familiar names were given to quite different birds by early European settlers and have stayed with us. New World sparrows are rounded but long-tailed, and have small, conical or triangular bills that are adapted to feed on grass seeds. While some birds are distinctive, especially the more brightly patterned males, many are small, "streaky-brown" species that present considerable identification difficulties. Range, habitat, behavior, and voice are all often used together as a suite of characteristics for identification. Not only are the species much alike, but studies conducted in recent years have revealed different relationships between them, with some subspecies being split as separate species and others being grouped together. Nevertheless, their neat, subtle patterns make even the duller species worth studying: the delicateness of a Sagebrush Sparrow or the exquisite streaking of Lincoln's Sparrow, for example, repay close observation.

**TYPICAL SPECIES**
A White-crowned Sparrow shows the typical stout bill of New World sparrows.

| Order **Passeriformes** | Family **Calcariidae** | Species *Calcarius lapponicus* |

# Lapland Longspur

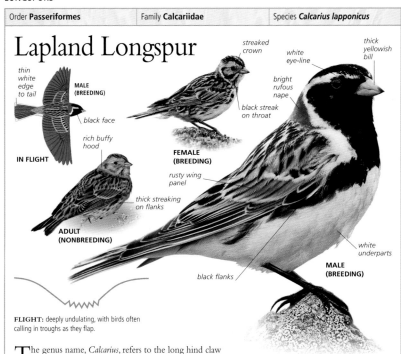

streaked crown

white eye-line

thick yellowish bill

thin white edge to tail

**MALE (BREEDING)**

black face

bright rufous nape

black streak on throat

rich buffy hood

**IN FLIGHT**

**FEMALE (BREEDING)**

rusty wing panel

**ADULT (NONBREEDING)**

thick streaking on flanks

white underparts

**MALE (BREEDING)**

black flanks

**FLIGHT:** deeply undulating, with birds often calling in troughs as they flap.

The genus name, *Calcarius*, refers to the long hind claw of this bird, hence "longspur" in American usage. The Lapland Longspur is one of the most numerous breeding birds in the Arctic tundra, from Labrador west to Alaska, and across northern Eurasia. In winter, they form huge flocks in open habitats of southern Canada and the US and are found on gravel roads and barren countryside immediately after heavy snowfall. The longspurs and the snow bunting were formerly part of the Emberizidae family but are now placed in a distinct family of their own.
**VOICE** Flight call a dry rattle, *tyew*, unlike other longspurs; song a series of thin tinklings and whistles, melodious, often in flight.
**NESTING** Cup of grass and sedges placed in depression on ground next to a clump of vegetation; 4–6 eggs; 1 brood; May–July.
**FEEDING** Eats insects during breeding season; seeds in winter.

**CONSPICUOUS SPECIES**
This longspur is one of the most conspicuous breeding birds of the Arctic tundra.

**OCCURRENCE**
Breeds in tundra right across the High Arctic of North America and Eurasia. Winters in open grasslands and barren fields, and on beaches across the northern and central US and parts of south-central and northeastern Canada.

## SIMILAR SPECIES

**SMITH'S LONGSPUR** ♀
see p.461

white bars on wing

thin bill

**CHESTNUT-COLLARED LONGSPUR** ♀ ✳
see p.460

more white in tail

dark cheek patch

| Length **6½in (16cm)** | Wingspan **10½–11½in (27–29cm)** | Weight **⅞–1¹⁄₁₆oz (25–30g)** |
| Social **Large flocks** | Lifespan **Up to 5 years** | Status **Secure** |

| DATE SEEN | WHERE | NOTES |
| --- | --- | --- |
| | | |
| | | |
| | | |
| | | |
| | | |

| Order **Passeriformes** | Family **Calcariidae** | Species ***Plectrophenax nivalis*** |

# Snow Bunting

*less white in wings*

*white outer tail feathers*

**MALE (NONBREEDING)**

*black back*

*yellow bill*

**IN FLIGHT**

*large white patches on black wings*

**MALE (BREEDING)**

**FEMALE (NONBREEDING)**

*white head and underparts*

*black bill*

**FEMALE (BREEDING)**

*pale rufous crown*

*white underparts*

*dark brown eyes*

*rusty orange cheek patch*

*black peeks through buffy feather edgings*

*rusty orange breast patch*

*gray body*

*white eye-ring*

**MALE (NONBREEDING)**

**JUVENILE**

The bold white wing patches of the Snow Bunting make it immediately recognizable in a whirling winter flock of dark-winged longspurs and larks. In winter, heavy snowfall forces flocks onto roadsides, where they can be seen more easily. To secure and defend the best territories, some males arrive as early as April in their barren High Arctic breeding grounds; these buntings breed further north than any other songbirds. The Snow Bunting is very similar in appearance to the rare McKay's Bunting, localized to western Alaska. Although McKay's Bunting generally has less black on the back, in the wings, and on the tail, the two species cannot always be conclusively identified. This is especially true as they sometimes interbreed, producing hybrids.

**VOICE** Flight call a musical, liquid rattle, also *tyew* notes and short buzz; song a pleasant series of squeaky and whistled notes.

**NESTING** Bulky cup of grass and moss, lined with feathers, and placed in sheltered rock crevice; 3–6 eggs; 1 brood; June–August.

**FEEDING** Eats seeds (sedge in Arctic), flies and other insects, and buds on migration.

**FLIGHT:** deeply undulating; flocks "roll" along as birds at back overtake those in front.

**ROCKY GROUND**
About the only perches in the Snow Bunting's barren breeding grounds are large boulders.

| SIMILAR SPECIES |
| --- |
| **McKAY'S BUNTING** see p.461 <br> *mostly white tail, back, and wings* |

**OCCURRENCE**
Breeds in rocky areas, usually near sparsely vegetated tundra, right across the Arctic in both North America and Eurasia. North American birds winter in open country and on shores across southern Canada and the northern US, and in southern and western coastal areas of Alaska.

| Length **6½–7in (16–18cm)** | Wingspan **12½–14in (32–35cm)** | Weight **1¼–2oz (35–55g)** |
| Social **Large flocks** | Lifespan **Unknown** | Status **Declining** |

| DATE SEEN | WHERE | NOTES |
| --- | --- | --- |
| | | |
| | | |
| | | |
| | | |

| Order **Passeriformes** | Family **Passerellidae** | Species *Peucaea cassinii* |

# Cassin's Sparrow

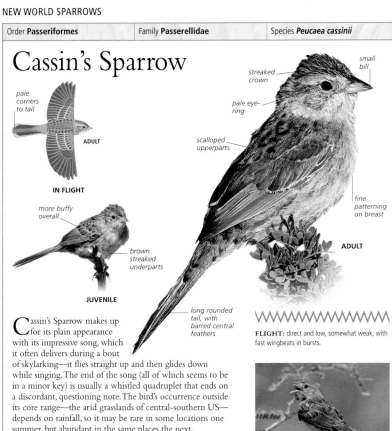

*small bill*

*streaked crown*

*pale corners to tail*

**ADULT**

**IN FLIGHT**

*pale eye-ring*

*scalloped upperparts*

*more buffy overall*

*fine patterning on breast*

**ADULT**

*brown streaked underparts*

**JUVENILE**

*long rounded tail, with barred central feathers*

**FLIGHT:** direct and low, somewhat weak, with fast wingbeats in bursts.

Cassin's Sparrow makes up for its plain appearance with its impressive song, which it often delivers during a bout of skylarking—it flies straight up and then glides down while singing. The end of the song (all of which seems to be in a minor key) is usually a whistled quadruplet that ends on a discordant, questioning note. The bird's occurrence outside its core range—the arid grasslands of central-southern US—depends on rainfall, so it may be rare in some locations one summer, but abundant in the same places the next.

**VOICE** Calls high *seeps* and *chips*, often in series; song *see-eee sii-ii-i-i-i-i-i-i-i zee-zooo' zee-ZWAAAY*, ending on questioning note.
**NESTING** Cup placed in grass on or near ground, often in prickly-pear cactus; 2–5 eggs; 1–2 broods; May–September.
**FEEDING** Scratches around on ground for seeds, flowers, buds, insects, insect larvae, and spiders.

**COMMON TUNE**
This sparrow's song is well known in the central-southern US, and is an easy way to identify the bird.

**OCCURRENCE**
Breeds in arid grasslands with scattered shrubs, yuccas, and low trees, from western Nebraska southward to central Mexico. Winters from US–Mexican border southward to central Mexico.

### SIMILAR SPECIES

**BACHMAN'S SPARROW**
*smaller overall*
*grayer overall*

**BOTTERI'S SPARROW**
see p.462
*no eye-ring*
*larger bill*
*dark tail*

| Length **6in (15cm)** | Wingspan **9in (23cm)** | Weight ⅝–¹¹⁄₁₆oz (18–20g) |
| Social **Solitary** | Lifespan **Unknown** | Status **Declining** |

| DATE SEEN | WHERE | NOTES |
|---|---|---|
| | | |
| | | |
| | | |
| | | |

| Order **Passeriformes** | Family **Passerellidae** | Species *Ammodramus savannarum* |

# Grasshopper Sparrow

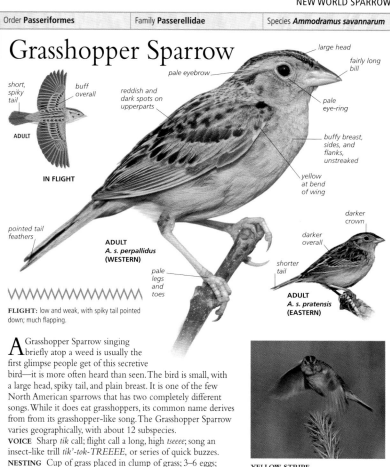

large head

fairly long bill

pale eyebrow

short, spiky tail

buff overall

reddish and dark spots on upperparts

**ADULT**

**IN FLIGHT**

pale eye-ring

buffy breast, sides, and flanks, unstreaked

yellow at bend of wing

pointed tail feathers

**ADULT
A. s. perpallidus
(WESTERN)**

pale legs and toes

darker crown

darker overall

shorter tail

**ADULT
A. s. pratensis
(EASTERN)**

**FLIGHT:** low and weak, with spiky tail pointed down; much flapping.

A Grasshopper Sparrow singing briefly atop a weed is usually the first glimpse people get of this secretive bird—it is more often heard than seen. The bird is small, with a large head, spiky tail, and plain breast. It is one of the few North American sparrows that has two completely different songs. While it does eat grasshoppers, its common name derives from from its grasshopper-like song. The Grasshopper Sparrow varies geographically, with about 12 subspecies.

**VOICE** Sharp *tik* call; flight call a long, high *tseeee*; song an insect-like trill *tik'-tok-TREEEE*, or series of quick buzzes.

**NESTING** Cup of grass placed in clump of grass; 3–6 eggs; 1–2 broods; April–August.

**FEEDING** Forages on ground for seeds and insects.

**YELLOW STRIPE**
The pale crown stripe is quite visible here as the bird faces the photographer.

## SIMILAR SPECIES

**LECONTE'S SPARROW**
see p.364

brighter overall

orange eyebrow

gray cheek patch

**BAIRD'S SPARROW**
see p.464

ocher crown

dark, lateral throat stripe

**OCCURRENCE**
Breeds in short grassland, pastures, and even mown areas across much of the US and in southern Canada. Locally distributed in the Southwest, also patchily through central US. Winters in similar habitats from southern US to Colombia; also in the West Indies.

| Length **5in (13cm)** | Wingspan **8in (20cm)** | Weight **½–¹¹⁄₁₆oz (15–20g)** |
| Social **Solitary/Flocks** | Lifespan **Up to 7 years** | Status **Declining** |

| DATE SEEN | WHERE | NOTES |
| --- | --- | --- |
| | | |
| | | |
| | | |
| | | |
| | | |

349

| Order **Passeriformes** | Family **Passerellidae** | Species *Amphispiza bilineata* |
| --- | --- | --- |

# Black-throated Sparrow

white-edged black tail

**ADULT**

white stripe along cheek

brownish gray upperparts

grayish overall

**IN FLIGHT**

bold white eyebrow

black throat

**ADULT**

faint streaking on breast

**JUVENILE**

B ecause of perceived similarities in their songs, the Black-throated Sparrow has been called "the Song Sparrow of the desert." They are easily identified as they possess a bold white eyebrow in all plumages, which prevents confusion with other species. It is possible, however, for first-time observers to misidentify juvenile Black-throated Sparrows for Bell's Sparrows. The Black-throated Sparrow is exclusively western. It lives in a variety of arid habitats, especially on hillsides covered with cactus, creosote, and ocotillo, but also in sagebrush and open pine woodlands.

**VOICE** Weak *tink* call; song consists of a few short, clear notes, followed by a high trill: *tink tink-tink treeeeee*, also *ti-ti-tink churrrrrrrrrr*.

**NESTING** Loose cup placed on or near ground in bush or grass; 3–4 eggs; 1–2 broods; March–September.

**FEEDING** Eats seeds, insects, and cactus fruit.

**FLIGHT:** direct with rapid wingbeats, flies low between shrubs and trees.

**CLEAR PLUMAGE**
No other sparrow comes close to equaling this species' bold head and throat patterning.

**SIMILAR SPECIES**

**BELL'S SPARROW** see p.362

lacks bold eyebrow

gray head

**SPRING SINGER**
In spring the male declares his territory by singing from the top of a yucca or other high perch.

**OCCURRENCE**
Found in desert scrub, from the Great Basin east and south to Texas, south to Baja California and central Mexico. Breeds sporadically in eastern Washington state. Withdraws from the Great Basin and much of the arid Southwest in winter. Resident in Mexico. Casual to the Pacific Coast and the East.

| Length **5½in (14cm)** | Wingspan **7¾in (19.5cm)** | Weight **⅜–⁹⁄₁₆oz (10–16g)** |
| --- | --- | --- |
| Social **Solitary** | Lifespan **Up to 6 years** | Status **Secure** |

| DATE SEEN | WHERE | NOTES |
| --- | --- | --- |
| .................. | .................. | .................. |
| .................. | .................. | .................. |
| .................. | .................. | .................. |
| .................. | .................. | .................. |
| .................. | .................. | .................. |

| Order **Passeriformes** | Family **Passerellidae** | Species *Chondestes grammacus* |

# Lark Sparrow

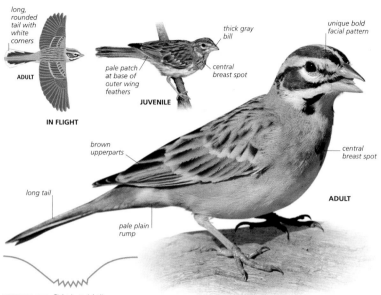

**long, rounded tail with white corners**

**ADULT**

**IN FLIGHT**

**thick gray bill**

**pale patch at base of outer wing feathers**

**central breast spot**

**JUVENILE**

**unique bold facial pattern**

**brown upperparts**

**central breast spot**

**long tail**

**ADULT**

**pale plain rump**

**FLIGHT:** strong flight, in straight lines; often perches when flushed.

The bold harlequin facial pattern, single central breast spot, and long, rounded, black tail with white outer corners make the Lark Sparrow one of the most easily identifiable of North American sparrows. It is commonly found singing from the top of a fencepost or small tree in the western US. Conversely, Lark Sparrow numbers have declined precipitously in the East, where the species is mostly associated with western-like sandy soils. It is likely, however, that its presence in the East was only possible because of the clearing of forests, so the species may in fact simply be retreating to its natural range. Males are strongly territorial at their nesting sites.

**VOICE** Thin, up-slurred *tseep* call, flight call sharp *tink*; song series of trills, whistles, and rattles on varying pitches.

**NESTING** Cup usually placed on ground at base of plant, or off-ground in tree or bush; 3–5 eggs; 1–2 broods; April–August.

**FEEDING** Eats seeds and insects.

**ON THE FENCE**
The Lark Sparrow is a common roadside bird, often found perching on barbed wire fences.

**OCCURRENCE**
In the West, breeds in a variety of open habitats, such as sagebrush flats and grasslands from British Columbia and Saskatchewan to Baja California and central Mexico. Localized breeder in the East, associated with well-drained soils, east to Ohio. Winters from southern US to southwestern and central Mexico.

| Length **6–6¾in (15–17cm)** | Wingspan **11in (28cm)** | Weight **¹¹⁄₁₆–1¹⁄₁₆oz (20–30g)** |
| Social **Large flocks** | Lifespan **Up to 8 years** | Status **Secure** |

| DATE SEEN | WHERE | NOTES |
|-----------|-------|-------|
| | | |
| | | |
| | | |
| | | |
| | | |

| Order **Passeriformes** | Family **Passerellidae** | Species ***Calamospiza melanocorys*** |

# Lark Bunting

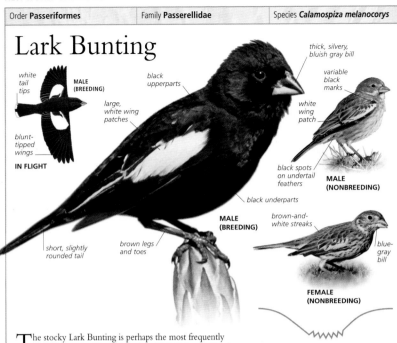

white tail tips

**MALE (BREEDING)**

black upperparts

large, white wing patches

blunt-tipped wings

**IN FLIGHT**

short, slightly rounded tail

brown legs and toes

**MALE (BREEDING)**

black underparts

thick, silvery, bluish gray bill

variable black marks

white wing patch

black spots on undertail feathers

**MALE (NONBREEDING)**

brown-and-white streaks

blue-gray bill

**FEMALE (NONBREEDING)**

**FLIGHT:** low and undulating, short glides alternating with stiff wingbeats.

The stocky Lark Bunting is perhaps the most frequently seen bird on the North American High Plains. Unlike the Chestnut-collared Longspur, which lives alongside it, it coped with the changes wrought on its habitat by humans, and occurs in extraordinarily high density throughout its range. Nomadic flocks of thousands of birds scour the high deserts, open grasslands, and sagebrush for seeds. Breeding-plumage males are unmistakable: black with large white wing patches. Females and immature birds are duller, with more subdued wing patches.
**VOICE** Call a low, soft, whistled *hwoik*; song partly melodious, partly "scratchy," with repetitions of phrases, then whistles.
**NESTING** Open cup of grass, lined with fine plant material, in depression in ground; 4–5 eggs; 1 brood; May–August.
**FEEDING** Mainly seeds in winter, a variety of insects in summer.

**CAUGHT BY ANY MEANS**
Lark Buntings hawk, glean, and forage insect prey throughout the breeding season.

### SIMILAR SPECIES

**PURPLE FINCH ♀**
see p.337

no white in notched tail

**VESPER SPARROW**
see p.363

no white wing patches

pink bill

longer, squarer tail

**OCCURRENCE**
Breeds in grasslands and sage flats on High Plains from Alberta south to the Texas panhandle. Winters in similar habitats—and also in deserts, cultivated plains, and open shrub-steppes—across interior southwestern US and northern Mexico. Migrants use similar open-country habitats.

| Length **7in (18cm)** | Wingspan **10½–11in (27–28cm)** | Weight **1¹⁄₁₆–1¾oz (30–50g)** |
| Social **Large flocks** | Lifespan **Unknown** | Status **Secure** |

| DATE SEEN | WHERE | NOTES |
|---|---|---|
| | | |
| | | |
| | | |
| | | |
| | | |

| Order **Passeriformes** | Family **Passerellidae** | Species *Spizella passerina* |

# Chipping Sparrow

**pale underparts**

**ADULT IN FLIGHT**

**rusty cast to crown**

**pinkish bill**

**ADULT (WINTER)**

**bright rufous crown**

**blackish bill**

**white eyebrow**

**black eye line**

**ADULT (BREEDING)**

**gray underparts**

**heavily streaked, especially on breast**

**JUVENILE**

**long tail**

The Chipping Sparrow is a common and trusting bird, which breeds in backyards across most of North America. While they are easily identifiable in the summer, "Chippers" molt into a drab, nonbreeding plumage during fall, at which point they are easily confused with the Clay-colored and Brewer's Sparrows they flock with. Most winter reports of this species in the North are actually of the larger American Tree Sparrow. In winter, Chipping Sparrows lack their bright, rusty crown and are restricted to the southern states.

**VOICE** Call a sharp *tsip*; flight call a sharp, thin *tsiiit*; song an insect-like trill of chip notes, variable in duration and intensity.
**NESTING** Neat cup usually placed well off the ground in tree or shrub; 3–5 eggs; 1–2 broods; April–August.
**FEEDING** Eats seeds of grasses and annuals, plus some fruit; when breeding, also eats insects and other invertebrates.

**FLIGHT:** lightly undulating, often to open perch when flushed.

**BACKYARD BIRD**
Chipping Sparrows are common in gardens and backyards all across the continent.

**SIMILAR SPECIES**

**CLAY-COLORED SPARROW**
see p.354

**heavy streaks**

**BREWER'S SPARROW**
see p.355

**partial "necklace"**

**streaked crown**

**pale under-parts**

**OCCURRENCE**
Found in a wide variety of habitats: open forest, woodlands, grassy park-like areas, seashores, and backyards. Breeds in North America south of the Arctic timberline southward to Mexico, and in Central America as far south as Nicaragua. Winters from southern states to Nicaragua.

| Length **5½in (14cm)** | Wingspan **8½in (21cm)** | Weight **⅜–½oz (10–15g)** |
| Social **Large flocks** | Lifespan **Up to 9 years** | Status **Secure** |

| DATE SEEN | WHERE | NOTES |
|---|---|---|
| | | |
| | | |
| | | |
| | | |
| | | |

| Order **Passeriformes** | Family **Passerellidae** | Species *Spizella pallida* |

# Clay-colored Sparrow

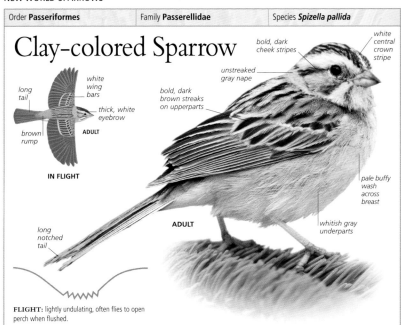

white central crown stripe

bold, dark cheek stripes

unstreaked gray nape

bold, dark brown streaks on upperparts

white wing bars

long tail

thick, white eyebrow

**ADULT**

brown rump

**IN FLIGHT**

pale buffy wash across breast

long notched tail

**ADULT**

whitish gray underparts

**FLIGHT:** lightly undulating, often flies to open perch when flushed.

The small Clay-colored Sparrow is best known for its mechanical, buzzy song. This bird spends much of its foraging time away from its breeding habitat; consequently, males' territories are very small, allowing for dense breeding populations. Clay-colored Sparrows have shifted their breeding range eastward and northward over the last century, most likely because of changes in land practices. During the nonbreeding season, they form large flocks in open country, associating with other *Spizella* sparrows, especially Chipping and Brewer's.

**VOICE** Call a sharp *tsip*; flight call a short, rising *sip*; song a series of 2–7 mechanical buzzes on one pitch.

**NESTING** Cup of grass placed just off the ground in shrub or small tree; 3–5 eggs; 1–2 broods; May–August.

**FEEDING** Forages on or near the ground for seeds and insects.

**CHRISTMAS PRESENT**
The Clay-colored Sparrow is fond of low conifers for breeding, so Christmas tree farms form a perfect habitat.

**SIMILAR SPECIES**

**CHIPPING SPARROW** ❄
see p.353

grayish rump

dark stripe through eye

**BREWER'S SPARROW**
see p.355

streaked nape

lacks bold, crown stripe

grayer breast

**OCCURRENCE**
Breeds in open habitats: prairies, shrubland, forest edges, and Christmas tree farms along the US/Canadian border and northward to the southern Northwest Territory. Winters in a large variety of brushy and weedy areas from south Texas to Mexico. Migration takes it to the Great Plains.

| Length **5½in (14cm)** | Wingspan **7½in (19cm)** | Weight **⅜–½oz (10–15g)** |
| Social **Large flocks** | Lifespan **Up to 5 years** | Status **Secure** |

| DATE SEEN | WHERE | NOTES |
|---|---|---|
| | | |
| | | |
| | | |
| | | |
| | | |

| Order **Passeriformes** | Family **Passerellidae** | Species *Spizella breweri* |

# Brewer's Sparrow

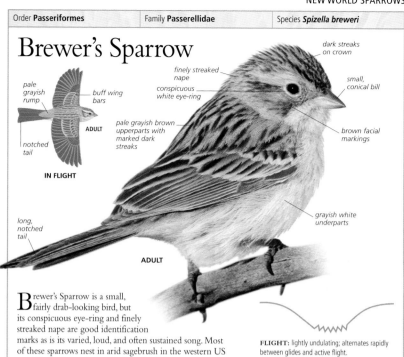

dark streaks on crown

finely streaked nape

conspicuous white eye-ring

small, conical bill

pale grayish rump

buff wing bars

**ADULT**

pale grayish brown upperparts with marked dark streaks

brown facial markings

notched tail

**IN FLIGHT**

grayish white underparts

long, notched tail

**ADULT**

Brewer's Sparrow is a small, fairly drab-looking bird, but its conspicuous eye-ring and finely streaked nape are good identification marks as is its varied, loud, and often sustained song. Most of these sparrows nest in arid sagebrush in the western US and Alberta, but an isolated subspecies *S. b. taverneri* ("Timberline Sparrow"), breeds in the Canadian Rockies and north Alaska. It is darker, more boldly marked, and longer billed with a slower, more musical song. This species was named to honor Thomas Mayo Brewer, a naturalist from Massachusetts.

**VOICE** Call a sharp *tsip*; flight call a short, rising *sip*; song a long series of descending trills, rattles, and buzzes on different pitches: quite a production.

**NESTING** Compact cup on or near ground in small bush; 3–4 eggs; 1–2 broods; May–August.

**FEEDING** Forages on ground for insects and seeds.

**FLIGHT:** lightly undulating; alternates rapidly between glides and active flight.

**CONTINUOUS SINGING**
Across its range in spring, male Brewer's Sparrows sing continuously to attract a mate.

**HIGH AND DRY**
These sparrows are fond of the arid brushlands and deserts of the High Plains and Great Basin.

**OCCURRENCE**
The "Timberline" subspecies breeds in mountain valleys of eastern Alaska and the western Yukon. The "Brewer's" subspecies breeds in brushlands, shrublands, and thickets, especially sagebrush, in the intermontane West. Winters in desert scrub and weedy fields in the Southwest, and northwestern and central Mexico.

**SIMILAR SPECIES**

**CHIPPING SPARROW** ✻
see p.353

lacks white eye-ring

dark stripe through eye

**CLAY-COLORED SPARROW**
see p.354

bold crown stripe

no eye-ring

| Length **5½in (14cm)** | Wingspan **7½in (19cm)** | Weight **⁵⁄₁₆–½oz (9–14g)** |
| Social **Solitary/Flocks** | Lifespan **Unknown** | Status **Declining** |

| DATE SEEN | WHERE | NOTES |
|-----------|-------|-------|
|  |  |  |
|  |  |  |
|  |  |  |
|  |  |  |
|  |  |  |

| Order **Passeriformes** | Family **Passerellidae** | Species *Passerella iliaca* |
| --- | --- | --- |

# Fox Sparrow 🔊

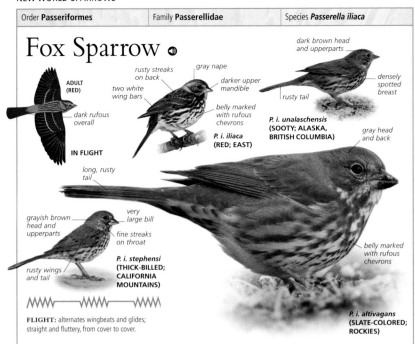

**ADULT (RED)**

dark rufous overall

**IN FLIGHT**

rusty streaks on back

gray nape

two white wing bars

darker upper mandible

belly marked with rufous chevrons

*P. i. iliaca* (RED; EAST)

dark brown head and upperparts

densely spotted breast

rusty tail

*P. i. unalaschensis* (SOOTY; ALASKA, BRITISH COLUMBIA)

gray head and back

long, rusty tail

grayish brown head and upperparts

very large bill

fine streaks on throat

rusty wings and tail

*P. i. stephensi* (THICK-BILLED; CALIFORNIA MOUNTAINS)

belly marked with rufous chevrons

*P. i. altivagans* (SLATE-COLORED; ROCKIES)

**FLIGHT:** alternates wingbeats and glides; straight and fluttery, from cover to cover.

Larger, more robust, and more colorful than its close relatives, the Fox Sparrow is a beautiful species. When it appears in backyards, its presence can be detected by its foraging habits; it crouches low in leaf litter, and hops back and forth, noisily, to disturb leaves, under which it finds seeds or insects. It varies considerably over its huge western range, from thick-billed birds in the Sierras to sooty ones in the Northwest, and distinctive Red Fox Sparrows in taiga forest from Newfoundland to Alaska.
**VOICE** Call is sharp, dry *tshak* or *tshuk;* flight call a high-pitched *tzeep!;* song is complex and musical with trills and whistles.
**NESTING** Dense cup of grasses or moss lined with fine material; usually placed low in shrub; 2–5 eggs; 1 brood; April–July.
**FEEDING** Forages for insects, seeds, and fruit.

**FOXY RED**
The Fox Sparrow gets its name from the rusty coloration of the eastern "Red" birds.

**SIMILAR SPECIES**

**HERMIT THRUSH** see p.317

unstreaked flanks

different bill shape

longer tail

**SONG SPARROW** see p.366

thinner bill

breast streaking less marked

**OCCURRENCE**
Encompasses the entire boreal forest zone, from Alaska in the West to Québec, Labrador, and Newfoundland in the East. In the West, it occurs in coastal and near-coast thickets within coniferous or mixed woodlands. Winters in the Pacific West, south to Baja California; also from Texas to Massachusetts.

| Length **6–7½in (15–19cm)** | Wingspan **10½–11½in (27–29cm)** | Weight **⅞–1⁹⁄₁₆oz (25–45g)** |
| --- | --- | --- |
| Social **Solitary/Small flocks** | Lifespan **Up to 9 years** | Status **Secure** |

| DATE SEEN | WHERE | NOTES |
| --- | --- | --- |
| | | |
| | | |
| | | |
| | | |
| | | |

| Order **Passeriformes** | Family **Passerellidae** | Species *Spizelloides arborea* |

# American Tree Sparrow

rufous crown

black-and-yellow bill

rusty tones on shoulder and wings

gray eyebrow and nape

rusty stripe behind eye

streaked underparts

**ADULT (BREEDING)**

**IN FLIGHT**

**JUVENILE**

black and rust streaking on back

two wing bars

rust patch at shoulder

dark central breast spot

tan, unstreaked flanks and underparts

streaked back

**ADULT (NONBREEDING)**

long square tail

**ADULT (BREEDING)**

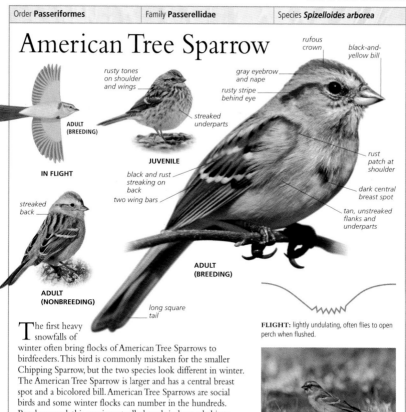

**FLIGHT:** lightly undulating, often flies to open perch when flushed.

The first heavy snowfalls of winter often bring flocks of American Tree Sparrows to birdfeeders. This bird is commonly mistaken for the smaller Chipping Sparrow, but the two species look different in winter. The American Tree Sparrow is larger and has a central breast spot and a bicolored bill. American Tree Sparrows are social birds and some winter flocks can number in the hundreds. Poorly named, this species actually breeds in boggy habitats of the Far North.

**VOICE** Call a bell-like *teedle-ee*; flight call a thin, slightly descending *tsiiiu*; song *seee seee di-di-di di-di-di dyew dyew*.

**NESTING** Neat cup on ground concealed within thicket; 4–6 eggs; 1 brood; June–July.

**FEEDING** Feeds on seeds, berries, and a variety of insects.

**WINTER HABITATS**
In winter this species frequents barren habitats, like old fields and roadsides, as well as feeders.

## SIMILAR SPECIES

**CHIPPING SPARROW**
see p.353

lacks rusty eye-line

**FIELD SPARROW**
see p.462

all-pale bill

bold white eye-ring

no central, black breast spot

smaller overall

**OCCURRENCE**
Breeds in scrubby thickets of birch and willows in the area between taiga and tundra across Alaska and north Canada. Nonbreeders choose open, grassy, brushy habitats. Winters across south Canada and the northern US. Casual to Pacific Coast and southern US.

| Length **6¼in (16cm)** | Wingspan **9½in (24cm)** | Weight **⁷⁄₁₆–⅞oz (13–25g)** |
| Social **Flocks** | Lifespan **Up to 11 years** | Status **Secure** |

| DATE SEEN | WHERE | NOTES |
|---|---|---|
| | | |
| | | |
| | | |
| | | |
| | | |

| Order **Passeriformes** | Family **Passerellidae** | Species *Junco hyemalis* |

# Dark-eyed Junco 🔊

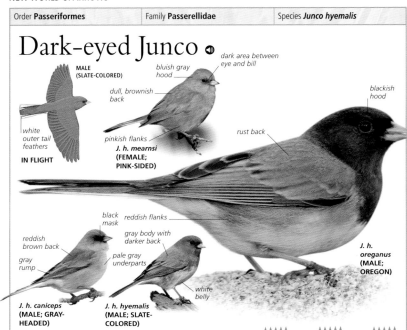

**MALE (SLATE-COLORED)**

dark area between eye and bill

bluish gray hood

dull, brownish back

blackish hood

white outer tail feathers

**IN FLIGHT**

pinkish flanks

**J. h. mearnsi (FEMALE; PINK-SIDED)**

rust back

**J. h. oreganus (MALE; OREGON)**

black mask

reddish flanks

reddish brown back

gray body with darker back

gray rump

pale gray underparts

white belly

**J. h. caniceps (MALE; GRAY-HEADED)**

**J. h. hyemalis (MALE; SLATE-COLORED)**

The Dark-eyed Junco's arrival at birdfeeders during winter snowstorms has earned it the colloquial name of "snowbird." The name "Dark-eyed Junco" is actually used to describe a group of birds that vary geographically in such a strikingly diverse way that 16 subspecies have been described. "Slate-colored" populations occur in central Alaska, Canada and the northeastern US. "White-winged" birds nest in the Black Hills of South Dakota; "Pink-sided" ones breed in Idaho, Montana, and Wyoming; and "Oregon" birds breed in the West, from coastal Alaska to British Columbia and the mountains of the western US in the Sierras south to Mexico. "Red-backed" populations (not illustrated) reside in the mountains of Arizona and New Mexico, and "Gray-headed" birds range between the "Red-backed" and "Pink-sided" populations.

**VOICE** Loud, smacking *tick* and soft *dyew* calls; flight call a rapid, twittering, and buzzy *zzeet*; song a simple, liquid, 1-pitch trill.

**NESTING** Cup placed on ground hidden under vegetation or next to rocks; 3–5 eggs; 1–2 broods; May–August.

**FEEDING** Eats insects and seeds; also berries.

**FLIGHT:** low and direct, staying within cover whenever possible.

**PINK-SIDED MALE**
Like most juncos, this male is brighter with greater contrasts, darker eye areas, and more vivid colors.

**SIMILAR SPECIES**

YELLOW-EYED JUNCO
see p.463

red back

yellow eyes

buff wash to belly

**OCCURRENCE**
Breeds in coniferous and mixed forests in Canada, south to the East Appalachians and Georgia; in the West, in mountains from Alaska and British Columbia to New Mexico and northern Baja California. Winters from southern Canada to northern Mexico except Florida.

| Length **6–6¾in (15–17cm)** | Wingspan **8–10in (20–26cm)** | Weight **⅝–1¹⁄₁₆oz (18–30g)** |
| Social **Flocks** | Lifespan **Up to 11 years** | Status **Secure** |

| DATE SEEN | WHERE | NOTES |
| --- | --- | --- |
| | | |
| | | |
| | | |
| | | |
| | | |

| Order **Passeriformes** | Family **Passerellidae** | Species ***Zonotrichia leucophrys*** |

# White-crowned Sparrow 🔊

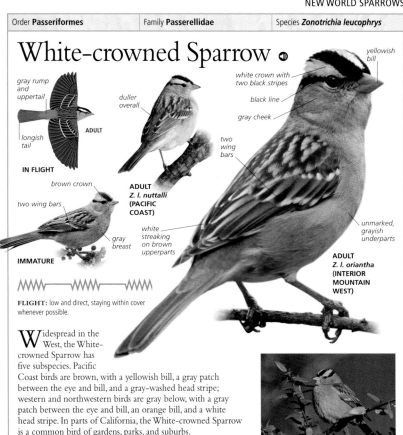

yellowish bill

white crown with two black stripes

black line

gray cheek

gray rump and uppertail

duller overall

**ADULT**

longish tail

**IN FLIGHT**

two wing bars

**ADULT**
**Z. l. nuttalli**
**(PACIFIC COAST)**

two wing bars

brown crown

gray breast

white streaking on brown upperparts

**IMMATURE**

two wing bars

unmarked, grayish underparts

**ADULT**
**Z. l. oriantha**
**(INTERIOR MOUNTAIN WEST)**

**FLIGHT:** low and direct, staying within cover whenever possible.

Widespread in the West, the White-crowned Sparrow has five subspecies. Pacific Coast birds are brown, with a yellowish bill, a gray patch between the eye and bill, and a gray-washed head stripe; western and northwestern birds are gray below, with a gray patch between the eye and bill, an orange bill, and a white head stripe. In parts of California, the White-crowned Sparrow is a common bird of gardens, parks, and suburbs.

**VOICE** Call a sharp *tink*; flight call a thin *seep*; song a buzzy whistle followed by buzzes, trills, and whistles.

**NESTING** Bulky cup of grass placed on or near the ground in bushes; 4–6 eggs; 1–3 broods; March–August.

**FEEDING** Forages for seeds, insects, fruit, buds, and even grass.

**LOOKING RESTED**
Perched on a shrub, this sparrow's white eyestreak is highly visible.

| SIMILAR SPECIES | | |
|---|---|---|
| **WHITE-THROATED SPARROW** see p.361<br>chunkier overall | yellow patch<br>gray bill<br>more reddish | **GOLDEN-CROWNED SPARROW** ☾<br>yellowish forecrown; see p.360 |
| | | plain face<br>gray bill |

**OCCURRENCE**
Widespread across the boreal forest and the taiga–tundra border, from Alaska eastward to Québec and Labrador, and southward from British Columbia to coastal California and the intermontane West. In the North, breeds in willow thickets, wet forest; in the West, habitats are more varied and include suburbs.

| Length 6½–7in (16–18cm) | Wingspan 9½–10in (24–26cm) | Weight 1¹⁄₁₆–1¼oz (20–35g) |
|---|---|---|
| Social **Flocks** | Lifespan **Up to 13 years** | Status **Secure** |

| DATE SEEN | WHERE | NOTES |
|---|---|---|
| | | |
| | | |
| | | |
| | | |
| | | |

| Order **Passeriformes** | Family **Passerellidae** | Species ***Zonotrichia atricapilla*** |

# Golden-crowned Sparrow

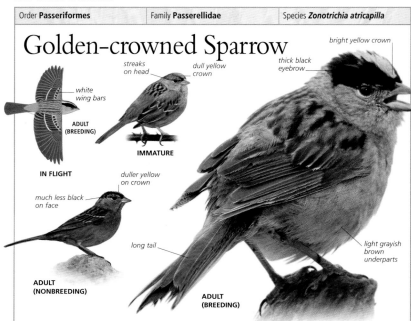

bright yellow crown

thick black eyebrow

streaks on head

dull yellow crown

white wing bars

**ADULT (BREEDING)**

**IMMATURE**

**IN FLIGHT**

duller yellow on crown

much less black on face

long tail

**ADULT (NONBREEDING)**

**ADULT (BREEDING)**

light grayish brown underparts

The large Golden-crowned Sparrow is common along the Pacific Coast of North America. It sings in a minor key and, as a result, has a reputation for sounding melancholic. Many late 19th-century Klondike gold prospectors called this bird "Weary Willie"—to them, its song sounded remarkably like *I'm so tired* or *No gold here*. It has been regarded as a pest in the past because of its habit of consuming crops in agricultural fields and gardens. Nonbreeding adults retain their distinctive golden crown in the winter, but it appears duller.

**VOICE** Call loud *tsik*; flight call soft, short *seeep*; song variable series of melancholic whistles, sometimes slurred or trilled.

**NESTING** Concealed bulky cup placed on ground at base of bush; 3–5 eggs; 1–2 broods; June–August.

**FEEDING** Predominantly forages on the ground for seeds, insects, fruit, flowers, and buds.

**FLIGHT:** low and direct, staying within cover whenever possible.

**GROUND FORAGER**
This sparrow can be found by listening for the noise it makes as it roots around in the leaf litter.

### SIMILAR SPECIES

**WHITE-CROWNED SPARROW** see p.359
white eyebrow / orange bill

**WHITE-THROATED SPARROW (TAN-STRIPED)** see p.361
lacks yellowish fore-crown / white throat

**OCCURRENCE**
Breeds in shrubby habitat along the tree line and open, boggy forests from Alaska east to the southwestern Northwest Territories, south to British Columbia and southwestern Alberta. Winters in dense thickets from south coastal British Columbia to northern Baja California.

| Length **7in (18cm)** | Wingspan **9–10in (23–25cm)** | Weight **$^{11}/_{16}$–1¼oz (20–35g)** |
| Social **Flocks** | Lifespan **Up to 10 years** | Status **Secure** |

| DATE SEEN | WHERE | NOTES |
| --- | --- | --- |
| | | |
| | | |
| | | |
| | | |
| | | |

| Order **Passeriformes** | Family **Passerellidae** | Species *Zonotrichia albicollis* |

# White-throated Sparrow 🔊

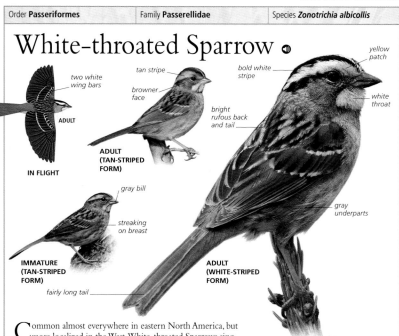

yellow patch

tan stripe

bold white stripe

two white wing bars

browner face

**ADULT**

bright rufous back and tail

white throat

**ADULT (TAN-STRIPED FORM)**

**IN FLIGHT**

gray bill

streaking on breast

gray underparts

**IMMATURE (TAN-STRIPED FORM)**

**ADULT (WHITE-STRIPED FORM)**

fairly long tail

Common almost everywhere in eastern North America, but more localized in the West, White-throated Sparrows sing all year round. Their distinctive song can be remembered with the popular mnemonics *Oh sweet Canada Canada Canada*, or the less accurate *Old Sam Peabody*. This species has two different color forms, one with a white stripe above its eye, and the other with a tan stripe. In the nonbreeding season, large flocks roam the leaf litter of woodlands in search of food. Often the only indication of their presence is the occasional moving leaf or thin, lisping flight call.
**VOICE** Call loud, sharp *jink*; flight call lisping *tssssst!*; song clear whistle comprising 1–2 higher notes, then three triplets.
**NESTING** Cup placed on or near ground in dense shrubbery; 2–6 eggs; 1 brood; May–August.
**FEEDING** Mainly forages on the ground for seeds, fruit, insects, buds, and various grasses.

**FLIGHT:** low and direct, staying within cover whenever possible.

**DIFFERENT COLOR FORMS**
The presence of white or tan stripes on White-throated Sparrows is not related to their sex.

| SIMILAR SPECIES | |
|---|---|
| **WHITE-CROWNED SPARROW** slimmer overall; see p.359 | **GOLDEN-CROWNED SPARROW** ⬮ see p.360 |
| no yellow patch | yellowish forecrown |
| orange or pink bill | plain, grayish breast |

**OCCURRENCE**
Breeds in forests from eastern Yukon to Newfoundland, south to the Great Lakes region and northern Appalachians. Nonbreeders prefer wooded thickets and hedges. Winters across the eastern US and extreme south of the Southwest. Rare but regular along the Pacific Coast.

| Length **6½–7½in (16–17.5cm)** | Wingspan **9–10in (23–26cm)** | Weight **¹¹⁄₁₆–1¼oz (20–35g)** |
| Social **Flocks** | Lifespan **Up to 10 years** | Status **Secure** |

| DATE SEEN | WHERE | NOTES |
|---|---|---|
| | | |
| | | |
| | | |
| | | |

| Order **Passeriformes** | Family **Passerellidae** | Species *Artemisiospiza nevadensis* |

# Sagebrush Sparrow

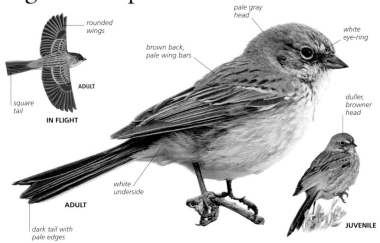

pale gray head

white eye-ring

rounded wings

brown back, pale wing bars

**ADULT**

square tail

**IN FLIGHT**

duller, browner head

white underside

**ADULT**

dark tail with pale edges

**JUVENILE**

In the dry, wide-open lands on high, rolling ground between western mountains, the Sagebrush Sparrow looks remarkably dapper. The males sing from bushtops in early mornings in spring, otherwise this long-tailed sparrow mostly sticks to the ground, foraging in and around the sagebrush with which it is so intimately associated. It mostly raises its tail clear off the ground while running between bushes. Often hard to find, these birds are more inconspicuous than rare—hiding under cover of the scrub. It forms a species pair with the nearly identical Bell's Sparrow, with which it was until recently grouped as one species, the Sage Sparrow.

**VOICE** Frequent bell-like tink call; song is a short series of low, musical, rolling notes.

**NESTING** Slender stems on or just above the ground in a shrub; 1–4 eggs, 1–3 broods, March–July.

**FEEDING** Small beetles, grasshoppers, spiders, and fallen seeds or berries from the ground.

**FLIGHT:** quick, undulating, bursts of quick wingbeats.

**SPRINGTIME PERFORMER**
This sparrow is calling for attention to itself with its repetitive territorial song in spring.

| SIMILAR SPECIES | | SUBSPECIES | |
|---|---|---|---|
|  **BLACK-THROATED SPARROW** see p.350 | stripe over eye / dark chest patch |  *A. belli* (Bell's Sparrow) / darker, plainer back | white line hooks under cheek |

**OCCURRENCE**
Rolling sagebrush steppe lands in western North America; winters in dry habitats that includes creosote and saltbush scrubs. Often found in mixed flocks with sparrows of other species.

| Length **6in (12–15cm)** | Wingspan **8½in (21cm)** | Weight **½– ¹¹/₁₆oz (15–22g)** |
| Social **Family groups/Winter flocks** | Lifespan **Up to 9 years** | Status **Secure** |

| DATE SEEN | WHERE | NOTES |
|---|---|---|
| | | |
| | | |
| | | |
| | | |
| | | |

| Order **Passeriformes** | Family **Passerellidae** | Species ***Pooecetes gramineus*** |

# Vesper Sparrow 🔊

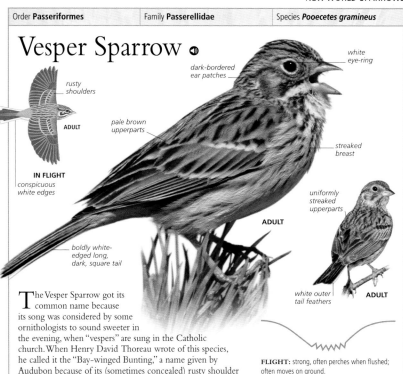

white eye-ring

dark-bordered ear patches

rusty shoulders

**ADULT**

pale brown upperparts

**IN FLIGHT**
conspicuous white edges

streaked breast

uniformly streaked upperparts

**ADULT**

boldly white-edged long, dark, square tail

white outer tail feathers  **ADULT**

The Vesper Sparrow got its common name because its song was considered by some ornithologists to sound sweeter in the evening, when "vespers" are sung in the Catholic church. When Henry David Thoreau wrote of this species, he called it the "Bay-winged Bunting," a name given by Audubon because of its (sometimes concealed) rusty shoulder patches. The Vesper Sparrow needs areas with bare ground to breed, so it is one of the few species that can successfully nest in areas of intensive agriculture; the bird's numbers seem to be declining in spite of this.

**VOICE** Full *tchup* call, flight call thin *tseent*; song consists of 2 whistles of same pitch, followed by 2 higher pitched ones, then trills, ends lazily.

**NESTING** Cup placed on patch of bare ground, against grass, bush, or rock; 3–5 eggs; 1 brood; April–August.

**FEEDING** Eats insects and seeds.

**FLIGHT:** strong, often perches when flushed; often moves on ground.

### SIMILAR SPECIES

**SAVANNAH SPARROW**
see p.365

smaller bill

**SAVANNAH SPARROW**
Eastern
see p.365

lacks white eye-ring

orange toes

**GIFTED SONGSTER**
The sweet song of the Vesper Sparrow is a characteristic sound of northern open areas.

**OCCURRENCE**
In the West, found in sagebrush, open pine woodlands, and subalpine grasslands. Occurs from the Maritimes westward to the Northwest Territories, and southward to California and Arizona. Winters in sparsely vegetated, open habitats from southern US to southwest Mexico.

| Length **6¼in (16cm)** | Wingspan **10in (25cm)** | Weight **¹¹⁄₁₆–1¹⁄₁₆oz (20–30g)** |
| Social **Flocks** | Lifespan **Up to 7 years** | Status **Declining** |

| DATE SEEN | WHERE | | NOTES |
|---|---|---|---|
| | | | |
| | | | |
| | | | |
| | | | |
| | | | |

| Order **Passeriformes** | Family **Passerellidae** | Species ***Ammospiza leconteii*** |

# LeConte's Sparrow

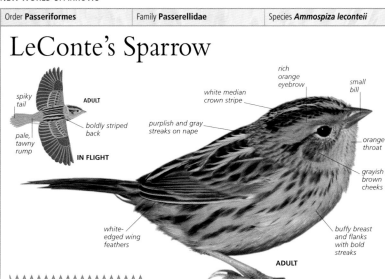

**IN FLIGHT**

spiky tail

**ADULT**

boldly striped back

pale, tawny rump

rich orange eyebrow

small bill

white median crown stripe

purplish and gray streaks on nape

orange throat

grayish brown cheeks

white-edged wing feathers

buffy breast and flanks with bold streaks

**ADULT**

**FLIGHT:** low and weak, with spiky tail pointed down; much fast flapping.

Intricately patterned in browns and buffs, LeConte's Sparrow is usually very difficult to see. Not only is it tiny—one of the smallest of all North American sparrows—but in its grassland and marsh habitats of interior North America, it darts for cover, hiding under grasses instead of flushing when disturbed. The flight call and song of this elusive little bird are remarkably insect-like. Many people who hear it believe that the unseen caller is a grasshopper. Its nest is even harder to find, making this bird a real challenge to study as well as to observe.

**VOICE** Call long, down-slurred *zheeep*; flight call similar to grasshopper; song insect-like, buzzy *tik'-uht-tizz-ZHEEEEEE-k.*

**NESTING** Concealed little cup placed on or near ground; 3–5 eggs; 1 brood; June–August.

**FEEDING** Forages on the ground and in grasses for insects, insect larvae, spiders, and seeds.

**HIDEAWAY BIRD**
LeConte's Sparrow is usually found skulking in medium-to-tall grass.

**OCCURRENCE**
Breeds in marshes, wet meadows, and bogs from the southern Yukon east to Lake Superior and western Québec. Migrants and wintering birds are found in tall grass and marshes in southwestern Kansas to southern Indiana, and from central Texas to the Carolinas.

**SIMILAR SPECIES**

**NELSON'S SPARROW** see p.463

gray nape

less streaked

**GRASSHOPPER SPARROW** see p.349

larger bill

duller overall

| Length **4½–5in (11.5–13cm)** | Wingspan **6½–7in (16–18cm)** | Weight **⁷⁄₁₆–⁹⁄₁₆oz (12–16g)** |
| Social **Solitary/Loose flocks** | Lifespan **Unknown** | Status **Secure** |

| DATE SEEN | WHERE | NOTES |
|---|---|---|
| ...................... | ...................... | ...................... |
| ...................... | ...................... | ...................... |
| ...................... | ...................... | ...................... |
| ...................... | ...................... | ...................... |
| ...................... | ...................... | ...................... |

| Order **Passeriformes** | Family **Passerellidae** | Species *Passerculus sandwichensis* |

# Savannah Sparrow 🔊

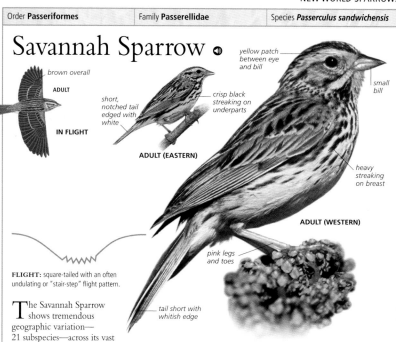

brown overall

**ADULT**

**IN FLIGHT**

short, notched tail edged with white

**ADULT (EASTERN)**

crisp black streaking on underparts

yellow patch between eye and bill

small bill

heavy streaking on breast

**ADULT (WESTERN)**

pink legs and toes

**FLIGHT:** square-tailed with an often undulating or "stair-step" flight pattern.

tail short with whitish edge

The Savannah Sparrow shows tremendous geographic variation— 21 subspecies—across its vast range, but it is always brown, with dark streaks above and white with dark streaks below. The "Large-billed Sparrow" (*P. s. rostratus* and *P. s. atratus*) breeds in Baja California, and Sonora, Mexico. The most distinct of all subspecies, these birds occur as nonbreeders near California's Salton Sea. Their distinct song consists of three buzzy trills, and their flight calls are lower and more metallic than those of other populations.

**VOICE** Call a sharp, but full *stip*; flight call a thin, weak, down-slurred *tseew*; song a *sit sit sit sit suh-EEEEE say*, from perch or in display flight with legs dangling.

**NESTING** Concealed cup of grass placed in depression on ground, protected by overhanging grass or sedges; 2–6 eggs; 1–2 broods; June–August.

**FEEDING** Forages on the ground, mostly for insects; in summer also eats seeds; in winter, berries and fruit when available; also small snails and crustaceans.

**BELDING'S SPARROW**
This darker, more heavily-streaked subspecies inhabits coastal saltmarshes in southern California.

**OCCURRENCE**
Breeds in meadows, grasslands, pastures, bushy tundra, and some cultivated land across northern North America. Also along the Pacific Coast and in Mexican interior. Nonbreeders use varied open habitats. Winters across southern US to Honduras, also Cuba, the Bahamas, and Cayman Islands.

| SIMILAR SPECIES | | |
| --- | --- | --- |

**SONG SPARROW** see p.366

larger overall

longer, rounded tail

**VESPER SPARROW** see p.363

rusty shoulder

dark tail

| Length 5½–6in (14–15cm) | Wingspan 6¾in (17cm) | Weight ½–1⅟₁₆oz (15–30g) |
| --- | --- | --- |
| Social **Solitary/Loose flocks** | Lifespan **Unknown** | Status **Secure** |

| DATE SEEN | WHERE | NOTES |
| --- | --- | --- |
| | | |
| | | |
| | | |
| | | |
| | | |

| Order **Passeriformes** | Family **Passerellidae** | Species ***Melospiza melodia*** |

# Song Sparrow 🔊

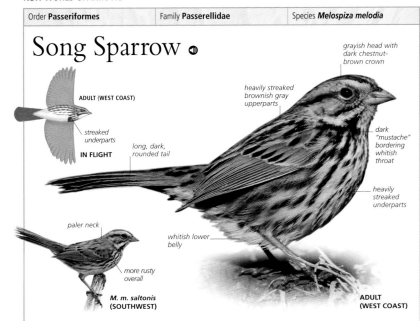

**ADULT (WEST COAST)**

*streaked underparts*

**IN FLIGHT**

*long, dark, rounded tail*

*heavily streaked brownish gray upperparts*

*grayish head with dark chestnut-brown crown*

*dark "mustache" bordering whitish throat*

*heavily streaked underparts*

*paler neck*

*whitish lower belly*

*more rusty overall*

**M. m. saltonis (SOUTHWEST)**

**ADULT (WEST COAST)**

The familiar song of this species can be heard in backyards across the continent, including in winter, although it varies both individually and geographically. In the southeastern US, where it does not breed, migrant birds start singing in early spring before departing for northern areas. The Song Sparrow may be the North American champion of geographical variation—about 40 subspecies have been described. These vary from the large, dark birds of the Aleutian Islands (*M. m. maxima*) to the smaller, paler birds of southern Arizona (*M. m. saltonis*). Eastern birds, such as *M. m. melodia*, fall between the two in size.
**VOICE** A dry *tchip* call; flight call a clear *siiiti*; song a jumble of variable whistles and trills, *deeep deeep deep-deep chrrrr tiiiiiiiiiiiii tyeeur* most common.
**NESTING** Bulky cup on or near ground, in brush or marsh vegetation; 3–5 eggs; 1–3 broods; March–August.
**FEEDING** In summer, feeds mainly on insects; in winter, eats mainly seeds, but also fruit.

**FLIGHT:** low and direct, staying within cover whenever possible.

**SIMILAR SPECIES**

**LINCOLN'S SPARROW** see p.367
*thinner black streaks*
*less rounded tail*

**SAVANNAH SPARROW** see p.365
*yellow eye-stripe*
*shorter, square tail*

**BREAST SPOT**
The Song Sparrow often sings from exposed perches, showing off its characteristic breast spot.

**OCCURRENCE**
Widespread in a range of habitats (although not in dense forests) across Canada and the US, from the Atlantic to the Pacific Coasts and north to Alaska. Some populations move south of their breeding range in winter.

| Length **5–7½in (13–19cm)** | Wingspan **8½–12in (21–31cm)** | Weight **⁷⁄₁₆–1¾oz (13–50g)** |
| Social **Solitary/Flocks** | Lifespan **Up to 9 years** | Status **Secure** |

| DATE SEEN | WHERE | NOTES |
| --- | --- | --- |
| | | |
| | | |
| | | |
| | | |

| Order **Passeriformes** | Family **Passerellidae** | Species *Melospiza lincolnii* |

# Lincoln's Sparrow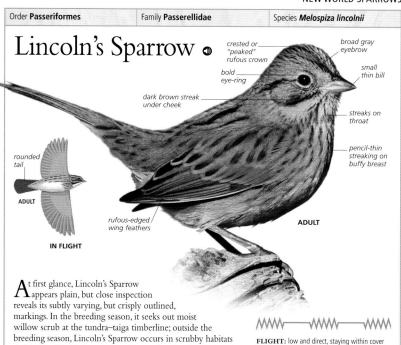

crested or "peaked" rufous crown

bold eye-ring

dark brown streak under cheek

broad gray eyebrow

small thin bill

streaks on throat

pencil-thin streaking on buffy breast

**ADULT**

rufous-edged wing feathers

rounded tail

**ADULT**

**IN FLIGHT**

At first glance, Lincoln's Sparrow appears plain, but close inspection reveals its subtly varying, but crisply outlined, markings. In the breeding season, it seeks out moist willow scrub at the tundra–taiga timberline; outside the breeding season, Lincoln's Sparrow occurs in scrubby habitats right across North America. It will occasionally visit backyard feeders in winter, but it is generally secretive and stays within fairly dense cover. Lincoln's Sparrow's rich, musical song is unmistakable, and it varies remarkably little from region to region. Audubon named this species in 1834 in honor of his collector Thomas Lincoln.

**VOICE** Call a variable, loud *tchip*, flight call a rolling *ziiiit*; song series of rich, musical trills, *ju-ju-ju dododoo didididi whrrrrr*.

**NESTING** Grass cup, lined with fine grass, and hidden in depression in ground under overhanging sedges or grasses; 3–5 eggs; 1 brood; June–August.

**FEEDING** Mainly seeds in winter; in summer, mostly insects, such as beetles, mosquitoes, and moths.

**FLIGHT:** low and direct, staying within cover whenever possible.

**RAISE THE ALARM**
When disturbed, Lincoln's Sparrow often raises its central crown feathers, which form a crest.

### SIMILAR SPECIES

**SONG SPARROW**
see p.366
larger overall

more coarse streaking

**SAVANNAH SPARROW**
see p.365

yellow stripe above eye

short, square, notched tail

**OCCURRENCE**
Breeds in muskeg and wet thickets across northern North America, also south into the western ranges of California and Arizona. Migrants and wintering birds use a variety of scrubby habitats. Winters in southern US (and farther south), and on Pacific Coast north to British Columbia.

| Length **5¼–6in (13.5–15cm)** | Wingspan **7½–8½in (19–22cm)** | Weight **½–⅞oz (15–25g)** |
| Social **Solitary/Small flocks** | Lifespan **Up to 7 years** | Status **Secure** |

| DATE SEEN | WHERE | NOTES |
| --- | --- | --- |
| | | |
| | | |
| | | |
| | | |

| Order **Passeriformes** | Family **Passerellidae** | Species ***Melospiza georgiana*** |
|---|---|---|

# Swamp Sparrow 🔊

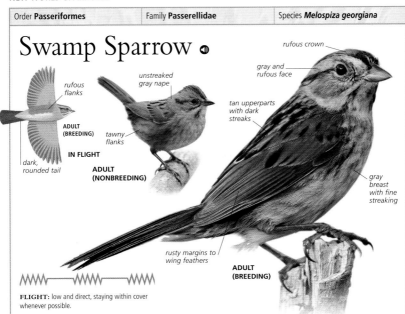

rufous crown

gray and rufous face

tan upperparts with dark streaks

rufous flanks

**ADULT (BREEDING)**

unstreaked gray nape

tawny flanks

**IN FLIGHT**

dark, rounded tail

**ADULT (NONBREEDING)**

gray breast with fine streaking

rusty margins to wing feathers

**ADULT (BREEDING)**

MMMM    MMMM    MMMM

**FLIGHT:** low and direct, staying within cover whenever possible.

The Swamp Sparrow is a common breeder in wet habitats across eastern North America and Canada west to the southern Yukon and eastern British Columbia. It is abundant in its preferred habitat of tall reed and cattail marshes. A somewhat skittish bird, the Swamp Sparrow is often seen darting rapidly into cover, but usually repays the patient observer with a reappearance, giving its characteristic *chimp* call. Though often confused with both the Song Sparrow and Lincoln's Sparrow, the Swamp Sparrow never shows more than a very faint, blurry streaking on its gray breast, and sports conspicuous rusty-edged wing feathers. Its song is also quite different.

**VOICE** Call a slightly nasal, forceful *chimp*, flight call a high, buzzy *ziiiiii*; song a slow, monotonous, loose trill of chirps.

**NESTING** Bulky cup of dry plants placed 1–4ft (30–120cm) above water in marsh vegetation; 3–5 eggs; 1–2 broods; May–July.

**FEEDING** Mostly insects in the breeding season, especially grasshoppers; seeds in winter; occasionally fruit.

**HIGH PERCH**
This male Swamp Sparrow is checking his territory from atop a seeding cattail flower.

**OCCURRENCE**
Breeds in marshes, cedar bogs, damp meadows, and wet hayfields, from the Yukon east to Newfoundland and south to Nebraska and the Delmarva Peninsula; winters in marshes in eastern US and south through Mexico; rare but regular along Pacific Coast.

**SIMILAR SPECIES**

**SONG SPARROW**
see p.366
brown tail
brown wings
streaked breast

**LINCOLN'S SPARROW**
see p.367
less red overall
fine breast streaks

| Length **5–6in (12.5–15cm)** | Wingspan **7–7½in (18–19cm)** | Weight **½–⅞oz (15–25g)** |
|---|---|---|
| Social **Solitary/Small flocks** | Lifespan **Up to 6 years** | Status **Secure** |

| DATE SEEN | WHERE | NOTES |
|---|---|---|
| | | |
| | | |
| | | |
| | | |
| | | |

| Order **Passeriformes** | Family **Passerellidae** | Species *Melozone fusca* |

# Canyon Towhee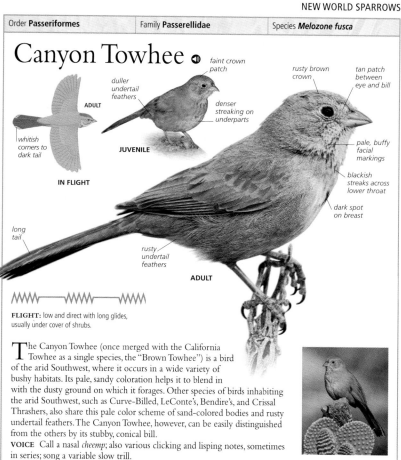

faint crown patch

duller undertail feathers

**ADULT**

denser streaking on underparts

**JUVENILE**

whitish corners to dark tail

**IN FLIGHT**

rusty brown crown

tan patch between eye and bill

pale, buffy facial markings

blackish streaks across lower throat

dark spot on breast

long tail

rusty undertail feathers

**ADULT**

**FLIGHT:** low and direct with long glides, usually under cover of shrubs.

The Canyon Towhee (once merged with the California Towhee as a single species, the "Brown Towhee") is a bird of the arid Southwest, where it occurs in a wide variety of bushy habitats. Its pale, sandy coloration helps it to blend in with the dusty ground on which it forages. Other species of birds inhabiting the arid Southwest, such as Curve-Billed, LeConte's, Bendire's, and Crissal Thrashers, also share this pale color scheme of sand-colored bodies and rusty undertail feathers. The Canyon Towhee, however, can be easily distinguished from the others by its stubby, conical bill.

**VOICE** Call a nasal *cheemp*; also various clicking and lisping notes, sometimes in series; song a variable slow trill.

**NESTING** Cup placed at about eye-level close to, or against trunk of tree or bush; 2–5 eggs; 1–2 broods; February–October.

**FEEDING** Forages on the ground for insects and seeds.

**DESERT LOVER**
The Canyon Towhee likes to perch high to survey its territory.

**OCCURRENCE**
Lives in a variety of habitats, including rocky hillside scrub, desert grasslands, and suburban areas from west Arizona, southeast Colorado, and central Texas to central Mexico. Largely resident, but some birds undertake local movements.

### SIMILAR SPECIES

**CALIFORNIA TOWHEE**
see p.464
darker overall

**ABERT'S TOWHEE**
see p.463
darker face
no central breast spot
unstreaked underparts

black mask
pale bill

| Length **8½in (21cm)** | Wingspan **11½in (29cm)** | Weight **1¼–1¾oz (35–50g)** |
| Social **Solitary/Small flocks** | Lifespan **Up to 7 years** | Status **Secure** |

| DATE SEEN | WHERE | NOTES |
|---|---|---|
| | | |
| | | |
| | | |
| | | |
| | | |

| Order **Passeriformes** | Family **Passerellidae** | Species *Aimophila ruficeps* |

# Rufous-crowned Sparrow

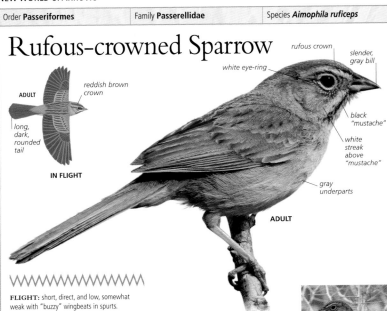

rufous crown

slender, gray bill

white eye-ring

reddish brown crown

**ADULT**

long, dark, rounded tail

**IN FLIGHT**

black "mustache"

white streak above "mustache"

gray underparts

**ADULT**

**FLIGHT:** short, direct, and low, somewhat weak with "buzzy" wingbeats in spurts.

This sparrow is a common resident of dry canyons and sparsely wooded hillsides in the southwestern US, locally up to 5,000ft (1,500m). The Rufous-crowned Sparrow is a real skulker, running and hiding at the first sign of danger. For this reason, it is often first detected by its characteristic *deeer* call note, which it gives sometimes in a laughter-like series. The Rufous-crowned Sparrow is quite similar to the rarer Rufous-winged Sparrow, but they have very different calls and live in separate habitats. Rufous-winged Sparrows live in flat desert.

**VOICE** Call a low, nasal *deeer*; song a jumble of chattering notes.

**NESTING** Cup of twigs and grass placed in bush or rocks on or near ground; 2–5 eggs; 1–3 broods; March–September.

**FEEDING** Forages on ground and in shrubs for seeds, insects, and insect larvae.

**BOLD MARKINGS**
This bird's bold white eye-ring and black "mustache" are good field marks.

**CATCHING A GLIMPSE**
Occasionally, this skulking bird will hop up to a perch to look at its surroundings.

**OCCURRENCE**
Resides in arid scrub and low trees on hillsides and in canyons in California, Colorado, Utah, Arizona, New Mexico, Oklahoma, Texas, and Arkansas; also in Mexico (Baja California, on mainland to Isthmus of Tehuantepec). In Mexico found in oak pine woodlands.

**SIMILAR SPECIES**

**CHIPPING SPARROW**
see p.353

black eye-line

notched tail

**RUFOUS-WINGED SPARROW**
see p.461

two-toned bill

rufous shoulder patch

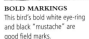

| Length **6in (15cm)** | Wingspan **7½in (19cm)** | Weight **½–⅞oz (15–25g)** |
| Social **Solitary** | Lifespan **Unknown** | Status **Secure** |

| DATE SEEN | WHERE | NOTES |
| --- | --- | --- |
| | | |
| | | |
| | | |
| | | |
| | | |

| Order **Passeriformes** | Family **Passerellidae** | Species *Pipilo chlorurus* |

# Green-tailed Towhee 🔊

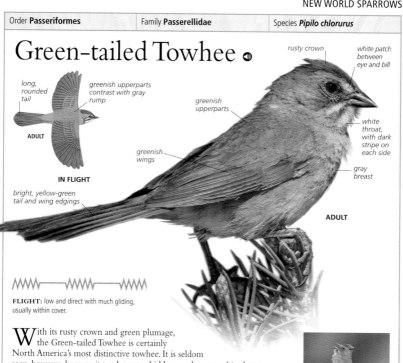

rusty crown

white patch between eye and bill

long, rounded tail

greenish upperparts contrast with gray rump

greenish upperparts

**ADULT**

white throat, with dark stripe on each side

gray breast

greenish wings

**IN FLIGHT**

bright, yellow-green tail and wing edgings

**ADULT**

**FLIGHT:** low and direct with much gliding, usually within cover.

With its rusty crown and green plumage, the Green-tailed Towhee is certainly North America's most distinctive towhee. It is seldom seen, however, because it tends to stay hidden on the ground in dense cover, both in the breeding season and in winter, although in that season, Green-tailed Towhees come out to feed on seeds on deserted, dusty roads. But generally you are more likely to hear this bird scratching about in the undergrowth than see it. Although the Olive Sparrow is superficially similar, the two seldom overlap in range or habitat.

**VOICE** Call a nasal mewing, rapid chips in excitement; flight call a high *tzhreeee*; song a slurred whistle followed by 1–2 trills.

**NESTING** Bulky cup of twigs and grasses placed on or near ground at base of sagebrush; 3–4 eggs; 1–2 broods; May–July.

**FEEDING** Forages under cover, often by "double-scratching" with both feet at the same time, for insects, insect larvae, seeds, and some fruit.

**WHERE TO SEE IT**
Finding a single male atop a bush or tree may be the easiest way to see this bird.

**OCCURRENCE**
Breeds in a variety of habitats, including chaparral, shrubby hillsides, sagebrush flats, and high-elevation creeks, in much of the western US and northern Baja California. Winters in desert thickets and shallow ravines from the US–Mexican border region southward to central Mexico.

**SIMILAR SPECIES**

**CHIPPING SPARROW**
see p.353

white wing bars

much smaller overall

**OLIVE SPARROW**
see p.462

smaller overall

no rufous on crown

lacks bold throat markings

| Length **7¼in (18.5cm)** | Wingspan **9½in (24cm)** | Weight **¹¹⁄₁₆–1¼oz (20–35g)** |
| Social **Solitary/Small flocks** | Lifespan **Up to 8 years** | Status **Secure** |

| DATE SEEN | WHERE | | NOTES |
|---|---|---|---|
| | | | |
| | | | |
| | | | |
| | | | |
| | | | |

| Order **Passeriformes** | Family **Passerellidae** | Species **Pipilo maculatus** |
|---|---|---|

# Spotted Towhee 🔊

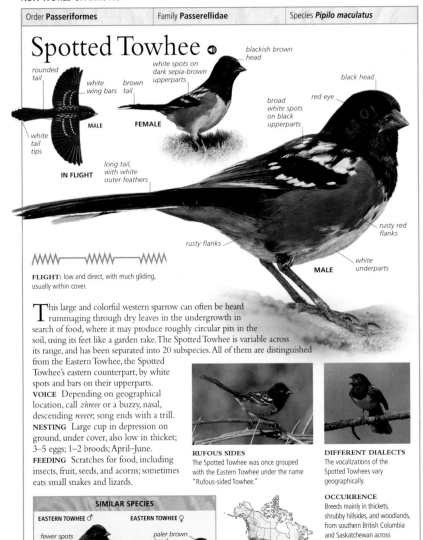

rounded tail

white wing bars

brown tail

**MALE**

white tail tips

**IN FLIGHT**

long tail, with white outer feathers

white spots on dark sepia-brown upperparts

**FEMALE**

blackish brown head

broad white spots on black upperparts

black head

red eye

rusty red flanks

rusty flanks

white underparts

**MALE**

**FLIGHT:** low and direct, with much gliding, usually within cover.

This large and colorful western sparrow can often be heard rummaging through dry leaves in the undergrowth in search of food, where it may produce roughly circular pits in the soil, using its feet like a garden rake. The Spotted Towhee is variable across its range, and has been separated into 20 subspecies. All of them are distinguished from the Eastern Towhee, the Spotted Towhee's eastern counterpart, by white spots and bars on their upperparts.

**VOICE** Depending on geographical location, call *zhreee* or a buzzy, nasal, descending *reeeer*; song ends with a trill.

**NESTING** Large cup in depression on ground, under cover, also low in thicket; 3–5 eggs; 1–2 broods; April–June.

**FEEDING** Scratches for food, including insects, fruit, seeds, and acorns; sometimes eats small snakes and lizards.

**RUFOUS SIDES**
The Spotted Towhee was once grouped with the Eastern Towhee under the name "Rufous-sided Towhee."

**DIFFERENT DIALECTS**
The vocalizations of the Spotted Towhees vary geographically.

**OCCURRENCE**
Breeds mainly in thickets, shrubby hillsides, and woodlands, from southern British Columbia and Saskatchewan across the western US, southward to southern Oaxaca, Mexico, but occurs in dense forests in coastal British Columbia. Winters in the south-central US and western Midwest.

**SIMILAR SPECIES**

**EASTERN TOWHEE ♂**

fewer spots on wing

no white spots on shoulder

**EASTERN TOWHEE ♀**

paler brown head

paler rusty flanks

| Length **8in (20cm)** | Wingspan **10½in (27cm)** | Weight **1¼–1⁹⁄₁₆oz (35–45g)** |
|---|---|---|
| Social **Solitary/Small flocks** | Lifespan **Up to 11 years** | Status **Secure** |

| DATE SEEN | WHERE | NOTES |
|---|---|---|
| | | |
| | | |
| | | |
| | | |
| | | |

# ORIOLES AND BLACKBIRDS

THE ICTERIDS EXEMPLIFY the wonderful diversity that exists among birds. Most members are common and widespread, occurring from coast to coast. They are present in nearly every habitat in North America, from the arid Southwest and Florida to the boreal forest zone in the North but do not live in the tundra. The species reveal a tremendous variety in color, nesting, and social behavior—from solitary orioles to vast colonies of blackbirds. One group of icterids, the cowbirds, are obligatory brood parasites, and make no nest, but lay their eggs in the nests of other species, mostly small songbirds.

## ORIOLES

Orioles are generally recognized by their contrasting black and orange plumage, although some species tend more toward yellow or chestnut shades. They are common tropical to subtropical seasonal migrants to North America, and their intricate hanging nests are an impressive combination of engineering and weaving. Most oriole species have a loud and melodious song and show tolerance of humans, a combination that makes them popular throughout their range. The Orchard Oriole and the Baltimore Oriole are widespread in the East, but the other North American species live either in the West, the Southwest, or in southern Texas. The Eastern North American orioles spend the winter in tropical America.

## COWBIRDS

These strictly parasitic birds have been known to lay eggs in the nests of nearly 300 different bird species in North and South America. The males of all three North American species are readily identified by their thick bills and dark, iridescent plumage. The females and immatures, however, are drab, brownish, or blackish birds. The eastern species, the Brown-headed Cowbird, has dramatically increased in recent years.

**SUBTLE BRILLIANCE**
Although its plumage is dark, the Common Grackle displays a beautiful iridescence.

## BLACKBIRDS & GRACKLES

This group of birds is largely covered with dark feathers, and has a streamlined appearance because of long, pointed bills and tails. Not as brilliantly colored as some of the other icterids, these are among the most numerous birds on the continent. After the breeding season they gather in huge flocks and form an impressive sight.

**BIG VOICE**
A Meadowlark's melodious voice is a defining feature in many rural landscapes.

## MEADOWLARKS

Meadowlarks occur in both North and South America. The North American species have yellow breasts; the South American species have bright red ones. Only one species breeds in the East. It can be distinguished from its western counterpart by its song.

**NECTAR LOVER**
The magnificently colored Baltimore Oriole inserts its bill into the base of a flower, taking the nectar but playing no part in pollination. Baltimore Orioles are rare in the West.

| Order **Passeriformes** | Family **Icteriidae** | Species *Icteria virens* |
|---|---|---|

# Yellow-breasted Chat

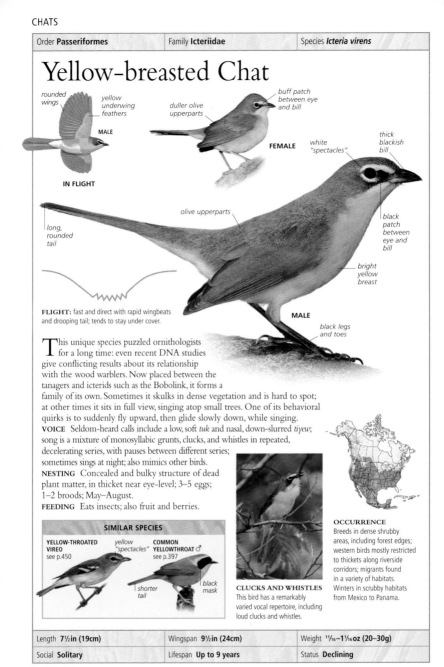

rounded wings

yellow underwing feathers

**MALE**

duller olive upperparts

buff patch between eye and bill

**FEMALE**

white "spectacles"

thick blackish bill

**IN FLIGHT**

olive upperparts

long, rounded tail

black patch between eye and bill

bright yellow breast

**FLIGHT:** fast and direct with rapid wingbeats and drooping tail; tends to stay under cover.

**MALE**

black legs and toes

This unique species puzzled ornithologists for a long time: even recent DNA studies give conflicting results about its relationship with the wood warblers. Now placed between the tangers and icterids such as the Bobolink, it forms a family of its own. Sometimes it skulks in dense vegetation and is hard to spot; at other times it sits in full view, singing atop small trees. One of its behavioral quirks is to suddenly fly upward, then glide slowly down, while singing.

**VOICE** Seldom-heard calls include a low, soft *tuk* and nasal, down-slurred *tiyew*; song is a mixture of monosyllabic grunts, clucks, and whistles in repeated, decelerating series, with pauses between different series; sometimes sings at night; also mimics other birds.

**NESTING** Concealed and bulky structure of dead plant matter, in thicket near eye-level; 3–5 eggs; 1–2 broods; May–August.

**FEEDING** Eats insects; also fruit and berries.

**CLUCKS AND WHISTLES** This bird has a remarkably varied vocal repertoire, including loud clucks and whistles.

**OCCURRENCE** Breeds in dense shrubby areas, including forest edges; western birds mostly restricted to thickets along riverside corridors; migrants found in a variety of habitats. Winters in scrubby habitats from Mexico to Panama.

### SIMILAR SPECIES

**YELLOW-THROATED VIREO** see p.450

yellow "spectacles"

shorter tail

**COMMON YELLOWTHROAT** ♂ see p.397

black mask

| Length **7½in (19cm)** | Wingspan **9½in (24cm)** | Weight **¹¹⁄₁₆–1¹⁄₁₆oz (20–30g)** |
|---|---|---|
| Social **Solitary** | Lifespan **Up to 9 years** | Status **Declining** |

| DATE SEEN | WHERE | NOTES |
|---|---|---|
| ...................... | ............................ | ................................................ |
| ...................... | ............................ | ................................................ |
| ...................... | ............................ | ................................................ |
| ...................... | ............................ | ................................................ |
| ...................... | ............................ | ................................................ |

| Order **Passeriformes** | Family **Icteridae** | Species *Xanthocephalus xanthocephalus* |

# Yellow-headed Blackbird 🔊

**MALE**

yellow head

conspicuous white wing patches

**IN FLIGHT**

black, conical bill

black mask and crown on yellow head

**JUVENILE MALE**

bright yellow head and chest

brownish overall

yellowish throat and facial patch

black overall

white wing patch

**MALE**

**FEMALE**

**FLIGHT:** direct with shallow rise and fall pattern; flaps and glides.

long tail

The male Yellow-headed Blackbird is unmistakable, with its conspicuous bright yellow head. Females, however, are more drab. Populations of this species fluctuate widely, in number but locally, depending on rainfall, which controls the availability and quality of its breeding marshland habitat. In some wetlands, the Yellow-headed Blackbird can be extremely abundant, and is easily noticed because of its amazing song, which once heard, can never be forgotten.

**VOICE** Call a nasal *whaah*; song a series of harsh, cackling noises, followed by a brief pause, and a high, long, wailing trill.

**NESTING** Cup of plant strips woven into standing aquatic vegetation; 3–4 eggs; 1 brood; May–June.

**FEEDING** Eats insects while breeding; agricultural grains and grass seeds in winter.

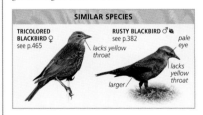

**SIMILAR SPECIES**

TRICOLORED BLACKBIRD ♀
see p.465

lacks yellow throat

RUSTY BLACKBIRD ♂
see p.382

pale eye

lacks yellow throat

larger

**YELLOW GARLAND**
Five evenly spaced Yellow-headed males watch over their wetland habitat from a twig.

**OCCURRENCE**
Widely distributed in western Canada and the central and western US, this species breeds in marshes with cattail and bullrush vegetation, and also, locally, in wetlands within wooded areas. Winters in Mexico; resident in Baja California.

| Length **8½–10½in (21–27cm)** | Wingspan **15in (38cm)** | Weight **2⅛–3½oz (60–100g)** |
| Social **Flocks/Colonies** | Lifespan **Up to 9 years** | Status **Localized** |

| DATE SEEN | WHERE | NOTES |
| --- | --- | --- |
| | | |
| | | |
| | | |
| | | |
| | | |

| Order **Passeriformes** | Family **Icteridae** | Species **Dolichonyx oryzivorus** |

# Bobolink

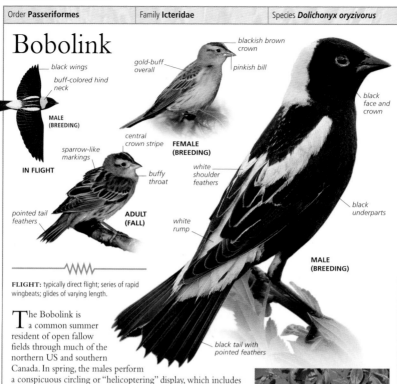

black wings

buff-colored hind neck

**MALE (BREEDING)**

**IN FLIGHT**

blackish brown crown

gold-buff overall

pinkish bill

**FEMALE (BREEDING)**

central crown stripe

sparrow-like markings

buffy throat

**ADULT (FALL)**

pointed tail feathers

black face and crown

white shoulder feathers

white rump

black underparts

**MALE (BREEDING)**

black tail with pointed feathers

**FLIGHT:** typically direct flight; series of rapid wingbeats; glides of varying length.

The Bobolink is a common summer resident of open fallow fields through much of the northern US and southern Canada. In spring, the males perform a conspicuous circling or "helicoptering" display, which includes singing, to establish territory and to attract females. Bobolink populations have declined on its breeding grounds and in wintering areas because of habitat loss and changing agricultural practices.

**VOICE** Calls like the end of its name *link*; song a long, complex babbling series of musical notes varying in length and pitch.

**NESTING** Woven cup of grass close to or on the ground, well hidden in tall grass; 3–7 eggs; 1 brood; May–July.

**FEEDING** Feeds mostly on insects, spiders, grubs in breeding season, but seasonally variable; also cereal grains and grass seeds.

**TAKING A BREAK**
This male has fled the sun of the open fields to seek shelter in the shade of a tree.

## SIMILAR SPECIES

**RED-WINGED BLACKBIRD** see p.380
red shoulder patches

lacks buff-colored hind neck

larger overall

**LARK BUNTING** see p.352
lacks buff-colored hind neck

white wing patches

larger

**OCCURRENCE**
Breeds in open fields with a mixture of tall grasses and other herbaceous vegetation, especially old hayfields. In Canada from British Columbia to the Atlantic Coast; in the US from Idaho to New England. Migrates through the southern US and the Caribbean; winters in northern South America.

| Length **6–8in (15–20cm)** | Wingspan **10–12in (25–30cm)** | Weight **1¹⁄₁₆–2oz (30–55g)** |
| Social **Winter flocks** | Lifespan **Up to 10 years** | Status **Declining** |

| DATE SEEN | WHERE | NOTES |
| --- | --- | --- |
| | | |
| | | |
| | | |
| | | |
| | | |

| Order **Passeriformes** | Family **Icteridae** | Species *Sturnella neglecta* |

# Western Meadowlark

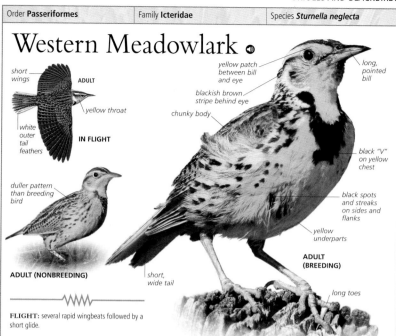

short wings

**ADULT**

yellow throat

white outer tail feathers

**IN FLIGHT**

yellow patch between bill and eye

blackish brown stripe behind eye

chunky body

long, pointed bill

black "V" on yellow chest

black spots and streaks on sides and flanks

yellow underparts

**ADULT (BREEDING)**

duller pattern than breeding bird

**ADULT (NONBREEDING)**

short, wide tail

long toes

**FLIGHT:** several rapid wingbeats followed by a short glide.

The Western Meadowlark is one of the most abundant and widespread grassland birds in North America. It inhabits open country in the western Great Plains, the Great Basin, and the Central Valley of California. It is frequently encountered along roadsides, singing its melodious song from atop a fencepost or utility pole. Although the range of the Western Meadowlark overlaps widely with that of its Eastern counterpart, hybrids between the two species are very rare and usually sterile.

**VOICE** Series of complex, bubbling, whistled notes descending in pitch.
**NESTING** Domed grass cup, well hidden in tall grasses; 3–7 eggs; 1 brood; March–August.
**FEEDING** Feeds mostly on insects, including beetles, grubs, and grasshoppers; also grains and grass seeds.

**A SHRUB WILL DO**
In spring and summer male Western Meadowlarks can be seen perching on shrubs to sing.

**OCCURRENCE**
Common in western North America, across much of southern Canada and the western US, south to Mexico. Breeds primarily in open grassy plains, but also uses agricultural fields with overgrown edges and hayfields. Partial migrant in US, winters south to Mexico.

**SIMILAR SPECIES**

**AMERICAN PIPIT**
see p.331

shorter bill

lacks yellow chest and black necklace

**EASTERN MEADOWLARK**

less yellow at corner of bill

slightly darker overall

| Length **7–10in (18–26cm)** | Wingspan **13–15in (33–38cm)** | Weight **2⅞–4oz (80–125g)** |
| Social **Pairs/Winter flocks** | Lifespan **Up to 10 years** | Status **Secure** |

| DATE SEEN | WHERE | NOTES |
|---|---|---|
| | | |
| | | |
| | | |
| | | |

| Order **Passeriformes** | Family **Icteridae** | Species *Icterus bullockii* |

# Bullock's Oriole 🔊

black eye stripe

black cap
and nape

orange
face

black
bib

large white
wing patch

**MALE**

black back
and wings

conspicuous
white wing
patch

pale yellow
underparts
**MALE (1ST FALL)**

**IN FLIGHT**

yellow face,
throat, and
breast

olive-brown
back and wings

olive
tail

orange
underparts

**MALE**

buffy gray
belly and
rump

**FEMALE**

black tail
with orange
outer
feathers

gray legs
and toes

Bullock's Oriole is the western counterpart of the Baltimore in both behavior and habitat. The two were considered to belong to a single species, the Northern Oriole (*I. galbula*), because they interbreed where they overlap in the Great Plains. Recent studies, however, suggest that they are separate species. Unlike many other orioles, Bullock's is more resistant to brood parasites and removes cowbird eggs from its nest.

**VOICE** Varied string of one- and two-part notes often mumbled or slurred at the end; similar to, but less melodious, than the Baltimore Oriole's song.

**NESTING** Hanging basket of woven plant strips located at the tips of branches; 4–5 eggs; 1 brood; March–June.

**FEEDING** Forages for insects, in particular grasshoppers and caterpillars, but also ants, beetles, and spiders; nectar and fruit when available.

**FLIGHT:** full, powerful wingbeats, resulting in a "heavier" flight aspect than similar species.

**OCCURRENCE**
Found in the western US; breeds commonly in riverside woodlands with willows and cottonwoods; also mixed hardwood forests, mesquite woodland, and groves of fruit trees. After breeding, Bullock's Orioles migrate southward and spend the winter from Mexico to Nicaragua.

### SIMILAR SPECIES

**HOODED ORIOLE**
see p.465

orange
head

long, slender
black tail

**BALTIMORE ORIOLE**
see p.465

black hood

black face

less white
in wings

**OBLIVIOUS TO THORNS**
This male Bullock's Oriole perches on a branch with long thorns, but it is not perturbed.

| Length 6½–7½in (16–19cm) | Wingspan 10–12in (25–30cm) | Weight 1¹⁄₁₆–1⁹⁄₁₆oz (30–45g) |
| Social **Pairs/Flocks** | Lifespan **Up to 8 years** | Status **Secure** |

| DATE SEEN | WHERE | NOTES |
| --- | --- | --- |
| | | |
| | | |
| | | |
| | | |

| Order **Passeriformes** | Family **Icteridae** | Species **Icterus parisorum** |

# Scott's Oriole

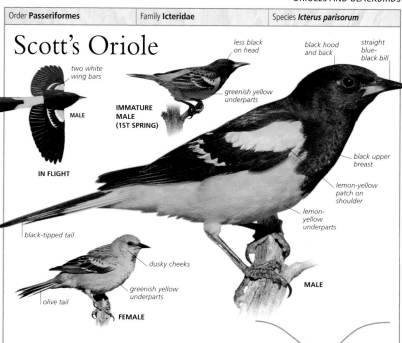

two white wing bars

**MALE**

**IN FLIGHT**

less black on head

**IMMATURE MALE (1ST SPRING)**

greenish yellow underparts

black hood and back

straight blue-black bill

black upper breast

lemon-yellow patch on shoulder

lemon-yellow underparts

black-tipped tail

dusky cheeks

greenish yellow underparts

olive tail

**FEMALE**

**MALE**

Scott's Oriole's Latin species name, *parisorum*, was coined by Prince Charles Bonaparte in 1838 for the Paris brothers, two French natural history specimen dealers. This oriole's bright yellow plumage is unusual among North American orioles, most of which are varying degrees of orange. It lives in semiarid and rocky slopes, a fact that is largely responsible for its colloquial names of "Desert" or "Mountain" Oriole. The species is often associated with yuccas, as it forages on yucca plants and uses fibers from their leaves to build its nest.

**VOICE** Call a sharp *chek*; song a musical series of loud whistles *tew-tew-treew*.
**NESTING** Shallow cup woven from thin plant strips, often yucca, hung from leaves or branches; 3–5 eggs; 1–2 broods; March–July.
**FEEDING** Eats insects, adults and larvae, such as flies, wasps, and beetles; feeds on nectar and fruit where available; visits feeders.

**FLIGHT:** quick wingbeats; more bouncing between flapping than other orioles.

**SIMILAR SPECIES**

**ORCHARD ORIOLE ♂** see p.464

olive upperparts

**AUDUBON'S ORIOLE**

greenish yellow back

black hood

all-black tail

**YUCCA LOVER** Found in all kinds of arid scrubland—yuccas are a favorite of Scott's Orioles.

**OCCURRENCE** Breeds in mid-elevation, semiarid open scrub on level ground or slopes with oak scrub, piñon pine, and yucca. Winters in pine oak scrub valleys of central Mexico. Individuals wander widely and have been reported as far away from their usual habitat as New York City.

| Length **8–9in (20–23cm)** | Wingspan **11–13in (28–33cm)** | Weight **1⅜oz (40g)** |
| Social **Pairs/Family groups** | Lifespan **Up to 6 years** | Status **Secure** |

| DATE SEEN | WHERE | | NOTES |
|---|---|---|---|
| | | | |
| | | | |
| | | | |
| | | | |
| | | | |

| Order **Passeriformes** | Family **Icteridae** | Species ***Agelaius phoeniceus*** |
|---|---|---|

# Red-winged Blackbird

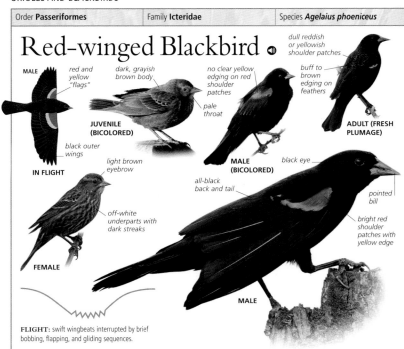

**MALE** red and yellow "flags"

dark, grayish brown body

no clear yellow edging on red shoulder patches

pale throat

dull reddish or yellowish shoulder patches

buff to brown edging on feathers

**JUVENILE (BICOLORED)**

**ADULT (FRESH PLUMAGE)**

black outer wings

**IN FLIGHT**

light brown eyebrow

**MALE (BICOLORED)**

black eye

all-black back and tail

pointed bill

off-white underparts with dark streaks

bright red shoulder patches with yellow edge

**FEMALE**

**MALE**

**FLIGHT:** swift wingbeats interrupted by brief bobbing, flapping, and gliding sequences.

One of the most abundant native bird species in North America, the Red-winged Blackbird is also one of the most conspicuous in wetland habitats. The sight and sound of males singing from the tops of cattails is a sure sign that spring is near. This adaptable species migrates and roosts in flocks that may number in the millions. There are 22 subspecies, one of the most distinctive being the "Bicolored" Blackbird (*A. p. gubernator*) from Mexico.

**VOICE** Various brusk *chek*, *chit*, or *chet* calls; male song a *kronk-a-rhee* with a characteristic nasal, rolling and metallic "undulating" ending.

**NESTING** Cup of grasses and mud woven into dense standing reeds or cattails; 3–4 eggs; 1–2 broods; March–June.

**FEEDING** Forages for seeds and grains; largely insects when breeding.

**DENSE FLOCKS**
The huge flocks of Red-winged Blackbirds seen in the fall and during migration are an amazing sight.

### SIMILAR SPECIES

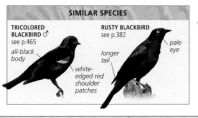

**TRICOLORED BLACKBIRD** ♂
see p.465

all-black body

white-edged red shoulder patches

**RUSTY BLACKBIRD**
see p.382

longer tail

pale eye

**OCCURRENCE**
Widespread across Canada and the US from Alaska to the Maritimes, and south to Mexico, Central America, and the Bahamas. Lives in wetlands, especially freshwater marshes with cattails, and also saltwater; wet meadows with tall grass and open woodlands with reeds. Migrates south in winter.

| Length **7–10in (18–25cm)** | Wingspan **11–14in (28–35cm)** | Weight **1⁹⁄₁₆–2½oz (45–70g)** |
|---|---|---|
| Social **Flocks** | Lifespan **At least 14 years** | Status **Secure** |

| DATE SEEN | WHERE | NOTES |
|---|---|---|
| | | |
| | | |
| | | |
| | | |
| | | |

| Order **Passeriformes** | Family **Icteridae** | Species *Molothrus ater* |

# Brown-headed Cowbird 🔊

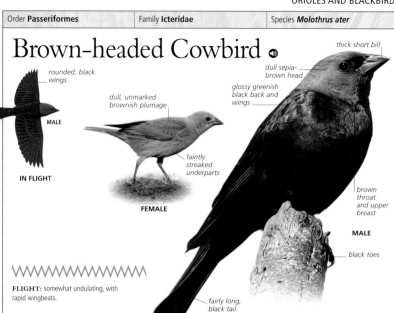

*rounded, black wings*

**MALE**

*dull, unmarked brownish plumage*

**IN FLIGHT**

*faintly streaked underparts*

**FEMALE**

*thick short bill*

*dull sepia-brown head*

*glossy greenish black back and wings*

*brown throat and upper breast*

**MALE**

*black toes*

**FLIGHT:** somewhat undulating, with rapid wingbeats.

*fairly long, black tail*

Nouth America's most common brood parasite, the Brown-headed Cowbird was once a bird of the Great Plains, following the vast herds of bison to feed on insects kicked up by their hooves. Now, most likely the result of forest clearance and suburban development, it is found continent-wide and north to the Yukon and Canada. It has become a serious threat to the breeding success of North American songbirds. It lays its eggs in the nests of more than 220 different species, and its young are raised to fledglings by more than 140 species, including the highly endangered Kirtland's Warbler.

**VOICE** High-pitched, squeaky whistles and bubbling notes, *dub-dub-come-tzeee*; also various clucks and *cheks*.

**NESTING** No nest, lays eggs in nests of other species; a female may lay an astounding 25–55 (or more) eggs per season; April–August.

**FEEDING** Primarily eats grass seeds and cereal grains, but also insects when available, especially grasshoppers and beetles.

**AT A FEEDER**
A female Brown-headed Cowbird enjoys a snack of seeds at a suburban feeder.

### SIMILAR SPECIES

**BRONZED COWBIRD ♂**
see p.465

*red eye*

*glossy blue-black wings and tail*

*longer, thicker bill*

**SHINY COWBIRD ♂**

*glossy purplish black*

*thinner, more pointed bill*

**OCCURRENCE**
Favors habitats modified by human activity, such as open wooded patches, low grass fields, fruit orchards, agricultural pastures with livestock, suburban gardens and areas. Widespread across North America except in Alaska and northern Canada. Western birds migrate south to Mexico.

| Length **6–8in (15–20cm)** | Wingspan **11–13in (28–33cm)** | Weight **1⁷⁄₁₆–1¾oz (40–50g)** |
| Social **Large flocks** | Lifespan **Up to 16 years** | Status **Secure** |

| DATE SEEN | WHERE | NOTES |
|---|---|---|
| | | |
| | | |
| | | |
| | | |
| | | |

| Order **Passeriformes** | Family **Icteridae** | Species **Euphagus carolinus** |
|---|---|---|

# Rusty Blackbird 🔊

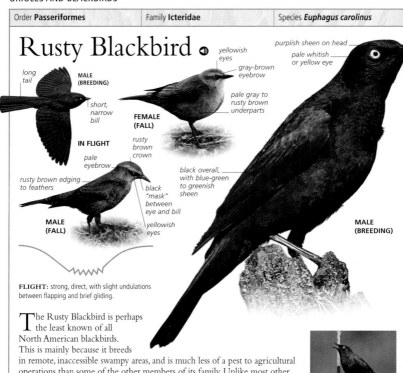

**MALE (BREEDING)**

long tail

short, narrow bill

**IN FLIGHT**

pale eyebrow

yellowish eyes

gray-brown eyebrow

**FEMALE (FALL)**

pale gray to rusty brown underparts

rusty brown crown

rusty brown edging to feathers

**MALE (FALL)**

black "mask" between eye and bill

yellowish eyes

black overall, with blue-green to greenish sheen

purplish sheen on head

pale whitish or yellow eye

**MALE (BREEDING)**

**FLIGHT:** strong, direct, with slight undulations between flapping and brief gliding.

The Rusty Blackbird is perhaps the least known of all North American blackbirds. This is mainly because it breeds in remote, inaccessible swampy areas, and is much less of a pest to agricultural operations than some of the other members of its family. Unlike most other blackbirds, the plumage on the male Rusty Blackbird changes to a dull, reddish brown during the fall—giving the species its common name. It is also during the fall migrations that this species is most easily observed, moving south in long flocks that often take several minutes to pass overhead.

**VOICE** Both sexes use *chuk* call during migration flights; male song a musical *too-ta-lee*.

**NESTING** Small bowl of branches and sticks, lined with wet plants and dry grass, usually near water; 3–5 eggs; 1 brood; May–July.

**FEEDING** Eats seasonally available insects, spiders, grains, seeds of trees, and fleshy fruit or berries.

**WIDE OPEN**
Seldom seen, the male's courtship display includes gaping and tail-spreading.

**OCCURRENCE**
Breeds in moist to wet forests up to the timberline in the far north from Alaska to NE Canada; but barely in the continental US (farther north than any other species of North American blackbird); winters in eastern US, in several kinds of swampy forests.

**SIMILAR SPECIES**

**BREWER'S BLACKBIRD** see p.383
purplish sheen on head
longer tail

**COMMON GRACKLE** see p.384
bill thicker at base
large tail

bluish sheen on head
glossy bronze body

| Length **8–10in (20–25cm)** | Wingspan **12–15in (30–38cm)** | Weight **1⁹/₁₆–2⁷/₈oz (45–80g)** |
|---|---|---|
| Social **Pairs/Winter flocks** | Lifespan **At least 9 years** | Status **Declining** |

| DATE SEEN | WHERE | NOTES |
|---|---|---|
| | | |
| | | |
| | | |
| | | |
| | | |

| Order **Passeriformes** | Family **Icteridae** | Species *Euphagus cyanocephalus* |
| --- | --- | --- |

# Brewer's Blackbird 🔊

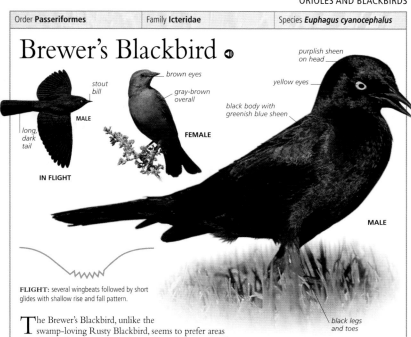

stout bill

brown eyes

gray-brown overall

**MALE**

long, dark tail

**IN FLIGHT**

**FEMALE**

purplish sheen on head

yellow eyes

black body with greenish blue sheen

**MALE**

black legs and toes

**FLIGHT:** several wingbeats followed by short glides with shallow rise and fall pattern.

The Brewer's Blackbird, unlike the swamp-loving Rusty Blackbird, seems to prefer areas disturbed by humans to natural ones throughout much of its range. It is likely that the relatively recent eastward range expansion of Brewer's Blackbird has been aided by changes in land practices. Interestingly, when the Brewer's Blackbird range overlaps with that of the Common Grackle, it wins out in rural areas, but loses out in urban areas. This species can be found feasting on waste grains left behind after the harvest.

**VOICE** Buzzy *tshrrep* song ascending in tone.

**NESTING** Bulky cup of dry grass, stem and twig framework lined with soft grasses and animal hair; 3–6 eggs; 1–2 broods; April–July.

**FEEDING** Forages on the ground for many species of insects during breeding season, also snails; seeds, grain, and occasional fruit in fall and winter.

**BROWN-EYED BIRD**
Brown eyes distinguish the female Brewer's from the yellow-eyed, female Rusty Blackbird.

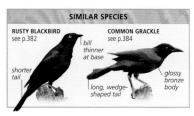

**SIMILAR SPECIES**

**RUSTY BLACKBIRD**
see p.382

shorter tail

bill thinner at base

**COMMON GRACKLE**
see p.384

glossy bronze body

long, wedge-shaped tail

**OCCURRENCE**
Breeds and winters in open areas, readily adapting to, and preferring, disturbed areas and human developments, such as parks, gardens, clear-felled forests, and fallow fields edged with dense trees or shrubs.

| Length **10–12in (25–30cm)** | Wingspan **13–16in (33–41cm)** | Weight **1¾–2½oz (50–70g)** |
| --- | --- | --- |
| Social **Flocks/Colonies** | Lifespan **Up to 13 years** | Status **Secure** |

| DATE SEEN | WHERE | | NOTES |
| --- | --- | --- | --- |
| | | | |
| | | | |
| | | | |
| | | | |
| | | | |

| Order **Passeriformes** | Family **Icteridae** | Species *Quiscalus quiscula* |

# Common Grackle 🔊

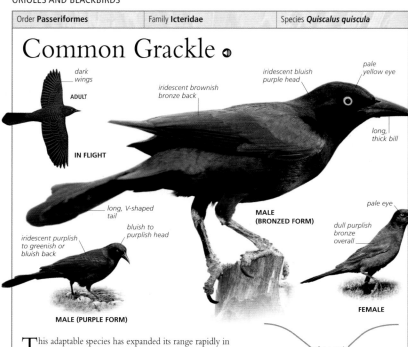

dark wings

**ADULT**

**IN FLIGHT**

iridescent brownish bronze back

iridescent bluish purple head

pale yellow eye

long, thick bill

long, V-shaped tail

**MALE (BRONZED FORM)**

bluish to purplish head

iridescent purplish to greenish or bluish back

**MALE (PURPLE FORM)**

pale eye

dull purplish bronze overall

**FEMALE**

This adaptable species has expanded its range rapidly in the recent past, thanks to human land clearing practices. The Common Grackle is so well suited to urban and suburban habitats that it successfully excludes other species from them. During migration and winter, Common Grackles form immense flocks, some of which may be made up of more than one million individuals. This tendency, combined with its preference for cultivated areas, has made this species an agricultural pest in some regions.

**VOICE** Call a low, harsh *chek*; loud song series of odd squeaks and whistles.

**NESTING** Small bowl in trees, with a frame of sticks filled with mud and grasses; 4–6 eggs; 1–2 broods; April–July.

**FEEDING** Eats beetles, flies, spiders, and worms, as well as small vertebrates; also seeds and grain, especially in nonbreeding season; an omnivore.

**FLIGHT:** straight, level, and direct without the up and down undulation of blackbird species.

**SIMILAR SPECIES**

**GREAT-TAILED GRACKLE**
larger; see p.385

very long, deeply wedged tail

**BOAT-TAILED GRACKLE**

purplish gloss to feathers

longer tail

bluish gloss on black feathers

**HIGHLY ADAPTABLE**
This grackle is comfortable near human developments, resulting in the expansion of its range.

**OCCURRENCE**
The Common Grackle lives in a wide variety of open woodlands, suburban woodlots, city parks, gardens, and hedgerows. It is absent west of the Great Plains. Wintering range extends south to the Gulf Coast.

| Length **11–13½in (28–34cm)** | Wingspan **15–18in (38–46cm)** | Weight **3⅛–4oz (90–125g)** |
| Social **Flocks** | Lifespan **Up to 20 years** | Status **Secure** |

| DATE SEEN | WHERE | NOTES |
| --- | --- | --- |
| | | |
| | | |
| | | |
| | | |

| Order **Passeriformes** | Family **Icteridae** | Species *Quiscalus mexicanus* |
|---|---|---|

# Great-tailed Grackle 🔊

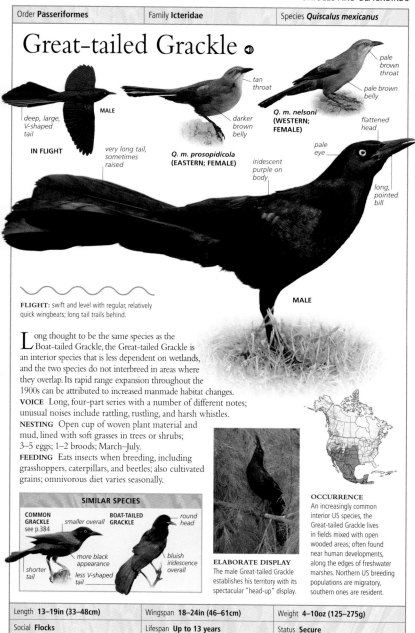

**MALE**

**IN FLIGHT**

deep, large, V-shaped tail

very long tail, sometimes raised

tan throat

*Q. m. prosopidicola* (EASTERN; FEMALE)

darker brown belly

pale brown throat

*Q. m. nelsoni* (WESTERN; FEMALE)

pale brown belly

flattened head

pale eye

iridescent purple on body

long, pointed bill

**MALE**

**FLIGHT:** swift and level with regular, relatively quick wingbeats; long tail trails behind.

Long thought to be the same species as the Boat-tailed Grackle, the Great-tailed Grackle is an interior species that is less dependent on wetlands, and the two species do not interbreed in areas where they overlap. Its rapid range expansion throughout the 1900s can be attributed to increased manmade habitat changes.

**VOICE** Long, four-part series with a number of different notes; unusual noises include rattling, rustling, and harsh whistles.

**NESTING** Open cup of woven plant material and mud, lined with soft grasses in trees or shrubs; 3–5 eggs; 1–2 broods; March–July.

**FEEDING** Eats insects when breeding, including grasshoppers, caterpillars, and beetles; also cultivated grains; omnivorous diet varies seasonally.

**SIMILAR SPECIES**

**COMMON GRACKLE** see p.384

smaller overall

**BOAT-TAILED GRACKLE**

round head

more black appearance

shorter tail

bluish iridescence overall

less V-shaped tail

**ELABORATE DISPLAY**
The male Great-tailed Grackle establishes his territory with its spectacular "head-up" display.

**OCCURRENCE**
An increasingly common interior US species, the Great-tailed Grackle lives in fields mixed with open wooded areas; often found near human developments, along the edges of freshwater marshes. Northern US breeding populations are migratory, southern ones are resident.

| Length **13–19in (33–48cm)** | Wingspan **18–24in (46–61cm)** | Weight **4–10oz (125–275g)** |
|---|---|---|
| Social **Flocks** | Lifespan **Up to 13 years** | Status **Secure** |

| DATE SEEN | WHERE | NOTES |
|---|---|---|
| | | |
| | | |
| | | |
| | | |

# WOOD WARBLERS

THE FAMILY PARULIDAE is restricted to the Americas, and is remarkable for its diversity in plumage, song, feeding, breeding biology, and sexual dimorphism. In general, however, wood warblers share similar shapes: all are smallish, slender birds with longish, thin bills (unlike thick vireo bills) used mostly for snapping up insects. Their varied colors and patterns make the lively, busy mixed groups seen on migration especially appealing and fascinating to watch. Ground-dwelling warblers tend to be larger and clad in olives, browns, and yellows, whereas many arboreal species are smaller and sport bright oranges, cool blues, and even ruby reds. The location and presence or absence of wingbars and tail spots is often a good identification aid. Warblers are especially diverse in the East, where more than 30 species may be seen in a single morning of spring birding, which may be the highlight of the year for some birdwatchers. Eastern species have three different migration routes to deal with the obstacle of the Gulf of Mexico when going to or coming from their Neotropical wintering grounds.

**PLASTIC PLUMAGE**
Some male *Setophaga* warblers (like this Blackburnian) are only brightly colored when breeding. This species is rare in the West.

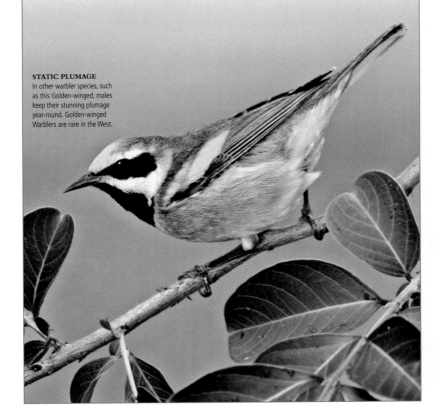

**FEEDING STRATEGIES**
Some warblers, such as this Black-and-White, probe the cracks in tree trunks for food.

Circum-Gulf migrants fly along the eastern shore of Mexico; Caribbean migrants travel through Florida then island-hop through the West Indies; and trans-Gulf migrants fly directly across the Gulf of Mexico, from the Yucatán Peninsula to the US Gulf Coast. Birds flying this third route are subjected to weather changes that sometimes result in spectacular fallouts at locations such as High Island, Texas.

**STATIC PLUMAGE**
In other warbler species, such as this Golden-winged, males keep their stunning plumage year-round. Golden-winged Warblers are rare in the West.

| Order **Passeriformes** | Family **Parulidae** | Species *Seiurus aurocapilla* |
|---|---|---|

# Ovenbird

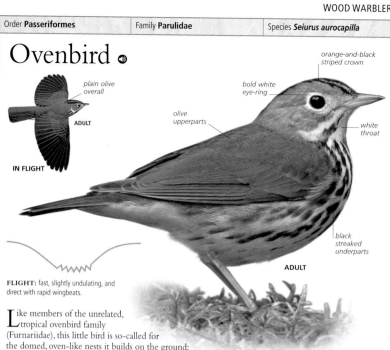

*orange-and-black striped crown*

*plain olive overall*

**ADULT**

**IN FLIGHT**

*bold white eye-ring*

*olive upperparts*

*white throat*

*black streaked underparts*

**ADULT**

**FLIGHT:** fast, slightly undulating, and direct with rapid wingbeats.

Like members of the unrelated, tropical ovenbird family (Furnariidae), this little bird is so-called for the domed, oven-like nests it builds on the ground; unique structures for a North American bird. The Ovenbird is also noted for its singing. Males flit about boisterously, often at night, incorporating portions of their main song into a jumble of spluttering notes. In the forest, one male singing loudly to declare his territory can set off a whole chain of responses from his neighbors, until the whole forest rings.

**VOICE** Call variably pitched, sharp *chik* in series; flight call high, rising *siiii*; song loud, ringing crescendo of paired notes *chur-tee' chur-tee' chur-tee' chur-tee' chur-TEE chur-TEE chur-TEE*.

**NESTING** Domed structure of leaves and grass on ground with side entrance; 3–6 eggs; 1 brood; May–July.

**FEEDING** Forages mainly on the forest floor for insects and other invertebrates.

**STRUTTING ITS STUFF**
The Ovenbird is noted for the way it struts across the forest floor like a tiny chicken.

### SIMILAR SPECIES

**NORTHERN WATERTHRUSH** much slimmer; see p.388
*dark brown upperparts*
*no eye-ring*

**LOUISIANA WATERTHRUSH** see p.471
*white eyebrow*
*dark brown upperparts*

**OCCURRENCE**
Breeds from parts of Yukon and British Columbia to the eastern US in closed-canopy mixed and deciduous forests with suitable amount of fallen plant material for nest building and foraging; migrants and wintering birds use similar habitats.

| Length **6in (15cm)** | Wingspan **9½in (24cm)** | Weight **⁹⁄₁₆–⁷⁄₈oz (16–25g)** |
|---|---|---|
| Social **Solitary/Flocks** | Lifespan **Up to 7 years** | Status **Declining** |

| DATE SEEN | WHERE | NOTES |
|---|---|---|
| | | |
| | | |
| | | |
| | | |
| | | |

**387**

| Order **Passeriformes** | Family **Parulidae** | Species *Parkesia noveboracensis* |

# Northern Waterthrush

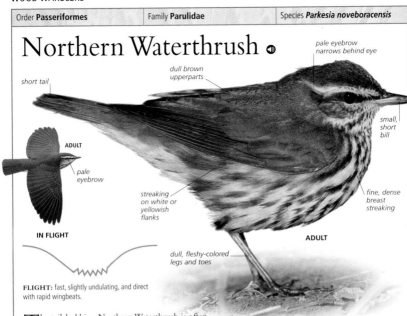

pale eyebrow
narrows behind eye

dull brown
upperparts

short tail

small,
short
bill

**ADULT**

pale
eyebrow

streaking
on white or
yellowish
flanks

fine, dense
breast
streaking

**IN FLIGHT**

**ADULT**

dull, fleshy-colored
legs and toes

**FLIGHT:** fast, slightly undulating, and direct
with rapid wingbeats.

The tail-bobbing Northern Waterthrush is often heard giving a *spink!* call as it swiftly flees from observers. Although this species may be mistaken for the closely related Louisiana Waterthrush, there are clues that are helpful in its identification. While the Northern Waterthrush prefers still water, its relative greatly prefers running water; in addition, its song is quite unlike that of the Louisiana Waterthrush.

**VOICE** Call a sharp, rising, ringing *spink!*; flight call a rising, buzzy *ziiiit*; song a loud series of rich, accelerating, staccato notes, usually decreasing in pitch *teet, teet, toh-toh toh-toh tyew-tyew!*.

**NESTING** Hair-lined, mossy cup placed on or near ground, hidden in roots of fallen or standing tree or in riverbank; 4–5 eggs; 1 brood; May–August.

**FEEDING** Mostly eats insects, such as ants, mosquitoes, moths, and beetles, both larvae and adult, plus slugs, and snails; when migrating, also eats small crustaceans, and even tiny fish.

**YELLOW FORM**
Many Northern Waterthrushes have yellow
underparts, like this one, while others have white.

### SIMILAR SPECIES

**OVENBIRD**
much rounder;
fatter; see p.387
*olive
upperparts*

bold
eye-ring

**LOUISIANA
WATERTHRUSH**
see p.471

eyebrow
widens behind
eye

thicker,
longer
bill

orange
wash to
flanks

**OCCURRENCE**
Breeds right across northern
North America in dark,
still-water swamps and bogs;
also in the still edges of rivers
and lakes; migrant birds
use wet habitats; winters in
shrubby marshes, mangroves,
and occasionally in crops, such
as rice fields and citrus groves.

| Length **6in (15cm)** | Wingspan **9½in (24cm)** | Weight **½–⅞oz (14–23g)** |
| Social **Solitary** | Lifespan **Up to 9 years** | Status **Secure** |

| DATE SEEN | WHERE | NOTES |
| --- | --- | --- |
| | | |
| | | |
| | | |
| | | |

| Order **Passeriformes** | Family **Parulidae** | Species *Mniotilta varia* |

# Black-and-white Warbler 🔊

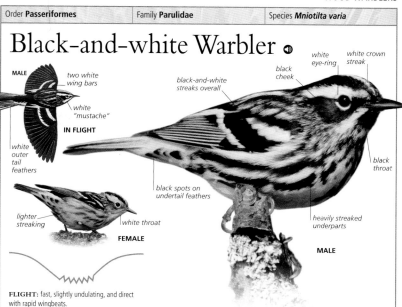

**MALE**

two white
wing bars

white
"mustache"

**IN FLIGHT**

white
outer
tail
feathers

white
eye-ring

white crown
streak

black
cheek

black-and-white
streaks overall

black
throat

black spots on
undertail feathers

lighter
streaking

white throat

**FEMALE**

heavily streaked
underparts

**MALE**

**FLIGHT:** fast, slightly undulating, and direct
with rapid wingbeats.

The Black-and-white Warbler is best known for its creeper-like habit
of feeding in vertical and upside-down positions as it pries into bark
crevices, where its relatively long, curved bill allows it to reach into tiny
nooks and crannies. These habits, combined with
a streaked plumage, make this bird one of the
most distinctive warblers in North America.
It is a long-distance migrant, with some birds
wintering in parts of northern South America.
**VOICE** Sharp *stik* call; flight call a very high, thin *ssiit*,
often doubled; song a thin, high-pitched, wheezy
series *wheesy wheesy wheesy wheesy wheesy wheesy.*
**NESTING** Cup on ground against stump, fallen
logs, or roots; 4–6 eggs; 1 brood; April–August.
**FEEDING** Creeps along branches and trunks,
probing into bark for insects and insect larvae.

**SQUEAKY WHEEL**
The high-pitched, wheezy song
of this warbler is said to be
reminiscent of a squeaky wheel.

**UPSIDE DOWN**
Black-and-white Warblers often
creep head-first along trunks
and branches of trees.

**OCCURRENCE**
Breeds in deciduous
and mixed mature and
second-growth woodlands;
migrants occur on a greater
variety of habitats; winters
in a wide range of wooded
habitats in southern US,
Mexico and into Central
and South America. Rare
along West Coast in winter.

**SIMILAR SPECIES**

**BLACKPOLL
WARBLER** ♂
see p.402

black
cap

white cheek
patch

**BLACK-THROATED
GRAY WARBLER** ♂
see p.405

yellow
patch

bright
orange legs

| Length **5in (13cm)** | Wingspan **8in (20cm)** | Weight **⁵⁄₁₆–¹⁄₂oz (9–14g)** |
| Social **Migrant/Winter flocks** | Lifespan **Up to 11 years** | Status **Secure** |

| DATE SEEN | WHERE | NOTES |
| --- | --- | --- |
| | | |
| | | |
| | | |
| | | |
| | | |

| Order **Passeriformes** | Family **Parulidae** | Species *Leiothlypis peregrina* |

# Tennessee Warbler

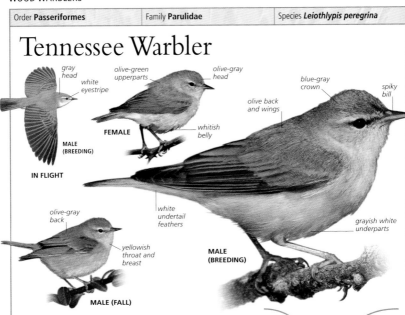

gray head

white eyestripe

olive-green upperparts

olive-gray head

blue-gray crown

spiky bill

olive back and wings

whitish belly

**FEMALE**

**MALE (BREEDING)**

**IN FLIGHT**

olive-gray back

white undertail feathers

yellowish throat and breast

grayish white underparts

**MALE (BREEDING)**

**MALE (FALL)**

The Tennessee Warbler was named on the basis of a specimen found in that state on migration, as this species breeds almost entirely in Canada and winters in Central America. These warblers inhabit fairly remote areas and their nests are difficult to find. It is one of a number of species that takes advantage of outbreaks of spruce budworms (actually tortricid moths); their populations tend to increase in years when budworms themselves increase.

**VOICE** Call a sharp *tzit*; flight call a thin slightly rolling *seet*; song usually three-part staccato series, *chip-chip-chip*, each series increasing in pitch and usually in tempo.

**NESTING** Nest woven of fine plant matter, in ground depression, concealed from above by shrubbery; 4–7 eggs; 1 brood; June.

**FEEDING** Searches outer branches of trees for caterpillars, bees, wasps, beetles, and spiders; also eats fruit in winter and drinks nectar by piercing base of flowers.

**FLIGHT:** fast, slightly undulating, and direct with rapid wingbeats.

**UNIQUE UNDERPARTS**
The breeding male is the only North American wood warbler with unmarked grayish white underparts.

### SIMILAR SPECIES

**PHILADELPHIA VIREO** see p.267

white eyebrow

yellowish underparts

**ORANGE-CROWNED WARBLER** see p.391

shorter wings

greenish yellow rump

muted markings

**OCCURRENCE**
Breeds in a variety of habitats, especially woodlands with dense understory and thickets of willows and alders. Very common in suburban parks and gardens during migration, particularly in the Midwest. Winters from southern Mexico to northern Ecuador and northern Venezuela; also Cuba.

| Length **4¾in (12cm)** | Wingspan **7¾in (19.5cm)** | Weight **⁹⁄₃₂–⅝oz (8–17g)** |
| Social **Flocks** | Lifespan **Up to 6 years** | Status **Secure** |

| DATE SEEN | WHERE | NOTES |
|-----------|-------|-------|
| | | |
| | | |
| | | |
| | | |
| | | |

| Order **Passeriformes** | Family **Parulidae** | Species *Leiothlypis celata* |

# Orange-crowned Warbler 🔊

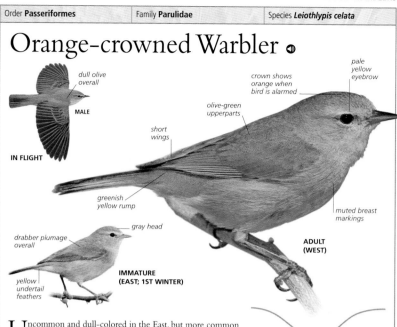

**MALE**

dull olive overall

**IN FLIGHT**

short wings

greenish yellow rump

gray head

crown shows orange when bird is alarmed

pale yellow eyebrow

olive-green upperparts

muted breast markings

**ADULT (WEST)**

drabber plumage overall

yellow undertail feathers

**IMMATURE (EAST; 1ST WINTER)**

Uncommon and dull-colored in the East, but more common and brightly coloured in the West, the Orange-crowned Warbler has a large breeding range. The 19th-century American naturalist Thomas Say described this species on the basis of specimens collected in Nebraska. He was struck by the tiny orange cap, but because it was so concealed in the plumage of the crown, he named it *celata*, which is Latin for "hidden." The orange cap is not usually visible in the field.

**VOICE** Call a clean, sharp *tsik*; flight call a high, short *seet*; song a loose, lazy trill; eastern birds lazier, western birds more emphatic.

**NESTING** Cup of grasses, fibers, and down, usually on ground under bush; 4–5 eggs; 1 brood; March–July.

**FEEDING** Gleans mostly arthropods, such as beetles, ants, spiders, and their larvae; also eats fruit; collects nectar by piercing base of flower.

**FLIGHT:** fast, slightly undulating, and direct with rapid wingbeats.

**FACE MARKINGS**
In eastern populations of this warbler, the birds have whitish facial markings during their first winter.

## SIMILAR SPECIES

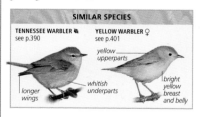

**TENNESSEE WARBLER** 🐦
see p.390

longer wings

whitish underparts

**YELLOW WARBLER** ♀
see p.401

yellow upperparts

bright yellow breast and belly

**OCCURRENCE**
Breeds in a variety of habitats across North America from Alaska eastward to Newfoundland, and in the West from British Columbia southward to California, New Mexico, and western Texas. Prefers streamside thickets. Some winter in the West, while others go to Mexico and Guatemala.

| Length **5in (13cm)** | Wingspan **7¼in (18.5cm)** | Weight **¼–⅜oz (7–11g)** |
| Social **Winter flocks** | Lifespan **Up to 6 years** | Status **Secure** |

| DATE SEEN | WHERE | NOTES |
| --- | --- | --- |
| | | |
| | | |
| | | |
| | | |
| | | |

| Order **Passeriformes** | Family **Parulidae** | Species *Leiothlypis ruficapilla* |
| --- | --- | --- |

# Nashville Warbler 🔊

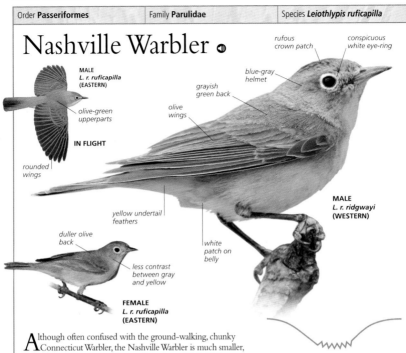

MALE
*L. r. ruficapilla*
(EASTERN)

olive-green
upperparts

IN FLIGHT

rounded
wings

rufous
crown patch

conspicuous
white eye-ring

blue-gray
helmet

grayish
green back

olive
wings

MALE
*L. r. ridgwayi*
(WESTERN)

yellow undertail
feathers

white
patch on
belly

duller olive
back

less contrast
between gray
and yellow

FEMALE
*L. r. ruficapilla*
(EASTERN)

Although often confused with the ground-walking, chunky Connecticut Warbler, the Nashville Warbler is much smaller, hops about up in trees, and has a yellow throat. Nashville has two subspecies: *L. r. ruficapilla* in the East and *L. r. ridgwayi* in the West. Differences in voice, habitat, behavior, and plumage hint that they may in fact be separate species. *L. r. ridgwayi* can be distinguished by more extensive white on the belly and a grayish green back.

**VOICE** Call sharp *tik*, sharper in West; flight call high, thin *siit*; eastern song two parts: first part lazy, second faster trill *tee-tsee tee-tsee tee-tsee tititititi*; western song slightly lower and fuller with lazier second part, a seldom trilled *tee-tsee tee-tsee tee-tsee weesay weesay way*.

**NESTING** Cup hidden on ground in dense cover; 3–6 eggs; 1 brood; May–July.

**FEEDING** Gleans insects and spiders from trees.

**FLIGHT:** fast, slightly undulating, and direct, with rapid wingbeats.

### SIMILAR SPECIES

**VIRGINIA'S WARBLER**
see p.393

lacks
yellow belly

**CONNECTICUT WARBLER** ♂
walks on ground;
see p.394

lacks
olive
wings

shorter
tail

chunky
pink bill

**FIELD MARKS**
The white eye-ring and belly are evident on this singing male.

**OCCURRENCE**
Western *ridgwayi* breeds in brushy montane habitats in the Sierras and northern Rockies and winters in coastal California and from southern Texas to Guatemala; Eastern *ruficapilla* breeds in wet habitats from Saskatchewan east to Newfoundland and south to Virginia; it winters in Mexico.

| Length **4¾in (12cm)** | Wingspan **7½in (19cm)** | Weight **¼–⁷⁄₁₆oz (7–13g)** |
| --- | --- | --- |
| Social **Migrant/Winter flocks** | Lifespan **Up to 7 years** | Status **Secure** |

| DATE SEEN | WHERE | NOTES |
| --- | --- | --- |
| | | |
| | | |
| | | |
| | | |

| Order **Passeriformes** | Family **Parulidae** | Species *Leiothlypis virginiae* |

# Virginia's Warbler

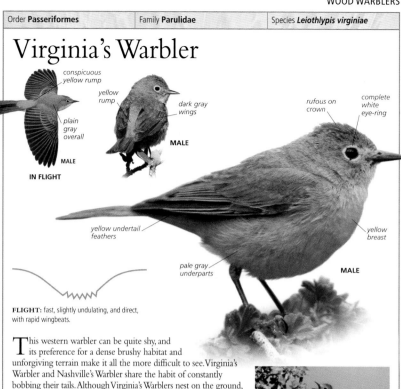

conspicuous yellow rump

plain gray overall

**MALE**
**IN FLIGHT**

yellow rump

dark gray wings

**MALE**

rufous on crown

complete white eye-ring

yellow undertail feathers

pale gray underparts

yellow breast

**MALE**

**FLIGHT:** fast, slightly undulating, and direct, with rapid wingbeats.

This western warbler can be quite shy, and its preference for a dense brushy habitat and unforgiving terrain make it all the more difficult to see. Virginia's Warbler and Nashville's Warbler share the habit of constantly bobbing their tails. Although Virginia's Warblers nest on the ground, singing males frequent the tops of junipers and pines. In the Davis Mountains of west Texas, a small population of Virginia's Warblers has been seen to interbreed with the rare Colima Warbler.

**VOICE** Call hard, sharp, yet hollow *ssink*; song lazy, sweet warble: *sweet sweet sweet sweet teedle-eedle-eedle-eedle tyew tyew.*

**NESTING** Cup of grassy material on steep slope, hidden in hole or vegetation; 3–5 eggs; 1 brood; May–July.

**FEEDING** Gleans a variety of insects, especially caterpillars, from branches and leaves.

**CONSPICUOUS BREAST PATCH**
The yellow breast patch on a singing male stands out against its overall gray plumage.

### SIMILAR SPECIES

**NASHVILLE WARBLER (WESTERN)** ♀
see p.392

blue-gray helmet

olive wings

more extensive yellow

**COLIMA WARBLER**
see p.466

orange upper- and undertail feathers

brownish back

brownish flanks

**OCCURRENCE**
Breeds in dense dry shrub on steep slopes, often with open pine canopy, in the southern Rockies, Great Basin, and the Black Hills; occupies similar habitats during migration and in winter. Wintering range extends southward to Oaxaca in Mexico.

| Length 4¾in (12cm) | Wingspan 7½in (19cm) | Weight ¼–⅜oz (7–10g) |
| Social **Flocks** | Lifespan **Up to 4 years** | Status **Secure** |

| DATE SEEN | WHERE | NOTES |
|---|---|---|
| .................. | .............................. | .............................................. |
| .................. | .............................. | .............................................. |
| .................. | .............................. | .............................................. |
| .................. | .............................. | .............................................. |
| .................. | .............................. | .............................................. |

| Order **Passeriformes** | Family **Parulidae** | Species *Oporornis agilis* |

# Connecticut Warbler

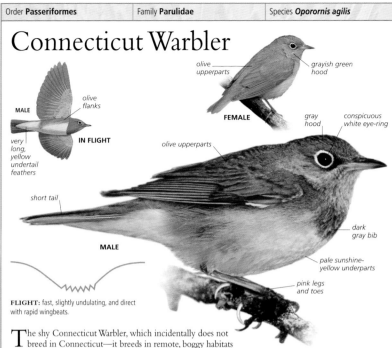

olive upperparts

grayish green hood

**FEMALE**

**MALE**

olive flanks

**IN FLIGHT**

very long, yellow undertail feathers

gray hood

conspicuous white eye-ring

olive upperparts

short tail

**MALE**

dark gray bib

pale sunshine-yellow underparts

pink legs and toes

**FLIGHT:** fast, slightly undulating, and direct with rapid wingbeats.

The shy Connecticut Warbler, which incidentally does not breed in Connecticut—it breeds in remote, boggy habitats in Canada and is hard to spot during its spring and fall migrations. It arrives in the US in late May and leaves its breeding grounds in August. It is the only warbler that walks along the ground in a bouncy manner, with its tail bobbing up and down.

**VOICE** Seldom-heard call a nasal *champ*, flight call a buzzy *ziiiit*; song a loud "whippy," accelerating series, often ending with upward inflection *tweet, chuh WHIP-uh chee-uh-WHIP-uh chee-uh-WAY*.

**NESTING** Concealed cup of grass or leaves, lined with fine plant matter and hair; placed near or on ground in damp moss or grass clump; 3–5 eggs; 1 brood; June–July.

**FEEDING** Gleans a variety of adult insects, insect larvae, and spiders from under leaves; also eats small fruit.

**EXCEPTIONAL UNDERTAIL**
The yellow undertail feathers nearly reach the tip of the Connecticut Warbler's tail.

**OCCURRENCE**
Breeds across Canada from British Columbia to Québec and in the US in Minnesota and the Great Lakes region, in bogs and pine forests. Winters in forest habitats of Amazonian Peru and Brazil.

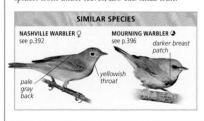

**SIMILAR SPECIES**

**NASHVILLE WARBLER ♀**
see p.392

**MOURNING WARBLER ♂**
see p.396

darker breast patch

pale gray back

yellowish throat

| Length **6in (15cm)** | Wingspan **9in (23cm)** | Weight **⁷⁄₁₆–¹¹⁄₁₆ oz (13–20g)** |
|---|---|---|
| Social **Solitary** | Lifespan **Up to 4 years** | Status **Secure (p)** |

| DATE SEEN | WHERE | NOTES |
|---|---|---|
| | | |
| | | |
| | | |
| | | |

| Order **Passeriformes** | Family **Parulidae** | Species *Geothlypis tolmiei* |

# MacGillivray's Warbler

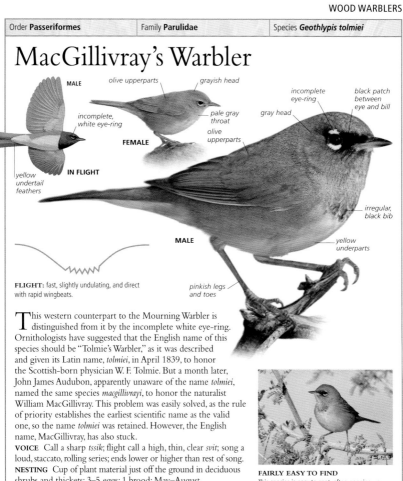

**MALE**

olive upperparts

grayish head

incomplete, white eye-ring

pale gray throat

olive upperparts

**FEMALE**

**IN FLIGHT**

yellow undertail feathers

incomplete eye-ring

black patch between eye and bill

gray head

irregular, black bib

**MALE**

yellow underparts

**FLIGHT:** fast, slightly undulating, and direct with rapid wingbeats.

pinkish legs and toes

This western counterpart to the Mourning Warbler is distinguished from it by the incomplete white eye-ring. Ornithologists have suggested that the English name of this species should be "Tolmie's Warbler," as it was described and given its Latin name, *tolmiei*, in April 1839, to honor the Scottish-born physician W. F. Tolmie. But a month later, John James Audubon, apparently unaware of the name *tolmiei*, named the same species *macgillivrayi*, to honor the naturalist William MacGillivray. This problem was easily solved, as the rule of priority establishes the earliest scientific name as the valid one, so the name *tolmiei* was retained. However, the English name, MacGillivray, has also stuck.

**VOICE** Call a sharp *tssik*; flight call a high, thin, clear *svit*; song a loud, staccato, rolling series; ends lower or higher than rest of song.
**NESTING** Cup of plant material just off the ground in deciduous shrubs and thickets; 3–5 eggs; 1 brood; May–August.
**FEEDING** Gleans beetles, flies, bees, caterpillars from low foliage.

**FAIRLY EASY TO FIND**
This species is easy to spot, often popping up onto a branch in response to some disturbance.

| SIMILAR SPECIES | | |
| --- | --- | --- |
| **MOURNING WARBLER** ♀ see p.396 | **COMMON YELLOWTHROAT** ♀ see p.397 | smaller, black bill |
| shorter tail | no bold eye markings | longer tail |

**OCCURRENCE**
Breeds in thickets within mixed and coniferous forests, often along streams from southeast Alaska and British Columbia south to California and Baja California, and across the western states. Winters in varied habitats with sufficient thickets in Mexico and in Central America.

| Length **5in (13cm)** | Wingspan **7.5in (19cm)** | Weight **⁵⁄₁₆–⁷⁄₁₆oz (9–12g)** |
| Social **Solitary** | Lifespan **Up to 4 years** | Status **Secure** |

| DATE SEEN | WHERE | NOTES |
| --- | --- | --- |
| | | |
| | | |
| | | |
| | | |
| | | |

| Order **Passeriformes** | Family **Parulidae** | Species *Geothlypis philadelphia* |

# Mourning Warbler

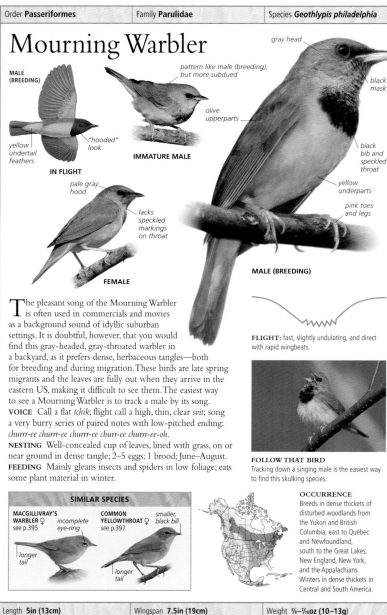

**MALE (BREEDING)**

gray head

black mask

black bib and speckled throat

yellow underparts

pink toes and legs

**MALE (BREEDING)**

pattern like male (breeding), but more subdued

olive upperparts

**IMMATURE MALE**

yellow undertail feathers

"hooded" look

**IN FLIGHT**

pale gray hood

lacks speckled markings on throat

**FEMALE**

The pleasant song of the Mourning Warbler is often used in commercials and movies as a background sound of idyllic suburban settings. It is doubtful, however, that you would find this gray-headed, gray-throated warbler in a backyard, as it prefers dense, herbaceous tangles—both for breeding and during migration. These birds are late spring migrants and the leaves are fully out when they arrive in the eastern US, making it difficult to see them. The easiest way to see a Mourning Warbler is to track a male by its song.

**VOICE** Call a flat *tchik*; flight call a high, thin, clear *svit*; song a very burry series of paired notes with low-pitched ending: *churrr-ee churrr-ee churrr-ee churr-ee churrr-ee-oh*.

**NESTING** Well-concealed cup of leaves, lined with grass, on or near ground in dense tangle; 2–5 eggs; 1 brood; June–August.

**FEEDING** Mainly gleans insects and spiders in low foliage; eats some plant material in winter.

**FLIGHT:** fast, slightly undulating, and direct with rapid wingbeats.

**FOLLOW THAT BIRD**
Tracking down a singing male is the easiest way to find this skulking species.

### SIMILAR SPECIES

**MACGILLIVRAY'S WARBLER** ♀
see p.395

incomplete eye-ring

longer tail

**COMMON YELLOWTHROAT** ♀
see p.397

smaller, black bill

longer tail

### OCCURRENCE
Breeds in dense thickets of disturbed woodlands from the Yukon and British Columbia, east to Québec and Newfoundland, south to the Great Lakes, New England, New York, and the Appalachians. Winters in dense thickets in Central and South America.

| Length **5in (13cm)** | Wingspan **7.5in (19cm)** | Weight **⅜–⁷⁄₁₆oz (10–13g)** |
| Social **Solitary** | Lifespan **Up to 8 years** | Status **Secure** |

| DATE SEEN | WHERE | NOTES |
| --- | --- | --- |
|  |  |  |
|  |  |  |
|  |  |  |
|  |  |  |

| Order **Passeriformes** | Family **Parulidae** | Species *Geothlypis trichas* |

# Common Yellowthroat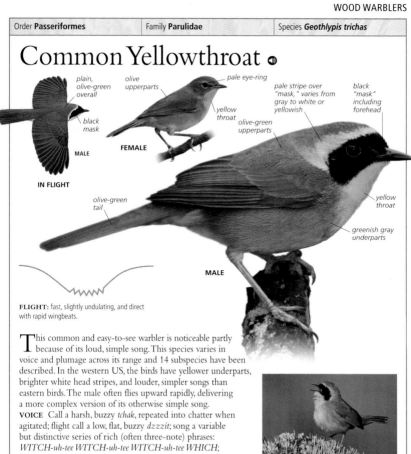

plain, olive-green overall

olive upperparts

pale eye-ring

pale stripe over "mask," varies from gray to white or yellowish

black "mask" including forehead

black mask

yellow throat

olive-green upperparts

**FEMALE**

**MALE**

**IN FLIGHT**

olive-green tail

yellow throat

greenish gray underparts

**MALE**

**FLIGHT:** fast, slightly undulating, and direct with rapid wingbeats.

This common and easy-to-see warbler is noticeable partly because of its loud, simple song. This species varies in voice and plumage across its range and 14 subspecies have been described. In the western US, the birds have yellower underparts, brighter white head stripes, and louder, simpler songs than eastern birds. The male often flies upward rapidly, delivering a more complex version of its otherwise simple song.

**VOICE** Call a harsh, buzzy *tchak*, repeated into chatter when agitated; flight call a low, flat, buzzy *dzzzit*; song a variable but distinctive series of rich (often three-note) phrases: *WITCH-uh-tee WITCH-uh-tee WITCH-uh-tee WHICH*; more complex flight song.

**NESTING** Concealed, bulky cup of grasses just above ground or water; 3–5 eggs; 1 brood; May–August.

**FEEDING** Eats insects and spiders in low vegetation; also seeds.

**UNFORGETTABLE CALL**
The song of the male Common Yellowthroat is an extremely helpful aid in its identification.

| SIMILAR SPECIES | | |
|---|---|---|
| **KENTUCKY WARBLER** ♂ much larger | **MOURNING WARBLER** ♀ see p.396 | gray head |
| yellow eyebrow | | pink-based bill |
| shorter tail | bright yellow belly | bright yellow on belly |

**OCCURRENCE**
Found south of the tundra, from Alaska and the Yukon to Québec and Newfoundland, and south to California, Texas, and to southeastern US. Habitats dense herbaceous understory, from marshes and grasslands to pine forest and hedgerows. Winters from Mexico to Panama and the Antilles.

| Length **5in (13cm)** | Wingspan **6¾in (17cm)** | Weight **29oz (825g)** |
| Social **Migrant/Winter flocks** | Lifespan **Up to 11 years** | Status **Secure** |

| DATE SEEN | WHERE | | NOTES |
|---|---|---|---|
| | | | |
| | | | |
| | | | |
| | | | |
| | | | |

| Order **Passeriformes** | Family **Parulidae** | Species *Setophaga ruticilla* |
| --- | --- | --- |

# American Redstart 🔊

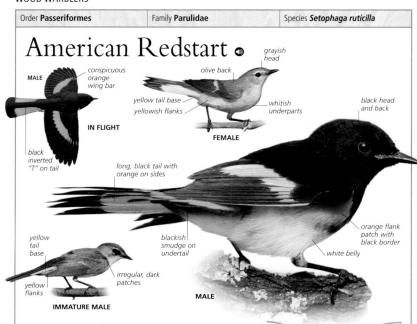

**MALE**

conspicuous orange wing bar

**IN FLIGHT**

black inverted "T" on tail

grayish head

olive back

yellow tail base
yellowish flanks

whitish underparts

**FEMALE**

black head and back

long, black tail with orange on sides

yellow tail base

yellow flanks

blackish smudge on undertail

irregular, dark patches

**IMMATURE MALE**

orange flank patch with black border

white belly

**MALE**

The American Redstart is a vividly colored, energetic and acrobatic warbler with a reasonably broad range across North America. One of its behavioral quirks is to fan its tail and wings while foraging, supposedly using the flashes of bold color to scare insects into moving, making them easy prey. It possesses well-developed rictal bristles, hair-like feathers extending from the corners of the mouth, which help it to detect insects.

**FLIGHT:** fast, slightly undulating, and direct with rapid wingbeats.

**VOICE** Harsh *tsiip* call; flight call a high, thin *sweep*; song a confusingly variable, high, thin, yet penetrating series of notes; one version burry, emphatic, and down-slurred *see-a see-a see-a see-a ZEE-urrrr*.

**NESTING** Cup of grasses and rootlets, lined with feathers; placed low in deciduous tree; 2–5 eggs; 1–2 broods; May–July.

**FEEDING** Gleans insects and spiders from leaves at mid-levels in trees; also catches moths, flies in flight; will also eat fruit.

**COMMON SONG**
This bird's short, ringing song is a common sound in the moist deciduous woods of the East and North.

**MALE CAREGIVER**
As with most warblers, male Redstarts help raise the young, though they may be polygamous.

**OCCURRENCE**
Breeds in moist deciduous and mixed woodlands; migrants and wintering birds use a wide range of habitats. Winters from Baja California and south Florida through Middle America and the Caribbean to northern South America. Rare along coast of Southern California, and Baja California in winter.

| Length **5in (13cm)** | Wingspan **8in (20cm)** | Weight **⁷⁄₃₂–³⁄₈oz (6–11g)** |
| --- | --- | --- |
| Social **Flocks** | Lifespan **Up to 10 years** | Status **Secure** |

| DATE SEEN | WHERE | NOTES |
| --- | --- | --- |
| | | |
| | | |
| | | |
| | | |

| Order **Passeriformes** | Family **Parulidae** | Species *Setophaga tigrina* |

# Cape May Warbler

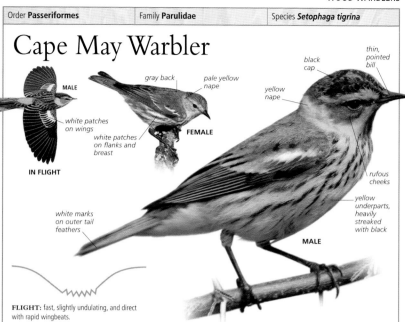

**MALE**

**IN FLIGHT**

white patches on wings

gray back

pale yellow nape

**FEMALE**

white patches on flanks and breast

white marks on outer tail feathers

black cap

thin, pointed bill

yellow nape

rufous cheeks

yellow underparts, heavily streaked with black

**MALE**

**FLIGHT:** fast, slightly undulating, and direct with rapid wingbeats.

The Cape May Warbler is a spruce budworm specialist, and its populations increase during outbreaks of this pest (which is a moth actually, not a worm). Cape May Warblers chase other birds aggressively from flowering trees, where they use their semitubular tongue to suck the nectar from blossoms. In its summer spruce forest habitat, the Cape May Warbler plucks insects from clumps of needles. The "Cape May" Warbler was named this way because the first specimen was collected there—it doesn't breed at Cape May!

**VOICE** Song a high, even-pitched series of whistles *see see see see*.

**NESTING** Cup placed near trunk, high in spruce or fir near top; 4–9 eggs; 1 brood; June–July.

**FEEDING** Gleans arthropods, especially spruce budworms, and also flies, adult moths, and beetles from mid-high levels in canopy; also fruit and nectar during the nonbreeding season.

**SPRING FLASH**
Magnificently colored, a male shows its chestnut cheek, yellow "necklace," and yellow rump.

### SIMILAR SPECIES

**YELLOW-RUMPED WARBLER (MYRTLE)** ♀
see p.404

yellow rump

yellow flank patches

thicker, heavier bill

**PALM WARBLER (WESTERN)** 
see p.403

browner overall

yellow undertail feathers

**OCCURRENCE**
Breeds from the Yukon and British Columbia to the Great Lakes, the Maritimes, and New England in mature spruce-fir forests. Migrants occur in a variety of habitats. Winters in varied habitats in Central America, as far south as Honduras.

| Length **5in (13cm)** | Wingspan **8in (20cm)** | Weight **⁹⁄₃₂–³⁄₈oz (8–11g)** |
| Social **Flocks** | Lifespan **Up to 4 years** | Status **Secure (p)** |

| DATE SEEN | WHERE | NOTES |
|-----------|-------|-------|
| | | |
| | | |
| | | |
| | | |

| Order **Passeriformes** | Family **Parulidae** | Species ***Setophaga magnolia*** |
|---|---|---|

# Magnolia Warbler 🔊

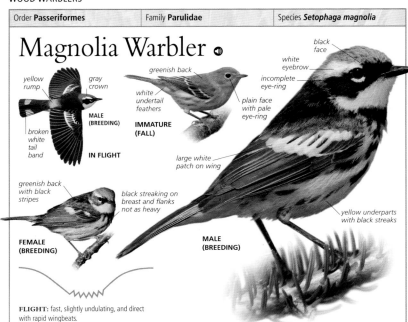

yellow rump

gray crown

greenish back

black face

white eyebrow

incomplete eye-ring

**MALE (BREEDING)**

**IN FLIGHT**

broken white tail band

white undertail feathers

**IMMATURE (FALL)**

plain face with pale eye-ring

large white patch on wing

greenish back with black stripes

black streaking on breast and flanks not as heavy

**FEMALE (BREEDING)**

**MALE (BREEDING)**

yellow underparts with black streaks

**FLIGHT:** fast, slightly undulating, and direct with rapid wingbeats.

The bold, flashy, and common Magnolia Warbler is hard to miss as it flits around at eye level, fanning its uniquely marked tail. This species nests in young forests and winters in almost any habitat, so its numbers have not suffered in recent decades, unlike some of its relatives. Although it really has no preference for its namesake plant, the 19th-century ornithologist Alexander Wilson discovered a Magnolia Warbler feeding in a magnolia tree during migration, which is how it got its name.

**VOICE** Call a tinny *jeinf*, not particularly warbler-like; also short, simple whistled series *wee'-sa wee'-sa WEET-a-chew*; short, distinctive, flight call a high, trilled *zeep*.

**NESTING** Flimsy cup of black rootlets placed low in dense conifer against trunk; 3–5 eggs; 1 brood; June–August.

**FEEDING** Gleans mostly caterpillars, beetles, and spiders.

**SPRUCE WARBLER**
The conspicuous male Magnolia Warbler can be found singing its distinctive, loud song, often throughout the day, in a spruce tree.

### SIMILAR SPECIES

**PRAIRIE WARBLER ♀**
yellowish undertail; see p.471

thinner streaks

**CANADA WARBLER ♀**
see p.409

greenish yellow upperparts

yellow patch between eye and bill

dark gray wings

**OCCURRENCE**
Breeds in dense, young mixed and coniferous forests from Yukon east to Newfoundland and south into Appalachians of Tennessee; migrates across the Gulf and Caribbean; winters in varied habitats in Caribbean and from southeast Mexico to Panama; rare vagrant in the West.

| Length **5in (13cm)** | Wingspan **7½in (19cm)** | Weight **⁷⁄₃₂–⁷⁄₁₆oz (6–12g)** |
|---|---|---|
| Social **Migrant/Winter flocks** | Lifespan **Up to 6 years** | Status **Secure** |

| DATE SEEN | WHERE | NOTES |
|---|---|---|
| | | |
| | | |
| | | |
| | | |
| | | |

| Order **Passeriformes** | Family **Parulidae** | Species ***Setophaga petechia*** |

# Yellow Warbler 🔊

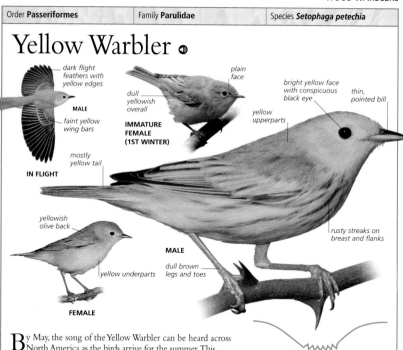

dark flight feathers with yellow edges

**MALE**

faint yellow wing bars

**IN FLIGHT**

mostly yellow tail

dull yellowish overall

plain face

**IMMATURE FEMALE (1ST WINTER)**

bright yellow face with conspicuous black eye

thin, pointed bill

yellow upperparts

yellowish olive back

yellow underparts

**MALE**

dull brown legs and toes

rusty streaks on breast and flanks

**FEMALE**

B y May, the song of the Yellow Warbler can be heard across North America as the birds arrive for the summer. This warbler is treated as a single species with about 35 subspecies, mostly in its tropical range (West Indies and South America). The Yellow Warbler is known to build another nest on top of an old one when cowbird eggs appear in it, which can result in up to six different tiers. The Yellow Warbler does not walk, but rather hops from branch to branch.

**VOICE** Call a variable *chip*, sometimes given in series; flight call buzzy *zeep*; song variable series of fast, sweet notes; western birds often add an emphatic ending.

**NESTING** Deep cup of plant material, grasses in vertical fork of deciduous tree or shrub; 4–5 eggs; 1 brood; May–July.

**FEEDING** Eats mostly insects and insect larvae, plus some fruit.

**FLIGHT:** fast, slightly undulating, and direct, with rapid wingbeats.

**ONE OF A KIND**
This species has more yellow in its plumage than any other North American wood warbler.

### SIMILAR SPECIES

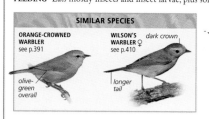

**ORANGE-CROWNED WARBLER** see p.391

olive-green overall

**WILSON'S WARBLER** see p.410

dark crown

longer tail

**OCCURRENCE**
Widespread in most shrubby and second-growth habitats of North America. Migrates to southern US and southward to Mexico, Central America, and South America. Resident populations live in Florida and the West Indies.

| Length **5in (13cm)** | Wingspan **8in (20cm)** | Weight **⁹⁄₃₂–¹⁄₂oz (8–14g)** |
| Social **Flocks** | Lifespan **Up to 9 years** | Status **Secure** |

| DATE SEEN | WHERE | NOTES |
|---|---|---|
| | | |
| | | |
| | | |
| | | |

| Order **Passeriformes** | Family **Parulidae** | Species *Setophaga striata* |

# Blackpoll Warbler 🔊

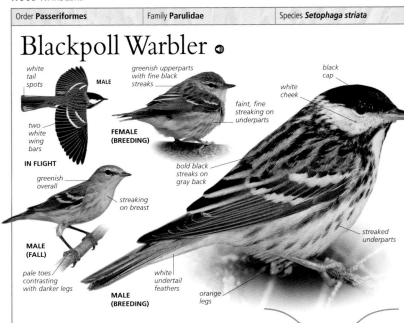

white tail spots

**MALE**

two white wing bars

**IN FLIGHT**

greenish upperparts with fine black streaks

**FEMALE (BREEDING)**

faint, fine streaking on underparts

black cap

white cheek

greenish overall

streaking on breast

**MALE (FALL)**

pale toes contrasting with darker legs

bold black streaks on gray back

white undertail feathers

orange legs

**MALE (BREEDING)**

streaked underparts

The Blackpoll Warbler is well known for undergoing a remarkable fall migration that takes it over the Atlantic Ocean from the northeastern US to northern Venezuela. Before departing, it almost doubles its body weight with fat to serve as fuel for the nonstop journey. With the return of spring, most of these birds travel the shorter Caribbean route back north.
**VOICE** Call piercing *chip*; flight call high, buzzy yet sharp *tzzzt*; common singing crescendo of fast, extremely high-pitched ticks, ending with a decrescendo *tsst tsst TSST TSST TSST tsst tsst*; less commonly, ticks run into even faster trill.
**NESTING** Well-hidden cup placed low against conifer trunk; 3–5 eggs; 1–2 broods; May–July.
**FEEDING** Gleans arthropods, such as worms and beetles, but will take small fruit in fall and winter.

**FLIGHT:** fast, slightly undulating, and direct, with rapid wingbeats.

**REACHING THE HIGH NOTES**
The song of the male Blackpoll is so high-pitched that it is inaudible to many people.

### SIMILAR SPECIES

**BAY-BREASTED WARBLER** 🔖 see p.466
greenish sides to neck
warm wash to flanks

**BLACK-AND-WHITE WARBLER** ♂ see p.389
black cheek
distinct black-and-white stripes

**OCCURRENCE**
Breeds in spruce-fir forests across the northern boreal forest zone from Alaska eastward to Newfoundland, southward to coastal coniferous forests in the Maritimes and northern New England. Migrants fly over the Atlantic Ocean to a landfall in the Caribbean and northern South America.

| Length **5½in (14cm)** | Wingspan **9in (23cm)** | Weight **⅜–⅝oz (10–18g)** |
| Social **Flocks** | Lifespan **Up to 8 years** | Status **Secure** |

| DATE SEEN | WHERE | NOTES |
|---|---|---|
| | | |
| | | |
| | | |
| | | |
| | | |

| Order **Passeriformes** | Family **Parulidae** | Species *Setophaga palmarum* |

# Palm Warbler ◉

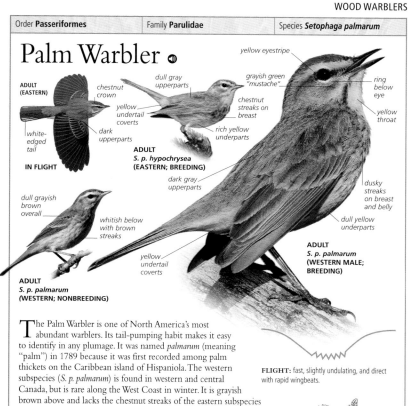

**ADULT (EASTERN)**

chestnut crown

yellow undertail coverts

dark upperparts

white-edged tail

**IN FLIGHT**

dull gray upperparts

yellow eyestripe

grayish green "mustache"

chestnut streaks on breast

rich yellow underparts

**ADULT *S. p. hypochrysea* (EASTERN; BREEDING)**

ring below eye

yellow throat

dark gray upperparts

dusky streaks on breast and belly

dull yellow underparts

**ADULT *S. p. palmarum* (WESTERN MALE; BREEDING)**

dull grayish brown overall

whitish below with brown streaks

yellow undertail coverts

**ADULT *S. p. palmarum* (WESTERN; NONBREEDING)**

The Palm Warbler is one of North America's most abundant warblers. Its tail-pumping habit makes it easy to identify in any plumage. It was named *palmarum* (meaning "palm") in 1789 because it was first recorded among palm thickets on the Caribbean island of Hispaniola. The western subspecies (*S. p. palmarum*) is found in western and central Canada, but is rare along the West Coast in winter. It is grayish brown above and lacks the chestnut streaks of the eastern subspecies (*S. p. hypochrysea*), which has a yellower face, and breeds in southeastern Canada and northeastern US.

**VOICE** Call a husky *chik* or *tsip*; flight call a light *ziint*; slow, loose, buzzy trill: *zwi zwi zwi zwi zwi zwi zwi zwi*.

**NESTING** Cup of grasses on or near ground in open area of conifers at forest edge of a bog; 4–5 eggs; 1 brood; May–July.

**FEEDING** Eats insects, sometimes caught in flight; also takes seeds and berries.

**FLIGHT:** fast, slightly undulating, and direct with rapid wingbeats.

### SIMILAR SPECIES

**CAPE MAY WARBLER ♀** see p.399

olive-gray back

thin patch of yellow on throat and neck

**YELLOW-RUMPED WARBLER (MYRTLE) ♀** see p.404

streaking on back

white throat

**FAR FROM THE PALMS** This male Palm Warbler is far north of the coastal palms where its kin spend the winter.

**OCCURRENCE** In North America, breeds in spruce bogs within the northern forest zone, across Canada from the Yukon to the Maritimes and Labrador, and in the US from Minnesota to Maine. Often migrates through central portions of eastern US; winters in southeastern US, Florida, and Central America.

| Length **5½in (14cm)** | Wingspan **8in (20cm)** | Weight **¼–⁷⁄₁₆oz (7–13g)** |
| Social **Flocks** | Lifespan **Up to 6 years** | Status **Secure** |

| DATE SEEN | WHERE | NOTES |
|-----------|-------|-------|
| | | |
| | | |
| | | |
| | | |
| | | |

| Order **Passeriformes** | Family **Parulidae** | Species *Setophaga coronata* |

# Yellow-rumped Warbler 🔊

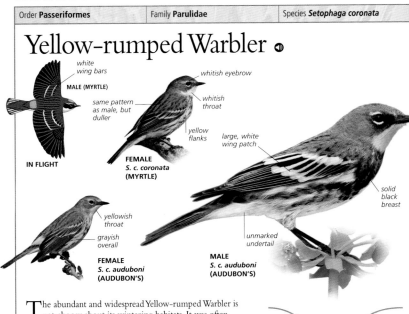

*white wing bars*

**MALE (MYRTLE)**

*same pattern as male, but duller*

**IN FLIGHT**

*whitish eyebrow*

*whitish throat*

*yellow flanks*

**FEMALE
S. c. coronata
(MYRTLE)**

*large, white wing patch*

*yellowish throat*

*grayish overall*

*unmarked undertail*

*solid black breast*

**FEMALE
S. c. auduboni
(AUDUBON'S)**

**MALE
S. c. auduboni
(AUDUBON'S)**

The abundant and widespread Yellow-rumped Warbler is not choosy about its wintering habitats. It was often considered to consist of two species, "Myrtle" (*S. c. coronata*) in the North, and "Audubon's" (*S. c. auduboni*) in the West. Because they interbreed freely in a narrow zone of contact in British Columbia and Alberta, the American Ornithologists Union merged them. The two forms differ in plumage and voice, and their hybrid zone appears stable.

**VOICE** Myrtle's call a flat, husky *tchik*; Audubon's a higher pitched, relatively musical, rising *jip*; flight call of both a clear, up-slurred *sviiit*; song loose, warbled trill with an inflected ending; Myrtle's song higher and faster, Audubon's lower and slower.

**NESTING** Bulky cup of plant matter in conifer; 4–5 eggs; 1 brood; March–August.

**FEEDING** Feeds mostly on flies, beetles, wasps, and spiders during breeding; takes fruit and berries at other times of the year, often sallies to catch prey.

**FLIGHT:** fast, slightly undulating, and direct with rapid wingbeats.

**WIDESPREAD WARBLER**
Yellow-rumped Warblers are widespread and are likely to be spotted often.

**OCCURRENCE**
Both northern and western populations are widespread across the continent from Alaska eastward to Québec and Newfoundland, and westward in the mountains south to Arizona, New Mexico, and Northern Mexico. Prefers coniferous and mixed hardwood coniferous forests.

**SIMILAR SPECIES**

**MAGNOLIA WARBLER** ♂
see p.400

*yellow throat and breast*

*more white in tail*

**CAPE MAY WARBLER** ♀
see p.399

*dark eye-line*

*thin, curved bill*

| Length **5in (13cm)** | Wingspan **9in (23cm)** | Weight **⅜–⅝oz (10–17g)** |
| Social **Flocks** | Lifespan **Up to 7 years** | Status **Secure** |

| DATE SEEN | WHERE | NOTES |
| --- | --- | --- |
| | | |
| | | |
| | | |
| | | |

| Order **Passeriformes** | Family **Parulidae** | Species *Setophaga nigrescens* |

# Black-throated Gray Warbler

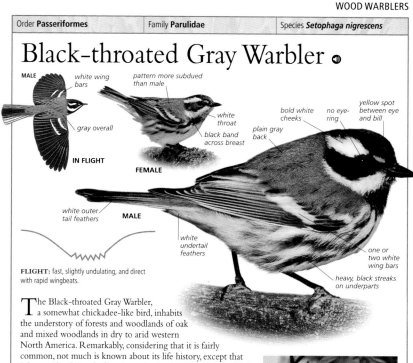

**MALE**
white wing bars
pattern more subdued than male
gray overall

**IN FLIGHT**

white throat
black band across breast

**FEMALE**

yellow spot between eye and bill
no eye-ring
bold white cheeks
plain gray back

white outer tail feathers   **MALE**

white undertail feathers

one or two white wing bars

heavy, black streaks on underparts

**FLIGHT:** fast, slightly undulating, and direct with rapid wingbeats.

The Black-throated Gray Warbler, a somewhat chickadee-like bird, inhabits the understory of forests and woodlands of oak and mixed woodlands in dry to arid western North America. Remarkably, considering that it is fairly common, not much is known about its life history, except that it has a rather leisurely foraging style, that its nest is built by both males and females, placed only a feet few away from the ground, and that it lingers in its breeding range until late fall, sometimes even wintering in California and Arizona.

**VOICE** Call a hard, flat *chep*; flight call a rising *siiit*; song a series of mid-range, paired, buzzy notes, slightly rising then dropping in pitch with the last note, *buzz-zu buzz-zu buzz-zu buzz-zo buzz-zo buzz-zee BEE-chu!*

**NESTING** Deep and compact cup of grass, lined with feathers, in brush; 3–5 eggs; 2 broods; May–July.

**FEEDING** A rather deliberate forager, gleans insects, especially caterpillars, from foliage at mid-levels.

**LIVELY SONG**
The buzzy song of this species is typical of the "black-throated" warbler group.

**SIMILAR SPECIES**

**BLACK-AND-WHITE WARBLER** ♂
see p.389
streaked undertail feathers

white eyebrow
black "V" mark on undertail feathers

**BLACK-AND-WHITE WARBLER** ♀
see p.389
black streaks on back

**OCCURRENCE**
Ranges from British Columbia south to California. Breeds in open coniferous and mixed woodlands with dense scrubby understory of piñon, juniper, and/or oak; migrants use a greater variety of habitats; winters in dry scrub and woodlands southward away from its breeding range.

| Length **5in (13cm)** | Wingspan **7½in (19cm)** | Weight **¼–⅜oz (7–10g)** |
| Social **Flocks** | Lifespan **Unknown** | Status **Secure** |

| DATE SEEN | WHERE | NOTES |
| --- | --- | --- |
| | | |
| | | |
| | | |
| | | |

| Order **Passeriformes** | Family **Parulidae** | Species ***Setophaga townsendi*** |
|---|---|---|

# Townsend's Warbler 🔊

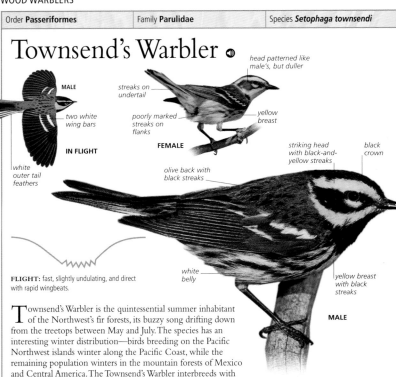

*head patterned like male's, but duller*

**MALE**

*streaks on undertail*

*two white wing bars*

**IN FLIGHT**

*white outer tail feathers*

*poorly marked streaks on flanks*

*yellow breast*

**FEMALE**

*striking head with black-and-yellow streaks*

*black crown*

*olive back with black streaks*

**FLIGHT:** fast, slightly undulating, and direct with rapid wingbeats.

*white belly*

*yellow breast with black streaks*

**MALE**

Townsend's Warbler is the quintessential summer inhabitant of the Northwest's fir forests, its buzzy song drifting down from the treetops between May and July. The species has an interesting winter distribution—birds breeding on the Pacific Northwest islands winter along the Pacific Coast, while the remaining population winters in the mountain forests of Mexico and Central America. The Townsend's Warbler interbreeds with the closely related Hermit Warbler in Washington and Oregon, resulting in varied-looking hybrids.

**VOICE** Song a series of buzzy notes that accelerate and increase in pitch; two examples are *wheezy wheezy wheezy zeee* and *zuuu dit-dit-dit zuuu dit-dit-dit zo ZEE zu ZAY.*

**NESTING** Bulky shallow cup of plant matter, hidden by needles on branch far from trunk, high in conifer trees; 3–7 eggs; 1 brood; May–July.

**FEEDING** Gleans insects, spiders, and caterpillars; will also take honeydew secreted by aphids and other insects.

**PALER JUVENILE**
Young Townsend's Warblers are paler than adults but show the same color pattern as adult females.

### SIMILAR SPECIES

**BLACK-THROATED GREEN WARBLER** ♂ see p.408

*larger bib*

*no yellow on breast*

**BLACK-THROATED GREEN WARBLER** ♀ see p.408

*paler cheek patch*

*lacks bright yellow breast*

**OCCURRENCE**
Breeds from southern Alaska to Wyoming in mature fir, coniferous, and mixed coniferous–deciduous forests; elevations range from sea level to subalpine. Populations winter either in Mexico and Central America or in California and Oregon in different habitats including coastal, woodland, and suburban parks and gardens.

| Length **5in (13cm)** | Wingspan **8in (20cm)** | Weight **¼–⅜oz (7–11g)** |
|---|---|---|
| Social **Flocks** | Lifespan **Up to 4 years** | Status **Secure** |

| DATE SEEN | WHERE | NOTES |
|---|---|---|
| | | |
| | | |
| | | |
| | | |
| | | |

| Order **Passeriformes** | Family **Parulidae** | Species *Setophaga occidentalis* |

# Hermit Warbler

**MALE**

two white wing bars  **FEMALE**

more olive upperparts

olive-green crown

pale throat

**IN FLIGHT**

white outer tail feathers

bright yellow head

narrow dark patch

plain face

grayish back

black throat

unstreaked white underparts

**MALE**

The yellow-headed Hermit Warbler is the southern counterpart of the Townsend's Warbler, which has a yellow head patterned with black and a yellow breast. In spite of differences in their markings, the two species interbreed where their ranges meet, in parts of Washington and Oregon. Their songs are nearly indistinguishable in the contact zone. Most hybrids resemble Hermit Warblers with greenish backs and yellow breasts. The Hermit Warbler lives in the canopy of tall conifers, including tall pines and douglas fir, and also in mixed conifer-hardwood forests. Its canopy-dwelling behavior makes this species difficult to observe.

**VOICE** Series of clear notes with down-slurred ending *wee-see wee-see wee-see seu*; another buzzier note, increasing in tempo and pitch: *zuuuu zoooh zeee zee-zee ZEEP*; similar to Black-throated Green Warbler of northeastern coniferous forests.

**NESTING** Cup of fine material in conifer on main horizontal branch near trunk; 4–5 eggs; 1 brood; May–July.

**FEEDING** Gleans a variety of insects, spiders, and caterpillars from branches and leaves; also catches insects in flight.

**FLIGHT:** fast, slightly undulating, and direct with rapid wingbeats, from treetop to treetop.

**EXCEPTIONAL VIEW**
Hermit Warblers spend nearly all their time in tree canopies and are rarely seen on the ground.

### SIMILAR SPECIES

| OLIVE WARBLER ♀ see p.458 | BLACK-THROATED GREEN WARBLER ♀ see p.408 |

dark patch beside eye

yellow extends further

darker underparts

bold streaks on flanks

**OCCURRENCE**
A conifer forest specialist preferring cool, old forests along the Pacific slope of its coastal ranges and sierras from Washington State to California. Winters in southern California as well as Mexico and Central America.

| Length **5in (13cm)** | Wingspan **8in (20cm)** | Weight **⁹⁄₃₂–³⁄₈oz (8–11g)** |
| Social **Flocks** | Lifespan **Up to 4 years** | Status **Secure (p)** |

| DATE SEEN | WHERE | | NOTES |
|---|---|---|---|
| | | | |
| | | | |
| | | | |
| | | | |

| Order **Passeriformes** | Family **Parulidae** | Species *Setophaga virens* |

# Black-throated Green Warbler 🔊

olive-green back

**MALE**

two white wing bars

same as male, but duller

greenish flanks

**FEMALE**

greenish cap

yellow face

**IN FLIGHT**

white outer tail feathers

yellowish flanks

**MALE**

black bib and chin

heavily streaked underparts

**FLIGHT:** fast, slightly undulating, and direct with rapid wingbeats; typical warbler flight.

This species is easy to distinguish as its bright yellow face is unique among birds inhabiting northeastern North America. It is a member of the *virens* "superspecies," a group of nonoverlapping species that are similar in plumage and vocalizations—the Black-throated Green, Golden-cheeked, Townsend's, and Hermit Warblers. Sadly, this species is vulnerable to habitat loss in parts of its wintering range.

**VOICE** Flat *tchip* call; flight call a rising *siii*; two high-pitched, buzzy songs, fast *zee zee zee zee zoo zee*; and lower, slower *zu zee zu-zu zee*.

**NESTING** Cup of twigs and grasses around 10–65ft (3–20m) on horizontal branch near trunk in the North, away from trunk in the South; 3–5 eggs; 1 brood; May–July.

**FEEDING** Gleans arthropods, especially caterpillars; also takes small fruit, including poison ivy berries, in nonbreeding season.

**YELLOW-AND-BLACK GEM**
From a high perch in a spruce tree, a male advertises his territory with persistent singing.

**SIMILAR SPECIES**

**GOLDEN-CHEEKED WARBLER ♂**
see p.467

black crown

**GOLDEN-CHEEKED WARBLER ♀**
see p.467

darker crown

darker upper breast

thin, black eye-line

**OCCURRENCE**
Breeds in many forest types, especially a mix of conifers and hardwoods, from British Columbia east to Newfoundland and the southeastern US along the Appalachians. Migrants and wintering birds use a variety of habitats. Winters from southern Texas into Venezuela; small numbers in Caribbean.

| Length **5in (13cm)** | Wingspan **8in (20cm)** | Weight **⁹⁄₃₂–³⁄₈oz (8–11g)** |
| Social **Migrant/Winter flocks** | Lifespan **Up to 6 years** | Status **Secure** |

| DATE SEEN | WHERE | NOTES |
| --- | --- | --- |
| | | |
| | | |
| | | |
| | | |

| Order **Passeriformes** | Family **Parulidae** | Species *Cardellina canadensis* |

# Canada Warbler

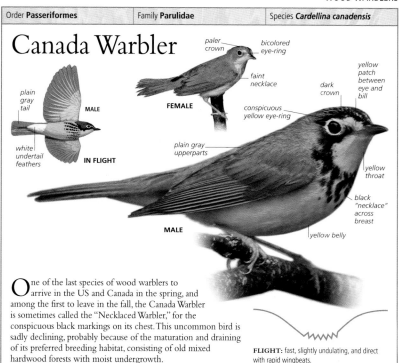

paler crown

bicolored eye-ring

faint necklace

**FEMALE**

plain gray tail

**MALE**

white undertail feathers

**IN FLIGHT**

plain gray upperparts

yellow patch between eye and bill

dark crown

conspicuous yellow eye-ring

yellow throat

black "necklace" across breast

**MALE**

yellow belly

Oone of the last species of wood warblers to arrive in the US and Canada in the spring, and among the first to leave in the fall, the Canada Warbler is sometimes called the "Necklaced Warbler," for the conspicuous black markings on its chest. This uncommon bird is sadly declining, probably because of the maturation and draining of its preferred breeding habitat, consisting of old mixed hardwood forests with moist undergrowth.

**VOICE** Call a thick *tchip;* flight call a variable, clear *plip;* song a haphazard jumble of sweet notes, often beginning with or interspersed with *tchip,* followed by a pause.

**NESTING** Concealed cup of leaves, in moss or grass, on or near ground; 4–5 eggs; 1 brood; May–June.

**FEEDING** Gleans at mid-levels for many species of insects; also flycatches and forages on ground.

**FLIGHT:** fast, slightly undulating, and direct with rapid wingbeats.

**TAKING FLIGHT**
This species often waits for prey to fly by, before launching into flight to pursue it.

**FAMILIAR MEAL**
Flying insects, including crane flies, make up the bulk of the Canada Warbler's diet.

### SIMILAR SPECIES

**MAGNOLIA WARBLER** ♀ see p.400

white eyebrow

streaked flanks

**KIRTLAND'S WARBLER** ♂

streaked mantle and flanks

**OCCURRENCE**
Breeds in moist deciduous, mixed, and coniferous forests with well-developed understory, especially swampy woods; migrants use well-vegetated habitats; winters in dense, wet thickets and a variety of tropical woodlands in South America.

| Length **5in (13cm)** | Wingspan **8in (20cm)** | Weight **⁹⁄₃₂–½oz (8–15g)** |
| Social **Flocks** | Lifespan **Up to 8 years** | Status **Declining** |

| DATE SEEN | WHERE | NOTES |
|---|---|---|
| | | |
| | | |
| | | |
| | | |
| | | |

| Order **Passeriformes** | Family **Parulidae** | Species **Cardellina pusilla** |
|---|---|---|

# Wilson's Warbler

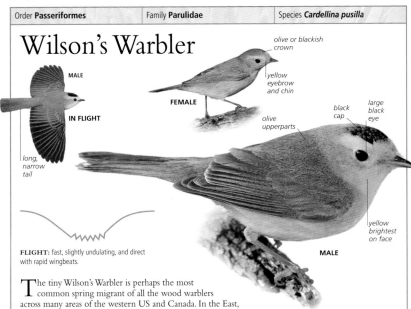

olive or blackish crown

**MALE**

**FEMALE**

yellow eyebrow and chin

**IN FLIGHT**

olive upperparts

black cap

large black eye

long, narrow tail

yellow brightest on face

**MALE**

**FLIGHT:** fast, slightly undulating, and direct with rapid wingbeats.

The tiny Wilson's Warbler is perhaps the most common spring migrant of all the wood warblers across many areas of the western US and Canada. In the East, however, it is much scarcer in spring. Wilson's Warblers have a wide range of habitats, yet their numbers are declining, especially in the West, as its riverside breeding habitats are gradually being destroyed by development. This species is named after the renowned early 19th-century ornithologist, Alexander Wilson.

**VOICE** Call a rich *chimp* or *champ;* flight call a sharp, liquid *tsik;* song a variable, chattering trill, often increases in speed *che che che che chi-chi-chi-chit.*
**NESTING** Cup of leaves and grass placed on or near ground in mosses or grass, higher along Pacific Coast; 4–6 eggs; 1 brood; April–June.
**FEEDING** Captures insects in foliage, leaf litter, or during flight; also takes berries and honeydew.

**BRIGHT WESTERN BIRD**
In its western range, male Wilson's Warblers have a glowing yellow-orange face; eastern birds are duller.

**EASY IDENTIFICATION**
The black cap and yellow face of the otherwise olive-colored Wilson's Warbler are good field marks.

**SIMILAR SPECIES**

**YELLOW WARBLER ♀** see p.401
yellow edges to wing feathers
shorter tail
yellow overall

**HOODED WARBLER ♀** see p.471
larger body
larger bill

**OCCURRENCE**
Breeds in wet shrubby thickets with no canopy, often along streams and lakes; Pacific slope birds use more varied habitats, including moist forests. Widespread in forests south of tundra, from Newfoundland to northern New England, west to Alaska and south through the western US to California and New Mexico.

| Length **4¾in (12cm)** | Wingspan **7in (17.5cm)** | Weight **⁷⁄₃₂–⁵⁄₁₆oz (6–9g)** |
|---|---|---|
| Social **Flocks** | Lifespan **Up to 6 years** | Status **Declining** |

| DATE SEEN | WHERE | NOTES |
|---|---|---|
| | | |
| | | |
| | | |
| | | |

# CARDINALS AND RELATIVES

BIRDS BELONGING to the cardinalidae family are visually stunning, noisy birds. Some tanagers (those in the genus *Piranga*) and grosbeaks and buntings (those in the genus *Passerina*) are grouped together with the Northern Cardinal and Pyrrhuloxia in this family. Tanagers are slender-bodied, cone-billed, finch-like birds that feed on insects, such as wasps and bees, and fruits in high foliage. Males are brightly colored, while the females are duller and greener. They have similar songs but more distinctive calls.

## CARDINALS

Cardinals are striking birds: the Northern Cardinal is almost entirely red, while the Pyrrhuloxia of the southwestern states is gray with vivid red patches. Both species have pointed, upstanding crests. Females are grayer, but still have the crest. Their bills are stout but short, adapted to feed on tough fruits, berries, and seeds.

## GROSBEAKS AND BUNTINGS

Grosbeaks in the genus *Pheucticus* are stocky, heavily built, sluggish species, with characteristically heavy, deeply triangular bills for splitting and peeling seeds. Again, males are bright and boldly colored, while females are duller but distinctively patterned. The colorful buntings in this family (with a preponderance of blues in their plumage) are similar to the grosbeaks, but more lightly built and with more delicate, triangular bills.

**MALE COLORS**
Male Western Tanagers are some of North America's most colorful birds.

| Order **Passeriformes** | Family **Cardinalidae** | Species *Piranga rubra* |

# Summer Tanager 🔊

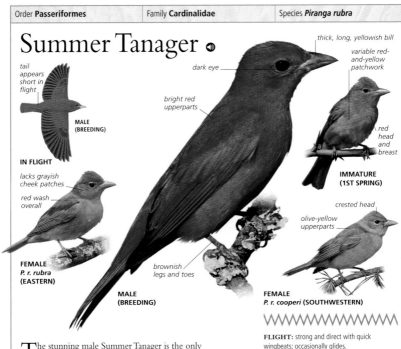

tail appears short in flight

**MALE (BREEDING)**

**IN FLIGHT**

dark eye

bright red upperparts

thick, long, yellowish bill

variable red-and-yellow patchwork

red head and breast

**IMMATURE (1ST SPRING)**

lacks grayish cheek patches

red wash overall

**FEMALE**
*P. r. rubra*
**(EASTERN)**

brownish legs and toes

**MALE (BREEDING)**

crested head

olive-yellow upperparts

**FEMALE**
*P. r. cooperi* (SOUTHWESTERN)

**FLIGHT:** strong and direct with quick wingbeats; occasionally glides.

**MAD FOR MULBERRIES**
All *Piranga* tanagers are frugivores in season and mulberries are one of their favorites.

The stunning male Summer Tanager is the only North American bird that is entirely bright red. Immature males in their first spring plumage are almost equally as striking, with their patchwork of bright yellow-and-red plumage. The two subspecies of the Summer Tanager are quite similar— *P. r. rubra* breeds in the East while *P. r. cooperi* breeds in the West. The latter is, on average, paler, larger, and longer-billed.
**VOICE** Call an explosive *PIT-tuck!* or *PIT-a TUK*; flight call a muffled, airy *vreee*; song similar to American Robin, but more muffled and with longer pauses.
**NESTING** Loosely built cup of grasses usually placed high up in tree; 3–4 eggs; 1 brood; May–August.
**FEEDING** Eats bees, wasps, and other insects; also consumes fruit.

## SIMILAR SPECIES

**HEPATIC TANAGER** ♀
see p.468
yellowish upperparts

reddish brown wings

**SCARLET TANAGER** ♀
greenish overall

smaller, grayish bill

darker, wings and tail

**OCCURRENCE**
*P. r. rubra* breeds in deciduous and mixed woodlands from New Jersey and Nebraska south to Texas; *P. r. cooperi* in cottonwood-willow habitats near streams and rivers from California and Utah to Texas and Mexico. Both winter from southern Texas and Mexico to Bolivia and Brazil, and the West Indies.

| Length **8in (20cm)** | Wingspan **12in (31cm)** | Weight **⅞–1⁷⁄₁₆oz (25–40g)** |
| Social **Solitary** | Lifespan **Unknown** | Status **Secure** |

| DATE SEEN | WHERE | NOTES |
| --- | --- | --- |
| | | |
| | | |
| | | |
| | | |

| Order **Passeriformes** | Family **Cardinalidae** | Species *Piranga ludoviciana* |

# Western Tanager

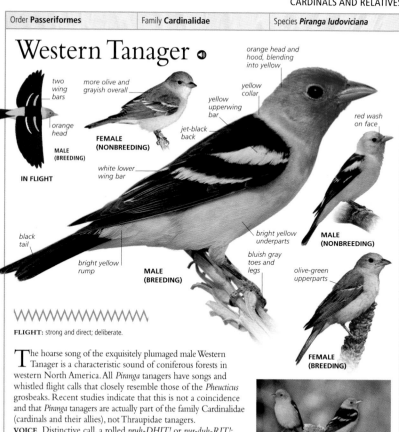

**IN FLIGHT**

two wing bars

orange head

**MALE (BREEDING)**

more olive and grayish overall

**FEMALE (NONBREEDING)**

jet-black back

orange head and hood, blending into yellow

yellow collar

yellow upperwing bar

red wash on face

white lower wing bar

black tail

bright yellow rump

**MALE (BREEDING)**

bright yellow underparts

bluish gray toes and legs

**MALE (NONBREEDING)**

olive-green upperparts

**FEMALE (BREEDING)**

**FLIGHT:** strong and direct; deliberate.

The hoarse song of the exquisitely plumaged male Western Tanager is a characteristic sound of coniferous forests in western North America. All *Piranga* tanagers have songs and whistled flight calls that closely resemble those of the *Pheucticus* grosbeaks. Recent studies indicate that this is not a coincidence and that *Piranga* tanagers are actually part of the family Cardinalidae (cardinals and their allies), not Thraupidae tanagers.
**VOICE** Distinctive call, a rolled *pruh-DHIT!* or *pur-duh-RIT!*; flight call a *hweee*; song similar to Scarlet Tanager, but less burry.
**NESTING** Loosely woven cup of grasses, lined with rootlets, high in tree; 3–5 eggs; 1 brood; May–August.
**FEEDING** Forages for insects, such as termites, flies, moths, and bees in breeding season; eats berries in nonbreeding season.

**ORANGE AND YELLOW**
Two Western Tanagers display their beautiful orange, yellow, and black plumage.

## SIMILAR SPECIES

**SCARLET TANAGER ♀**

greener overall

lacks bold wing bars

**BRIGHT BLEND**
This colorful bird blends into its surroundings surprisingly well.

**OCCURRENCE**
Breeds farther north than any other tanager, in open coniferous and mixed forests of the West, from southeastern Alaska and southwestern Northwest Territories to northern Baja California and western Texas. Winters from southern California and southward to Mexico.

| Length **7½in (19cm)** | Wingspan **11½in (29cm)** | Weight **⅞–1¼ oz (25–35g)** |
| Social **Solitary** | Lifespan **Up to 8 years** | Status **Secure** |

| DATE SEEN | WHERE | NOTES |
|-----------|-------|-------|
|  |  |  |
|  |  |  |
|  |  |  |
|  |  |  |
|  |  |  |

| Order **Passeriformes** | Family **Cardinalidae** | Species *Pheucticus ludovicianus* |
| --- | --- | --- |

# Rose-breasted Grosbeak 🔊

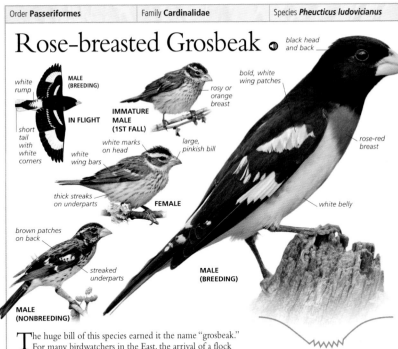

black head and back

white rump

**MALE (BREEDING)**

**IN FLIGHT**

short tail with white corners

white wing bars

white marks on head

thick streaks on underparts

brown patches on back

streaked underparts

**MALE (NONBREEDING)**

rosy or orange breast

**IMMATURE MALE (1ST FALL)**

large, pinkish bill

**FEMALE**

bold, white wing patches

rose-red breast

white belly

**MALE (BREEDING)**

The huge bill of this species earned it the name "grosbeak." For many birdwatchers in the East, the arrival of a flock of dazzling male Rose-breasted Grosbeaks in early May signals the peak of spring songbird migration. Adult males in their tuxedo attire with rose-red ties are unmistakable, but females and immature males are more somber. In the fall, immature males often have orange breasts, and may be mistaken for female Black-headed Grosbeaks. The difference is in the pink wing lining usually visible on perched birds, pink bill, and streaking across the center of the breast.

**FLIGHT:** undulating but powerful flight with bursts of wingbeats.

**VOICE** Call a high, sharp, explosive *sink* or *eeuk*, flight call an airy *vreee*; song a liquid, flute-like warble, rather slow in delivery, almost relaxed.

**NESTING** Loose, open cup or platform, usually in deciduous saplings, mid- to high level; 2–5 eggs; 1–2 broods; May–July.

**FEEDING** Eats arthropods, fruit, seeds, and buds.

**SIMILAR SPECIES**

**PURPLE FINCH ♀** see p.337

much smaller

thick, lateral throat stripe

smaller, dark bill

**BLACK-HEADED GROSBEAK ♀** see p.415

tawny breast

pencil-thin streaks on underparts

**STUNNING MALE**
A striking male Rose-breasted Grosbeak in springtime is quite unmistakable on a tree.

**OCCURRENCE**
Uncommon in the western US; breeds in western Canada in deciduous and mixed woods, parks, and orchards. Found across the northeastern US, and across Canada westward from Newfoundland through Ontario to southeastern Yukon. Winters from Mexico and the Caribbean, south to Guyana and Peru.

| Length **8in (20cm)** | Wingspan **12½in (32cm)** | Weight **1¼–2oz (35–55g)** |
| --- | --- | --- |
| Social **Solitary/Small flocks** | Lifespan **Up to 13 years** | Status **Secure** |

| DATE SEEN | WHERE | NOTES |
| --- | --- | --- |
| | | |
| | | |
| | | |
| | | |
| | | |

| Order **Passeriformes** | Family **Cardinalidae** | Species *Pheucticus melanocephalus* |

# Black-headed Grosbeak

**MALE (BREEDING)**

large, white wing patch

**IN FLIGHT**

brown head and upperparts

white eyebrow

tawny breast

**FEMALE**

fine brown streaks on underparts

orange rump

blackish brown cheek patch

white tip to feathers

pencil-thin streaks on breast

black upperparts

**MALE (1ST FALL)**

two white wing bars

black head

thick gray-and-black bill

orange hind collar

orange breast

**MALE**

short tail, with white corners

**FLIGHT:** undulating but powerful, with few rapid wingbeats followed by glides.

Well-known and widespread across the West, this orange-breasted grosbeak is the western counterpart of the Rose-breasted Grosbeak. The two species are closely related, despite their color differences, and interbreed where their ranges meet in the Great Plains. The Black-headed Grosbeak is aggressive on its breeding grounds, with both sexes fighting off intruders.

**VOICE** Call a *hwik*, similar to Rose-breasted Grosbeak, but flatter, "hollow," and less squeaky; song generally higher, faster, less fluid, and harsher.

**NESTING** Loose, open cup or platform, usually in deciduous sapling, not far above eye level; 3–5 eggs; 1–2 broods; May–September.

**FEEDING** Gleans insects and spiders; also eats seeds and fruit.

**STREAMSIDE SONGSTER**
Through much of its range, this species is common along riverside corridors containing a variety of trees.

### SIMILAR SPECIES

**CASSIN'S FINCH ♀** *smaller,* see p.338 *dark bill*

*much smaller overall*

*lacks bold wing markings*

**ROSE-BREASTED GROSBEAK ♀** *pink* see p.414 *bill*

*dense, thick streaking below*

*white belly*

**OCCURRENCE**
Breeds in dense deciduous growth—old fields, hedgerows, woodlands along waterways, disturbed forests, and hillside thickets—from British Columbia and Saskatchewan, south to Baja California and central Mexico. Winters in interior, highland, and Pacific slope of Mexico.

| Length **8½in (21cm)** | Wingspan **12½in (32cm)** | Weight **1¹⁄₁₆–2oz (40–55g)** |
| Social **Solitary/Small flocks** | Lifespan **Up to 9 years** | Status **Secure** |

| DATE SEEN | WHERE | NOTES |
|---|---|---|
| | | |
| | | |
| | | |
| | | |
| | | |

| Order **Passeriformes** | Family **Cardinalidae** | Species *Passerina caerulea* |
|---|---|---|

# Blue Grosbeak 🔊

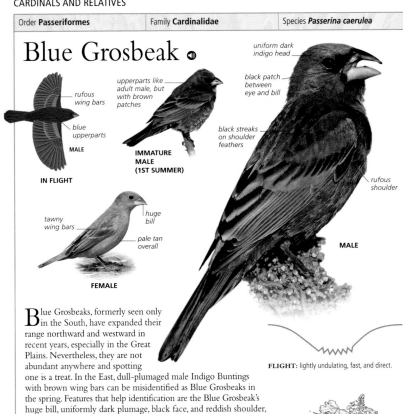

**MALE** — blue upperparts, rufous wing bars

**IN FLIGHT**

**IMMATURE MALE (1ST SUMMER)** — upperparts like adult male, but with brown patches

uniform dark indigo head

black patch between eye and bill

black streaks on shoulder feathers

rufous shoulder

**MALE**

**FEMALE** — tawny wing bars, huge bill, pale tan overall

**B**lue Grosbeaks, formerly seen only in the South, have expanded their range northward and westward in recent years, especially in the Great Plains. Nevertheless, they are not abundant anywhere and spotting one is a treat. In the East, dull-plumaged male Indigo Buntings with brown wing bars can be misidentified as Blue Grosbeaks in the spring. Features that help identification are the Blue Grosbeak's huge bill, uniformly dark plumage, black face, and reddish shoulder, which the buntings lack.

**VOICE** Call a loud, sharp, metallic *tchink*; similar to Indigo Bunting, but lower-pitched, louder, and burrier; song rambling, husky.

**NESTING** Compact cup placed low in deciduous tangle; 3–5 eggs; 1–2 broods; April–July.

**FEEDING** Eats seeds in winter, insects such as beetles, caterpillars, and grasshoppers in summer, and fruit.

**FLIGHT:** lightly undulating, fast, and direct.

### SIMILAR SPECIES

**INDIGO BUNTING ♂ 1ST ⚥**
see p.469 — pale blue markings overall

**LAZULI BUNTING ♀**
see p.417 — pale brown upperparts, much smaller bill

**TRUE INDIGO**
The Blue Grosbeak is actually indigo in color, with rufous shoulders and wing bars.

**OCCURRENCE**
Breeds in dense undergrowth of disturbed habitats: old fields, hedgerows, and desert scrub across the southern US from California to New Jersey, and southward to northwestern Costa Rica; breeders are trans-Gulf migrants; winters from Mexico to Panama and West Indies.

| Length **6¾in (17cm)** | Wingspan **11in (28cm)** | Weight **⅞ –1¹⁄₁₆oz (25–30g)** |
|---|---|---|
| Social **Large flocks** | Lifespan **Up to 6 years** | Status **Secure** |

| DATE SEEN | WHERE | NOTES |
|---|---|---|
| | | |
| | | |
| | | |
| | | |
| | | |

| Order **Passeriformes** | Family **Cardinalidae** | Species *Passerina amoena* |

# Lazuli Bunting 🔊

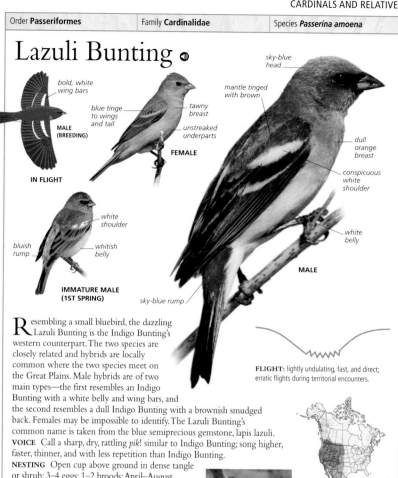

**MALE (BREEDING)**

bold, white wing bars

blue tinge to wings and tail

**IN FLIGHT**

sky-blue head

mantle tinged with brown

tawny breast

unstreaked underparts

**FEMALE**

dull orange breast

conspicuous white shoulder

white belly

**MALE**

white shoulder

bluish rump

whitish belly

**IMMATURE MALE (1ST SPRING)**

sky-blue rump

Resembling a small bluebird, the dazzling Lazuli Bunting is the Indigo Bunting's western counterpart. The two species are closely related and hybrids are locally common where the two species meet on the Great Plains. Male hybrids are of two main types—the first resembles an Indigo Bunting with a white belly and wing bars, and the second resembles a dull Indigo Bunting with a brownish smudged back. Females may be impossible to identify. The Lazuli Bunting's common name is taken from the blue semiprecious gemstone, lapis lazuli.

**VOICE** Call a sharp, dry, rattling *pik!* similar to Indigo Bunting; song higher, faster, thinner, and with less repetition than Indigo Bunting.
**NESTING** Open cup above ground in dense tangle or shrub; 3–4 eggs; 1–2 broods; April–August.
**FEEDING** Eats seeds and fruit; insects if breeding.

**FLIGHT:** lightly undulating, fast, and direct; erratic flights during territorial encounters.

### SIMILAR SPECIES

**BLUE GROSBEAK ♀**
see p.416

reddish rust on shoulder

larger overall

bigger bill

**INDIGO BUNTING ♀**
see p.469

lacks bold wing bars

streaking on breast

**DAPPLED AND DAPPER**
Brightly colored males blend into their surroundings surprisingly well in dappled sunlight.

**OCCURRENCE**
Breeds in various open, disturbed habitats, especially alongside waterways and in thickets from southern British Columbia and southern Saskatchewan to northern Baja California and northern New Mexico. Winters from southern Arizona to southwestern Mexico. Casual in the East.

| Length **5½in (14cm)** | Wingspan **8½in (22cm)** | Weight **⁷⁄₁₆–⅝oz (13–18g)** |
| Social **Large flocks** | Lifespan **Up to 10 years** | Status **Secure** |

| DATE SEEN | WHERE | NOTES |
|-----------|-------|-------|
| | | |
| | | |
| | | |
| | | |
| | | |

# RARE SPECIES

| Family **Anatidae** | Species ***Dendrocygna autumnalis*** |
|---|---|

## Black-bellied Whistling-Duck

With its distinctive red bill, black belly, and long, pink legs, this Whistling-Duck is unmistakable. Unlike most other waterfowl, it has an upright posture when perched. Whistling-ducks are also known as "tree-ducks" because they perch on trees when roosting, and build their nests in tree holes.

**OCCURRENCE** Prefers shallow, freshwater habitats; rice fields are a common foraging habitat; also occurs along shorelines and mud bars. Casual west to southeastern California and occasionally east as far as Florida.

**VOICE** Soft wheezy series of 5–6 notes *pit pit weee do dew*; flight calls include a *chit-chit-chit*.

red bill

black belly

**ADULT**

pink legs

| Length **18½–20in (47–51cm)** | Wingspan **34–36in (86–91cm)** |
|---|---|

| Family **Anatidae** | Species ***Dendrocygna bicolor*** |
|---|---|

## Fulvous Whistling-Duck

Although sometimes thought of as dabbling ducks, whistling-ducks behave more like swans, as they form long-term pairs, but without elaborate courtship displays, and the males help to raise the brood. The Fulvous Whistling-Duck is widespread in tropical regions, but in the US it is found in coastal Texas, where it is associated with rice fields. The Fulvous Whistling-Duck is rare in California.

**OCCURRENCE** Permanent resident in southern Texas and Florida; range expands in summer to coastal Texas and Louisiana. Casual vagrant as far west as British Columbia and east as Nova Scotia.

**VOICE** High-pitched squeaky *pi-teeeew*; often calls in flight.

tawny buff head and neck

**ADULT**

| Length **16½–20in (42–51cm)** | Wingspan **33–37in (85–93cm)** |
|---|---|

| Family **Anatidae** | Species *Anser canagicus* |
|---|---|

# Emperor Goose

With its white head, black throat, and scalloped silvery-gray body and wings, the Emperor Goose is a distinctive bird. During migration, they congregate to feed in large estuaries along the Alaska Peninsula. The Alaskan population of Emperor Geese declined drastically during the 1960s–80s, but has remained stable since then.

**OCCURRENCE** Breeds in Arctic and subarctic coastal saltmarsh habitats in Alaska and eastern Russia. Majority winter along the Alaska Peninsula and on ice-free beaches in the Aleutian Islands.

**VOICE** Calls rapid high-pitched *kla-ha kla-ha kla-ha*, deep ringing *u-lugh u-lugh* when alarmed.

white head

silver-gray plumage with black-and-white edges

**MALE**

| Length **26in (66cm)** | Wingspan **4ft (1.2m)** |
|---|---|

| Family **Anatidae** | Species *Branta hutchinsii* |
|---|---|

# Cackling Goose

Arctic populations of the Canada Goose, long considered a subspecies, *Branta canadensis hutchinsii*, are now believed by many ornithologists to be a distinct but closely related species, *Branta hutchinsii*, the Cackling Goose. The populations breeding in the Aleutian Islands winter in California; those from the Canadian Arctic winter in the Great Plain and the Gulf Coast. Cackling Geese are smaller and thicker-necked than Canada Geese.

**OCCURRENCE** Breeds in rocky tundra from the Aleutians east to Baffin Island and Hudson Bay. Winters in pastures and agricultural fields; in the West, from British Columbia to California.

**VOICE** Male call a *honk* or *bark*; females have higher pitched *hrink*; also high-pitched yelps.

white chin strap

**ADULT**

| Length **21½–30in (55–75cm)** | Wingspan **4¼–5ft (1.3–1.5m)** |
|---|---|

| Family **Anatidae** | Species *Cygnus buccinator* |
|---|---|

# Trumpeter Swan

North America's quintessential swan and heaviest waterfowl, the magnificent Trumpeter Swan has made a remarkable comeback after its numbers were severely reduced by hunting in the 1800s. By the mid-1930s, fewer than a hundred birds were known to exist. Successful reintroduction efforts were made in the upper Midwest and Ontario to reestablish the species to its former breeding range. Its typical far-reaching call is usually the best way to identify it.

**OCCURRENCE** Alaskan and northern Canadian breeders go south in winter; others remain year-round at places such as Yellowstone National Park. Found on freshwater lakes and marshes with plenty of vegetation and on estuaries in winter.

**VOICE** Call nasal, resonant *oh-OH* reminiscent of French horn.

all-white plumage

**ADULT**

| Length **4¼–5ft (1.3–1.5m)** | Wingspan **6½ft (2m)** |
|---|---|

| Family **Anatidae** | Species *Aythya marila* |
|---|---|

# Greater Scaup

A great swimmer and diver, the Greater Scaup is the only diving duck of the genus *Aythya* that breeds both in North America and Eurasia. More restricted to coastal breeding and wintering habitats, it is less numerous in North America than its close relative, the Lesser Scaup. Greater Scaups can form large, often sexually segregated flocks outside the breeding season.

**OCCURRENCE** Most birds breed in western coastal Alaska on tundra wetlands; also in lower densities in northwestern and eastern Canada. Almost all birds winter offshore, along the Atlantic and Pacific Coasts, or on the Great Lakes.

**VOICE** During courtship, male call a soft, fast, wheezy *week week wheew*; female gives a series of growled monotone *arrrr* notes.

smooth, round black head with greenish-purple gloss

**MALE (BREEDING)**

wavy-patterned gray back

| Length **15–22in (38–56cm)** | Wingspan **28–31in (72–79cm)** |
|---|---|

| Family **Anatidae** | Species *Polysticta stelleri* |

# Steller's Eider

With its steep forehead, flat crown, and the way it floats high on the water, Steller's Eider resembles a dabbling duck. Steller's Eiders are the synchronized swimmers of the duck clan. The Arctic and Pacific populations of this species have recently declined in numbers, and are classified as vulnerable.

**OCCURRENCE** Pacific population breeds mainly in Russia's far northeast; small numbers breed in Alaska. About half the Russian population molts and winters in large groups along the Alaska Peninsula and in the Aleutian Islands.

**VOICE** Female a rapid, harsh growling call; also loud *qua-haaa* or *cooay*; males growl but are rarely heard.

**MALE**

pointed tail

| Length **17–18in (43–46cm)** | Wingspan **28–30in (70–76cm)** |

| Family **Anatidae** | Species *Somateria fischeri* |

# Spectacled Eider

In order to see the striking Spectacled Eider one needs to travel to remote tundra in the far north of Alaska. Much of their life is spent offshore, with males spending up to 11 months of the year at sea. In flight, male Spectacled Eiders reveal more black extending up the breast than the other eiders, and the females have gray, rather than white, underwings.

**OCCURRENCE** Arctic coastal breeding sites are remote and isolated; most birds breed in northern Russia, few in Alaska. They winter in dense flocks in small ice-free areas in the Bering Sea.

**VOICE** Males a faint *ho HOOO* during display, otherwise silent; females a rapid clucking call *buckbuck buckbuck* with emphasis on second syllable; also guttural rolled *gow gow gow*.

large white cheek patch

mossy green nape

**MALE (SUMMER)**

| Length **20½–22½in (52–57cm)** | Wingspan **33in (83cm)** |

| Family **Anatidae** | Species *Somateria spectabilis* |

# King Eider

The scientific name of the King Eider, *spectabilis*, means "remarkable," and its gaudy marking and coloring around the head and bill make it hard to misidentify. Female King Eiders, however, can be hard to distinguish from female Common Eiders. King Eiders can dive down to 180ft (55m) when foraging for mollusks.

**OCCURRENCE** Nests along coasts and inland in the High Arctic, in a variety of habitats; prefers well-drained areas. During winter, found mostly in coastal waters along the southern edge of the ice pack.

**VOICE** Courting males give a repeated series of low, rolled dove-like *arrrrooooo* calls, each rising, then falling, followed by softer *cooos*; females give grunts and croaks.

green cheek

reddish orange bill

**MALE (BREEDING)**

| Length **18½–25in (47–64cm)** | Wingspan **37in (94cm)** |

| Family **Anatidae** | Species *Somateria mollissima* |

# Common Eider

The Common Eider is the most numerous and widespread of the eiders. Males show considerable seasonal plumage changes, and do not acquire their striking adult plumage until their third year.

**OCCURRENCE** Arctic breeder on coastal islands and peninsulas. One population stays in the Hudson and James Bays region. Others winter in the Bering Sea, Hudson Bay, northern British Columbia, Gulf of St. Lawrence, and along the Atlantic Coast.

**VOICE** Repeated hoarse, grating notes *korr-korr-korr*; male's owl-like *ah-WOO-ooo*; female's low, guttural notes *krrrr-krrrr-krrrr*.

**ADULT (MALE)**

white upperparts

| Length **19½–28in (50–71cm)** | Wingspan **31–42in (80–108cm)** |

Family **Odontophoridae** | Species *Oreortyx pictus*

# Mountain Quail

The most diagnostic field marks of this quail are its deep-gray body offset by a chestnut-colored throat and "zebra-striped" flanks edged in black and buff, and its thin, usually vertical head plumes. The largest quail found in the US, it is an adept runner, even uphill, and often prefers running to flying.

**OCCURRENCE** Resident in Washington, Oregon, California, Idaho, and Nevada; in mixed evergreen and oak forests at mid- to high elevations.

**VOICE** Males emit crowing *qu-ook* to attract mates; scattered coveys reunite using whistled *kow, kow*.

long head plumes

chestnut throat

striped flanks

**ADULT**

Length **9–11in (23–28cm)** | Wingspan **14–16in (35–41cm)**

Family **Odontophoridae** | Species *Colinus virginianus*

# Northern Bobwhite

This small, plump, chicken-like bird is loved by hunters. When flushed it erupts in "coveys" of 10 to 20 individuals, bursting from groundcover and dispersing in many directions. Large numbers are raised in captivity and released to supplement wild populations for hunting.

**OCCURRENCE** Widely distributed in much of the eastern US, and in Mexico, southward to Guatemala. Occurs in a patchwork of young forests, fields, and brushy hedges. Very local in the West; introduced in the Northwest and Colorado.

**VOICE** Characteristic *bob-WHITE* or *bob-bob-WHITE* whistled by males in breeding season; call to reunite flock includes *hoi-lee* and *hoi*.

**MALE**

short wings

fine streaking on breast

Length **8–10in (20–25cm)** | Wingspan **11–14in (28–35cm)**

Family **Odontophoridae** | Species *Callipepla squamata*

# Scaled Quail

Named for the scale-like appearance of its chest, neck, and belly feathers, this quail is also called the "Blue Quail," because of its bluish sheen in some lights, or "Cottontop," because of the fluffy white tip to its crest. Its population periodically experiences a "boom and bust" cycle that may be tied to rainfall and subsequent food shortages or abundance, but is also influenced by grazing practices.

**OCCURRENCE** Locally common in arid rangelands and semideserts of western Texas, New Mexico, and eastern Arizona, preferring less dense vegetation than other quails.

**VOICE** Flushed or separated covey (flock) uses 2-syllable *CHE-kar* call to reunite.

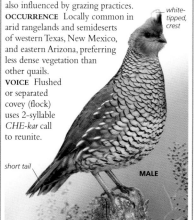

white-tipped, crest

short tail

**MALE**

Length **10–12in (25–30cm)** | Wingspan **13–15in (33–38cm)**

Family **Odontophoridae** | Species *Cyrtonyx montezumae*

# Montezuma Quail

When seen, the male Montezuma Quail is unmistakable with its "clown-like" black-and-white face and white-spotted underparts, but its secretive nature makes this species difficult to spot. When threatened, it prefers to crouch, walk, and then run away, but it may also crouch and freeze in place, then suddenly burst into flight.

**OCCURRENCE** Habitat is a mixture of grassy and open pine oak woodlands at 4,000–6,000ft (1,200–1,800m); also found in arid scrubland. Predominantly a Mexican species.

**VOICE** Males produce a loud, descending buzzy whistle *wheeerrr*, sometimes compared to the sound of a bomb falling; female emits low descending hoots.

**MALE**

streaked back

Length **8½–9in (21–23cm)** | Wingspan **11–12in (28–30cm)**

| Family **Phasianidae** | Species ***Centrocercus urophasianus*** |
|---|---|

# Greater Sage-Grouse

The Greater Sage-Grouse is the largest native North American grouse. Each spring, males gather on communal sites, known as "leks," where they compete for females with spectacular courtship displays. As many as 40 males may gather at a lek for these events. Once numerous, Greater Sage-Grouse populations have declined, as human encroachment on sagebrush habitats has increased.

**OCCURRENCE** Present distribution in North America is a fraction of its formerly large range in the vast sagebrush plains of the West. Breeds in a variety of habitats, the ideal being composed of several sagebrush species of varying heights.

**VOICE** Clucks repeatedly when flushed; male makes odd popping sounds with throat sacs when displaying.

spiky tail, fanned out in display

fluffy white neck

**MALE**

| Length **19½–30in (50–76cm)** | Wingspan **32–39in (81–99cm)** |
|---|---|

| Family **Phasianidae** | Species ***Centrocercus minimus*** |
|---|---|

# Gunnison Sage-Grouse

In the 1990s, ornithologists discovered differences between the populations of the Gunnison Basin, Colorado, and other Sage-Grouse populations. This led to the description of a new species, *C. minimus*, in 2001. Fewer than 10 breeding populations of *C. minimus* occur within this restricted area. Continued loss of its habitat because of cultivation and development puts this species at risk of extinction.

**OCCURRENCE** Prefers areas of mixed, tall sagebrush with significant overhead cover and ground-based succulent plant foliage, especially in areas along river corridors. Also found where there is deciduous scrub and fruit-bearing trees.

**VOICE** Clucks repeatedly when flushed; male makes about nine booming sounds when displaying.

long, spiky, pointed tail, fanned in display

black nape plume

**MALE**

| Length **21–23in (53–58cm)** | Wingspan **33–36in (83–91cm)** |
|---|---|

| Family **Phasianidae** | Species ***Tympanuchus cupido*** |
|---|---|

# Greater Prairie-Chicken

Once common in prairie and woodland areas across central North America, numbers of Greater Prairie-Chicken have been greatly reduced as their native habitats have given way to agriculture. During the breeding season, males aggressively defend communal areas called "leks" and perform dramatic displays to entice females to mate with them.

**OCCURRENCE** Breeds in openings mixed with oak-forested river corridors with areas of native tallgrass prairie; resident year-round. Local in the west-central states.

**VOICE** During courtship, males emit "booming" sounds like a three-part low hoot; also cackling calls.

bright orange skin of "air sac"

**MALE (DISPLAYING)**

| Length **15½–17½in (40–45cm)** | Wingspan **26–29in (66–74cm)** |
|---|---|

| Family **Phasianidae** | Species ***Tympanuchus pallidicinctus*** |
|---|---|

# Lesser Prairie-Chicken

Destruction of its native shortgrass prairie and oak scrub habitat has drastically reduced the range and numbers of the Lesser Prairie-Chicken. The species is sensitive to fences, buildings, and power line towers, and females do not nest near such structures, further reducing its already restricted habitat.

**OCCURRENCE** Primarily native shortgrass prairie mixed with shrub woodlands; fallow fields; occasional agricultural properties.

**VOICE** Males "boom" or "gobble" in series of high, hooting notes during courtship display; females occasionally "boom" on lek.

**MALE**

barred upperparts

hornlike feathers during displays

| Length **15–17in (38–43cm)** | Wingspan **23–26in (58–66cm)** |
|---|---|

| Family **Phasianidae** | Species ***Tetraogallus himalayensis*** |
|---|---|

# Himalayan Snowcock

Introduced from Asia in the 1960s to overcome Nevada's lack of upland galliforms, it took the Himalayan Snowcock nearly 20 years to become successfully established. This large, wary species with its whitish head and brownish body appears gray when viewed from a distance. The very restricted range and high elevation habitat make this bird unlikely to be mistaken for anything else.

**OCCURRENCE** At high elevations near the snow line in the Ruby Mountains of northwestern Nevada.

**VOICE** Variety of low and high whistles; clucks, cackles, and chuckles to signal food, alarm, or mating.

gray background with mottled brown-and-gray streaks

dark brown stripes on each side of neck

**ADULT**

| Length **23½–29in (60–74cm)** | Wingspan **28–31in (71–79cm)** |
|---|---|

| Family **Columbidae** | Species ***Streptopelia decaocto*** |
|---|---|

# Eurasian Collared-Dove

A stocky bird, the Eurasian Collared-Dove can be identified by the black collar on the back of its neck and its pale body color. First released in the Bahamas in the mid-1970s, this species is now spreading rapidly across the mainland. Very tolerant of humans, it regularly nests and feeds in urban and suburban areas. Eurasian Collared-Doves have a high reproductive rate, as they raise several broods a year from March to November.

**OCCURRENCE** In North America south of the northern forest zone in suburban and urban areas; agricultural areas. In the West, less widespread, mostly in the Southwest and California.

**VOICE** Repeated 4-note *coo-hoo-HOO-cook* that is quick and low-pitched; also harsh, nasal *krreeew* in flight.

black collar on hind neck

**ADULT**

pale gray

| Length **11½–12in (29–30cm)** | Wingspan **14in (35cm)** |
|---|---|

| Family **Columbidae** | Species ***Streptopelia chinensis*** |
|---|---|

# Spotted Dove

Originally from southern and eastern Asia, the Spotted Dove was introduced to urban areas of California over a century ago. More chunky and with broader wings and tail than the Mourning Dove, this medium-sized species has grayish brown upperparts and pinkish brown underparts. A characteristic feature is a broad, black neck patch with white spots. The Spotted Dove lives in parks, gardens, and suburbs.

**OCCURRENCE** Found in southern California from Santa Barbara and Bakersfield south to Baja California, uncommon.

**VOICE** Hoarse *coo-coo-croooo* call with emphasis on the middle and last notes.

broad black-and-white neck patch

**ADULT**

| Length **12in (30cm)** | Wingspan **19½in (50cm)** |
|---|---|

| Family **Columbidae** | Species ***Columbina inca*** |
|---|---|

# Inca Dove

A small, brownish gray dove that forages on the ground, the Inca Dove can be identified by the scaly pattern of its plumage. It has expanded its distribution northward to the US in the last 100 years, from its Central American and Mexican range. It now breeds in the Southwest from California, Nevada, and Arizona, eastward all the way to the Mississippi River. It is secretive, yet tame, and is often found in human settlements. Inca Doves commonly flush from almost underfoot, revealing the chestnut color of their wings.

**OCCURRENCE** Resident in cities, towns, and farms. Forages on lawns and in barnyards; occasionally near rivers and streams but favors drier areas in the south of its range.

**VOICE** Repeated 2-note chant, *pol-pah*, which can sound like the words "no hope;" sometimes low, trilling *coo*.

**ADULT**

scaly plumage pattern

| Length **7–9in (18–23cm)** | Wingspan **11in (28cm)** |
|---|---|

| Family **Columbidae** | Species *Columbina passerina* |
|---|---|

# Common Ground Dove

The Common Ground Dove, the smallest of the North American doves, is only slightly larger than a sparrow. It retains its pair-bond throughout the year and tends not to form flocks: birds in a pair usually remain within a few yards of each other. Besides its diminutive size, the Common Ground Dove is recognizable by prominent black spots on its reddish-looking wings, scaly underparts (seen when perched), and its square, blackish tail while in flight.

**OCCURRENCE** In the US, has a disjointed population in the Southwest, Texas, and Florida. Lives in dry, sandy areas with open vegetation and also shrubby habitats.

**VOICE** Simple, repeated, ascending double-note *wah-up* given every 2–3 seconds.

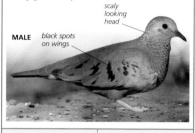

scaly looking head

**MALE** black spots on wings

| Length **6–7in (15–18cm)** | Wingspan **11in (28cm)** |
|---|---|

| Family **Columbidae** | Species *Columbina talpacoti* |
|---|---|

# Ruddy Ground Dove

The female Ruddy Ground Dove is similar to the Common Ground Dove with its black wing spots. It lacks the scaly neck pattern, however. Male Ruddy Ground Doves are more colorful, with an overall rusty-red color and contrasting pale-gray head. Common in tropical America north to Mexico, the Ruddy Ground Dove is mostly a winter visitor to the US Southwest (Arizona) and southern California, but it occasionally breeds there.

**OCCURRENCE** Localized in California, Arizona, New Mexico, and Texas; occurs in woodlands, gardens, fields, forest edges, and shrubbery.

**VOICE** Monotonous, endlessly repeated 2-syllable *ca-whoop* given every second or so.

**ADULT (FEMALE)** marked bars on wings

pale gray head

| Length **6¾in (17cm)** | Wingspan **11in (28cm)** |
|---|---|

| Family **Cuculidae** | Species *Crotophaga sulcirostris* |
|---|---|

# Groove-billed Ani

Anis, members of the cuckoo family, have black plumage, long tails, and high, narrow, blackish bills. They always appear dishevelled—as if their feathers were about to fall off. Two of their toes point forward and two backward. These social birds exhibit an unusual communal nesting behavior— several females lay eggs in the same nest, and both males and females share incubation duties.

**OCCURRENCE** Breeds along the Rio Grande Valley, but leaves the area in the winter. Widely distributed, and resident, from Mexico to South America.

**VOICE** Call a liquid *Tee-ho,* accented on first syllable, given in flight and when perched, chorus-like when many birds call together.

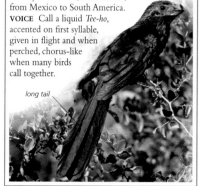

long tail

| Length **13½in (34cm)** | Wingspan **17in (43cm)** |
|---|---|

| Family **Caprimulgidae** | Species *Chordeiles acutipennis* |
|---|---|

# Lesser Nighthawk

The Lesser Nighthawk is a wide-ranging airborne forager, and is well camouflaged while resting on the ground in daytime. Most active at dawn and dusk, it swoops low over water, bush, and desert in pursuit of insect prey, which it tracks with agile and abrupt changes in direction. This species was formerly known as the Trilling Nighthawk because of its distinctive call, which distinguishes it from the similar looking Common Nighthawk where the two species occur together.

**OCCURRENCE** Breeds in desert and open scrub and along watercourses. Occurs from the southern US to Central and South America as far south as Paraguay and Peru.

**VOICE** Low, trilled whistle lasting up to 12 seconds and resembling a calling toad.

white band close to wing tips

**MALE** white throat

| Length **8–9in (20–23cm)** | Wingspan **21–23in (53–58cm)** |
|---|---|

| Family **Caprimulgidae** | Species *Antrostomus carolinensis* |
|---|---|

# Chuck-will's-widow

The largest North American nightjar, the Chuck-will's-widow is also one of the least known. It is tolerant of human development and often nests in suburban and even urban areas. It captures its insect prey in flight, and has occasionally been observed chasing down and swallowing bats and small birds whole. Chuck-will's-widows hunt mostly at dawn and dusk, as well as being active during a full moon.

**OCCURRENCE** Breeds in forests composed of a mixture of deciduous and evergreen trees, and in open fields. Winters in Mexico and northern Central America.

**VOICE** Whistled *chuck-will's-wid-ow*; beginning softly, then increasing in volume, with emphasis on the two middle syllables.

long, grayish eyebrow

ADULT

| Length **11–12½in (28–32cm)** | Wingspan **25–28in (63–70cm)** |
|---|---|

| Family **Caprimulgidae** | Species *Antrostomus vociferus* |
|---|---|

# Eastern Whip-poor-will

More often heard than seen, the Eastern Whip-poor-will's camouflage makes it extremely difficult to spot on the forest floor. It flies away only when an intruder is just a few feet away. This species has an unusual breeding pattern—the male feeds the first brood until fledging, while the female lays eggs for a second brood. Both eggs from one brood may hatch simultaneously during a full moon, when there is most light at night, perhaps allowing the parents more time to forage for food.

**OCCURRENCE** Mixed mature forests with oaks and pines on dry upland sites. Breeds north to southern Canada and south to Mexico. Eastern and southwestern populations are widely separated.

**VOICE** Loud, 3-syllable whistle *WHIP-perrr-WIIL.*

MALE

tawny patch on cheeks

| Length **9–10in (23–26cm)** | Wingspan **17–20in (43–51cm)** |
|---|---|

| Family **Apodidae** | Species *Cypseloides niger* |
|---|---|

# Black Swift

The Black Swift is the largest of the North American swifts, and also the most enigmatic. It forages at high altitudes and nests on sea cliffs or behind waterfalls in mountains, meaning it can be difficult to observe. On cold and cloudy days, when aerial insect prey occurs closer to the ground, Black Swifts forage lower, and are easier to see.

**OCCURRENCE** Breeds from British Columbia in Canada south to Mexico, Costa Rica, and the West Indies. Found in mountains from May or June to early October. Wintering areas still largely unknown.

**VOICE** Generally silent, but gives twittering chips, sometimes in fast series, during interactions with other swifts; sharp *cheep* when approaching nest.

blackish upperparts

ADULT

| Length **7in (18cm)** | Wingspan **18in (46cm)** |
|---|---|

| Family **Apodidae** | Species *Chaetura pelagica* |
|---|---|

# Chimney Swift

A familiar sight and sound during the summer months, Chimney Swifts race through the skies over town and country, their rolling twitters often very loud. These birds feed, drink, and bathe on the wing. Chimney Swifts used not to nest in tree holes, but have taken to many kinds of human structures. Although some populations have declined, they remain common in many places.

**OCCURRENCE** Widespread over many habitats; regular in summer in southern California. Winters in Amazonian South America.

**VOICE** High, rapid chips and twittering; notes from individuals in a flock run together into a rapid, descending chatter.

dark brown upperparts

| Length **5in (13cm)** | Wingspan **14in (36cm)** |
|---|---|

| Family **Trochilidae** | Species *Eugenes fulgens* |
| --- | --- |

# Rivoli's Hummingbird

Although smaller than the showy Blue-throated Mountain-gem, this species is more spectacular. Living in the "sky islands" of Arizona and New Mexico, it is less territorial and aggressive than other hummingbirds, often utilizing more nectar sites.
**OCCURRENCE** Breeds at mid altitudes in woodlands of the Southwest; forages and migrates in drier habitats away from breeding areas.
**VOICE** Call a loud, sharp *chip*; chase call an accelerating series of squeaky *dee* or *dik* notes; song a quiet, buzzy warbling.

MALE

long, straight, black bill

| Length **5in (13cm)** | Wingspan **7½in (19cm)** |
| --- | --- |

| Family **Trochilidae** | Species *Lampornis clemenciae* |
| --- | --- |

# Blue-throated Mountain-gem

The largest hummingbird in North America, the Blue-throated Mountain-gem strikes an imposing figure when seen near one of its smaller relatives. Its large size and a two-striped facial pattern distinguish it from other hummingbirds in its range. It is a specialist of the isolated "sky island" mountaintops of the Southwest.
**OCCURRENCE** Breeds locally in Arizona, New Mexico, and Texas; winters in Mexico. Sometimes winters at feeding stations in the Southwest.
**VOICE** Call a loud, high squeak, *seep*; common song a steady, slow series of *seep* notes given by perched male; song a whisper of mechanical hissing notes.

MALE

blue throat

| Length **5in (13cm)** | Wingspan **8in (20cm)** |
| --- | --- |

| Family **Trochilidae** | Species *Calothorax lucifer* |
| --- | --- |

# Lucifer Hummingbird

A specialist of the Chihuahuan desert, the Lucifer Hummingbird can be recognized by its long, curved bill. Males perform an impressive display in front of females at the nest, diving repeatedly and producing a vibrating sound with their wings.
**OCCURRENCE** Breeding range barely reaches Arizona, New Mexico, and Texas. Resident in Mexico.
**VOICE** A dry, hard *chit*, often doubled or rolled into series when agitated; a sweeter *chi-chip* in territorial interactions; chase call a rapid series of sharp *chit* notes.

MALE

long, decurved bill

| Length **3½in (9cm)** | Wingspan **4in (10cm)** |
| --- | --- |

| Family **Trochilidae** | Species *Archilochus colubris* |
| --- | --- |

# Ruby-throated Hummingbird

The only hummingbird breeding east of the Mississippi River, this species can only be confused with other species during migration, when the others are present in its range. Before migration, these birds add about ¹⁄₁₆oz (2g) of fat to their weight; this provides enough fuel for their nonstop 800-mile (1,300km) flight across the Gulf of Mexico.
**OCCURRENCE** Occurs in a variety of woodlands and gardens; leaves breeding range by November, returns as early as February. The bulk of the population migrates to Central America.
**VOICE** A soft, thick *chic*, sometimes doubled; twittered notes in interactions; chase call a fast, slightly buzzy *tsi-tsi-tsi-tsi-tsi-tsi-*; soft, rattling song rarely heard.

orange-red throat

MALE

| Length **3½in (9cm)** | Wingspan **4¼in (11cm)** |
| --- | --- |

| Family **Trochilidae** | Species *Calypte costae* |
|---|---|

# Costa's Hummingbird

Costa's Hummingbird lives in the Sonoran and Mojave Deserts, where it is common locally. The male Costa's Hummingbird performs an acrobatic dive display, which includes up to 40 narrow vertical loops, a whistled song, followed by a back-and-forth shuttle display in front of the female.

**OCCURRENCE** Found in desert scrub, sage scrub, and dense shrubs in southern California and adjacent areas of the Southwest. Most birds migrate to Mexico for the winter.

**VOICE** Call a soft, metallic *tik*; chase call rapid series of *tik*, often mixed with high, buzzy *tssrr* notes; song a thin, high-pitched, buzzing whistle *tseee-seeeeeeew*.

straight, black bill

MALE

| Length  3¼in (8.5cm) | Wingspan  4¾in (12cm) |
|---|---|

| Family **Trochilidae** | Species *Cynanthus latirostris* |
|---|---|

# Broad-billed Hummingbird

The iridescent blue of an adult male Broad-billed Hummingbird qualifies it as one of North America's most beautiful birds. During courtship, males perform a pendulum-like display, accompanied by zinging wingbeats and chattering calls. The bird's bill is broader at the base than that of many other hummingbird species.

**OCCURRENCE** Lives in dry shrubby washes and riverside areas. Winters in Mexico.

**VOICE** Common call dry *tch-chk*, sometimes with 1–3 syllables; chase call squeaky twittering; song short, rapid series of high *tsi* notes with buzzy ending.

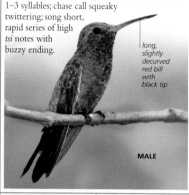

long, slightly decurved red bill with black tip

MALE

| Length  4in (10cm) | Wingspan  5½in (14cm) |
|---|---|

| Family **Trochilidae** | Species *Amazilia violiceps* |
|---|---|

# Violet-crowned Hummingbird

Its white underparts, red bill, and violet-blue crown make the Violet-crowned Hummingbird the most distinctive hummingbird in North America. In the US, it is restricted to riverside sycamore woodlands in Arizona and New Mexico, which it leaves in winter. It is resident in its Mexican range.

**OCCURRENCE** Localized breeder in Arizona and New Mexico, vagrant in California and Texas. Resident breeder in Mexico.

**VOICE** Call a hard, dry *tek*, often in short series; chase call a squeaky series of *twi* notes; song a steady series of descending *chew* notes.

white throat and underparts

MALE

| Length  4¼in (11cm) | Wingspan  6in (15cm) |
|---|---|

| Family **Trochilidae** | Species *Amazilia beryllina* |
|---|---|

# Berylline Hummingbird

Named after the glittering green gemstone, this hummingbird lives up to its name, with extra colors added by its rufous wing patch and buff belly. This species is easy to identify in its limited North American range.

**OCCURRENCE** Rare in southeastern Arizona in summer; nests in very small numbers in high-elevation canyons and pine oak woodlands; very rare in the mountains of western Texas. Its main range is in central Mexico.

**VOICE** Call rough, buzzy *tzrrr*; song a series of high-pitched, squeaky chips and twitters.

ADULT

glittering green upperparts

| Length  4in (10cm) | Wingspan  5½in (14cm) |
|---|---|

| Family **Trochilidae** | Species *Hylocharis leucotis* |
|---|---|

# White-eared Hummingbird

The bold black-and-white facial pattern of this species distinguishes it from other hummingbirds in its limited US range. A resident of Mexico, it did not establish itself in the US until 1989. It is aggressive even for a hummingbird defending its nectar sources and chasing away larger species. Males are very vocal during the breeding season.

**OCCURRENCE** Breeds in mountain forests of southeastern Arizona and southwestern New Mexico.

**VOICE** Call a metallic *tchink*, often doubled; chase call a rapid series of high chip notes; song a fast series of chips with up-slurred rattles.

white
ear
patch

**MALE**

| Length  3¾in (9.5cm) | Wingspan  5½in (14cm) |
|---|---|

| Family **Rallidae** | Species *Laterallus jamaicensis* |
|---|---|

# Black Rail

This tiny, mouse-sized rail is very secretive, with the result that its life history is still poorly known. Its presence is confirmed when it gives its territorial call during the breeding season, from the dense cover of its marshy habitat. Its distribution in the US is very local, except along the Eastern Seaboard. In the West, the Black Rail breeds in isolated populations in California, Arizona, Colorado, and Kansas.

**OCCURRENCE** Patchy distribution across the US in freshwater and brackish marshes or wet meadows; occurs locally in the West Indies, Central and South America.

**VOICE** Distinctive, 3-note *kik-kee-do* given by male, mostly at night, during breeding season; makes low growl when agitated.

small,
straight
bill

**ADULT
(SUMMER)**

| Length  6in (15cm) | Wingspan  9in (23cm) |
|---|---|

| Family **Rallidae** | Species *Rallus obsoletus* |
|---|---|

# Ridgway's Rail

A relative of the more widespread Clapper and King Rails, Ridway's Rail comprises a group previously considered subspecies of the Clapper Rail. It inhabits open muddy areas where it can feed, but with tall vegetation close by, particularly cordgrass, pickleweed, and bulrush, so that it can run for cover if threatened. One population, the "Yuma Rail," lives in freshwater marshes. Ridgway's Rail is most frequent in San Francisco Bay, but numbers remain low throughout its range. It can exploit even small, isolated patches of suitable muddy marsh, especially as juveniles disperse in late summer and fall.

**OCCURRENCE** Forages in tidal marshes, especially at the upper edge of coastal mudflats. The precarious nature of this habitat in regions subject to coastal development threatens its survival.

**VOICE** Both sexes make loud, fast *kak-kak-kak* calls.

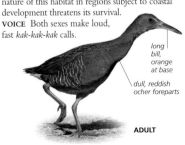

long
bill,
orange
at base

dull, reddish
ocher foreparts

**ADULT**

| Length  14½in (37cm) | Wingspan  19in (48cm) |
|---|---|

| Family **Rallidae** | Species *Rallus crepitans* |
|---|---|

# Clapper Rail

The Clapper Rail is common in tidal marshes along the entire seaboard of the Atlantic and Gulf Coasts. In the West its distribution is more localized; it is found in coastal marshes of California and in freshwater marshes, inland, in Arizona. The Clapper Rail's loud, endlessly repeated "song" consists of sharp *kek, kek, kek...* notes that indicate its presence in dense marshes. It is rarely seen running across patches of marsh grass at low tide.

**OCCURRENCE** Breeds in saltwater and brackish marshes along the Atlantic Seaboard. Isolated populations are found inland in Arizona, along the lower Colorado River. Winters south of its breeding range.

**VOICE** Grunting calls; repeated loud *kek* notes.

gray cheeks

long,
down-
curved
bill

**R. c. saturatus
(GULF COAST)**

| Length  14½in (37cm) | Wingspan  19in (48cm) |
|---|---|

| Family **Rallidae** | Species *Rallus elegans* |
|---|---|

# King Rail

This chicken-sized marsh bird is the freshwater counterpart of the saltmarsh-dwelling Clapper Rail. The King Rail depends on freshwater marshes with tall, emergent reeds and cattails. Its distribution is centered on the eastern and southeastern US; in the West, local populations can be found in Kansas, Oklahoma, and Texas, but it is rare farther west. Like the Clapper Rail, the King is rarely seen and is most often detected by its loud calls.

**OCCURRENCE** Mostly freshwater marshes in the eastern US and in southern Ontario. Also found throughout the year along the southern coast of the US, including Florida, and in central Mexico and Cuba. Rare in the West.

**VOICE** Male call similar to Clapper Rail but lower; loud *kik kik kik* in breeding season.

**ADULT**

long, yellow-orange bill

| Length **15in (38cm)** | Wingspan **20in (51cm)** |
|---|---|

| Family **Gruidae** | Species *Grus americana* |
|---|---|

# Whooping Crane

The majestic Whooping Crane is one of the most compelling success stories that resulted from passing the US Endangered Species Act. The species has rebounded from just a few dozen birds in the mid-20th to hundreds of individuals in the early 21st century. It still remains endangered, however, because it reproduces slowly in a restricted area and migrates along a narrow corridor to winter in coastal Texas, risking mortality along the way.

**OCCURRENCE** Breeds in country with scattered ponds and prairies in a very small area of the Northwest Territories and Alberta; winters in coastal Texas; uses both agricultural fields and marshland on migration.

**VOICE** Piercing and trumpeting, *kerloo!* and *kerleeyew*, bugling calls during courtship dances.

white overall

**ADULT**

| Length **4–4½ft (1.2–1.4m)** | Wingspan **7¼ft (2.2m)** |
|---|---|

| Family **Haematopodidae** | Species *Haematopus palliatus* |
|---|---|

# American Oystercatcher

This large, noisy, and conspicuous shorebird breeds along beaches and coastal dunes of the Atlantic and Gulf Coasts. In the West, it is restricted to coastal southern California, and is replaced along the Pacific Coast by the Black Oystercatcher. American Oystercatchers are social birds that can be observed in flocks, from a few birds to several hundred, especially in winter, at preferred feeding and roosting locations.

**OCCURRENCE** Saltwater coastal habitats, along the Atlantic Seaboard from Massachusetts to Argentina, and along the Pacific Seaboard from Baja California to Chile.

**VOICE** Whistled, loud, clear descending *wheeu* call; alarm call sharp *wheep*; flight display call several sharp whistles accelerating into a series of descending piping notes.

**ADULT**

thick, pinkish legs

| Length **15½–17½in (40–44cm)** | Wingspan **29–32in (73–81cm)** |
|---|---|

| Family **Charadriidae** | Species *Pluvialis fulva* |
|---|---|

# Pacific Golden-Plover

The Pacific Golden-Plover and American Golden-Plover were formerly considered to belong to the same species. The Pacific Golden-Plover breeds in western Alaska and migrates over the ocean to wintering grounds on remote South Pacific Islands. Its nest is a shallow depression lined with lichens in the tundra.

**OCCURRENCE** Nests primarily in Arctic tundra; during migration and in winter, found in a variety of habitats, including prairies, pastures, mudflats, shorelines, mangroves, parks, lawns and gardens in urban areas, and roadsides. About 12 percent of the world's population nests in Alaska.

**VOICE** Flight call a clearly 2-syllabled *chu-EEt*, with emphasis on second note; breeding song a clear, haunting, low whistle *pEE-prr-EE*.

tan, black, and white upperparts

off-white underparts

**ADULT (NONBREEDING)**

| Length **9–10½in (23–27cm)** | Wingspan **21–24in (53–61cm)** |
|---|---|

| Family **Charadriidae** | Species *Charadrius wilsonia* |
|---|---|

# Wilson's Plover

Slightly smaller than the well-known Killdeer, Wilson's Plover is a coastal species, common in the East, but rare in the West. It has a relatively "heavy-looking" belly, which gives it a characteristic upright posture when it pauses after a run. This plover's populations may be declining; it was called a species of "high concern" in 2000.

**OCCURRENCE** Beaches, sand dunes, coastal lagoons, and saltwater flats along the Atlantic Coast, south to Mexico, and in the West Indies; along the Pacific Coast from Baja California southward to Peru.

**VOICE** Flight call a short *pip*, or *pi-dit*; alarm calls include slurred whistle *tweet*, and short whistled *peet*; common distraction call a descending buzzy rattle, given in series.

*heavy, black bill*

**MALE**

| Length 6½–8in (16–20cm) | Wingspan 15½–19½in (39–49cm) |
|---|---|

| Family **Charadriidae** | Species *Charadrius montanus* |
|---|---|

# Mountain Plover

Unlike most other North American shorebirds, this rather plain-looking plover is rarely found near water. Unusually wary by nature, the Mountain Plover often faces away from danger and squats motionless on the ground, virtually disappearing into the landscape and earning its nickname "Prairie Ghost." It is declining, and endangered because of habitat loss from overgrazing and pesticides.

**OCCURRENCE** Localized in west-central North America in dry, flat, short grass prairies and semidesert areas with sparse vegetation; winters south to Mexico.

**VOICE** Generally silent; flight call grating *kirrp*; wintering birds in flight give short *kip* call; courtship song rolling, drawled, whistled *wee-wee*.

*white forehead*

*tan-colored overall*

**ADULT (BREEDING)**

| Length 8½–9½ in (21–24cm) | Wingspan 21½–23½in (54–60cm) |
|---|---|

| Family **Scolopacidae** | Species *Bartramia longicauda* |
|---|---|

# Upland Sandpiper

Unlike other sandpipers, this graceful bird spends most of its life away from water. Its brownish coloration is a good camouflage in grasslands, especially when nesting. It is known for landing on fence posts and raising its wings while giving its tremulous, whistling call. Because of the disappearance of its grassland habitat, the species has suffered substantial population losses, and is currently listed as endangered.

**OCCURRENCE** Breeds in tallgrass or mixed-grass prairies. During migration found in grazed pastures, turf farms, and cultivated fields. Uncommon along the West Coast and inland in the Southwest. Winters in South America, south to Argentina.

**VOICE** Flight call a low *qui-pi-pi-pi*; song consists of gurgling notes followed by long, descending "wolf whistle" *whooooleeeeee, wheeelooooo*.

*brownish, spotted back*

**ADULT (BREEDING)**

*straight, mostly yellow bill*

| Length 11–12½in (28–32cm) | Wingspan 25–27in (64–68cm) |
|---|---|

| Family **Scolopacidae** | Species *Numenius tahitiensis* |
|---|---|

# Bristle-thighed Curlew

This rare and localized curlew is one of the world's most unusual shorebirds. It winters on oceanic islands, becomes flightless during its molting period on its wintering grounds, and uses "tools" when foraging, such as rocks to break open eggs. Nesting in only two areas of western Alaska, it migrates about 4,000 miles (6,500km) over the Pacific Ocean to reach its wintering grounds on South Pacific islands. The world population of Bristle-thighed Curlews may number as few as 3,500 pairs.

**OCCURRENCE** Breeds in hilly tundra with scattered vegetation in western Alaska; winters on remote South Pacific islands; occasional in California.

**VOICE** Flight call a clear whistle *ee-o-weet*; flight song a whistled phrase, *wiwiwi-chyoo*.

*strongly patterned head*

**ADULT (BREEDING)**

| Length 16–17½in (41–45cm) | Wingspan 30–35in (75–90cm) |
|---|---|

| Family **Scolopacidae** | Species *Limosa lapponica* |
| --- | --- |

# Bar-tailed Godwit

Primarily a Eurasian species, the Bar-tailed Godwit is a summer visitor to western Alaska. After breeding, it migrates a distance of over 7,000 miles (11,250km) to Australia and New Zealand, a non-stop overwater flight. Before this amazing journey, the Bar-tailed Godwit doubles its body weight with fat that will be used as fuel, and shrinks its digestive tract as a weight-saving measure. Almost 100,000 birds make this journey in September and early October.

**OCCURRENCE** Breeds in lowland tundra, coastal wetlands, foothills, and uplands of Arctic and subarctic. Only Alaska in North America.

**VOICE** Flight call a slightly nasal *kirruc, kurruc* or *kirrik*; display song *ta-WEA, ta-WEA, ta-WEA.*

streaked head and breast

off-white underparts

**ADULT (WINTER)**

| Length **14½–15½in (37–39cm)** | Wingspan **28–32in (72–81cm)** |
| --- | --- |

| Family **Scolopacidae** | Species *Limosa haemastica* |
| --- | --- |

# Hudsonian Godwit

This large sandpiper undertakes a remarkable annual migration from its tundra breeding grounds in Alaska and Canada all the way to extreme southern South America, a distance of at least 10,000 miles (16,000km) in one direction, with few stopovers. There are perhaps 50–80,000 breeding pairs. Counts in Tierra del Fuego indicate totals of perhaps 30,000 to 40,000. Hudsonian Godwits spend six months wintering, two breeding, and four flying between the two locations.

**OCCURRENCE** Breeds in the High Arctic in sedge meadows and bogs in tundra; locally found in flooded rice fields, pastures, and reservoirs in spring. Winters in extreme southern Chile and Argentina.

**VOICE** Flight call emphatic *peed-wid*; also high *peet* or *kwee*; display song *to-wida to-wida to-wida*, or *to-wit, to-wit, to-wit.*

long, orange-based bill

**MALE (BREEDING)**

| Length **14–16in (35–41cm)** | Wingspan **27–31in (68–78cm)** |
| --- | --- |

| Family **Scolopacidae** | Species *Calidris ptilocnemis* |
| --- | --- |

# Rock Sandpiper

Breeding in Siberia and western Alaska, and wintering along the Pacific Coast south to California, the Rock Sandpiper is the western counterpart of the Purple Sandpiper. Both species are closely related to each other. In the winter, look for Rock Sandpipers along rocky shores, which they share with Surfbirds and Black Turnstones.

**OCCURRENCE** Breeds in Arctic coastal tundra and mountain tundra. During migration and in winter is common along rocky shores from Alaska south to southern California.

**VOICE** Call short squeaking *chreet, cheet,* or *cheerrt*; song *di-jerr, di-jerr, di-jerr* and more melodic *quida-se-quida-we-quida.*

**ADULT (NONBREEDING)**

greenish yellow on base of bill

slightly darker, uniform gray upperparts

| Length **7¼–9½in (18.5–24cm)** | Wingspan **13–18½in (33–47cm)** |
| --- | --- |

| Family **Scolopacidae** | Species *Calidris subruficollis* |
| --- | --- |

# Buff-breasted Sandpiper

This sandpiper has a remarkable mating system. On the breeding grounds in the Arctic, each male flashes his white underwings to attract females for mating. After mating, the female leaves and performs all nest duties alone, while the male continues to display and mate with other females. Once nesting is over, the Buff-breasted Sandpiper leaves the Arctic and covers an astonishing 16,000 miles (26,000km) to winter in temperate South America.

**OCCURRENCE** Breeds in moist to wet, grassy, or sedge coastal tundra; during migration favors pastures, sod farms, meadows, rice fields, or farm lands. Winters in the pampas region of South America in short, wet grass habitats.

**VOICE** Flight call soft, short *gert,* or longer, rising *grriit.*

scaly upperparts

rich buff wash to breast

**JUVENILE**

| Length **7¼–8in (18.5–20cm)** | Wingspan **17–18½in (43–47cm)** |
| --- | --- |

| Family **Scolopacidae** | Species *Tringa incana* |
|---|---|

# Wandering Tattler

While "Wandering" refers to this species' remarkable migration, "tattler" highlights the loud songs it makes in its breeding haunts in Alaska and western Canada. The Wandering Tattler also breeds in eastern Siberia. The total population size of this species is small, of only about 10,000 to 25,000 birds. After long overwater flights, Wandering Tattlers spend the winter on Pacific islands, including the Galápagos and New Zealand.

**OCCURRENCE** Breeds in shrubby mountain tundra near water bodies. During migration and winter, uses rocky coastlines; also reefs, jetties, and piers along the California Coast in fall and winter.

**VOICE** Flight call a ringing, trilled *didididididi*; song a sharp, 3–4 note whistle *treea-treea-treea-tree.*

white stripe above eye

**IMMATURE (1ST FALL)**

| Length **10½–12in (27–30cm)** | Wingspan **20–22in (51–56cm)** |
|---|---|

| Family **Scolopacidae** | Species *Phalaropus fulicarius* |
|---|---|

# Red Phalarope

The Red Phalarope spends about ten months each year over deep ocean waters. Many Red Phalaropes winter in cold oceanic areas, with large concentrations in the Humboldt Current off Peru and Chile, and in the Benguela Current off southwestern Africa. During migration in Alaskan waters, flocks of Red Phalaropes feed on crustaceans in the mud plumes created by gray and bowhead whales that forage on the ocean floor.

**OCCURRENCE** Breeds in coastal Arctic tundra in Canada and Alaska; small numbers are seen in coastal California in fall and winter. It is rare inland.

**VOICE** Flight call a sharp *psip* or *pseet*, often in rapid succession; alarm call a drawn-out, 2-syllabled *sweet.*

black cheek patch and nape

mostly gray upperparts

**ADULT (NONBREEDING)**

white neck and head

| Length **8–8½in (20–22cm)** | Wingspan **16–17½in (41–44cm)** |
|---|---|

| Family **Stercorariidae** | Species *Stercorarius maccormicki* |
|---|---|

# South Polar Skua

A regular visitor to US waters, the Antarctic-breeding South Polar Skua is a large relative of the jaegers. It is a perpetual threat to penguins on their breeding grounds, patrolling around their colonies and waiting to pinch an egg or snatch a chick. Outside the breeding season, South Polar Skuas roam both the Atlantic and Pacific Oceans, reaching high latitudes in each.

**OCCURRENCE** Spends southern winters (northern summer) offshore in the North Atlantic and Pacific; breeds in the South Shetland Islands and along the coast and islands of the Antarctic.

**VOICE** Deep gull-like burbling; generally silent at sea.

hooked bill

**IMMATURE**

| Length **21in (53cm)** | Wingspan **4¼ft (1.3m)** |
|---|---|

| Family **Alcidae** | Species *Alle alle* |
|---|---|

# Dovekie

Also known as the Little Auk, the stocky and diminutive Dovekie is a bird of the High Arctic. Most Dovekies breed in Greenland in large, noisy, crowded colonies (some contain 15–20 million birds), others breed in northeastern Canada, and smaller numbers on a few islands in the Bering Sea off Alaska. On their breeding grounds in Greenland, both adult and immature Dovekies are hunted by Glaucous Gulls and Arctic foxes.

**OCCURRENCE** Breeds on islands inside the Arctic Circle. Many birds remain south of the Arctic pack ice in the winter; others fly farther south to winter off the northeastern seaboard of North America. The wintering grounds of the Bering Sea population are still unknown.

**VOICE** Variety of calls at breeding colony, including high-pitched trilling that rises and falls; silent at sea.

**ADULT (NONBREEDING)**

white collar

small bill

| Length **8½in (21cm)** | Wingspan **15in (38cm)** |
|---|---|

| Family **Alcidae** | Species *Uria lomvia* |
|---|---|

# Thick-billed Murre

A large and robust auk, the Thick-billed Murre is one of the most abundant seabirds at high latitudes in Eurasia and North America. Some cliff colonies can number upward of a million birds, breeding side by side on narrow ledges. Chicks leave the colony when their weight is only 25 percent that of the adults, and they mature at sea, fed by the male parent. Thick-billed Murres can dive for fish and squid down to a depth of 600ft (180m).
**OCCURRENCE** Away from High Arctic colonies, Thick-billed Murres remain at sea off the Atlantic and Pacific Coasts, usually far offshore. Regular off the coast of California in winter.
**VOICE** Roaring, groaning, insistent sounding *aoorrr*, lower-pitched than the Common Murre.

white line along bill

**ADULT (BREEDING)**

| Length **18in (46cm)** | Wingspan **28in (70cm)** |
|---|---|

| Family **Alcidae** | Species *Cepphus grylle* |
|---|---|

# Black Guillemot

The Black Guillemot, which is primarily a North Atlantic seabird found in both the Old and New Worlds, is largely replaced along the Pacific Coast, from Alaska southward to California, by its close relative, and almost look-alike, the Pigeon Guillemot. Black Guillemots breed along the northern coast of Alaska, and occur in the Bering Sea during the winter. A Guillemot seen along the Pacific Coast of North America is sure to be a Pigeon Guillemot.
**OCCURRENCE** Breeds in deep crevices on remote rocky islands. When foraging for food, prefers shallow waters close to shore.
**VOICE** Very high-pitched whistles and squeaks on land and water near nesting habitat that resonate like an echo.

thin, straight bill

**ADULT (BREEDING)**

| Length **13in (33cm)** | Wingspan **21in (53cm)** |
|---|---|

| Family **Alcidae** | Species *Brachyramphus brevirostris* |
|---|---|

# Kittlitz's Murrelet

This small, North Pacific-breeding auk was described by Vigors as *brevirostris* ("short-billed") in 1828, and later by Brandt as *kittlitzii*. Because of the rules of scientific names, the latter name was not retained, but Kittlitz's name remained in the vernacular. Little is known about it, other than that it does not breed in colonies, and lays its single egg hidden under a slab of rock, at inland locations high above the sea and far away from seashores.
**OCCURRENCE** Occurs where glaciers calve into the sea. When breeding feeds at sea around icebergs or close to coast; after breeding moves out to sea; winter location unknown. Breeds in the Bering Sea and along the Aleutian Island chain.
**VOICE** Quiet, low, groaning *urrrrn* call; also short quacking.

short bill

**ADULT (BREEDING)**

mottled upperparts

| Length **9½in (24cm)** | Wingspan **17in (43cm)** |
|---|---|

| Family **Alcidae** | Species *Synthliboramphus scrippsi* |
|---|---|

# Scripps's Murrelet

Among the world's most threatened seabird species, Scripps's Murrelets breed on islands in southern California and Baja California. However, they are rarely seen from shore; instead, they prefer deep, warm, offshore waters. Two days after hatching, chicks leap into the water from cliffs as high as 200ft (60m). Parents then rear their young (usually only one per pair) in family groups offshore.
**OCCURRENCE** Nests in sheltered areas on California's and Baja California's islands, then, after breeding, disperses along the Pacific Coast, offshore, northward as far as Washington State and, rarely, British Columbia.
**VOICE** Series of several high pitched *seeep* notes by southern Californian birds; Baja California birds give a rattling call.

slender, black bill

**ADULT**

| Length **10in (25cm)** | Wingspan **15in (38cm)** |
|---|---|

| Family **Alcidae** | Species **Synthliboramphus hypoleucus** |
| --- | --- |

# Guadalupe Murrelet

Until 2012, Guadalupe and Scripps's Murrelets were treated as one species, Xantus's Murrelet, but where the two overlap they never interbreed. Moreover, genetic differences as well as variation in bill shape and face pattern have been identified. Guadalupe Murrelets feed at sea, diving deeply and taking advantage of the disturbance caused by large predatory fish to catch anchovies and sardines.

**OCCURRENCE** Offshore rocks and rocky islands in warm seas off Baja California; disperses northward, as far as Californian seas, after breeding.

**VOICE** Rattled trill, unlike the even trill of piping notes from Scripps's Murrelet.

eye surrounded by white

**ADULT**

short, slim bill

| Length **10in (27cm)** | Wingspan **15in (38cm)** |
| --- | --- |

| Family **Alcidae** | Species **Synthliboramphus craveri** |
| --- | --- |

# Craveri's Murrelet

It was the German zoologist Johann Friedrich von Brandt (1802-1879) who gave such long scientific names to the tiny murrelets. The genus name, *Synthliboramphus,* actually simply means "compressed bill." Craveri's Murrelet breeds on a number of islands in the Gulf of California, Mexico, and wanders as far north as San Francisco afterward. After breeding it forages offshore and is not normally seen from shorepoints. Craveri's Murrelet was named after Frederico Craveri, who discovered the bird.

**OCCURRENCE** Warm waters of the Gulf of California and the Pacific Coast of Baja California during breeding season. Rare visitor, mostly from fall through spring, to pelagic waters off the coast of California.

**VOICE** Adult at sea gives high rattling or trilling *sreeeer*. Other calls unknown.

**ADULT**

long bill

| Length **9½in (24cm)** | Wingspan **15in (38cm)** |
| --- | --- |

| Family **Alcidae** | Species **Aethia psittacula** |
| --- | --- |

# Parakeet Auklet

This robust, pot-bellied auklet has a bright orange, conical bill—a unique feature among alcids. Its range spans the North Pacific, the widest of any auklet species, but breeding is concentrated at colonies in the Bering Sea and the Aleutians. Like other auklets, Parakeet Auklets are monogamous, and pairs perform conspicuous vocal and visual courtship displays when breeding.

**OCCURRENCE** Breeds in rocky habitats on islands of the northern Gulf of Alaska and the Bering Sea.

**VOICE** Whinnying by males to attract a mate, followed by duet-whinnying by a mated pair during courtship; squeal calls when alarmed.

conical orange bill

**ADULT (NONBREEDING)**

white flanks

| Length **10in (25cm)** | Wingspan **18in (46cm)** |
| --- | --- |

| Family **Alcidae** | Species **Aethia pusilla** |
| --- | --- |

# Least Auklet

The smallest of the auklets, Least Auklets often form huge flocks, roosting on boulders along the edge of nesting islands. In the air, these flocks swirl around with great coordination. The Least Auklet's underparts vary individually from white to spotted or even solid gray—a possible status signal during the breeding season. The Least Auklet has a low survival rate compared to other auks. It is vulnerable to rats and foxes and sensitive to human disturbance.

**OCCURRENCE** Bering Sea islands and Aleutians; forages in areas with turbulent waters and concentrated food sources; winters at sea near breeding sites.

**VOICE** Pulsing series of high, grating trills, chirps, or chatters; silent at sea.

well-defined white throat

spotted underparts

**BREEDING (DARK FORM)**

| Length **6½in (16.5cm)** | Wingspan **12in (31cm)** |
| --- | --- |

| Family **Alcidae** | Species *Aethia pygmaea* |
|---|---|

# Whiskered Auklet

This compact, dark-plumaged auklet lives along the outer islands of the Aleutian chain and in eastern Russia. Compared with other North Pacific auks, it is relatively scarce and lives in smaller colonies. During the nesting season, the birds become nocturnal, and huge numbers congregate after dark. The long head plumes help the birds feel their way to their underground nests. This nocturnal arrival keeps them safe from predatory birds such as large gulls and falcons, and crevice-nesting protects the eggs and chicks against predation in daylight hours.

**OCCURRENCE** Occurs locally in Alaska's Aleutian Islands. Forages in shallow waters off rocky coasts, especially in areas of rapid tidal currents.

**VOICE** Kitten-like *meew* and rapid, harp *beedeer, beedeer, beedeer* call; silent at sea.

**ADULT (BREEDING)**

dark sooty brown overall

thin, black crest

| Length **8in (20cm)** | Wingspan **14in (36cm)** |
|---|---|

| Family **Alcidae** | Species *Aethia cristatella* |
|---|---|

# Crested Auklet

Male and female Crested Auklets have a forward-curling tuft of feathers on the forehead that varies in size among individuals. Both sexes prefer mates with large tufts. Pairs are typically monogamous and compete intensely for nest sites. Crested Auklets fly in large, tight flocks and are usually active only at night at the colonies. Like their close relative, the Whiskered Auklet, their plumage has a distinctive citrus-like odor.

**OCCURRENCE** Forages in turbulent waters around remote islands in the Bering Sea and the Aleutian Islands. Winters in the Gulf of Alaska. Very rare along Pacific Coast south to California.

**VOICE** In colonies, variable barking *kyow* call, reminiscent of small dog; rapid series of honks; silent at sea.

bushy tuft that curls forward

**ADULT (BREEDING)**

| Length **10½in (27cm)** | Wingspan **17in (43cm)** |
|---|---|

| Family **Alcidae** | Species *Fratercula corniculata* |
|---|---|

# Horned Puffin

Similar to, but larger than, its close relative the Atlantic Puffin, the Horned Puffin lives in the North Pacific Ocean and Bering Sea, where it breeds on remote, rocky, offshore islands. Outside the breeding season, Horned Puffins spend much time far out at sea, hundreds of miles from the nearest land. Remarkably, when birds return to their breeding grounds, they go directly to the very same rock crevice they used the previous year.

**OCCURRENCE** Winters far from land in the North Pacific. Rare along Pacific Coast, south to California.

**VOICE** Low-pitched, rumbling growls in rhythmic phrases.

fleshy "horn" above eye

**ADULT (BREEDING)**

| Length **15in (38cm)** | Wingspan **23in (59cm)** |
|---|---|

| Family **Laridae** | Species *Rissa brevirostris* |
|---|---|

# Red-legged Kittiwake

More than 65 percent of the world's Red-legged Kittiwake population nests on St. George Island, in the Pribilofs. Research has indicated that this species was once more widespread in the Aleutians than it is today. It is found accidentally south to Oregon. The Red-legged Kittiwake, when outside its normal range, can be mistaken for the Black-legged Kittiwake since the latter may also, occasionally, have red legs.

**OCCURRENCE** Spends life out at sea, mostly over deep waters. Restricted almost totally to the Bering Sea and vicinity.

**VOICE** Calls similar to Black-legged Kittiwake, but higher pitched; vocal at breeding colony, generally silent elsewhere.

gray upperparts

**ADULT**

| Length **14–15½in (35–39cm)** | Wingspan **33–36in (84–92cm)** |
|---|---|

| Family **Laridae** | Species ***Xema sabini*** |
|---|---|

# Sabine's Gull

This striking-looking gull has a distinctive black, white, and gray wing pattern and a notched tail, which make it unmistakable in all plumages—only juvenile kittiwakes are superficially similar. Previously thought to be related to the larger, but similarly patterned, Swallow-tailed Gull of the Galápagos, recent research indicates that Sabine's Gull is more closely related to the all-white Ivory Gull.

**OCCURRENCE** In the summer, breeds near the Arctic Coast and on wet tundra in Arctic Canada and Alaska. Winters offshore in tropical and subtropical waters; widespread in Pacific and Atlantic Oceans during migration

**VOICE** Raucous, harsh *kyeer, kyeer, kyeer*, tern-like.

yellow-tipped bill

red eye-ring

**ADULT (BREEDING)**

| Length **13–14in (33–36 cm)** | Wingspan **35–39in (90–100cm)** |
|---|---|

| Family **Laridae** | Species ***Larus livens*** |
|---|---|

# Yellow-footed Gull

First described as a species in 1919, the Yellow-footed Gull was long considered to be a subspecies of the Western Gull. It is now thought to be related to the Kelp Gull of South America. It has yellow legs, but if its leg color is not visible, it is hard to distinguish from the Western Gull. The best place outside of the Sea of Cortez, Mexico, to see the Yellow-footed Gull is the Salton Sea in southern California.

**OCCURRENCE** Breeds in the Sea of Cortez, Mexico, on offshore islands and rocks; in the US, nonbreeders found at Salton Sea, June–September; occasional in Utah, Arizona, coastal California.

**VOICE** Call a *keow*, repeated in series, speeding up slightly toward the end.

large, red spot

**ADULT**

| Length **21½–28in (55–72cm)** | Wingspan **5ft (1.5m)** |
|---|---|

| Family **Laridae** | Species ***Rhodostethia rosea*** |
|---|---|

# Ross's Gull

Named for the great British Polar explorer, James Clark Ross, this small, delicate gull is unmistakable in adult breeding plumage. Dove-gray upperparts, pale-pink underparts, red legs, and a black collar contribute to make it elegant and beautiful. In winter it lacks the distinctive black neck ring and the delicate pink blush on the underside.

**OCCURRENCE** Siberian breeder found along Alaskan north coast in fall; expanded recently as a breeding bird to Arctic Canada; winter strays found across Canada, northeastern and northwestern US.

**VOICE** Rarely heard in winter; tern-like *kik-kik-kik* on the breeding grounds.

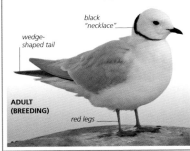

black "necklace"

wedge-shaped tail

**ADULT (BREEDING)**

red legs

| Length **11½–12in (29–31cm)** | Wingspan **35–39in (90–100cm)** |
|---|---|

| Family **Laridae** | Species ***Onychoprion aleuticus*** |
|---|---|

# Aleutian Tern

The Aleutian Tern was the last North American tern to be described. Discovered on Kodiak Island in 1868, it was not found nesting there again until 1944. This tern received its scientific and English names from the assumption that it must nest somewhere in the Aleutian Islands, although it was not actually found nesting there until the mid-20th century.

**OCCURRENCE** Breeds in coastal Alaska, in areas with low vegetation, marshes, meadows, sandy spits, lagoons, and tundra. Winter range is mostly unknown, but suspected to be in the southwestern Pacific. Migrants reported from Hong Kong and Indonesia. Also breeds in Siberia.

**VOICE** Vocal around colonies; no information elsewhere; shorebird-like 3-note whistle, unlike other tern species.

gray wings

**ADULT (BREEDING)**

| Length **12½–15in (32–38cm)** | Wingspan **30–31in (75–80cm)** |
|---|---|

| Family **Laridae** | Species ***Sternula antillarum*** |
| --- | --- |

# Least Tern

The Least Tern, the smallest of the North American terns, is, in addition, distinguished from them by its black cap, white forehead, and short yellow legs. In the 19th century the species suffered a dramatic decline, as its feathers were prized fashion accessories. Protected by the Migratory Bird Treaty of 1916, Least Tern numbers have increased, but continued protection is needed because of the loss of its breeding habitat because of development in coastal areas, especially sand dunes.

**OCCURRENCE** Breeds along beaches, in sand dunes and sandbars along sea coasts, rivers, lakes, reservoirs, and wetlands. Winters from Mexico to South America.

**VOICE** Extremely vocal during breeding; a high-pitched *ki-deek, ki-deek*; also a rapid, almost nonstop chatter.

yellow bill

**ADULT (BREEDING)**

| Length 8½–9in (21–23cm) | Wingspan **19–21in (48–53cm)** |
| --- | --- |

| Family **Laridae** | Species ***Gelochelidon nilotica*** |
| --- | --- |

# Gull-billed Tern

With its relatively heavy build, thick bill, and broad wings, the Gull-billed Tern is indeed more gull-like than other North American terns. Also, unlike many other terns, its diet is not restricted to fish, but also includes insects and lizards. It often nests in colonies with other tern species and with skimmers, and will occasionally hunt their chicks and steal their prey. During the 19th century, Gull-billed Terns were hunted ruthlessly for their eggs and feathers. Their numbers have now partially recovered.

**OCCURRENCE** Breeds on sandy beaches and barrier islands. Common along the East Coast; rare in California and Arizona. Worldwide in distribution.

**VOICE** Short, 2-note, nasal yapping, *kay-wek, kay-wek.*

thick, black bill

**ADULT (BREEDING)**

| Length 13–15in (33–38cm) | Wingspan **3¼–4ft (1–1.2m)** |
| --- | --- |

| Family **Laridae** | Species ***Sterna paradisaea*** |
| --- | --- |

# Arctic Tern

The majority of these remarkable migrants breed in the Arctic and subarctic, then migrate to the Antarctic pack-ice for the Southern Hemisphere summer before returning north. On this round-trip, Arctic Terns travel at least 25,000 miles (40,000km). Apart from migration periods, it spends its life in areas of near continuous daylight and rarely comes to land, except to nest. It looks similar to the Common Tern, but the Arctic has a comparatively smaller bill, shorter legs, and a shorter neck.

**OCCURRENCE** Breeds across North America in unforested areas near water and along coasts; generally migrates far offshore. Winters on edge of pack ice in Antarctica. Also breeds across northern Eurasia.

**VOICE** Descending call; nearly all calls similar to Common Tern, but higher pitched and harsher.

**ADULT (BREEDING)**

short neck

| Length **11–15½in (28–39cm)** | Wingspan **26–30in (65–75cm)** |
| --- | --- |

| Family **Laridae** | Species ***Thalasseus maximus*** |
| --- | --- |

# Royal Tern

Royal Terns have a full black cap for only a very short time at the beginning of the breeding season; for most of the year, they have white foreheads. The color of a Royal Tern's bill is quite variable, ranging from yellowish orange to red. Some possess a reddish bill similar to that of the Caspian Tern, but the latter does not have a pure white forehead and its bill is thicker. Perhaps it was these red-billed Royal Terns that caused the renowned ornithologist, John James Audubon, to confuse the two species.

**OCCURRENCE** Breeds in dense colonies, often on barrier islands. Widespread along the Atlantic Coast; in the West, southern California; occasional elsewhere.

**VOICE** Call *keer-reet*, usually during courtship; higher pitched and less raspy than Caspian Tern; more vocal around colonies.

black forehead and crown

**ADULT (BREEDING)**

| Length 17½–19½in (45–50cm) | Wingspan **4–4¼ft (1.2–1.3m)** |
| --- | --- |

| Family **Laridae** | Species **Thalasseus elegans** |

# Elegant Tern

The Elegant Tern is not a geographically widespread species. By the mid-20th century its population had declined because of the demand for its eggs and the introduction of predators; at one point it was confined to only five nesting colonies. This bird nests in tight groups within colonies of Heermann's Gulls and Caspian Terns, taking advantage of the other birds' aggressive behavior toward predators. Elegant Terns nest in remarkable synchrony, most birds in a colony laying eggs within 24 hours of each other.

**OCCURRENCE** Southern California and Baja California; more than 90 percent of world's population nests on one island, Isla Raza in the Gulf of California. After breeding, many fly to the coast of central California.

**VOICE** Nasal *karrreeek, karrreek*; very vocal at nesting colonies.

shaggy black crest

**ADULT (BREEDING)**

| Length **15½–16½in (39–42cm)** | Wingspan **30–32in (76–81cm)** |

| Family **Laridae** | Species **Rynchops niger** |

# Black Skimmer

With its very long, orange-red and black bill, the Black Skimmer is unmistakable. Compressed laterally into a knife-like shape, the lower mandible is about 1in (2.5cm) longer than the upper mandible. This extraordinary bill allows Black Skimmers to "cut" the waters—they fly with the lower mandible in the water, then snap the bill shut when prey is caught.

**OCCURRENCE** East Coast from Massachusetts to Mexico; West Coast in southern California. Rarely found far from saltwater. Winters in Central America. Resident populations breed in South America.

**VOICE** Calls given by both sexes, more often at night; distinctive sound like the yapping of a small dog.

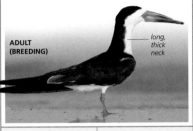

**ADULT (BREEDING)**

long, thick neck

| Length **15½–19½in (40–50cm)** | Wingspan **3½–4¼ft (1.1–1.3m)** |

| Family **Diomedeidae** | Species **Phoebastria nigripes** |

# Black-footed Albatross

The most frequently seen albatross in North American waters, this distinctive all-dark bird breeds mainly on the Hawaiian Islands, and regularly visits the Pacific Coast during the nonbreeding season. Unfortunately, a tendency to scavenge around fishing boats can cause them to drown when they are accidentally hooked on long lines or tangled in drift nets. This is a major conservation concern for this species.

**OCCURRENCE** Breeds on sandy beaches, almost exclusively on remote, uninhabited islands in Hawaii.

**VOICE** Generally silent outside the breeding season, but utters weak squeals while scavenging; makes a variety of noises during courtship.

long, slender wings

white undertail feathers

**ADULT**

| Length **25–29in (64–74cm)** | Wingspan **6¼–7¼ft (1.9–2.2m)** |

| Family **Procellariidae** | Species **Puffinus opisthomelas** |

# Black-vented Shearwater

An inshore feeder, the Black-vented Shearwater is one of the few species of tubenoses that can be seen easily from land. Flocks of hundreds can be observed from various points along the coast of California. Black-vented Shearwaters vary in color from ghostly pale beige to very dark.

**OCCURRENCE** Breeds on islands off Baja California, Mexico; spends August–January off the Pacific Coast from southern California south to Mexico (as far as Oaxaca). Northernmost and southernmost extent of post-breeding range not well known.

**VOICE** Silent at sea; breeding ground vocalizations unknown.

dark smudging on head and breast

dark undertail feathers

**ADULT**

| Length **14in (36cm)** | Wingspan **34in (86cm)** |

| Family **Hydrobatidae** | Species *Hydrobates homochroa* |

# Ashy Storm-Petrel

The Ashy Storm-Petrel is one of four species of all-dark storm-petrels that breed on islands in the waters of California and Baja California. In California, these islands include Farallon, San Miguel, Santa Barbara, Santa Clara, and Santa Cruz. Ashy Storm-Petrels molt during the breeding season, a double expenditure of energy. In flight, this species looks noticeably long-tailed.

**OCCURRENCE** Breeds on islands off the coast of California and northern Baja California. Post-breeding dispersal takes some birds north to waters off Humboldt County, others south to waters off central Baja California.

**VOICE** Usually silent at sea; coos and makes other calls at colonies.

*forked tail*

**ADULT**

| Length 7½in (19cm) | Wingspan **16–18in (41–46cm)** |

| Family **Hydrobatidae** | Species *Hydrobates melania* |

# Black Storm-Petrel

The Black Storm-Petrel, the largest storm-petrel occurring off the coast of southern California, breeds on islands free from predators such as rats, along the coasts of Baja California. After the breeding season, the population of the Black Storm-Petrel splits into two wintering populations—half head to the coast of Central and South America and half stay off the coasts of California and northern Mexico.

**OCCURRENCE** A warm-water species, breeding on a number of small islands off both the Pacific and Gulf Coasts of Baja California.

**VOICE** Silent at sea; in colonies, emits long, undulated, chattering and purring sounds.

*long, deeply forked tail*

**ADULT**

| Length 9in (23cm) | Wingspan **19–21in (48–53cm)** |

| Family **Hydrobatidae** | Species *Hydrobates microsoma* |

# Least Storm-Petrel

The smallest storm-petrel in North American waters, the all-dark Least Storm-Petrel is numerous in flocks of tubenoses off the southern California Coast in fall. These petrels are very susceptible to predation by introduced cats and rats on their Pacific nesting islands. The Least Storm-Petrel is dark and similar in appearance to the Black Storm-Petrel, but the latter flies with slower wingbeats interrupted by glides.

**OCCURRENCE** Breeds on a small number of islands along the Pacific and Gulf Coasts of Baja California, Mexico. After the breeding season, many birds disperse north to waters off southern California.

**VOICE** Silent at sea; whirring and purring at breeding sites.

*dark underwing coverts*

*pale underside of flight feathers*

*all-dark body*

**ADULT**

| Length 5½in (14cm) | Wingspan **13in (33cm)** |

| Family **Ardeidae** | Species *Ixobrychus exilis* |

# Least Bittern

The smallest species of heron in North America, the Least Bittern is also one of the most colorful, but its secretive nature makes it easy to overlook in its habitat of reeds and cattails. Widely distributed in the East, the Least Bittern is local in several western states, including Oregon, California, and Nevada.

**OCCURRENCE** Breeds in lowland freshwater marshes, occasionally brackish marshes. In winter in tropical American also found in saltwater marshes. Its breeding distribution ranges from eastern Canada through Central and South America, south to Argentina.

**VOICE** During courtship displays, a soft series of *ku, ku, ku, ku, ku* notes; calls are harsh and loud, *kak, kak, kak*.

*long, yellow bill*

*black back*

**MALE**

| Length 11–14in (28–36cm) | Wingspan **15½–18in (40–46cm)** |

| Family **Fregatidae** | Species *Fregata magnificens* |
|---|---|

# Magnificent Frigatebird

One of North America's most-skilled aerialists, the Magnificent Frigatebird is not seen perched, except when nesting in mangroves or roosting on buoys. It is usually seen flying gracefully above bays, lagoons, or open ocean. This species is well known for its piratical behavior—it pursues birds such as boobies, making them disgorge their food.
**OCCURRENCE** Usually seen flying high in the sky over open water. In the West, rare along the coast of Southern California.
**VOICE** Male call consists of whirring, rattling, and drumming sounds, only at breeding sites.

long bill

white
underparts

**FEMALE**

| Length  **3ft 3in (100cm)** | Wingspan  **4½ft (1.4m)** |
|---|---|

| Family **Phalacrocoracidae** | Species *Phalacrocorax brasilianus* |
|---|---|

# Neotropic Cormorant

The slender Neotropic Cormorant ranges widely in the Western Hemisphere. In the US, it breeds and winters along the Gulf Coast and in the lower Rio Grande Valley. In the West, it breeds locally in Arizona and New Mexico, and is a rare visitor to California.
**OCCURRENCE** Breeds in coastal marshes, swamps, and inland reservoirs from southeastern Texas and western Louisiana to the far south of South America; winters close inshore in protected bays, inlets, estuaries, and lagoons.
**VOICE** Series of low, pig-like grunts; croaks in alarm.

dull orange
base to bill

**ADULT**

| Length  **24in (61cm)** | Wingspan  **3¼ft (1m)** |
|---|---|

| Family **Phalacrocoracidae** | Species *Phalacrocorax urile* |
|---|---|

# Red-faced Cormorant

The Red-faced Cormorant's breeding distribution stretches from the Aleutian Islands southward to British Columbia. Within this range, it occurs in small and isolated colonies on rocky outcrops and cliffs, usually in remote locations. The Red-faced Cormorant's bare facial skin varies from yellow to orange, and to red. Its crest is relatively prominent, even in nonbreeding birds.
**OCCURRENCE** Found in the Aleutian Islands and the Pacific Coast of Alaska. Nests on steep cliffs on rocky marine islands and headlands; seldom seen far out at sea.
**VOICE** Low groans and croaks; alarmed birds hiss.

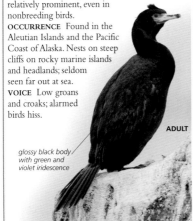

**ADULT**

glossy black body
with green and
violet iridescence

| Length  **30in–3ft 3in (75–100cm)** | Wingspan  **3½ft (1.1m)** |
|---|---|

| Family **Cathartidae** | Species *Coragyps atratus* |
|---|---|

# Black Vulture

Common in southern and eastern states but rare in the West, the Black Vulture can be seen in large communal roosts in the evening. Maintaining long pair bonds, these vultures remain together year-round. According to one study, parents will continue to feed their young for as long as eight months after fledging. When not feeding on roadkills along highways, they spend time soaring above the landscape, in search of carrion.
**OCCURRENCE** Breeds in dense woodlands, caves, old buildings; forages in open habitats, near roads and highways; found year-round throughout its range.
**VOICE** Usually silent; hisses and barks occasionally.

naked
grayish
skin

short tail
**ADULT**

| Length  **24–27in (61–68cm)** | Wingspan  **4½–5ft (1.4–1.5m)** |
|---|---|

| Family **Cathartidae** | Species *Gymnogyps californianus* |

# California Condor

With more than 500 individuals, 300 or so flying freely, the California Condor is one of the world's rarest birds. In 1987, only 27 birds remained, and were taken into breeding programs in San Diego and Los Angeles. They once occupied much of western North America from Canada to Mexico, and east to Florida. Condors' heads are bare of feathers, and may flush bright red, orange, or purplish at times of intense interaction with others. Otherwise, the bird is largely black, except for its striking white wing linings.
**OCCURRENCE** Found in wild, rocky, upland areas with open shrubland, and scattered conifers and oak trees.
**VOICE** Hisses and grunts.

*bare head for probing inside carcasses*

*bunched wings create hump-backed shape*

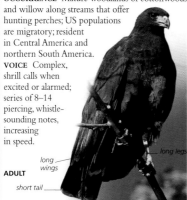

**ADULT**

| Length **43–55in (109–140cm)** | Wingspan **8–10ft (2.5–3m)** |

| Family **Accipitridae** | Species *Ictinia mississippiensis* |

# Mississippi Kite

The locally abundant Mississippi Kite nests in colonies in the central and southern Great Plains. Foraging flocks of 25 or more birds are common, and groups of ten or more roost near nests. In the West, the species nests in urban habitats, including city parks and golf courses, westward to New Mexico, and, locally, in Arizona and Colorado. This graceful bird pursues and eats its insect prey in flight. Mississippi Kites are long-distance migrants, wintering in South America.
**OCCURRENCE** Western birds use both rural woodland and suburban or urban habitat.
**VOICE** High-pitched *phee-phew;* also multisyllabled *phee-ti-ti.*

*orange-red eye*

*pale gray head with dark eye patch*

*long wings*

**SUBADULT**

| Length **13–15in (33–38cm)** | Wingspan **35in (89cm)** |

| Family **Accipitridae** | Species *Buteogallus anthracinus* |

# Common Black Hawk

Although it is found in several US States (southwestern Utah, Arizona, New Mexico, and Texas), the Common Black Hawk is actually relatively uncommon north of Mexico. This long-legged, short-tailed, and broad-winged hawk is all black except for a broad white band across its tail. Almost always found near water, the Common Black Hawk is fond of frogs and fishes.
**OCCURRENCE** Mature woodlands of cottonwoods and willow along streams that offer hunting perches; US populations are migratory; resident in Central America and northern South America.
**VOICE** Complex, shrill calls when excited or alarmed; series of 8–14 piercing, whistle-sounding notes, increasing in speed.

*long legs*

*long wings*

**ADULT**

*short tail*

| Length **21in (53cm)** | Wingspan **4¼ (1.3m)** |

| Family **Accipitridae** | Species *Parabuteo unicinctus* |

# Harris's Hawk

Named by the renowned ornithologist John James Audubon in honor of his friend and patron, Edward Harris, Harris's Hawks nest in social units, unlike other North American birds of prey. These groups engage in cooperative hunting: members take turns leading the chase to wear down their prey and share in the kill. This species has become popular with falconers all over the world.
**OCCURRENCE** Forages and breeds year-round in semi-open desert scrub, savanna, grassland, and wetlands containing scattered larger trees and cacti. Occasionally appears in suburban areas. Essentially a Central and South American species, with a small range north of the Rio Grande.
**VOICE** Main territorial alarm call a prolonged, harsh growl lasting about 3 seconds; also chirps, croaks, and screams.

*chestnut shoulder patch*

**ADULT**

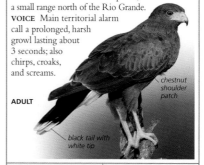

*black tail with white tip*

| Length **18–23in (46–59cm)** | Wingspan **3½–4ft (1.1–1.2m)** |

| Family **Accipitridae** | Species *Buteo plagiatus* |
|---|---|

# Gray Hawk

The elegant Gray Hawk is found from Mexico south to Argentina, but in North America is only seen in southwestern Texas and southeastern Arizona. The Gray Hawk's breeding system can include trios, one female and two males, all of whom cooperate with chick rearing. While only about 100 pairs breed in the US, their numbers are stable and possibly even increasing. Cottonwood and mesquite woodlands are key to their survival.

**OCCURRENCE** Breeds in riverside woodlands of mesquite and cottonwoods, especially along streams in the Gila River (Arizona) and Rio Grande (Texas) drainages. Little information exists about its winter habitats.

**VOICE** High-pitched whistled alarm, *creee*, rising and descending.

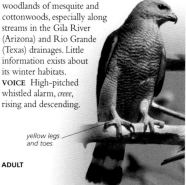

*yellow legs and toes*

**ADULT**

| Length **16–17in (41–43cm)** | Wingspan **35in (89cm)** |
|---|---|

| Family **Accipitridae** | Species *Buteo platypterus* |
|---|---|

# Broad-winged Hawk

A common species in the eastern US and Canada, the Broad-winged Hawk reaches British Columbia in the northwest, but otherwise is rare in the western US, usually in the fall. Broad-winged Hawks are a spectacular sight during fall migration at some eastern hawk-watching localities, when hundreds, and sometimes even thousands, of birds soar and glide in rising thermals. Most of these birds average 70 miles (110km) a day, and, after more than 4,000 miles (6,500km), reach their wintering quarters in Bolivia and Brazil.

**OCCURRENCE** Breeds across Canada (west to British Columbia) and the eastern US, in forested areas with clearings and water.

**VOICE** High-pitched *peeoweee* call, first note shorter and higher pitched.

**ADULT**

*one to two broad, white tail bands*

*black trailing wing edge*

| Length **13–17in (33–43cm)** | Wingspan **32–39in (81–100cm)** |
|---|---|

| Family **Accipitridae** | Species *Buteo albonotatus* |
|---|---|

# Zone-tailed Hawk

Widely distributed in Central and South America, the Zone-tailed Hawk is more localized in the US, where it breeds in Arizona, New Mexico, and Texas, sharing its riverside woodland habitat with the Common Black Hawk. It has been suggested that the Zone-tailed Hawk "mimics" the Turkey Vulture. The hawk, like the vulture, has a long tail, and flies with its wings held up at an angle, called a dihedral. The hawk uses the vulture's ability to spot prey on the ground, but, unlike the vulture, it catches live prey.

**OCCURRENCE** Breeds in riverside woodland, desert uplands, and mixed-conifer forest in mountains. Winters in central South America. Found in South America southward to Paraguay.

**VOICE** Harsh *kreeee*; also another harsh 2-syllable *kreeee-arr*.

*barred flight feathers*

*long, broad wings*

**ADULT**

| Length **17½–22in (45–56cm)** | Wingspan **4–4½ft (1.2–1.4m)** |
|---|---|

| Family **Strigidae** | Species *Megascops asio* |
|---|---|

# Eastern Screech-Owl

This widespread little owl has adapted well to suburban areas, and its "rolled" trill is a familiar sound across the eastern US. In the West, it is replaced by the Western Screech-Owl, which has a different call, a series of hoots accelerating and descending in pitch.

**OCCURRENCE** Distribution reaches westward to Idaho in the North and western Texas in the South.

**VOICE** Most familiar call a descending whinny; also an even trill; occasional barks and screeches; female higher pitched than male.

**ADULT (GRAY FORM)**

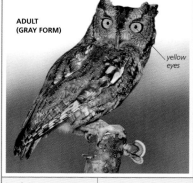

*yellow eyes*

| Length **6½–10in (16–25cm)** | Wingspan **19–24in (48–61cm)** |
|---|---|

| Family **Strigidae** | Species **Megascops trichopsis** |
|---|---|

# Whiskered Screech-Owl

The Whiskered Screech-Owl is more often heard than seen, and has a distinctive voice of hoots and trills. It can be heard on still nights in mountain canyons of southeastern Arizona and southwestern New Mexico. This small owl feeds largely on insects and insect larvae.

**OCCURRENCE** Resident at about 8,000ft (2,400m) in oak pine woodlands in canyons, along rivers, deciduous woodlands. Ranges southward through Mexico to Nicaragua.

**VOICE** Series of toots and trills; also single hoots, barks, screeches; pairs may sing duets; female higher pitched.

small "ear" tufts

ADULT

| Length **6–7½in (15–19cm)** | Wingspan **17½in (44cm)** |
|---|---|

| Family **Strigidae** | Species **Micrathene whitneyi** |
|---|---|

# Elf Owl

One of the smallest owls in the world, the Elf Owl is probably the most common bird of prey in the deserts of the Southwest. Being strictly nocturnal, however, it is more often heard than seen, and its distinctive voice is easy to recognize once heard. Elf Owls defend their nests aggressively, and several can get together to mob an intruder.

**OCCURRENCE** Breeds in southern Nevada, Arizona, California, New Mexico, and Texas, and adjacent areas of Mexico. Occurs in thorn-scrub, woodlands along rivers, and suburban areas.

**VOICE** Call a loud chatter of 5–6 notes; also trills and barks.

no "ear" tufts

thin white eyebrow

ADULT

| Length **4¾–5½in (12–14cm)** | Wingspan **15in (38cm)** |
|---|---|

| Family **Strigidae** | Species **Strix occidentalis** |
|---|---|

# Spotted Owl

In the Pacific Northwest, the Spotted Owl is threatened by competition from the Barred Owl and by habitat loss from clear cutting. Spotted Owls breed in old-growth forests, which the forestry industry covets, while conservationists argue that old-growth forests are not a renewable resource. These conflicting views have led to hot debates.

**OCCURRENCE** British Columbia, the US Pacific Northwest, California; Rocky Mountains south to Mexico. Breeds in forested areas.

**VOICE** Typical call of four notes, *whoo hoo-hoo hooo*, emphasis on the last syllable. Also whistles and barks.

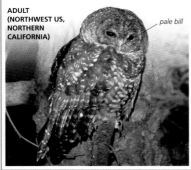

ADULT (NORTHWEST US, NORTHERN CALIFORNIA)

pale bill

| Length **18–19in (46–48cm)** | Wingspan **3½ft (1.1m)** |
|---|---|

| Family **Strigidae** | Species **Glaucidium brasilianum** |
|---|---|

# Ferruginous Pygmy-Owl

Quite widespread in the tropics, from Mexico to Argentina, this owl reaches the US only in Arizona and Texas, where it can be found close to rivers and in desert areas at lower elevations than the similar-looking Northern Pygmy-Owl. The Ferruginous species has an orange, not brown, tail, and its belly and crown are streaked, not spotted like the Northern Pygmy-Owl's.

**OCCURRENCE** Rare north of Mexico. Extreme southeastern Arizona and southern Texas. Occurs in riverside areas, and mesquite scrub; nests in cavities.

**VOICE** Call a quick series of repeated single rising notes.

streaked crown

brown bars in orange-rusty tail

ADULT

| Length **5½–7in (14–18cm)** | Wingspan **15in (38cm)** |
|---|---|

| Family **Trogonidae** | Species *Trogon elegans* |
|---|---|

# Elegant Trogon

Although widely distributed in Mexico and Central America, the well-named Elegant Trogon reaches the US only in the Southwest, where it occurs in wooded canyons. Rather sluggish, Elegant Trogons can remain perched for long periods.

**OCCURRENCE** Breeds in wooded canyons with pine oak or oak juniper; widely distributed in Mexico and Central America.

**VOICE** Alarm call a rapid, hoarse *bekekekekek*; varying croaking or *churr* notes; song a series of deep, croaking, *Ko-ah Ko-ah*.

MALE

finely-marked gray upper wings

| Length **11½in (29cm)** | Wingspan **16in (41cm)** |
|---|---|

| Family **Alcedinidae** | Species *Megaceryle torquata* |
|---|---|

# Ringed Kingfisher

The largest of the three species of North American kingfishers, the Ringed Kingfisher is easily identified by its size and color. Although it is brightly colored, and perches conspicuously on trees and branches over the water, its shy nature makes it difficult to spot. It flies off at the least suspicion of intrusion, with a loud rattle signalling its presence. Like other kingfishers it nests in a burrow, which it digs in a muddy or sandy riverbank.

**OCCURRENCE** Ranges from southern Texas to southern South America. At the northernmost part of range, in Texas, occurs along the Rio Grande Valley.

**VOICE** Loud rattle; also loud, double-syllabled *ktok-ktok* in flight.

blue breast

FEMALE

white band between breast and chestnut belly

| Length **16in (41cm)** | Wingspan **25in (63cm)** |
|---|---|

| Family **Alcedinidae** | Species *Chloroceryle americana* |
|---|---|

# Green Kingfisher

The Green Kingfisher is identified by its small size, proportionately large bill, conspicuous white collar, and green underparts. This species is the smallest of the three North American kingfishers. It is found in small numbers in southern Arizona and southern Texas, but its range is vast, and reaches as far south as Chile and Argentina.

**OCCURRENCE** Breeds and winters near wooded shorelines of lakes, ponds, and streams; in southern Texas and Arizona in US, and from Mexico all the way to southern South America (Chile and Argentina).

**VOICE** Staccato "ticking" call; also a harsh, buzzy scold; quieter than other two North American kingfishers.

MALE

long, thick, black bill

| Length **8½in (22cm)** | Wingspan **11in (28cm)** |
|---|---|

| Family **Picidae** | Species *Melanerpes erythrocephalus* |
|---|---|

# Red-headed Woodpecker

Widespread in the East, but rare west of the Great Plains, the Red-headed Woodpecker is the only member of its family, and its completely red head makes it easy to identify. It stores its food—insects and nuts—to eat at a later time. A truly North American species, the Red-headed Woodpecker does not occur south of the Rio Grande.

**OCCURRENCE** Occurs in deciduous woodlands, orchards, municipal parks, agricultural areas, forest edges, and forests affected by fire.

**VOICE** Primary call an extremely harsh and loud *churr*, also produces breeding call and alarm; no song; active drummer.

bluish gray bill

ADULT

| Length **8½–9½in (22–24cm)** | Wingspan **16–18in (41–46cm)** |
|---|---|

| Family **Picidae** | Species *Melanerpes uropygialis* |
|---|---|

# Gila Woodpecker

The Gila Woodpecker has characteristic heavily barred upperparts, with a tan head and underparts—only the male has a red crown patch. It is a common inhabitant of southern Arizona's desert and semidesert areas, which are covered sparsely with a variety of cactus species. Both male and female excavate a nest hole in a live cactus, but they may not use that hole until its walls have hardened.

**OCCURRENCE** From the southwestern US to central Mexico, this species is attracted to cacti and dead trees in riverside woodlands; it is also found in suburban areas.

**VOICE** Noisy, loud *churr-churr* and a series of *pip-pip* or *yip-yip* notes; drumming is prolonged.

tan-rust neck and underparts

**MALE**

| Length **8–10in (20–25cm)** | Wingspan **16–17in (41–43cm)** |
|---|---|

| Family **Picidae** | Species *Melanerpes aurifrons* |
|---|---|

# Golden-fronted Woodpecker

The yellow forehead, red crown, and bright orange nape give the male Golden-fronted Woodpecker a tricolored head pattern, while the female has only two color patches. This Mexican species reaches Texas and Oklahoma in the US, where it lives in a variety of open woodlands, including mesquite, riverside thickets, and subtropical scrub.

**OCCURRENCE** Southern Oklahoma and Texas in US, Mexico, and Central America, south to Nicaragua.

**VOICE** A noisy, basic *churr* closely resembling that of other *Melanerpes* woodpeckers, especially the Red-bellied, but harsher; a rather short "drum."

yellow forehead

**MALE**

| Length **10–12in (25–30cm)** | Wingspan **17in (43cm)** |
|---|---|

| Family **Picidae** | Species *Melanerpes carolinus* |
|---|---|

# Red-bellied Woodpecker

A quintessentially eastern species, the Red-bellied Woodpecker is common from the Mississippi Valley eastward to the Atlantic Seaboard, north to Minnesota and New York, and south to eastern Texas and Florida. Since the early 20th century it has expanded its range both northward into Canada and westward toward the Rockies. Its English name, "Red-bellied Woodpecker" is misleading, as its belly is pale buff, not red. Its presence is often given away by its rolling call, which is similar to that of the Gray Tree Frog.

**OCCURRENCE** Eastern and southeastern US; forests, swamps, suburbs, and gardens.

**VOICE** Rather soft, clearly rolling, slightly quivering *krrurrr* call.

red forehead to nape

**MALE**

| Length **9–10½in (23–27cm)** | Wingspan **16in (41cm)** |
|---|---|

| Family **Picidae** | Species *Dryobates nuttallii* |
|---|---|

# Nuttall's Woodpecker

Named for the famous British naturalist Thomas Nuttall, Nuttall's Woodpecker is resident in California and nearby Mexico. It resembles the Ladder-backed Woodpecker, with black-and-white barring on the back, and the male's red crown. Interestingly, although Nuttall's Woodpecker prefers oak woodlands, acorns are not part of its diet. It excavates a new nest cavity each year and it is likely that earlier nest sites are used by other species.

**OCCURRENCE** Mainly oak woodlands, but also pine oak and woodlands near rivers; also willows, sycamores, maple, and pine trees; occasionally found in Oregon.

**VOICE** Two calls; single note contact call *pweek* and 2-note call *pir-it-pir-it-pir-it*.

white breast with dark spots

**MALE**

| Length **7–7½in (18–19cm)** | Wingspan **16in (41cm)** |
|---|---|

| Family **Picidae** | Species ***Dryobates arizonae*** |
|---|---|

# Arizona Woodpecker

A resident of southeastern Arizona, southwestern New Mexico, and the western mountains of Mexico, the Arizona Woodpecker is the only brown-backed woodpecker species in North America. In addition, it has a conspicuous white neck patch, and brown-and-white spots and bars on its underparts. It inhabits inaccessible areas, is well camouflaged, and is remarkably secretive during the nesting period, which makes it difficult to observe. It uses quite a range of calls, except when nesting.

*short, thin, pointed bill*

**OCCURRENCE**
Oak and pine oak woodlands, at 4,000–7,000ft (1,200–2,150m). Winters at lower elevations if food is scarce.
**VOICE** Main call long *peep*; also lengthy, loud, and harsh rattling call; also a *kweek* call.

**MALE**

| Length **7–8in (18–20cm)** | Wingspan **14in (36cm)** |
|---|---|

| Family **Picidae** | Species ***Colaptes chrysoides*** |
|---|---|

# Gilded Flicker

The Gilded Flicker was long considered a subspecies of the Northern Flicker. Where the ranges of these two species overlap, in parts of the Southwest, there is interbreeding between them. Gilded Flickers have golden undertail coverts, yellow underwing coverts, and a white rump. They have a preference for saguaro cacti as nesting sites.

**OCCURRENCE**
Resident in deserts with giant cacti in Arizona and southeastern California. Also resident in Baja California and continental areas of northwestern Mexico.

*red "mustache"*

**VOICE** Two common calls, loud *kew-kew-kew* with each note ascending at end, and softer *wicka-wicka-wicka*.

**MALE**

| Length **11–11½in (28–29cm)** | Wingspan **18–19in (46–48cm)** |
|---|---|

| Family **Falconidae** | Species ***Caracara cheriway*** |
|---|---|

# Crested Caracara

In North America, the hawk-like Crested Caracara is only found in Texas, southern Arizona, and central Florida. Crested Caracara pairs are monogamous and highly territorial. Known locally as the "Mexican Buzzard," the Crested Caracara is actually a member of the falcon family, not the hawk family.
**OCCURRENCE** Ranges widely in Central and South America. Breeds and winters in open areas ranging from desert to grasslands with scattered tall trees. Has been recorded in California.
**VOICE** Adults disturbed at the nest emit cackles, hollow rattles, and high-pitched screams; nestlings utter high-pitched screams and raspy *swee-swee* calls.

*yellow to orange naked facial skin*

*dark bars on breast and upper back*

**ADULT**

| Length **19–23in (48–58cm)** | Wingspan **4ft (1.2m)** |
|---|---|

| Family **Falconidae** | Species ***Falco rusticolus*** |
|---|---|

# Gyrfalcon

The majestic Gyrfalcon breeds in the Arctic and the Subarctic in Eurasia and North America, and rarely occurs south of its breeding range, except during years with peaks in population numbers. For centuries, the Gyrfalcon has been sought by falconers for its power and gentle nature, and is the mascot of the US Air Force Academy. Variable in color, Gyrfalcons range from almost pure white to gray and dark forms.
**OCCURRENCE** Breeds in Alaska and Arctic Canada. In winter some birds move south as far as the northern US.
**VOICE** Loud, harsh *KYHa-KYHa-KYHa*.

*dark back*

*white underparts*

*yellow toes*

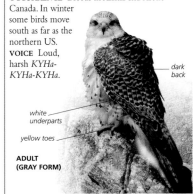

**ADULT (GRAY FORM)**

| Length **22in (56cm)** | Wingspan **4ft (1.2m)** |
|---|---|

| Family **Tityridae** | Species *Pachyramphus aglaiae* |
|---|---|

# Rose-throated Becard

The Rose-throated Becard is a grayish or brownish bird with a large head. The male's pink throat and the female's charcoal cap and brown body are distinctive. Its roundish, foot-long nest hangs from a high tree limb, and is a reliable cue to its presence. It forages mainly on fruit and insects, sallying short distances from a perch.

**OCCURRENCE** This Central American species reaches southeastern Arizona and the lower Rio Grande Valley in Texas.

**VOICE** Plaintive *tseeeuuuu*, and *pik* or *pidik* calls; song repeated *see-cheeu, wee-chew.*

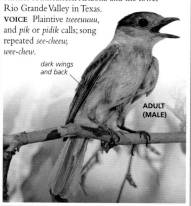

dark wings and back

**ADULT (MALE)**

| Length **7¼in (18.5cm)** | Wingspan **12in (30cm)** |
|---|---|

| Family **Tyrannidae** | Species *Camptostoma imberbe* |
|---|---|

# Northern Beardless-Tyrannulet

This tiny flycatcher is uncommon along streams in southeastern Arizona, southeastern New Mexico, and southern Texas. Its whistled calls often reveal its presence before it is seen. "Beardless" refers to the lack of bristles at the base of its bill, and "tyrannulet" to its diminutive size for a flycatcher.

**OCCURRENCE** Found especially in riverside vegetation, including sycamores and cottonwoods; local in Arizona, New Mexico, and Texas; more common from Mexico to Costa Rica.

**VOICE** Calls include clear, piping *peeeuuu* and *peeut di-i-i-i;* song *pee-pee-pee-pee,* a descending series of whistles given by males.

stubby bill

**ADULT**

| Length **4½–5½in (11.5–14cm)** | Wingspan **7in (18cm)** |
|---|---|

| Family **Tyrannidae** | Species *Myiarchus tuberculifer* |
|---|---|

# Dusky-capped Flycatcher

One of four species of flycatchers of the genus *Myiarchus* found in North America, the Dusky-capped breeds in Arizona and New Mexico. It inhabits dense woodlands, where it forages for insects in the foliage below the canopy. As in other *Myiarchus* species, the sexes are similar, and juveniles are slightly darker than adults. The species is mainly silent, except when it sings at dawn.

**OCCURRENCE** Southeastern Arizona and southwestern New Mexico. Migrates to Mexico. Resident populations occur all the way south to South America.

**VOICE** Dawn song a *whit, peeur,* or *wheeeeu* alternated with *huit* notes.

bushy crest

**ADULT**

| Length **7¼in (18.5cm)** | Wingspan **10in (25cm)** |
|---|---|

| Family **Tyrannidae** | Species *Myiarchus crinitus* |
|---|---|

# Great Crested Flycatcher

The only species of *Myiarchus* flycatchers breeding in the eastern region, the Great Crested Flycatcher occurs in the West only in Canada, where it reaches Alberta. However it is sometimes seen farther west and north in the fall, when it can be identified by the pale base of its bill and the sharp definition between its gray breast and yellow belly.

**OCCURRENCE** From Alberta eastward to the Maritimes in Canada, southward to Texas and Florida. Migrates to Mexico, Central America, and northern South America. Breeds in woodlands.

**VOICE** Main call a loud, abrupt *purr-it* given by both sexes; male song repeated *whee-eep,* occasionally *wheeyer.*

**ADULT**

long, thin bill

| Length **7–8in (18–20cm)** | Wingspan **13in (33cm)** |
|---|---|

| Family **Tyrannidae** | Species **Myiarchus tyrannulus** |
|---|---|

# Brown-crested Flycatcher

This is the largest of the three western *Myiarchus* species. It is a slender-looking, long-tailed flycatcher, with a thick bill and a ragged-looking, tan-brown crest. In flight, the rufous outer tail feathers are quite noticeable. Although mostly an insect catcher, it will sometimes pluck a hummingbird from a perch.

**OCCURRENCE** Found only in the southwestern US, north to Nevada and east to Texas; breeds in riverside woodlands. Migrates to Mexico and Guatemala, resident south to Honduras.

**VOICE** Call *huit* singly or repeated, also distinctive *rasp*; dawn song loud *come-here, come-here* or *whit-will-do, whit-will-do*.

ragged crest

**ADULT**

| Length **8½in (22cm)** | Wingspan **13in (33cm)** |
|---|---|

| Family **Tyrannidae** | Species **Myiodynastes luteiventris** |
|---|---|

# Sulphur-bellied Flycatcher

In North America, this large and boldly marked flycatcher breeds in the mountain canyons of southeastern Arizona. It is heavily streaked on both back and belly, its tail is rufous, and its loud squeaky calls are distinctive. Sulphur-bellied Flycatchers are cavity nesters, using holes in trees, or, occasionally, nest boxes.

**OCCURRENCE** Southeastern Arizona; widely distributed from Mexico to Costa Rica. Winters from Ecuador to Bolivia and Brazil.

**VOICE** Calls *p'p'pe-ya, p'p'p'pe-ya, weel-yum, weel-yum, chu-eer*; male song soft *tre-le-re-re, tre-le-re-re, chu-eer, chee-a-leet s-lik*.

streaked chest

**ADULT**

rufous tail

| Length **8–9in (20–23cm)** | Wingspan **14½in (37cm)** |
|---|---|

| Family **Tyrannidae** | Species **Tyrannus melancholicus** |
|---|---|

# Tropical Kingbird

The Tropical Kingbird is another of the widespread tropical American species of flycatchers that barely reach the US as a breeder. It nests in open areas of southeastern Arizona, but can be seen as far north as British Columbia in the fall.

**OCCURRENCE** In the US, regularly found in residential areas, such as golf courses, farmland, and gardens. In the tropics breeds in a wide variety of habitats, including evergreen forest edges and mangroves.

**VOICE** Twittering calls given throughout the day and all year long; song tremulous *tere-ee-ee-tril-il-iil-l* or *tre-e-e-e-eip*.

**ADULT**

grayish olive upperparts

| Length **7–9in (18–23cm)** | Wingspan **14½in (37cm)** |
|---|---|

| Family **Tyrannidae** | Species **Tyrannus crassirostris** |
|---|---|

# Thick-billed Kingbird

Though it is similar in size and color to other kingbirds of the western region, the Thick-billed Kingbird has a noticeably thicker bill, and a darker head, both of which give it a somewhat "beefy" look. In North America, Thick-billed Kingbirds breed locally in southern Arizona and New Mexico, mostly in sycamore groves along streams.

**OCCURRENCE** Prefers cottonwoods and sycamores in wooded canyons, close to water. Reported from California and Texas.

**VOICE** Harsh and raspy *tch tchee* and *tch-uhreeeE* calls; vocal through the day while breeding; dawn song consists of two phrases *T-t-t-t-t, t-T-tt-rwheeuh -t-t-t*, or a loud whistled *pwaareeet*.

thick bill

**ADULT**

| Length **9–9½in (23–24cm)** | Wingspan **16in (41cm)** |
|---|---|

| Family **Tyrannidae** | Species ***Tyrannus forficatus*** |

# Scissor-tailed Flycatcher

The long tail streamers of the Scissor-tailed
Flycatcher are seen in all their glory when males
display in flight over their breeding territory.
Scissor-tailed Flycatchers often incorporate manmade
debris into their nests, including pieces of string,
cloth, or bits of wrapping. This flycatcher forms
large pre-migratory roosts in late summer, often
of more than 100, and even up to 1,000 birds.
**OCCURRENCE** Breeds in open areas in south-
central US states and adjacent Mexico. Reported
widely in western North America. Winters from
Mexico to Costa Rica.
**VOICE** Males vocalize in breeding territories and
communal roosts; song a variable number of *pups*
followed by *perleep* or *peroo*.

pale gray head

**ADULT
(BREEDING)**

| Length **9–15in (23–38cm)** | Wingspan **15in (38cm)** |

| Family **Tyrannidae** | Species ***Contopus pertinax*** |

# Greater Pewee

First identified by its whistled song, the Greater
Pewee, when seen, looks like a plain grayish
flycatcher with a tufted crest. Primarily a Mexican
and Central American species, it reaches Arizona
and New Mexico across the US border. Greater
Pewees vigorously defend their nests against
potential predators like jays and squirrels.
US breeders move south after breeding.
**OCCURRENCE** Breeds in open pine
woodland with oak understory
at elevations of 7,000–10,000ft
(2,100–3,000m) along
steep-sided canyons.
**VOICE** A repeated *pip*,
*peep*, or *beep-beep*;
male territorial
song a plaintive
*ho-say ma-ree-ah*.

tufted crest

**ADULT**

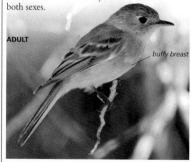

| Length **7in (18cm)** | Wingspan **13in (33cm)** |

| Family **Tyrannidae** | Species ***Contopus virens*** |

# Eastern Wood-Pewee

The Eastern Wood-Pewee, common in woodlands
in the eastern US and southern Canada, is
replaced in the West by the very similar Western
Wood-Pewee. Their ranges overlap slightly at
the margins of their respective distributions. The
Eastern Wood-Pewee looks somewhat like
the Eastern Phoebe, but does not flick its tail.
**OCCURRENCE** Woodlands in the eastern US
and southern and eastern Canada; also along
rivers in the Midwest. Winters in shrubby,
second-growth forests of South America.
**VOICE** Call terse *chip*; song
slurred *pee-ah-wee*, plaintive
*wee-ooo*, or *wee-ur*, and
slurred *ah di dee*.

**ADULT**

slightly ragged crest

| Length **6in (15cm)** | Wingspan **9–10in (23–26cm)** |

| Family **Tyrannidae** | Species ***Empidonax fulvifrons*** |

# Buff-breasted Flycatcher

The smallest of the genus *Empidonax*, the
Buff-breasted Flycatcher has a rusty or buffy wash
on its breast. The other *Empidonax* species are
grayish or yellow below. A resident in Mexico
and Central America, the Buff-breasted Flycatcher
reaches the US locally in Arizona and Texas, where
it lives at high elevations in pine oak woodlands.
**OCCURRENCE** Southern Arizona and New Mexico
to Mexico, and south to Honduras. US populations
migratory, resident in Mexico and Central America.
**VOICE** Call *pit*, and alarm call *quit-*
*quit-qui-r-r*; song on breeding grounds
*chee-lick* or *chee-lick-chou* by
both sexes.

**ADULT**

buffy breast

| Length **5in (13cm)** | Wingspan **8½in (22cm)** |

| Family **Tyrannidae** | Species *Sayornis phoebe* |
|---|---|

# Eastern Phoebe

An early spring migrant, the Eastern Phoebe often nests under bridges and culverts, as well as on buildings. Not shy, it is also familiar because of its *fee-bee* vocalization and constant tail wagging. Ornithologist John James Audubon tied threads on several birds' legs and established that individuals return from the South to a previously used nest site.

**OCCURRENCE** Occurs in open woodlands, forest edges, and parks, often near water. Breeds across Canada and in the eastern half of the US. Winters in the southeastern US and Mexico.

**VOICE** Common call a clear, weak *chip*; song an emphatic *fee-bee* or *fee-b-be-bee*.

ADULT (BREEDING)

round, dark head

| Length **5½–7in (14–17cm)** | Wingspan **10½in (27cm)** |
|---|---|

| Family **Tyrannidae** | Species *Pyrocephalus rubinus* |
|---|---|

# Vermilion Flycatcher

Contrasting with all other North American species of flycatcher, the Vermilion Flycatcher well deserves its English name. Beware, however, that only the male is red; the female, brownish above and streaked below, is drab by comparison. Males advertise their territories during spectacular flight displays accompanied by loud vocalizations.

**OCCURRENCE** Breeds mostly along rivers, in woodlands with cottonwoods, willows, and sycamores. In the US, found only in the South; south of the border, occurs south to Argentina.

**VOICE** Contact call *peeent*; male song an excited *p-p-pik-zee*, *pit-a-zee*, or *ching-tink-a-link*.

MALE (BREEDING)

red plumage

| Length **5–6in (13–15cm)** | Wingspan **10in (25cm)** |
|---|---|

| Family **Vireonidae** | Species *Vireo atricapilla* |
|---|---|

# Black-capped Vireo

The only vireo to show a sexually dimorphic (different) plumage, the Black-capped Vireo is restricted to central and southern Texas and Mexico. Despite its broad, white "spectacles" and a red eye, it is not easy to spot as it forages in dense shrubby vegetation. It sings persistently from near the top of bushes, often long into the day. Habitat changes and Brown-headed Cowbird parasitism have caused declines in the bird's population.

**OCCURRENCE** Breeds only in the Hill Country of central southern Texas and adjacent Mexico, casually in Oklahoma. Winters in the foothill country of western Mexico.

**VOICE** Calls are variable scolds; song an extensive repertoire of trills, whistles, chips, and squeaks, with individual variations.

red eye

MALE

| Length **4½in (11.5cm)** | Wingspan **7½in (19cm)** |
|---|---|

| Family **Vireonidae** | Species *Vireo flavifrons* |
|---|---|

# Yellow-throated Vireo

This large and robust vireo of eastern US woodlands is usually found foraging and singing high in the canopy. It is distinctly patterned, with a bright yellow throat, breast, and "spectacles," and a white belly and flanks. The fragmentation of forests, spraying of insecticides, and cowbird parasitism have led to regional declines in its populations, but the bird's range, as a whole, has actually expanded.

**OCCURRENCE** Breeds in deciduous and mixed woodlands in the eastern half of the US, and extreme southern Canada. Winter range from wooded areas of southern Mexico to northern South America.

**VOICE** Scolding, hoarse, rapid calls; male song a slow, repetitive, 2- or 3-note phrase, separated by long pauses.

yellow "spectacles"

ADULT

| Length **5½in (14cm)** | Wingspan **9½in (24cm)** |
|---|---|

| Family **Corvidae** | Species *Cyanocitta cristata* |
| --- | --- |

# Blue Jay

One of the best-known birds in North America because of its abundance and beautiful plumage, the Blue Jay is largely an eastern species, although in Canada it occurs westward to Alberta and British Columbia. In the West, it is replaced by the equally spectacular Steller's Jay.

**OCCURRENCE** In the West, breeds in British Columbia, Alberta, Saskatchewan, and Montana. Rare elsewhere (California, Oregon, Washington) in winter. Found in a variety of woodlands, suburban areas, and gardens.

**VOICE** Harsh, screaming *jay! jay!*; other common call an odd ethereal, chortling *queedle-ee-dee;* soft clucks when feeding.

ADULT
blue wings and tail

| Length 9½–12in (24–30cm) | Wingspan 16in (41cm) |
| --- | --- |

| Family **Corvidae** | Species *Aphelocoma californica* |
| --- | --- |

# California Scrub-Jay

Western Scrub-Jays have recently been separated into two distinct species. The California Scrub-Jay is a brighter blue, with a more distinct buff-gray back and dark breastband, than the Woodhouse's Scrub-Jay. These birds are active and vocal, moving in jerky hops and jumps, often in groups of up to 30 birds, most of which are immatures. Established pairs defend their territories year-round. California Scrub-Jays are easily attracted to suburban backyards with feeders.

**OCCURRENCE** From British Columbia to southern California, typically in dry, open woodland, especially oak, scrubby chaparral, orchards, and backyards.

**VOICE** Short, harsh, rising shriek and quicker, repeated *chirr chirr chirr chirr chirr.*

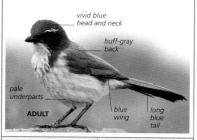

vivid blue head and neck

buff-gray back

pale underparts

ADULT

blue wing

long blue tail

| Length 11–12in (27–31cm) | Wingspan 15in (39cm) |
| --- | --- |

| Family **Corvidae** | Species *Aphelocoma wollweberi* |
| --- | --- |

# Mexican Jay

The bell-like calls from a flock of Mexican Jays can be heard in the pine oak canyons of Mexico and adjacent Arizona, New Mexico, and Texas. These birds have a fascinating social system. Instead of territorial pairs, they form territorial flocks, within which females mate with several males. Nestlings are not fed only by their parents, but also by other members of the flock, including those that have failed to breed.

**OCCURRENCE** Occurs in mountains with rugged slopes, covered with oaks and pines.

**VOICE** Rapid-fire, ringing *wink, wink*; harsher and less bell-like in Texas population, which also gives rattle call similar to scrub-jays.

ADULT
(A. u. couchii)

pale gray back

| Length 11–12½in (28–32cm) | Wingspan 19½in (50cm) |
| --- | --- |

| Family **Corvidae** | Species *Pica nuttalli* |
| --- | --- |

# Yellow-billed Magpie

Found only in California, where it is common locally, the Yellow-billed Magpie is very similar to the more widely distributed Black-billed Magpie. Its yellow bill, small bare yellow patch underneath the eye, and slightly different calls all help to distinguish it from the Black-billed Magpie. The Yellow-billed Magpie occasionally nests in loose colonies, but never with more than one pair to a tree.

**OCCURRENCE** Oak savanna, orchards, and other open habitats with widely spaced trees; also areas near rivers and streams.

**VOICE** Whining *mag* call; also a series of *kwah-kwah-kwah*; similar to Black-billed Magpie, but higher pitched and less harsh.

yellow bill

ADULT

| Length 15–17½in (38–45cm) | Wingspan 24in (61cm) |
| --- | --- |

| Family **Corvidae** | Species **Corvus caurinus** |

# Northwestern Crow

Very similar to the widespread American Crow, the Northwestern Crow's range is restricted to a coastal strip from Alaska to Washington State, where the American Crow does not appear to occur. Northwestern Crows often congregate in large flocks in tidal areas, where they dig for clams, pry open barnacles, chase crabs, and catch small fish in tidal pools, at low tide.

**OCCURRENCE** Coastal areas from Alaska to Washington state; avoids dense forests; along rivers at higher elevation inland.

**VOICE** Varied, but most common call a loud, familiar *caw!* lower, raspier, and more rapid than most American Crows.

ADULT

bluish black
upperparts

| Length **13–16in (33–41cm)** | Wingspan **34in (86cm)** |

| Family **Corvidae** | Species **Corvus cryptoleucus** |

# Chihuahuan Raven

Smaller than the Common Raven but larger than the American Crow, the Chihuahuan Raven was previously called the White-necked Raven. This name alludes to its concealed white neck feathers, which may come into view in the bird's windswept habitat. A gregarious and vocal species, the Chihuahuan Raven may be seen wheeling about in flocks of hundreds of birds.

**OCCURRENCE** Breeds in south-central and southwestern US and in Mexico, in grasslands, scrub, and deserts. Northern populations winter in Mexico.

**VOICE** High-pitched croaks, less varied than the highly diverse repertoire of the Common Raven.

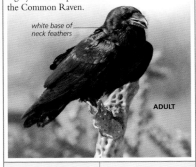

white base of
neck feathers

ADULT

| Length **17½–20in (44–51cm)** | Wingspan **3½ft (1.1m)** |

| Family **Alaudidae** | Species **Alauda arvensis** |

# Eurasian Skylark

The Eurasian Skylark was introduced to Vancouver Island, British Columbia in the 1900s, and still breeds there in small numbers. Wild individuals of an Asian subspecies are occasional visitors to islands in the Bering Sea Region of Alaska; and vagrants occur south to California. Eurasian Skylarks are similar to pipits and American sparrows, but have a short crest, white outer tail feathers, and different calls.

**OCCURRENCE** Likes windswept, hilly, and grassy areas near the ocean; stays close to the ground and is hard to see unless flushed; fluttery flight.

**VOICE** Flight call a sudden *jeeup*; aerial song consists of endless trills and buzzes, heard only on the breeding grounds.

prominent
crest

ADULT

short tail with
white outer
feathers

| Length **7¼in (18.5cm)** | Wingspan **12–14in (30–36cm)** |

| Family **Hirundinidae** | Species **Petrochelidon fulva** |

# Cave Swallow

Its orange throat and rufous forehead distinguish the Cave Swallow from its close relative, the Cliff Swallow. This species breeds locally in parts of Arizona, New Mexico, Texas, and southern Florida. Cave Swallows cement their cup nests to the walls of caves, bridges, culverts, and buildings. This adaptation, of building nests on manmade structures, has led to the species' geographical and numerical expansion.

**OCCURRENCE** Breeds in arid areas, preferably near water. Also breeds in Mexico and the Greater Antilles.

**VOICE** Call a low *wheet*; song a series of bubbly sounds blending into warbling trill, ending in series of double-toned notes.

orange
cheeks
and
throat

ADULT

| Length **5½in (14cm)** | Wingspan **13in (33cm)** |

| Family **Paridae** | Species ***Poecile carolinensis*** |
|---|---|

# Carolina Chickadee

This eastern and southeastern species is very similar to the Black-capped Chickadee, which is widespread in the West. In parts of the central and eastern US, both species have adjacent ranges and hybridize locally. The western range of the Carolina Chickadee is limited to parts of Kansas, Oklahoma, and Texas, where the Black-capped does not normally occur. The Carolina's characteristic call is the easiest way to distinguish it from the Black-capped.

**OCCURRENCE** Mixed woodlands, orchards, gardens; often at feeders.

**VOICE** Fast *dee-dee-dee* call; song clear, whistled, 4–note sequence *wee-bee wee-bay*, second note lower in pitch.

ADULT

white cheeks

| Length **4¾in (12cm)** | Wingspan **7½in (19cm)** |
|---|---|

| Family **Paridae** | Species ***Poecile sclateri*** |
|---|---|

# Mexican Chickadee

Although widespread in the mountains of Mexico, the Mexican Chickadee's range in the US is restricted to mountaintops in southern Arizona and New Mexico, known as "sky islands." These high elevation habitats include forests of conifers separated from one another by valleys.

**OCCURRENCE** High-elevation coniferous forests of southeastern Arizona, and southwestern New Mexico; mountains of Mexico; occurs as high as 12,800ft (3,900m). Some move lower down in winter.

**VOICE** Variety of rapid warbles, including *tse-tse tse-tse tse-tse*; also harsh *churr-churr* notes.

large bib extending to chest

ADULT

| Length **5in (13cm)** | Wingspan **8in (20cm)** |
|---|---|

| Family **Paridae** | Species ***Baeolophus wollweberi*** |
|---|---|

# Bridled Titmouse

This species, the smallest of the North American titmice, is especially agile, capable of acrobatics and of hanging upside down to catch insects. Its striking black-and-white facial marks and tall, dark crest distinguish it from other titmice. Its voice is also softer and more chickadee-like than those of other titmice. It forms flocks in fall and winter that include chickadees, nuthatches, and kinglets.

**OCCURRENCE** Primarily a Mexican species, in US lives in the mountain oak and pine oak forests up to 7,200ft (2,130m) in southeastern Arizona and southwestern New Mexico. Winters at lower elevations.

**VOICE** High-pitched *cheer cheer cheer* call; song a fast series of whistled *peet peet peet* notes.

conspicuous crest

ADULT

| Length **5¼in (13.5cm)** | Wingspan **8in (20cm)** |
|---|---|

| Family **Paridae** | Species ***Baeolophus inornatus*** |
|---|---|

# Oak Titmouse

The Oak Titmouse and its look-alike relative, the Juniper Titmouse, are the least colorful species of titmice. The two species were previously united in a single species, the Plain Titmouse. The Oak Titmouse, as its English name suggests, favors a habitat where oaks are present, especially the Coast Live Oaks of California.

**OCCURRENCE** Year-round resident in oak or oak pine woodlands on dry foothills of the Pacific slope.

**VOICE** Rough *see-see-see-chrr* or *tsicka-tsicka jeer-jeer* call; song a series of clear, whistled double notes, *peedle peedle peedle* or *pe-er pe-er pe-er*.

blackish bill

ADULT

| Length **5¾in (14.5cm)** | Wingspan **9in (23cm)** |
|---|---|

| Family **Paridae** | Species ***Baeolophus atricristatus*** |
|---|---|

# Black-crested Titmouse

Only found in Texas and southwestern Oklahoma in the US, where it is resident, the Black-crested Titmouse much resembles the Tufted Titmouse, except for its noticeably taller, black crest. Because of this striking difference, the two were once considered separate species, but as the two interbreed in a wide area of Texas, ornithologists merged them into a single species in 1983. Still later studies in 2002 suggested, once again, that they should be considered distinct.

**OCCURRENCE** Scrubby oak woodlands; frequents feeders in winter. Occurs as high as 6,000ft (2,000m) in the mountain forests of Mexico.

**VOICE** Call a rasping, scolding *jhree jhree jhree*; song a loud series of clear notes *pew, pew, pew*.

tall, black crest

**ADULT**

| Length **6½in (16.5cm)** | Wingspan **10in (25cm)** |
|---|---|

| Family **Troglodytidae** | Species ***Cistothorus platensis*** |
|---|---|

# Sedge Wren

A shy bird, the Sedge Wren is difficult to see except when singing atop a sedge stalk or a shrub. If spotted, it flies a short distance away, drops down, and runs off through the vegetation. In the West, it reaches Alberta in western Canada, and northeastern Montana in the US. The male, like other species of wrens, builds up to 8–10 unlined "dummy" nests before the female builds the real, better-concealed, nest.

**OCCURRENCE** In North America, breeds in wet meadows and sedge marshes. Winters in drier habitats. Occurs south to South America.

**VOICE** Call a loud *chap*; song a dry, staccato two-part chatter: *cha cha cha cha ch'ch'ch ch'ch'ch'ch'*.

faint, white barring on chest

**ADULT**

| Length **4½in (11.5cm)** | Wingspan **5½–6in (14–15.5cm)** |
|---|---|

| Family **Troglodytidae** | Species ***Thryothorus ludovicianus*** |
|---|---|

# Carolina Wren

The Carolina Wren is a popular and common suburban and backyard bird in much of its range. It is rarely still, often flicking its tail and looking around nervously. Harsh winters at the edge of its range in New England can cause a decline in numbers, as food resources dwindle. At such times, food and shelter from humans may aid survival.

**OCCURRENCE** Breeds in woodlands, parks, and yards, from northeastern Mexico to the Great Lakes, northeast to New England. A separate population is found from Mexico to Nicaragua.

**VOICE** Calls variable; often a sharp *chlip* or long, harsh chatter; song a loud, long, fast *whee'dle-dee whee'dle-dee whee'dle-dee*.

**ADULT**

tough-looking, bluish bill

| Length **5¼in (13.5cm)** | Wingspan **7½in (19cm)** |
|---|---|

| Family **Polioptilidae** | Species ***Polioptila californica*** |
|---|---|

# California Gnatcatcher

Scarce and threatened in its patchy, localized habitat in southern California, this species is highly sought-after by birders. To spot it, listen for its odd "mewing" call and then wait patiently for it to fly between patches of sage scrub. Formerly classified together with the more widespread Black-tailed Gnatcatcher, the two were separated in 1989, on the basis of plumage, vocal, and molecular differences.

**OCCURRENCE** Year-round resident in Baja California, Mexico, and scattered breeding localities in coastal sage scrub in southern California. In Baja California, breeds in desert scrub and thorn thickets.

**VOICE** Characteristic call an odd "mewing" sound *wee-eeew*, *ch-ch-ch* when disturbed.

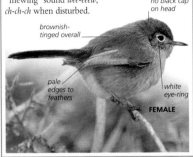

no black cap on head

brownish-tinged overall

pale edges to feathers

white eye-ring

**FEMALE**

| Length **4¼in (11cm)** | Wingspan **5½in (14cm)** |
|---|---|

| Family **Phylloscopidae** | Species *Phylloscopus borealis* |
|---|---|

# Arctic Warbler

The Arctic Warbler is a small, slender, olive-colored bird with a prominent buffy yellow eyestripe and a faint, single wing bar. Predominantly Eurasian, it occurs in North America in willow thickets in Alaska, where it breeds. Its biology in Alaska is not as well known as its habits are in Eurasia. Vagrant birds occur as far south as California.

**OCCURRENCE** Breeds in stands of dwarf willow, often along streams. Winters in open rain forests, grasslands, gardens, and mangroves in the Philippines and in Indonesia.

**VOICE** Alarm call a short hard metallic *dzik*; male's song a loud, vigorous, monotonous slow trill *chingingingingining*.

dull green upperparts

**ADULT (SPRING)**

thin, pointed bill

| Length 4¼–5in (11–13cm) | Wingspan 8in (20cm) |
|---|---|

| Family **Sylviidae** | Species *Chamaea fasciata* |
|---|---|

# Wrentit

Much easier to hear than to see, the Wrentit is neither a wren nor a chickadee. It is the sole New World representative of a large and diverse Old World family that includes species formerly classified as babblers. Wrentits are not especially sociable; pairs are rather aloof, guarding their territories, and rarely foraging with other birds. Affected by the destruction of coastal brushwood, their numbers have nevertheless increased locally where logging has opened up new habitats.

**OCCURRENCE** Pacific Coast and dense foothill shrubs with chamise, manzanita, sagebrush, and poison oak. Nonmigratory; generally stay close to their breeding areas.

**VOICE** Calls varied, agitated-sounding *jrrr, krrrrt*; sings a loud accelerating series all year long: *pip… pip… pip… pi'pi'pi'pi'pi'pi'pi*.

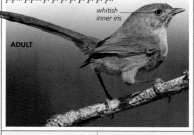

whitish inner iris

**ADULT**

| Length 6½in (16cm) | Wingspan 7in (17.5cm) |
|---|---|

| Family **Muscicapidae** | Species *Cyanecula svecica* |
|---|---|

# Bluethroat

Widespread in Eurasia, the Bluethroat is found in North America only in Alaska and the Yukon. The male's iridescent blue throat adorned with a rufous spot is rarely seen because it spends most of its time in thick vegetation, except during its flight songs.

**OCCURRENCE** Breeds in willow thickets in the tundra of northern Alaska and the western Yukon.

**VOICE** Calls are sharp, dry *krak*, often repeated; also a soft *whooit*. Song is melodious, lengthy, and may include the calls of other bird species, as the Bluethroat is a gifted mimic.

blue throat with rufous center spot

**MALE (BREEDING)**

| Length 6in (15cm) | Wingspan 9in (23cm) |
|---|---|

| Family **Muscicapidae** | Species *Oenanthe oenanthe* |
|---|---|

# Northern Wheatear

The largely Eurasian Northern Wheatear visits North America during a brief breeding season, and nests in the tundra of Alaska and northeastern Canada. The two subspecies breeding in North America, *O. o. leucorhoa* in the Northeast and *O. o. oenanthe* in the Northwest both migrate to wintering grounds in sub-Saharan Africa, but use different routes: *oenanthe* across Asia, and *leucorhoa* across the Atlantic.

**OCCURRENCE** Breeds in the Yukon (*O. o. oenanthe*) and the Arctic archipelago (*O. o. leucorhoa*).

**VOICE** Multiple calls, a sharp *tuc* or *tek* common; three types of songs—territorial, conversational, and perched—mixtures of sweet and harsh notes; imitates other species.

black bill

**MALE (BREEDING)**

| Length 5½–6in (14–15cm) | Wingspan 10¾in (27cm) |
|---|---|

| Family **Turdidae** | Species *Sialia sialis* |

# Eastern Bluebird

The blue and chestnut Eastern Bluebird has made a remarkable comeback in the past 30 years. After much of the bird's habitat was eliminated by agriculture in the mid-1900s, nest boxes were readily accepted as alternatives to their tree cavities. The Eastern Bluebird's complex mating system involves multiple partners.

**OCCURRENCE** Found in clearings and woodland edges; occupies open habitats in rural, urban, and suburban areas; orchards, parks, and spacious lawns; westward to the 100th meridian.

**VOICE** Main song a melodious series of soft, whistled notes; *churr-wi* or *churr-li*.

blue upperparts

chestnut breast

**MALE**

| Length **6–8in (15–20cm)** | Wingspan **10–13in (25–33cm)** |

| Family **Turdidae** | Species *Catharus minimus* |

# Gray-cheeked Thrush

The Gray-cheeked Thrush breeds in remote areas of Canada, westward all the way to Alaska. During migration, this bird is more likely to be heard in flight at night than seen on the ground by birdwatchers.

**OCCURRENCE** Breeds in densely vegetated areas with small shrubs; prefers spruce forests in northern and western Canada and Alaska. Winters in northern South America.

**VOICE** Call a thin *kweer*, sometimes doubled; song flute-like, somewhat nasal, several notes ending on a lower pitch.

olive-gray upperparts

**ADULT**

| Length **6½–7in (16–18cm)** | Wingspan **11½–13½in (29–34cm)** |

| Family **Turdidae** | Species *Hylocichla mustelina* |

# Wood Thrush

The Wood Thrush, an eastern breeder, has seen its populations decrease markedly over the past 30 years, largely because of forest destruction and fragmentation. Its susceptibility to brood parasitism by the Brown-headed Cowbird has also affected its numbers.

**OCCURRENCE** Hardwood forests in the East, from Texas and Florida to Minnesota and the Canadian Maritimes. Breeds in deciduous and mixed forests. Winters from eastern Mexico south through Central America to Panama. Rare in the West.

**VOICE** Rapid *pip-pippipip* or *rhuu-rhuu*; a three-part flute-like song—first part indistinct, second part loudest, third part trilled.

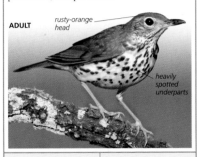

rusty-orange head

**ADULT**

heavily spotted underparts

| Length **7½–8½in (19–21cm)** | Wingspan **12–13½in (30–34cm)** |

| Family **Turdidae** | Species *Turdus rufopalliatus* |

# Rufous-backed Thrush

This secretive Mexican species is rare to uncommon in the southwestern US, especially in the winter. More colorful than the American Robin, it has a gray head, wings, and tail, reddish back and flanks, white abdomen, and long and thin dark streaks on its throat extending all the way to the breast.

**OCCURRENCE** Occurs in a variety of scrubby or woodland habitats in southern California, southern Arizona, southwest New Mexico, and western Texas.

**VOICE** Repeated warbling of cheery phrases; call is a *tche-tche-che*.

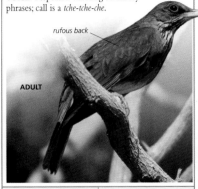

rufous back

**ADULT**

| Length **8½–9½in (21–24cm)** | Wingspan **15in (38cm)** |

| Family **Mimidae** | Species *Toxostoma longirostre* |

# Long-billed Thrasher

In the US, this largely Mexican species is found only in southern Texas, where its habitat of semiarid thickets and riverside woodlands has been much altered or destroyed by mechanized land-clearing practices. This habitat loss may be offset by the increase in area of invasive scrubby vegetation in other parts of its range.

**OCCURRENCE** Sedentary in scrubby vegetation in the lowlands along the Gulf of Mexico, along woodlands near the Rio Grande, and on the slopes of western mountains at up to 3,300ft (1,100m).

**VOICE** Call a harsh *tchek*; song a loud, harsh series of notes, usually repeated 2–4 times in succession.

two conspicuous wing bars

**ADULT**

| Length **10–11in (25–28cm)** | Wingspan **12–13in (30–33cm)** |

| Family **Mimidae** | Species *Toxostoma bendirei* |

# Bendire's Thrasher

This small and rather nondescript thrasher of southwestern US deserts was named in 1873 in honor of Charles Bendire, the US army officer who discovered it. In spite of its early discovery, much remains to be learned about this species, including the number of broods it can raise per season, and whether it winters in Baja California.

**OCCURRENCE** In the US, breeds in dry areas and sparse cover of cactus, thorn-scrub, and Joshua trees. Winters in Mexico; Mexican populations resident.

**VOICE** Call a hoarse *krrh*; song a clear, continuous series of notes, repeated 2–4 times, but not broken into distinct phrases.

**ADULT**

fine, dark olive-brown spots on chest

| Length **8–10in (20–25cm)** | Wingspan **11–13in (28–33cm)** |

| Family **Mimidae** | Species *Toxostoma redivivum* |

# California Thrasher

This thrasher's Latin name, *redivivum*, means "resurrected." It was already known in the 16th century, but "rediscovered" in 1845. This is the largest of the North American thrashers, and a real Californian native. It likes the dense undergrowth of arid or semiarid vegetation along the slopes of canyons, a habitat that is unfortunately used for suburban development, posing a threat to its survival.

**OCCURRENCE** Prefers arid to semiarid, brushy canyons; also suburban parks and gardens; needs dense undergrowth vegetation.

**VOICE** Call a dry *tchek*; song a loud, clear series of repeated phrases; often includes songs of other species.

long, deeply curved bill

**ADULT**

| Length **11–13in (28–33cm)** | Wingspan **15–17in (38–43cm)** |

| Family **Mimidae** | Species *Toxostoma lecontei* |

# LeConte's Thrasher

This species is the real desert thrasher, in terms of its habitat preference and sandy color, which is rather similar to its surroundings. LeConte's Thrasher prefers a more open and sparsely vegetated habitat than any other member of its genus. This hardy and adaptable species regularly endures temperature extremes ranging from -4 to +133°F (-20 to +56°C). Increased irrigation of desert areas has caused loss of its habitat.

**OCCURRENCE** Resident in the southwestern US and Mexico, in sheltered areas along desert washes, with clumps of grass.

**VOICE** Call *ti-WHIP*; song a long, squeaky musical series of varied notes or phrases, often repeated two or three times.

**ADULT**

orangish buff undertail

| Length **10–12in (25–30cm)** | Wingspan **12–14in (30–36cm)** |

| Family **Mimidae** | Species *Toxostoma crissale* |
|---|---|

# Crissal Thrasher

Although locally common, little is known about the life history of this secretive bird, which lives in dense mesquite thickets and shrubland. Its distinctive melodious songs set it apart from other, similar-looking southwestern thrashers. Its Latin name refers to the color of its undertail feathers in an otherwise pretty uniformly gray plumage. Although loss of habitat at lower elevations may restrict its numbers, its preference for high-elevation habitats insulate the species from much human encroachment.
**OCCURRENCE** Breeds in the arid southwestern US and Mexico, especially in dense shrubbery at mid-elevations, but can occur up to 6,500ft (2,000m).
**VOICE** Call a soft *Krrrt*; song a strong numerical note, or group of notes, with double repetitions, delivered softly.

long, dark tail

ADULT

| Length **10–13in (25–33cm)** | Wingspan **13–16in (33–41cm)** |
|---|---|

| Family **Ptiliogonatidae** | Species *Phainopepla nitens* |
|---|---|

# Phainopepla

The name Phainopepla, Greek for "shiny robe," refers to the species' glossy plumage. Phainopeplas like to perch high up in trees and shrubs, from which they sally to catch flying insects. When in flight, the conspicuous white wing patches contrast with the black of body and tail. The somewhat similar Northern Mockingbird also has white wing patches, but also has white in its tail, and is gray, not black.
**OCCURRENCE** Inhabits the southwestern US and adjacent Mexico, in a variety of dry to arid habitats, including oak scrub, open mesquite woodlands, and patches of juniper on rocky slopes.
**VOICE** Call a mellow *wurp*, with upward inflection; song a long series of short phrases, overall soft and halting delivery.

prominent crest

MALE

| Length **7¾in (19.5cm)** | Wingspan **11in (28cm)** |
|---|---|

| Family **Peucedramidae** | Species *Peucedramus taeniatus* |
|---|---|

# Olive Warbler

Although its appearance and behavior are warbler-like, this orange-headed and black-masked species differs from warblers in the family Parulidae in its song, breeding habits, and genetic make-up. It is placed in its own family, the Peucedramidae, and lives at high elevations in coniferous forests.
**OCCURRENCE** Found in pine oak woodlands, and forests with ponderosa pines and douglas firs. US birds winter in Mexico; Central American birds are resident.
**VOICE** Calls include a smack-like *bit* and a softer, bluebird-like *view*; song is a loud and repeated series of *peetar-peetar-peetar*, somewhat similar to the Tufted Titmouse.

green edges to wing feathers

ADULT

| Length **5¼in (13.5cm)** | Wingspan **9in (23cm)** |
|---|---|

| Family **Motacillidae** | Species *Motacilla tschutschensis* |
|---|---|

# Eastern Yellow Wagtail

Like its relative the White Wagtail, the Eastern Yellow Wagtail is widely distributed in Eurasia, with a nesting foothold in Alaska and the Yukon. Until recently, the Eastern Yellow Wagtail was treated as one of about 17 subspecies of the Yellow Wagtail *(M. flava)*, the race *tschutschensis* having been described as long ago as 1789, but it has now been separated as a species in its own right. It also breeds in eastern Russia.
**OCCURRENCE** In Western Alaska and extreme western Yukon found in tundra with scattered shrub, especially along watercourses. Winters in eastern Asia, south to Indonesia.
**VOICE** Call a short, "outgoing" *tzeep*!; song a thin, musical, *tzee-ouee-sir*, often in flight.

greenish gray back

MALE

yellow underparts

| Length **5–7in (13–18cm)** | Wingspan **7–9in (18–23cm)** |
|---|---|

| Family **Motacillidae** | Species *Motacilla alba* |
| --- | --- |

# White Wagtail

Only one (*M. a. ocularis*) of the 11 subspecies of the wide-ranging Eurasian White Wagtail breeds in North America, in a very small geographical area of northwestern Alaska and on St. Lawrence Island. It arrives in Alaska in late May or early June, and leaves after only about two months, in August, migrating to wintering areas in tropical southeast Asia.

**OCCURRENCE** Found near water, either coastal areas or along rivers; also commonly associated with human structures.

**VOICE** Call a single, sharp *tzzip* or double *tzzizzip*; song is an extension of its call, the notes blending into a warble.

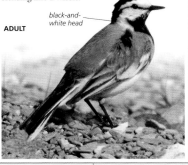

black-and-white head

**ADULT**

| Length **6–8in (15–20cm)** | Wingspan **9–10in (23–25cm)** |
| --- | --- |

| Family **Motacillidae** | Species *Anthus spragueii* |
| --- | --- |

# Sprague's Pipit

Sprague's is the only wholly North American pipit. Males perform an extraordinary fluttering display flight, circling high above the ground while singing an unending series of high-pitched calls, for periods up to an hour. The current decline in its population is quite likely the result of the conversion of tall-grass native prairie to extensive farmland.

**OCCURRENCE** Breeds along and across the US-Canada border, in dry, open, grassland habitats, especially native prairies in the northern part of the Great Plains; most birds winter in Mexico.

**VOICE** Call a high *squeeek*; song a high, repetitive series of *szee-szee-szee*, usually given during lengthy aerial displays.

**ADULT**

pale, whitish flanks and belly

| Length **4–6in (10–15cm)** | Wingspan **6–8in (15–20cm)** |
| --- | --- |

| Family **Motacillidae** | Species *Anthus cervinus* |
| --- | --- |

# Red-throated Pipit

The heavily streaked upperparts, and pale legs of this rare Alaskan breeder help to distinguish it from the American Pipit. The extent of the red on the throat varies among individual birds from rusty brick red to tan. Nonbreeding birds are usually heavily streaked on the breast.

**OCCURRENCE** Tundra and low scrub along the coasts of northern and western Alaska. Occasionally along the coast of California in winter. Widespread in northern Eurasia, it winters in Africa and southeast Asia.

**VOICE** Two-syllable *tzee-zeep*, somewhat like White or Yellow Wagtails. Song is varied, musical, often in flight.

**ADULT (BREEDING)**

reddish to tan throat

heavily streaked

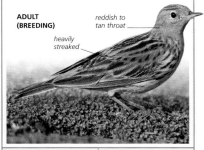

| Length **5–7in (12–17cm)** | Wingspan **7–8in (20–23cm)** |
| --- | --- |

| Family **Fringillidae** | Species *Leucosticte atrata* |
| --- | --- |

# Black Rosy-Finch

Actually deep-brown in color, this bird appears black when seen against its snowy background. Black Rosy-Finches, the darkest of the North American Rosy-Finch species, are nevertheless similar in appearance to the much more widely distributed Gray-crowned Rosy-Finch.

**OCCURRENCE** Found in Rocky Mountain and Great Basin mountaintop habitats above timberline. Breeds from central Idaho and southwestern Montana, south through northwestern Nevada and most of Utah. Winters at lower elevations.

**VOICE** Call a low, raspy *brrrt* and descending *peew*; song a long series of *peew* notes of variable composition and pitch.

dark cheeks

pinkish shoulder patch

**MALE (NONBREEDING)**

| Length **5½–6½in (14–16cm)** | Wingspan **13in (33cm)** |
| --- | --- |

| Family **Fringillidae** | Species *Leucosticte australis* |
|---|---|

# Brown-capped Rosy-Finch

This southernmost member of the rosy-finch genus *Leucosticte* is more pink and less gray than the other two North American species. Despite its name, the "cap" of this species is almost black, similar to those of the other rosy-finches, and contrasts with the brown of the rest of the head and upper back.

**OCCURRENCE** Restricted to high elevations in the Medicine Bow range of Wyoming and the high mountains of Colorado and northern New Mexico. Lower down in winter.

**VOICE** High-pitched *peee*, raspy *brrt*, and descending and repeated *peew* calls.

grayish brown head

**MALE**

| Length  5½–6¾in (14–17cm) | Wingspan  13in (33cm) |
|---|---|

| Family **Fringillidae** | Species *Acanthis hornemanni* |
|---|---|

# Hoary Redpoll

Closely related to the Common Redpoll, the Hoary Redpoll is more conspicuously white, has a stubbier bill, and looks more fluffy. These two species often breed in the same areas, but do not interbreed. The Hoary Redpoll is a bird of the High Arctic, breeding in extreme northern Canada westward to Alaska.

**OCCURRENCE** Breeds in low, scrubby trees of the open tundra, and winters in the boreal forest belt from the Canadian Maritimes to Alaska, south of the tundra.

**VOICE** Flight calls dry *zit-zit-zit-zit* and rattling *chirr*; also high *too-ee* call while perched; song series of rapid trills.

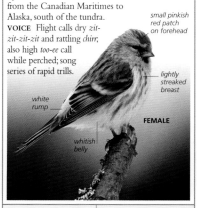

small pinkish red patch on forehead

lightly streaked breast

white rump

whitish belly

**FEMALE**

| Length  5–5½in (12.5–14cm) | Wingspan  8½–9¼in (21–23.5cm) |
|---|---|

| Family **Fringillidae** | Species *Spinus lawrencei* |
|---|---|

# Lawrence's Goldfinch

John Cassin of Philadelphia's Academy of Natural Sciences described this species in 1850, to honor G.N. Lawrence, who worked on birds collected during the Pacific Railroad Surveys. The large yellow patches on the wings are characteristic of this species, which breeds in dry habitats like chaparral, grassy slopes, and open ranchland.

**OCCURRENCE** Breeds in open foothills and valleys of California at elevations up to 9,000ft (2,750m). Most migration is east and west rather than north and south.

**VOICE** Single, bell-like call notes and harsh *kee-urr*; song canary-like; may imitate other species.

black face

large, conspicuous yellow patches

**MALE**

| Length  4–4¾in (10–12cm) | Wingspan  6–6½in (15–16cm) |
|---|---|

| Family **Calcariidae** | Species *Calcarius ornatus* |
|---|---|

# Chestnut-collared Longspur

Once quite common and widespread, the Chestnut-collared Longspur bred where huge herds of bison disturbed its prairie habitat. After the elimination of bison and the "farming" of the prairies, such areas were hard to find, and the longspur declined. A distinguishing feature of this species is the large amount of white on its outer tail feathers.

**OCCURRENCE** Breeds in shortgrass prairie in south-central Canada and central US. Winters in grasslands and other barren areas in the southern Great Plains.

**VOICE** Flight call a chortling *KTI-uhl-uh*, often in series; also a soft rattle and short *buzz*; song a sweet, rich, whistled series, in fluttering, circular flights over the prairies.

chestnut neck

**MALE (BREEDING)**

black belly

| Length  5½–6in (14–15cm) | Wingspan  10–10½in (25–27cm) |
|---|---|

| Family **Calcariidae** | Species *Calcarius pictus* |
|---|---|

# Smith's Longspur

With its pumpkin-colored breast and black-and-white "helmet," Smith's Longspur in its breeding colors contrasts strongly with its drab winter plumage. On its Arctic breeding grounds and shortgrass prairie range in winter, this longspur remains hidden on the ground, and is hard to spot. Smith's Longspurs breeds communally: males mate with several females; they, in turn, mate with several males.

**OCCURRENCE** Breeds along the tundra-taiga timberline from northern Alaska south and east to northern Ontario. Winters in open areas with shortgrass.

**VOICE** Flight call a mechanical, sharp rattle; also a nasal *nief* when squabbling; song a series of thin, sweet whistles.

black-and-white "helmet"

**MALE (BREEDING)**

| Length **6–6½in (15–16cm)** | Wingspan **10–11½in (25–29cm)** |
|---|---|

| Family **Calcariidae** | Species *Rhynchophanes mccownii* |
|---|---|

# McCown's Longspur

Like other longspurs, this range-restricted species inhabits native shortgrass prairies from Alberta and Saskatchewan southward to Nebraska and Colorado. In this windswept habitat males perform flight displays, hovering and floating, wings held in a "V" position, looking surprisingly dark against the pale sky.

**OCCURRENCE** Breeds in shortgrass prairies of the High Plains. Winters in grasslands from southeastern Colorado southward to Texas and westward to southeastern Arizona.

**VOICE** Flight call a short, liquid *rit-up*; also an abrupt *poink* and metallic *tink*; song melodious; high-pitched tinklings in flight.

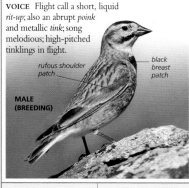

rufous shoulder patch

black breast patch

**MALE (BREEDING)**

| Length **6in (15cm)** | Wingspan **10–11in (25–28cm)** |
|---|---|

| Family **Calcariidae** | Species *Plectrophenax hyperboreus* |
|---|---|

# McKay's Bunting

A close relative of the widespread and similar-looking Snow Bunting, with which it occasionally interbreeds, McKay's Bunting numbers fewer than 20,000 individuals, which breed on two isolated islands in the Bering Sea.

**OCCURRENCE** Breeds in rocky areas on Hall Island and St. Matthew Island in the Bering Sea. Occasional visitor to St. Lawrence Island and the Pribilof Islands.

**VOICE** Like Snow Bunting, flight call musical, liquid rattle; also *tyew* notes and short *buzz*; song squeaky repetitive whistle.

**FEMALE (NONBREEDING)**

frosty gray streaks on back

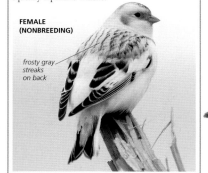

| Length **6¾in (17cm)** | Wingspan **14in (36cm)** |
|---|---|

| Family **Passerellidae** | Species *Peucaea carpalis* |
|---|---|

# Rufous-winged Sparrow

This sparrow is very localized within its restricted US range, as it lives in grassland with thornbushes, a habitat that has largely been lost to grazing. Rufous-winged Sparrows depend on the greening of their habitat that follows irregular rains. Male sparrows "respond" to this uncertainty by maintaining their territory all year round, and are thus ready to breed as soon as the rains begin.

**OCCURRENCE** Resident in Sonoran Desert scrub and bunchgrass from south-central Arizona southward to central Sinaloa, Mexico.

**VOICE** Call high, strident *tseeep*!; song a couple of *chips* or whistles followed by long, loose trill, or accelerating series of *chips*.

rufous eye-line

**ADULT**

| Length **5¾in (14.5cm)** | Wingspan **7½in (19cm)** |
|---|---|

| Family **Passerellidae** | Species *Peucaea botterii* |
|---|---|

# Botteri's Sparrow

Essentially a bird of Mexican grasslands, Botteri's Sparrow reaches the US in two areas, coastal southern Texas and the Southwest. In Texas, its habitat includes gulf cordgrass, whereas in the Southwest it lives in grasslands and open mesquite woodlands with a grass understory. When alarmed, Botteri's Sparrows run rather than fly.

**OCCURRENCE** Breeds in grasslands of southeastern Arizona and southwestern New Mexico, and in coastal prairies of southern Texas. Winters in Mexico.

**VOICE** Call a *chip* or double *tsip*; song starts with stuttering, mechanical *chips* and ends in an accelerating trill.

bill thick at base

rusty and gray streaks on upperparts

**ADULT**

| Length **18–20in (46–51cm)** | Wingspan **27–38in (68–96cm)** |
|---|---|

| Family **Passerellidae** | Species *Arremonops rufivirgatus* |
|---|---|

# Olive Sparrow

The rather drab and shy Olive Sparrow spends much of its time hopping in and out of the undergrowth of dense, tropical woodlands and thorn scrub. In the Lower Rio Grande Valley in winter, this tough-to-spot species does not sing at this time of the year, but its lisping calls will often lead to a birdfeeder, where tamer individuals may be observed at leisure.

**OCCURRENCE** From southern Texas and northwestern Mexico south to northwestern Costa Rica. Often found at backyard feeders in southern Texas in the winter.

**VOICE** Dry *chip* call, also a drawn-out *sreeeeee*; song a series of chips accelerating to a level.

**ADULT**

dull olive upperparts

| Length **6½in (16cm)** | Wingspan **8in (20cm)** |
|---|---|

| Family **Passerellidae** | Species *Spizella atrogularis* |
|---|---|

# Black-chinned Sparrow

This gray, yet elegant, bird is a locally common but secretive inhabitant of dense shrubbery on steep hillsides of the southwestern US and California. In the breeding season the loudly-singing and brightly-plumaged males are easy to spot, but in the winter their plumage is quite drab and they are not easy to see. The plumage pattern and pink bill of the Black-chinned Sparrow are reminiscent of those of juncos, but they are not closely related.

**OCCURRENCE** Breeds in California, southwestern Utah, and northeastern New Mexico southward to central Mexico.

**VOICE** Call a high *tsip*; song an accelerating, bouncy trill climaxing in a rapid, metallic, ascending echo.

brownish black wings

**MALE (BREEDING)**

| Length **5¾in (14.5cm)** | Wingspan **7¾in (19.5cm)** |
|---|---|

| Family **Passerellidae** | Species *Spizella pusilla* |
|---|---|

# Field Sparrow

The distinctive, accelerating trilled song of the Field Sparrow is a characteristic sound in shrubby fields and scrub of the eastern US and adjacent Canada. Westward, this species reaches Montana, the Dakotas, and Nebraska. The Field Sparrow's pink bill, rusty cheek patch, and pale eye-ring are good field marks. Westernmost birds are paler than eastern ones.

**OCCURRENCE** Breeds in overgrown fields, woodland edges, roadsides. Casual in Atlantic Canada and along the Pacific Coast.

**VOICE** Call a sharp *tsik*; flight call a strongly descending *tsiiiu*; song a series of sweet, down-slurred whistles accelerating to a rapid trill.

pink bill

rusty cheek patch

**ADULT (REDDISH FORM)**

| Length **5½in (14cm)** | Wingspan **8in (20cm)** |
|---|---|

| Family **Passerellidae** | Species *Junco phaeonotus* |
|---|---|

# Yellow-eyed Junco

This common and confident bird, the Mexican representative of the Dark-eyed Junco, lives at high elevations in pine and oak pine forests from Arizona and New Mexico to south-central Mexico. Its "glaring" yellow eyes set off by a black mask are distinguishing characters. Yellow-eyed Juncos often forage for food under picnic tables.
**OCCURRENCE** Southeastern Arizona and southwestern New Mexico, and more widely in Mexico.
**VOICE** Loud *dip*, soft *dyew*; flight call a twittering, buzzy *zzeet*; song 2–3 whistles followed by various trills and buzzes.

**ADULT**

rusty back

yellow eye

| Length 6½in (16cm) | Wingspan 9½–10in (24–25cm) |
|---|---|

| Family **Passerellidae** | Species *Zonotrichia querula* |
|---|---|

# Harris's Sparrow

The only North American species to breed only in Canada, Harris's Sparrow migrates southward and winters in the US Great Plains. Its scientific name, *querula*, was given because of the plaintive quality of its whistled song. Its nest was first discovered in 1907 in the Northwest Territories.
**OCCURRENCE** Breeds in scrub-tundra along the taiga-tundra timberline. Winters in the Great Plains from South Dakota and Iowa south to northern Texas. Nonbreeders are found in thickets and hedges. Casual to rare in East and West.
**VOICE** Call a sharp *weeek*; song a melancholy series of 2–4 whistles on the same pitch.

**ADULT
(BREEDING)**

gray rump and undertail feathers

| Length 6¾–7½in (17–19cm) | Wingspan 10½–11in (27–28cm) |
|---|---|

| Family **Passerellidae** | Species *Ammospiza nelsoni* |
|---|---|

# Nelson's Sparrow

This shy species includes three subspecies that differ in plumage, breeding habitat, and range. The brightly colored *A. n. nelsoni* is found from the Northwest Territories south to Wisconsin. The duller *A. n. subvirgatus* breeds in coastal Maine, the Maritimes, and along the St. Lawrence River. The intermediate *A. n. alterus* breeds along the southern and western coasts of Hudson Bay.
**OCCURRENCE** Breeds in a variety of marsh habitats across North America.
**VOICE** Sharp *tik* call; song a husky *t-SHHHHEE-uhrr*.

smaller bill

brighter upperparts

**ADULT
*A. n. nelsoni***

| Length 4¾in (12cm) | Wingspan 7in (17.5cm) |
|---|---|

| Family **Passerellidae** | Species *Melozone aberti* |
|---|---|

# Abert's Towhee

Restricted to the southwestern US and adjacent Mexico, Abert's Towhee, named after Major James W. Abert, was originally found in the dense undergrowth of cottonwood-willow stands along the Colorado River and its tributaries. It has declined since its description in 1852, because of habitat destruction, overgrazing, and invasive plant species.
**OCCURRENCE** Resident in dense brush, remnant patches of mesquite woodland close to rivers and streams, and desert scrub; also suburban areas. Prefers the proximity of water, even small streams. Occurs up to about 3,280ft (1,000m).
**VOICE** Sharp *peek* call; song short, accelerating *peeks* followed by harsh, squeaky chatter; pairs often duet.

pale grayish blue bill

**ADULT**

dark face

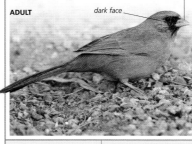

| Length 9½in (24cm) | Wingspan 11in (28cm) |
|---|---|

| Family **Passerellidae** | Species ***Melozone crissalis*** |
|---|---|

# California Towhee

This fairly large and grayish-colored towhee is common around human settlements, including suburban gardens, parks, and riverside woodlands, from northern California to Baja California. Once considered, together with the Canyon Towhee of the Southwest, to form a single species (the "Brown Towhee"), they are now split into separate species because of morphological and molecular differences.
**OCCURRENCE** Along California's Pacific Coast and throughout Baja California in Mexico, in a variety of bushy habitats with open areas for foraging and bush for cover.
**VOICE** Call a ringing, metallic *tink*; song an accelerating trill of ringing *chips*, occasionally ending with squeaky chatter.

rich tan facial markings

ADULT

| Length **9in (23cm)** | Wingspan **11½in (29cm)** |
|---|---|

| Family **Passerellidae** | Species ***Amphispiza quinquestriata*** |
|---|---|

# Five-striped Sparrow

The Five-striped Sparrow is one of the rarest of the breeding sparrows of North America, with perhaps as few as 100 pairs, which are found only in southern Arizona. The Five-striped Sparrow is a large, handsome sparrow with gray underparts, olive-brown upperparts, a blackish head with the stripes for which it is named and eye crescents, a black central breast spot, and a long, thick bill.
**OCCURRENCE** Breeds on steep, arid mountain slopes, up to about 6,500ft (2,000m); locally in southern Arizona, and more commonly in Mexico, southward to Chihuahua and Sonora.
**VOICE** Call a low *turp*; song a series of musical chirps, tinklings, and trills interspersed with second-long pauses.

white stripes on head

ADULT

| Length **6in (15cm)** | Wingspan **8in (20cm)** |
|---|---|

| Family **Passerellidae** | Species ***Centronyx bairdii*** |
|---|---|

# Baird's Sparrow

The sweet, tinkling song of Baird's Sparrow is a sure sign of high-quality mixed-grass prairie in the Northern Plains. Its musical song and square, pale-edged tail are unique in its genus. Like other species that depend on native grasslands, it has not coped well with the intensive agriculture that has swept across the Northern Plains during the last century.
**OCCURRENCE** Breeds in light mixed-grass prairie of central US and adjacent Canada. Migrates through the High Plains. Winters in grasslands in Mexico.
**VOICE** Call soft, metallic *tsink*; flight call insect-like *tisk*; song *tsk tsk tsuck tsooweeeeee.*

fine streaks on nape

ADULT

| Length **5½in (14cm)** | Wingspan **8½–8¾in (21–22.5cm)** |
|---|---|

| Family **Icteridae** | Species ***Icterus spurius*** |
|---|---|

# Orchard Oriole

The way Orchard Orioles flit among leaves when foraging for insects recalls the behavior of wood warblers. In addition, and unlike other orioles, it flutters its tail. A late arrival in spring, it is also an early species to leave in the fall. The foothills of the Rocky Mountains correspond approximately to its range border in the West.
**OCCURRENCE** Breeds in open forest and woodland edges with a mixture of evergreen and deciduous trees; also found in parks and gardens. Winters in Mexico, Central America, and South America.
**VOICE** Fast, not very melodious, series of high warbling notes mixed with occasional shorter notes ending in slurred *shheere.*

rich chestnut shoulders

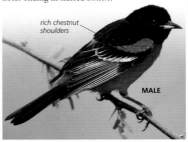

MALE

| Length **7–8in (18–20cm)** | Wingspan **9in (23cm)** |
|---|---|

| Family **Icteridae** | Species *Icterus cucullatus* |
| --- | --- |

# Hooded Oriole

Tall palm trees in suburban gardens and urban parks, especially in California, have become popular nesting sites for the Hooded Oriole. Increasing numbers of palm trees, combined with the offerings of nectar intended for hummingbirds have contributed to the expansion of its range from California to the Southwest. By contrast, its numbers in Texas have been shrinking, in part because of its susceptibility to brood parasitism by Brown-headed and Bronzed Cowbirds.

**OCCURRENCE** Breeds in open woodlands along water courses, especially those containing palm trees. Winters in Mexico.

**VOICE** A harsh *weeek* call; song a weakly whined and rapid series of whistles where notes often run together; imitates other birds.

long, curved bill

**MALE (BREEDING)**

| Length **7–8in (18–20cm)** | Wingspan **9–11in (23–28cm)** |
| --- | --- |

| Family **Icteridae** | Species *Icterus galbula* |
| --- | --- |

# Baltimore Oriole

The brilliantly colored Baltimore Oriole, the eastern counterpart of the Bullock's Oriole, ranges westward in Canada to Alberta and, locally, eastern British Colombia. At the edge of their respective distributions, in the Great Plains, Baltimore and Bullock's Orioles interbreed. Ornithologists have, at times, considered them to be a single species.

**OCCURRENCE** A variety of woodlands, also parks and gardens. Most winter in Central and South America.

**VOICE** Loud, clear, melodious song comprising several short notes in series, often of varying lengths.

straight, blue-gray bill

**MALE**

| Length **8–10in (20–26cm)** | Wingspan **10–12in (26–30cm)** |
| --- | --- |

| Family **Icteridae** | Species *Agelaius tricolor* |
| --- | --- |

# Tricolored Blackbird

A close relative of the widespread Red-winged Blackbird, the Tricolored occurs primarily in California, where it breeds in marshes in large colonies, sometimes containing more than 100,000 pairs. After breeding, flocks of Tricolored Blackbirds move to agricultural areas.

**OCCURRENCE** Found in cattail marshes, also in a variety of human-altered upland and wetland habitats; found in western California, northward to Washington State and southward to Baja California.

**VOICE** Both sexes call a *chip*, *chuk*, and *chu-aah* when alarmed; male song a grave, nasal *kera-oooow* or *kerrrraaaa*.

dark red shoulders edged with white

**MALE**

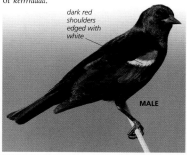

| Length **7–9½in (18–24cm)** | Wingspan **10–13in (26–33cm)** |
| --- | --- |

| Family **Icteridae** | Species *Molothrus aeneus* |
| --- | --- |

# Bronzed Cowbird

The range of this species has been expanding in the US ever since it was first recorded in the early 1900s. This could be the result of human clearing of native habitats and replacing them with agricultural crops. A brood parasite, it has been recorded to lay its eggs in the nests of more than 80 bird species, and their young have fledged from more than 30 of these. The females may work cooperatively to identify and parasitize the nests of other birds.

**OCCURRENCE** Inhabits open fields, pastures, scattered scrub, and suburban parks. In the US occurs along the Mexican border from California to Texas, from Mexico to Panama and Colombia.

**VOICE** High and metallic with short notes, can be described as *gug-gub-bub-tzee-pss-tzee*.

bright red eye

**MALE**

| Length **8in (20cm)** | Wingspan **13–14in (33–36cm)** |
| --- | --- |

| Family **Parulidae** | Species *Leiothlypis crissalis* |
|---|---|

# Colima Warbler

Big Bend National Park in Texas is home to the only breeding population of Colima Warblers in the US—numbers vary but may reach 200 pairs. The scientific name, *crissalis*, refers to this bird's bright orange undertail coverts, or "crissum." Its common name, Colima, refers to the state in Mexico, which is one of its wintering grounds.

**OCCURRENCE** Breeds in the Chisos Mountains of Texas and in north Mexico, in canyons with pine oak woodland with brushy understory, normally above about 4,900ft (1,500m). Almost never detected on migration. Winters in similar but more humid habitats of southwestern Mexico.

**VOICE** Song a rapid trill, descending in pitch and ending with one or two emphatic motives *titititititutututu eet-choo eet-choo*.

ADULT

orange-yellow tail feathers

| Length **6in (15cm)** | Wingspan **8in (20cm)** |
|---|---|

| Family **Parulidae** | Species *Leiothlypis luciae* |
|---|---|

# Lucy's Warbler

Named for Lucy Baird, daughter of the eminent ornithologist Spencer Fullerton Baird, this species, small and unassuming, lacks any yellow coloration and could be mistaken for a gnatcatcher, an immature Verdin, or a Bell's Vireo. It is locally common in mesquite woodlands near watercourses.

**OCCURRENCE** Breeds in riverside woodlands of the southwestern US and adjacent northern Mexico. Winters along the western seaboard of Mexico south to Oaxaca.

**VOICE** A sharp, metallic *vink*; flight call a soft *tsit*; song a loose trill, modulated in pitch and with variably emphatic ending.

dark gray upperparts

reddish rump

MALE

| Length **4¼in (11cm)** | Wingspan **7in (18cm)** |
|---|---|

| Family **Parulidae** | Species *Setophaga castanea* |
|---|---|

# Bay-breasted Warbler

A male Bay-breasted Warbler in breeding plumage is a striking sight. By contrast, fall females look very different with their dull greenish color. The Bay-breasted Warbler depends largely on outbreaks of spruce budworms (a moth larva) and its population fluctuations are related to those of this food source. Overall, Bay-breasted Warbler numbers have decreased in the last decade or so.

**OCCURRENCE** Breeds in mature spruce-fir-balsam forests from the Yukon east to the Maritimes, south to the Great Lakes and northern New England. Winters in wet forests in central America.

**VOICE** Call a somewhat up-slurred *tsip*; flight call a high, buzzy, short, and sharp *tzzzt*; song of very high, thin notes, often ending on lower pitch: *wee-si wee-si wee-si wee*.

MALE (BREEDING)

yellowish buff belly

| Length **5½in (14cm)** | Wingspan **9in (23cm)** |
|---|---|

| Family **Parulidae** | Species *Setophaga fusca* |
|---|---|

# Blackburnian Warbler

Its brilliant orange throat makes this species one of the most beautiful members of the North American warblers. Blackburnian Warblers coexist with other *Setophaga* warblers in the coniferous and mixed woodlands of the North and East, but exploit a slightly different niche for foraging—the treetops. They also seek the highest trees for nesting.

**OCCURRENCE** Breeds in coniferous and mixed forests of the eastern US and Canada, west to Alberta. Winters in wet forests in Costa Rica and Panama, and southward as far as Peru.

**VOICE** Call a slightly husky *chik*; flight-call a high, thin *zzee*; song variable, but always high-pitched; swirling series of lisps, spiraling upward to end in an almost inaudible trill.

black-and-orange facial pattern

MALE

| Length **5in (13cm)** | Wingspan **8½in (21cm)** |
|---|---|

| Family **Parulidae** | Species *Setophaga pensylvanica* |

# Chestnut-sided Warbler

One of the few wood warbler species that has benefited from deforestation, the Chestnut-sided Warbler depends on second-growth and forest edges for breeding. In all plumages, two conspicuous wing bars and a whitish belly are distinguishing characteristics. Its pleasant song has long been transcribed as *pleased pleased pleased to MEET'cha*.
**OCCURRENCE** Breeds in successional deciduous woodlands, from Alberta to the Great Lakes, Nova Scotia, and the Appalachians. Winters in the West Indies, Mexico, and Central America.
**VOICE** Call a sweet *chip*; flight call a low, burry *brrrt*; song a series of fast, sweet notes, usually ending with an emphatic *WEET-chew*.

two conspicuous wing bars

MALE (BREEDING)

| Length **5in (13cm)** | Wingspan **8in (20cm)** |

| Family **Parulidae** | Species *Setophaga graciae* |

# Grace's Warbler

Named for Grace Coues, sister of the well-known ornithologist Elliott Coues, this warbler is the western counterpart of the Yellow-throated Warbler. It lives in the tops of tall pines, and tends to have large territories, making it a difficult bird to spot and study. Its range has been expanding northward in recent years.
**OCCURRENCE** Breeds in mature, open pine and pine oak mountain forests of the southwestern US and Mexico.
**VOICE** Call soft *chip*; flight call very high, thin *ssss*; song loose trill, louder toward the end and at times ending with a change in pitch: *chew chew chew chew chew CHEW CHEW CHEE-DEED-DEED-DEED*.

bright yellow throat

MALE

| Length **5in (13cm)** | Wingspan **8in (20cm)** |

| Family **Parulidae** | Species *Setophaga chrysoparia* |

# Golden-cheeked Warbler

The male of this beautiful species often sings throughout the day from conspicuous perches. It breeds in a restricted area of Texas, near, and on, the Edwards Plateau in woodlands where junipers are common. Habitat loss has made this scarce species even scarcer. It has been on the Endangered Species list since 1990.
**OCCURRENCE** Breeds in oak juniper woodlands mixed with hardwood species like maple and ash. Winters in high-elevation pine oak woodlands from Mexico to Nicaragua.
**VOICE** Dry *tsk* call; song a variable series of relatively low, buzzy notes, often ending on a high, clear note *zo zu zu zo zu zhray ZHEE*; another version ends at a lower pitch *ZOH zu ZO-ZOH zhray*.

black and yellow facial pattern

MALE

| Length **5in (13cm)** | Wingspan **8in (20cm)** |

| Family **Parulidae** | Species *Cardellina rubrifrons* |

# Red-faced Warbler

A dazzling-looking bird, with its red-and-black face and white nape, the Red-faced Warbler is a favorite of birdwatchers visiting mountains in the southwestern US. Because its closest relatives are uncertain at present, the Red-faced Warbler is related to two very differently colored species also of the *Cardellina* genus, the Wilson's and Canada Warblers.
**OCCURRENCE** Breeds in Arizona, New Mexico, and Mexico, in high-elevation fir, pine, and pine oak forests. Winters in mountain pine oak and pine forests from Mexico southward to Honduras.
**VOICE** Call a sharp *chik*; song a variable, sweet warble; often has emphatic ending: *swee-wee-wee tuh-wee-wee-wee WEE-chee-chew*.

red and black facial pattern

ADULT

| Length **5½in (14cm)** | Wingspan **8½in (21cm)** |

| Family **Parulidae** | Species ***Myioborus pictus*** |

# Painted Redstart

White, red, and black, the Painted Redstart (*pictus* means "painted" in Latin) is fairly common locally in the wooded canyons of Arizona, New Mexico, and western Texas. It flicks open its wings and tail, showing off white wing patches and undertail feathers, which has been interpreted as a behavior meant to flush out insect prey. Ten other species of *Myioborus* live from Mexico to South America.

**OCCURRENCE** Breeds at high elevations in oak and pine oak forests in canyons of the southwestern US. Winters south of its breeding range in Mexico.

**VOICE** Call a distinctive, down-slurred, bisyllabic *TSHEE-ew*; song a rich, whistled series of paired notes, at times with emphatic ending: *wee-dee wee-dee wee-dee chichi-chichi-tyew*.

white wing patch

**ADULT**

| Length **5¾in (14.5cm)** | Wingspan **8½in (22cm)** |

---

| Family **Cardinalidae** | Species ***Piranga flava*** |

# Hepatic Tanager

This species ranges widely in the Americas, from California (very locally) and Colorado south to Mexico, central America, and South America (to Argentina). In the US, the Hepatic Tanager is the western counterpart of the Summer Tanager, which it replaces at higher elevations in oak pine woodlands. It is slightly more orange-colored than the Summer Tanager.

**OCCURRENCE** Found in southwestern US in mountain woodlands of pine and pine oak. Winters away from US, except in extreme southeastern Arizona.

**VOICE** Single *chuk* or *chup* call; flight call an up-slurred, slightly burry *veet*; song less burry than other tanagers, more robin-like.

flat crown

**ADULT**

| Length **8in (20cm)** | Wingspan **12½in (32cm)** |

---

| Family **Cardinalidae** | Species ***Cardinalis cardinalis*** |

# Northern Cardinal

The state bird of seven different states in the US, the Northern Cardinal, or "redbird," is a familiar sight across the eastern US. In the West, it is restricted to Arizona, New Mexico, and Colorado.

**OCCURRENCE** Resident in thickets of various relatively moist habitats, such as deciduous woodland, scrub, desert washes, and backyards. Range spans across the eastern US, southernmost Canada, the extreme Southwest, and south into Mexico, northern Guatemala, and northern Belize.

**VOICE** Sharp, metallic *tik* call, also bubbly chatters; song a loud, variable, sweet, slurred whistle, *tsee-ew-tsee-ew-whoit-whoit-whoit-whoit-whoit*.

thick, orange-red bill

**MALE**

| Length **8½in (22cm)** | Wingspan **12in (30cm)** |

---

| Family **Cardinalidae** | Species ***Cardinalis sinuatus*** |

# Pyrrhuloxia

The "Pyro" is considered to be the Southwest's equivalent of the Northern Cardinal and was once known as the "Arizona Cardinal." Their ranges do overlap and, although the two birds share very similar habits and vocalizations, they seem to tolerate each other's presence well.

**OCCURRENCE** Desert scrub of southwest US and Mexico. Where they occur together, prefers drier, more upland habitats than the Northern Cardinal, at elevations up to 6,500ft (2,000m).

**VOICE** Call a distinctive dry, low *chik*, often accelerating into chatter; song generally higher, thinner, and less musical than the Northern Cardinal's.

**MALE**

red outer wing feathers

| Length **8½in (22cm)** | Wingspan **12in (30cm)** |

| Family **Cardinalidae** | Species *Passerina cyanea* |
|---|---|

# Indigo Bunting

Brilliantly colored, this bird however is not really indigo but rather a vibrant, almost cyan-blue. Only a part of the male's head is colored indigo. Dependent on tree-falls within forests and the grassland-forest edge, they are specialists of disturbed habitats. Human activity has greatly benefited them with a radical increase in suitable habitats for their breeding.
**OCCURRENCE** Breeds in moist disturbed habitats, such as weedy fields, forest edges, and areas of heavy cultivation. Winters in small numbers along the Gulf Coast and in Florida.
**VOICE** Call a sharp, dry, rattling *pik!*; flight call a long *buzz* ; song a series of high-pitched "*fire!-fire!*, *where?-where?, there!- there!, put-it-out!, put-it-out!*"

indigo neck

**MALE (BREEDING)**

| Length **5½in (14cm)** | Wingspan **8in (20cm)** |
|---|---|

| Family **Cardinalidae** | Species *Passerina versicolor* |
|---|---|

# Varied Bunting

It is the only purple-and-red songbird in North America. When seen in good light, males are a rich plum color with ruby-red napes and sparkling, sapphire-blue foreheads and rumps. The female, by contrast, is the dullest member of the Cardinalidae group. A largely Mexican species with a small US range, it is localized and hard to find.
**OCCURRENCE** Breeds in dense desert scrub in canyons and washes and in thorn forests of southwest US. In winter, most migrate to the coastal slopes of Mexico.
**VOICE** Call a sharp, dry, rattling *pik!*; song a pleasant, rambling burry warble.

purple breast

**MALE**

| Length **5½in (14cm)** | Wingspan **7½–8in (19–20cm)** |
|---|---|

| Family **Cardinalidae** | Species *Passerina ciris* |
|---|---|

# Painted Bunting

With its violet-blue head, red underparts, and vibrant lime-green back, the adult male Painted Bunting is the most brightly-colored bunting in North America. The female is dull yet distinctive as one of the few truly green songbirds of the region. There are two populations that differ in molt pattern. Western birds molt after leaving the breeding grounds, while eastern molt before they depart for the 'winter.
**OCCURRENCE** Breeds in dense thickets, and other disturbed areas, across south-central US and northern Mexico and along the East Coast. Western birds winter from tropical Mexico to western Panama.
**VOICE** A soft, ringing, upward slurred *pwip!*; flight call slurred, softer, and flatter than Indigo Bunting; song a sweet, relatively clear warble.

red-and-green wings

**MALE**

| Length **5½in (14cm)** | Wingspan **8½in (22cm)** |
|---|---|

| Family **Cardinalidae** | Species *Spiza americana* |
|---|---|

# Dickcissel

A tallgrass prairie resident, the Dickcissel seldom breeds outside this core range. Known for its spectacular seasonal movements, this bird winters in Venezuela, with flocks of tens of thousands ravaging rice fields and damaging seed crops.
**OCCURRENCE** Breeds in tallgrass prairie, grasslands, hayfields, unmown roadsides, and untilled cropfields across the eastern central US. Casual in the West.
**VOICE** A flat *chik*; flight call a low, electric buzz *frrrrrrt*; song a short series of sharp, insect-like stutters followed by few longer chirps or trill *dick-dick-dick-SISS-SISS-suhl.*

yellow eyebrow

**MALE (BREEDING)**

| Length **6½in (16cm)** | Wingspan **9½in (24cm)** |
|---|---|

# VAGRANTS AND ACCIDENTALS

T HE LIST THAT FOLLOWS INCLUDES species that occur rarely in western North America (defined in this book as Canada and the continental United States *west* of the 100th Meridian). These species can reach North America from Eurasia, Central or South America, Africa, and even Oceania, and Antarctica. The US and Canada can receive birds that drift off course, during migration, from eastern Asia across the Pacific Ocean, or from Europe across the Atlantic. Western Alaska has a high concentration of "vagrants" because the southwesternmost tip of the state forms a series of islands, the Aleutians, that

reach almost all the way across the Bering Sea to the Russian Far East.

The occurrence of "vagrant" species is classified by the American Birding Association, depending on their relative frequency, and this terminology is followed in the "status" column for each species. **Rare** species are reported every year in small numbers. **Casual** visitors have been reported at least a dozen times. **Accidental** species have been recorded no more than five times. However, because of climatological, biological, and other factors, the status of "vagrant" species is constantly changing.

| COMMON NAME | SCIENTIFIC NAME | FAMILY NAME | STATUS |
|---|---|---|---|
| **Ducks, Geese, and Swans** | | | |
| Whooper Swan | Cygnus cygnus | Anatidae | Rare visitor from Eurasia to Aleutians, south to California |
| Garganey | Spatula querquedula | Anatidae | Rare visitor from Eurasia to the Pribilofs; casual in California |
| Eurasian Wigeon | Mareca penelope | Anatidae | Rare visitor from Eurasia to West Coast |
| American Black Duck | Anas rubripes | Anatidae | Introduced to British Columbia and Washington state |
| Tufted Duck | Aythya fuligula | Anatidae | Rare visitor from Eurasia to Alaska; casual along the West Coast |
| Smew | Mergellus albellus | Anatidae | Rare visitor from Eurasia to Alaska; casual to California |
| **Cuckoos** | | | |
| Common Cuckoo | Cuculus canorus | Cuculidae | Casual visitor from Eurasia to islands off Alaska |
| Oriental Cuckoo | Cuculus optatus | Cuculidae | Casual visitor from Asia to Aleutian and Pribilof Islands |
| **Hummingbirds** | | | |
| Xantus's Hummingbird | Hylocharis xantusii | Trochilidae | Accidental from Baja California to S California and British Columbia |
| **Shorebirds, Gulls, Auks, and Relatives** | | | |
| Common Ringed Plover | Charadrius hiaticula | Charadriidae | Casual visitor from Eurasia to the Aleutian and Pribilof Islands |
| Lesser Sand-Plover | Charadrius mongolus | Charadriidae | Rare visitor from Asia to West Alaska and Pacific Coast |
| Red-necked Stint | Calidris ruficollis | Scolopacidae | Rare visitor from Siberia to both coasts in summer and fall |
| Temminck's Stint | Calidris temminckii | Scolopacidae | Casual visitor from Eurasia to Alaska and Pacific Northwest |
| Long-toed Stint | Calidris subminuta | Scolopacidae | Rare visitor from Asia to Aleutians, Pribilofs, Pacific Coast to California |
| Sharp-tailed Sandpiper | Calidris acuminata | Scolopacidae | Rare visitor from eastern Asia to Alaska and Pacific Coast to California |
| Curlew Sandpiper | Calidris ferruginea | Scolopacidae | Rare visitor from Eurasia in Alaska and Pacific Coast |
| Ruff | Calidris pugnax | Scolopacidae | Rare visitor from Eurasia to Alaska and Pacific Coast |
| American Woodcock | Scolopax minor | Scolopacidae | Casual visitor from the East to the West and Southwest |
| Common Sandpiper | Actitis hypoleucos | Scolopacidae | Casual visitor from Eurasia to western Alaska and the Aleutian Islands |
| Black-tailed Godwit | Limosa limosa | Scolopacidae | Casual visitor from Eurasia to the Aleutian and Pribilof Islands |
| Wood Sandpiper | Tringa glareola | Scolopacidae | Rare visitor from Eurasia to Alaska and south to California |
| Gray-tailed Tattler | Tringa brevipes | Scolopacidae | Rare visitor from Asia to Alaska, southward to California |
| Great Black-backed Gull | Larus marinus | Laridae | Casual visitor from the East to several western states |
| Laughing Gull | Leucophaeus atricilla | Laridae | Rare visitor from Mexico to SouthCalifornia; casual from the East to Colorado and West Texas |
| Slaty-backed Gull | Larus schistisagus | Laridae | Casual visitor from Asia to Alaska and West Coast |
| Ivory Gull | Pagophila eburnea | Laridae | Casual visitor from the Arctic to Colorado, California, and British Columbia |

| COMMON NAME | SCIENTIFIC NAME | FAMILY NAME | STATUS |
|---|---|---|---|
| **Tubenoses** | | | |
| Wedge-rumped Storm-Petrel | *Hydrobates tethys* | Hydrobatidae | Rare visitor to California coast; breeds on Galapagos and islands off Peru |
| Cook's Petrel | *Pterodroma cookii* | Procellariidae | Regular visitor from New Zealand off the coast of California |
| Flesh-footed Shearwater | *Ardenna carneipes* | Procellariidae | Rare visitor from New Zealand and Australia to California |
| **Storks** | | | |
| Wood Stork | *Mycteria americana* | Ciconiidae | Accidental from Mexico to California |
| **Ibises and Herons** | | | |
| Little Blue Heron | *Egretta caerulea* | Ardeidae | Rare visitor from Mexico to West Coast from California to British Columbia |
| Tricolored Heron | *Egretta tricolor* | Ardeidae | Rare visitor from Mexico to southern California |
| Reddish Egret | *Egretta rufescens* | Ardeidae | Rare visitor from Mexico to California |
| Yellow-crowned Night Heron | *Nyctanassa violacea* | Ardeidae | Casual visitor from Mexico to California |
| Glossy Ibis | *Plegadis falcinellus* | Threskiornithidae | Casual visitor from the East or Central America to California |
| **Pelicans and Relatives** | | | |
| Brown Booby | *Sula leucogaster* | Sulidae | Rare visitor to southern California |
| **Eagles** | | | |
| Steller's Sea Eagle | *Haliaeetus pelagicus* | Accipitridae | Casual visitor from eastern Asia to Alaska |
| **Trogons** | | | |
| Eared Quetzal | *Euptilotis neoxenus* | Trogonidae | Casual visitor from Mexico to Southeast Arizona; may be resident |
| **Chickadees** | | | |
| Gray-headed Chickadee | *Poecile cincta* | Paridae | Eurasian species resident from northern Alaska to Northwest Yukon |
| **Wrens** | | | |
| Sinaloa Wren | *Thryothorus sinaloa* | Troglodytidae | Accidental from Mexico to Arizona |
| **Old World Warblers** | | | |
| Willow Warbler | *Phylloscopus trochilus* | Sylviidae | Casual visitor from Eurasia to Alaska |
| **Mockingbirds** | | | |
| Blue Mockingbird | *Melanotis caerulescens* | Mimidae | Casual visitor from Mexico to southeastern Arizona |
| **Pipits** | | | |
| Olive-backed Pipit | *Anthus hodgsoni* | Motacillidae | Rare visitor from eastern Asia to Alaska (Aleutians); accidental to California |
| **Finches** | | | |
| Brambling | *Fringilla montifringilla* | Fringillidae | Casual visitor in West Canada, south to California; regular visitor to Alaska (Aleutians) |
| **Wood Warblers** | | | |
| Louisiana Waterthrush | *Parkesia motacilla* | Parulidae | Casual to rare visitor from the East to Arizona and California |
| Golden-winged Warbler | *Vermivora chrysoptera* | Parulidae | Casual visitors from the East to many western states |
| Hooded Warbler | *Setophaga citrina* | Parulidae | Casual to rare visitor from the East to California and southwestern states |
| Northern Parula | *Setophaga americana* | Parulidae | Rare visitor from the East to the western states to California |
| Pine Warbler | *Setophaga pinus* | Parulidae | Casual visitor from the East to California, also other western states |
| Yellow-throated Warbler | *Setophaga dominica* | Parulidae | Casual visitor from the East to many western states |
| Prairie Warbler | *Setophaga discolor* | Parulidae | Casual to rare visitor from the East to California, also other western states |
| Rufous-capped Warbler | *Basileuterus rufifrons* | Parulidae | Casual visitor from Mexicoto Texas and Arizona |
| Slate-throated Redstart | *Myioborus miniatus* | Parulidae | Casual visitor from Mexico to the Southwest |

# GLOSSARY

Many terms defined here are illustrated in the general introduction (pp.10–21).

**adult** A fully developed, sexually mature bird. It is in its final plumage, which no longer changes pattern with age and remains the same after yearly molt, although it may change with season. *See also* **immature, juvenile.**

**aerie** The nest of birds of prey, like eagles or peregrine falcons, usually on a cliff, and often used by the same pair of adult birds in successive years.

**alarm call** A call made by a bird to signal danger. Alarm calls are often short and urgent in tone, and a few species use different calls to signify the precise nature of the threat. *See also* **call.**

**allopreening** Mutual preening between two birds, the main purpose of which is to reduce the instinctive aggression when birds come into close contact. In the breeding season, allopreening helps to strengthen the pair bond between the male and female. *See also* **preening.**

**altitudinal migrant** *see* **vertical migrant**

**alula** A small group of two to six feathers projecting from a bird's "thumb," at the bend of its wing that reduces turbulence when raised.

**Audubon, John James (1785–1851)** American naturalist and wildlife illustrator, whose best known work was his remarkable collection of prints, *Birds of North America.*

**axillary** A term describing feathers at the base of the underwing. Axillary feathers often form small patches, with coloration differing from the rest of the underwing.

**barred** With marks crossing the body, wing, or tail; the opposite of streaked. *See also* **streaks.**

**bastard wing** *see* **alula**

**beak** *see* **bill**

**bill** A bird's jaws. A bill is made of bone, with a hornlike outer covering of keratin.

**bird of prey** Any of the predatory birds in the orders Accipitriformes (eagles, hawks, kites, and ospreys), Falconiformes (falcons), and Strigiformes (owls). They are characterized by their acute eyesight, powerful legs, strongly hooked bill, and sharp talons. Also known as raptors. *See also* **raptor, raptor.**

**body feather** *see* **contour feather**

**booming** A sound produced by bitterns and some species of grouse. The booming of male bitterns is a deep, resonant, hollow sound that can carry for several miles. The booming of male grouse is produced by wind from air pouches in the sides of the bird's neck.

**brackish** Containing a mixture of saltwater and freshwater.

**breeding plumage** A general term for the plumage worn by adult birds when they display and form breeding pairs. It is usually (but not always) worn in the spring and summer. *See also* **nonbreeding plumage.**

**brood (noun)** The young birds produced from a single clutch of eggs and incubated together. *See also* **clutch. (verb)** In birds, to sit on nestlings to keep them warm. Brooding is usually carried out by the adult female. *See also* **incubate.**

**brood parasite** A bird that lays its eggs in the nest of other species. Some brood parasites always breed this way, while others do so only occasionally.

**brood patch** An area of bare skin on the belly of a parent bird, usually the female, that is richly supplied with blood vessels and thus helps keep the eggs warm during incubation. This area loses its feathers in readiness for the breeding season and is fully feathered at other times.

**caged-bird** A species of bird commonly kept in captivity.

**call** A sound produced by the vocal apparatus of a bird to communicate a variety of messages to other birds. Calls are often highly characteristic of individual species and can help to locate and identify birds in the field. Most bird calls are shorter and simpler than songs. *See also* **alarm call, booming, contact call, song.**

**casque** A bony extension on a bird's head.

**cere** A leathery patch of skin that covers the base of a bird's bill. It is found only in a few groups, including birds of prey, pigeons, and parrots.

**claw** In birds, the nail that prolongs their toes.

**cloaca** An opening toward the rear of a bird's belly. It is present in both sexes and is used in reproduction and excretion.

**clutch** The group of eggs in a single nest, usually laid by one female and incubated together.

**cock** A term sometimes used to describe the adult male in galliforms and songbirds. *See also* **hen.**

**collar** The area around a bird's neck, which in some species is a prominent feature of its plumage pattern and can be used for identification.

**color form** One of two or more clearly defined plumage variations found in the same species. Also known as a color morph or phase, a color form may be restricted to part of a species's range or occur side by side with other color forms over the entire range. Adults of different color forms are able to interbreed, and these mixed pairings can produce young of either form.

**comb** A fleshy growth of bare skin usually above the eyes.

**contact call** A call made by a bird to give its location as a means of staying in touch with others of the same species. Contact calls are used by birds in flocks and by breeding pairs. Contact calls are crucial for nocturnal migrants. *See also* **call.**

**contour feather** A general term for any feather that covers the outer surface of a bird, including its wings and tail. Contour feathers are also known as body feathers, and help streamline the bird.

**cooperative breeding** A breeding system in which a pair of parent birds are helped in raising their young by several other birds, which are often related to them and may be young birds from previous broods.

**courtship display** Ritualized, showy behavior used in courtship by the male, and sometimes by the female, involving plumage, sound (vocal and non-vocal), and movements.

**covert** A small feather covering the base of a bird's flight feather. Together, coverts form a well-defined feather tract on the wing or at the base of the tail. *See also* **feather tract.**

**creche** A group of young birds of about the same age, produced by different parents but tightly packed together. One or more adults guards the entire creche.

**crepuscular** Relating to the period just before dawn, when many birds are active, especially during courtship. When used in connection with birds, the term is often used to refer to both dawn and twilight.

**crest** A group of elongated feathers on top of a bird's head, which may be raised during courtship or to indicate alarm.

**crown** The area on top of a bird's head. It is often a prominent plumage feature, with a different color from the feathers on the rest of the head.

**dabble** To feed in shallow water by sieving water and obtain food through comb-like filters in the bill; used mostly for ducks (dabbling ducks or dabblers).

**decurved** A term describing a bird's bill that curves downward from the forehead toward the tip.

**dimorphism** *see* **sexual dimorphism**

**display** *see* **courtship display, distraction display, threat display**

**distraction display** A display in which a bird deliberately attempts to attract a predator's attention in order to lure it away from its nest or nestlings.

**diurnal** Active during the day.

**down feather** A soft, fluffy feather, lacking the system of barbs of contour or flight feathers, that provides good insulation. Young birds are covered by down feathers until they molt into their first juvenile plumage. Adult birds have a layer of down feathers under their contour feathers. *See also* **contour feather, juvenile.**

**drake** An adult male duck. The adult female is known as the duck.

**drift** The diversion of migrating birds from their normal migration route by strong winds.

**dynamic soaring** *see* **soaring**

**ear tuft** A distinct tuft of feathers on each side of a bird's forehead, with no connection to the true ears, which can be raised as a visual signal. Many owls have ear tufts.

**echolocation** A method of sensing nearby objects using pulses of high-frequency sound. Echoes bounce back from obstacles, enabling the sender to build up a "picture" of its surroundings.

**eclipse plumage** A female-like plumage worn in some birds, especially waterfowl, by adult males for a short period after the breeding season is over. The eclipse plumage helps camouflage them during their molt, when they are flightless.

**elevational migrant** *see* **vertical migrant**

**endemic** A species (or subspecies) native to a particular geographic area—such as an island, a forest patch, a mountain, or state, or country—and found nowhere else.

**escape** An individual bird that has escaped from a zoo or other collection to live in the wild. *See also* **exotic**

**eye-ring** A ring of color, usually narrow and well defined, around the eye of a bird.

**eyestripe** A stripe of color running as a line through the eye of a bird.

**eyrie** *see* **aerie**

**exotic** A bird found in a region from which it is not native. Some of these are escapees, or were originally, but now live as wild birds.

**feather tract** A well-defined area on a bird's skin where feathers grow, leaving patches of bare skin inbetween.

**fledge** In young birds, to leave the nest or acquire the first complete set of flight feathers. Known as fledglings, these birds may still remain dependent on their parents for some time. *See also* **flight feather.**

**fledging period** The average time taken by the young of a species to fledge, timed from the moment they hatch. Fledging periods in birds range from 11 days in some small songbirds to as long as 280 days in the Wandering Albatross.

**fledgling** *see* **fledge**

**flight feather** A collective term for a bird's wing and tail feathers, used in flight. More specifically, it refers to the largest feathers on the outer part of the wing, the primaries and secondaries.

**forewing** The front section of a bird's wing, including the primary coverts and secondary coverts. *See also* **hindwing.**

**gamebird** Generally, any bird that is legally hunted, including some doves and waterfowl. This name is generally used for members of the order Galliformes.

**gular sac** Also known as a gular pouch, it is a large, fleshy, extendable sac just below the bill of some birds, especially fish-eaters such as pelicans. It forms part of the throat.

**habitat** The geographical and ecological area where a particular organism usually lives.

**hen** A term sometimes used to describe the adult female in galliforms, especially grouse and songbirds. *See also* **cock.**

**hindwing** The rear section of a bird's spread wing, including the secondary feathers, especially when it has a distinctive color or pattern. *See also* **forewing.**

**hybrid** The offspring produced when two species, sometimes from different genera, interbreed. Hybrids are usually rare in the wild. Among birds, they are most frequent in gamebirds and waterfowl, especially ducks. Hybrid progeny may or may not be fertile.

**immature** In birds, an individual that is not yet sexually mature or able to breed. Some birds pass through a series of immature plumages over several years before adopting their first adult plumage and sexual maturity. *See also* **adult, juvenile.**

**incubate** In birds, to sit on eggs to keep them warm, allowing the embryo inside to grow. Incubation is often carried out by the female. *See also* **brood.**

**incubation period** In birds, the period when a parent incubates its eggs. It may not start until the clutch is completed.

**injury feigning** *see* **distraction display.**

**inner wing** The inner part of the wing, comprising the secondaries and rows of coverts (typically marginal, lesser, median, and greater coverts).

**introduced species** A species that humans have accidentally or deliberately brought into an area where it does not normally occur.

**iridescent plumage** Plumage that shows brilliant, luminous colors, which seem to sparkle and change color when seen from different angles.

**irruption** A sporadic mass movement of animals outside their normal range. Irruptions are usually short-lived and occur in response to food shortage. Also called irruptive migration.

**juvenile** A term referring to the plumage worn by a young bird at the time it makes its first flight and until it begins its first molt. *See also* **adult, immature.**

**keratin** A tough but lightweight protein. In birds, keratin is found in the claws, feathers, and outer part of the bill.

**kleptoparasite** A bird that gets much of its food by stealing it from other birds, usually by following them in flight and forcing them to disgorge their food.

**lamellae** Delicate, comb-like structures on the sides of the bill of some birds used for filtering tiny food particles out of water.

**leap-frog migration** A pattern of migration in which some populations of a species travel much further than the other populations, by "leap-frogging" over the area where these sedentary (nonmigratory) birds are found. *See also* **migration.**

**lek** An area, often small, used by males as a communal display arena, where they show off special plumage features accompanied by vocal and non-vocal sounds, to attract females. Females wait along the lek and select the male or males that they will mate with.

**lobed feet** Feet with loose, fleshy lobes on the toes, adapted for swimming.

**lore** A small area between a bird's eye and the base of its upper bill.

**mandible** The upper or lower part of a bird's bill, known as the upper or lower mandible respectively.

**mantle** The loose term used to define the back of a bird, between its neck and rump.

**migrant** A species that regularly moves between geographical areas. Most migrants move on an annual basis between a breeding area and a wintering area. *See also* **partial migrant, sedentary.**

**migration** A journey to a different region, following a well-defined route. *See also* **leap-frog migration, partial migrant, reverse migration, sedentary, vertical migrant.**

**mobbing** A type of defensive behavior in which a group of birds gang up to harass a predator, such as a bird of prey or an owl, swooping repeatedly to drive it away.

**molt** In birds, to shed old feathers so that they can be replaced. Molting enables birds to keep their plumage in good condition, change their level of insulation, and change their coloration or markings so that they are ready to breed or display.

**monogamous** Mating with a single partner, either in a single breeding season or for life. *See also* **polygamous.**

**morph** *see* **color form**

**nape** The back of the neck.

**nestling** A young bird still in the nest.

**New World** The Americas, from Alaska to Cape Horn, including the Caribbean and offshore islands in the Pacific and Atlantic Oceans. *See also* **Old World.**

**nictitating membrane** A transparent or semiopaque "third eyelid," which moves sideways across the eye. Waterbirds often use the membrane as an aid to vision when swimming underwater.

**nocturnal** Active at night.

**nomadic** Being almost constantly on the move. Birds of deserts, grasslands, and the coniferous forests of the far north are commonly nomadic.

**nonbreeding plumage** The plumage worn by adult birds outside the breeding season. In many species, particularly in temperate regions, it is also known as winter plumage. *See also* **breeding plumage.**

**nonmigrant** *see* **sedentary**

**nonpasserine** Any bird that is not a member of the order Passeriformes (or passerines). *See also* **passerine.**

**oil gland** Also called the preen gland, a gland at the base of a bird's tail that secretes oils that are spread over the feathers for waterproofing them during preening.

**Old World** Europe, Asia, Africa, and Australasia. *See also* **New World.**

**orbital ring** A thin, bare, fleshy ring around the eye, sometimes with a distinctive color. *See also* **eye-ring.**

**outer wing** The outer half of the wing, comprising the primaries, their coverts, and the alula (the "thumb").

**partial migrant** A species in which some populations migrate while others are sedentary. This situation is common in widely distributed species that experience a wide range of climatic conditions. *See also* **migration, sedentary.**

**passerine** A bird belonging to the vast order Passeriformes (the passerines). This group contains more species than all other orders of birds combined. Passerines are also called songbirds or perching birds. *See also* **nonpasserine.**

**pelagic** Relating to the open ocean. Pelagic birds spend most of their life at sea and only come to land to nest.

**phase** *see* **color form**

**polygamous** Mating with two or more partners during the course of a single breeding season. *See also* **monogamous.**

**population** A group of individual birds of the same species living in a geographically and ecologically circumscribed area.

**preening** Routine behavior by which birds keep their feathers in good condition. A bird grasps a feather at its base and then "nibbles" upward toward the tip, and repeats the process with different feathers. This helps smooth and clean the plumage. Birds often also smear oil from their preen gland onto their feathers at the same time. *See also* **allopreening.**

**primary feather** One of the large outer wing feathers, growing from the digits of a bird's "hand." *See also* **secondary feather.**

**race** *see* **subspecies**

**range** A term to indicate the geographical distribution of a species or population

**raptor** A general name for birds belonging to the orders Falconiformes and Accipitriformes, often used interchangeably with bird of prey. *See also* **bird of prey.**

**ratite** A member of an ancient group of flightless birds that includes the ostrich, cassowaries, emus, rheas, and kiwis. In the past, the group was larger and more diverse.

**resident** *see* **sedentary**

**reverse migration** A phenomenon that occurs when birds from a migratory species mistakenly travel in the opposite direction from normal, causing birds to turn up in places far outside their normal range. *See also* **migration.**

**roost** A place where birds sleep, either at night or by day.

**rump** The area between a bird's back and the base of its upper tail coverts. In many species, the rump is a different color from the rest of the plumage and can be a useful diagnostic character for identification.

**sally** A feeding technique (sallying), used especially by tyrant flycatchers, in which a bird makes a short flight from a perch to catch an insect, often in midair, followed by a return to a perch, often the same one.

**salt gland** A gland located in a depression of the skull, just above the eye of some birds, particularly seabirds. This enables them to extract the fluids they need from saltwater and then expel the excess salts through the nostrils.

**scapular** Any one of a group of feathers on the "shoulder," forming a more or less oval patch on each side of the back, at the base of the wing.

**scrape** A simple nest that consists of a shallow depression in the ground, which may be unlined or lined with material such as feathers, bits of grass, or pebbles.

**secondary feather** One of the row of long, stiff feathers along the rear edge of a bird's wing, between the body and the primary feathers at the wingtip. *See also* **primary feather.**

**sedentary** Having a settled lifestyle that involves little or no geographic movement. Sedentary birds are also said to be resident or nonmigratory. *See also* **migration.**

**semipalmated** The condition in which two or more of the toes are partially joined by an incomplete membrane at their base.

**sexual dimorphism** The occurrence of physical differences between males and females. In birds, the most common differences are in size and plumage.

**shorebird** Also known as a wader, any member of several families in the order Charadriiformes, including plovers, sandpipers, godwits, snipe, avocets, stilts, oystercatchers, and curlews. Not all species actually wade in water and some live in dry habitats.

**soaring** In birds, flight without flapping of the wings. A soaring bird stays at the same height or gains height. Updraft soaring is a type of soaring in which a bird benefits from rising currents that form at cliffs or along mountain ridges. Seabirds are expert at dynamic soaring, repeatedly diving into the troughs between waves and then using the rising air deflected off the waves to wheel back up into the air.

**song** A vocal performance by a bird, usually the adult male, to attract and impress a potential mate, advertise ownership of a territory, or drive away rival birds. Songs are often highly characteristic of individual species and can be a major aid in locating and identifying birds in the field. *See also* **call.**

**songbird** A general term used to describe a member of the suborder Passeri (or oscines), a subdivision of the largest order of birds, the Passeriformes (passerines).

**species** A group of similar organisms that are capable of breeding among themselves in the wild and producing fertile offspring that resemble themselves, but that do not interbreed in the wild with individuals of another similar group, are called a species. *See also* **subspecies, superspecies.**

**speculum** A colorful patch on the wing of a duck, formed by the secondary feathers. *See also* **secondary feather.**

**spur** A sharply pointed, claw-like structure at the back of the leg of some birds, like the Wild Turkey.

**staging ground** A stopover area where migrant birds regularly pause while on migration, to rest and feed.

**stoop** A near-vertical and often very fast dive made by falcons and some other birds of prey when chasing prey in the air or on the ground.

**streaks** Marks that run lengthwise on feathers; opposite of bars.

**subspecies** When species show geographical variation in color, voice, or other characters, these differentiated populations are recognized by ornithologists as subspecies (formerly also called races). *See also* **species.**

**superspecies** Closely related species that have different geographical ranges. *See also* **species.**

**syrinx** A modified section of a bird's trachea (windpipe), equivalent to the voicebox in humans, that enables birds to call and sing.

**talon** One of the sharp, hooked claws of a bird of prey.

**territory** An area that is defended by an animal, or a group of animals, against other members of the same species. Territories often include useful resources, such as good breeding sites or feeding areas, which help a male attract a mate.

**tertial** Any one of a small group of feathers, sometimes long and obvious, at the base of the wing adjacent to the inner secondaries.

**thermal** A rising bubble or column of warm air over land that soaring birds can use to gain height with little effort. *See also* **soaring.**

**threat display** A form of defense in which a bird adopts certain postures, sometimes accompanied by loud calls, to drive away a rival or a potential predator.

**trachea** The breathing tube in animals, also known as the windpipe.

**tubenose** A general term used to describe members of the order Procellariiformes, including albatrosses, petrels, and shearwaters; their nostrils form two tubes on the upper mandible.

**underwing** The underside of a bird's wing, usually visible only in flight or when a bird is preening, displaying, or swimming.

**upperwing** The upper surface of a bird's wing clearly exposed in flight but often mostly hidden when the bird is perched.

**vagrant** A bird that has strayed far from its normal range. Usually, vagrants are long-distance migrants that have been blown off course by storms, have overshot their intended destination because of strong winds, or have become disoriented.

**vent** Also called the crissum, the undertail feathers between the lower belly feathers and tail feathers, which in some species are differently colored from either belly or tail feathers. Can be helpful in identification.

**vertical migrant** A species that migrates up and down mountains, usually in response to changes in the weather or food supply. *See also* **migration.**

**wader** *see* **shorebird.**

**waterfowl** A collective term for members of the family Anatidae, including ducks, geese, and swans.

**wattle** A bare, fleshy growth that hangs loosely below the bill in some birds. It is often brightly colored, and may play a part in courtship.

**wildfowl** *see* **waterfowl**

**Wilson, Alexander (1766–1813)** A contemporary of J.J. Audubon, Wilson's seminal American Ornithology marks the start of scientific ornithology in the US.

**wingbar** A line or bar of color across the upper surface of a bird's wing. Wingbars can often be seen when a bird is on the ground or perched and its wings are in the closed position, but they are normally much more obvious in flight. Wingbars may be single or in groups of two or more.

**wingspan** The distance across a bird's outstretched wings and back, from one wingtip to the other.

# INDEX